Dictionary of Munster Women Writers
1800–2000

Dictionary of
Munster Women Writers

1800–2000

General Editor
Tina O'Toole

Scríbhneoirí Ban na Mumhan

1800–2000

Eagarthóirí Gaeilge
Gearóidín Nic Carthaigh
agus Síle Ní Chochláin

Foreword
Patricia Coughlan
and
Éibhear Walshe

CORK **c u p** UNIVERSITY PRESS

In memory of
Sheelagh O'Toole (1943–1993)

First published in 2005 by
Cork University Press
Youngline Industrial Estate
Pouladuff Road, Togher
Cork
Ireland

British Library Cataloguing in Publication Data
A CIP catalogue record for this book is available from the British Library
A CIP record for this publication is available from the Library of Congress

ISBN 1-85918-388-3

Typeset by Tower Books, Ballincollig, Co. Cork
Printed by Betaprint Ltd., Dublin

www.corkuniversitypress.com

Contents

Acknowledgements

This dictionary has been a collaborative effort, and I would like to begin by acknowledging the contribution made by our two Irish language scholars – Gearóidín Nic Carthaigh and Síle Ní Chochláin – without whom our list of Munster women writers would be very much the poorer. Similarly, the work of part-time postgraduate researchers has been invaluable throughout, and I would like to thank in particular June O'Sullivan and Kalene Kenefick for their efforts.

I would like to express appreciation of the Advisory Panel to the Munster Women Writers Project who were very generous with their expertise, time, and in some cases their own research: Angela Bourke, Mary Breen, Claire Connolly, Roz Cowman, Jennifer FitzGerald, Anne Fogarty, Margaret Kelleher, Clíona Ó Gallchóir, Gerardine Meaney, Antoinette Quinn, Shaun Richards, Pádraigín Riggs and Elizabeth Tilley. Our University College Cork colleagues in the other strands of the Women in Irish Society Project – Linda Connolly, Liz Kiely and Máire Leane – lent invaluable interest and support throughout the research process.

The human resources we consulted throughout this project have been its lifeblood, and I would like to thank a number of people whose knowledge, skill and generosity supported and facilitated all of us throughout the research process. In the Cork libraries, I would like to thank the staff at the Boole Library, UCC, particularly Julian Walton, Carol Quinn, the Special Collections staff and Margaret Clayton; and the City Library staff, particularly Tom McCarthy and Kieran Burke. I would also like to say a special word of thanks to the local studies librarians who provide a really vital service throughout the Munster region, particularly Eamonn Browne in Kerry County Library, and Mike Maguire in Limerick, whose enthusiasm for the project, as well as his advice, were a great source of inspiration.

Joan Murphy at the RTÉ Sound Archive has been a good friend to the project, and her unstinting patience and support was, as ever, much appreciated. The help of Elizabeth Kirwan and Eilís Ní Dhuibhne at the National Library contributed greatly to the finished dictionary, and Ann Butler's bibliography of Una Troy's papers there also proved extremely helpful. I would also like to mention the volunteers who staff the library of the Society of Friends at Swanbrook in Dublin, who were unfailingly generous with their time on each of my research visits.

A number of local scholars and book dealers have been very helpful to all of us: I thank in particular Seán Spellissy in Clare, Marcus Bourke and Mary Guinan Darmody in relation to Tipperary writers, Naughton's Books in Dun Laoghaire, and Mary Mackey of Fuchsia Books in Schull. Local writers' groups throughout the region were also generous in their support of the project, especially Mary Johnston and Paddy Galvin of the Munster Literature Centre, The Works in Waterford, Listowel Writers' Centre, and Liz Willows and Máire Bradshaw at Tigh Filí.

I would like to thank Tom Dunne, Mike Collins and Caroline Somers at Cork University Press for their commitment to bringing this research to publication stage. We would also like to acknowledge the generous assistance of the Irish Research Council for the Humanities and Social Sciences Programme for Research in Third-Level Institutions and the Cork City of Culture 2005 Committee for providing funding. I would like to say a particular word of thanks to Tom McCarthy for his enthusiastic support of the project.

The Department of English at UCC was the context within which this project was carried out, and several colleagues and students there contributed greatly to our ongoing research. I would like to say a special word of thanks to Anne Fitzgerald, Jennifer Crowley, Elaine Hurley, Janet Milner and Teresa Murphy, administrative staff of the Department during the various phases of the life of the project, who assisted us greatly in many of the practical tasks involved in getting this project ready for publication and who could not have been more supportive and tolerant.

We are indebted to the "techies" who gave us so much of their time and advice over the course of the project: Catherine Sanborne, Orla Murphy, and particularly Diane Searls, who customized the database. Petra Stone did a top-class job with our web design, and the two programmers, Jonathan Neville and Albert Williams, were worth their weight in gold, not least for their patience in explaining the basics to the rest of us.

Two conferences held during the lifetime of this research process proved to be vital spaces for discussion and elaboration of the ideas within the project. I thank all of those who presented at our 2001 conference, "Munster Women Writers: Towards a Feminist Literary History", specifically: Janet Todd, Eiléan Ní Chuilleanáin, Magda Stouthamer-Loeber, Jackie Belanger, Silvia Diez Fabre, Biling Chen, Gaye Shortland, Jessie Lendennie, Róisín Conroy, Mary Mulcahy, Jo O'Donoghue, Catherine Rose, Rolf Loeber and Christine St Peter, in addition to those scholars already mentioned. In the last phase, while we conceived and wrote the Introduction, the organizers of the 2004 IASIL conference at NUI Galway – Riana O'Dwyer and Patrick Lonergan – were most flexible and supportive in facilitating our panels on "Contemporary Feminist Scholarship and Irish Women's Writing". The following scholars are owed thanks for their generous participation in these panels, which helped our thinking greatly: Gerardine Meaney, Heidi Hansson, Margaret Kelleher, Claire Connolly, Joanna Wydenbach, Kalene Kenefick, Claire Bracken, Moynagh Sullivan and Borbála Farágo.

Thanks to the generous advice and assistance of a number of people, from a wide range of contexts, the dictionary is considerably larger than any of us expected at the outset. I would like to thank all of the writers and scholars who took the time to fill out our questionnaire and pass on information to us about other writers. I would also like to acknowledge a number of individuals who have been very good to us over the course of the project: Lia Mills, David Rose, Sara Wilbourne, Gerard Dineen, Lis Pihl, Carmel Quinlan, Edward Power, Mary Leland, Dolores Dooley, Michael Coady, Sinéad McCoole, Alan Hayes and Kieran Halpin. Piaras Mac Éinrí was, as always, generous with his time and expertise on a number of fronts – not least his knowledge of the geographical aspect of the research. Margaret Mac Curtain was an invaluable early informant to the project, and is always a role model for those engaged in all Irish feminist projects. I would like to thank my colleagues at the Institute of Irish Studies, Queen's University Belfast, for their friendship and support over the past year. I'd also like to say a special thanks to Siobhán O'Dowd.

Without the expertise and commitment of Patricia Coughlan and Éibhear Walshe, the Munster Women Writers Project would never have been initiated in the first place. In addition to his knowledge of Munster women writers, Éibhear's skills as a project manager were invaluable, and he kept us all on the financial straight and narrow throughout the lifetime of the project. Pat Coughlan's scholarly work in this field both in English and Irish was the backbone of the project. Her role as project leader for the overall Women in Irish Society Project is testament to her commitment to interdisciplinary feminist research in Irish studies and her belief that such research can and should be supported within academe. On a personal level, she has been a great source of support and friendship to me over a number of years in Cork, and I'd like to thank her for that.

Tina O'Toole
Cork, February 2005

Foreword

Patricia Coughlan and
Éibhear Walshe

The idea for this dictionary arose from the constellation of research, writing, teaching and supervision in which we had been engaged for several years in the Department of English at University College Cork. We have had long-standing and strong literary and historical interests, some shared, some contiguous, in the work of several prominent Munster women writers. These interests are closely connected with our shared engagement in feminist criticism and in advancing ideological and aesthetic enquiry into representations of gender and sexuality in Irish ideologies over the last two centuries.[1] When we conceived this project, we had already taught and supervised undergraduate and postgraduate students carrying out research on writers about whom we had ourselves lectured, written and broadcast.[2] The Introduction discusses at greater length the numerous and distinguished cohort of female writers, in both its languages, which the province of Munster has produced since 1800.

Against this intellectual background, the dictionary owes its existence to the provision by the Government of funding for collaborative original research projects under the Programme for Research in Third-Level Institutions, which awarded us a three-year grant of €75,000 in 1999, for which we thank the Irish Research Council for the Humanities and Social Sciences.[3] This project in literary history was part of a larger one on "Women in Irish Society: Understanding the Past and Present through Social Research and Archives". The other two strands were based in UCC's Departments of Sociology (led by Dr Linda Connolly, on "Documenting Irish Feminisms") and Applied Social Studies (an oral history project, led by Dr Máire Leane and Dr Elizabeth Kiely, on "Women in Paid Employment in Munster 1936–60"). The project as a whole constituted an important interdisciplinary initiative to develop feminist research in humanities and social sciences. A strong regional emphasis linked the literary and social aspects of this parallel research: the investigation of women's life experience, and contributions to culture and society in this region, carried out by the Departments of English and of Applied Social Studies, shared an empirical focus and involved the detailed collection of data, with a long historical compass in the case of the dictionary.[4]

We were fortunate in being able to recruit Dr Tina O'Toole as the project's principal researcher and General Editor of the dictionary. Tina had already written on Kate O'Brien, and was completing important and original doctoral research on two Irish "New Woman" writers of the Victorian period.[5] Tina's own work and her supervision of several other postgraduate researchers were exemplary, and we would like to pay the warmest tribute here to her talent, acumen and dedication to what turned out to be a far more extensive project than any of us had initially envisaged. She leaves not only feminist but Irish literary scholarship in general in her debt for the provision of this new resource to set beside existing materials for scholars and critics in the field, and also for general readers with an interest in Munster, in women's creative and intellectual work, or in the social history of writing in the province since 1800.

From the outset it was an essential part of our conception that the dictionary should include writing in the Irish language, so that its readers could gain a more unified vision of the cultural life of the province and of the interpenetration of its two languages. To that end we recruited two specialist scholarly researchers in that field, Gearóidín Nic Carthaigh and Síle Ní Chochláin, who worked successively on the material and are joint Editors of the Irish-language entries. Gearóidín and Síle have provided their own explanation of the specific challenges presented by their research, and of their editorial policy decisions about how to approach material from the oral traditions of Munster (see Réamhrá, below). We wish, however, as leaders of the dictionary project, to express our deep appreciation of the quality of their scholarship and the extent of their dedication to a project which sometimes strained the boundaries of conventional disciplinary thinking, and to which they gave much time and thought.[6]

Many others, both within and outside this and other academies, made contributions to the compilation of this volume, to solving the many editorial questions which arose, and to the protracted assembly of the material. These debts are recorded in detail in the Acknowledgements. We apologize here for any inadvertent omissions.

We inaugurated the project with a seminar in early 2000, drawing on a panel of scholarly experts recruited from Ireland and Britain, and began the three-year process of tracking down and recording biographical and bibliographical details for some 560 Munster women who had written or (in Irish) contributed to the oral tradition, or both. In July 2001, we hosted at UCC a multi-national conference with papers on many of these writers, in which scholars based in Spain, Britain and North America participated; the project concluded in 2003 with a joint exhibition, with the two other strands of the larger "Women in Irish Society" project. It is appropriate that this volume should be launched in the year that Cork is Capital of European Culture, and we are delighted to acknowledge funding to aid its publication from the Cultural Committee of Cork 2005.[7] We believe that the dictionary is not just a record of, but itself a fitting contribution to, the celebration of Munster's cultural heritage: many of the writers here being acknowledged were vital and influential voices in the making of modern Ireland over the past 200 years, and all of them deserve to be commemorated.

Notes

1   The Introduction further develops the underlying intellectual and ideological aims of such feminist recovery work. See Coughlan (1991), Kilfeather and Walshe.

2   The Department of English MA course on "Gender and Sexuality in Irish

Writing" which, together with our colleague Clíona Ó Gallchoir, we developed and taught from 2000, played a role also, in parallel with the dictionary compilation, in generating further projects in feminist criticism and literary history, and in training researchers, two of whom – Kalene Kenefick and June O'Sullivan – became dictionary contributors and doctoral researchers in the field.

3   We are also grateful to the staff of the Research Office and the Boole Library in UCC for their assistance throughout the project, to our colleagues in the Department of English, especially Dr Ó Gallchoir and Mary Breen, for their consultations and encouragement, and to the dedicated administrative staff of the Department who always actively facilitated us in the carrying out of the project; to Anne Fitzgerald, the outstanding Administrator, a particular vote of thanks is owing.

4   "Documenting Irish Feminisms" had a countrywide extent, thanks to its basis in the Attic Press Archive, held in the Boole Library at UCC. See Connolly and O'Toole. We thank Máire, Liz and Linda for their warm cooperation and fellowship throughout.

5   One was "George Egerton" (Mary Chavelita Dunne), who herself had significant associations with Co. Cork, where she lived while producing some of her best-known work (see O'Toole 2001). Tina's parallel work on the sociology project also helped to unify the strands and to develop all of our thinking about the conduct of feminist research.

6   We also thank An tOllamh Seán Ó Coileáin of Roinn na Nua-Ghaeilge, UCC, for his advice and friendly assistance.

7   We also warmly thank the National University of Ireland and the UCC Faculty of Arts for grants in aid of publication.

Works cited

Connolly, Linda, and Tina O'Toole (eds.), *Documenting Irish Feminisms* (Dublin: Woodfield Press, 2004).

Coughlan, Patricia, "'Bog Queens': The Representation of Femininity in the Poetry of Seamus Heaney and John Montague" (1991), reprinted in Claire Connolly (ed), *Theorizing Ireland* (Houndsmills: Palgrave Macmillan, 2003), 41–60.

—, "An Léiriú ar Shaol na mBan in dTéacsanna Dírbheathaisnéise Pheig Sayers", in Máire Ní Chéileachair (ed.), *Peig Sayers Scéalaí 1873–1958* (Baile Átha Cliath: Coiscéim, 1999), 20–57.

Kilfeather, Siobhán, and Éibhear Walshe, "Contesting Ireland: The Erosion of the Heterosexual Consensus, 1940–2001", in Angela Bourke *et al.* (eds.), *Field Day Anthology of Irish Writing Vol. IV: Irish Women's Writing and Traditions* (Cork: Cork University Press, 2002), 1039–41.

O'Toole, Tina. "Narrating the New Woman: The Feminist Fictions of Sarah Grand and George Egerton", unpub. PhD dissertation, University College, Cork, 2001.

Walshe, Éibhear (ed.), *Ordinary People Dancing* (Cork: Cork University Press, 1993).

—, *Sex, Nation and Dissent* (Cork: Cork University Press, 1997).

— (ed.), *Selected Plays of Irish Playwright Teresa Deevy, 1894–1963* (Lewiston: Edwin Mellen Press, 2003).

Introduction

Main aims of the project

This book is the outcome of a research project with a small number of inter-related principal aims. These were: to advance literary and cultural – as distinct from primarily historical – research on the region of Munster over the last two centuries; to enable a new view, as a whole, of the work of women writers, a few well-known, many forgotten or neglected, in this place and time; to juxtapose the work of Irish, English-language and bilingual writers, and thereby help to develop an understanding of the province of Munster as a diverse cultural milieu, and focus on the role of regionality in the process of cultural creation. The Munster Women Writers Project is the first research project of its kind to bring feminist scholarship to bear on the cultural and social work of Irish women writers as a group and in one region, and thus the project makes a unique contribution to literary schol-arship in Ireland.[1]

When once we look at Munster, however tentatively, as a unit in terms of literary history, the truly extraordinary wealth of excellent writings by women in the field of literary fiction and poetry becomes newly visible. From Eibhlín Dubh Ní Chonaill and Edith Somerville to Nuala Ní Dhomh-naill via Elizabeth Bowen, Peig Sayers and Molly Keane, to the Limerick and Clare O'Briens Kate and Edna, and contemporary Cork poet Eiléan Ní Chuilleanáin, to name some of the most distinguished, a striking constella-tion of world-class work has emanated from Munsterwomen. This work involves both of Ireland's vernacular languages, and its authors come from a range of social classes and places: from the subsistence-farming Blasket milieu of Sayers, outstanding twentieth-century performer of narratives in the Irish oral tradition, through the comfortably bourgeois environments of Kate O'Brien and Ní Chuilleanáin, to the native-gentry background of Ní Chonaill, Kerry kinswoman of the Liberator Daniel O'Connell and author of the beautiful eighteenth-century love-lament for her murdered husband Art Ó Laoghaire, and Somerville's, Bowen's and Keane's Big House upbringing in Cork and Waterford amid the slow but terminal decline of their life-world.[2] Confining ourselves for the moment to the literary genres, a further host of somewhat lesser, but often able and lively, writers surrounds these principals, all under-researched and relatively neglected: Una Troy, Teresa Deevy, Eilís Dillon, Katherine Cecil Thurston, L.T. Meade and Regina Maria Roche, to name but a few.

It is to be hoped that this book may stimulate further enquiry into the complex identities of Munster, towards which our list merely gestures. Many interesting cultural questions, and future projects for research and criticism, arise. For instance, Bowen and Kate O'Brien were exact contemporaries whose difference of social milieu markedly separated them in life. Paradoxically, however, both were culturally and geographically amphibious: the Catholic and broadly nationalist O'Brien made her literary life in London, thus following the pattern of generations of Irish writers since 1800 and before, but wrote of the Limerick bourgeoisie, whereas Bowen, the descendant of Cromwellian incomers, constructed a life, an imaginative world, and a cultural appartenance which shifted between southern England (especially the Kent coast and London) and the Co. Cork of her Ascendancy childhood. There are several such paradoxes and parallels to be explored among the interlinked and diverse cohort of writers whose many voices are invoked by this book. In the case of the whole list, one might argue that a focus on the region in which their differing identities were generated might help us to avoid the usual bi-national dualities which bedevil Irish literary – and broader – history; perhaps it is precisely at the level of region that some of the dichotomies which apparently both constitute and fracture Irishness might be both revealed and provisionally resolved.

Bowen's and Keane's novels offer classic representations of the lifestyles, social history and decline of the landed gentry, in their long, in Keane's case mainly retrospective, glance over the period from the land agitations and reforming legislation of the 1880s well into the Free State regime. We believe that by juxtaposing these writings, mostly familiar to mainstream literary history, with other less well-known women's work – literary and other – readers, scholars and critics can gain a much deeper understanding of this extraordinary flourishing of the creative imagination among the daughters of the Ascendancy. We take the view that Somerville, Bowen and Keane are daughters also of Munster, and belong with Peig Sayers, Edna O'Brien and Nuala Ní Dhomhnaill in that region of the imagination, as well as in the physical territory of the province.[3]

On an island where issues of region, location and local community are frequently invoked in any number of contexts, including the discussion of painful political divides, socioeconomic differences, language use, community development and traditional music, it seems curious to us that in Irish literary history there has been so little research specific to region. There are a number of possible reasons for this. Developing from the Revival period and continuing after the foundation of the Irish Free State till at least the 1970s, the western seaboard was privileged in official ideology as the locus of both an Irish imaginary landscape and the origin of an authentic Irish identity, a notion which was powerful and pervasive in the culture of the Republic for a good part of the twentieth century. As a counterpoint to this, the position of Dublin and Dublin-based writers as a kind of cultural magnet in the recent literary history of the island – partly through the concentration on the work of Joyce, but also via the more recent emphasis on the writing of the 1980s Dublin realists – has tended to obscure any examination of the cultural heritage of other parts of the island by instituting a binary perspective. Today, much of the available material dealing with the question of regionalism, specifically in relation to Irish *literature* within the island, appears to relate only to the North of Ireland.[4] This seems to suggest that the literary history and culture of the remaining twenty-six counties is homogeneous, an assumption we hope that this project, in tandem with further research in this field, will help to cast in doubt. By concentrating on Munster in our research, we wish to re-examine a different kind of "hidden Ireland", using the combined perspective of literary and women's history within the region. Furthermore, we hope that our research has raised questions about the influence of location and regionality in the work of these writers which may give materials and direction to further research. Women's social lives, in almost all classes, tend to be more rooted and fixed than those of men, certainly than those of elite male writers; hence the role of place is especially interesting in women's writing.

To answer what may appear to be a remarkably obvious question – yet one raised by many people during the course of the project – Munster is, of course, the southern province of Ireland, and consists of (in alphabetical order) the six counties of Clare, Cork, Kerry, Limerick, Tipperary and Waterford. Clare has often tended to be associated more with the west of Ireland, so its inclusion in this list may be a surprise to some. This example underlines the fact that, as geographers are well aware, rather than being a culturally and socially unified monolith, the province is quite diverse. This research tended to show it as a series of sub-regions, each with their own traditions, from the long-established urban districts of Cork, Limerick and Waterford to the great agricultural heartlands of East Limerick, North Cork and Tipperary, the Golden Vale; from uplands and hinterlands where the Irish language has survived, such as Coolea, Ballyvourney, Corca Dhuibhne and Ring, to the "planted" or planned towns, such as Bandon, Bantry and Mitchelstown. Each of these districts brings with it characteristic inflexions of a shared Irish identity, and in many cases a specific tradition of narrative, derived from song, folktale, family and social history and variations of language, dialect or accent. For many centuries, Munster enjoyed substantial economic prosperity, with a flourishing trade in agricultural exports and a variety of imported goods (and some smuggled) coming in from the south-west of England, as well as from France, Spain and further afield through various points along the coast. Over some centuries before 1800, several port towns grew up around this kind of trade, such as Dungarvan, Youghal, Cobh, Kinsale, Cahersiveen and Dingle, among others. Coming into these towns alongside imported goods were a variety of non-native traditions, cultures, people and tongues (for example the German spoken by Palatine settlers in Co. Limerick and Huguenot French in eighteenth-century Cork.) This is evident in particular in the houses of old Munster families, such as the O'Connell house at Derrynane, Co. Kerry, from where sons were sent to Catholic France and Spain to be educated, bringing back with them continental tastes in furniture, art, political ideas and culture generally. During the eighteenth century, some Munster Catholic families established wealthy merchant dynasties, and the cities saw elegant architectural development and gained a sophisticated civic culture.[5]

Corkery claimed in *The Hidden Ireland* that seventeenth- and eighteenth-century Munster poets turned to address mainland Europe in an attempt imaginatively to bypass English power in Dublin and London.[6] The sturdy continuance of Irish-language literary culture up to the end of the seventeenth century did dwell more or less uneasily alongside the strengthening planter tradition in Munster.[7] Elizabeth Bowen wrote, in tones of romantic retrospection, about Doneraile Court: "The demesne was dear to several Elizabethans – Raleigh, Spenser and Sidney all conversed here, strolling along the lime walk or reclining 'among the coolly shade of the green alders', Edmund Spenser recalls."[8]

Women's cultural work throughout this period also contributes to the region in more diffuse ways. For example, we can discern the development of the planter tradition in women's historical and memoir writing about houses and families from within this milieu itself, such as Castle Freke near Rosscarbery in West Cork, and Bowen's Court in North Cork. The genres of letters, memoirs, history and fiction are all involved in this complex and rich literary development. We have already mentioned its fictional culmination in the famous Big House novels with strongly imagined Munster settings, but as readers of the dictionary can see, a wealth of prior writing leads up to, and can enrich our reception of, these familiar texts.

One might select many individually distinctive aspects of the region. For instance, the port of Cobh was not only a central site in the history of Irish emigration, famine, exile and loss – as is evident in the work of Charlotte Grace O'Brien among many others – but also a Royal Naval base, and one of the few Irish districts included in the Contagious Diseases Acts.[9] Although Cobh has a very distinctive history of its own, the importance of other towns in the region should not be underestimated, particularly in terms of the history of women's writing, towns such as Clonmel, Ennis, Tralee and Skibbereen, as well as the three cities in the region. As we have noted, women's lives were relatively constrained within small local areas by family responsibilities and social mores; in many ways, it is the intimate social history of such towns we find writ large in the narratives of many of the writers included here. Provincial life is rendered particularly memorably in the work of Katherine Cecil Thurston, whose novel *The Fly on the Wheel* (1908) opens with the following setting in Waterford:

> For it is here, in Lady Lane, – a thoroughfare as long and narrow as a continental street, composed of tall, old houses with square-paned windows and mysterious hall doors giving entry to vast and rambling interiors, – that the story, comedy or tragedy, is to find its stage; here, in the dining room of one of the flat-fronted houses, that the student of human nature is to take his first glance at Stephen Carey – hero, so far as middle-class Irish life produces heroes, of the anticipated romance.[10]

The work of writers such as Thurston, along with Kate O'Brien, Una Troy and others, brings to life the social milieu of the Catholic middle classes in mid-twentieth-century Munster, in much the same way as Keane,

Somerville and Ross, and Bowen did the Big House world. The town of Mellick, based on Limerick, plays a central role in most of O'Brien's narratives, and the landscape of the surrounding countryside is depicted particularly clearly in the opening pages of *Without My Cloak* (1931). She captured the essential atmosphere of prosperous middle-class provincial Ireland in the fictional world of the Considine family in that early novel, and, in darker shades, in *The Ante Room* (1934), with its anatomy of moral dysfunctionality and social exploitation. In the late, non-fictional *My Ireland* (1962) she captures the essence of Limerick at mid-century, changed to be sure from her youth, but well before the extensive modernization of later decades:

> Todd's is gone, of course – fine, Victorian Todd's where every stitch that everyone wore was always bought – and charged! And where an old man in a top hat opened the doors [...] Cannock's clock is still above our heads and still keeps time and chime. Lloyd's is ended – all untidy mahogany within, with grapes standing round in barrels of bran, and the air sedative with smells of spilt port and brandy; but a little up the street where once there was a tea merchant's the life-size Chinese mandarin still stands against the old façade. There is a long-shaped kiosk near Tait's Clock that hasn't been repainted since I was twelve years old and where comics are still called *Tiger Tim* and *The Magnet*. And the coachmen on the carriage boxes when the funerals cross the bridge from St Munchin's are the same coachmen of all the generations, as are their horses and their very high top hats. Also Limerick still has, dominating proudly all the new drugstore-style chemists' shops, two lofty marbled mahogany-ed Medical Halls that inspired awe in childhood and still in Victorian calm can do the same through evocation. How peculiar, how delicate the smell of a Medical Hall![11]

A central feature of such settings as these in various writers is the local convent – and again Kate O'Brien's *The Land of Spices* (1941) is a good fictional example of this institution, present without exception in Munster towns. Religious communities form the backdrop for the work of several women writers listed in the dictionary, where the brilliant eccentric Margaret Ann Cusack (better known as "the Nun of Kenmare") joins many less prominent sisters, engaged in writing and publishing prayer books, hymns, church histories and lives of the saints through local and convent printing presses, some in Irish, some in English.

The dictionary as a feminist recovery project

In the last few decades, a number of major feminist projects in many countries have been seeking by original research to make women's contribution to literary culture, in both past and present, more visible. This dictionary is another such project, with the specific regional focus we have already described. As well as gathering brief accounts of the famous figures mentioned above, it recovers the work of heretofore forgotten or neglected female writers. Prompted by a shared background in feminist literary history among the project members, we sought by our research to address questions such as: How can we best develop and enrich the state of knowledge about these writers? What kinds of writings did they produce, and in what genres? Who collected or published their work, when and if it was published; what factors inhibited its non-publication? What prompted them to write, or, a much more difficult question, what may have prevented some from writing and others from writing more? Why do we not know more about them? In taking a feminist approach, we were aware that many of the writers we focused on were working in periods when the surrounding society and culture had a distinctly patriarchal character. We knew that, in line with what research has unquestionably demonstrated concerning the fate of women's work in other locales, especially between 1800 and the latter decades of the last century, women's writing was consistently under-valued and frequently unpublished, that it rarely reached a wide audience and, even when it did, the reputation of the author rarely lasted much longer than a generation or two.[12] In seeking out these local women writers, in publishing short biographies of each of them and in reproducing bibliographies of their writings, we intended to contribute to the continuing process by which women are reinstated as active and vital contributors to Irish literary culture. Many visitors to Ireland, particularly students from abroad, comment on a widely available poster in tourist offices country-wide with pictures of Ireland's great writers, all of them men. Young visiting students often ask: were there no women writers? As the editors and compilers of the *Field Day Anthology Vols. IV and V: Women's Writing and Traditions* have now amply demonstrated, academic literary history and criticism unfortunately tend to replicate the sexism of that poster.[13] If such published literary history is a primary vehicle for current Irish studies, then what happens to groups and identities which have been rendered wholly or partly invisible in the mainstream culture, and have little or no officially sanctioned voice? In compiling this dictionary we have sought to answer these questions, and to provide interesting and easily accessible material for those who wish to hear some of those muted voices. We have put in place some of the stepping stones necessary for future researchers, scholars and readers to explore in more depth the work of these writers and, in so doing, to question the master narratives of Irish literary history.

Other larger enterprises, such as the Irish Women's History Project, in addition to a number of individual and local research projects, have focused critical attention on the importance of feminist research for the field of Irish studies. Contemporary scholarship such as that of Angela Bourke, Gerardine Meaney, Ailbhe Smyth, Margaret Kelleher, Anne Fogarty, Eavan Boland, Christine St Peter and Elizabeth Butler Cullingford has opened up the field of literary and cultural criticism on this island to feminist scrutiny. Yet, despite the major contribution made by feminism to the intellectual, literary and political traditions of Ireland, as Margaret Kelleher has noted: "Irish studies as a discipline remains singularly ill-informed of (and by) the debates and concerns that have occupied Irish feminist criticism in the past decade."[14] Within Irish literary scholarship, it is important that we maintain a focus on feminist aims, both to stimulate ideological diversity and to redress the structure dividing "writing" (i.e. mainstream or men's work) from "women's writing" (received as a kind of supplement). Furthermore, searching for women's part in Irish literary history *and* in contemporary culture, studies such as this mean to provoke interesting questions about the very categories "women" and "Irish women", and thus challenge what Gerardine Meaney has described as "the generalisation of all Irish women into one type, one history, one 'figure'",[15] instead recovering the differences between women on this island. In this sense, by focusing on the work of Munster women as active cultural producers and agents, the dictionary develops the resistance in Irish feminist thought to the appropriation of Irish femininity evident in Mother Ireland, Róisín Dubh and the other such stereotyped constructions which dominate the representation of femininity in Irish writing.

One of the realities facing any researcher working on the recovery of women's work from earlier time periods is that much of the documentary evidence of this work has disappeared. As elsewhere, Munster women writers during the nineteenth century frequently presented their work for publication using male pseudonyms, such as George Egerton (Mary Chavelita Dunne), or used ambiguous initials, such as L.T. (Elizabeth Thomasina) Meade, and others still left their work unsigned, which has made it difficult to know whether or not "Anonymous" is a woman writer. During the early nineteenth century, most Munsterwomen had no access to books and couldn't read; some didn't speak English. Literacy skills themselves, and, much more, the confidence and the material resources to write and to attempt publication of one's work, were limited to a small proportion of the privileged classes, attributes of a particular rank in the earlier period of our study. In the case of Irish-language lore, stories, poems, prayers and songs, of course, oral transmission was common, and many districts of Munster possessed a rich vein of such traditional creation. It is important to acknowledge the different configuration of verbal skill and creativity between written and oral traditions and conventions, and the relative difficulty and indeed questionable desirability of identifying oral material with the figures of individual performers. The "writer" – oral performer – of such "texts" is as much channel as originator of the poem, song, or stories transmitted by her agency.[16] Furthermore, the process of collection for the Irish Folklore Commission was itself dominated by men: of 300 collectors in Co. Cork, mainly in the period 1930–60, fewer than fifty were women.[17] Commenting on the "male orientation" of this enterprise, Gearóid Ó Crualaoich has observed:

> Since folklore is an expression of the popular world-view of both women and men [...] and since much folklore is gender-specific for both genders, it follows that the female side of [...] folklore is severely under-represented in the archive. (926)

For reasons of both class and gender disadvantage, we decided it was important in the earlier period of our list to note unpublished works – diaries, journals, letters and of course women's recorded contributions to the oral tradition in Irish – in the dictionary. For example, we include Eliza Dalton (1796–1874) for her 1853 letter to emigrants Ned and Johanna Hogan from Co. Tipperary, which gives us a vivid glimpse of the social history of that period, as well as of the concerns of a mother for her own emigrant son. We also mention the unpublished diaries of a number of Quaker women, collected by the Dublin Friends' Historical Library, such as Jane Abell's (1787–1852) spiritual diary, and the journal of Elizabeth Clibborn (1780–1861), kept from 1807 to 1818. This provides a social diary of the Quaker community in Munster during the early years of the nineteenth century, as the Clibborns' house in Clonmel was a convenient resting-point for Quakers travelling to meetings in various parts of the region. The journal also gives us insights into a woman's experience of the world and sense of her life-prospects at that time. For example, in 1810 she wrote: "I am thirty years of age, it is an awful consideration, even if it should be a long life the prime is over" (42). Including unpublished writers such as these, and the later jail journals of women such as Hannah Moynihan from her period of internment in Kilmainham in 1923, enables us to come nearer to realizing how many different kinds of writing women have done over the past 200 years.

Those who did break through the barriers which the patriarchal system put around women's aspirations and efforts to write and publish often did so because of encouragement from within their communities, such as the Quaker women mentioned above who often began writing by taking the minutes at their meetings according to the Friends' tradition of equality, at a time when literacy skills were not always considered a priority among female members of the family. In other cases, women perhaps began to write because female relatives were writers of one kind or another. This affords an example of the direct influence of female role models on women's aspirations towards cultural activity and self-expression. Sometimes, women found a way into writing through the initially ancillary role of editing the letters of their ancestors or writing a biography of a well-known family member. For example, the first literary venture of Mary Carbery (1867–1949), author of the distinguished memoir *The Farm by Lough Gur* (1923) and of a novel, was the editing of diaries written by Elizabeth Freke (1641–1714), who, like Mary herself, was an Englishwoman who married into the Carbery family. Elizabeth Freke's experiences of married life and West Cork were not entirely happy: her diary was sub-titled "Some Few Remembrances of My Misfortuns which have Attended Me in my Unhappy Life since I were Marryed: whc was Novemer the 14, 1671". This work inspired Mary Carbery to keep a journal of her own, which she began following her husband's death. This remained unpublished until 1998, when her grandson edited and published it.

Given that the most recent adult-literacy report carried out in this country tells us that 25 per cent of the adult population have literacy difficulties, perhaps the issue of who has access to literacy and to books of any kind, let alone the literary institution, is not confined to the distant past.[18] Women are still placed lower than men in terms of earning power and on various indexes of social deprivation. Despite the relative exclusion of the poor from the whole social system of writing and publication, not all of the works mentioned in the dictionary are located either within the confines of the gentry estate, or among the middle-class milieu experienced and represented by convent-educated authors. This, of course, is particularly true of the Irish-language writers and oral performers who are recorded in the dictionary and who, certainly in the earlier periods, are overwhelmingly of rural origin, many from places remote from the city, such as the Beara peninsula or West Waterford. Especially in the past thirty years, we find a much wider range of settings in the fictional works of women writers, including those coming from social spaces outside the "mainstream". Maeve Kelly's description of a Travellers' encampment in the 1980s, in her classic story "Orange Horses", is an example:

> Elsie leaned on the caravan door while she spoke, staring out at the twisted remains of a bicycle, a rusty milk churn, a variety of plastic containers, three goats, two piebald ponies, all tethered to an iron stake, and a scattering of clothes hanging on the fence that separated her domain from the town dump.[19]

On the whole, however, representations of urban working-class, Traveller and of some ethnic minorities – particularly those from within refugee and asylum-seeker communities – are still slender enough within the published work of these women writers. As Borbála Faragó has noted, this may in part be due to a lack of dialogue between the "mainstream" and the marginal in Irish culture more generally.[20] However, we are beginning to catch initial glimpses of such counter-cultural writing, and over the next twenty years this may prove to be a whole new area of development within women's writing in Ireland, in Munster as elsewhere.

The dictionary consists essentially of an alphabetical list of Munster women writers working, whether in Irish or English, in the period 1800–2000.[21] Each writer's entry is made up of two sections: a biographical note, detailing her life, and a bibliography, or list of her works. As can be seen from the following example, the name of the author is given first, followed by her dates, the place in Munster with which she is associated and a list of the genres – or kinds of writing – she worked in:

Clerke, Ellen Mary. 1840–1906. Skibbereen, Co. Cork. Poetry, religious writing, journalism, science.

Some writers have written under a pen-name, and, where this is the case, the pseudonym is followed in brackets by her given name. Following this top line, then, is a biography, which in most cases is brief:

> Older sister of the astronomer Agnes Clerke, she was also born in Skibbereen. She lived with Agnes in Italy from 1870 to 1877, and while there

studied Italian language and culture, contributing short stories in Italian to periodicals in Florence. She also published essays and studies, translated Italian poetry into English in the original metre and contributed to Garnett's *History of Italian Literature* (1898). She was a talented musician, particularly noted for her guitar playing. Her understanding of the religious and political discourses of the Europe of her day became apparent in her later writing. Ellen also had an intellectual interest in astronomy, although geology was her specialism. A member of the Manchester Geographical Society, she contributed to their *Journal*.

On moving to London, she began to write for the London Catholic magazine, *The Tablet*, and became known as a writer of religious poetry. Her collection, *The Flying Dutchman, and Other Poems* (1881), was her best-known work. Her association with *The Tablet* continued throughout her life, and she wrote a weekly leader on Catholic activities abroad for the last twenty years of her life. She also published articles in German, Italian and Arabic for other newspapers and journals.

Like her sister, Ellen Clerke was also interested in science, and her pamphlets, "Jupiter and His System" and "The Planet Venus", contributed to the literature of popular astronomy in the late nineteenth century. Ellen contributed entries to the *Dictionary of National Biography* on Mary Somerville and others. One article written by her in *Observatory* combines her interest in astronomy with her knowledge of Arabic – examining links between Arabian astronomical observations and the mathematical process Algol.

Then follows a list of the main writings of this author, which includes information about the genres within which she worked:

Select bibliography:

Clerke, Ellen Mary.

—. *The Flying Dutchman, and Other Poems*. Poetry. London: Satchell, 1882.
—. *Jupiter and His System*. Science. London: Edward Stanford, 1892.
—. *The Planet Venus*. Science. London: Witterby, 1893.
—. *History of Italian Literature*. Poetry, translations. Ed. R. Garrett. N.p.: n.p., 1898.
—. *Fable and Song in Italy*. Poetry, translations. London: Grant Richards, 1899.
—. *Flowers of Fire*. Novel. London: Hutchinson, 1902.

The final part of the dictionary entry is a list of secondary sources, a list of the main works written by others *about* the writer in question – these may be biographical or scholarly works on their writing:

Secondary Sources

Huggins, Lady Margaret. *Agnes Mary Clerke and Ellen Mary Clerke, An Appreciation*. N.p.: self-published, 1907.

Our aim was to include rather than exclude useful information about each writer. We wanted to recover knowledge of, and attract interest to, the work of women whose writing lives have, in many cases, been hidden from history, rather than creating another more or less exclusive canon. Concerning the question of place, the geographical criteria for inclusion were frequently discussed at our meetings and seminars. Who could and could not reasonably be considered a Munster writer? There are of course scores of women writers for whom this question did not arise, who were born, lived and worked here all their lives. In other cases, we took a decision to include both those who were born and brought up in the province, but then went to live abroad or elsewhere in Ireland, and those who came here from abroad to live and work for any significant period of time, long enough to have been influenced by a place in Munster, or who made long stays on a regular basis: anyone whom we felt to have taken some area of the region into their mental and imaginative life, and contributed in turn to its cultural imaginary. We therefore defined two categories of inclusion: place of birth and place of association. We decided for or against the inclusion of an individual figure based on the existence of such a real influence as we have defined: did the author's own sense of regional identity, or her use of language, knowledge of local customs and stories, education or background in local history and culture, or the social group or milieu she moved in, or the material reality of the landscape itself leave a mark on her writing? For example, George Egerton (Mary Chavelita Dunne), whose 1893 collection *Keynotes*, an important contribution to the "New Woman" literature at the end of the nineteenth century, was written and published while she was living in Millstreet, Co. Cork, is included, as elements of the local landscape and oral popular culture are clearly discernible in her work. Where earlier writers were concerned, it sometimes proved impossible to trace biographical information as to specific regional background, which partly relates to the ways in which women felt constrained to conceal their origins, as well as their gender identities, when overcoming strong taboos against female appearance in the public domain. At the other end of the scale, in the writing scene of the late 1990s and early 2000s, we invited female writers with strong Munster connections to fill out a questionnaire, and thus self-identify as Munster, or not. Most chose to do so, though there was a minority who did not.

   In terms of genre, a wide range of different kinds of writing is listed in the dictionary (see Appendix 1 for a full list of genres). Apart from such obvious categories as "novels", "poetry", "plays" and "short stories", we used more specific headings where there were a number of texts in a sub-genre, including "historical novels" (such as Deborah Alcock's 1871 *The Spanish Brothers*), "family history" (like Olga Bonaparte-Wyse's 1969 *The Spurious Brood*) and "travel writing" (such as Suzanne R. Day's 1933 *Where the Mistral Blows*). The aim of this is to make it easier for the reader or researcher to locate titles by an individual author within a specific area. Thus, for example, if a scholar is interested only in the plays of Máirín Cregan, they can easily isolate these works within her bibliography. We used more general headings such as "academic writing" to cover many diverse areas of the work of scholars, mainly contemporary. Similarly, we employed the category "political writing" to refer broadly to *all* kinds of writing within the political sphere, such as socialist, republican and feminist writings, as well as those relating to affairs of government and public policy. We might make a broader point here: there is a tendency, not confined to Irish historiography, to imagine that "women don't do politics", and especially that they scarcely stretch to political writing; much material in this book gives the lie to this view, as we shall see. This category contains works such as Anna Haslam's 1898 "Irishwomen and the Local Government Act", Mary MacSwiney's 1932 *Poblacht na hÉireann: The Republic of Ireland* and social activist Sr Stanislaus Kennedy's 1996 *Focus on Residential Child Care in Ireland*.

We also wished to reflect the diversity of the material, and so, in addition to published books, we have included radio plays, documentaries, film scripts and journalism. Some aspects of women's literary work cannot be strictly described as textual, which reflects the difficulty of access to formal culture often experienced even by creative women. For this reason, in the case of English-language writers we have used the category "folklore" to describe some of this material. We have listed songwriters such as Eibhlís Uí Chróinín (Bess Cronin) and Nóirín Ní Nuadháin, among others, in the dictionary. We wished not to confine the range of reference to "high" literature: given the importance of popular creative acts and of domestic production in the repertoire of women's roles, we included the categories "cookbooks", "handcrafts" and "manuals", in recognition of the fact that these too are part of the cultural and social work that women do. With regard to writing for children, we divided this important category into three distinct categories, to register how the genre has changed over time. The general categories of "children's writing" is here, but we have also included "young adult fiction" and the category "fiction for girls", which refers to the particular late-nineteenth- and early-twentieth-century sub-genre of stories written for adolescent girls, of which girls' school stories are a prominent part.

There has been a tendency in literary scholarship to see women's writing as being confined to a small range of genres to the exclusion of others. However, browsing entries at random lets the reader see that these writers have covered a surprising variety of genres, not just collectively, but often in the case of an individual. There are poetry and novels, but also journalism, science writing, memoirs, diaries and letters, travel and religious writing as well as writing for children, manuals and educational works, and political writing. For example, the very prolific late-nineteenth-century novelist L.T. Meade has tended to be dismissed as "merely" a writer of schoolgirl fiction, yet she also wrote extensively across the genres of fiction for adults, including several works which can only be characterized as "social protest" fiction. Thus, the dictionary demonstrates clearly that women in Ireland, even in one province, have been and are much more versatile contributors to culture than is sometimes supposed.

The sheer amount of material we uncovered as the project progressed surprised us greatly. We have already mentioned some of the best-known poets and novelists, but there are scores of others, ranging between the internationally known, such as the travel writer Dervla Murphy, and authors of nationally popular reminiscences, such as Alice Taylor. Some are playwrights – Teresa Deevy, Una Troy, Margaret O'Leary, Geraldine Cummins, Susanne

R. Day and the contemporary Lahinch playwright Ursula Rani Sarma. There are prolific and influential writers of fiction for children such as Patricia Lynch, Eilís Dillon, Mary Arrigan and Bernadette Leach; children's literature is a genre which extends that vital work of acculturation which is begun in the home, and in which mothers still take the major part. Then there is a variety of other kinds of writers – journalists, sociologists, philosophers, historians, literary critics, writers of cookbooks, as well as the diarists and letter-writers mentioned above. Where a publication was unseen, or we had no other information about it, we have left the 'genre' field blank.

Several Munster writers were remarkable travellers. The many and geographically wide-ranging works of Dervla Murphy, Kate O'Brien's writing on Spain and Bowen's on Rome are possibly the best-known examples of such work. But we also found that the Wilmot sisters from Glanmire were well-known travellers in the early nineteenth-century, in mainland Europe and on into Russia, where they stayed for some time in 1803 at the court of Princess Daschkaw. Throughout their journeys they kept diaries, and also wrote letters home describing their travels and the people they encountered. Their maid Eleanour Cavanagh also wrote letters home to her father in Cork in 1805, giving us a different class perspective on Europe in the early nineteenth century. Other travel writers became familiar names in the countries they settled in, such as Daisy Bates, who emigrated from Roscrea, Co. Tipperary, to Australia in the 1880s and became an anthropologist and expert on the indigenous tribes of northwest Australia.

It is worth noting here that some of the nineteenth- and early-twentieth-century writers listed worked in less traditional areas, such as science. The best-known of these, Agnes Clerke (1842–1907) from Skibbereen, was a celebrated scientist of the nineteenth century, achieving fame as an astronomer. Cynthia Longfield (1896–1991) from Cloyne in Co. Cork became an experienced entomologist whose particular interest and area of knowledge was the dragonfly. Longfield travelled widely during the 1920s and 1930s, participating in many expeditions, where her sense of adventure and survival skills came to the fore. One of her trips was an expedition to the Pacific Ocean in 1924 which replicated Darwin's journey. Ellen Hutchins (1785–1815) from Bantry suffered much illness as a child, and she was encouraged by a family friend, Whitley Stokes, a keen naturalist, to take up botany in order to give her a healthy outdoor hobby. She went on to meet many leading botanists of the day – such as James Townsend Mackay, curator of Trinity's first botanic garden in Ballsbridge. Mackay encouraged her growing interest in collecting and identifying specimens, and she became an expert on mosses, lichens, liverwort and particularly seaweed. Because women were discouraged from publishing their own scientific findings during this period, Hutchins's discoveries were passed on to her male peers for publication in their studies (a pattern echoed in the collection of narratives and other material in the Irish tradition; see Réamhrá). Nonetheless, she is credited with having written many reports on particular species in their publications, and several species bear her name – such as the *Hutchinsia* alpine flowering plant. Even after her death, the algae expert, William Henry Harvey, based some of his drawings in *Phycologia Britannica* (1846–61) on her work, and he credits her with finding and recording a number of new species. As a child, Mary Everest already had a serious interest in mathematics which led her to continue her study of calculus by herself, using her father's books. In 1850 when visiting her uncle and aunt in West Cork she was introduced to the mathematician George Boole, whom she married five years later. She attended her husband's lectures at the then Queen's College Cork (which were, of course, officially open only to men at that time), and edited his *Laws of Thought*. She went on to become a teacher and writer of science textbooks for children, such as *The Preparation of the Child for Science* (1904). She described herself as a mathematical psychologist, who made efforts to analyse how people might learn, or be taught, mathematics and science – and she invented curve stitching, or string geometry, in order to teach children the geometry of angles and spaces. Her daughters both became well known in their own fields: Alicia Boole Stott became a mathematician and Ethel was later well known as the fiction writer E.L. Voynich, which in some ways underlines the point we made earlier about role models.

There have been several female political writers in Munster, starting with Anna Doyle Wheeler's move to France to join a group of socialists and free thinkers in 1816. Wheeler was a close friend of Jeremy Bentham, the utilitarian leader. Dooley describes her at this point in her life as: "a translator, a collaborator between French and English co-operators, a liaison person facilitating introductions to both Owen and Fourier, and a diplomatic ombudswoman among highly competitive men" (71). Today, Wheeler is probably best known for her collaboration with William Thompson on the first socialist feminist manifesto, *Appeal of One-Half the Human Race, Women, Against the Pretensions of the Other Half, Men, to Retain Them in Political and thence in Civil and Domestic Slavery* (1825). Although her name is not given as co-author of this work, Thompson explains in the introduction, a "Letter to Mrs. Wheeler", that the project was a joint effort: "our joint property, I being your interpreter and the scribe of your sentiments" (xxiii). This explanation of the kind of project undertaken by Thompson and Wheeler acknowledges Wheeler's part in it, and does set out her intellectual contribution to the finished work, though in terms which themselves unconsciously reveal contemporary assumptions about the limited capacity of women to be the authors of thought (the implication is that Wheeler needed Thompson to "interpret" her thinking, while this is described as "sentiments", also a somewhat stereotypical characterization of women's ideas). We know, however, that she actually did write some sections of the *Appeal*, and Wheeler's arguments and ideas were well known to those in the cooperative movement in the period, and would have been recognizable as hers to those familiar with her work, even in the sections actually composed by Thompson.

Another political writer, Anna Haslam (1829–1922), came from a middle-class Quaker background in Youghal, Co. Cork. Described by her contemporaries as "one of the giants of the women's cause" (Cullen, 161), she founded the Dublin Women's Suffrage Association in 1876. She was involved in every first-wave campaign for women's rights in Ireland and her work as an organizer and a leader within the feminist movement was widely recognized. Haslam's contribution to politics in Ireland has been discussed by Munster historian Carmel Quinlan.[22]

In the 1920s, sisters Cis and Jo Power from Tralee were members of the Kerry branch of Cumann na mBan. As Republicans, they actively opposed the Treaty and co-edited a Republican newsletter, *The Invincible*, during the Civil War. They were interned in Kilmainham along with their cousin Han Moynihan, another *Invincible* writer, and during their imprisonment they kept a jail journal with the somewhat alarming title of "Blaze Away with Your Little Gun: A Memoir of Three Jails". Thus, just as we find a diversity of subject matter among these writers, their political and ideological motivation to write is equally varied.

Compiling the dictionary

The key editorial decisions during the compilation of the dictionary were all made in consultation with the panel of literary historians and critics from Ireland and Britain who helped to oversee the project, and we also benefited from the advice and assistance of a wider international group of scholars.[23] Exchanges with international research projects working in the same field proved enormously helpful, as was the contribution of expert bibliographers who came to the workshop on bibliographical work and feminist literary research during our 2001 international conference on Munster women writers at University College Cork. The project also benefited from study visits made to the Centre for Editorial and Intertextual Research at Cardiff University, the Fawcett Women's Library (now the National Women's Library) in London and the Canadian Women's Movement Archive at Ottawa University.

After some initial discussion about the form our research would take, we ruled out, as beyond our resources, an attempt to produce an anthology of writings and agreed to construct a biographical dictionary. The book is intended to have a range of uses: in it, readers, scholars, local historians and students can follow up their various interests and gain more knowledge and understanding of the contexts within which the writers they admire or wish to study lived and worked. We have tacitly acknowledged the spectrum of achievement, in terms of literary and intellectual quality as well as of sheer quantity of production, among the writers, by providing more extended or briefer biographical notes. The information provided also, of course, reflects the sometimes very scant facts available. We hope that the dictionary will act as a base and an incentive for the subsequent researches of others. We have already argued that the juxtaposition of well known and largely unknown figures is itself useful: for instance, the information we provide about playwright Margaret O'Leary will help the development of critical thinking about the better known work of Teresa Deevy, plays by both were written and performed in the same period.

We approached the category "writer" with some flexibility, being aware, as noted above, of the problems women faced in all but the most recent decade or two in being accorded the status of authorship. Very many women writing in the nineteenth and even up to the mid- twentieth century encountered formidable difficulties in this respect, and the related phenomenon of writers producing work which was promising but small in extent also needed to be acknowledged. For instance, there were authors of able short stories in periodicals such as *The Bell* who had never published a full-length collection.[24] However, in the case of late-twentieth-century authors we tried to adhere to the "one published work" guideline as a minimum criterion for inclusion, given the far more favourable circumstances of publication. The question posed itself differently in relation to academic writers. We wished to give as representative an account as possible of the range of women writing in diverse areas in the current period, and academic writing in many fields tends to appear in specialist journals rather than full-length studies. In these cases we set the minimum at three essays or articles in well known journals.

An important question arises for bibliographers in relation to material listed in such a dictionary as this: were the publications "seen" or "unseen"? In other words, did those of us listing the books actually hold a copy of the article or book in our hands before we wrote it down in the list? The most desirable procedure is only to list "seen" material, so that one can be sure the book actually exists and was not, for example, merely listed in a list of forthcoming publications but either never completed or not in the event published. However, given the short time frame for our project, and our limited labour force, we decided to include some "unseen" material, such as titles listed in the National Library catalogue, for example, or in other reputable library lists.

The assembling of facts in any empirical project such as this is, of course, error-prone. We encountered much variation among our sources in, for example, dates and in the form and spelling of names, while carrying out the primary research and cross-checking in different sources. Some sources conflated two distinct authors into one entry because of a similarity in their names. We found that such errors and inaccuracies were particularly common where online databases were concerned, an important point in an era when electronic sources are relied on for so much basic information. We have endeavoured to arrive at correct dates and places of origin for all of our authors, but in a work of this nature, with several hundred individual listings, it is unfortunately probable that we ourselves may have either perpetuated other people's mistakes or introduced others of our own.

Sources used

One of the main aims of this research has been to make available the tools for further reading and work in the field. Our approach is not to see the dictionary as an end in itself, but rather as a future-oriented research resource for scholars, students and critics, both of literary history and literary criticism in general, as well as those interested in women's social, and cultural history. Thus, in addition to the entries themselves, the list of documentary sources used will, we hope, contribute to the knowledge base for any scholar in the field of Irish literary and cultural enquiry (see Works Cited). Additional resources include a list of libraries and archives (see Appendix 2) and a list of selected web addresses relating to this field (Appendix 3).

In briefly addressing some methodological issues relating to the research, we also hope to provide here a series of signposts for future research in the field. Most of the sources we consulted during the project were documentary, and involved time spent at computer screens, in library stacks, working through card catalogues and newspaper archives, or excavating library collections not yet fully catalogued and in cardboard boxes. However, we soon realized that not all the information we sought to collect was available in the public domain, and that in order to get beyond a name to a corpus of writing, in the case of less well known writers, we had to rely on oral or written information from people living locally in an area who were able to connect up the publications with the life histories. The research process itself was a collaborative one, and the informants consulted throughout were invaluable as sources both of information and of support to those of us directly engaged in the work. Following the initial meeting with our advisory panel, we compiled a questionnaire for the project (see Appendix 4), which we distributed widely and posted on a variety of websites (listed in Appendix 3). We initially carried out research in the local studies sections of libraries in Limerick, Waterford, Cork, Kerry, Clare and Tipperary, where the librarians were willing and invaluable sources of information, much of which is unavailable elsewhere. Through these and a variety of other contacts, and those within our panel, we gained the assistance of scholars both locally and internationally who had worked or were working on specific writers, such as Una Troy, or on areas of women's history such as the membership of Cumann na mBan, and gradually lists of further informants and further sources of information grew. Our editors did broadcast interviews on local radio and Radio na Gaeltachta at different times during the lifetime of the project, and the project was also covered in the national press. Material consulted in larger libraries – at the National Library of Ireland, the British Library, the Fawcett Women's Library (now the National Women's Library) in London, the Quaker library at Swanbrook in Dublin and the RTÉ Sound Archive – helped us to make further local links relating to individual authors (see Appendix 2 for further information). The practice followed by some authors of signing the introduction to a work and also naming the place where they were based at the time of writing gave us leads about places of association. We also contacted local writers' groups and centres throughout the region, independent scholars, booksellers, publishers, local historians, journalists and many contemporary Munster women writers, among others, all of whom pointed us in the direction of writings and biographical material on authors. As the project developed, local interest in it grew, and we gradually built up a large correspondence, as a result of which the research has benefited from the knowledge, advice and hospitality of a wide range of people both at home and abroad. The network of those who have contributed to the project stretches from Copenhagen to Schull, from Philadelphia to Dunmore East and from Burgos to Lahinch, taking in a considerable number of other places along the way.

In the initial stages of the project, we consulted existing dictionaries such as Hogan's *Dictionary of Irish Literature* (1979, 1996), Welch's *Oxford Companion to Irish Literature* (1996), Brown's *Guide to Books in Ireland* (1912, 1969) and *Ireland in Fiction* (1919, 1968). In comparison to these expansive works, at first glance the slight paperback dictionaries produced by Cleeve in the late 1960s seemed to hold out little promise, but in fact they proved some of the most reliable and useful sources. Similarly, the much earlier *Cabinet of Irish Literature* anthology, particularly the fourth volume, edited by Katharine Tynan (1905), turned up vital pieces of biographical information about many women authors not represented in later and apparently more comprehensive sources. More general works of reference such as *Burke's Irish Family Records* (1976) and Cross's *The Royal Literary Fund 1790–1918* (1984), as well as local histories of the various towns and counties, also proved helpful. Specialist works such as Butler's *Irish Botanical Illustrators and Flower Painters* (2000) and Leland's *The Lie of the Land: Journeys through Literary Cork* (1999) threw up some interesting leads. Where we derive information from an already published source, we have cited this source and listed it in the Works Cited section at the back.

A number of dictionaries specifically of women's writing were consulted, such as Buck's *Bloomsbury Guide to Women's Literature* (1992), McBreen's *The White Paper/An Bhilleog Bhán: Twentieth-Century Irish Women Poets* (1999), and Owens Weekes's *Unveiling Treasures: The Attic Guide to the Published Works of Irish Women Literary Writers* (1993), as well as many literary anthologies such as Madden Simpson's *Woman's Part: An Anthology of Short Fiction by and about Irish Women, 1890–1960* (1984), and Kelly's *Pillars of the House* (1987, 1997). One of the key resources was Colman's *Dictionary of Nineteenth-Century Irish Women Poets* (1996). This was useful to us in practical terms, but it also provided us with a rigorously researched model for our own work in this field. In addition to published dictionaries, many local libraries hold their own lists of local authors and their works which are compiled in-house and, as we have noted, these proved invaluable to our research, as they list many otherwise obscure authors who were connected with a given locality.

With regard to Irish feminist literary scholarship, our work drew on a number of sources, some of which we have already mentioned. B.G.

MacCarthy's pioneering study *The Female Pen: Women Writers, Their Contribution to the Novel* (1944, 1994) bears the distinction, along with a few other texts, of being both an entry in the dictionary and a reference point for our research.[25] In terms of more recent research, volumes IV and V of the *Field Day Anthology of Irish Writing* unfortunately only appeared at the very concluding stage of this project, which meant that the overall direction taken by our research was determined in the absence of this very valuable contribution to scholarship in this field. However, we have revisited our writer entries in the light of any new information made available by the new volumes and made a few appropriate revisions. In printing excerpts from the work of so many women writers which has been unavailable for many generations, the contribution of *Field Day Vols. IV* and *V* to further scholarship in this field cannot be overstated. More importantly, in calling attention to the ways in which the canon of Irish writing has been constructed and maintained, and in the interrogation of the kinds of material which constitute Irish women's textual production – from letters and diaries to songs to Big House novels to science and journalism – many of the decisions we made relating to the inclusions in this dictionary find common cause with those of the *Field Day Anthology* project. For readers interested in engaging with the current field of Irish feminist literary research, Margaret Kelleher's recent essay in *Irish Review* 30 (2003) provides a thorough history of publications in this field.

Apart from these sources, many other monographs, literary-critical essays and books, as well as writer biographies and autobiographies, were consulted, as well as other publications too numerous to mention. We drew on a number of online sources, such as local history websites, and corresponded with those maintaining them, which proved very fruitful to our research (a full list of these sources, and further information about cognate international projects, is available in Appendix 3). Working on a research project of this scale, despite the geographically circumscribed nature of the coverage, can induce a sense of being overwhelmed by the sheer masses of information. Yet, while we aspired to totality of coverage, no doubt we have missed much in the course of the research. We hope others will fill these gaps and make productive and various uses of the material we have made available.

In conclusion, we hope that this volume will make an important contribution to our knowledge of the history of writing in the southern region of Ireland over the past 200 years. The presence of this detailed local study will increase the visibility and reputation of Munster's culture and creativity. It also illuminates the role in that culture of women from many different social backgrounds, places and communities in the region, as well as juxtaposing the work of Irish and English-language writers in the province, and focusing on issues of regionality in the creative process.

Notes

1 We kept close contact throughout this research with the other strands of the 2000–2003 Women and Irish Society Project at UCC, where colleagues from other disciplines were working on the history of the second-wave Irish Women's Movement 1970–90, and on women and work in Munster 1930–60. The project was funded by the state's Programme for Research in Third-Level Institutions, as detailed in the Foreword, above. Project outcomes have included seminars, international conferences, an exhibition, and *Documenting Irish Feminisms*, ed. Linda Connolly and Tina O'Toole (Dublin: Woodfield Press, 2004). For further information, see the project website at www.ucc.ie/wisp.

2 The classic lament performed by Eibhlín Dubh falls just before the starting date of our research: her husband Art Ó Laoghaire was murdered in the 1770s.

3 Despite the recent contestation in some quarters of the Irishness of Bowen, in particular (see *Irish Times* letters page, 17 May 2004).

4 The model of Ulster identities proposed by poet John Hewitt could be one inspiration for such future cultural work. John Wilson Foster's *Forces and Themes in Ulster Fiction* (Dublin: Gill & Macmillan, 1974) and *Across a Roaring Hill: Northern Ireland and the Protestant Imagination*, ed. Gerald Dawe and Edna Longley (Belfast: Blackstaff, 1985), are examples of regional criticism. The case of the province of Ulster, paradoxically as a result of the very febrile contestation of identities there, has prompted a cultivation of regional consciousness, in part as an antidote to the divisions in the polity.

5 See Maureen Wall's classic essay on "The Rise of a Catholic Middle Class in Eighteenth-Century Ireland", in Gerard O'Brien and Tom Dunne (eds.), *Catholic Ireland in the Eighteenth Century* (Dublin: Geography Publications, 1989), 73–84.

6 Yet it is also true that the distinguished work in Irish of Co. Limerick poet Dáibhí Ó Bruadair repeatedly celebrates marriages in the later seventeenth century between young people from the two traditions, Irish or Hiberno-Norman and New English.

7 On the flourishing of Irish poetry in non-syllabic metres in this period, despite the large-scale destruction of the Gaelic order, see Breandán Ó Buachalla, *Na Stíobhartaigh agus an t-Aos Léinn* (Baile Átha Cliath: An Clóchomhar, 1996). Toby Barnard has vividly described the culture of improvement among increasingly well-to-do Munster Protestants during the seventeenth and early eighteenth century (see "Gardening, diet and 'improvement' in later 17th-century Ireland". *Journal of Garden History* 10 (1990): 71–85). His trenchant observation that "the English might garden while the Irish starved" pinpoints the social injustices of landlord culture and prefigures the structure of marked inequities between richer and poorer parts of Munster replicated in later periods, not always with the same ethnic character as in the seventeenth century (xx).

8 *Bowen's Court* (London: Longmans, 1942), 4. The importance to Bowen of Spenser's writing, and of his example as a North Munster writer and planter, is echoed in the revisiting and interrogation of the paradoxes of his combined cultural and political roles, together with that of English incomers in Munster generally, in academic work by Munster academics Eiléan Ní Chuilleanáin, Patricia Coughlan and Anne Fogarty, and more particularly in Ní Chuilleanáin's remarkable poetry, which explores connections between the two poles of colonized Munster and native topographical, poetic and Catholic traditions.

9 These 1864 Acts were a response to the devastating effects of venereal disease on British troop strength during the Crimean War. The Acts enabled the

compulsory examination and hospitalization for three months of any woman suspected of being a prostitute in "protected districts" (i.e. areas around army and naval barracks, such as Cobh and the Curragh). Any woman found alone in these areas late at night could be committed on the evidence of a policeman for examination, which meant that any unchaperoned woman was a legitimate target of the Acts.

10 Katherine Cecil Thurston, *The Fly on the Wheel* (London: Blackwood, 1908), 1–2.

11 Kate O'Brien, *My Ireland* (London: Batsford, 1962), 30–31.

12 A point underscored in feminist literary criticism such as Janet Todd, *The Sign of Angelica: Women, Writing and Fiction 1660–1800* (London: Virago, 1989); Margaret Ezell, *Writing Women's Literary History* (Baltimore: John's Hopkins University Press, 1993); Susie Tharu and K. Lalita, *Women Writing in India* (London: Pandora, 1991).

13 *Field Day Anthology of Irish Literature Vols. IV and V: Irish Women's Writing and Traditions*, ed. Angela Bourke *et al.* (Cork: Cork University Press, 2002).

14 Margaret Kelleher, "The *Field Day Anthology* and Irish Women's Literary Studies", *The Irish Review* 30 (2003): 82–94.

15 Gerardine Meaney, "Writing the Unread: Canons, Anthologies, and Feminist Editing", Contemporary Feminist Scholarship and Irish Women's Writing Panels, IASIL NUI Galway, 21 July 2004.

16 This is exemplified primarily in the Irish-language entries, and some of the issues arising, in particular the more complex categories required by the richness of the Irish-language material, and of the peculiar difficulties encountered by our researchers in that field, are further addressed in the Réamhrá, below. Angela Bourke has usefully discussed these and related questions as they affect our attempt to understand and weigh women's role especially in Irish traditions: see for instance "Performing – Not Writing: The Reception of an Irish Woman's Lament", in Yopi Prins and Maeera Shreiber (eds), *Dwelling in Possibility: Women Poets and Critics on Poetry* (Ithaca: Cornell University Press, 1997), 132–46).

17 Gearóid Ó Crualaoich, "County Cork Folklore and Its Collection", in Patrick O'Flanagan and Cornelius G. Buttimer (eds.), *Cork: History and Society* (Dublin: Geography Publications, 1993), 919–41.

18 International Adult Literacy Survey 1997, http://www.nala.ie.

19 Maeve Kelly, "Orange Horses", in Ailbhe Smyth (ed.), *Wildish Things* (Dublin: Attic Press, 1990), 41–52.

20 Borbála Faragó, "'Even the Grass Grows at an Alien Angle': Invisible Immigrants of Ireland", Contemporary Feminist Scholarship and Irish Women's Writing Panels, IASIL NUI Galway, 23 July 2004.

21 In relation to the time frame of the project, we have allowed a little overspill at either end of this period: for instance, we have listed some works published during the working period of the project, usually in cases where authors had been publishing shorter works, essays or individual poems, and only more recently brought out a longer work.

22 Carmel Quinlan, *Genteel Revolutionaries* (Cork: Cork University Press, 2002).

23 See Acknowledgements for a full list of these and of all others who gave their time to advise and help the work.

24 The even lighter footprints left by women performers and transmitters of oral material in Irish necessitated a still more sensitive attitude to their productions (as for example "Cailíní Óga na Muiri" or "Bean chéile Neddy", whose given names have not been handed down).

25 Born in Cork in 1904, Bridget G. MacCarthy wrote a PhD thesis for Cambridge University in 1940 which was the basis of *The Female Pen,* a literary history of women writers and their works from the early 1600s to the early 1800s. As Janet Todd points out in the 1994 reissue of this book by Cork University Press, MacCarthy's work remains useful today despite the developments in research and especially in feminist consciousness since the 1940s. MacCarthy later became Professor of English at UCC, a post she held until her death in 1966.

Réamhrá

Gearóidín Nic Carthaigh agus
Síle Ní Chochláin

Conas ar Cuireadh Cumadóireacht as Gaeilge san Áireamh?

Mar atá ráite cheana sa chuid Bhéarla den Réamhrá seo, ba faoi choimirce Roinn an Bhéarla i gColáiste na hOllscoile, Corcaigh a thosaigh an tionscnamh "Scríbhneoirí Ban na Mumhan, 1800–2000". Tar éis comhairle a fháil ó phainéal saineolaithe agus ón taighde luath a deineadh, ba léir nach raibh aon easpa scríbhneoirí Béarla ann ar bhaineannaigh iad agus ceangal acu le Cúige Mumhan. Cén fáth, mar sin, ar tosaíodh ar thaighde faoi chumadóireacht as Gaeilge? Tá cúpla freagra ar an gceist sin. I dtosach báire, ní bhíonn deighilt shoiléir i gcónaí ann idir scríbhneoirí Béarla agus scríbhneoirí Gaeilge; is é sin le rá, go bhfuil mná ann a scríobhann, nó a scríobhadh, sa dá theanga – Deirdre Brennan agus Eithne Strong, cuir i gcás – agus níor theastaigh ó na taighdeoirí neamhaird a thabhairt ar na téacsanna Gaeilge a bhí cruthaithe acu siúd agus ag mná mar iad. Chomh maith leis sin, cé go raibh an tionscnamh á stiúradh i Roinn an Bhéarla, bhí blas trasroinne air ó thosach toisc gur bhain sé le dhá thionscnamh thaighde eile a bhí á reáchtáil i gColáiste na hOllscoile, Corcaigh, agus iad go léir dírithe ar mhná i sochaí na hÉireann. Ina theannta sin, cé go bhfuil An tOllamh Pat Coughlan lonnaithe i Roinn an Bhéarla, deineann sí taighde ar litríocht an Bhéarla, ar an litríocht Angla-Éireannach, agus ar litríocht na Gaeilge. Tuigeann sí féin agus Éibhear Walshe, mar sin, go bhfuil dhá thaobh an traidisiúin ceangailte go dlúth dá chéile.

Fuarthas amach go luath san aimsir go raibh go leor ábhar ann faoi scríbhneoirí Béarla agus Gaeilge, ach go raibh sé scaipthe agus go raibh sé deacair teacht air dá dheasca. Toisc nár deineadh aon mhóriarracht roimhe seo ar íomhá iomlán a chur le chéile de shaol cruthaitheach na mban i gCúige Mumhan le dhá chéad bliain anuas, ceapadh go raibh gá le bunachar sonraí chun an t-eolas go léir a bhailiú agus a léiriú i slí ina mbeadh sé éasca don phobal teacht air. Bhí an dealramh ar an scéal ó thosach go mbeadh an bunachar sonraí níos cuimsithí agus gur mhó an éifeacht a bheadh leis dá mbeadh cumadóireacht as Gaeilge curtha san áireamh ann. Mar sin, chomh maith leis na taighdeoirí a bhí ag obair ar an litríocht as Béarla, ceapadh Gearóidín Nic Carthaigh ina taighdeoir lánaimseartha ar ábhar as Gaeilge agus chuaigh sí i mbun oibre i mBealtaine na bliana 2001. Nuair a bhí uirthi éirí as lean Síle Ní Chochláin ar aghaidh leis an obair ó Dheireadh Fómhair 2001 i leith.

Foinsí

Ba é ár bpointe tosaigh ná *1882–1982 Beathaisnéis a hAon* le Diarmuid Breathnach agus Máire Ní Mhurchú. Is é atá déanta acu ná cuntais bheathaisnéise a sholáthar ar dhaoine a raibh baint acu le saol na Gaeilge agus a fuair bás idir 1882–1982. Tháinig an saothar seo amach i gcúig cinn d'imleabhair idir 1986 agus 1997. Bhaineamar tairbhe as an séú ceann chomh maith, ina raibh cur síos orthu siúd a cailleadh idir 1782–1881 (1999). Bhí an seachtú ceann lasmuigh de scóip ár dtaighde toisc é a bheith ag plé leis an tréimhse ama 1560–1781, ach bhí an t-ochtú ceann an-chabhraitheach arís, *1983–2002 Beathaisnéis* (2003). Foinsí eile a bhí áisiúil agus sinn ag tosú amach ná *Scríbhneoirí na Gaeilge 1945–1995* (Ó Cearnaigh, 1995) agus *Eolaire Chló Iar-Chonnachta de Scríbhneoirí Gaeilge* (Uí Nia, 1998). Díríonn Ó Cearnaigh ar an leathchéad bliain i ndiaidh an tarna cogadh domhanda agus ar scríbhneoirí cruthaitheacha don chuid is mó. Daoine is ea iad a bhfuil leabhar amháin ar a laghad curtha i gcló acu, agus bhí a bhformhór beo an uair a bhí an leabhar á ullmhú ag Mac Uí Chearnaigh. Is le scríbhneoirí comhaimseartha Gaeilge a phléann Uí Nia, agus brí leathan á baint aici as an bhfocal "scríbhneoir". Cé gurb é bunchuspóir an eolaire ná bheith ina áis do lucht taighde agus do na scríbhneoirí féin ionas go mbeadh teacht acu go léir ar a chéile, bhaineamar leas nach beag as an saothar. Maidir leis na mná a chruthaigh téacsanna laistigh den traidisiún béil an chéad uair ach go bhfuil na téacsanna sin ar fáil i gcló anois, is í an fhoinse is mó a ndeinimid tagairt di ná *Béaloideas*. Dá mhéid an t-eolas saibhir ar scéalaithe agus ar sheanchaithe ban atá san fhoilseachán luachmhar seo, níl aon innéacs ag gabháilt leis agus dá bhrí sin, ní féidir teacht ar aon eolas ach amháin trí phóirseáil agus tochailt a dhéanamh. Tá súil againn, tar éis dúinn na mná a bhaineann le Cúige Mumhan atá luaite ann a aimsiú, go bhfuilimid tar éis dua éigin a spáráilt ar léitheoirí an tsaothair seo. Baineadh feidhm as leabhair agus as irisleabhair inar bailíodh seanchas agus scéalaíocht i gceantair Ghaeltachta chomh maith – mar shampla, *Duanaire Duibhneach* (Ó Dubhda, eag. [1933] 1969) a bhaineann le Gaeltacht Chorca Dhuibhne i gCo. Chiarraí, *An Linn Bhuí, Iml. 1-6* (Ó Macháin agus Nic Dhonnchadha, eag. 1997-2002) a bhaineann le Gaeltacht na Rinne, sna Déise i gCo. Phort Láirge, – a bhaineann le Múscraí, Co. Chorcaí, *Béarrach Mná ag Caint* (Verling, eag. 1999) ina bhfuil seanchas a bailíodh ó Mháiréad Ní Mhionacháin, agus *Céad Fáilte go Cléire* (Marion Gunn, eag. 1990) a bhaineann le hOileán Chléire ar chósta iarthair Chorcaí. Maidir le scéalaithe agus seanchaithe ban na Gaeltachta in Uíbh Ráthach, tá tagairt déanta do roinnt acu in *An File: Staidéar ar Osnádúrthacht na Filíochta sa Traidisiún Gaelach* (Ó hÓgáin,1982).

Saintréithe an Tionscnaimh Seo

Bhí eolas le fáil ar théacsanna a chruthaigh mná i gCúige Mumhan sna foinsí thuas, mar a bhí i leabhair ar chúrsaí scríbhneoireachta in Éirinn trí chéile, i leabhair thaighde, in innéacsanna, i ndíolamí filíochta, i gcnuasaigh phróis, i leabhair bhéaloidis, in irisí áitiúla, i dtráchtais neamhfhoilsithe, agus ar shuímh idirlín. Chomh maith leis sin, bhí gach ar scríobh na mná féin le fáil. Tá saintréithe ag baint leis an tionscnamh seo, áfach, a fhágann go bhfuil sé difriúil ó na foinsí eile. I dtosach báire, is le Cúige Mumhan amháin a phléann sé, rud a chuireann ar chumas na léitheoirí féachaint go

mion ar an réigiún sin dá mba mhian leo é. Rud eile de, cé go bhfuil
iontrálacha againn ar scríbhneoirí móra cáiliúla i saol na Gaeilge – Nuala Ní
Dhomhnaill nó Máire Mhac an tSaoi, mar shampla – tá an-chuid eolais
bailithe againn ar scríbhneoirí nach bhfuil aon cháil rómhór bainte amach
acu, agus tá cuntais againn ar mhná nach bhfuil a oiread sin foilsithe acu –
aiste ghairid in iris áitiúil acu, b'fhéidir, nó aistriúchán go Gaeilge ar aon
leabhar amháin déanta acu. Sa chás go raibh eolas faoin mbean le fáil faoi
ainm a céile, faoina deartháir nó faoina hathair sna foinsí ar thángamar
orthu, táimidne tar éis an bhean féin a chur 'i lár an aonaigh' – is é sin le rá,
tiocfar uirthi sa tionscnamh seo faoina hainm féin. Maidir leis na saothair
léirmheastóireachta ar fhéachamar orthu – mar shampla, *B'ait Leo Bean*
(Nic Eoin, 1998) agus *An tÚrscéal Gaeilge* (Titley, 1991) bhí eolas
luachmhar iontu ar scríbhneoirí, agus is minic gur foinsí iontacha iad i
dtaobh an bhéaloidis, ach de ghnáth bhí an t-eolas scaipthe tríd an leabhar
mar is dual do leabhair den saghas sin. Táimidne tar éis an t-eolas a eagrú ar
mhalairt slí, is é sin alt beathaisnéise faoin mbean a chur ar fáil, mar aon le
leabhar liosta agus le liosta na bpríomhthagairtí.

Daoine a Roinn Eolas Linn

Ní i dtaobh le leabhair nó le hirisí amháin a bhíomar. Cuireadh ceistneoir le
chéile, a bhí bunaithe, a bheag nó a mhór, ar an gceann a úsáideadh chun
taighde a dhéanamh ar na scríbhneoirí Béarla, ach gur cuireadh in oiriúint é
do phobal na Gaeilge. Deineadh é a dháileadh ar léachtóirí Gaeilge sna
hinstitiúidí tríú leibhéal, ar eagrais Ghaeilge, agus ar shiopaí leabhar. Chomh
maith leis sin, chuaigh Gearóidín faoi agallamh ar Raidió na Gaeltachta i
samhradh na bliana 2001 chun aidhmeanna an tionscnaimh a mhíniú agus
chun cabhair an lucht éisteachta a lorg. Ba mhaith linn an deis a thapú anso
ár mbuíochas a ghabháil le gach éinne a labhair linn nó a scríobh chugainn.
Ní mór dúinn, leis, an Dr. Pádraigín Riggs (Coláiste na hOllscoile,
Corcaigh) agus an Dr. Angela Bourke (Coláiste na hOllscoile, Baile Átha
Cliath) a lua, a bhí ina mbaill den phainéal comhairleach, agus a bhí i gcónaí
ar fáil chun tacaíocht a thabhairt dúinn.

Mná ón traidisiún béil

Deineadh an cinneadh go gcuirfí mná san áireamh a chruthaigh – nó a
d'athchruthaigh – téacsanna laistigh den traidisiún béil an chéad lá, ach gur
foilsíodh na téacsanna sin i leabhair nó in irisí ina dhiaidh sin. Is baolach go
raibh sé lasmuigh de scóip an taighde mná a bhfuil a gcuid téacsanna á
gcoimeád i gcartlann a liostáil, bíodh is go bhfuil a leithéidí ann chomh
maith. Is i láithriú[1] ó bhéal a tháinig na téacsanna seo go léir ar an saol ar
dtúis, rud a dtabharfar éachtaint air sna paragraif a leanas. Déanfar cúram ar
leith den ghné chruthaitheach den láithriú, agus ansan féachfar ar an tslí a
ndeineann an bailitheoir taifead – idir thaifead scríofa agus thaifead fuaime
– ar scéalta, ar bhlúirí seanchais, agus ar amhráin. Ar deireadh cíorófar
"turas" an bhéaloidis ón láithriú go dtí an leathanach, agus pléifear na
daoine éagsúla a mbíonn lámh acu sa phróiseas sin.

Amach ar aghaidh a chéile na scéalta, na heachtraí agus araile sa traidisiún béil. Téann siad i bhfeidhm ar an tsúil sa tslí is go mbíonn an lucht éisteachta ag féachaint ar chuntanós agus ar gheáitsí an scéalaí. Ach is ar an gcluais is mó a théann siad i gcion – idir fhuaim na bhfocal agus ghuth an scéalaí. Thar aon ní eile, téann teacht i láthair nó pearsantacht an scéalaí i bhfeidhm ar an éisteoir. Is as nithe mar sin a bhaintear an sásamh sa traidisiún béil.

Deirtear scéalta, seanchas, agus amhráin ar chúiseanna cinnte. Roghnaítear an píosa go cúramach chun freagairt don ócáid agus don éisteoir. Bíonn feidhm nó feidhmeanna ag an bpíosa: fuascailt a sholáthar ó leadrán nó ó bhuairt an tsaoil, dlisteanú a dhéanamh ar nósa agus ar luachanna an phobail, teagasc a chur ar an bpobal i gcúrsaí praiticiúla nó móráltachta, agus an pobal a aontú ina shaoldearcadh agus ina iompar (feic Bascom agus Ó Héalaí). Tá an Dr. Angela Bourke tar éis mórán a scríobh faoi fheidhm na caointeoireachta agus na síscéalta, dhá *genre* a shamhlaítí le mná de ghnáth (feic Bourke 1988, 1993, 1996, 1997). Tá líon nach beag de mhná aimsithe againn sa tionscnamh seo a luaitear caointe leo. Tá an-léiriú curtha ar fáil ag Bourke ina haiste "The Irish Traditional Lament and the Grieving Process" ar an gcaointeoireacht mar láithriú agus mar dheasghnáth ina gcuireann an bhean chaointe síos ar an mbuairt mhór a bhíonn ar an dream a fhágtar tar éis céile, cara, nó comharsa a chailliúint. Ba í an bhean chaointe a chabhraigh leis an bpobal an brón sin a chur in iúl, agus é a chur díobh ar deireadh. Seo í feidhm na fuascailte arís a ndeineann Bascom agus Ó Héalaí tagairt di.

Pé acu scéal nó caoineadh é, amhrán nó paidir, ní téacsanna dochta iad. Ní fhoghlaimítear iad "focal ar fhocal" faoi mar a thuigtear a leithéid dúinne a bhfuil níos mó taithí againn ar thraidisiún na léitheoireachta agus na scríbhneoireachta. Mura mbeadh ann ach an méid sin, ní bheadh sa duine – an scéalaí, an bhean chaointe, an t-amhránaí nó an seanchaí – ach mar a bheadh téipthaifeadán daonna. Téacsanna solúbtha is ea téacsanna an traidisiúin bhéil ar féidir, agus ar gá, cur leo nó baint díobh, ag brath ar mhianta an chainteora agus an éisteora. Deintear an scéal a chur in oiriúint don ócáid agus do théama na cainte a thagann roimh an scéal agus ina dhiaidh sa chomhrá. Cé go gcaitheann an scéalaí feidhmiú de réir dlithe an traidisiúin, leis – scaoilfear athruithe áirithe leis, ach ní scaoilfear a thuilleadh acu nó an iomad acu – tugtar scóip dó nó di a stampa féin a bhualadh ar an scéal. Is ansan a fhaigheann sé nó sí deis a c(h)ruthaitheacht féin a chur in iúl. Tá an scoláire Albert B. Lord tar éis aird mhór a dhíriú ar an taobh cruthaitheach den láithriú (Lord, 1974 [1960]). Tá áitithe aige go mbíonn cumadóireacht fite fuaite san aithris; nó i bhfocail eile, go mbíonn athchruthú ar siúl le linn an láithrithe. Is ar an bhfilíocht eipiciúil a chanadh amhránaithe Slavacha atá saothar Lord bunaithe, ach is léir ó thaighde David C. Rubin go bhfuil an tsolúbthacht a thuig Lord a bheith in aithris na filíochta eipiciúla ag baint le *genres* éagsúla eile leis, bíodh is go mbíonn cuid acu níos solúbtha ná a chéile gan dabht (Rubin, 1995).

Táimid tar éis féachaint ar eiliminтí den bhéaloideas go dtí seo faoi mar a chuirtear i láthair iad sa phobal. Dírímis anois ar obair an bhailitheora agus ar thaifeadadh an bhéaloidis, mar is é sin an chéad chéim i dturas an scéil ón láithriú go dtí an leagan foilsithe. Nuair a théann an bailitheoir go dtí an faisnéiseoir, bíonn de rogha aige taifead scríofa nó taifead fuaime a dhéanamh. Mar sin, pé leagan den scéal nó den amhrán a thugann an faisnéiseoir dó ar an lá sin, "beirtear" air – ar pháipéar, ar spól, ar théip nó ar fhístéip. Murab ionann agus traidisiún na litríochta ina n-áirítear an leagan foilsithe de théacs mar leagan údarásach nó deifnídeach, níl sa scéal a eascraíonn ón traidisiún béil ach insint amháin as sraith fhada acu. Ní hann don bhunleagan.

An chéad chéim eile i dturas an bhéaloidis óna phobal féin go dtí lucht a léite ná nuair a bheartaítear ar é a fhoilsiú. Bunaítear an leagan seo ar dheachtú an bhailitheora nó ar thras-scríobh na téipe. Tharlódh sé go ndéanfadh an bailitheoir féin nó eagarthóir eile athruithe air – os ard nó os íseal. Tharlódh sé, leis, go ndéanfadh duine acu siúd, nó duine eile arís, an píosa a aistriú ó Ghaeilge go teanga eile. Mar sin, is próiseas é seo a mbíonn lámh ag a lán daoine ann, agus is minic nach mbíonn aon bhaint ag an bhfaisnéiseoir féin leis an bpíosa a ullmhú don chló.

Agus canathaobh ar cuireadh mná san áireamh a chum lasmuigh de – agus go neamhspleách ar – thraidisiún na scríbhneoireachta? Measadh nach bhféadfaí pictiúr iomlán de chruthaitheacht na mban i gCúige Mumhan le dhá chéad bliain anuas a sholáthar gan tagairt a dhéanamh dóibh. Bhain na mná seo leas as meán eile seachas meán na scríbhneoireachta, meán a bhí sofaisticiúil agus ealaíonta. Ba ghá do na mná sin a gcuid dintiúirí a bheith go maith acu nó gan an scéalaíocht (an seanchas, an amhránaíocht, agus araile) a tharraingt orthu féin in aon chor. "Coláistí cois tine" a bhíodh acu; is é sin, gur chaitheadar a saol, geall leis, ag síoréisteacht leis an seandream ag scéalaíocht, ag eachtraí, ag amhrán, ag caint ar luibheanna is ar leigheasanna, ar chócaireacht is ar chomharthaí aimsire, ar phúcaí, ar phúireanna móra, ar na daoine maithe; an chaint á polladh ag blúirí filíochta mar a bhainfidís le hábhar, agus an seanfhocal á shníomh isteach ann chun an argóint a bhuachtaint nó chun ciall a chur sa duine eile. Is beag an radharc a fhaighimid ar an saol sin anois, saol ina raibh meas an domhain ar an ardchainteoir agus níos mó measa arís ar an scéalaí, toisc go gcaithfeadh bua ar leith a bheith aige nó aici siúd, anuas ar an deisbhéalaíocht, ar an nGaeilge shaibhir agus ar an gcruinneas cainte (feic Bourke 1991–2).

Crot na n-iontrálacha

Tá liosta de na mná in ord aibítre de réir sloinne. Níl na hiontrálacha Gaeilge scartha amach ó na cinn Bhéarla; mar shampla, tagann "Mhic Néill, Seosaimhín" roimh "Michael, Christine". Toisc gur cuireadh cnámha an leabhair seo le chéile mar bhunachar sonraí an chéad lá is ea a cuireadh béim ar aimsir, áit, agus *genre*; is ar na critéir sin a bhí na modhanna cuardaigh ríomhaireachta bunaithe. Mar sin, leagtar amach gach iontráil mar a leanas: ainm na mná, an aimsir inar fhás sí aníos, na háiteanna lenar bhain sí, agus na *genres* a chleachtaigh sí. Ina theannta sin, cuirtear alt beathaisnéise ar an mbean ar fáil, mar aon le "Select bibliography" – is é sin, liosta de na téacsanna is mó a luaitear léi. Ina dhiaidh sin, faoin teideal "Secondary sources", faightear na príomhthagairtí – leabhair agus ailt inar deineadh tagairt do shaothar na mná nó dá saol, agus is ionann roinnt acu siúd agus na foinsí a d'úsáideamar chun an iontráil a ullmhú.

Ainm

Tugtar an t-ainm baiste agus an sloinne as Béarla idir lúibíní cearnógacha má d'úsáid an bhean an dá leagan dá hainm, m.sh. "Ní Bhriain, Neilí [O'Brien, Ellen]". Tugtar an litriú caighdeánach den ainm idir na lúibíní sa chás gur úsáid an bhean an seanlitriú, m.sh. Maighréad [Máiréad], Clíodhna [Clíona]. Tugtar leasainm nó ainm ceana na mná idir lúibíní nuair a bhíonn a leithéid againn, m.sh. "Ní Chríodáin, Nóra ['Nóra an tSleasa']". Tríd is tríd, deintear iarracht ar a oiread eolais agus is féidir a sholáthar; cuir i gcás, tugtar sloinne a céile, sloinne a muintire agus an leagan dá hainm a chítear ar a cuid foilseachán de ghnáth sa sampla seo a leanas: "Uí Dhálaigh, Máirín [Nic Dhiarmada / O Daly, Máirín]". Níor thángamar ach ar aon sampla amháin de bhean anaithnid laistigh de thraidisiún na scríbhneoireachta Gaeilge i gCúige Mumhan; b'in í an bhean rialta a d'aistrigh dráma le Robert Benson – níl d'eolas uirthi féin ar an leathanach teidil dá saothar ach 'Bean Riaghalta i gCorcaigh'. Maidir le mná an traidisiúin bhéil, is beag an t-eolas ar chuid acu atá sna leabhair agus sna hirisí, m.sh. 'Bean Chéile Neddy' ó Bhaile na Curtaí, Co. Chiarraí, 'Bean de mhuintir Chéileachair' ó Chluan Droichead, Co. Chorcaí, nó 'Cailín Óg ó Bhaile na bPoc', Co. Chiarraí. Sloinnte a bhfear céile amháin atá sna foilseacháin uaireanta, m.sh. Bean Uí Cheárna ó Mhúscraí nó Bean Uí Chiabháin (An Charraig) ó Chorca Dhuibhne. I gcás nó dhó, tugtar ainm baiste an fhir chéile agus a shloinne, m.sh. 'Bean Sheáin Uí Chonaill'. Bréag a chur ar an gcóras dúchais ab ea a leithéid seo d'úsáid; agus é bunoscionn leis an nós a bhí riamh sa Ghaeltacht (agus i gcuid mhaith de Ghalltacht na hÉireann, leis) go gcoimeádadh an bhean sloinne a muintire féin. "Peig Sayers", mar shampla, a thugtaí riamh ar an mbean sin ina ceantar dúchais, cé gur faoi "Uí Ghuithín, Peig" atá sí cláraithe i gcartlann Choimisiún Bhéaloideas Éireann.

Tá cuid mhór de na hiontrálacha sa leabhar seo faoi "sheanchas / béaloideas" nó faoi "scéalaíocht / béaloideas" le fáil faoi láthair sna foinsí eile faoi ainm an bhailitheora nó faoi ainm an eagarthóra agus b'fhir iad a bhformhór, de ghnáth. Mar shampla, nuair a foilsíodh ábhar ó Pheig Sayers in *Béaloideas 2* (1929–30) is faoi ainm an bhailitheora, Robin Flower, a bhí sé, agus faoin teideal 'Sgéalta ón mBlascaod'. Cuireadh dhá scéal eile uaithi i gcló in *Béaloideas 4* (1934) faoi ainm Kenneth Jackson agus faoi theideal den saghas céanna. Ciallaíonn sé seo nach léir ar an gcéad amharc gur scéalaí mná an faisnéiseoir. Soláthraíonn an leabhar seo againne an béaloideas ón mbean faoina hainm féin agus cé nach bhfuil ann ach véarsa nó dhó i gcásanna, tá seans ann go dtiocfaidh níos mó ábhar chun solais san am atá romhainn.

Aimsir

Nuair ab eol dúinn dáta breithe agus báis na mná tugadh an t-eolas sin. Má bhí amhras faoi na dátaí, nó mura raibh ach aon dáta amháin againn, tugadh dáta foilsithe an téacs agus aon dáta eile a bhain leis an mbean san alt beathaisnéise. Sa chás nach raibh aon dáta beathaisnéise againn níor tugadh ach dáta foilsithe an téacs, agus léiríodh é sin le *fl.*, *.i. floruit*, focal Laidne a chiallaíonn "bhí sí faoi bhláth". Fágann sé sin go bhfuil an chuma ar an scéal i gcás nó dhó go bhfuil an bhean beo i láthair na huaire, cé go mbaineann sí siúd agus a téacs le haimsir i bhfad níos luaithe. Tarlaíonn sé sin i gcás Shíle Ní Dhonnchú, mar shampla, ar tógadh ábhar béaloidis uaithi i 1935. Cuireadh i dtaisce é i gCartlann Roinn Bhéaloideas Éireann, ach níor-foilsíodh aon chuid de go dtí 1990, nuair a chuir Marion Gunn seanchas uaithi i gcló ina leabhar *Céad Fáilte go Cléire* (1990, 40 agus 175). Maidir leis na mná beo, úsáideadh an téarma "comhaimseartha" agus tugadh an dáta breithe san alt beathaisnéise má bhí sé ar eolas againn.

Áit

Nuair ab eol dúinn áit chónaithe na mná, tugadh an leagan ab iomláine a bhí againn. Nuair a bhí ceangal ag bean le níos mó ná áit amháin, luadh na háiteanna go léir agus míníodh an ceangal san alt beathaisnéise. I ngach cás, luadh an chathair nó an contae i gCúige Mumhan ina bhfuil na háiteanna sin. Saolaíodh agus tógadh formhór na mban atá sa saothar seo i gCúige Mumhan, ach má chaith bean tréimhse fhada nó tréimhsí rialta leanúnacha i gCúige Mumhan cuireadh san áireamh, leis, í. Sa chás sin, ba mhinic a bhí baint faoi leith ag an mbean le scríbhneoireacht na Mumhan: Marie-Louise Sjoestedt (–Jonval) ón bhFrainc, a dhein staidéar ar chanúint Chiarraí agus Caoilfhionn Nic Pháidín ó Bhaile Átha Cliath, a bhfuil staidéar déanta aici ar chanúintí Chorca Dhuibhne, Uíbh Ráthaigh agus Chléire, mar shampla.

Genre

Deineadh iarracht ar na *genres* a choimeád chomh simplí agus ab fhéidir. Uaireanta ní raibh ach iontráil nó dhó faoi *genre* áirithe agus cuireadh faoi scáth *genre* níos mó é; mar shampla, ní raibh ach trí nó ceithre iontráil ag plé le hiriseoireacht as Gaeilge agus cé nach mbaineann siad go díreach leis an scríbhneoireacht acadúil, is faoin *genre* sin a cuireadh iad toisc go mbaineann siad le scríbhneoireacht fhoirmeálta agus le léirmheastóireacht don chuid is mó. Thángamar ar líon mór scríbhneoirí a raibh leabhair de shaghsanna difriúla tiontaithe go Gaeilge acu, agus tá *genre* faoi leith againn d'aistriúchán dá thoradh. Mar sin féin, is minic a bhaineann na haistriúcháin le *genre* eile chomh maith, le litríocht leanaí nó le scríbhneoireacht acadúil mar shampla. Mar sin, is annamh a thagtar ar iontráil faoi "aistriúchán" gan an tarna *genre* a bheith luaite ina theannta.

Clúdaíonn an *genre* "scríbhneoireacht acadúil" scríbhneoireacht fhoirmeálta de gach saghas: aistí, ailt, fileolaíocht, léirmheastóireacht, eagarthóireacht ar sheanlitríocht, léachtaí, taighde, leabhair theagaisc agus, mar a luadh thuas, iriseoireacht. Cé go bhfuil leabhair theagaisc ar imeall an *genre* seo, cuireadh san áireamh iad toisc go ndíríonn siad ar scoláirí teangan de ghnáth agus go mbaineann an-chuid scríbhneoireachta acadúla as Gaeilge le cúrsaí teangan.

"Dírbheathaisnéis" a thabharfaí ar an leabhar *Peig* le Peig Sayers de ghnáth, ach toisc go raibh daoine eile ag scríobh síos agus ag cur oird agus eagair ar a cuid focal, tá tionchar an bhailitheora le brath ar an scéal chomh maith. D'fhonn an díospóireacht seo a sheachaint cuireadh dírbheathaisnéisí agus beathaisnéisí faoi aon *genre* amháin, "beathaisnéis". Ciallaíonn sé sin go bhfuil dírbheathaisnéis nó dhó – an ceann leis an tSiúr de Lourdes Stac, cuir i gcás – curtha faoin *genre* "beathaisnéis". Tá na *genres* "litríocht leanaí", "úrscéalaíocht", "gearrscéalaíocht", agus "drámaíocht" soiléir go leor. Uaireanta cuireadh taobh le *genre* eile iad – "aistriúchán" nó "scríbhneoireacht acadúil", mar shampla, chun níos mó eolais a sholáthar.

Nuair a tosaíodh ar an taighde bhí "béaloideas" mar aon *genre* amháin againn, ach tar éis tamaillín deineadh idirdhealú idir sheanchas agus scéalaíocht toisc go raibh an-chuid iontrálacha ann. Is ionann "scéalaíocht / béaloideas" agus scéalta a insíodh ó bhéal an chéad lá, agus cuireadh seanchas, cuimhní cinn, agus paidreacha faoi "seanchas / béaloideas". Deineadh deighilt idir fhilíocht ó thraidisiún na scríbhneoireachta agus fhilíocht ón traidisiún béil. Mar sin, cuireadh na hiontrálacha faoi "filíocht" nó faoi "filíocht / béaloideas" chun an difear seo a thabhairt amach. S minic a chuirtear eolas breise ann cosúil le "filíocht, caoineadh / béaloideas."

Focail scoir

Tá súil againn go mbainfidh idir scoláirí, mhic léinn, agus chriticeoirí leas as an saothar seo san am atá le teacht. Ba mhaith linn go mbeadh sé ina áis, ní amháin don lucht léinn i ngort na litríochta, ach dóibh siúd atá ag saothrú i réimsí na staire, na socheolaíochta agus an bhéaloidis, freisin. Dheineamar iarracht ar an dúshraith a chur síos, ionas go bhféadfadh taighdeoirí eile bheith ag tógáil uirthi sna blianta atá amach romhainn.

Notes

1   Is é is brí le "láithriú" anseo ná "performance".

Tagairtí

Bascom, William R. "Four Functions of Folklore" in Alan Dundes (eag.), *The Study of Folklore* (Englewood Cliffs, NJ: Prentice-Hall, 1965), (279–98).

Bourke, Angela. "The Irish Traditional Lament and the Grieving Process", *Women's Studies International Forum* 11.4 (1988), 287–91.

Bourke, Angela. "Performing – Not Writing." *Graph: Irish Literary Review*.11 (1991–2): 28–31.

Bourke, Angela. "'Performing, Not Writing': The Reception of an Irish Woman's Lament", in Prins, Yopie agus Maeera Schreiber (eag.), *Dwelling in Possibility: Women Poets and Critics on Poetry* (Ithaca: Cornell University Press, 1997), 132–46.

Breathnach, Diarmuid agus Máire Ní Mhurchú. *1882–1982 Beathaisnéis a hAon*. Baile Átha Cliath: An Clóchomhar Tta, 1986.

—. *1882–1982 Beathaisnéis a Dó* (Baile Átha Cliath: An Clóchomhar Tta, 1990).

—. *1882–1982 Beathaisnéis a Trí* (Baile Átha Cliath: An Clóchomhar Tta, 1992).

—. *1882–1982 Beathaisnéis a Ceathair* (Baile Átha Cliath: An Clóchomhar Tta, 1994).

—. "Beathaisnéis 1–4 Ceartúcháin agus Eolas Breise". *1882–1982 Beathaisnéis a Cúig* (Baile Átha Cliath: An Clóchomhar Tta, 1997).

—. *1782–1891 Beathaisnéis* (Baile Átha Cliath: An Clóchomhar Tta, 1999).

Gunn, Marion (eag.), *Céad Fáilte go Cléire* (Baile Átha Cliath: An Clóchomhar Tta, 1990).

Lord, Albert, *The Singer of Tales* [Cambridge, Mass.: Harvard University Press, 1960.] New York, Atheneum, 1974.

Ó Cearnaigh, Seán, *Scríbhneoirí na Gaeilge 1945–1995* (Baile Átha Cliath: Comhar Teoranta, 1995).

Ó Dubhda, Seán (eag.), *Duanaire Duibhneach: bailiú d'amhránaibh agus de phíosaibh eile filidheachta a ceapadh le tuairim céad bliain i gCorca Dhuibhne, agus atá fós i gcuimhne agus i mbéaloideas na ndaoine ann* ([1933]. Baile Átha Cliath: Oifig Dhíolta Foilseacháin Rialtais, 1969).

Ó Héalaí, "Fiúntas an Bhéaloidis do Phobal Chorca Dhuibhne in aimsir Jeremiah Curtin", in eag. Pádraig Ó Fiannachta, *Thaitin Sé Le Peig. Iris na hOidhreachta 1* (Baile an Fheirtéaraigh: Oidhreacht Chorca Dhuibhne, 1989) 17–30.

Ó hÓgáin, Daithí, *An File: Staidéar ar Osnádúrthacht na Filíochta sa Traidisiún Gaelach* (Baile Átha Cliath: Oifig an tSoláthair, 1982).

Ó Macháin, Pádraig, agus Aoibheann Nic Dhonnchadha (eag.), "Cáit M. Ní Ghráinne", *An Linn Bhuí: Iris Ghaeltacht na nDéise* (Baile Átha Cliath, 1999). 130.

Rubin, David C. *Memory in Oral Traditions: The Cognitive Psychology of Epic, Ballads and Counting-out Rhymes* (New York agus Oxford: Oxford University Press, 1995).

Titley, Alan, *An tÚrscéal Gaeilge*. Leabhair Thaighde 67 (Baile Átha Cliath: An Clóchomhar Tta, 1991).

Uí Nia, Gearóidín (eag.), *Eolaire Chló Iar-Chonnachta de Scríbhneoirí Gaeilge* (Indreabhán: Cló Iar-Chonnachta, 1998).

Verling, Máirtín (eag.), *Béarrach Mná ag Caint: Seanchas Mháiréad Ní Mhionacháin.* Tadhg Ó Murchú a bhailigh (Indreabhán: Cló Iar-Chonnachta, 1999).

Abbreviations

To a large extent, we have endeavoured to avoid using abbreviations in the dictionary. Where there are abbreviations (in the bibliographies, for example), we follow the guidelines of the Modern Language Association of America (MLA) system. Thus, scholarly abbreviations used in the dictionary include:

arr.	arranged
BA	Bachelor of Arts
cf.	compare – i.e. see another entry or source
comp.	compiler / compiled by
DIAS	Dublin Institute of Advanced Studies
dir.	director / directed by
ed.	editor / edited by / edition
ESRC	Economic and Social Research Council
ESRI	Economic and Social Research Institute
et al.	and others (*et alii*)
fl.	floruit / flourished – we have used this with a date to indicate the period during which an author's work was published in cases where we do not have the dates of birth or death of a writer
fwd.	foreword / foreword by
intro.	introduction / introduced by
illus.	illustrator / illustrated by
MA	Master of Arts
MLitt	Master of Literature
n.d.	there is no date of publication listed for the book in question
n.p.	no place of publication; no publisher name on the book in question
PhD	Doctor of Philosophy
rev.	review of / reviewer / reviewed by
sel.	selected by
ser.	series
sic	"thus in the source" - i.e. we have reproduced a quotation exactly as it is in the original source, including spelling or other differences from standard English
trans.	translator / translated by / translation
unpub.	unpublished
q.v.	quod vide [Latin: "which see"] refers the reader to a related dictionary entry
U	university [see below for a list of specific universities]
UP	university press
vol.	volume

Most of the Irish universities referred to are abbreviated, and they are:

UCC	University College Cork, recently renamed NUI Cork (National University of Ireland Cork). In one or two bibliographical entries UCC is referred to by its original name, Queen's College Cork or QCC.
UCG	University College Galway, also NUI Galway (National University of Ireland Galway)
DIT	Dublin Institute of Technology (similarly, Waterford Institute of Technology, etc.)
UL	University of Limerick
UCD	University College Dublin
TCD	Trinity College Dublin
QUB	Queen's University Belfast

References in the biographical entries to secondary material – such as other dictionaries of Irish Literature, or works relating to specific writers – can be found in full in the Bibliography, which contains a list of all the material we used in compiling the dictionary.

Dictionary of Munster Women Writers 1800–2000

Abell, Jane. 1787–1852. Cork. Diaries.

A Cork Quaker, whose unpublished diary (1824–52) is held by the Dublin Friends Historical Library. Her diary entries chiefly consist of spiritual matters.

Select bibliography
Abell, Jane.
—. *Journal.* 1824–58. (Unpub.) diary. Notes: Held at Dublin Friends Historical Library.

Adshead, Maura. Contemporary. Limerick. Academic writing, political writing.

Born in Cork in 1967, she received a BA from UL and a PhD from Liverpool University. She is a lecturer in politics and public administration at UL.

Select bibliography
Adshead, Maura.
—. "European Community – Development, Progress and Prospects." *Regional and Local Development.* Political writing. Ed. G.P. Sweeney. Dublin: DIT, 1995. 101–31.
—. "Sea-Change on the Isle of Saints and Scholars? The 1995 Irish Referendum on Divorce." Political writing. *Electoral Studies* 15.1 (1996): 138–42.
—. *Developing European Regions? Comparative Governance, Policy Networks and European Integration.* Political writing. Aldershot: Ashgate, 2002.
—. and Michelle Millar. *Public Policy in Ireland: Theory and Methods.* Academic writing. London: Routledge, 2003.

Alcock, Deborah. 1825–1913. Waterford. Novels.

Daughter of John Alcock, Archdeacon of Waterford, she lived with her father throughout her life. She wrote stories published by the Religious Truth Society in the 1870s–80s, many of which were written for children or young adults and possibly intended for Sunday school use. Her best-known work is *The Spanish Brothers* (1871), a narrative of Protestant martyrdom set in the sixteenth century, which details the rise and fall of the Protestant Church in Spain. Other works include *The Czar* (1891), set during the Napoleonic invasion of Russia; and *Archie's Chances* (1886).

Select bibliography
Alcock, Deborah.
—. *The Spanish Brothers.* Historical novel. London: T. Nelson, 1871.
—. *Lessons on Early Church History.* Religious writing. London: Church of England 1879.
—. *She Hath Done What She Could.* Religious writing. London: Church of England 1880.
—. *The Roman Students; or, On the Wings of the Morning: A Tale of the Renaissance.*

1

Historical novel. London: T. Fisher Unwin, 1883.

—. *Archie's Chances – and the Child's Victory*. London: T. Nelson, 1886.

—. *The Cross and the Crown*. Religious writing. London: Religious Truth Society, 1886.

—. *Walking with God: A Memoir of the Venerable John Alcock (Late Archdeacon of Waterford)*. Memoir. London: Hodder & Stoughton, 1887.

—. *Genevieve, or, The Children of Port Royal*. London: Religious Truth Society, 1889.

—. *Arthur Erskine's Story: A Tale of the Days of Knox*. 1890.

—. *The Seven Churches of Asia*. Religious writing. Edinburgh: T. & T. Clarke, 1890.

—. *Crushed, Yet Conquering*. Religious writing. London: Religious Truth Society, 1891.

—. *The Czar: A Tale of the Time of the First Napoleon*. Historical novel. London: Nelson, 1891.

—. *Prisoners of Hope. A Story of the Faith*. Religious writing. London: Religious Truth Society, 1894.

—. *The Well in the Orchard*. Historical novel. London: Religious Truth Society, 1895.

—. *By Far Euphrates: A Tale*. Historical novel. London: Hodder & Stoughton, 1897.

—. *Doctor Adrian. A Story of Old Holland*. Children's writing. London: Religious Truth Society, 1897.

—. *The Little Captives, and Other Stories*. Religious writing. London: Religious Truth Society, 1898.

—. *Not for Crown or Sceptre*. London: Hodder & Stoughton, 1902.

—. *Under Calvin's Spell*. Religious writing. London: Religious Truth Society, 1902.

—. "John Frith." "Claude Brousson." *Six Heroic Men*. Biography. London: Religious Tract Society, 1906.

—. *Done and Dared in Old France*. Religious writing. London: S.W. Partridge, 1907.

—. *The Romance of Protestantism: Tales of Trials and Victory*. History. London: Hodder & Stoughton, 1908.

—. *Robert Musgrave's Adventure. A Story of Old Geneva*. London: S.W. Partridge, 1909.

—. *The King's Service. A Story of the Thirty Years' War*. Historical novel. London: Religious Truth Society, 1910.

—. *No Cross, No Crown*. London: T. Nelson, 1910.

—. "Preface." *Songs of Faith and Freedom*. Songs. L.H. Dalton. London: Elliot Stock, 1910.

—. *The Friends of Pascal*. Historical novel. London: Religious Truth Society, n.d.

Allen, Darina, née O'Connell. Contemporary. Cork. Cookbooks.

Born in 1948, she runs and owns the Ballymaloe Cookery School, which was established in 1983 in Shanagarry, Co. Cork. Allen trained in Hotel and Catering Management at DIT, Cathal Brugha St. She is a member of the International Association of Cooking Professionals, Euro-Toques, the Irish Food Writers Guild and the Guild of Food Writers in Britain. In 1992 she was awarded the Gilbeys of Ireland Gold Medal of Excellence jointly with Myrtle Allen and in 2001 was named the Veuve Clicquot Business Woman of the Year. She has achieved international recognition for her range of Irish cookbooks and the televised series *Simply Delicious*.

Select bibliography
Allen, Darina.

—. *Simply Delicious*. Cookbook. Dublin: Gill & Macmillan, 1989.

—. *A Simply Delicious Christmas*. Cookbook. Dublin: Gill & Macmillan, 1989.

—. *Simply Delicious 2*. Cookbook. Dublin: Gill & Macmillan, 1990.

—. *Simply Delicious Fish*. Cookbook. Dublin: Gill & Macmillan, 1991.

—. *Simply Delicious France and Italy*. Cookbook. Dublin: Gill & Macmillan, 1992.
—. *Simply Delicious Recipes*. Cookbook. Dublin: Gill & Macmillan, 1992.
—. *Simply Delicious Food for Family and Friends*. Cookbook. Dublin: Gill & Macmillan, 1993.
—. *Simply Delicious Versatile Vegetables*. Cookbook. Dublin: Gill & Macmillan, 1994.
—. *Simply Delicious Meals in Minutes*. Cookbook. Dublin: Gill & Macmillan, 1996.
—. *Darina Allen's Complete Cookery Course*. Cookbook. Gill & Macmillan, 2001.

Secondary sources
Power, Vincent. *Voices of Cork*. Dublin: Blackwater Press, 1997.

Allen, Myrtle, née Hill. Contemporary. Cork. Cookbooks, journalism.

Born in 1924. she grew up in Monkstown, Co. Cork. Her father was an academic in UCC and designed the Dairy Science Building where Myrtle later studied. Following her marriage to Ivan Allen she moved to Shanagarry, to the fourteenth-century estate of Ballymaloe House. By 1962 she was a regular cookery correspondent for the *Irish Farmer's Journal* and shortly after opened a restaurant at Ballymaloe. Following periods of study at the Cordon Bleu in London and in Paris she began cookery courses during the 1960s along with her daughter-in-law Darina Allen (*q.v.*). She was a constant ambassador for Irish food and hospitality abroad. During the 1980s she participated in a promotional project called "A Taste of Ireland" in Brussels. The project was hugely successful and as a result was brought to New York and Amsterdam. From 1981 to 1985 she ran La Ferme Irlandaise, an Irish restaurant in Paris, in collaboration with the FBD. In 2000 Myrtle Allen was awarded an Honorary Doctorate of Laws in UCC.

Select bibliography
Allen, Myrtle.
—. *The Ballymaloe Cook Book*. Cookbook. Dublin: Agri-Books, 1977.
—. *Myrtle Allen's Cooking at Ballymaloe House*. Cookbook. Dublin: Gill & Macmillan, 2000.

Anson, Clodagh, née Beresford. *fl.*1930–60. Lismore, Co. Waterford. Memoir, family history.

A social activist and traveller, she lived in Lismore, Co. Waterford. Much of her writing consists of memoirs and family histories of her own family, the Beresfords.

Select bibliography
Anson, Clodagh.
—. *Book: Discreet Memoirs*. Memoir. London: Bateman Blackshaw, 1931.
—. *Another Book*. Memoir. London: Burnett (self-published), 1937.
—. *Victorian Days*. Memoir. London: Richards, 1957.

Ardilaun, Lady Olive [Lady Olive White]. *fl.*1914. Bantry, Co. Cork. Family history.

Wrote a history of her grandfather, the Earl of Bantry.

Select bibliography
Ardilaun, Lady Olive.
—. *Richard White, First Earl of Bantry: Tales of a Grandfather*. Family history. N.p.: n.p., 1914.

Armitage, Marigold. *fl.* 1952–61. Tipperary, Limerick. Novels.

Born in 1920 on a Royal Air Force base in Lincolnshire, she moved to Tipperary after her marriage and subsequently to Limerick.

Select bibliography
Armitage, Marigold.
—. *A Long Way to Go: An Anglo-Irish Near-Tragedy*. Novel. London: Faber & Faber, 1952. London: Robin Clark, 1989.
—. *A Motley to the View*. Novel. London: Faber & Faber, 1961. London: Robin Clark, 1990.

Arrigan, Mary. Comhaimseartha. Ros Cré, Co. Thiobraid Árann. Litríocht leanaí.

Tá Mary ag cur fúithi i Ros Cré, Co. Thiobraid Árann. "Bhí *Lá le Mamó* ar ghearrliosta Bisto Book Awards 1994 agus *Mamó Cois Trá* ar ghearrliosta Readers' Association Awards 1995." (Uí Nia 1998, 1). Bronnadh an "Hennessey Literary Award" agus an "Sunday Times/CWA Short Story Award" uirthi i 1991 chomh maith leis an "International White Ravens Title" i 1997. Mhaisigh sí an leabhar *Daisy Bates* (An Gúm, 1999), a scríobh Elisabeth Monkhouse agus Emmet Arrigan.

Mary Arrigan, a prolific and internationally well-received children's novelist since the early 1990s, comes from Kildare and lives in Roscrea. She writes in both Irish and English. Originally trained as an artist, she is also an illustrator and a regular reviewer of children's literature. Her *Lá le Mamó* (1993) was shortlisted for the Bisto Book Awards in 1994, and *Mamó Cois Trá* (1994) for the Readers' Association awards in 1995. She won both the Hennessy Literary Award and the Sunday Times/CWA Short Story Award in 1991, as well as the International White Ravens Title in 1997.

Select bibliography
Arrigan, Mary.
—. *Lá le Mamó*. Litríocht leanaí. Baile Átha Cliath: An Gúm, 1993.
—. *Andy, Zeph and the Flying Cottage*. Children's writing. London: Hamish Hamilton, 1994.
—. *Mamó Cois Trá*. Litríocht leanaí. Baile Átha Cliath: An Gúm, 1994.
—. *An Scáth Báistí*. Litríocht leanaí. Baile Átha Cliath: An Gúm, 1994.
—. *Dead Monks and Shady Deals*. Children's writing. Dublin: Children's, 1995.
—. *An Maicín Cliste*. Litríocht leanaí. Baile Átha Cliath: An Gúm, 1995.
—. *Saving the Dark Planet*. Young adult fiction. Bright Sparks. Dublin: Attic, 1995.
—. *Searching for the Green*. Young adult fiction. Bright Sparks. Dublin: Attic, 1995.
—. *An Bhó Fhionn*. Litríocht leanaí. Aist. Eilís Ní Anluain. Baile Átha Cliath: An Gúm, 1996.
—. *The Dwellers Beneath*. Young adult fiction. Bright Sparks. Dublin: Attic, 1996.
—. *Landscape with Cracked Sheep*. Children's writing. Dublin: Children's, 1996.

—. *Mamó ar an Fheirm.* Litríocht leanaí. Baile Átha Cliath: An Gúm, 1996.
—. *Mamó ag an Sorcas.* Litríocht leanaí. Baile Átha Cliath: An Gúm, 1997.
—. *Seascape with Barber's Harp.* Children's writing. Dublin: Children's, 1997.
—. *The Spirits of the Bog.* Children's writing. Dublin: Children's, 1998.
—. *Maeve and The Long-Arm Folly.* Children's writing. Dublin: Children's, 1999.
—. *Nutty Knut.* Children's writing. Dublin: Poolbeg, 1999. Notes: Illus. the author.
—. *Siúlóid Bhreá [A Great Walk].* Litríocht leanaí. Baile Átha Cliath: An Gúm, 1999.
—. *Grimstone's Ghost.* Children's writing. London: HarperCollins, 2000.
—. *Mamó ag an Zú.* Litríocht leanaí. Baile Átha Cliath: An Gúm, 2000.
—. *The Spirits of the Attic.* Children's writing. Dublin: Children's, 2000.
—. *Baldur's Bones.* Children's writing. London: HarperCollins, 2001.
—. *Ghost Bird.* Children's writing. London: Random House, 2001.
—. *Maeve and the Goodnight Trail.* Children's writing. Dublin: Children's, 2001.
—. *The Goodnight Trail.* Children's writing. Dublin: Children's, 2002.
—. *Knut and Freya in Wales.* Children's writing. Dublin: Poolbeg, 2002. Notes: Illus. the author.
—. *Lawlor's Revenge.* Children's writing. London: HarperCollins, 2002.
—. *Pa Jinglebob, The Fastest Knitter in the West.* Children's writing. London: Egmont, 2002.

Secondary sources
Ní Ghlinn, Áine. "Léirmheas ar *An Bhó Fhionn.*" *The Irish Times* (24ú Aibreán 1997).
Uí Nia, Gearóidín, eag. "Arrigan, Mary." *Eolaire Chló Iar-Chonnachta de Scríbhneoirí Gaeilge.* Indreabhán: Cló Iar-Chonnachta, 1998.

Astaire-McKenzie, Ava. Contemporary. Cork. Cookbook.
Daughter of Fred Astaire, spent her childhood in Hollywood. She visited Ireland during her youth and in 1975 she and her husband decided to relocate to West Cork with their two young sons. They received frequent visits from Fred Astaire and his sister Adele, who was living in Co. Waterford at the time. Ava's husband, Richard, is also a writer and has published a memoir of their journey from Hollywood to Cork.
Select bibliography
Astaire-McKenzie, Ava.
—. *At Home In Ireland: Cooking and Entertaining with Ava Astaire-McKenzie.* Cookbook. Colorado: Roberts Rinehart, 1998.

Aylward, Margaret. 1810–89. Waterford. Letters, religious writing.
Daughter of a Catholic merchant in Waterford, she was educated by the Ursulines in Thurles, Co. Tipperary. She was a philanthropist, doing charity work in Waterford before entering the Sisters of Charity in 1834. However, her novitiate was not a success and she returned to her charity work in Waterford. Again in 1846 she entered a convent, this time the Ursuline convent in Waterford, but left soon after. She went to live in Dublin and became a member of the Ladies Association of the St Vincent de Paul. In 1856 she set up an orphanage, St Brigid's, and some time later she established schools to educate disadvantaged children in Dublin, which she also named after St Brigid. In 1868 her work in the schools led her to establish a congregation, the Sisters of the Holy Faith, to continue

this educational project. She died in 1889 (*Field Day V*, 704).

Secondary sources

Gibbon, Margaret. *The Life of Margaret Aylward*. London: Sands, 1928.

Prunty, Jacinta. "Margaret Aylward 1810–1889." *Women, Power and Concsiousness in 19th Century Ireland*. Ed. Mary Cullen and Maria Luddy. Dublin: Attic, 1995.

Prunty, Jacinta. *Lady of Charity, Sister of Faith: Margaret Aylward 1810–1889*. Dublin: Four Courts, 1999.

Barnes, Edel. Contemporary. Cork. Academic writing.

A lecturer in the Department of Accounting and Finance, UCC, since 1992, her research interests include capital structure, and takeovers and mergers.

Select bibliography

Barnes, Edel.

—. "SWAPS, An Accidental Discovery?" Academic writing. *Studies in Accounting and Finance* 2.3 (1995): 56–60.

—. and J. Bogue. *Enterprise Skills for Development Workers*. Academic writing. Cork: Centre for Cooperative Studies, 1997.

—. "The Impact of Free Cashflow on Target and Bidder Probability, a Study of UK Firms." Academic writing. *Irish Accounting Review* 7.2 (2000): 1–37.

Barrington, Margaret. 1896–1982. West Cork. Short stories, novels, journalism.

Born 10 May 1896 at Malin, Co. Donegal, where her father was an RIC inspector, she was educated in Dungannon, at Alexandra College Dublin, before going to school in Normandy and on to TCD. Her first marriage was to Edmund Curtis, the historian, but, following its dissolution, she married the short-story writer Liam O'Flaherty in 1926, with whom she had one daughter. They separated in 1932. During the 1930s she lived in England, where she supported the republican side in the Spanish civil war and also helped refugees from Nazi Germany. She was by profession a freelance journalist and wrote for Irish, English and American newspapers and periodicals. She also contributed a woman's page to the *Tribune*. During the Second World War she moved to Kilmacabe House in Leap, Co. Cork, but later moved to Kinsale, where she died in 1982. Her last years were spent quietly pursuing her interest in walking, collecting wild flowers, bird-watching and fishing. She also continued to write short stories and essays based on her interests for *The Bell* magazine and other journals. Her literary output consists of one novel, *My Cousin Justin* (1939), and a collection of short stories, *David's Daughter, Tamar* (1982), which was published posthumously.

Select bibliography

Barrington, Margaret.

—. "Miss Baby." Short story. *Dublin Magazine* 1.5 (1923): 377–81.

—. "The Bear." Play. *Dublin Magazine* 1.8 (1924): 731–5.

—. *My Cousin Justin*. Novel. London: Jonathan Cape, 1939.

—. "The Death of My Father." Short story. *The Bell* 2.3 (1941): 52–60.

—. "The Funeral." Short story. *The Bell* 3.4 (1942): 257–60.

—. "A Writer's Day in Carbery." Memoir. *The Bell* 8.1 (1944): 65–75.

—. "Public Opinion: Censorship." Letter. *The Bell* 9.6 (1945): 528–30.
—. "Spider in Love." Short story. *The Bell* 11.6 (1946): 1038–42.
—. "The Corbies." Essay. *The Bell* 14.1 (1947): 40–4.
—. "'Degrees of Evil.' Rev. of *Comrade O Comrade*, by Ethel Mannin, and *All Hallows' Eve*, by Charles Williams." *The Bell* 15.5 (1947): 71–3.
—. "'People and Books.' Rev. of novels by twelve authors." *The Bell* 14.2 (1947): 68–73.
—. "To Ethel Mannin." Letter. *The Bell* 15.2 (1947): 67–8.
—. "Wild Flowers of West Cork and Kerry." *Countrygoer: Introducing Ireland*. Science. Ed. Cyril Moore. N.p.: n.p., 1947. 48–50.
—. "Fable." Essay. *The Bell* 17.1 (1951): 63–7.
—. "Rev. of *The Betrothed*, by Alessandro Manzoni, trans. by Archibald Colquhoun." *The Bell* 17.7 (1951): 62–3.
—. "The Bishop's Turkey." Short story. *The Bell* 18.7 (1952): 405–13.
—. *David's Daughter, Tamar*. Short stories. Dublin: Wolfhound, 1982. Notes: Intro. William Trevor.
—. "Village Without Men." *Territories of the Voice: Contemporary Stories by Irish Women Writers*. Short story. Ed. Louise DeSalvo *et al*. N.p.: n.p., 1989. Boston: Beacon, 1999. 228–38.
—. "The End of a Hero." *Best Broadcast Stories*. Short story. Ed. H. Brown. London: Faber & Faber, 1944. 72–9.

Barry, Kate. Contemporary. Cork. Short stories.
Born in Cork in 1975, she grew up in Midleton. A graduate of English at UCC, she received an MPhil in Anglo-Irish Literature from TCD in 1998. In 1993 Barry won a commendation in the Prudential Irish Schools Writing Awards and was twice nominated for a Hennessy/*Sunday Tribune* Award, in 1997 and 1999.
Select bibliography
Barry, Kate.
—. "Gabriel Malkin." *Social and Personal* (Nov. 1996).
—. "The Insomniac." *Sunday Tribune* (Dec. 1996).
—. "Snow." *Metropolitan* (Sept. 1996).
—. contributor. *Snow*. Short stories. BBC (Jan. 1997).
—. "A Death in the Family." *Sunday Tribune* (Oct. 1998).

Barry, M. *fl.*1840–50. Cork. Poetry.
O'Donoghue tells us that "a lady of this name wrote a good deal of verse for the *Cork Southern Reporter* in the earlier half of the nineteenth century. Eight of her pieces are in *Echoes from Parnassus*, selected from the original poetry of the *Southern Reporter*, Cork, 1849" (20).
Select bibliography
Barry, M.
—. *Echoes from Parnassus*. Poetry. Cork: *Southern Reporter*, 1849. (20)

Bary, Valerie. Contemporary. Co. Kerry. History.
Born in New Zealand, she now lives in Killorglin, Co. Kerry. Her interest is in historical research and her published work is on old houses in Co. Kerry.

She has written several articles for the *Kerry Magazine*, the journal of the Kerry Archaeological and Historical Society, for the *Irish Ancestor* (1979) and for local magazines. Her current projects are biographical accounts of the Godfrey family from Kilcolman Abbey and of the Leeson-Marshall/Ruth family of Callinafercy House, whose family documents are now in her possession.

Select bibliography
Bary, Valerie.
—. "National Monuments: An Endangered Species." Essay. *Kerry Magazine* 4 (1993): 9–10.
—. "Flesk Castle." History. *Kerry Magazine* 5 (1994): 9–11.
—. *Historical, Genealogical, Architectural Notes of Some Houses of Kerry*. History. Whitegate, Co. Clare: Ballinakella, 1994.
—. "Gortnaglough House." History. *Kerry Magazine* 6 (1995): 40–2.
—. "Dromin House." History. *Kerry Magazine* 8 (1997): 35–6.
—. "Molahiff House." History. *Kerry Magazine* 9 (1998): 28–30.
—. "Caragh Cottage." History. *Kerry Magazine* 10 (1999): 17–19.
—. "Annamore House." History. *Kerry Magazine* 11 (2000): 6–10.

Bates, Daisy May, née O'Dwyer. 1861–1951. Roscrea, Co. Tipperary. Travel writing, social history.

Her origins are a little obscure, her birthdate is variously given as 1861 and 1863. She tells us herself that she was the daughter of James Edward O'Dwyer and Margaret Hunt, and was raised by grandparents in Roscrea, Co. Tipperary, but other accounts suggest that she was from Ballychrine, Co. Tipperary, and that she may have grown up in an orphanage. She left Ireland in her early twenties, and is best known for her life and travels in Australia. She emigrated to Townsville in 1883, working first as a governess on a North Queensland cattle ranch, and then she married a stockman, Edwin Henry Morant, in 1884. This man was the infamous "Breaker Morant" executed by a British firing squad during the Boer War – when Daisy met him he was a flamboyant horseman and womanizer, and their marriage barely lasted a year (Kelly, 1995, 119–20). Daisy then married Jack Bates, another tough cattleman, in 1885, and he taught her how to survive in the outback. They had a son, Albert, but again, this marriage was not a success. Leaving Jack, Daisy travelled widely throughout Australia, staying with friends as she moved about.

She was financially ruined in the economic crash of the 1890s, and left for England, leaving her son with his father. She lived with a cousin in Ireland, and following an introduction to W.T. Stead began to write articles for *Review of Reviews* and the *Pall Mall Gazette*. She moved to London and lived in a women's hostel, and although her lifestyle conformed to the New Woman stereotype, she was no fan of these early feminists. When she recovered some of her lost money she paid her fare back to Australia. Her interest in Australia's indigenous tribes dates from this period; we are variously told that she was sent by *The Times* to write on these peoples, or that while making her own way back to Australia she met a Catholic priest who worked with aborigines, and this was the origin of her interest in recording the languages and customs of those tribes.

Bates was reunited with her son, but less than twelve months later set off on her travels again – this time for Australia's north-west coast. Her first visit to the Trappist Mission in north-west Australia is recounted in *The Passing of the Aborigines* (1938). She went on to study the Koolarrubulloo tribes while living at Broome, and later lived with the Bibbulmun tribe near Perth for two years. By the late 1890s Bates was a recognized authority on Australian aboriginal tribes; she gave lectures to the Royal Geographical Society and was consulted by anthropologists. She understood the importance of place and kin to these tribes, and came to be known as Kabbarli, the Grandmother, to the natives of Shark Bay. In 1910 she was appointed as a travelling protector to the aborigines on an expedition with Radcliffe Brown, Australia's first professor of anthropology. He intended to study the habits of a variety of tribes, but Bates was necessary to the expedition as she had already built up links with these tribes and she was a gifted linguist. Their trip was a controversial one, and Bates accused Brown of stealing and plagiarizing her notes. She studied aspects of language, myth, religion and kinship on this and other expeditions, and she also compiled a "southern zodiac" based on her observations of the night sky.

In between her long spells of living in the bush she and Jack lived together on his ranch at Glen Carrick, but they finally separated in 1912. During the First World War I, she lived with the tribes near Fowler's Bay, and from 1919 till 1935 she occupied a pitched tent at Ooldea, on the Nullarbor Plain. She became a familiar sight to travellers in the region, cutting an odd figure in that landscape wearing her Edwardian ankle-length skirts, high starched collar and voluminous fly-veil.

In the 1920s she wrote for Mee's *Children's Newspaper* and the *Australasian*. However, her best-known work, based on her life's work, was *The Passing of the Aborigines* (1938). She believed that contact with Western civilization was fatal to the aborigines, that they needed their traditional environment. Natives journeyed to visit her from long distances, and she clothed them, nursed them and settled their disputes. She has been something of a folk hero in Australia, and is the subject of an opera (Margaret Sutherland's *The Young Kabbarli*) and a film (Andrew Taylor's 2002 *Kabbarli*). The latter depicts Bates as a contradictory figure, whose tireless work on behalf of aborigines is at odds with her snobbery and devotion to the British Empire – in 1933 she was created a Commander of the Order of the British Empire by King George V.

When she was more than eighty years of age she went back to live with tribal aborigines at Wynbring, but illness compelled her to return to Adelaide, where she died in 1951. Much of her research remains unpublished.

Select bibliography
Bates, Daisy May.
—. *The Passing of the Aborigines*. Social history. N.p.: n.p., 1938. Melbourne: Heine-
    mann, 1966.

Secondary sources
Hill, Ernestine. *Kabbarli: A Personal Memoir of Daisy Bates*. Sydney: Angus & Robertson, 1973.
Monkhouse, Elisabeth, and Emmet Arrigan. *Daisy Bates*. Trans. Ciardha Ní Mháirtín. Baile Átha Cliath: An Gúm, 1999.

Beamish, Florence F. *fl.*1850–55. Cork. Poetry, short stories.

O'Donoghue tells us that she was a native of Cork, and notes that she was a "contributor of prose and verse to *Duffy's Fireside Magazine* [... and] Hayes' *Ballads of Ireland* (1855)" (23).

Bean chéile Neddy. *fl.*1933. Baile na Curtaí, Co. Chiarraí. Filíocht, caoineadh / béaloideas.

Ní fios go baileach cérbh é Neddy, ach amháin gur Chonnachtach é, agus gur chum a bhean caoineadh ar ócáid a bháis, uair éigin idir 1833–1933. Bhí sé féin agus a bhean ag cur fúthu i mBaile na Curtaí, Co. Chiarraí. Bhí sé ag obair ar an mbóthar idir Trá Lí agus an Daingean, ach d'éirigh sé breoite agus cailleadh é. Tá blúire den chaoineadh i gcló in *Duanaire Duibhneach* (Ó Dubhda 1933, 140). Ba é Seán Mac Criomhthain, Cill Maoilchéadair, a thug do Sheán Ó Dubhda é (162).

Select bibliography
Bean chéile Neddy.
—. "Caoine Neddy." *Duanaire Duibhneach: bailiú d'amhránaibh agus de phíosaibh eile filidheachta a ceapadh le tuairim céad bliain i gCorca Dhuibhne, agus atá fós i gcuimhne agus i mbéaloideas na ndaoine ann*. Filíocht / béaloideas. Eag. Seán Ó Dubhda. 1933. Baile Átha Cliath: Oifig Dhíolta Foilseacháin Rialtais, 1969.

Bean de mhuintir Chéileachair. *fl.*1926. Cluan Droichead agus Ceann Toirc, Co. Chorcaí. Filíocht / béaloideas.

Bhreac Séamas Lankford síos beagnach caoga líne de "Caoineadh Airt Uí Laoghaire" ón mbean seo, agus foilsíodh sa *Lóchrann* é i 1926. Saolaíodh í i gCluan Droichead, Co. Chorcaí agus bhí sí ag maireachtáil i gCeann Toirc nuair a bailíodh an caoineadh uaithi (Ó Tuama 1961, 47).

Select bibliography
Bean de mhuintir Chéileachair.
—. a d'aithris. "Caoineadh Airt Uí Laoghaire." Filíocht / béaloideas. *An Lóchrann*. Meitheamh (1926): 50.

Secondary sources
Ó Tuama, Seán, eag. *Caoineadh Airt Uí Laoghaire*. 1961. Baile Átha Cliath: An Clóchomhar Tta, 1963.

Bean Riaghalta i gCorcaigh [Bean Rialta i gCorcaigh]. *fl.*1934. An Charraig Dhubh, Cathair Chorcaí. Aistriúchán, drámaíocht.

Bean rialta i gClochar na nUrsalach, An Charraig Dhubh, Corcaigh ab ea an t-aistritheoir. Chuir sí Gaeilge ar dhráma le Robert Hugh Benson, *Maighdean Orléans* (Ó Droighneáin 1937, 247).

Select bibliography
Bean Riaghalta i gCorcaigh.
—. aist. *Maighdean Orléans*. Drámaíocht. Le Robert Hugh Benson. Cluichí Gearra
XVI. Baile Átha Cliath: Oifig Dhíolta Foilseacháin Rialtais, 1934.
Secondary sources
Ó Droighneáin, Muiris. *Taighde i gComhair Stair Litridheachta na Nua-Ghaedhilge ó
1882 anuas*. 1936. Baile Átha Cliath: Oifig Dhíolta Foilseacháin Rialtais, 1937.

Beasley, Maureen, née Horgan. Contemporary. Finuge, Co. Kerry. Poetry,
memoirs.
Born in 1918 near Listowel, Co. Kerry, on a farm that has been in her family
for generations, she was educated locally, worked in Dublin for a while and
returned to her native townland to marry and raise her family. Writing has
always been an integral part of her life and her books recount her childhood
and the changes that have come about in her community during her long life.
Select bibliography
Beasley, Maureen.
—. *The Echoes of Maureen*. Memoirs.Self-published, 1974.
—. *The River Echoes*. Memoirs. Self-published, 1975.
—. *Maureen's Meanderings*. Memoirs. Self-published, 1982.
—. *A Gabháil of Life*. Memoirs. Self-published, 1987.
—. *The Homes of Killocrim*. Memoirs. Self-published, 1989.
—. *Farewell to Bygone Days*. Memoirs. Self-published, 1998.

Beatty, Bertha, née Creagh. *fl.*1939. Listowel, Co. Kerry. Memoirs.
Born in Listowel, Co. Kerry, in 1879, she was the daughter of Francis
Creagh, a well known solicitor and racehorse owner. She was educated at
home, and following her marriage to Richard Beatty from Wexford she went
to live in Wiltshire.
   She records her time there in her first book, *West-Country Thoughts* (n.d.),
which was followed by a memoir of her childhood in Kerry, *Kerry Memories*
(1939).
Select bibliography
Beatty, Bertha.
—. *West-Country Thoughts*. Memoirs. Dawlish, Devon: Channing, n.d.
—. *Kerry Memories*. Memoirs. Dawlish, Devon: Channing, 1939.

Benn, Mary [Wilhelm]. *fl.*1850–60. Co. Cork. Poetry.
It is thought that Mary Benn was the wife of the Rev. John Watkins Benn,
Rector of Carrigaline and Douglas, Co. Cork. Her father William Dunn was
rector of Charleville, Co. Cork and she appears in some services as Mary
Dunn. O'Donoghue tells us that she was "fervently Irish and distinguished
for her Latin poems", and that she "wrote a couple of poems for the *Nation*
under the signature of 'Wilhelm'" (25).
Select bibliography
Benn, Mary.
—. *The Solitary, or A Lay from the West, with Other Poems in English and Latin*. Poetry.
   Dublin: James McGlashan, 1853.
—. *Lays of the Hebrews and Other Poems*. Poetry. London: Joseph Masters, 1854.

Bennett, Isabel. Contemporary. Co. Kerry. Academic writing.

An archaeologist, she lives in Ballyferriter, Co. Kerry. She is a graduate of UCG. Since 1964 she has edited at least nine summary accounts of the archaeological excavations carried out in Ireland each year.

Select bibliography
Bennett, Isabel.
—. "Archaeological Excavations in County Kerry 1985–1993." Academic writing. *Kerry Magazine* 5 (1994): 19–22.
—. "Museum Chorca Dhuibhne." Journalism. *Kerry Magazine* 6 (1995): 24–5.
—. ed. *Ogham Stones of the Dingle Peninsula* [*Clocha Oghaim Chorca Dhuibhne*]. Academic writing. Ballyferriter: Oidhreacht Chorca Dhuibhne, 1995.
—. "Note on the Re-Location of Rock Art from Killelton Townland." Academic writing. *Kerry Magazine* 11 (2000): 38–9.

Bernard, Kathleen. Contemporary. Mitchelstown, Co. Cork. Poetry.

Raised in Mitchelstown, she was living in Paris in 1985. She had poetry published in *Poetry Ireland Review* that year.

Select bibliography
Bernard, Kathleen.
—. "The Moon." Poetry. *Poetry Ireland Review* 14 (1985): 75–6.

Bewick, Harry. *fl.* **1958.** Kenmare, Co. Kerry. Autobiography.

Mother of the artist Pauline Bewick (*q.v.*), she led a peripatetic existence living at various times in a houseboat, a caravan, a railway carriage, a gate lodge and, later, in a boardinghouse she ran in Dublin while Pauline was a student at the National College of Art. She wrote an account of living in Kerry in *A Wild Taste* (1958).

Select bibliography
Bewick, Harry.
—. *A Wild Taste*. Memoir. London: Peter Davies, 1958.

Bewick, Pauline. Contemporary. Kerry. Autobiography, travel writing.

One of Ireland's best-known artists, she was born in 1935 in Northumberland. Following her father's death her mother brought her to live in Kenmare, Co. Kerry, but they returned to England after the war, where Pauline attended a number of progressive schools. They returned to Kerry in 1950, and Pauline commenced her studies at the National College of Art in Dublin while she and her mother lived in a caravan behind an advertisement hoarding in Kilmainham. Later they moved to a nearby house in Rathmines where they let rooms to art students. After college Pauline worked for the Pike Theatre as stage designer and actor, and also did illustrations for Liam Miller at Dolmen Press and other publishers in Dublin and London. One of these was a collection of Irish tales written by Ulick O'Connor. In 1962 she married Pat Melia, and continued to hold exhibitions in Dublin and Cork. In 1974 they moved to Kerry, where they built a house and studio.

Bewick's work has been exhibited all over the world, and her paintings can be found in many prestigious collections at home and abroad. In addition to this work, she has published illustrations and articles in a wide range of magazines and journals. She has also written a number of books based on her travels and her art. James White, the former director of the National Gallery of Ireland, has written her biography, *Painting a Life* (1985), and she was also the subject of a film, *A Painted Diary*, directed by David Shaw Smith in 1984.

Select bibliography
Bewick, Pauline.
—. *Ireland: An Artist's Year*. Diary. London: Methuen, 1990.
—. *The Yellow Man*. Autobiography. Dublin: Wolfhound, 1995.
—. *The South Seas and a Box of Paints*. Autobiography. London: Art Books International, 1996.

Secondary sources
White, James. *Painting a Life*. Dublin: Wolfhound, 1985.

Blackburn, Helen. 1842–1903. Valentia Island, Co. Kerry. Political writing, history.

Born in 1842, in Valentia, Co. Kerry. Her father, Bewicke Blackburn, was a civil engineer who managed the Knight of Kerry's slate quarries, and her mother, Isabella Lamb, came from Durham. The family moved to London when Helen was seventeen, and she went on to become involved in the suffrage movement. From 1874 to 1895 she was secretary for the National Society for Women's Suffrage. She published widely on feminist issues, and edited *The Englishwoman's Review* from 1881. In 1895 she gave up her political activism to look after her father, whose health suffered following a riding accident. After his death she began to write full-time, her main areas of interest being women's rights and working conditions for women in industry.

Her best-known work, *Women's Suffrage: A Record of the Movement in the British Isles* (1902), remains an important source for feminists and scholars today. In addition to her writing, Blackburn became an unofficial archivist of the women's suffrage movement, as she collected pamphlets and newspaper clippings relating to women's political activism during the period. She began her collection in memory of Lydia Becker and Caroline Ashurst Biggs (each book contains a bookplate to the memory of Becker and Biggs designed by Edith Mendham and printed by the Women's Printing Society) and it consists of books, pamphlets, periodicals and newspaper cuttings which relate to the nineteenth-century women's movement internationally. She kept the collection in a mahogany bookcase of her own design and on her death she bequeathed it to Girton College, with the proviso that the books be kept together.

Select bibliography
Blackburn, Helen.
—. *Some of the Facts of the Women's Suffrage Question*. Political writing. London: Central Committee of the National Society for Women's Suffrage, 1878.
—. *A Handy Book of Reference for Irishwomen*. Political writing. London: n.p., 1888.

Notes: Published in relation to the Irish Exhibition of 1888.

—. *A Handbook for Women Engaged in Social and Political Work*. Political writing. Bristol: J.W. Arrowsmith, 1895.

—. and E.J. (Jessie) Boucherett. *The Condition of Working Women*. Political writing. London: Elliot Stock, 1896.

—. ed. and comp. *Words of a Leader: Being Extracts from the Writings of the Late Miss L. Becker*. Political writing, history. Bristol: J.W. Arrowsmith, 1897.

—. and Edith Palliser. *The Way the World Went Then: The Story of Evolution for Children*. Children's writing, science. London: Stanford, 1898.

—. *Women's Suffrage: A Record of the Movement in the British Isles*. Political writing, history. London: Williams & Norgate, 1902.

—. and N. Vynne. *Women Under the Factory Acts*. Political writing. London: Williams & Norgate, 1903.

Blake, Carla. Contemporary. Cork. Handbooks, cookbooks, social history.

Trained and worked as a staff nurse on the children's ward of the Groote Hospital in South Africa before she travelled to Wales to study midwifery. There, she met and married an Irishman, and moved to Careysville, Fermoy, Co. Cork, in 1951 where they had four children. Blake began to work as a journalist in 1970, writing for the *Irish Press*, the (then) *Cork Examiner*, and a range of other newspapers and magazines. She continues to write freelance newspaper articles. Many of her early articles concerned child welfare and protection, and she addressed issues such as breastfeeding and Down syndrome in the 1970s, when such matters were not publicly discussed. She frequently incorporated recipes in her pieces. Her articles are a unique record of Irish social history, providing glimpses of Irish rural life throughout the 1970s and 1980s. Her more recent pieces address issues such as ecology and rural incomes. She published two books in the 1970s dealing with childcare and cookery.

Select bibliography
Blake, Carla.
—. *The Irish Cookbook*. Cookbook. Cork: Mercier, 1971.
—. *The Irish Mother's Baby Book*. Handbook. Cork: Mercier, 1974.

Blake, Lady Edith, née Bernal Osborne. 1845–1926. Clonmel. Botany, political writing.

A close friend of Anna Parnell, she was deeply interested in Irish political issues of the day. In the early years of her married life in Clonmel she wrote *The Realities of Freemasonry* (1879), which included details of the society's history and secret ceremonies. Her husband was the head of the Clonmel RIC, and went on to serve as a magistrate in Ireland, and then to take up the position of Governor, first in the Bahamas and later in Newfoundland, Jamaica, Hong Kong and Ceylon. In each of these countries Edith sketched and painted the flora, fauna and landscape, and she became well known as a botanical artist. Her outstanding collection of drawings, annotated by her, is held in the Entomology Library at the British Museum. In 1907 the couple returned to live in Myrtle Grove, Co. Cork, once the home of Sir Walter Ralegh, where she died in 1926. Some examples of her work, and her sketch books, are still in the house.

Select bibliography
Blake, Lady Edith.
—. *The Realities of Freemasonry.* History. London, 1879.

Boddington, Mary, née Comerford. *fl.*1836–39. Cork. Poetry, travel writing.

Born in Cork, 1776. According to O'Donoghue, she may have been one of the Boddingtons mentioned in Thomas Moore's diary (30). Her poetry was published in the Cork newspapers, and she wrote travel literature. She married a wealthy West Indian merchant in London.

Select bibliography
Boddington, Mary.
—. *The Gossip's Week.* Short stories. 2 vols. N.P.: n.p., 1836.
—. *Sketches in the Pyrenees, With Some Remarks on Languedoc, Provence and the Corniche.* Travel writing. London: n.p., 1837.
—. *Slight Reminiscences of the Rhine, Switzerland, and a Corner of Italy.* Travel writing. 2 vols. London: John Rodwell, 1837.
—. *Poetry.* Poetry. London: Longmans, 1839.

Boland, Bridget. 1913–88. Kerry. Memoir, novels, plays, screenplays.

Born in London in 1913, she was the daughter of John Pius Boland, an Irish barrister who represented the South Kerry constituency at Westminster from 1900 to 1918. When Bridget was a child she spent several years at Daniel O'Connell's family residence in Derrynane on the Ring of Kerry, and she refers to the impact of this place on her formative years, in her auto-biography. She was educated at Roehampton and graduated from Oxford in 1935. She worked as a screenwriter and playwright, wrote a number of novels as well as two books on gardening. The National Library holds a poster of another play written by Bridget Boland, *The Return*, which was staged at the Gate Theatre in May/June 1966.

Select bibliography
Boland, Bridget.
—. *Gardener's Magic.* Handbook. N.p.: n.p., n.d.
—. *Gaslight.* (Unpub.) screenplay. N.d.
—. and Maureen Boland. *Old Wives' Lore for Gardeners.* Handbook. N.p.: n.p., n.d.
—. *The Prisoner.* (Unpub.) play. N.d.
—. *The Wild Geese.* Novel. London: Heinemann, 1938. London: Virago, 1988.
—. *Portrait of a Lady in Love.* Novel. London: Heinemann, 1942.
—. *Caterina.* Novel. London: Souvenir, 1975.
—. *At My Mother's Knee.* Memoir. London: Bodley Head, 1978.
—. sel. and arr. *The Lisle Letters: An Abridgement.* Ed. Muriel St Clare Byrne. Chicago: UP, 1983.

Boland, Rosita. Contemporary. Ennis, Co. Clare. Poetry, travel writing.

Born in 1965 in Ennis, Co. Clare, she graduated from TCD with a BA in

English and History. She travelled for a year in Australia, and on her return to London worked in publishing for two years. Her work had already appeared in several anthologies and magazines while she was a student, and in 1991 she published her first book of poetry, *Muscle Creek*. The following year she wrote a travel book based on three months she had spent hitchhiking around the coast of Ireland on a tight budget. She also translated some of the Irish poems of Cathal Ó Searcaigh for inclusion in *The Bright Wave: An Tonn Geal* (Ed. Dermot Bolger, 1986). She is currently working as a journalist with the *Irish Times*.

Select bibliography
Boland, Rosita.
—. *Muscle Creek*. Poetry. Dublin: Raven Arts, 1991.
—. *Sea Legs: Hitch-Hiking the Irish Coast Alone*. Travel writing. Dublin: New Island, 1992.
—. *Dissecting the Heart*. Poetry. Oldcastle: Gallery Press, 2003.

Bolster, Evelyn [Sr. Angela Bolster]. 1925–2005. Cork. History, religious writing.

Born in Mallow in 1925, she was educated locally at St Marie's of the Isle in Cork and UCC. She became a member of the Mercy community of nuns and pursued an academic career, specializing in religious and ecclesiastical history. She was the first nun to receive a PhD degree from NUI in 1963, and taught at UCC from 1950 to 1968, when she was appointed Assistant Lecturer in Modern History. Bolster wrote a four-volume history of the diocese of Cork, and she was appointed by the Irish church authorities to investigate the cause for the canonization of Catherine McAuley, foundress of the Sisters of Mercy. She travelled extensively throughout the world researching her work.

Select bibliography
Bolster, Evelyn.
—. "Ecclesiastical Cork." History. *The Fold* 13 (1965): 28–31.
—. *The Sisters of Mercy in the Crimean War*. History. Cork: Mercier, 1965.
—. "The Diocese of Cork and the Great Eastern Schism." History. *Journal of Cork Historical and Archaeological Society* 71 (1966): 92.
—. "The Parish of Kilmichael." History. *The Fold* 14 (1967): 48–51.
—. "Blackpool Community Service Centre." Essay. *The Fold* 16 (1969): 8–11.
—. "Focus on the Philippines." Essay. *The Fold* 16 (1969): 7–10, 13–18.
—. *A History of Mallow*. History. Cork: Cork Historical Guides Committee, 1971.
—. *A History of the Diocese of Cork from the Earliest Times to the Reformation*. History. Shannon: Irish University, 1972.
—. ed. *Catherine McAuley 1778–1978: Bi-Centenary Souvenir Book*. History. Dublin: Irish Messenger, 1978.
—. *Catherine McAuley in Her Own Words*. History. Dublin: Diocesan Office for Causes, 1978.
—. *The Knights of Saint Columbanus*. History. Dublin: Gill & Macmillan, 1979.
—. and John Coolahan. *Carysfort 1877–1977: Two Centenary Lectures*. History. Blackrock, Co. Dublin: Our Lady of Mercy College, 1981.
—. "Catherine McAuley: Her Educational Thought and Its Influence on the Origin and

Development of an Irish Training College." *Carysfort 1877–1977: Two Centenary Lectures*. Lecture. Blackrock, Co. Dublin: Our Lady of Mercy College, 1981. 1–19.

—. *Catherine McAuley: The Story of a Woman of Prayer and Compassion*. History. Strasbourg: Editions SADIFA, 1982.

—. *A History of the Diocese of Cork from the Reformation to the Penal Era*. History. Vol. 2. Cork: Tower, 1982.

—. *My Song is of Mercy and Justice*. Religious writing. Ballincollig, Co. Cork: Tower, 1984.

—. *The Correspondence of Catherine McAuley 1827–1841*. Letters. Cork: Sisters of Mercy, 1988.

—. *A History of the Diocese of Cork from the Penal Era to the Famine*. History. Vol. 3. Ballincollig, Co. Cork: Tower, 1989.

—. *Catherine McAuley: Venerable for Mercy*. History. Dublin: Dominican, 1990.

—. *A History of the Diocese of Cork: The Episcopate of William Delany 1847–1886*. History. Vol. 4. Ballincollig, Co. Cork: Tower, 1993.

—. "The Knights of Saint Columbanus." *The Limerick Compendium*. History. Ed. Jim Kemmy. Dublin: Gill & Macmillan, 1997. 35.

Secondary sources
Forde, Rev. R. "Sister M. Angela Bolster." *A History of Mallow* (1971): 20.

Bonaparte-Wyse, Olga. *fl.* 1969. Waterford. Family history.

Wrote a history of the Bonaparte-Wyse family of Waterford, based on collections of family documents.

Select bibliography
Bonaparte-Wyse, Olga.
—. *The Spurious Brood: Princess Letitia Bonaparte and Her Children*. Biography, memoir. London: Victor Gollancz, 1969.

Boole, Mary Everest. 1832–1916. Cork. Science.

Born in England in 1832, she moved at a young age to Poissy in France because of her father's ill health. Dr Thomas Everest, a minister, was an adherent of homeopathy and a firm believer in preventive medicine. Her uncle, George Everest, had made the family name famous, having led the expedition to the mountain which has since borne his name. As a child, Mary Everest's first language was French, and her interest in mathematics and philosophy was fostered by the family tutor, M. Deplace, whose methods may have been based on Rousseau's teachings. When Mary was in her early adolescence the Everest family returned to England, where Mary went to school, but she left when still quite young to teach Sunday school and help her father with his sermons. She continued to study calculus by herself, using her father's books. In 1850, when visiting her uncle and aunt in West Cork, she was introduced to the mathematician George Boole, and the two became friends – Boole tutored Everest in maths for two years. In 1855 they married, and lived together in Cork, where George Boole had a post at the then QCC. His young wife attended his lectures (which were only open to men at the time). She helped him to edit his *Laws of Thought* (1854) and he encouraged her study. The couple had five daughters (Alicia Boole Stott followed in her parents' footsteps to become a mathematician, and another daughter, Ethel, better known as E.L. Voynich (*q.v.*), went on to become a fiction writer). However, in 1864, when their youngest daughter was six months old, George Boole died of pneumonia, which forced his wife to manage alone and find employment. A year after her husband's death she found a post as a librarian at a women's college in England.

This was the start of Everest Boole's own career as a teacher and writer. Becoming first an unofficial student adviser, she discovered an aptitude for teaching and began to teach children. This led to her writing textbooks for children, the first of which was *The Preparation of the Child for Science* (1904). She invented curve stitching, or string geometry, in order to teach children the geometry of angles and spaces. Always interested in the psychic world, efforts to get *The Message of Psychic Science for Mothers and Nurses* (1883) published became controversial, and she was forced to quit her job as a result of her beliefs. She took another job as a secretary to a family friend, James Hinton, who encouraged her interest in philosophy. Now fifty, Everest Boole began to write in earnest, penning a number of books and articles on a variety of subjects. She described herself as a mathematical psychologist, who made efforts to analyse how people might learn, or be taught, mathematics and science. Mary Everest Boole died in 1916.

Select bibliography
Boole, Mary Everest.

—. *The Message of Psychic Science to Mothers and Nurses*. Spiritualism. London: Trulbner, 1883.

—. *Symbolical Methods of Study*. Science. London: Kegan Paul, 1884.

—. *Logic Taught by Love*. Science. London: C.W. Daniel, 1890.

—. *The Mathematical Psychology of Gratry and Boole, Translated from the Language of the Higher Calculus into that of Elementary Geometry*. Science. London: Swan Sonnenschein, 1897.

—. *The Preparation of the Unconscious Mind for Science*. Science. London: S.H. Cowell, 1899. Notes: Paper read at the Parents National Education Union (P.N.E.U.) conference, 1899.

—. *Boole's Psychology as a Factor in Education*. Science, philosophy. Colchester: Benham, 1902.

—. *The Cultivation of the Mathematical Imagination*. Science. Colchester: Benham, 1902.

—. *Lectures on the Logic of Arithmetic*. Science. London: Clarendon Press, 1903.

—. *The Preparation of the Child for Science*. N.p.: n.p., 1904.

—. *Miss Education and Her Garden. A Short Summary of the Educational Blunders of Half a Century*. Academic writing. London: C.W. Daniel, 1908.

—. *Mistletoe and Olive: An Introduction for Children to the Life of Revelation*. Science. London: C.W. Daniel, 1908.

—. *Philosophy and the Fun of Algebra*. N.p.: Daniel, 1909.

—. *Suggestions for Increasing Ethical Stability*. London: C.W. Daniel, 1909.

—. *A Woodworker and a Tentmaker*. London: C.W. Daniel, 1909.

—. *The Forging of Passion into Power*. London: C.W. Daniel, 1910.

—. *Some Master-Keys of the Science of Notation*. Science. London: C.W. Daniel, 1911. Notes: Sequel to *Philosophy and the Fun of Algebra*.

—. *What One Might Say to a Schoolboy*. Science. London: C.W. Daniel, 1911.

—. *At the Foot of the Cotswolds: Reminiscences of the Parish of Wickwar*. Memoir. London: C.W. Daniel, 1923.

—. *Collected Works*. Science. Ed. E.M. Cobham. London: C.W. Daniel, 1931.

Secondary sources

Daniel, Florence. *A Teacher of Brain Liberation (Mary Everest Boole)*. London: C.W. Daniel, 1923.

Cobham, Eleanor Meredith. *Mary Everest Boole: A Memoir with Some Letters*. London: C.W. Daniel, 1951.

Tahta, D.G. ed. *A Boolean Anthology: Selected Writings of Mary Boole on Mathematical Education*. N.p.: Association of Teachers of Mathematics, 1972.

Bowen, Elizabeth. 1899–1973. Kildorrery, Co. Cork. Novels, short stories, essays, memoir, family history, literary criticism, children's writing.

Born in Dublin, the last descendant of an Anglo-Irish landowning family based at Bowen's Court, in North Cork near Fermoy, she was educated at home, then at Downe House school for girls, in Kent. She lived with her mother in south-eastern England until the latter's death. As a child, she was much affected by the major mental illness suffered by her father, then by the death from cancer of her mother when she was thirteen. After this she was looked after by various female relatives during adolescence, a period when she divided her time between Dublin, London and Bowen's Court (after her father's recovery). In early adulthood, Bowen lived partly in London and partly in Italy. Her first short story collection was published in 1923, when she also married Alan Cameron, who was employed by the BBC. The marriage lasted companionably till his death, but seems not to have precluded other sexual attachments by Bowen with both men and women. Settling in Oxford upon their marriage, Bowen and Cameron had friendships with many members of the English literary and social elite of the period, notably including Virginia Woolf, an important influence on Bowen's sensibility. They later lived in Regent's Park, a location memorably invoked in several of the works.

Bowen is the most significant Irish woman writer of the first half of the twentieth century. Her work is wide-ranging in nature and shows influences from the major modernists who just preceded her: Proust and James are obvious examples. A writer of marked intelligence and irony, she weaves together these rather anti-realist influences with those of nineteenth-century English realism and comedy of manners, especially Austen. One of the great Anglo-Irish stylists, Bowen is a novelist of sexualities who specializes in ambiguous sexual adherence. Expertly adapting the *Bildungsroman* genre, her representations of lesbian characters, ranging from the comic (Theodora in *Friends and Relations* (1931)) through the undecided ingénue (Sidney in *The Hotel* (1927), Lois in *The Last September* (1929)) to the doomed (in the late novel *Eva Trout* (1969)) have recently begun to be recognized as important contributions to lesbian literature. She is also a major English novelist of the Second World War as it was experienced in London, where she continued to live throughout the Blitz and worked as an air-raid warden. Her representation of children, especially intelligent and emotionally solitary ones, is also one of the glories of her work.

Deeply influenced by nineteenth-century Irish Gothic writing, especially that of J.S. Le Fanu, another notable writer of Munster landscapes, Bowen frequently deploys effects of haunting and otherworldliness, especially in some of her finest short stories. She used material from her own family and childhood to write the definitive "Big House novel" of the century, *The Last September*, which is justly celebrated for its elegant, penetrating and haunting representation of the decline of her own community and its complex, quizzical intersections with the rising forces of Irish self-determination after long colonial rule. Bowen also conducted striking and elegant interrogations of Irish and Anglo-Irish culture and psychology in other works: both *The House in Paris* (1935) and *The Heat of the Day* (1949) contain episodes set in Munster, and a decaying gentry house is the principal setting of her quasi-Gothic novel *A World of Love* (1955). This aspect of her vision is perhaps most fully realized in the brilliant opening sections of *Bowen's Court* (1942), her family history: she always showed an intense imaginative attraction to the North Cork countryside, and in many works she explores its history and its changing guises with unparalleled vividness and sympathy. She is a great writer of region and place, including Kent and London. Above all she celebrates, and to a degree interrogates, the rich wooded landscape of North Cork, so marked by its history of landed estates, with its many demesnes and Norman castle keeps. In this paradoxical representation her half-questioning relationship with her own family's planter history is evident. The complexity of her relation to independent Ireland as a whole is shown by her engaging, on the one hand, in official British intelligence-gathering about Irish attitudes to neutrality during the Second World War, and on the other in a well known love-affair with Cork writer Seán O'Faoláin, also during the 1940s.

Perhaps the most persistent and unifying quality of Bowen's vision is the pursuit of moral enquiry against a background of the dissolution of nineteenth-century certainties, ideological and historical as well as ethical. She repeatedly places modern characters, especially female ones, in a milieu which is denuded of formerly firm structures, and stages their bewildered, often transgressive, actions and responses. The cultural and ideological distance between Munster and London afforded her an important point of leverage in exploring this characteristically twentieth-century loss of direction. Her prose is distinguished by balance, subtle and dry humour, exact beauty of diction, and clear-sighted penetration of moral and psychological dilemmas. In her last two novels she was altering her style towards greater complexity; in its sheer resistance to ready decoding her late work is formidably experimental and vividly expresses post-war *anomie*. With a reputation hitherto fractured by her very variousness (war novelist, "women's novelist", novelist of childhood, Ascendancy writer), Bowen is only now beginning to be granted the high stature and distinguished place in the traditions of Irish and English writing which her work deserves.

Select bibliography
Bowen, Elizabeth.

—. *Encounters*. Short stories. London: Sidgwick & Jackson, 1923.
—. *Ann Lee's and Other Stories*. Short stories. London: Sidgwick & Jackson, 1926.
—. *The Hotel*. Novel. N.p.: n.p., 1927. London: Penguin, 1996.
—. *Joining Charles and Other Stories*. Short stories. London: Constable, 1929.
—. *The Last September*. Novel. N.p.: n.p., 1929. London: Penguin, 1987.
—. *Friends and Relations*. Novel. N.p.: n.p., 1931. London: Jonathan Cape, 1951.
—. *To the North*. Novel. N.p.: n.p., 1932. London: Penguin, 1997.
—. *The Cat Jumps and Other Stories*. Short stories. London: Victor Gollancz, 1934.
—. *The House in Paris*. Novel. London: Victor Gollancz, 1935.
—. *The Death of the Heart*. Novel. N.p.: n.p., 1938. London: Vintage, 1999.
—. *Look at All Those Roses*. Short stories. London: Victor Gollancz, 1941.
—. *Bowen's Court*. Family history. London: Longmans, 1942.
—. *Seven Winters: Memories of a Dublin Childhood*. Memoir. Dublin: Cuala Press, 1942.
—. *The Demon Lover and Other Stories*. Short stories. London: Jonathan Cape, 1945.
—. *English Novelists*. Literary criticism. London: Collins, 1945.
—. *The Heat of the Day*. Novel. N.p.: n.p., 1949. London: Vintage, 1998.
—. *Collected Impressions*. Essays. London: Longmans, Green, 1950.
—. *Early Stories*. Short stories. New York: Alfred Knopf, 1951.
—. *The Shelbourne: A Centre in Dublin Life for More than a Century*. History. London: Harrap, 1952.
—. *A World of Love*. Novel. London: Jonathan Cape, 1955.
—. *Stories by Elizabeth Bowen*. Short stories. New York: Vintage Books, 1959.
—. *A Time in Rome*. Essays. London: Longmans, 1960.
—. *Afterthoughts: Pieces on Writing*. Essays. London: Longmans, 1962.
—. *The Little Girls*. Novel. 1964. London: Vintage, 1999.
—. *A Day in the Dark and Other Stories*. Short stories. London: Jonathan Cape, 1965.
—. contributor. *Writer in Conflict*. Radio programme. RTÉ Radio 1. 7 May 1967. Notes: Documentary on E.M. Forster.
—. *Eva Trout or Changing Scenes*. Novel. 1969. London: Penguin, 1983.
—. *The Good Tiger*. Children's writing. London: Jonathan Cape, 1970.
—. contributor. *Quiet Novelist*. Radio programme. Prod. Donnacha O Dúlaing. RTÉ Radio 1. 11 June 1970. Notes: Documentary about E.M. Forster.
—. *Pictures and Conversations*. Essays. 1975. London: Jonathan Cape, 1975.
—. *Elizabeth Bowen's Irish Stories*. Short stories. Dublin: Poolbeg, 1978.
—. *Collected Stories*. Short stories. London: Jonathan Cape, 1980.
—. *Bowen's Court and Seven Winters*. Family history, memoir. London: Virago, 1984.
—. *The Mulberry Tree: Writings of Elizabeth Bowen*. Essays. Ed. Hermione Lee. London: Vintage, 1999.

Secondary sources
Coughlan, Patricia. "Women and Desire in the Work of Elizabeth Bowen." *Sex, Nation and Dissent in Irish Writing*. Ed. Éibhear Walshe, Cork: Cork UP, 1997.
Glendinning, Victoria. *Elizabeth Bowen: Portrait of a Writer*. London: Weidenfeld & Nicholson, 1977.
Greenwood, Jane, prod. *Sunday Feature: Elizabeth Bowen*. Documentary. BBC Radio 3. 13 June 1999.
Hoogland, Renée. *Elizabeth Bowen: A Reputation in Writing*. New York: New York UP, 1994.
Hosey, Séamus, prod. *Book on One*. Reading: *World of Love* by Elizabeth Bowen. RTÉ Radio 1. 7–11 June 1999.
Jordan, Heather Bryant. *How Will the Heart Endure: Elizabeth Bowen and the Landscape of War*. Michigan: MUP, 1992.

Lassner, Phyllis. *Elizabeth Bowen*. London: Macmillan, 1990.

Lee, Hermione. *Elizabeth Bowen*. London: Vintage, 1999.

McCormack, W.J. "Infancy and History: Beckett, Bowen and Critical Theory." *From Burke to Beckett: Ascendancy, Tradition and Betrayal in Literary History*. Cork: Cork UP, 1994. 375–433.

O Dúlaing, Donnacha, interviewer. Interview with Molly O'Brien about Bowen's Court and Elizabeth Bowen. *Highways and Byways*. RTÉ Radio 1. 15 Oct. 1980.

Ó Mórdha, Seán, prod. *Bookmark: Death of the Heart*. Documentary. BBC 2. 7 Feb. 1999.

Rule, Jane. *Lesbian Images*. Trumansburg: Crossing Press, 1975.

Sellery, J'nan, and William O. Harris. *Elizabeth Bowen: A Bibliography*. Austin: Texas UP, 1977.

Bowen, Muriel. *fl.* 1950. History.

Wrote a history of Irish hunting, in which a chapter is devoted to each of the hunts in Ireland, from Avondhu to Wexford.

Select bibliography
Bowen, Muriel.

—. *Irish Hunting*. History. Tralee: *Kerryman*, 1950. Notes: Illus. by Lionel Edwards R.I.

Bracken, Pauline. Contemporary. Waterford. Novels, memoir, handbook.

Born in Dublin, she is a modern languages graduate from UCD. She is the daughter of Charles E. Kelly, who was Director of Broadcasting in Radio Éireann and editor of the *Dublin Opinion* magazine. Her account of her early life is contained in *Light of Other Days: A Dublin Childhood* (1992), in which she documents the many prominent people of the time who visited her family home, including visiting musicians and conductors of the Radio Éireann Symphony Orchestra. She has worked as a translator at home and abroad, as a tour guide in Ireland, France and the Middle East, in journalism and public relations, and latterly as an author. Bracken is also an associate of the Royal Irish Academy of Music. She moved to Waterford in 1998, where she continues to live and write.

Select bibliography
Bracken, Pauline.

—. *Light of Other Days: A Dublin Childhood*. Memoirs. Cork: Mercier, 1992.

—. *Indian Summer*. Novel. Cork: Collins, 1994.

—. and Niall Bracken. *The Dalkey Persuaders*. Novel. Dublin: Blackwater, 1999.

—. *Get Happy Now!* Handbook. Dublin: Swan, 2001.

Bradshaw, Máire, née Harrison. Contemporary. Limerick, Cork. Poetry.

Born in Limerick in 1943, she now lives in Cork, where she is closely involved with Tigh Filí (House of Poets) and runs a publishing company, Bradshaw Books.

Select bibliography
Bradshaw, Máire.

—. "Brodsky." "No Photograph as Evidence." "A Poet Woman." *Poets Aloud Abu*. Poetry. Cork: Ink Sculptors, 1988.

—. *Instinct*. Poetry. Cork: Ink Sculptors, 1988.
—. *High Time for All the Marys*. Poetry. Comp. Patricia Scanlon. Cork: Ink Sculptors, 1992.
—. "High Time for All the Marys." *The Cork Anthology*. Poetry. Ed. Seán Dunne. Cork: Cork UP, 1993. 223–6.

Breathnach, Máire. Comhaimseartha. Na Déise, Co. Phort Láirge. Scríbhneoireacht acadúil, aiste.

Is Riarthóir Aosoideachais le Coiste Gairmoideachais Chontae Phort Láirge í agus is ón tSráidbhaile í ó dhúchas. Chaith sí scór blianta ag obair mar mhúinteoir i gCo. Uíbh Fhailí.

Select bibliography
Breathnach, Máire.
—. "Aosoideachas i nGaeltacht na Rinne." *An Linn Bhuí: Iris Ghaeltacht na nDéise*. Aiste. Eag. Pádraig Ó Macháin agus Aoibheann Nic Dhonnchadha. Vol. 5. Baile Átha Cliath: Leabhair na Linne, 2001.

Breathnach, Máire Seó. Comhaimseartha. An Chúil Rua, An Seanphobal, Na Déise, Co. Phort Láirge. Scríbhneoireacht acadúil, aiste.

Is sa Seanphobal a saolaíodh Máire. Bhain sí céim amach sa Tráchtáil ó Choláiste na hOllscoile, Corcaigh, agus tá sí ag obair faoi láthair mar Oifigeach Caidrimh Phoiblí le hÚdarás na Gaeltachta (Ó Macháin agus Nic Dhonnchadha 1999, 146–7). Scríobh sí faoi fhorbairt an Údaráis sna Déise, agus faoi thodhchaí na Gaeltachta agus na Gaeilge ina haiste in *An Linn Bhuí* 3 (1999, 83–7).

Select bibliography
Breathnach, Máire Seó.
—. "Údarás na Gaeltachta agus Gaeltacht na nDéise." *An Linn Bhuí: Iris Ghaeltacht na nDéise*. Scríbhneoireacht acadúil, aiste. Eag. Pádraig Ó Macháin agus Aoibheann Nic Dhonnchadha. Vol. 3. Baile Átha Cliath: Leabhair na Linne, 1999.

Breatnach, Bríd. Comhaimseartha. An Rinn, Na Déise, Co. Phort Láirge. Scríbhneoireacht acadúil, aiste.

Sa Rinn a saolaíodh Bríd. Bhain sí céim amach ó Ollscoil Luimnigh agus is ceoltóir í. Tá sí ag obair mar mhúinteoir i mBaile Átha Cliath faoi láthair. Tá taighde déanta aici ar bhéaloideas na nDéise.

Select bibliography
Breatnach, Bríd.
—. "Nioclás Tóibín." *An Linn Bhuí: Iris Ghaeltacht na nDéise*. Aiste. Eag. Pádraig Ó Macháin agus Aoibheann Nic Dhonnchadha. Vol. 6. Baile Átha Cliath: Leabhair na Linne, 2002.

Breatnach, Úna. c.1915–2000. Maol an Chóirnigh agus Baile Uí Dhuibh, Dún Garbhán, Co. Phort Láirge. Scríbhneoireacht acadúil, aistí.

Saolaíodh Úna i mBaile Uí Dhuibh, Dún Garbhán. Thosaigh sí ag múineadh i Scoil Náisiúnta na Rinne sa bhliain 1935 (Ó Macháin agus Nic

Dhonnchadha 1997, 95–6; 1999, 146–7). Scríobh sí aiste ar an Ardeaspag Mícheál Ó Síothcháin in *An Linn Bhuí I* (1997, 36–42), fear a raibh aithne phearsanta aici air. In *An Linn Bhuí 3* (1999, 19–24) scríobh sí faoi Dhiarmuid Stócs (1885–1910), comharsa léi, a bhí ina mhúinteoir Gaeilge agus ina fhile. Bhí aiste eile aici in uimhir a ceathair den iris chéanna.

Select bibliography
Breatnach, Úna.
—. "An tArdeaspag Mícheál Ó Síothcháin." *An Linn Bhuí: Iris Ghaeltacht na nDéise.* Aiste. Eag. Pádraig Ó Macháin agus Aoibheann Nic Dhonnchadha. Vol. 1. Baile Átha Cliath: Leabhair na Linne, 1997.
—. "Diarmuid Stócs." *An Linn Bhuí: Iris Ghaeltacht na nDéise.* Aiste. Pádraig Ó Macháin agus Aoibheann Nic Dhonnchadha. Vol. 3. Baile Átha Cliath: Leabhair na Linne, 1999.
—. "Håkon Melberg." *An Linn Bhuí: Iris Ghaeltacht na nDéise.* Aiste. Eag. Pádraig Ó Macháin agus Aoibheann Nic Dhonnchadha. Vol. 4. Baile Átha Cliath: Leabhair na Linne, 2000.

Breen, Mary. Contemporary. Cork. Academic writing, literary criticism.

Born in Co. Wexford and a graduate of TCD, she received an MA in English from UCC in 1998. She is currently the academic adviser for visiting students in the Department of English, UCC, and coordinator for the Adult Education Certificate and Diploma in Women's Studies. Her research interests include late-eighteenth- and nineteenth-century Irish women writers, especially Dorothea Herbert, and twentieth-century Irish novelists, in particular Molly Keane, Kate O'Brien, Edna O'Brien and John Banville.

Select bibliography
Breen, Mary.
—. "Something Understood? Kate O'Brien and *The Land of Spices*." *Ordinary People Dancing: Essays on Kate O'Brien.* Academic writing. Ed. Éibhear Walshe. Cork: Cork UP, 1993.
—. "Piggies and Spoilers of Girls, the Representation of Sexuality in the Novels of Molly Keane." *Sex, Nation and Dissent.* Academic writing. Ed. Éibhear Walshe. Cork: Cork UP, 1997.

Brennan, Deirdre. Comhaimseartha. Cluain Meala agus Durlas, Co. Thiobraid Árann. Filíocht.

Saolaíodh i mBaile Átha Cliath í sa bhliain 1934, ach tá sí ag cur fúithi i gCeatharlach le beagnach daichead bliain anuas. Chaith sí tréimhsí ina cónaí i gCluain Meala, Co. Thiobraid Árann agus i dTuaim, Co. na Gaillimhe. Bhí ceathrar sa chlann, agus ba í Deirdre an duine ba shine. Fuair sí a cuid oideachais i gClochar na nUrsalach, Durlas. Ghnóthaigh sí céim BA sa Bhéarla agus sa Laidin chomh maith leis an Ardteastas san Oideachas ó Choláiste na hOllscoile, Baile Átha Cliath. Tá saothar dá cuid foilsithe in *The Irish Times*. Scríobhann sí i mBéarla freisin, agus tá cuid dá saothar foilsithe i dtréimhseacháin dhifriúla, in *Passages 10* mar shampla. Bhuaigh *Scothanna Geala* Rogha Éigse Éireann i 1989 (Ó Cearnaigh 1995, 38–9). Bhí sí mar rannpháirtí ar an gclár raidió *The Arts Show* ar RTÉ ar an

7ú lá d'Aibreán 1992, agus arís ar *Éigse an Aeir* ar an 4ú lá de Mheán Fómhair, 1998.

Select bibliography
Brennan, Deirdre.
—. *I Reilig na mBan Rialta*. Filíocht. Baile Átha Cliath: Coiscéim, 1984.
—. *Scothanna Geala*. Filíocht. Baile Átha Cliath: Coiscéim, 1989.
—. rannpháirtí. *The Arts Show: Galway Poetry Festival*. Filíocht. Láithreoir. Séamus Hosey. Radio 1. RTÉ. 1992.
—. *Thar cholbha na mara*. Filíocht. Baile Átha Cliath: Coiscéim, 1993.
—. rannpháirtí. *Éigse an Aeir*. Filíocht. Láithreoir. Cathal Póirtéir. Raidió 1. RTÉ. 1998.
—. *Ag Mealladh Réalta*. Filíocht. Baile Átha Cliath: Coiscéim, 2000.

Secondary sources
Ó Coigligh, Ciarán, eag. *An Fhilíocht Chomhaimseartha 1975–1985*. Baile Átha Cliath: Coiscéim, 1987.
Donovan, Katie, A. N. Jeffares and Brendan Kennelly, eag. *Ireland's Women*. Dublin: Gill & Macmillan, 1994.
Ó Cearnaigh, Seán. "Brennan, Deirdre." *Scríbhneoirí na Gaeilge 1945–1995*. Baile Átha Cliath: Comhar, 1995.
Nic Fhearghusa, Aoife. *Glór Baineann, Glór an Léargais: an tsochaí, an bheith agus dánta Dheirdre Brennan*. Baile Átha Cliath: Coiscéim, 1998.

Brennan, Elizabeth. *fl.* **1945–84.** Clonmel, Co. Tipperary. Novels.

Born in 1922 in Clonmel, Co. Tipperary, she was educated in Blackrock, Co. Dublin. Her earlier work consisted of retellings of Irish legends in prose and verse, as in *The Wind Fairies* (1946). She later turned to novels, writing mainly light romantic and mystery fiction, for which she received little critical attention. A contemporary reviewer described her first novel, *Out of the Darkness* (1945), as "a promising first book". Several of her works have been translated. One novel, *Girl on an Island* (1984), won the Irish Countrywomen's Association Award in 1984. A recent compilation of creative writings based on articles written for the association's monthly magazine in the 1950–70 period includes four such articles attributed to an Elizabeth Brennan, which are listed in the bibliography. Her later years were spent in Lecarrow, Co. Sligo.

Select bibliography
Brennan, Elizabeth.
—. *Out of the Darkness*. Novel. Dublin: Metropolitan, 1945.
—. *Am I My Brother's Keeper?* Novel. Dublin: Metropolitan, 1946.
—. *The Wind Fairies*. Children's writing. Dublin: Metropolitan, 1946.
—. *The Mystery of the Hermit's Cave*. Children's writing. Dublin: Metropolitan, 1948.
—. *Whispering Walls*. Novel. Dublin: Metropolitan, 1948.
—. *The Wind Fairies Again*. Children's writing. Dublin: Metropolitan, 1948.
—. *Wind over the Bogs*. Poetry. Dublin: Metropolitan, 1950.
—. *The Children's Book of Irish Saints*. Children's writing. London: Harrap, 1963.
—. *His Glamorous Cousin*. Novel. London: Hale, 1963.
—. *Her Lucky Mistake*. Novel. London: Hale, 1966.

—. *Love in the Glade*. Novel. London: Hale, 1967.
—. *Retreat from Love*. Novel. London: Hale, 1967.
—. *Patrick's Women*. Novel. London: Hale, 1969.
—. *Mountain of Desire*. Novel. London: Hale, 1970.
—. *Innocent in Eden*. Novel. London: Hale, 1971.
—. *No Roses for Jo*. Novel. London: Hale, 1972.
—. *Love's Loom*. Novel. London: Hale, 1973.
—. *A Girl Called Debbie*. Novel. London: Hale, 1975.
—. *Sweet Love of Youth*. Novel. London: Hale, 1978.
—. *Girl on an Island*. Novel. London: Hale, 1984.
—. "Far from the Madding Crowd." *Miscellany of Creative Writings*. Essay. Ed. Sarah McNamara. Parteen, Co. Limerick: self-published, 1997. 124–6.
—. "Fine China." *Miscellany of Creative Writings*. Short story. Ed. Sarah McNamara. Parteen, Co. Limerick: Self-published, 1997. 22–5.
—. "Go West Woman!" *Miscellany of Creative Writings*. Political writing. Ed. Sarah McNamara. Parteen, Co. Limerick: self-published, 1997. 64–7.
—. "A Woman's Reach Should Exceed Her Grasp." *Miscellany of Creative Writings*. Political writing. Ed. Sarah McNamara. Parteen, Co. Limerick: self-published, 1997. 53–4.

Secondary sources
J.E. "Rev. of *Out of the Darkness* by Elizabeth Brennan." *The Bell* 10.2 (1945): 179.

Brennan, Lucy. Contemporary. Cork. Poetry.

Born in Dublin in 1931, she spent her childhood in Cork, where she was educated. She emigrated to Montreal in 1957, and now lives in Whitby, Ontario. Her poetry has been published in various Canadian journals, such as *Poetry Canada Review*, *Poetry Toronto*, *Canadian Woman Studies*, *Intangible* and *The Antigonish Review*. In Ireland her work has appeared in *Poetry Ireland Review*, *Irish University Review*, *New Irish Writing* and *Salmon*. She has participated in television programmes in Ontario and has read her works both in Ireland and in Canada. Her collection of poetry, *Migrants All*, was published in Toronto in 1999.

Select bibliography
Brennan, Lucy.
—. *Migrants All*. Poetry. Toronto: Watershed, 1999.
—. "When All Is Said and Done." *Slow Time: 100 Poems to Take You There*. Poetry. Ed. Niall MacMonagle. Dublin: Marino, 2000. 78.

Brew, Margaret [M.W. Brew]. *fl.*1880–91. Co. Clare. Poetry, short stories, novels.

Biographical information on Margaret Brew is scanty, although her autobiographical writings suggest that she was from a landowning Catholic background, and Brown tells us that she was from Co. Clare. She contributed poetry and essays to *The Irish Monthly*, and other periodicals (1968. 41).

Her 1891 essay "An Unknown Hero" deals with Catholic Emancipation. She also published two novels under the name M.W. Brew, *The Burtons of Dunroe* (1880), and *The Chronicles of Castle Cloyne; or Pictures of the Munster People* (1884). The latter, set during the Famine, was favourably received by critics from *The Times* and other established periodicals of the late nineteenth century including *The Athenaeum*, although the reviewer for the latter assumed the unknown author was a man. The *Irish Monthly* discussed it in the following terms: "When a tale of Irish scenes is honoured with long eulogistic reviews in *The Times*, *The Standard*, *The Morning Post*, *The Scotsman* and many other journals of the sort, we are by no means inclined to look upon it with favour, but rather to expect distorted views of Ireland [...] and Irish social life as outrageously unreal [...]. Yet, Miss Brew's "Chronicles of Castle Cloyne" has received these perilous commendations and nevertheless is an excellent Irish tale [...] and altogether [...] is one of the most satisfactory additions to the story of *Irish* fiction from *Castle Rackrent* to *Marcella Grace*" (*Irish Monthly* 14 (1886): 455–6).

Select bibliography
Brew, Margaret.
—. *The Burtons of Dunroe*. Novel. 3 vols. London: Samuel Tinsley, 1880.
—. *The Chronicles of Castle Cloyne; or Pictures of the Munster People*. Novel. 3 vols. London: Chapman & Hall, 1884.
—. "The Soul's Offering." Poetry. *Irish Monthly* 14 (1886): 679–80.
—. "A Poor Traveller." Short stories. *Irish Monthly* 15.Jan. (1887): 42–56.
—. "The Soul's Choice." Poetry. *Irish Monthly* 15.May (1887): 276–7.
—. "Tomorrow at the Breaking of the Day." Poetry. *Irish Monthly* 15.Dec. (1887): 708–9.
—. "Before I Die." Poetry. *Irish Monthly* 16.July (1888): 401.
—. "The Memorial Tablet." Poetry. *Irish Monthly* 17.Apr. (1889): 185–6.
—. "An Unknown Hero." Essay. *Irish Monthly* 19.Feb. (1891): 57–68.

Secondary sources
Wolff, Robert Lee. Intro. *The Burtons of Dunroe*. New York: Garland, 1979.

Brogan, Patricia Burke. Contemporary. Co. Clare. Poetry, plays.

Born in Co. Clare, she spent some years at the Sisters of Mercy convent, where she supervised women working in the infamous Magdalen laundries. Later she taught art at primary and secondary levels and exhibited her own paintings in the 1960s. Her first play, *Eclipsed*, was staged in Galway, Dublin and in Edinburgh, where it received the Scotsman Fringe First Award. She published her first collection of poems, illustrated by herself, in 1994.

Select bibliography
Brogan, Patricia Burke.
—. *Above the Waves*. Poetry. Galway: Salmon, 1994.
—. *Eclipsed*. Play. Galway: Salmon, 1994.

Budds, Bridget. 1869–98. Kilcockan, Co. Waterford. Poetry.

Published about fifty poems in local Waterford newspapers, particularly in the *Weekly Herald*. Her papers are in the County Library, Lismore.

Butler, Kathleen T. [Blake Butler, Kathleen Teresa]. 1833–1950.
Wrote a history of French literature in two volumes while she was Director
of Studies in Modern and Medieval Languages at Girton College and an
Associate of Newnham College in Cambridge, England.
Select bibliography
Butler, Kathleen T.
—. *A History of French Literature.* Academic writing. London: Methuen, 1923.

Butler, Mary E.L. [Máire de Buitléir]. 1874–1920. Co. Clare. Short
stories, novel.

Born in Co. Clare and educated at Alexandra College, Dublin, she was the
editor of a women's page in the *Irish Weekly Independent* 1889–1903. She was
involved in the Gaelic League, at executive level, also in Sinn Féin – in fact,
she was said to have suggested the name "Sinn Féin" for Arthur Griffith's
ideologies. She married Tomás Ó Nualláin in 1907 (*Field Day V*, 118).
Select bibliography
Butler, Mary E.L.
—. *A Bundle of Rushes.* Short stories. London: Sealy Bryers, 1899.
—. *The Ring of Day.* Novel. London: Hutchinson, 1906.
Secondary sources
Ní Chinnéide, Máire. *Máire de Buitléir: Bean Athbheocana.* Baile Átha Cliath:
    Comhar Teoranta, 1993.

Cailín ó Bhaile na bPoc. fl.1933. Baile na bPoc, Paróiste Múrach, Corca
Dhuibhne, Co. Chiarraí agus Co. Thiobraid Árann. Filíocht, béaloideas.

Saolaíodh an cailín i mBaile na bPoc, Paróiste Múrach. Cumadh "Má's
Buairt Rómhór" uair éigin idir 1833–1933, agus foilsíodh é in *Duanaire
Duibhneach* (Ó Dubhda 1933, 105). Is amhlaidh a bhí an cailín agus a
deirfiúr ag obair i gCo. Thiobraid Árann. Theip an tsláinte ar an deirfiúr,
agus chum an cailín roinnt véarsaí chun uchtach a thabhairt di nuair a bhí
an bheirt acu ag siúl abhaile go Co. Chiarraí. Ba í Bean Uí Mhurchadha, An
Baile Loiscthe, a d'aithris do Sheán Ó Dubhda é.
Select bibliography
Cailín ó Bhaile na bPoc.
—. "Má's Buairt Rómhór." *Duanaire Duibhneach: bailiú d'amhránaibh agus de phíosaibh
    eile filidheachta a ceapadh le tuairim céad bliain i gCorca Dhuibhne, agus atá fós i
    gcuimhne agus i mbéaloideas na ndaoine ann.* Filíocht / béaloideas. Eag. Seán Ó
    Dubhda. 1933. Baile Átha Cliath: Oifig Dhíolta Foilseacháin Rialtais, 1969. 105.

Cailíní Óga na Muirí. fl.1934. Corca Dhuibhne, Co. Chiarraí. Ní fios cé
acu *genre*.

In aiste leis "An Scoláire Scairte" (Pádraig Ó Coileáin) in *Agus* cáineann sé
alt a bhí, de réir dealraimh in *Nuacht Chorca Dhuibhne*, inar fágadh a lán
scríbhneoirí de bhunadh an cheantair sin ar lár: "Agus féach go raibh cailíní
óga na Muirí chomh maith le dream ar bith eile níorbh fhiú le *Nuacht
Chorca Dhuibhne* a n-ainm a lua, gan trácht ar iad a mholadh..." (1974, 22).

Is baolach nár ainmnigh Pádraig Ó Coileáin iad ach an oiread.

Select bibliography
Cailíní Óga na Muirí.

Secondary sources
An Scoláire Scairte. "Scríbhneoirí Móra is Beaga Chorca Dhuibhne." *Agus* XIV.6 (1974): 18–22.

Callanan, Helena. *fl.*1879–99. Cork. Poetry.

Born in 1864, she was a Cork poet whose address in the preface to her 1899 collection, *Verses Old and New*, was given as "Asylum for the Blind, Infirmary Road, Cork". Her first collection, *Gathered Leaflets* (1884), was dedicated to Richard Dowden, a patron of the home she lived in. Much of the response to this collection seems to have concentrated on her blindness: "the work of an inmate of the Cork Blind Asylum who, deprived of heaven's greatest gift, has devoted her hours of darkness to the improvement of those intellectual qualities with which she is more than ordinarily gifted" (*Cork Daily Herald*, 31 Jan. 1885). She was a frequent contributor to Irish and Catholic periodicals, such as the *Irish Monthly*, whose editor, Matthew Russell, edited her second collection.

Select bibliography
Callanan, Helena.
—. "Summer: A Poem." Poetry. *Irish Monthly* 7.Aug. (1879): 404–5.
—. "Grandmamma's Boy: A Poem." Poetry. *Irish Monthly* 8.Jan. (1880): 46.
—. "No Room: A Poem." Poetry. *Irish Monthly* 8.Oct. (1880): 571–2.
—. "Widowed Flowers: A Poem." Poetry. *Irish Monthly* 9.Aug. (1881): 418.
—. "Another Sonnet to St Agnes." Poetry. *Irish Monthly* 10.Jan. (1882): 46.
—. "The Last of an Old Friend: A Poem." Poetry. *Irish Monthly* 10.May (1882): 368–9.
—. "One Link: A Poem." Poetry. *Irish Monthly* 11.Feb. (1883): 89–90.
—. *Gathered Leaflets*. Poetry. Cork: Purcell, 1884.
—. "A Promise: A Poem." Poetry. *Irish Monthly* 13.June (1885): 324.
—. "True to the Dead: A Poem." Poetry. *Irish Monthly* 14.Nov. (1886): 611–12.
—. "A Shamrock: A Poem." Poetry. *Irish Monthly* 18.Mar. (1890): 130–1.
—. "In the Starlight: A Poem." Poetry. *Irish Monthly* 24.Apr. (1896): 219.
—. *Verses Old and New*. Poetry. Cork: self-published, 1899.

Campbell, Lady Colin, née Blood [G.E. Brunefille, Q.E.D., Vera Tsaritsyn]. 1861–1911. Cratloe, Co. Clare. Novels, journalism, plays.

From Cratloe, she was the daughter of Edmond Maghlin Blood, who was the High Sheriff of Clare. Her first article was published by *Cassell's Magazine* when she was fourteen. Gertrude Elizabeth published her first book, *Topo: A Tale About English Children in Italy* (1878), under the pen name "G.E. Brunefille". This contained forty-four pen-and-ink drawings by the famous illustrator Kate Greenaway. In 1881 she married Lord Colin Campbell, the eighth Duke of Argyll, but they separated three years later.

Following her divorce from Campbell she became a journalist, contributing regular columns on art and travel to a variety of publications, including

Pall Mall Gazette, National Review and *The World,* for which she wrote a weekly column "In the Picture Galleries", which she signed "Q.E.D." According to Fleming, she penned two or three articles a week for *Saturday Review,* on a variety of subjects, under a variety of names. Her knowledge of French, German, Spanish and Italian enabled her to review much of the foreign-language material submitted to the periodical (205). Her collection *A Book of the Running Brook and of Still Waters* (1886) consisted of seven pieces she had written for the *Saturday Review.* In addition to this extremely prolific journalistic output, she edited the *Ladies' Field* and co-founded a periodical, *The Realm,* with Earl Hodgson.

She mixed in a circle of artists and writers including Whistler, Shaw and Henry James, and was a campaigner for women's rights. In addition to writing four more novels, she also wrote some plays, one of which, *St Martin's Summer: A Play Written by Ladies for Ladies,* was written in collaboration with Clothilde Graves.

Select bibliography
Campbell, Lady Colin.
—. *Topo: A Tale About English Children in Italy.* Children's writing. London: Marcus Ward, 1878. Notes: With forty-four pen-and-ink illus. by Kate Greenaway.
—. *A Book of the Running Brook and Still Waters.* Journalism. London: Sampson, Low, 1886. Notes: A collection of seven pieces she wrote for *Saturday Review.*
—. *Darrell Blake: A Study.* London: Trischler, 1889.
—. trans. *The Lady's Dressing-Room.* London: Cassell, 1892.
—. *Etiquette of Good Society.* Handbook. London: Cassell, 1893.
—. *A Woman's Walks: Studies in Colour Abroad and at Home.* Journalism. London: Eveleigh Nash, 1903. Notes: Reprinted pieces from *The World.*
—. *Bud and Blossom.* (Unpub) play. N.d.

Secondary sources
Fleming, G. H. *Victorian Sex Goddess.* Oxford: Oxford UP, 1990.

Canavan, Rosemary. Comhaimseartha. Alba / Tuaisceart na hÉireann / Cathair Chorcaí / Réidh na nDoirí, Co. Chorcaí / Co. Chiarraí. Úrscéalaíocht, litríocht leanaí.

Saolaíodh Rosemary in Albain i 1949 agus tógadh i dTuaisceart na hÉireann í, ach tá sí ina cónaí i gCúige Mumhan ó 1975 i leith. Foilsíodh a céad chnuasach filíochta i 1994 agus foilsíodh dhá scéal do leanaí léi chomh maith. Chaith sí bliain mar Scríbhneoir Cónaitheach i gCo. Chiarraí agus foilsíodh obair a cuid scoláirí in *Breacadh* (2001). Tá sí ag obair ar úrscéal nua faoi láthair, *Foxy Hugh,* agus foilsíodh sliocht as an leabhar sin in *Southword* (2001).

Rosemary Canavan was born in Scotland in 1949 and brought up in Northern Ireland, but has lived in various parts of Munster since 1975. Her first collection of poems was published in 1994 and she has also written two children's stories in Irish. She spent a year as Writer in Residence in Co. Kerry and the results of her students' work were published in *Breacadh* (2001). She is currently working on a new novel, *Foxy Hugh,* from which an extract 'The Wife', was published in *Southword* (2001).

Select bibliography
Canavan, Rosemary.
—. *The Island.* Filíocht. Oregon: Story Line, 1994.
—. *Caitríona agus an tÉinin Óir.* Litríocht leanaí. Baile Átha Cliath: An Gúm, 1999.
—. eag. *Breacadh: An Anthology of Kerry Voices.* Litríocht leanaí. Tralee: Kerry County Council, 2001.
—. "Learning Irish near Ballyferriter." *Breacadh: An Anthology of Kerry Voices.* Filíocht. Eag. Rosemary Canavan. Tralee: Kerry County Council, 2001. 95–6.
—. "A Wife." Scríbhneoireacht acadúil, aiste. *Southword* 3.1 (2001): 47–53.
—. *Lios Chaitríona.* Litríocht leanaí. Baile Átha Cliath: An Gúm, c.1999.

Carbery, Mary, née Toulmin. 1867–1949. Castle Freke, Co. Cork. Diaries, social history.

Born near St Albans, England, she enjoyed a privileged upbringing which included musical training and an involvement in philanthropy. She started to write at the age of twelve and these reminiscences (completed in adulthood) formed the basis of *Happy World* (1941). In November 1890 she married Algernon, ninth Baron Carbery, and came to live on his estate in Castle Freke in West Cork. They had two sons. Her husband died in 1898. Her first literary venture was the editing of diaries written by Elizabeth Freke (1641–1714), an Englishwoman who married a Carbery forefather, like Mary. This was published in Cork in 1913 with the sub-title "Some Few Remembrances of My Misfortuns which have Attended Me in my Unhappy Life since I were Marryed: whc was Novemer the 14, 1671". This inspired Mary to write her own journal, which she began following her husband's death, at which point she became mistress of the estate until her eldest son came of age. This journal remained unpublished until 1998 when her grandson Jeremy Sandford edited and published it as *Mary Carbery's West Cork Journal*.

In 1917 she was the author of a series of satirical letters published anonymously under the title *The Germans in Cork: Being the Letters of His Excellency the Baron von Kartoffel (Military Governor of Cork in the Year 1918) and Others.* Another anonymous publication is thought to be the novel *The Light in the Window.* In 1923 she wrote *Children of the Dawn*, a novel based on the Tuatha de Danaan. Mary Carbery familiarized herself with many aspects of Irish literature and folklore, an interest she retained even after she left Castle Freke. While seeking the words of a lost song in Co. Limerick in 1904 she met Mary Fogarty, with whom she had become acquainted in 1901. An extensive correspondence ensued between the two women as Mary Fogarty wrote down the old stories and legends of Lough Gur and Mary Carbery formed them into a continuous narrative. The resulting publication was *The Farm by Lough Gur* (1937). The introduction was written by Shane Leslie and the book remains in print today. Mary Carbery spent the latter part of her life travelling extensively in Europe with her second husband and she died in England in 1949.

Select bibliography
Carbery, Mary.

—. ed. *The Diaries of Elizabeth Freke (1641–1714): Some Few Remembrances of My Misfortuns which have Attended me in my Unhappy Life since I were Marryed: whc was November the 14, 1671.* Diaries. Cork: n.p., 1913.

—. *The Germans in Cork: Being the Letters of His Excellency the Baron von Kartoffel (Military Governor of Cork in the year 1918) and Others.* Dublin: Talbot, 1917.

—. *Children of the Dawn.* Novel. London: Heinemann, 1923.

—. *The Farm by Lough Gur: The Story of Mary Fogarty (Sissy O'Brien).* Social history. Cork: Mercier, 1923. London: Longmans, 1937. Notes: Intro. Shane Leslie.

—. *Happy World: The Story of a Victorian Childhood.* Memoir. London: Longmans, 1941.

Secondary sources
Sandford, Jeremy, ed. *Mary Carbery's West Cork Journal 1898–1901.* Dublin: Lilliput, 1998.

Carew, Dorothea Petrie, née Townshend. 1895–1968. Waterford. Autobiography.

Born in London, her life was very much bound up with the south of Ireland. Her father, a naval man, was a Townshend from Garrycloyne, Co. Cork, and her mother came from Blackrock, Co. Dublin. In many ways, Dorothea Townshend could be described as a "New Woman", as her life bore all the visible hallmarks of these first-wave feminists: she was rumoured to be a suffragette during her schooldays at Eastbourne, and was encouraged by enlightened parents to attend Somerville College, Oxford, in the early years of the century. As a young woman, she travelled to Paris and the Scandinavian countries with her lifelong friend Bryher and her parents. Like many women of her class, she became a temporary civil servant during the First World War, living at a women's hostel in Bloomsbury. She went on to join *The New Witness*, a literary newspaper, as an editorial assisant, during which time she became friends with the novelist Rose Macaulay. She subsequently worked for a variety of other magazines including *The Queen* and *Femina*, before going to work as editor of the women's page of the *Sunday Dispatch*.

Dorothea continued to travel after the war, visiting Italy and climbing in the Pyrenees. In later life she would travel extensively in North America, riding trails in the Rockies, as well as visiting Paris regularly, where she numbered Adrienne Monnier and Sylvia Beach among her friends. On her return from America, she began to study and later practise psychoanalysis, working mostly with children. She took up a joint editorship, with Robert Herring of the literary journal *Life and Letters Today*.

She married Maj. Robert Carew in 1936 and moved to his family estate at Ballinamona Park, Waterford (*Burke's Irish Family Records*). At this point her autobiography, *Anything Once* (n.d.), ends, but, according to the afterword (written by her friend Sylva Norman), Dorothea "threw herslf eagerly into the planning of her daughter's upbringing and education" (117). She died suddenly in 1968 before her autobiography was published.

Select bibliography
Carew, Dorothea Petrie.
—. *French Education for English Girls*. Handbook. N.p.: Wells, Gardner & Darton, 1930.
—. *Many Years, Many Girls: The History of a School 1862–1949*. History. N.p.: Browne & Nolan, 1967.
—. *Anything Once: An Autobiography*. Autobiography. London: Wordens, n.d.

Carew, Joan Pollard. Contemporary. Thurles, Co. Tipperary. Poetry.

Born in 1950 in the Slieveardagh hills near Thurles in North Tipperary, she spent a lot of time on her grandparents' farm as a child, wandering the fields and chatting with her granddad, who passed on to her his love of reading. This love of poetry was later nurtured during her schooldays and she has been writing poetry since her early childhood. She has broadcast her work on local radio and published in various local anthologies, magazines and newspapers. In 2000 she published her first collection, *Moll Strings & Others*. Her other interest is Irish set dancing and she contributes regular articles to *Set Dancing News*, the magazine for Irish set dancers.

Select bibliography
Carew, Joan Pollard.
—. *Moll Strings & Others*. Poetry. Roscrea, Co. Tipperary: Lisheen, 2000.

Carson, Katherine, née Corcoran. *fl.* **1880–1900.** Skibbereen.

Listed in the 1956 *Cork County Library List* as a Skibbereen author who spoke Irish, French and Italian: "She wrote excellent verse, some of which was published." Patricia Egan, in her 1978 bibliography *Nineteenth Century Cork Authors* (held in Cork City Library Special Collection), notes that none of these publications could be traced.

Casey, Maeve. Contemporary. Dublin. Sociology, short stories, fiction.

A lecturer in social policy and psychology at the Women's Education Research and Resource Centre (WERRC), UCD, since 1990. She worked at the Social and Organisational Psychology Research Unit at UCD during the 1980s, researching topics including gender issues, women in the workplace and domestic violence. During the 1990s Casey worked with the New Opportunities for Women (NOW) and Politically Organised Women Educating for Representation (POWER) programmes addressing inner-city community leadership and North–South political education. She is currently a WERRC delegate to the National Women's Council of Ireland. Other research interests include Third World development, as a result of which Casey visited refugee resettlements in Nepal and Mozambique and development projects in Ethiopia, Belize and Tanzania.

Select bibliography
Casey, Maeve.
—. *Blood, Birth and Sacrifice*. (Unpub.) novel. N.d.
—. contributor. Short stories. Radio programme. BBC Radio 4. 1987.

Cavanagh, Eleanor. Cork. Letters.

A maid in the service of Katherine Wilmot (*q.v.*), she accompanied her mistress to Russia in the early 1800s. While in Troitskoe she wrote long letters home to her father, which have survived, possibly because they were later given to the Wilmots. In one of her letters, in October 1805, she describes Russian life: "From Moscow to the Country Palace where we now are & where we have been 3 weeks is more than 80 mile (*sic*) [...] I druve with the Princess's first maid Natasia. At night the devil an inn we came to, but a big palace belonging to a Count! [...] up we went upstairs until we got into a playhouse [...] There was an old man with a trumpet in his mouth & his two eyes looking at me. 'Come here,' says Miss Anna Petrovna, the P[rince]ss niece [...] 'I'm frightened Ma'am', says I [...] I looked thro' a little hole & faith there I seen London & Petersburg & cartloads of grand towns, but 'twas very quair Cork did not come anyhow" (Kelly, 1995, 23). Notes: These letters are now in the library of the Royal Irish Academy.

Chatterton, Lady Georgiana. 1806–76. Novels, poetry, travel writing, memoir.

Born Georgiana Iremonger in London, she married Sir William Chatterton of Castle Mahon, Co. Cork, in 1824 (cf. Kelly, 2003). Her first book, *Aunt Dorothy's Tales*, was published anonymously in 1837 and was followed two years later by *Rambles in the South of Ireland*. This was a huge success and the first edition sold out in a few weeks. She went on to write several novels and books of travel. After Sir William died, she married Edward Dering, who converted to Catholicism a few weeks later. She became a Catholic herself six months before her death in 1876.

Select bibliography
Chatterton, Georgiana.
—. *Aunt Dorothy's Tales, or, Geraldine Morton, A Novel*. Novel. 2 vols. London: Richard Bentley, 1837.
—. *Rambles in the South of Ireland*. Travel writing. London: Saunders & Otley, 1839.
—. *Country Coteries*. Novel. 3 vols. London: Hurst & Blackett, 1868.
—. *Lady May: A Pastoral*. Poetry. London: T. Richardson, 1869.

Secondary sources
Dering, Edward Heneage, ed. *Memoirs of Georgiana, Lady Chatterton*. London: Hurst & Blackett, 1878.

Chetwode, [Anne?]. *fl.*1827.

Daughter of Rev. John Chetwode of Glanmire, Co. Cork, and granddaughter of Knightley Chetwode, a friend of Jonathan Swift, she travelled in Russia in the early part of the nineteenth century. She was part of a circle of Irish women, which included Katherine and Martha Wilmot (*q.v.*), who stayed with the Princess Daschkaw (Daschkoff) near Moscow (her sister Elizabeth married Robert Wilmot – brother of the Wilmot sisters). Daschkaw, a Russian intellectual of the period, went on to become Director of the Academy of Arts and Sciences in St Petersburg and first President of the Russian Academy. She travelled throughout Ireland in 1779–80, and this was presumably the beginning of her association with this group of Irish friends, which also included Catherine Hamilton of Edgeworthstown, Co. Longford.

Chetwode believed in equal rights to education for women, and she is said to have written four novels, only two of which survive. *Bluestocking Hall* (1827) has been attributed to William Pitt Scargill, but Chetwode was identified as its author by Windele (the Cork antiquarian) in 1839. It is an epistolary novel, set mostly in Kerry. As suggested by its title, the novel advocates education for women. Maria Edgeworth writes approvingly of it: "notwithstanding its horrid title [...] I thought that there was a great deal of good, and of good sense in it" (Loeber and Stouthamer-Loeber, 1998).

Select bibliography
Chetwode, [Anne?].
—. *Bluestocking Hall*. Novel. N.p.: n.p., 1827.

Secondary Sources
Windele, John. *Historical and Descriptive Notes of Cork City and its Environs*. N.p.: n.p., 1839.

Cilligriú, Eibhlín [Uí Churraoin, Eibhlín Bean]. 1895–1983. Ráth na mBiríneach, An Rinn, Na Déise, Co. Phort Láirge agus Cathair Phort Láirge. Seanchas, aistriúchán.

Saolaíodh Eibhlín i Ráth na mBiríneach. Ceathrar a bhí sa chlann. Bhuaigh sí scoláireacht Ollscoile agus bhain BA amach ó Choláiste na hOllscoile, Corcaigh. Dhein sí an tArdteastas san Oideachas agus mhúin sí i gColáiste na Rinne agus i Scoil na Leanbh. Phós sí Pádraig Ó Curraoin ó Bhaile Uí Churraoin sa Rinn, agus d'aistríodar go Cathair Phort Láirge mar ar mhúin sí sa Cheardscoil Láir. Bhí cúigear muirear orthu. Is é *Fir Mhóra an tSean-Phobail* a saothar is mó cáil, scríbhneoireacht atá bunaithe ar sheanchas áitiúil a bhí cloiste aici. D'aistrigh sí leabhar le Jerome K. Jerome go Gaeilge chomh maith.

Select bibliography
Cilligriú, Eibhlín.
—. aist. *Smaointe Fáin an tSuathramáin: Leabhar le hAghaidh an Lae Leisce* [*Idle Thoughts of an Idle Fellow*]. Litríocht. Le Jerome K. Jerome. Baile Átha Cliath: Oifig an tSoláthair, 1938.
—. *Fir Mhóra an tSean-Phobail*. Seanchas. Baile Átha Cliath: Oifig an tSoláthair, 1941.

Secondary sources
Breathnach, Diarmuid, agus Máire Ní Mhurchú. "Cilligriú, Eibhlín (1895–1983) [Uí Churraoin]." *1882–1982 Beathaisnéis a Cúig*. Baile Átha Cliath: An Clóchomhar, 1997.

Clarke, Kathleen, née Daly. 1878–1972. Limerick. Political writing.

Born into a well known Limerick political family in 1878, she was educated locally, and managed her own dressmaking business until she met Thomas J. Clarke in 1899. He was a Fenian who had spent many years living in the United States. Kathleen joined him there in 1901 and married him. They both threw themselves wholeheartedly into the movement for Irish independence, raising funds and printing a newspaper, until they returned to Dublin in 1907 where they continued their political activities. Clarke founded the Irish Volunteers and Kathleen was a founder member of Cumann na mBan. She had a key role in the organization of the 1916 rebellion and, following the execution of her husband, the first signatory of the Proclamation of Independence, she set up the Irish Volunteers' Dependants' Fund.

As an executive member of Sinn Féin under Éamonn de Valéra, Kathleen Clarke maintained her political activities and was arrrested and jailed in Holloway Women's Prison in north London. Her fellow prisoners were Countess Constance Markievicz and Madame Maud Gonne Mac Bride. Following her release, she remained active in the political sphere, joining de Valéra's Fianna Fáil party. She failed to be elected to the Dáil but served on the Senate for about eight years. In 1939 she was elected Lord Mayor of Dublin, the first woman to hold the office. This was her last political role, as she resigned from Fianna Fáil in 1943. She was honoured with a doctorate from the NUI in 1966 and was accorded a State funeral in Dublin in 1972. Her writings have been edited and published by her grandniece, Helen Litton.

Select bibliography
Clarke, Kathleen.
—. *Revolutionary Woman: My Fight for Irish Freedom, Kathleen Clarke 1878–1972.* Political writing. Ed. Helen Litton. Dublin: O'Brien, 1991.

Secondary sources
Broderick, Marian. *Wild Irish Women: Extraordinary Lives from Irish History.* Dublin: O'Brien, 2001. 186–91.

Clear, Caitriona. Contemporary. Cork. History.

A native of Co. Limerick, she is a lecturer in history at NUI Galway. Her research interests include the history of women and the social history of Ireland and Europe in the eighteenth and nineteenth century.

Select bibliography
Clear, Caitriona.
—. *Nuns in Nineteenth Century Ireland.* Academic writing. Dublin: Gill & Macmillan, 1987.
—. *Women of the House: Women's Household Work in Ireland 1926–1961: Discourses, Experiences, Memories.* Academic writing. Dublin: Irish Academic Press, 2000.

Cleary, Rose M. Contemporary. Cork. Academic writing.

Graduated from UCC in 1980 with an MA, she has worked since then as an archaeologist and lecturer in the Department of Archaeology, UCC. Her research interests include prehistoric pottery and the Late Neolithic/Beaker period assemblage from Newgrange. She is currently engaged in research for a PhD degree.

Select bibliography
Cleary, Rose M.
—. "Archaeological Investigation of the Site of a Star-shaped Fort at Singland, Garryowen, Limerick City." Academic writing. *North Munster Antiquarian Journal* 37 (1996): 131–4.

—. "Christ Church Site Excavation." *Skiddy's Castle and Christ Church, Cork. Excavations 1974–77 by D.C. Twohig.* Academic writing. Ed. R.M. Cleary, M.F. Hurley and E. Shee Twohig. Cork: Cork Corporation in assoc. with the Department of Archaeology, UCC, 1997. 26–100.

—. and T.B. Barry, eds. *Late Viking Age and Medieval Waterford Excavations 1986–92.* Academic writing. Waterford: Waterford Corporation, 1997.

—. M.F. Hurley and E. Shee Twohig, eds. *Skiddy's Castle and Christ Church, Cork. Excavations 1974–77 by D.C. Twohig.* Cork: Cork Corporation in assoc. with the Department of Archaeology, UCC, 1997.

—. "Stone Artefacts." *Skiddy's Castle and Christ Church, Cork. Excavations 1974–77 by D.C. Twohig.* Academic writing. Ed. R.M. Cleary, M.F. Hurley and E. Shee Twohig. Cork: Cork Corporation in assoc. with the Department of Archaeology, UCC, 1997. 206–22.

—. "A Vertical-Wheeled Water-Mill at Ardcloyne, Co. Cork." Academic writing. *Journal of the Cork Historical and Archaeological Society* 104 (1999): 37–56.

Clerke, Agnes. 1842–1907. Skibbereen, Co. Cork. Science.

One of the best-known scientists of the nineteenth century, she achieved fame as an astronomer and a popularizer of science. She was born in Skibbereen, Co. Cork. Her family moved to Dublin in 1861, and then back to Cobh, Co. Cork, in 1863, spending winters in Italy from 1867 on. Her parents, Catherine Deasy, a well-educated woman and a talented musician, and William Clerke, a bank manager who was interested in chemistry and astronomy, enabled their daughters to pursue their various academic interests. Educated at home by their parents, the Clerke sisters became accomplished in a variety of fields of study. Agnes' sister, Ellen Clerke (*q.v.*), was a well known writer, and the two lived together all their lives, dying within a year of each other.

Agnes was widely travelled, having lived in Italy 1867–77, studying astronomy and writing articles on the subject, which were published in British journals such as the *Edinburgh Review* and *Observatory* magazine. In total, she published over fifty articles in the fields of science and literature during her life. She moved to London in 1877, where she continued her research at the Royal Observatory. She visited the Cape of Good Hope to make astonomical observations in 1888, and in 1890 she sailed to Copenhagen, Stockholm and St Petersburg on the yacht *Palatine.*

She began her *Popular History of Astronomy during the 19th Century* (1885) at the age of fifteen, and some chapters in the existing text were written at that age. It was to become a standard work. Her research consisted of material both on the history of astronomy and on modern developments in the science. Her employment of new technology such as the camera and the spectroscope enabled her to use photographs to legitimize her scientific endeavours in the eyes of her Victorian audience. She was awarded the Actonian Prize of a hundred guineas for her work in 1893, and wrote the Hodgkins Essay on Low Temperature Research at the Royal Institution in 1901. She became an honorary member of the Royal Astronomical Society in 1903, a rank previously held only by two other women, Caroline Herschel and Mary Somerville.

An important contributor to the *Encyclopaedia Britannica*, Agnes also wrote for the *Dictionary of National Biography*, penning almost all the lives of astronomers, including an entry for Caroline Herschel. Fenwick lists her among eight women she considers "major contributors" to the *DNB* – that is to say – those who wrote more than eighty articles, and she is one of only six of the overall forty-five women contributors to also have an entry about her in the dictionary. Agnes also published journal articles about classical literature throughout her life, and she was a renowned musician.

Select bibliography
Clerke, Agnes.
—. *Familiar Studies in Homer*. Academic writing. N.p.: n.p., 1892.
—. *The Herschels and Modern Astronomy*. Science, history. Century Science ser. N.p.: n.p., 1895.
—. co-author, with J.E. Gore and A. Fowler. *Astronomy*. Science. Concise Knowledge ser. N.p.: n.p., 1898.
—. *Problems in Astrophysics*. Science. London: A. & C. Black, 1903.
—. *Modern Cosmogonies*. Science. London: A. & C. Black, 1905.
—. *System of the Stars*. Science. London: Longmans, 1905.
—. *Popular History of Astronomy during the 19th Century*. Science. London: A. & C. Black, 1885. N.p.: n.d., 1908.

Secondary sources
Bruck, M.T. "Agnes Mary Clerke: Chronicler of Astronomy." *Quarterly Journal of the Royal Astronomical Society* (1994): 59.
—. "Agnes Clerke's Work as a Scientific Biographer." *Irish Astronomical Journal* 24.2 (1997): 193.
Huggins, Lady Margaret. *Agnes Mary Clerke and Ellen Mary Clerke, An Appreciation*. Self-published, 1907.
Lightman, Bernard. "Constructing Victorian Heavens: Agnes Clerke and Gendered Astronomy." *Natural Eloquence: Women Reinscribe Science*. Ed. Barbara T. Gates and Ann B. Shteir. Madison: Wisconsin UP, 1997.
Weitzenhoffer, K. "The Prolific Pen of Agnes Clerke." *Sky & Telescope* 70 (1985): 211–12.

Clerke, Ellen Mary. 1840–1906. Skibbereen, Co. Cork. Poetry, religious writing, journalism, science.

Older sister of the astronomer Agnes Clerke, she was also born in Skibbereen. She lived with Agnes in Italy from 1870 to 1877, and while there studied Italian language and culture, contributing short stories in Italian to periodicals in Florence. She also published essays and studies, translated Italian poetry into English in the original metre and contributed to Garnett's *History of Italian Literature* (1898). She was a talented musician, particularly noted for her guitar playing. Her understanding of the religious and political discourses of the Europe of her day became apparent in her later writing. Ellen also had an intellectual interest in astronomy, although geology was her specialism. A member of the Manchester Geographical Society, she contributed to their *Journal*.

On moving to London, she began to write for the London Catholic magazine *The Tablet*, and became known as a writer of religious poetry. Her collection *The Flying Dutchman, and Other Poems* (1881) was her best-known work. Her association with *The Tablet* continued throughout her life, and she wrote a weekly leader on Catholic activities abroad for the last twenty years of her life. She also published articles in German, Italian and Arabic for other newspapers and journals.

Like her sister, Ellen Clerke was also interested in science, and her pamphlets, *Jupiter and His System* and *The Planet Venus*, contributed to the literature of popular astronomy in the late nineteenth century. Ellen contributed entries to the *Dictionary of National Biography* on Mary Somerville and others. One article written by her in *Observatory* combines her interest in astronomy with her knowledge of Arabic – examining links between Arabian astonomical observations and the mathematical process, Algol.

Select bibliography
Clerke, Ellen Mary.
—. *The Flying Dutchman, and Other Poems*. Poetry. London: Satchell, 1882.
—. *Jupiter and His System*. Science. London: Edward Stanford, 1892.
—. *The Planet Venus*. Science. London: Witterby, 1893.
—. contributor. *History of Italian Literature*. Poetry, translations. Ed. R. Garnett. N.p.: n.p., 1898.
—. *Fable and Song in Italy*. Poetry, translations. London: Grant Richards, 1899.
—. *Flowers of Fire*. Novel. London: Hutchinson, 1902.

Secondary sources
Huggins, Lady Margaret. *Agnes Mary Clerke and Ellen Mary Clerke, An Appreciation*. Self-published, 1907.

Clibborn, Elizabeth, née Grubb. 1780–1861. Clonmel, Co. Tipperary. Diary.

Writer of an unpublished journal (1807–18), the manuscript of which is in the Dublin Friends Historical Library. This journal gives an insight into the day-to-day life and concerns of a woman of the period; for example, in 1810 she writes: "I am thirty years of age, it is an awful consideration, even if it should be a long life the prime is over" (42). Her journal also provides a social diary of the Quaker community in Munster during the early years of the nineteenth century. The Clibborns' house in Clonmel seems to have been a convenient resting-point for Quakers travelling to meetings in various parts of the region.

Select bibliography
Clibborn, Elizabeth.
—. *Journal*, 1807–18. (Unpub.) diary. Notes: Held at Dublin Friends Historical Library.

Coakley, Catherine. Contemporary. Cork. Short stories.

Born in Mallow in 1957, she received a degree in sculpture and photography from the Cork College of Art and Design. She has taught art in Cork Prison since 1980 and is currently Deputy Principal there. Coakley won the Hennessy Award in 1980 for her short story "That Evening", and the Listowel Writers' Week Short Story Award for "A Clear Night" in 1989. She was nominated for the Hennessy Award for "Rembrandt and Escher" in 1991. Her writing has also been published in various anthologies.

Select bibliography
Coakley, Catherine.
—. "That Evening." *Irish Press*. Short story. 1980.
—. "A Clear Night." *Writers' Week: Award-Winning Short Stories 1973–1994*. Short story. Ed. David Marcus. 1989. Dublin: Marino, 1995. 226–47.
—. "Rembrandt and Escher." *Sunday Tribune*. Short story. 1991.

Cockburn, Patricia, née Arbuthnot. 1914–89. Youghal, Co. Cork. Autobiography, political writing.

Born in Rosscarbery in 1914, she moved shortly afterwards to her grandmother's home at Myrtle Grove near Youghal, Co. Cork. This had been the home of Sir Walter Ralegh when he was an English government official in 1588. She described her childhood there as "privileged". She was educated in England, and studied design at art college there before marrying her first husband at the age of eighteen. Together they travelled extensively in Canada, Tahiti, Australia and the Far East. Some time later they went to live in Central Africa, where she carried out research on various tribal languages for the Royal Geographical Society. She described her experiences there: "The amount of human suffering I had seen, against a background of nature in its most powerful and dramatic form, affected the whole of the rest of my life. I have never forgotten it, nor ceased to relate the condition of its people to that of the Western world I live in." (1985, 155)

Her next trip took her to Ruthenia (now the Ukraine), from where she sent reports to the *Evening Standard*. By then her marriage was over and she joined in the war effort in London, where she met her second husband, Claud Cockburn, controversial owner of the magazine *The Week* and also foreign editor of the Communist *Daily Worker*. This marriage caused her to be disinherited by her family but relations were restored with the birth of her first son. While Cockburn was in the United States to cover the founding of the United Nations for the *Worker*, Patricia became editor of *The Week*. This publication focused mainly on poltiical events from 1933 to 1946. The couple spent some time in Eastern Europe working as journalists, following which they decided to live in Ireland in her old home. While Claud continued writing, his wife started breeding horses and sheep to supply the post-war shortages. In later years she became an artist in seashell collages based on eighteenth-century crafts and held twelve solo exhibitions in Ireland, England and America. Her latter years were spent in Ardmore, Co. Waterford.

Select bibliography
Cockburn, Patricia.
—. *The Years of "The Week"*. Memoir. London: Macdonald, 1968. Notes: Intro. by Claud Cockburn.
—. *Figure of Eight*. Autobiography. London: Chatto & Windus, 1985. Dingle: Brandon, 1989.

Coll, Mary. Contemporary. Limerick. Poetry, journalism.

Born in Limerick City, where she currently lives, she took a BA at UCG, followed by an MA in English focusing on the works of Kate O'Brien. Coll also completed an HDip in Education and taught for a short time in Limerick. During the nine years when she worked as administrator for the Belltable Arts Centre, Coll became involved in theatre reviewing, and has broadcast regularly on Radio 1's *Rattlebag* and Lyric FM and written for the *Irish Theatre Magazine*. She is currently working on a second volume of poetry.

Select bibliography
Coll, Mary.
—. *All Things Considered*. Poetry. The Cliffs of Moher: Salmon Publishing, 2002.

Colthurst, E. *fl.*1830–50. Cork. Poetry, novels.

Listed in O'Donoghue as "A Cork lady of marked poetical ability", (75) much of whose work was published anonymously. O'Donoghue lists *The Irish Scripture Reader* (1841) and *The Little Ones of Innisfail* (1841) as being among her publications. In the 1836 publication of a slender volume of her poetry, *Home*, it is noted that she is living at Danesfort, Killarney, and she may have moved to Kilkenny at some point in the late 1830s. Colthurst was also associated with the Rev. E. Nangle's mission to Achill. According to Brown her work has religious overtones; for example, he tells us that *Irrelagh; or The Last of the Chiefs* (1845) introduces Protestant ideologies and, from his perspective, Catholic doctrine is disapproved of in her work (1968, 65).

Select bibliography
Colthurst, E.
—. *Home*. Poetry. Cork: John Bolster, 1836.
—. *Emmeline; or, Trials Sanctified*. Poetry. Cork: self-published, 1838.
—. *The Little Ones of Innisfail, or, The Children of God*. Novel. London: Houlston & Stoneman, 1841.
—. *Irrelagh; or, The Last of the Chiefs*. Novel. London: Houlston & Stoneman, 1849.
—. *Emmanuel*. Poetry. N.p.: n.p., n.d.
—. *Inishfail, or The Irish Scripture Reader*. Religious writing. N.p.: n.p., 1841.
—. *Life*. Poetry. 1835. N.p.: n.p., n.d.

Condell, Frances, née Sheppard. 1916–86. Limerick. Poetry, journalism, radio scripts.

Born in Limerick, she was educated in Dublin at the Church of Ireland Training College and at TCD. She taught at Villiers School in Limerick and also held various posts in social and public-relations fields, becoming involved in organizations for older people. She was elected Lord Mayor of Limerick in 1962, the first woman to hold the office in the 850-year history of the city, and was re-elected for a second term. She was also closely involved with the Red Cross movement. A collection of her poems was published posthumously.

Select bibliography
Condell, Frances.
—. "Welcome to John F. Kennedy." *The Limerick Compendium*. Lecture. Ed. Jim Kemmy. Dublin: Gill & Macmillan, 1997. 216.
—. *Poems: A Selection*. Poetry. N.p.: n.p., n.d.

Conlon, Lil. *fl.* 1969. Cork.

Born in Cork city, she was closely linked with the period of the national revival before 1916. She joined Cumann na mBan in 1914 and remained with the organization until 1925. Her early working life was in the civil service in Dublin but she later took up a post on the clerical staff of UCC. In 1969 she wrote a history of Cumann na mBan "as a tribute to those Women, organised and unorganised, who rendered such gallant and heroic assistance during the years 1913–25" (title page).

Select bibliography
Conlon, Lil.
—. *Cumann na mBan and the Women of Ireland, 1913–1925*. History. Kilkenny: Kilkenny People, 1969.

Connolly, Claire. Contemporary. Cork. Academic writing, literary criticism.

Born in Cork in 1967. she grew up in Tipperary. A graduate of UCC, she was awarded a PhD from Cardiff University, Wales. She has held the position of lecturer in English literature and cultural criticism in Cardiff University since 1993. Her research interests focus on the writings of Edmund Burke, Maria Edgeworth and Sydney Owenson, and on post-colonial and feminist theory. She is a co-editor of the *European Journal of English Studies*.

Select bibliography
Connolly, Claire.
—. "Uncanny *Castle Rackrent*." *The Supernatural and the Fantastic in Irish Literature*. Literary criticism. Ed. Bruce Stewart. Gerrards Cross, Bucks: Colin Smythe, 1998. 205–20.
—. "(Be)longing: The Strange Place of Elizabeth Bowen's *Eva Trout*." *Borderlands: Negotiating Boundaries in Post-Colonial Writing*. Literary criticism. Ed. Monika Reif-Hülser. Amsterdam: Rodopi, 1999. 135–43.
—. and Marilyn Butler, eds. *Manoeuvring and Vivian. The Novels and Selected Works of Maria Edgeworth*. Literary criticism. Vol. 4. London: Pickering & Chatto, 1999.
—. "Reading Responsibility in *Castle Rackrent*." *Ireland and Cultural Theory: The Mechanics of Authenticity*. Literary criticism. Ed. Richard Kirkland and Colin Graham. Basingstoke: Macmillan, 1999. 136–61.
—. ed. *Theorizing Ireland: A Reader in Cultural Criticism*. Literary criticism. Harlow: Palgrave Macmillan, 2003.

Connolly, Eileen. Comhaimseartha. An Neidín, Co. Chiarraí. Filíocht.

Is as An Neidín Eileen agus tá sí ina cónaí ann fós. Saolaíodh í i 1944. Oibríonn sí i Scoil Phroinsias Naofa sa Neidín agus sa leabharlann i gCill

Airne. Tá sí mar bhall de ghrúpa scríbhneoirí darb ainm "Clann na Farraige." Tá filíocht as Béarla agus as Gaeilge foilsithe aici i mbailiúcháin éagsúla.

Connolly, Linda. Contemporary. Cork. Academic writing, sociology.

Awarded a PhD from NUI Maynooth, where she was a researcher and teacher at the Centre for Adult and Community Education, she has been a lecturer in the Department of Sociology, UCC, since 1997. Her research interests include social movements theory, feminist theory and sociology of the family.

Select bibliography
Connolly, Linda.
—. "As Long as there are Women there will be Feminism." Journalism. *The Irish Reporter* 22 (1996).
—. "The Women's Movement in Ireland, 1970–1995: A Social Movements Analysis." Academic writing. *Irish Journal of Feminist Studies* 1.1 (1996).
—. "The Contemporary Irish Women's Movement: Case Study of New European Social Movement." *Aspects of Europe: Conference Proceedings*. Academic writing. Ed. Nicholas Rees and Ben Tora. Dublin: Irish Association for Contemporary European Studies, 1997.
—. "From Revolution to Devolution: Mapping the Contemporary Women's Movement in Ireland." *Women and Irish Society: A Sociological Reader*. Academic writing. Ed. Madeleine Leonard and Anne Byrne. Belfast: Beyond the Pale, 1997.
—. "The Current Challenges Facing Feminist Education in the Academy." *Gender and Education in Ireland*. Political writing. Ed. Brid Connolly and Anne B. Ryan. Vol. 2. Maynooth: Maynooth Adult Continuing Education (MACE), 1999.
—. "Theorising 'Ireland'." Political writing. *Sociology* (2001).
—. *The Irish Women's Movement: From Revolution to Devolution*. Academic writing. Basingstoke: Palgrave, 2002.
—. and Tina O'Toole. *Documenting Irish Feminisms*. Dublin: Woodfield Press, 2005.

Connolly, Margaret. Contemporary. Cork. Academic writing, literary criticism.

A native of Wigan, she graduated from the University of St Andrews with a PhD in 1991. She lectured at the University of St Andrews from 1990 to 1992, when she was appointed to lecture in the Department of English, UCC, on Medieval and Renaissance literature. Her research interests include Middle English literature, Chaucer translation theory and practice and the study of later medieval manuscripts.

Select bibliography
Connolly, Margaret.
—. *Contemplations of the Dread and Love of God*. Academic writing, literary criticism. Oxford: Oxford UP, 1994.
—. "Public Revisions or Private Responses? The Oddities of Arundel 197, with special reference to the *Contemplations of the Dread and Love of God*." Academic writing. *British Library Journal* 20 (1994): 55–64.
—. "A Newly Identified Letter in the Hand of John Shirley." Academic writing. *The Library, Sixth Series* 19.3 (1997): 47.

—. *John Shirley: Book Production and the Noble Household in Fifteenth-Century England*. Academic writing. Aldershot: Ashgate, 1998.

—. "Some Unrecorded Middle English Verse in a Nijmegen Manuscript." Academic writing. *Notes and Queries* 244 (1999): 442–4.

—. *The Middle English Mirror: Sermons from Advent to Lent*. (Unpub.) academic writing. N.d.

Conrick, Maeve. Contemporary. Munster. Academic writing.

Currently a senior lecturer and director of the MA in Applied Linguistics in the Department of French, UCC, she was awarded the NUI Travelling Studentship in 1974 and studied for three years at the Université d'Aix-Marseilles 1, obtaining a doctorate in General and Applied Linguistics. In 1998 Conrick was awarded the Prix du Québec in recognition of her contribution to Quebec studies. She is a former President of the Association of Canadian Studies in Ireland. Her research interests include French language and linguistics, sociolinguistics, applied linguistics and Canadian studies.

Select bibliography

Conrick, Maeve.

—. *How to Win Competitions*. Handbook. Dublin: Marino Books, 1997.

—. "Linguistic Intervention, Prescriptivism and Purism: Some Issues in the Non-Sexist Language Debate." Academic writing. *Teangeolas, Journal of the Linguistics Institute of Ireland* 36 (1997): 22–8.

—. "Norm and Standard as Models in Second Language Acquisition." *Intercultural Communication and Language Learning*. Academic writing. Ed. A. Chambers, and D. Ó Baoill. Dublin: Royal Irish Academy/Irish Association for Applied Linguistics (IRAAL), 1998. 176–86.

—. *Womanspeak*. Academic writing. Dublin: Mercier Press, 1999.

—. "The Feminisation Process in Francophone Countries: Principle and Practice." Academic writing. *International Journal of Francophone Studies* 3.2 (2000): 89–105.

—. "Problem Solving in a University Setting: the Role of the Ombudsperson." Academic writing. *Perspectives: Policy and Practice in Higher Education* 4.2 (2000): 50–4.

—. "Linguistics." *The Routledge International Encyclopedia of Women*. Academic writing. Ed. C. Kramarae and D. Spender. Vol. 3. New York and London: Routledge, 2001. 1241–5.

Conyers, Dorothea, née Blood Smith. 1871–1949. Co. Limerick. Novels, short stories.

From Castle Conyers, near Rathkeale, Co. Limerick, she wrote many novels, most of which had a background of horses and hunting in Ireland. Brown describes her novels as "humorous, lively stories of Irish sport, full of incident [...]. Her dramatis personae are hunting people, garrison officers, horse dealers, and the peasantry seen more or less from their point of view" (1968, 55). He goes on, in a description of *The Strayings of Sandy* (1909), to say: "the brogue is not overdone, and we are not, on the whole, caricatured" (56). In his reading of *Some Happenings of Glendalyne* (1911), Brown points out the influence of Sheridan LeFanu on Conyers' work.

Select bibliography

Conyers, Dorothea.

—. *The Thorn Bit*. Novel. London: Hutchinson, 1900.

—. *Aunt Jane and Uncle James*. Novel. N.p.: n.p., 1908. London: Hutchinson, 1917.
—. *The Boy, Some Horses, and a Girl*. Novel. N.p.: n.p., 1908. London: Arnold, 1917.
—. *Three Girls and a Hermit*. Novel. London: Hutchinson, 1908.
—. *The Conversion of Con Cregan*. Novel. London: Hutchinson, 1909.
—. *Lady Elverton's Emeralds*. Novel. London: Hutchinson, 1909.
—. *The Strayings of Sandy*. Novel. London: Hutchinson, 1909.
—. *Two Imposters and a Tinker*. Novel. London: Hutchinson, 1910.
—. *Some Happenings of Glendalyne*. Novel. London: Hutchinson, 1911.
—. *The Arrival of Anthony*. Novel. London: Hutchinson, 1912.
—. *Sally*. Novel. London: Methuen, 1912.
—. *Sally Married*. Novel. London: Methuen, 1913.
—. *Old Andy*. Novel. London: Methuen, 1914.
—. *Maeve*. Novel. London: Hutchinson, 1915.
—. *A Mixed Pack*. Short stories. London: Methuen, 1915.
—. *The Financing of Fiona*. Novel. London: Allen & Unwin, 1916.
—. *The Scratch Pack*. Novel. London: Hutchinson, 1916.
—. *The Experiments of Ganymede Bunn*. Novel. London: Hutchinson, 1917.
—. *Peter's Pedigree*. Novel. 1917. London: Arnold, 1904.
—. *The Blighting of Bartram*. Novel. London: Methuen, 1918.
—. *Sporting Reminiscences*. Social history. London: Methuen, 1920.
—. "Wild Duck." *Irish Short Stories*. Short stories. Ed. George A. Birmingham. 1932.
   London: Faber & Faber. 233–54.
—. *Kicking Foxes*. Novel. London: Hutchinson, n.d.
—. *The Witch's Samples*. Novel. London: Hutchinson, n.d.

Cooke, Emma [Enid Blanc]. Contemporary. Limerick, Killaloe. Novels, short stories.

Born in Portarlington, Co. Laois, in 1934, she was educated in Dublin and at teacher-training college in Limerick. Following her marriage in 1959 she moved to Killaloe in Co. Clare, where she founded the Killaloe Writers' Group. Her writing career began in 1970 followed by publication of *Female Forms* in 1980. Her stories have been anthologized in Ireland, England and the USA and also translated into German and Dutch. Her work espouses many of the aims of the women's movement in Ireland.

Select bibliography
Cooke, Emma.
—. *A Single Sensation*. Novel. Dublin: Poolbeg, 1981.
—. *Eve's Apple*. Novel. Belfast: Blackstaff, 1985.
—. *Female Forms*. Dublin: Poolbeg, 1986.
—. "The Foundress." *Territories of the Voice: Contemporary Stories by Irish Women Writers*. Short story. Ed. Louise DeSalvo *et al*. Boston: Beacon, 1989. Boston: Beacon, 1999. 191–200.
—. *Wedlocked*. Novel. Dublin: Poolbeg, 1994.

Cooke, Hester. *fl.*1935–53. Carrick-on-Suir, Waterford. Poetry, journalism.

Born in Waterford, she spent her early childhood at Moyglass, near Fethard, Co. Tipperary. Her father was a Church of Ireland clergyman, Canon Alfred Cooke, who became the rector of Carrick-on-Suir, where she was to live for twenty-eight years. Her uncle, W.C. Cooke, was a UCC lecturer in Spanish, and he provided his niece and her brother, Hewitt, with gifts of books, mostly natural history books, as the children were deeply interested in this subject. Thus she grew up with a love of the Irish natural landscape, which is reflected in her poetry. Her brother, to whom she was devoted, went away to Aravon School at twelve, followed by Sandhurst and a career in the army. Cooke remained unmarried, and following her mother's sudden death in 1932 she lived at home with her father, taking on many of the tasks which had been done by her mother in the church.

Her recently published memoir, *Rectory Days*, gives an autobiographical account of her life and illustrates the excitement occasioned in Carrick by a letter from Hewitt, who spent many years posted in Burma. While her brother travelled all over the East with the army, Hester Cooke led a quiet life at home, preparing food parcels for the families of ex-army men, and reading and writing poetry. She wrote many articles for local newspapers and periodicals, often about the natural world, and her poems appeared in the *Blarney Magazine*. She published three collections, all of which she prepared for publication on a Remington typewriter brought back from Burma. Her correspondence reveals that she wrote at some length to Temple Lane (*q.v.*) once or twice a year. She comments: "She and I have much in common and we both draw our sword against Philistinism!!" Her brother died of a tropical disease in Malta in 1954, and her father died in 1958. Cooke then moved to Cathedral Close in Waterford, where she died in 1986.

Select bibliography
Cooke, Hester.
—. *Fallen Petals*. Poetry. Dublin: Talbot, 1935.
—. *Hazel Leaves*. Poetry. Dublin: Talbot, 1939.
—. *The Mountain Road*. Poetry. Waterford: Carthage, 1948.
—. "The Little Roads of Ireland." Poetry. *Blarney Annual* 2 (1949–50): 54.
—. "My Early Home." Poetry. *Blarney Annual* 2 (1949–50): 54.
—. "June Blossoms." *Blarney Annual of Fact & Fancy*. Poetry. Vol. 3. Cork: Woodlands Press, 1951. 18.
—. "Autumn Evening." Poetry. *Blarney Magazine* 5 (1953): 37.
—. "Autumn Evening." Poetry. *Blarney Magazine* 5 (1953).
—. *Rectory Days*. Memoir. Portlaw, Co. Waterford: Rectory Press, 2002.

Secondary sources
Power, Edward. "Waterford's Hester Cooke." *Ireland's Own* 4.574 (1997).

Cotter, Máire. *fl.* **1946–57.** Cork. Poetry, short stories, journalism.

Born in Cork *c.* 1900, she was an elected member of the London Incorporated Society of Authors in 1947. She had planned to pursue a musical career but was prevented from this by ill health. She lived for many years in Europe and during this time much of her poetry was published. She also wrote freelance articles for Irish and American publications, specializing in literary articles, book reviews and short stories. The writers featured in these articles included G.K. Chesterton, the Brontës, Alice Meynell, Rene Bazin, James Barry and Matt Talbot.

Select bibliography
Cotter, Máire.
—. *To Victory*. Poetry. Dublin: Talbot, 1936.
—. *Westward by Command: The Life of St Francis Xavier Cabrini*. Biography. Cork: Mercier, 1947.
—. "When I'm Old." Poetry. *Blarney Annual of Fact & Fancy* 3 (1951): 74.
—. *What Peter Did: Written in Ribeauville, Lower Rhine, Alsace and Completed in Cork*. Poetry. Blarney, Co. Cork: Woodlands, 1953. Notes: Illus. Gladys Leach.
—. *Little Nellie of Holy God: A Lily Aflame*. Biography. Dublin: Clonmore & Reynolds, 1956.

Coughlan, Patricia. Contemporary. Cork. Academic writing, literary criticism.

Born in Limerick in 1948, she graduated from UCC with an MA in 1969. She was awarded an NUI Travelling Studentship in 1970, and studied at London University, gaining a PhD in 1980 with a thesis on Andrew Marvell. She lectured at Maynooth College 1973–77, then returned to join the staff in the Department of English at UCC, where she currently holds the position of Associate Professor. She was elected to the UCC Governing Body in 2000 and again in 2003 by the college professors.

Select bibliography
Coughlan, Patricia.
—. ed. *Spenser and Ireland: An Interdisciplinary Perspective*. Academic writing. Cork: Cork UP, 1990.
—. "Bog Queens: The Representation of Women in the Poetry of Seamus Heaney and John Montague." Literary criticism. *Gender in Irish Writing*. Ed. David Cairns and Toni O'Brien-Johnston. Milton Keynes: Open UP, 1991. 89–111.
—. and Alex Davis, eds. *Modernism and Ireland: The Poetry of the 1930s*. Academic writing. Cork: Cork UP, 1995.
—. "Women and Desire in the Work of Elizabeth Bowen." *Sex, Nation and Dissent in Irish Writing*. Academic writing, literary criticism. Ed. Éibhear Walshe. Cork: Cork UP, 1996.
—. "Counter-Currents in Colonial Discourse: The Political Thought of Vincent and Deniel Gookin". *Political Thought in 17th-Century Ireland*. Academic writing. Ed. Jane Ohlmeyer. Cambridge: Cambridge UP, 2000.
—. "'Does a man die at your feet...': Gender, History and Representation in *The Catastrophist*." Literary criticism. *Irish University Review* 33.2 (Autumn-Winter 2003): 371–91.
—. "Rereading Peig Sayers: Self, Social History and Narrative Art." *Feminist Approaches to Irish Texts*. Academic writing. Ed. Christine St Peter and Patricia Boyle Haberstroh. Madison: Wisconsin UP, 2004.

Courtney, Sister Marie Thérèse. *fl.* 1956. Limerick. Academic writing.

Graduated with a BA from UCC in 1947, and took a PhD from the University of Fribourg in Switzerland in 1952. Her 1956 study of Edward Martyn and the Irish theatre was based on that doctoral thesis. She was a lecturer at Mary Immaculate Teacher Training College in Limerick during the 1950s. She also co-authored a history of the Mercy order in Limerick.

Select bibliography
Courtney, Sister Marie Thérèse.
—. *Edward Martyn and the Irish Theatre*. Academic writing. New York: Vantage, 1956.

Couturié, Sylvia. *fl.*1939. Dungarvan, Co. Waterford. Autobiography.

In August 1939, she arrived in Ireland for a holiday with her sister, Marguerite, and their Irish governess. The plan was that their parents were to join them shortly and the whole family would return to France together. However, when war broke out it became impossible for them to return, and so they remained in Dungarvan throughout the war. Sylvia's autobiography, *No Tears in Ireland* (1999), tells the story of her experiences as an "alien" in Ireland during the war years.

Select bibliography
Couturié, Sylvia.
—. *No Tears in Ireland*. Autobiography. Ballivor, Co. Meath: Hannon, 1999.

Cowman, Roz [Ros, Róisín]. Contemporary. Clonmel, Cork. Poetry, literary criticism.

Born in Cork in 1942, she grew up in Clonmel, Co. Tipperary. Educated locally at the Loreto Convent, she graduated from UCC with a BA. She travelled to Africa in the 1960s and taught in Kenya and Nigeria, 1963–70. In 1990 she moved to Cork where she now lives and works. She was first published in 1975 in the *Cork Examiner*, since when she has published poetry and reviews in a variety of periodicals including *Poetry Ireland*, the *America Women's Review of Books*, *Graph*, *Southword* and the *Examiner*. She won the Patrick Kavanagh Award for poetry in 1985 and was granted Arts Council bursaries in 1982 and 1990. Her collection, *The Goose Herd*, was published in 1989. Most recently, she gained an MA at UCC, carrying out research on George Moore. She continues to teach literature and creative writing to adult students.

Select bibliography
Cowman, Roz.
—. "Medea Ireland." *The Adultery and Other Stories and Poems*. Poetry. Dublin: Arlen, 1982. 67.
—. "Medea Ireland." *Pillars of the House: An Anthology of Verse by Irish Women from 1690 to the Present*. Poetry. Ed. A.A. Kelly. Dublin: Wolfhound, 1987. 133–4.
—. *The Goose Herd*. Poetry. Galway: Salmon, 1989.
—. "Lost Time: The Smell and Taste of Castle T." *Sex, Nation and Dissent in Irish Writing*. Academic writing. Ed. Éibhear Walshe. Cork: Cork UP, 1997. 87–102.

Cregan, Máirín. 1891–1975. Killorglin, Co. Kerry. Novels, plays, children's writing.

Born in 1891 in Killorglin, Co. Kerry, she went to school locally. She was also educated in Carrickmacross and later taught in a number of Dublin schools. In 1919 she married Dr James Ryan, one of the founders of the Fianna Fáil political party, who held several ministerial roles in successive governments. She undertook many dangerous missions during the War of

Independence and was imprisoned in Waterford for defying a British soldier's order.

She wrote two novels, plays and short stories, and her work was reviewed in the *Dublin Magazine* during the 1930s and 1940s. At least one of her novels, *Old John*, which was published in New York and London (1937), was translated into Irish in 1938 with illustrations by Jack B. Yeats. It was serialized on BBC radio, and later the author did readings of her stories on national radio. Her 1942 novel *Rathina* (which centres on a sixteen-year-old girl's love for her horse) won the Downey Award for the finest children's book of the year in the USA in 1943. In a review of the book, fellow-author Patricia Lynch described it as having "more reality" than the Somerville and Ross books. In 1933 Cregan published a play, *Hunger-Strike*, and a second play, *Curlew's Call*, was published in the *Capuchin Annual* (1940). She also wrote articles on different topics for the *Father Mathew Record*. She died in 1975.

Select bibliography
Cregan, Máirín.
—. *Hunger-Strike*. Play. Dublin: M.H. Gill, 1933, 1963.
—. *Old John*. Children's Writing. London: Allen & Unwin, 1937. Dublin: Browne & Nolan, 1938.
—. 'Curlew's Call'. *Capuchin Annual*. 1940, 177–89.
—. *Sean-Eoin* [*Old John*]. Children's writing. Dublin: Oifig an tSoláthair, 1938. Trans. Tomás Ó Faoláin. Dublin: Oifig an tSoláthair, 1974.
—. *Rathina*. Children's writing. London: Allen & Unwin, 1942.
—. "The Bog Fairy Tells about Star-People." Short story. *Dublin Magazine* new series 23.4 (1948): 30–9.

Secondary sources
Anon. "Rev. of *Old John*, by Máirín Cregan." *Dublin Magazine* new series 7.3 (1937): 91.
Nic Gh., E. "Rev. of *Hunger-Strike*, by Máirín Cregan." *Dublin Magazine* new series 7.2 (1933): 86–7.
Lynch, Patricia. "Rev. of *Rathina*, by Máirín Cregan." *Dublin Magazine* new series 20.2 (1945): 61–2.

Crottie, Julia. *fl.* **1900–1920.** Lismore, Co. Waterford. Novels, short stories.
Born in 1853, in Lismore, Co. Waterford, where she was educated at the Presentation Convent there. She was a frequent contributor to Catholic periodicals, particularly American-published magazines. She lived for many years in Ramsay, Isle of Man, but is buried in Lismore. Her short-story collection, *Neighbours* (1900), was described by the *Glasgow Herald* as being in the same vein as work by Carleton, Lover and Maria Edgeworth.

Tynan says of this author: "Miss Crotty (*sic*) lived out the years of her early girlhood in the stagnant atmosphere of an Irish country town, receiving impressions which are rendered, sometimes with appalling faithfulness, in her books [...] Her output is small but very remarkable. She is no Irish idealist, and is not afraid of making the black really black and not only the dimmed white of a dusty angel. She is the first writer since Carleton who has shown fearless realism in her portrayal of Irish character, and that is not to say that she does not love her people and deal tenderly with them as well. Miss Crotty bids fair to be one of the most considerable figures in Irish literature" (362).

Select bibliography
Crottie, Julia.
—. *Neighbours.* Short stories. London: Fisher Unwin, 1900.
—. *The Lost Land.* Novel. London: Fisher Unwin, 1901.

Crowe, Úna. Contemporary. Tipperary. Poetry.

Born in Tramore, Co. Waterford, in 1948, she has published one collection of poetry, *Waiting for the Beasts* (1999), and is currently working as a learning-support teacher in Thurles, Co. Tipperary.

Select bibliography
Crowe, Úna.
—. *Waiting for the Beasts.* Poetry. Tipperary: Lisheen Publications, 1999.

Crowley, Louise. Contemporary. Cork. Academic writing.

Born in Cork in 1975, she is a graduate of UCC, who qualified as a solicitor and began to lecture in the Law Department, UCC, in 2000. Her research interests include family law, welfare law, and the law of business and financial transactions.

Select bibliography
Crowley, Louise.
—. "Recent Developments in the Law of Succession." Academic writing. *Irish Journal of Family Law* 2.5 (1998).
—. "The Slicing of the Marital Cake – Separation Agreements and Property Adjustment Orders." Academic writing. *Irish Journal of Family Law* 2.8 (1999).
—. "Pre-Nuptial Agreements – Have They Any Place in Irish Law?" Academic writing. *Irish Journal of Family Law* 4.3 (2001).

Crowley, Roz. Contemporary. Cork. Journalism, cookbooks.

Born in Cork in 1952, she writes a regular column for the *Irish Examiner* newspaper, and has published a number of cookbooks.

Select bibliography
Crowley, Roz.
—. *Kinsale Good Food Circle: Recipes from Ireland's Gourmet Capital.* Cookbook. Cork: Forum, 1990.
—. *The Examiner Cookbook.* Cookbook. Cork: Onstream, 1997.

Crumpe, M.G.T. [Miss Crumpe]. *fl.*1823–51. Limerick. Novels.

Daughter of Dr Crumpe, a well known physician in Limerick, she published several novels in the first half of the nineteenth century.

Select bibliography
Crumpe, M.G.T.
—. *Isabel St Albe; or, Vice and Virtue, a Novel.* Novel. Edinburgh: Archibald Constable, 1823.
—. *Geraldine of Desmond, or Ireland in the Reign of Elizabeth, An Historical Romance.* Historical novel. 3 vols. London: Henry Colburn, 1829.
—. *The Death Flag; or, The Irish Buccaneers.* Novel. N.p.: n.p., 1851.

Cullen, Sylvia. Contemporary. Waterford. Plays.

Raised in West Waterford, she now lives in Co. Wicklow. She studied drama at the Samuel Beckett Centre in TCD, graduating in 1989. A number of her plays have been performed at different venues around Ireland and she also scripted two devised shows, *Owl*, at Cork City Hall, and *Broken Ground*, which went on a national tour. She has received a number of Arts Council awards and was appointed Writer in Residence at Wicklow hospital in 2000. One of her plays, *The Thaw*, was published in 2001. This play centres on a rural farming family, visited by two strangers during the cold winter of 1947 and remaining isolated for several weeks. Unpublished plays include *Crows Falling*, *Crysalis*, *Flood* and *Hunting the Strawberry Tree*.

Select bibliography
Cullen, Sylvia.
—. *Crows Falling*. (Unpub.) Play.
—. *Crysalis*. (Unpub.) Play.
—. *Flood*. (Unpub.) Play.
—. *Hunting the Strawberry Tree*. (Unpub.) Play.
—. *The Thaw*. Play. Dublin: New Island, 2001.

Cullimore, Claudine. Contemporary. Waterford. Novels.

Born in Waterford, she worked as a nanny in France and Belgium for ten years before returning to live in Winchester, England. *Lola Comes Home* (2000), aimed at 18–30-year-old readers, is her first novel.

Select bibliography
Cullimore, Claudine.
—. *Lola Comes Home*. Novel. London: Penguin, 2000.

Cummins, Geraldine. 1890–1969. Cork. Plays, novels, short stories, spiritualism.

The fifth child in a large family, she was the daughter and granddaughter of "two overworked physicians" (*Unseen Adventures* 12). Her father was Professor of Medicine at UCC, and her uncles all followed medical careers, as did four of her siblings. Her own career was varied, but she is principally known as a writer, suffragist and spiritualist. She co-founded the Munster Women's Franchise League with Suzanne R. Day (*q.v.*). Describing her experiences during the suffrage campaigns, she wrote: "One spring morning in 1914 my advocacy of 'Votes for Women' led to my being stoned through the streets of my native city by sweated women factory workers whose cause I so ardently espoused" (18).

In terms of her writing, Cummins is best known for her collaborative partnership with Suzanne R. Day, with whom she had travelled throughout Cork and Kerry, "speaking in little village halls on the desirability of no longer classing women with imbeciles [...] through withholding the vote from them" (20). Cummins and Day wrote plays together, which were performed at the Abbey and in London. The best known of these was *Fox and Geese* (1917). Her short stories were published in the *Pall Mall* magazine and other journals of the period. Her fiction evokes a very strong sense of place: she specifically locates some of her stories in such places as Garryvoe, Dingle and Gougane Barra. For example, she sets "The Last of the Aristocrats" in the Coal Quay in Cork, writing about the shawlies, whom she describes as: "a tribe of Amazons who wore shawls and lived in the slums of Cork during the first quarter of this century" (31). She also wrote a biography of Edith Somerville (*q.v.*) in 1952.

Following her political activism in the early twentieth century, much of Geraldine Cummins' energies were subsequently devoted to psychic research and automatic writing. As in her earlier writing, she continued to work in a collaborative way, experimenting and publishing several works with E. Beatrice Gibbes. Some of her writing in this field includes *Beyond Human Personality* (1935), *Perceptive Healing* (1945) and *Mind in Life and Death* (1956). Despite her curiosity about the afterlife, she writes that she herself had no wish to exist beyond the grave: "My own experience of this life, of two world-wars and the Irish civil war, has led me to desire extinction for myself at its close" (*Mind in Life and Death*, 17).

Select bibliography

Cummins, Geraldine.

—. and Susanne R. Day. *Broken Faith.* (Unpub.) play. 1912.

—. and Susanne R. Day. *The Way of the World.* (Unpub.) play. 1914.

—. and Susanne R. Day. *Fox and Geese.* Play. Dublin: Maunsel, 1917.

—. *The Land They Loved.* Novel. London: Macmillan, 1919.

—. *The Scripts of Cleophas.* Religious writing. London: Psychic Press, 1928.

—. *The Road to Immortality.* Spiritualism. N.p.: n.p., 1932.

—. *The Great Days of Ephesus.* Religious writing. London: Rider, 1933. Notes: Intro. E.B. Gibbes.

—. *Beyond Human Personality.* Spiritualism. N.p.: n.p., 1935.

—. *Fires of Beltane.* Novel. London: Michael Joseph, 1936.

—. *The Childhood of Jesus.* Religious writing. London: Frederick Muller, 1937.

—. *After Pentecost.* Religious writing. London: Rider, 1944.

—. *Perceptive Healing.* Spiritualism. London: Rider, 1945.

—. "Mad Sheoogue." Short story. *Irish Writing* 3 (Nov. 1947): 40–9.

—. *The Resurrection of Christ.* Religious writing. London: LSA Publications, 1947.

—. co-written by E. Beatrice Gibbes. *Travellers in Eternity.* Spiritualism. London: n.p., 1948.

—. *The Manhood of Jesus.* Religious writing. London: Andrew Dakers, 1949.

—. *I Appeal Unto Caesar.* Religious writing. London: Psychic Press, 1950.

—. *Unseen Adventures.* Spiritualism, autobiography. London: Rider, 1951.

—. with preface by Lennox Robinson. *Dr E.OE. Somerville.* Biography. London: Andrew Dakers, 1952.

—. *Fate of Colonel Fawcett.* Spiritualism. London: Aquarian, 1955.

—. *Mind in Life and Death.* Spiritualism. London: Aquarian, 1956.

—. *Variety Show.* Short stories. London: Barrie & Rockcliff, 1959.

—. *Swans on a Black Sea.* Spiritualism. N.p.: n.p., 1965.

—. *Paul in Athens.* Religious writing. London: Rider, n.d.

—. "The Stone of Destiny." *Cummins and the Lia Fail.* Spiritualism. Ed. John Kerr. 1967. Enniskillen: self-published, n.d.

—. and E. Beatrice Gibbes. *They Survive.* Spiritualism. London: Psychic Book Club, n.d.

—. *Till Yesterday Comes Again.* (Unpub.) play. N.d.
—. *When Nero Was Dictator (St Paul's Last Years).* Religious writing. N.p.: n.p., n.d.

Cummins, Mary. 1944–19. Ballybunion, Co. Kerry. Journalism, political writing.

Born in Castletownshend, Co. Cork, in 1944, she moved with her family to Ballybunion in the late 1950s, where she went to St Joseph's School. She went to Cardiff to train as a nurse and midwife, and then came back to the Rotunda Hospital, Dublin. In 1970 she was appointed as a journalist with the *Irish Times*, and in 1991 became women's correspondent there, writing the regular column "About Women". She died of cancer in 1999 (*Field Day V*, 319).

Select bibliography
Cummins, Mary.
—. *The Best of "About Women".* Journalism. Dublin: Marino Books, 1999.

Curtayne, Alice. 1901–1981. Tralee, Co. Kerry. History, biography, religious writing, literary criticism.

A lecturer, broadcaster and historian, she was born in Tralee and lived for three years in Milan in her teens. She learned the art of public speaking in the Catholic Evidence Guild in Liverpool, an organization founded to teach the faith through outdoor and indoor lectures. Its pitches at Hyde Park Corner, Birmingham Bull Ring and Liverpool Pier Head were renowned. Curtayne's first two books, *St Catherine of Siena* (1929) and *A Recall to Dante* (1932), were the result of her studies during this period. In 1935 she married the writer and philosopher Seán Rynne, and they raised their family in Prosperous, Co. Kildare, where Rynne farmed. Known primarily as a Catholic writer, Curtayne published many books and pamphlets on the lives of the saints. She went on lecture tours of the USA in 1953 and 1955, reading from her books, and speaking on her career as a writer and on general themes relating to Ireland. Her biography of Francis Ledwidge (1972) won much critical acclaim.

Select bibliography
Curtayne, Alice.
—. *St Catherine of Siena.* Biography. London: Sheed & Ward, 1929.
—. "St Francis in Dante." Religious writing. *Capuchin Annual* (1930): 141–5.
—. "For the Septcentenary of St Anthony of Padua: A Study of St Anthony the Preacher." Religious writing. *Capuchin Annual* (1931): 18–25.
—. *Saint Patrick: Apostle of Ireland.* Religious writing. Dublin: Anthonian Press, 1931.
—. *St Philomena.* Religious writing. Dublin: Anthonian Press, 1931.
—. "The Grey Eye of Columcille." Religious writing. *Irish Monthly* 60.June (1932): 316–23.
—. "The Ignorance of St Patrick." Religious writing. *Irish Monthly* 60.Feb. (1932): 61–4.
—. "The Pompeii of Ireland." *Irish Monthly* 60.Mar. (1932): 133–7.
—. *A Recall to Dante.* Biography. London: Sheed & Ward, 1932.
—. "St Patrick and the Pecuniary Reward." Religious writing. *Irish Monthly* 60.May (1932): 257–61.

—. "The Twilight of Tara." History. *Irish Monthly* 60.Apr. (1932): 187–91.

—. *Borne on the Wind.* Essays, religious writing. Dublin: Brown & Nolan, 1933.

—. *Saint Brigid of Ireland.* Biography. Dublin: Brown & Nolan, 1933.

—. *St Brigid: The Mary of Ireland.* Religious writing. Dublin: Anthonian Press, 1933.

—. *St Patrick's Purgatory: The Sanctuary of Station Island, Lough Derg.* Religious writing. Dublin: Anthonian Press, 1933.

—. "The Story of the Eucharistic Congress." History. *Capuchin Annual* (1933): 74–88.

—. *The New Woman.* Essay. Dublin: Anthonian Press, 1934.

—. *Patrick Sarsfield.* Biography. Dublin: Talbot Press, 1934.

—. "Peter Michael's Tír na nÓg." Short story. *Irish Monthly* 63.Feb. (1935): 106–10.

—. "The Rediscovery of Saint Brigid." Essay. *Irish Monthly* 63.July (1935): 412–20.

—. *The Servant of God: Mother Mary Aikenhead, Foundress of the Irish Sisters of Charity 1787–1858.* Biography. Dublin: Anthonian Press, 1935.

—. *Jean-Baptiste Debrabant.* Biography. Paterson, NJ: St Anthony Guild Press, Franciscan Monastery, 1936.

—. "In Memoriam Rev. C.J. Brennan." Biography. *Capuchin Annual* (1938): 240–5.

—. *House of Cards.* Novel. Dublin: n.p., 1940.

—. "Swan-Song of a Hagiologist." Essay. *Irish Ecclesiastical Record* 60.Mar. (1940): 254–9.

—. *Lough Derg, St Patrick's Purgatory.* Religious writing. 1944. Tralee: *The Kerryman*, 1956.

—. "Five Irish Saints." Religious writing. *Capuchin Annual* (1945): 269–77.

—. "Five More Irish Saints." Religious writing. *Capuchin Annual* (1946): 381–92.

—. "Five More Irish Saints." Religious writing. *Capuchin Annual* (1948): 364–75.

—. "Saints and Scholars: The Spade-Work." Religious writing. *Irish Ecclesiastical Record* 70.Jan (1948): 33–9.

—. "Tara." History. *Capuchin Annual* (1950): 305–19.

—. *St Catherine of Siena.* Religious writing. Dublin: Dominican Publications, 1951.

—. *The Trial of Oliver Plunkett.* History. 1953. London: Sheed & Ward.

—. "The Trial of Oliver Plunkett." History. *Irish Ecclesiastical Record* 82.July (1954): 36–41.

—. *Irish Saints for Boys and Girls.* Religious writing. 1955. Dublin. Notes: Illus. Eileen Coughlan.

—. *Saint Brigid of Ireland.* Religious writing. Dublin: Brown & Nolan, 1955.

—. *More Tales of Irish Saints.* Religious writing. 1957. Dublin: Talbot. Notes: Illus. Brigid Rynne

—. *The Irish Story: A Survey of Irish History and Culture.* History. Dublin: Clonmore & Reynolds, 1962.

—. "Dante." Biography. *Studies* 54.Summer–Autumn (1965): 217–26.

—. *Francis Ledwidge: A Life of the Poet.* Biography. London: Martin, Brian & O'Keefe, 1972.

—. ed. *Complete Poems of Francis Ledwidge.* Literary criticism. London: Martin, Brian & O'Keefe, 1974.

—. *The Holy Man of Dublin; or The Silence of Matt Talbot.* Religious writing. Dublin: Anthonian Press, n.d.

—. *Saint Bernard: Abbot of Clairvaux and Doctor of the Church.* Religious writing. Dublin: Anthonian Press, n.d.

—. *Saint Columcille: The Dove of the Church.* Religious writing. Dublin: Anthonian Press, n.d.

—. *St Francis of Assisi.* Religious writing. Dublin: Anthonian Press, n.d.

Secondary sources
Anon. "Rev. of 'The Irish Story'." *The Irish Sword* 6.22 (1963): 60–1.
Brady, Rev. John. "Rev. of *The Trial of Oliver Plunkett.*" *Irish Ecclesiastical Record* 80.Oct. (1953): 286–7.
—. "Why was Oliver Plunkett Arrested? (Commentary on "The Trial of Oliver Plunkett" by Curtayne)." *Irish Ecclesiastical Record* 83.Jan. (1955): 41–7.
de Blacam, Aodh. "Mary of the Gael (Rev. of Curtayne's *St Brigid of Ireland*)." *Irish Monthly* 67.Aug. (1939): 577–86.
F. "Rev. of 'St Anthony of Padua'." *Capuchin Annual* (1932): 258.
Gwynn, Rev. Aubrey. "Rev. of *Lough Derg.*" *Studies* 33.Dec. (1944): 550–4.
Hickey, Des, presenter. Appraisal of biography of Francis Ledwidge by Alice Curtayne. RTÉ Radio 1. 29 Mar. 1972.
M.G. "Rev. of *Lough Derg.*" *Irish Ecclesiastical Record* 65.June (1945): 430–1.
MacGiobúin, Pól. "Rev. of 'St Brigid of Ireland'." *Irish Book Lover* 21.Nov.–Dec. (1933): 141.
Nic N. "Rev. of *Patrick Sarsfield.*" *Irish Book Lover* 23.Mar–Apr. (1935): 56.
S. "The Greatest Catholic Poet (Rev. of Curtayne's 'A Recall to Dante')." *Catholic Bulletin* 27.Aug. (1937): 622–3.
—. "Rev. of *House of Cards.*" *Dublin Magazine* new series 16.1 (Jan.–Mar. 1941): 76–7.
T.F. "Rev. of "St Brigid of Ireland"." *Irish Ecclesiastical Record* 85.Feb. (1956): 144–5.

Curtin, Teresa. Contemporary. Limerick. Science, academic writing.

Born in Cork, she is currently lecturer in Environmental Science at UL. Her publications are based on research carried out at UL and the Université Catholique de Louvain, Belgium.

Select bibliography
Curtin, Teresa.
—. "Rearrangement of Cyclohexanone Oxime to Caprolactam over Solid Acid Catalysts." Science. *Stud. Surf. Sci. Catal.* 59.531 (1991).
—. "Influence of Boria Loading on the Acidity of B_2O_3/Al_2O_3 Catalysts for the Conversion of Cyclohexanone Oxime to Caprolactam." Science. *Appl. Catal.* 93 (1992): 91–101.
—. "The Catalytic Oxidation of Ammonia: Influence of Water and Sulfur on Selectivity to Nitrogen over Promoted Copper Oxide/Alumina Catalysts." Science. *Catalysis Today* 55 (2000): 189–95.

Cusack, Margaret Anne [Nun of Kenmare, Mother Mary Francis Cusack]. 1832–99. Kenmare, Co. Kerry. History, biography.

Daughter of Protestant parents in Dublin, her father Samuel was a doctor to the poor in Coolock, and was, like her mother, Sarah Stoney, a member of the Anglo-Irish aristocracy. Cusack had an independent education. Inspired by the Oxford Movement, it is said, she was prompted to join an Anglican order of nuns following the death of her fiancé, Charles Holmes. She then converted to Catholicism and entered the Poor Clares, an enclosed order of nuns, in 1858. Having inherited a substantial fortune, she was obliged to relinquish this under Canon Law, and voluntarily donated it to her order.

Moving to Kenmare, she became involved in writing and publishing at the order's press there. She was an extremely prolific writer during her years in Kenmare. Beginning with a biography of St Francis, Cusack wrote a series of lives of the saints, as well as other devotional material. An ardent researcher, she gained access to the family libraries in many of the local Big Houses, as well as communicating with members of the Royal Irish Academy, such as William Wilde and Denis McCarthy. She published *The Illustrated History of Ireland* (1868) and *A History of the Kingdom of Kerry* (1871), to universal acclaim. The O'Connell family at Derrynane facilitated her in her biography of Daniel O'Connell (1872) and in an edition of his speeches and letters (1875). Originally she published under the name Mother Francis Clare, but she became widely known through her writing and publishing as "the Nun of Kenmare". She wrote everything by hand with pen and ink, and her output was prodigious, although the quality of her writing often suffered as a result.

Following the famine of 1879 Mother Francis Clare set up a famine appeal. Given the connections she had built up during her research, and the lists of subscribers to her publications, she was perfectly placed to organize an efficient campaign. Ultimately the fund brought in £15,000, a substantial amount of money at that time. In 1880 she wrote a controversial pamphlet, *The Present Case of Ireland Plainly Stated: A Plea for My People and My Race*, blaming landlords for Irish problems. This pamphlet caused an outcry: she was openly criticized by the Archbishop of Dublin, a well known opponent of Home Rule, and in an 1882 pastoral letter he forbade women to participate in politics.

As a direct result of this quarrel, Cusack left the Kenmare house, going first to Newry in 1881 and then to Rome in 1884. There she obtained permission from the Pope to establish her own order, the Sisters of Peace. She founded two houses at Nottingham in England and in Jersey City, USA, where she went to live. This order was pioneering at the time in that it provided lodging for factory workers away from home, as well as training girls in domestic service. Cusack advocated equal education for women, and later published works such as *Advice to Irish Girls in America* (1872), which publication was encouraged by Fanny and Anna Parnell.

However, as a publicly prominent and outspoken woman she continued to have difficulties with the patriarchal character of the church. The doctrine of papal infallibility also seems to have aroused her particular ire. She continued to clash with bishops in the USA, and in 1888 she retired from her order and returned to England. The effect of working for so long within the power structures of the church had taken its toll on her, and near the end of her life she had a heightened sense of persecution, evident in her autobiography, *The Nun of Kenmare* (1889). She reverted to Protestantism before she died in Warwickshire in 1899.

Select bibliography
Cusack, Margaret Anne.

—. *An Illustrated History of Ireland: From the Earliest Period.* History. London: Longmans, 1868.

—. *Five Years in a Protestant Sisterhood and Ten Years in a Catholic Convent.* Autobiography. London: Longmans, 1869.
—. *The Patriot's History of Ireland.* Local history. Kenmare, Co. Kerry: National Publication Office, 1869.
—. *The Student's Manual of Irish History.* History. London: Longmans, Green, 1870.
—. *A History of the Kingdom of Kerry.* Local history. London: Longmans, Green, 1871.
—. *The Life of St Patrick, Apostle of Ireland.* Religious writing. London: Longmans, Green, 1871.
—. *Ned Rusheen, or Who Fired the First Shot?* Novel. London: Burns & Oates, 1871.
—. *Advice to Irish Girls in America.* Handbook. New York: J.A. McGee, 1872.
—. *Hornehurst Rectory.* New York: J. & D. Sadleir, 1872.
—. *The Liberator (Daniel O'Connell): His Life and Times, Political, Social and Religious.* Biography. London: Longmans, Green, 1872.
—. *The Life of Father Mathew, the People's Soggart Aroon.* Religious writing. Dublin: James Duffy, 1874.
—. *A History of the City and County of Cork.* Local history. Cork: Guy, 1875.
—. *In Memoriam Mary O'Hagan, Abbess and Foundress of the Convent of Poor Clares, Kenmare.* Religious writing. London: Burns, 1876.
—. *Good Reading for Girls: Good Readings for Sundays and Festivals.* Religious writing. London: Burns & Oates, 1877.
—. *A Nun's Advice to Her Girls.* Handbook. Kenmare, Co. Kerry: Kenmare Publication Agency, 1877.
—. *Tim O'Halloran's Choice, or, From Killarney to New York.* Novel. London: Burns, 1877.
—. *The Trias Thaumaturga: or, The Three Wonder-Working Saints of Ireland, St Patrick, St Bridget, and St Columba.* Religious writing. London: J.G. Murdoch, 1877.
—. *The Life of the Most Rev. Joseph Dixon, D.D., Primate of All Ireland.* Religious writing. London: Burns, 1878.
—. *The Present Case of Ireland Plainly Stated: A Plea for My People and My Race.* Political writing. New York: P.V. Kennedy, 1881.
—. *The Question of Today: Anti-Poverty and Progress, Labour and Capital.* Political writing. Chicago & New York: Belford, Clarke, 1887.
—. *Life Inside the Church of Rome.* Religious writing. London: Hodder & Stoughton, 1889.
—. *The Nun of Kenmare.* Autobiography. London: Hodder & Stoughton, 1889.
—. *The Story of My Life.* Autobiography. London: Hodder & Stoughton, 1891.
—. *What Rome Teaches.* Religious writing. London: Marshall, 1892.
—. *The Black Pope: A History of the Jesuits.* Religious writing. London: Marshall, Russell, 1896.
—. *Is There a Roman Catholic Church?* Religious writing. London: Marshall, Russell, 1897.
—. *An Open Letter to Lord Halifax.* Political writing. London: Marshall, Russell, 1897.
—. *Revolution and War: The Secret Conspiracy of the Jesuits in Great Britain.* History. London: Swan, Sonnenschein, 1910.

Dalton, Eliza. 1796–1874. Athassel Abbey, Co. Tipperary. Letters, social history.

Wife of a prosperous farmer at Athassel Abbey, Co. Tipperary, she wrote, with her husband William, a number of letters to emigrants in the mid-nineteenth century, which are included in Fitzpatrick's 1994 study of migration to Australia, *Oceans of Consolation*. In 1853 Dalton wrote a letter to Ned and Johanna Hogan, who had worked for the Daltons and who had emigrated to New South Wales the previous year. Like many other letters of the period, this reflects the number of people from all classes emigrating in the post-famine years. She writes: "Mr. John [Dalton] is at home Since last April you never saw him looking better. He does not like the climate of America. Mr. Willy was well when last I heard from him. Father Matthew saw him and Said he is a credit to his country [...] You can also say that two of James Ryans Sisters left Abbey for Melbourn last June. James Magrath, the Coopers daughter is also in Melbourn. Julia Kennedy left for America her Sister has an excellent situation in England. The Turners who lived with Mr. Wayland are in your old habitation. Mr. Wayland gone to Austrilia his family in Dublin [...] Mart [Margaret] Dwyers best wishes to you all. She is sorry that those of her family who went to America Are not in your Country" (*sic*) (Fitzpatrick, 290–91).

Daltúin, Eibhlín. *fl.*1936. Sliabh gCua, Na Déise, Co. Phort Láirge. Filíocht, seanchas / béaloideas.

Bhí Eibhlín ina cónaí i Sráid an Chnuic Bhuidhe i Sliabh gCua. Bhí an-chuid amhrán aici agus bhí cáil uirthi mar fhile. Tá rannta léi agus seanchas fúithi in eagar ag Pádraig Ó Milléadha in *Béaloideas* 6. Fuair sí bás i 1876.

Select bibliography
Daltúin, Eibhlín.
—. Rannta léi in "Seanchas Sliabh gCua". Eag. Pádraig Ó Milléadha. Filíocht / béaloideas. *Béaloideas* 6 (1936): 194–5.

Daly, Kathleen [Margaret Hassett]. *fl.* 1937–49. Novels.

Born in Kanturk, Co. Cork, she was educated locally, before attending Notre Dame High School in Glasgow and the University of Glasgow. She became a lecturer in Education and English literature (cf. 1957 *Catalogue of Books by Cork Writers in the Twentieth Century*) but no further information is available about her life. She published under the pseudonym "Margaret Hassett".

Select bibliography
Daly, Kathleen.
—. *Educating Elizabeth*. Novel. London: Longmans, 1937.
—. *Next to These Ladies*. Novel. London: Longmans, 1940.
—. *Sallypark*. Novel. London: Longmans, 1946.
—. *Beezer's End*. Novel. London: Longmans, 1949.

Daunt, Alice O'Neill. 1874–1914. Kilscascan, Co. Cork. Short stories, poetry.

Only daughter of W.J. O'Neill Daunt, she wrote many serial stories for periodicals such as The Lamp and Ireland's Own. Some of her work included Catholic stories for children, such as Eva (1882), "The White Rose of

Koncic", "In Norway o'er the Foam", and "Watch and Hope". She edited her father's autobiography, A Life Spent for Ireland (1896), and also left a collection of poetry in manuscript.

Select bibliography
Daunt, Alice O'Neill.
—. *Eva, or, As the Child, so the Woman.* Short stories. London: Richardson, 1882.
—. ed. *A Life Spent for Ireland. Selections from the Journals of the late W.J. O'Neill Daunt.* London: T. Fisher Unwin, 1896.

Davis-Goff, Annabel. Contemporary. Waterford. Autobiography, novels, academic writing.

Born in Waterford in 1942, and educated at the local Bishop Foy School. She worked in television and films in London and Hollywood before moving to New York. Her more recent work, *The Literary Companion to Gambling* (1996), includes an eclectic collection of excerpts from Dickens, D.H. Lawrence, Maria Edgeworth, Benjamin Franklin, Edith Wharton, Blaise Pascal and George Eliot. She is the daughter of Cynthia O'Connor (*q.v.*), an expert in antiques and paintings, who wrote a history of the first Earl of Charlemont.

Select bibliography
Davis-Goff, Annabel.
—. *Night Tennis.* Novel. New York: Coward McCann & Geoghegan, 1979. London: Hutchinson, 1979.
—. *Walled Gardens: Scenes from an Irish Childhood.* Autobiography. New York: Alfred A. Knopf, 1989. London: Barrie & Jenkins, 1990.
—. *The Literary Companion to Gambling: An Anthology of Prose and Poetry.* Academic writing. London: Sinclair-Stevenson, 1996.
—. *The Dower House.* Novel. New York: St Martin's, 1998.

Secondary sources
Kirwan, Elizabeth M. "Rev. of *Walled Gardens*, by Annabel Davis-Goff." *Old Waterford Society's Decies* 44 (1991): 43–5.

Davitt, Deirdre. Comhaimseartha. Cathair Chorcaí. Aistriúchán.

Saolaíodh Deirdre i gCathair Chorcaí. Oibríonn sí i mBaile Átha Cliath le Foras na Gaeilge. Is deirfiúr í leis an bhfile Michael Davitt, a raibh baint aige le bunú na hirise liteartha, *Innti* i gColáiste na hOllscoile, Corcaigh. D'aistrigh Deirdre agus Cormac de Barra *The Boy Who Cried Wolf* go Gaeilge. Gabhann dlúthcheirnín leis an leabhar, ar a bhfuil an scéal á eachtraí ag Liam Ó Maonlaí.

Select bibliography
Davitt, Deirdre.
—. agus Cormac de Barra, aist. *Peadar agus an Mac Tíre* [*Le Serge Prokofiev*] Litríocht leanaí, aistriúchán. Baile Átha Cliath: Coiscéim, 1998.

Day, Suzanne R. 1890–1964. Cork. Plays, novels, social history.

Playwright, novelist and travel writer, Suzanne Rouvier Day, of Myrtlehill House, Cork, also collaborated with Geraldine Cummins (*q.v.*), with whom she wrote plays for the Abbey Theatre. The best known of these was *Fox and Geese*, performed by the Abbey 1917. Other Abbey plays which she co-wrote were *Broken Faith* (1912) and *The Way of the World* (Abbey 1914). We know that she wrote plays before and after this collaborative period, but very little information about these exists.

She was involved in setting up the Cork branch of the Irish Women's Franchise League (IWFL) in 1910 (*Field Day V*, 118). When the IWFL rejected a militant stance Day co-founded the Munster Women's Franchise League (MWFL) with Geraldine Cummins in 1911. Edith Somerville (*q.v.*), whom they invited to be President of the MWFL, credits her with doing most of the work in the organization. In letters to her brother Cameron, Somerville describes Day as a super-efficient secretary. In a pamphlet entitled *Women in the New Ireland*, Day sets out a series of reasons behind women's demand for suffrage which include the struggle for equal pay: "Politics and economics go hand in hand. Women having no political status are not protected in industry, and their wage rate is depreciated accordingly." In 1911 she went forward as a candidate for the Cork Board of [Poor Law] Guardians, and topped the poll in the North-East ward (*Field Day V*, 88). Welch tells us that she devoted much of her energies to local politics and her work on the Poor Law Board after 1912 (136). Her controversial novel *The Amazing Philanthropists* (1916), written in epistolary form, was based on her time as a Poor Law Guardian. This satire caused controversy, as it too closely identified members of the Board with whom she worked.

In 1914 Day left Cork to work with refugees in northern France, and *Round about Bar-le-Duc* (1918) was based on her experiences there during the First World War. Luddy tells us that she worked in the London Fire Service during the Second World War, and she died in London in 1964 (*Field Day* V, 118).

Select bibliography
Day, Suzanne R.
—. and Geraldine Cummins. *Broken Faith*. (Unpub.) play. 1912.
—. *Women in the New Ireland*. Political writing. Cork: Munster Women's Franchise League, 1912.
—. and Geraldine Cummins. *The Way of the World*. (Unpub.) play. 1914.
—. *The Amazing Philanthropists*. Novel. London: Sidgwick & Jackson, 1916.
—. and Geraldine Cummins. *Fox and Geese*. Play. Dublin: Maunsel, 1917.
—. *Round about Bar-le-Duc*. Memoir. London: Skeffington, 1918.
—. *Where the Mistral Blows: Impressions of Provence*. Travel writing. London: Methuen, 1933. Notes: Illus. with photographs by the author.

de Barra, Eibhlís. *fl.* 1997. Memoirs.

Born in Cork city in the 1930s, she was one of a family of seven whose father died at a young age. Her book, *Bless 'Em All* (1997), describes the poverty, hunger and unemployment that was a feature of her childhood. She acquired a reputation as a well known storyteller, which is evident in her memoir. She also wrote for local magazines and newspapers and has contributed to radio and television.

Select bibliography
de Barra, Eibhlís.
—. *Bless 'Em All: The Lanes of Cork*. Memoirs. Cork: Mercier, 1997.

Deevy, Teresa. 1894–1963. Waterford, Dublin. Plays.

Born in Waterford, the thirteenth and last child of Edward and Mary Deevy, she was educated at the Ursuline Convent in Waterford and UCD. However, her university education was cut short when she developed Ménière's disease, and by the time she transferred to UCC to complete her Arts degree Deevy was profoundly deaf. She returned to her family home in Waterford to pursue her dramatic writing, and in 1930 she had her first professional success when the Abbey Theatre accepted and staged her play, *Reapers*. The success of the play led to an association between Deevy and the Abbey, as a result of which she moved from Waterford to Dublin. Her later plays included *A Disciple* (1931), *Temporal Powers* (1932), *The King of Spain's Daughter* (1935), *Katie Roche* (1936) and *The Wild Goose* (1936), all of which were staged at the Abbey.

Deevy's strongest dramatic writing centred on young working-class Irish women, and *Katie Roche* proved to be her most popular play of this genre. However, much to Deevy's dismay, in 1942 the Abbey rejected her play *Wife to James Whelan* and made it clear that her future writing would no longer be staged. After her break with them, a number of her plays were produced by experimental theatre companies, and Deevy turned to radio drama. The BBC and Radio Éireann produced many of her plays between 1936 and 1957, some on historical themes, and she also began to review for various Irish literary journals. In the late 1950s she retired to her native Waterford, where she died in January 1963.

Select bibliography
Deevy, Teresa.
—. *The Reapers*. (Unpub.) Play. 1930.
—. *A Disciple*. (Unpub.) Play. 1931. Notes: Held at Abbey Theatre Archive; later published in *Dublin Magazine* 12.1 (1937): 29–47.
—. *Temporal Powers*. (Unpub.) Play. 1932.
—. *Katie Roche*. (Unpub.) Play. 1936. Notes: Held at Abbey Theatre Archive.
—. *Wife to James Whelan*. Play. 1937. Dublin: Irish University Press Review, 1995.
—. *Three Plays*. Plays. London: Macmillan, 1939. Note: Contains *Katie Roche, The Wild Goose* and *The King of Spain's Daughter*.
—. "Strange Birth." Play. *Irish Writing* 1 (1946): 40–8.
—. *The King of Spain's Daughter, and Other One-Act Plays*. Plays. Dublin: New Frontiers, 1947.
—. *Light Falling*. (Unpub.) play. 1948.
—. *Dignity*. Radio play. Prod. Seán O Briain. RTÉ Radio 1. 10 July 1977.
—. "Rev. of *Teresa of Avila* by Kate O'Brien." Review. *Irish Writing* 18 (1952): 54–5.
—. *The King of Spain's Daughter*. Radio play. Prod. Paul Murray. RTÉ Radio 1. Radio play. 1 Feb. 1979.
—. *Temporal Powers*. Play. Delaware: Journal of Irish Literature, 1985.
—. *Inion Rí na Spainne*. Radio play. Prod. Breandán Ó Dúill. RTÉ Radio 1. 2 Apr. 1994.
—. *Selected Plays*. Plays. Ed. Éibhear Walshe. Lampeter: Mellen, 2003.

Secondary sources

Becket, Fiona. "A Theatrical Matrilineage? Problems of the Familial in the Drama of Teresa Deevy and Marina Carr. *Ireland in Proximity: History, Gender, Space.* Ed. D. Alderson, *et al.* London: Routledge, 1999. 80–93.

Dunne, Seán. "Rediscovering Teresa Deevy." *Cork Examiner* (1984).

—. ed. *A Teresa Deevy Number.* Special issue. *Journal of Irish Literature* 14.2 (1985).

Feeley, Pat, prod. Seán Dunne talks about Teresa Deevy. RTÉ Radio 1. 2 Nov. 1988.

Johnston, Denis, interviewer. Interview with Deevy's nephew, Kyle Deevy. RTÉ Radio 1. 3 June 1975.

Lane, Temple. "The Dramatic Art of Teresa Deevy." *The Dublin Magazine* 21.4 (1946): 35–42.

Leeney, Cathy. "Deevy's Leap: Teresa Deevy Re-membered in the 1990s." *The State of Play: Irish Theatre in the Nineties.* Ed. E. Bort. Trier: Wissenschaftlicher Verlag Trier, 1996. 39–49.

Murray, Christopher, ed. *Teresa Deevy and Irish Women Playwrights.* Special issue. *Irish University Review* 32 (1995).

Riley, J.D. "On Teresa Deevy's Plays." *Irish Writing* 32 (1955).

T.S. "Rev. of *The King of Spain's Daughter and Other One-Act Plays* by Teresa Deevy." *Irish Writing* 4 (1948): 89–90.

Walshe, Éibhear. "Lost Dominions: European Catholicism and Irish Nationalism in the Plays of Teresa Deevy." *Irish University Review* 25.1 (1995): 133–42.

—. ed. *Selected Plays of Irish Playwright Teresa Deevy 1894–1963.* Foreword by Shaun Richards. Lampeter: Edwin Mellen Press, 2003.

Waterford City History. *Teresa Deevy: Playwright.* 2001. Web page. URL: http://members.tripod.com/waterfordhistory/teresa_deevy.htm (2 Sept. 2004).

Welch, Robert. "On Teresa Deevy's Plays." *The Abbey Theatre 1899–1999: Form and Pressure.* Oxford: Oxford UP, 1999. 124–7.

de hÓir, Nóra. Comhaimseartha. Co. Luimnigh. Scríbhneoireacht acadúil, stair.

Saolaíodh Nóra i Luimneach agus tá sí ina cónaí sa Ghaillimh anois. Is neacht í le Edward Daly, duine de cheannairí Éirí Amach na Cásca a cuireadh chun báis. Scríobh sí *Laochra Luimnigh: Uí Dhálaigh Luimnigh agus Éirí Amach na Cásca 1916.*

Select bibliography
de hÓir, Nóra.

—. *Laochra Luimnigh: Uí Dhálaigh Luimnigh agus Éirí Amach na Cásca 1916.* Scríbhneoireacht acadúil, stair. Baile Átha Cliath: Cló Saoirse – Irish Freedom Press, 2001.

Deirfiúr le Muiris 'ac Gearailt. fl. 1933. Corca Dhuibhne, Co. Chiarraí. Filíocht, caoineadh / béaloideas.

Cumadh "Caoine ar Mhuiris 'ac Gearailt" uair éigin idir 1833–1933. "De Ghearaltaigh Mhururagán dob eadh Muiris seo. Níl deimhin arbh é Muiris a' Chipín é nó nárbh é. Ba leis na Gearaltaigh úd ó Mhullach Bhéal go Sróin Bhroin tráth. Driofúr do Mhuiris is do Ghearróid a cheap an caoine deirtéar" (Ó Dubhda 1933, 138). Seán Ó Loinsigh ón gClochán a thug an leagan seo den chaoineadh do Sheán Ó Dubhda (1933, 163).

Select bibliography
Deirfiúr le Muiris 'ac Gearailt.
—. "Caoine ar Mhuiris 'ac Gearailt." *Duanaire Duibhneach: bailiú d'amhránaibh agus de phíosaibh eile filidheachta a ceapadh le tuairim céad bliain i gCorca Dhuibhne, agus atá fós i gcuimhne agus i mbéaloideas na ndaoine ann.* Filíocht / béaloideas. Eag. Seán Ó Dubhda. 1933. Baile Átha Cliath: Oifig Dhíolta Foilseacháin Rialtais, 1969. 138.

Delap, Maude. 1866–1953. Valentia Island, Co. Kerry. Science.

Daughter of Rev. Alexander Delap, a Church of Ireland clergyman based in Kerry. On her father's death in 1906 the Knight of Kerry allowed Mrs Delap and her three unmarried daughters, Constance, Mary and Maude, to live in a large house in Knightstown on Valentia Island, Co. Kerry, for the duration of their lifetimes. Although they had no formal education, Maude and Constance began to study the marine life in the seas around the island. Maude, in particular, was encouraged and supported by E.T. Browne of University College London, and she discovered a number of rare or new species of jellyfish and medusae. One of her findings, a new species of sea anemone, was called after her in recognition of her work. She contributed papers on the archaeology of the region to the proceedings of the Royal Irish Academy and also provided data for Dr Scully's *Flora of Co. Kerry* (1916).

Select bibliography
Delap, Maude.
—. "Some Holy Wells in Valencia and Portmagee." Local history. *Kerry Archaeological Magazine* 7 (1911): 403–14.

de Paor, Eibhlín. Comhaimseartha. An Seanphobal, Na Déise, Co. Phort Láirge. Scríbhneoireacht acadúil, aiste.Is ceoltóir í agus údar ar bhéaloideas an tSeanphobail.

Select bibliography
de Paor, Eibhlín.
—. "Cúrsaí Ealaíne i gCeantracha Gaeltachta na Mumhan." *An Linn Bhuí: Iris Ghaeltacht na nDéise.* Aiste. Eag. Pádraig Ó Macháin agus Aoibheann Nic Dhonnchadha.Vol. 2. Baile Átha Cliath: Leabhair na Linne, 1998.
—. "Cúrsaí Brúscair: Cad í an Réiteach?" *An Linn Bhuí: Iris Ghaeltacht na nDéise.* Aiste. Eag. Pádraig Ó Macháin agus Aoibheann Nic Dhonnchadha.Vol. 5. Baile Átha Cliath: Leabhair na Linne, 2001.

de Róiste, Máire Aodha. *fl.*1944. Múscraí, Co. Chorcaí. Scéalaíocht / béaloideas.

D'inis Máire an scéal "Sgeilmis" do Nóra Ní Scanail, a scríobh síos é. Scéal claidhreachta is ea é. Foilsíodh é in *An Músgraigheach* 7 (1944).

Select bibliography
de Róiste, Máire Aodha.
—. "Sgeilmis." Scéalaíocht / béaloideas. *An Músgraigheach* 7. Nodlaig (1944): 4–6.

Desplanques, Marie-Annick. Contemporary. Cork. Academic writing.

Awarded a PhD from the Memorial University of Newfoundland and a post-doctoral fellowship from the Institute of Social and Economic Research, St John's, Newfoundland, she joined the Department of Folklore, UCC, in 1995, where she set up the Folklore and Ethnology Archive and helped to establish the Northside Folklore Project. Her research interests include urban ethnology, oral history and the digitization of multimedia folklore archive resources.

Select bibliography
Desplanques, Marie-Annick.
—. ed. and comp. *A Critically Annotated Bibliography of Published and Unpublished Sources of Relevance to Family Life in Newfoundland Labrador.* Academic writing. St John's, Newfoundland: Family Life Institute, 1989.
—. "Gary Butler, Saying Isn't Believing." Book review. *Culture and Tradition* 14 (1992): 75–8.
—. "Contemporary Folk Women and the Recording Industry." Academic writing. *Journal of American Folklore* 106 (1993): 338–45.
—. "Folklore and Ethics." *The Heritage of Ireland.* Academic writing. Ed. Neil Buttimer, Helen Guerin and Colin Rynne. 2000. 178–87.
—. "'Urban Ethnology' and 'Legend'." *The Encyclopedia of Ireland.* Academic writing. Dublin: Gill & Macmillan, 2005. 178–87.

Devas, Nicolette, née MacNamara. 1912–87. Ennistymon, Co. Clare. Novels, memoirs.

Born in Co. Clare, she was the daughter of a landlord, Francis MacNamara. She and her sister, Caitlin (*q.v.*), were brought to England by their mother when their parents separated. Caitlin subsequently married the Welsh poet Dylan Thomas. The two sisters lived near the family home of Augustus John. Nicolette studied at the Slade art school and in 1931 she married the artist Anthony Devas. They had two sons and a daughter. She published novels initially and these were followed by two volumes of memoirs, *Two Flamboyant Fathers* (1966) and *Susannah's Nightingales* (1978). In 1965 she married Rupert Shephard, a contemporary at Slade; he illustrated her last novel, *Pegeen Crybaby* (1986).

Select bibliography
Devas, Nicolette.
—. *Bonfire.* Novel. London: Chatto & Windus, 1958.
—. *Nightwatch.* Novel. London: Chatto & Windus, 1961.
—. *Two Flamboyant Fathers: Reminiscences of Francis MacNamara and Augustus John.* Memoir. London: Collins, 1966.
—. *Black Eggs.* Novel. London: Collins, 1970.
—.*Susannah's Nightingales: A Companion to Two Flamboyant Fathers.* Memoir. London: Collins & Harvill, 1978.
—. *Footprints upon Water.* Novel. Belfast: Blackstaff, 1983.
—. *Pegeen Crybaby.* Novel. London: Gronow, 1986. Notes: Illus. Rupert Shephard.

de Vere, Joan. 1913–89. Co. Limerick, Buttevant, Co. Cork, Cork city. Memoirs, journalism.

Born in Scotland in 1913, she was adopted as a child by Robert Stephen de Vere and his wife, from Curragh Chase near Adare, Co. Limerick. Robert de Vere's grand-uncle was the famous poet, Aubrey de Vere, friend of Tennyson, who spent five weeks at Curragh Chase in 1848. Joan, who remained an only child, was brought to Curragh Chase after the First World War, where she spent a solitary childhood while her parents were abroad on colonial service. She was educated at home before moving to Cyprus with her parents in 1925. She continued her education through a correspondence course. Later the family moved to the Seychelles, where Joan was educated at a local convent. A brief spell at Alexandra College, in Dublin, completed her formal education. From a young age, Joan took a keen interest in all forms of wildlife, and while in Africa she collected butterflies and orchids for the British Museum. She wrote on topics relating to naturalism for several newspapers and magazines, as well as book reviews.

She then went to live with her godmother in London and commenced training as an almoner. She rejoined her parents in the West Indies, where she met her future husband, Martin Wynne-Jones, a Welsh teacher. Following their marriage they lived abroad for several years, until her husband was invalided home. He went on to become a clergyman of the Church of Ireland. Joan joined him in his work in parishes in Co. Limerick until his retirement, when they moved to Buttevant and later to Cork city. Her fondness for Curragh Chase rings clear in her autobiography. She writes: "From an early stage I was keenly aware of being cut out of the inheritance because of my sex. Curragh Chase had been entailed for generations, and although after my father's death it would probably have been possible to break the entail, my mother would never have done so. I loved Curragh Chase dearly and, ironically, in later life became the only person in the family who continued to really care about it." The house at Curragh Chase was accidentally burnt down in 1941and is now the property of the State and a forestry park has been made there.

Select bibliography
de Vere, Joan.
—. *The Abiding Enchantment of Curragh Chase.* Memoir. Dublin: Cló Duanaire, 1983.
—. *In Ruin Reconciled: A Memoir of Anglo-Ireland 1913–1959.* Memoir. Dublin: Lilliput, 1990. Notes: Fwd. by Mary Leland.

Dillon, Eilís. 1920–94. Cork. Novels, children's writing.

Born in Galway, into an academic family. Her father, Thomas Dillon, was Professor of Chemistry at UCG, and her Cork-born great-grandfather had been Professor of Chemistry at UCC and the college president from 1873 to 1890. The latter was also known as a scholar of Irish (Leland, 229). Her mother, Geraldine Plunkett, was the sister of the poet Joseph Mary Plunkett, who was executed at the end of the 1916 Easter Rising. Eilís Dillon was educated at the Ursuline Convent in Sligo, and she trained as a cellist, later performing with the Cork Symphony Orchestra. She was also a fluent Irish speaker, as is evident in the fact that her first publication, *An Choill bheo* (1948), was written in Irish.

In 1940, following some years working in the catering trade in Dublin, she married Cormac Ó Cuilleanáin, who went on to become Professor of Irish at UCC. As the wife of the Warden of the Honan Hostel at UCC, Dillon's responsibilities to the live-in students left her very little time for writing: "Fifty people had to be fed three times a day [...] [in addition to which] I had to think of a housekeeper and a children's nurse and three children, including a baby who was born after we went to live in the Warden's House. When all this was in order, after a tour of inspection of the hostel, by half-past ten in the morning I was sitting at my desk beginning my other life as a professional writer [...] I had exactly two and a half hours for this, because at a quarter-past one my husband and I went into the students' dining room and sat at a separate table for lunch, with the College chaplain" (Leland, 230).

Dillon is best known for her writing for children and teenagers; books such as *The Bitter Glass* (1958) and *The Singing Cave* (1959) were widely read at home and abroad. She won the Bisto Book of the Year Award for *The Island of Ghosts* (1990). She also wrote adult fiction, much of which was historical; her novel *Across the Bitter Sea* (1973), set against the backdrop of Irish independence, was a bestseller. She was also a noted linguist, a co-founder of the Dante Alghieri Society in Cork, and translator of Eibhlín Dubh Ní Chonaill's *Lament for Art O'Leary* (1973).

Her husband's illness in the 1960s prompted the family to move to Rome, and Ó Cuilleanáin died some years later. In 1974 she remarried, and moved to the USA when her husband, the literary critic Vivian Mercier, was appointed to a chair at the University of California, Santa Barbara. However, Dillon continued to spend each summer in Ireland. She invested much of her energies in public bodies supporting writers and the arts, such as the Arts Council, the International Commission for English in the Liturgy, the Irish Writers' Union and the Irish Writers' Centre. She was a Fellow of the Royal Society of Literature and a member of Aosdána. UCC conferred an honorary doctorate on her in 1992.

Mercier's death in 1989 was followed by the death in 1990 of Eilís's daughter Máire, who was a violinist with the London Philharmonic Orchestra. Despite these blows, and her own declining health, she continued to write until the last months of her own life (Ó Cuilleanáin and Ní Chuilleanáin). At the end of her life she worked on editing Vivian Mercier's posthumous *Modern Irish Literature: Sources and Founders* (1994), leaving unfinished a last novel of her own. Eilís Dillon died on 19 July 1994. Her daughter is the distinguished contemporary poet Eiléan Ní Chuilleanáin (*q.v.*).

Select bibliography

Dillon, Eilís.

—. *An Choill Beo*. Children's writing. Dublin: Government Publications Sale Office, 1948.

—. *Midsummer Magic.* Children's writing. London: Macmillan, 1950.
—. *The Lost Island.* Children's writing. London: Faber & Faber, 1952.
—. *Oscar agus an Cóiste sé nEasóg.* Children's writing. Dublin: Government Publications Sale Office, 1952.
—. *Death at Crane's Court.* Novel. London: Faber & Faber, 1953.
—. *The San Sebastian.* Children's writing. London: Faber & Faber, 1953.
—. *Sent to His Account.* Novel. London: Faber & Faber, 1954.
—. *Ceol na Coille.* Children's writing. Dublin: Government Publications Sale Office, 1955.
—. *The House on the Shore.* Children's writing. London: Faber & Faber, 1955.
—. *The Wild Little House.* Children's writing. London: Faber & Faber, 1955.
—. *Death in the Quadrangle.* Novel. London: Faber & Faber, 1956.
—. *The Island of Horses.* Children's writing. London: Faber & Faber, 1956.
—. *Plover Hill.* Children's writing. London: Hamish Hamilton, 1957.
—. *Aunt Bedelia's Cats.* Children's writing. London: Hamish Hamilton, 1958.
—. *The Bitter Glass.* Historical novel. London: Faber & Faber, 1958.
—. *The Singing Cave.* Children's writing. London: Faber & Faber, 1959.
—. *Bold John Henebry.* Historical novel. London: Faber & Faber, 1960.
—. *The Head of the Family.* Novel. London: Faber & Faber, 1960.
—. *The Fort of Gold.* Children's writing. London: Faber & Faber, 1961.
—. *King Big-Ears.* Children's writing. London: Faber & Faber, 1961.
—. *The Cat's Opera.* Children's writing. London: Faber & Faber, 1962.
—. *A Pony and Trap.* Children's writing. London: Hamish Hamilton, 1962.
—. *The Coriander.* Children's writing. London: Faber & Faber, 1963.
—. *A Family of Foxes.* Children's writing. London: Faber & Faber, 1964.
—. *The Sea Wall.* Children's writing. London: Faber & Faber, 1965.
—. *A Page of History,* 1966. (Unpub.) play. 1966.
—. *The Road to Dunmore.* Children's writing. London: Faber & Faber, 1966.
—. *The Cruise of the Santa Maria.* Children's writing. London: Faber & Faber, 1967.
—. *The Lion Cub.* Children's writing. London: Hamish Hamilton, 1967.
—. *The Seals.* Children's writing. London: Faber & Faber, 1968.
—. *Two Stories: The Road to Dunmore and The Key.* Children's writing. New York: Meredith, 1968.
—. *Under the Orange Grove.* Children's writing. London: Faber & Faber, 1968.
—. *A Herd of Deer.* Children's writing. London: Faber & Faber, 1969.
—. *The Voyage of Mael Duin.* Children's writing. London: Faber & Faber, 1969.
—. *The Wise Man on the Mountain.* Children's writing. London: Hamish Hamilton, 1969.
—. *The King's Room.* Children's writing. London: Hamish Hamilton, 1970.
—. *The Five Hundred.* Children's writing. London: Hamish Hamilton, 1972.
—. *Across the Bitter Sea.* Historical novel. New York: Simon & Schuster, 1973. London: Hodder & Stoughton, 1974.
—. trans. *The Lament for Art O'Leary.* Translation. By Eibhlín Dhubh Ní Chonaill. London: Anvil Press Poetry, 1973.
—. *Living in Imperial Rome.* Historical novel. London: Faber & Faber, 1974.
—. ed. *The Hamish Hamilton Book of Wise Animals.* Children's writing. 1975. London: Hamish Hamilton.
—. *The Shadow of Vesuvius.* Historical novel. New York: Nelson, 1977. London: Faber & Faber, 1978.
—. *Blood Relations.* Historical novel. London: Hodder & Stoughton, 1978.
—. *Wild Geese.* Historical novel. London: Hodder & Stoughton, 1981.

—. *Inside Ireland*. Memoir, history. London: Hodder & Stoughton, 1982.
—. *Down in the World*. Children's writing. London: Hodder & Stoughton, 1983.
—. *Citizen Burke*. Historical novel. London: Hodder & Stoughton, 1984.
—. *The Horse-Fancier*. Children's writing. London: Macmillan, 1985.
—. ed. *The Lucky Bag: Classic Irish Children's Stories*. Children's writing. Dublin: O'Brien, 1985.
—. *The Seekers*. Children's writing. New York: Scribner, 1986. Dublin: Poolbeg, 1991.
—. *The Interloper*. Historical novel. London: Hodder & Stoughton, 1987.
—. *The Island of Ghosts*. Children's writing. London: Faber & Faber, 1990.
—. *Children of Bach*. Children's writing. London: Faber & Faber, 1993.
—. ed. *Modern Irish Literature: Sources and Founders*. Oxford: Clarendon, 1994.

Secondary sources
Cormac Ó Cuilleanáin and Eiléan Ní Chuilleanáin. *The Eilís Dillon Irish Writing Pages*. Web page. URL: http://homepage.tinet.ie/~writing (2002).

Donegan, Maureen. Contemporary. Cork. Fiction, television drama, radio plays.

A professional writer for thirty years, her works include radio and television drama, Irish myths and fables, magazine articles and general fiction. Donegan worked as scriptwriter for eight years on *The Riordans*, a very popular television serial of Irish country life. She is currently writing a novel dealing with the Irish War of Independence.

Select bibliography
Donegan, Maureen.
—. *Fables and Legends of Ireland*. Folklore. Cork: Mercier, 1976.
—. contributor. *Ransom!* Radio play. RTÉ Radio 1. 1979.
—. *The Bedside Book of Irish Fables and Legends*. Folklore. Dublin: Mercier, 1980.
—. contributor. *Her Second Cousin*. Radio play. RTÉ Radio 1. 1982.
—. contributor. *The Emigrant*. Radio play. RTÉ Radio 1.. 1995.

Donnelly, Mary. Contemporary. Cork. Academic writing.

A graduate of UCD, she received an MA from UCC in 1993 and an MLitt from TCD in 1995. She practised as a solicitor in Dublin until 1993, when she came to UCC as a lecturer in the Department of Law. Her research interests include medical law, equality and banking law. She is a member of the editorial board of the *Dublin University Law Journal*.

Select bibliography
Donnelly, Mary.
—. "A Gendered View of Law and Policy-Making Processes in Ireland." *Making Women Count: Integrating Gender into Law and Policy Making*. Academic writing. Ed. Sue Nott, Fiona Beveridge and Kylie Stephen. London: Ashgate, 2000.
—. *The Law of Banks and Credit Institutions in Ireland*. Academic writing. Dublin: Round Hall, Sweet & Maxwell, 2000.
—. "Decision Making for Mentally Incompetent People: The Empty Formula of Best Interests." Academic writing. *Medicine and Law* 20 (2001).
—. *Consent: Bridging the Gap Between Doctor and Patient*. Academic writing. Cork: Cork UP, 2002.

Dooley, Dolores. Contemporary. Cork. Academic writing, philosophy.

Born in the USA, she is a senior lecturer in the Department of Philosophy in UCC, where she has taught since 1975. She was Visiting Professor at the University of Notre-Dame, 1982–3, and a Visiting Researcher at the library of the European University at Fiesole, Florence, 1987–8. From 2000 to 2002 she was involved in an Associate Partnership with the University of Athens on a two-year project, "Tempe". She has done editorial work on the *Irish Journal of Feminist Studies* and the *Journal of Medical Ethics*. Her research interests include bio-medical ethics, nineteenth-century utilitarian thought, the philosophy of Thomas Nagel and feminist theory.

Select bibliography
Dooley, Dolores.
—. "Anna Doyle Wheeler." *Women, Power and Consciousness in Nineteenth Century Ireland.* Academic writing. Ed. Mary Cullen and Maria Luddy. Dublin: Attic Press, 1995. 19–54.
—. "The History of Medical Ethics in the Republic of Ireland." *Encyclopedia of Bioethics.* Philosophy. Ed. Warren T. Reich. Vol. 3. 1995. 1576–79.
—. *Annotated Edition: Appeal of One Half the Human Race, by William Thompson (1825).* Philosophy. Cork: Cork UP, 1997.
—. *Equality in Community: the Philosophy of Sexual Equality in the Writings of William Thompson and Anna Doyle Wheeler.* Philosophy. Cork: Cork UP, 1997.
—. "Gendered Citizenship in the Irish Constitution." *Ireland's Evolving Constitution.* Academic writing. Ed. Tim Murphy and Patrick Twomey. Oxford: Hart Publishing, 1998. 121–33.
—. "Assisted Procreation: the Pursuit of Consensus?" Academic writing. *Medico-Legal Journal of Ireland* 5 (1999): 65–9.
—. "Ethics and Genetic Screening in the Republic of Ireland." *The Ethics of Genetic Screening.* Academic writing. Ed. Ruth Chadwick. Dordrecht: Kluwer, 1999. 95–105.
—. "Reconciling Liberty and the Common Good?" *The Ethics of Genetic Screening.* Academic writing. Ed. Ruth Chadwick. Dordrecht: Kluwer, 1999. 191–205.

Dorman, Nora, née Robinson. *fl.* **1938.** Co. Cork. Autobiography, play.

Born near Cork city in 1880, she was the only sister of Lennox Robinson, the noted playwright and director of the Abbey Theatre. Their father retired from his stockbroking position to become a Church of Ireland clergyman and consequently the family lived in three parishes, all within a thirty-mile radius of Cork city.

Together with Lennox and their brother Tom, in 1938 Nora published a co-authored autobiography based on their memories of the three houses that they had lived in as children. The book has three voices and from Nora's passages the reader learns that she became close to her older brother when the other children had left home, as they both loved books and both began to write at that time. Following her marriage to Stuart Dorman in 1907 she went to live in India, where she continued to live until the publication of her memoir. The only other piece of writing that is recorded is a one-act comedy co-authored with W.G. Fay.

Select bibliography
Dorman, Nora.
—. Lennox Robinson and Tom Robinson. *Three Homes*. Autobiography. London: Michael Joseph, 1938.
—. and W.G. Fay. *On the Road to Cork: A Comedy in One Act*. London: French, n.d.

Downing, Ellen ["Mary" of *The Nation*, E.M.P.D.]. 1828–69. Cork. Poetry, religious writing.

Raised in the Cork Fever Hospital, where her father was the resident medical officer and her mother the matron, she began to write in her teens, sending her poetry to *The Nation*, as was later noted by the *Irish Monthly*: "Charles Gavan Duffy, in his recently published sequel to *Young Ireland*, notes that when a certain Cork girl of seventeen, then known to a few as Ellen Downing, and afterwards known to many as 'Mary' of *The Nation*, sent her first poem to that famous journal, it was in such a scrawl as boys write in their teens – we have seen a great many of her letters, and we think her writing was very much worse than this – and he adds he would probably have looked no further if experience had not taught him to distrust appearances in such cases" (11 (1883): 280). Colman tells us that her first poem was published on 10 May 1845, under the pseudonym "Kate" (69). These poems included "By the Blackwater", "Conal and Eva", "A Dream of Other Years", "The Parting" and "Past and Present", and she continued to publish her work in *The Nation* until 1848, when she began to write for the more radical *United Irishman*.

Downing is the subject of an oft-repeated myth about her relationship with one of the "Young Ireland" writers, the Cork-born Joseph Brennan. According to popular sources, when her lover was forced to become a fugitive abroad in 1848, he soon forgot their attachment, and she died young, never having recovered from this loss. However, Colman, who has investigated the origins of this narrative, points out that Downing lived for twenty years after the departure of her so-called beau, and continued to write (70). In fact, according to Colman, the strain on her health centred on her politics. Her work for the *United Irishman* was much more radical in tone than her earlier material, and it is clear that she was an adherent of Mitchel. Following political struggles and the arrest of Mitchel, Downing suffered a complete breakdown in her health from which she did not recover until 1849.

Possibly as a result of this, she entered the North Presentation Convent in the same year. However, her ill-health caused doctors to declare her unfit for convent life, her condition being marked by lengthy bouts of paralysis. She continued to use her religious name throughout her life, and spent many hours each day in prayer. She died in 1869 at the Mercy Hospital in Cork.

Select bibliography
Downing, Ellen.
—. *Voices of the Heart*. Poetry. 1868. Ed. Most Rev. J.P. Leahy, Bishop of Dromore. Dublin: n.p., 1868.

—. *Novenas and Meditations.* Poetry. Ed. J.P. Leahy. Dublin: n.p., 1879.

—. *Poems for Children.* Poetry. Dublin: n.p., 1881.

Secondary sources

Anton, Brigitte. "Women of *The Nation.*" *History Ireland* 1.3 (1993): 34–7.

Cumming, G.F. "Mary of *The Nation.*" *Irish Rosary* 28 (1924): 649–55.

Ghall, Seán. "An Irish Woman Poet." *United Irishmen* Mar.–Apr. (1902).

Markham, Thomas. *Ellen Mary Downing: Mary of the Nation.* Dublin: Catholic Truth Society of Ireland, 1913.

O'Delany, M. Barry. "The Centenary of 'Mary' of *The Nation.*" *Irish Rosary* 32 (1928): 175–82.

Russell, Matthew. "Ellen Downing: 'Mary' of *The Nation.*" *Irish Monthly* 6.Aug.–Oct. (1878): 459–65; 506–12; 573–80; 621–30; 661–7.

—. "Unpublished Relics of Ellen Downing." *Irish Monthly* 12 (1884): 315–20; 425–32; 534–40.

—. "More about 'Mary' of *The Nation.*" *Irish Monthly* 36 (1908): 69–82.

Downing, Mary, née McCarthy [Mary McCarthy, Christabel Myrrha C**1 M.F.D.]. 1815–81. Cork. Poetry.

Born in Kenmare, Co. Kerry, *c.*1815, she married Washington Downing from Cork. A nationalist, she was involved in assisting James Stephens and Michael Doheny to escape from Ireland. She is remembered as "Claribel" in James Stephens's *Reminiscences* (1884). Her poetry appears in several anthologies of the period. Downing lived in London from 1871 until her death (Colman, 148). Her only published collection was *Scraps from the Mountains* (1840), published under the pseudonym "Christabel".

Select bibliography

Downing, Mary.

—. *Scraps from the Mountains, and Other Poems.* Poetry. Dublin: William Curry, 1840.

Doyle, Eleanor. Contemporary. Cork. Academic writing.

Born in Cork in 1971. She has lectured in the Department of Economics, UCC, since 1993. Doyle received an MA from UCC in 1993 and a PhD from the University of Birmingham in 2001. Her research interests include sources of Irish growth, organizational architecture and governance, and the efficiency of Irish industry.

Select bibliography

Doyle, Eleanor.

—. "Export-output Causality: the Irish Case 1953–93." Academic writing. *Atlantic Economic Journal* 26.2 (1998): 147–62.

—. "Labour Productivity Convergence Among EU Countries, 1970–1990: The Role of Structural Change." Academic writing. *Journal of Economic Studies* 26.2 (1999): 106–20.

—. "The Economy as a System." *Irish Cases.* Academic writing. Ed. E. Doyle. McGraw-Hill, 2001. 1–4.

—. "Exchange Rate Volatility and Irish–UK Trade: 1979–1992." Academic writing. *Applied Economics* 33.2 (2001): 249–65.

—. "Export-output Causality and the Role of Exports in Irish Growth, 1950–1997." Academic writing. *International Economic Journal* 15.3 (2001): 31–55.

—. "Creating the Celtic Tiger and Sustaining Economic Growth: A Business Perspective." *Quarterly Economic Commentary.* Academic writing. Ed. D. McCoy. Economic and Social Research Institute, 2002.

Dreyer, Dympna. Contemporary. Tipperary, Waterford. Poetry, short stories, journalism.

Born in Tipperary, she grew up in the Glen of Aherlow. She lived in London, Boston, New York and Paris at various stages, a factor which she believes influences her work. She lives in Waterford now where she has taught for the past thirty years. She was nearly sixty when she started writing, and her best known work is a collection of poetry, *Come Sun, Come Snow* (1999). She has also had individual poems anthologized in *Poetry Ireland, Oxford Magazine, The Shop, Waterford Review, Cork Literary Review* and others.

Select bibliography
Dreyer, Dympna.
—. *Come Sun, Come Snow.* Poetry. Cork: Bradshaw Books, 1999.

The Duchess [Margaret Wolfe Hamilton Hungerford]. 1854–97. Bandon, Co. Cork. Novels.

Born in West Cork, *c.*1854, she was the daughter of Rev. Canon Hamilton, rector and vicar choral of St Faughnan's Cathedral in Rosscarbery. Many of the male members of her family were in the army. When her first husband, Edward Argles, a Dublin solicitor, died in the sixth year of their marriage, she was widowed with three children. In 1883 she married Henry Hungerford of Cahermore, Bandon, and they had three more children. She wrote from a very early age, and her first publication, *Phyllis*, was written while she was in her teens and published in 1877. She went on to write over fifty novels under a variety of pseudonyms, primarily "The Duchess". Her works were sentimental and romantic, consisting of love stories, ghost storiesand humour, and were hugely popular in England and the USA, selling as far afield as Australia. In *Notable Women Authors of the Day* (1893), Helen C. Black attests to Hungerford's popularity at the time of their interview: "She is, as usual, over-full of work, sells as fast as she can write, and has at the present time more commissions than she can get through during the next few years" (112). Her best known work was *Molly Bawn* (1878). Its popularity was often used to market her subsequent material (for example, "The Author of *Molly Bawn*" was considered sufficient on the title page of new novels, instead of the author's name). She died of typhoid fever in Bandon in 1897.

Select bibliography
Duchess, The.
—. *Phyllis, a Novel.* Novel. 3 vols. London: n.p., 1877.
—. *Airy Fairy Lillian.* Novel. 3 vols. London: Smith & Elder, 1879.

—. *Beauty's Daughters*. Novel. London: Smith & Elder, 1880.

—. *The Hon. Mrs Vereker*. Novel. 2 vols. London: n.p., 1880. New York: Lovell, 1888.

—. *Faith and Unfaith*. Novel. 3 vols. London: Smith & Elder, 1881.

—. *Mrs Geoffrey*. Novel. 3 vols. London: n.p., 1881.

—. *Monica*. Novel. London: Smith & Elder, 1883.

—. *Moonshine and Marguerites*. Novel. London: Smith & Elder, 1883.

—. *Rossmoyne*. Novel. 3 vols. London: n.p., 1883.

—. *Doris*. Novel. 3 vols. London: Smith & Elder, 1884.

—. *Loÿs, Lord Berresford, and Other Tales*. Short stories. 3 vols. London: Smith & Elder, 1884.

—. *Sweet is True Love*. Novel. London: Smith & Elder, 1884.

—. *Twitching Horn and Other Stories*. Short stories. 3 vols. New York: G. Munro, 1884.

—. *A Week in Killarney*. Novel. London: n.p., 1884. New York: J.W. Lovell, 1886. Notes: Reissued as *Her Week's Amusement*.

—. *The Witching Hour*. Novel. London: Smith & Elder, 1884.

—. *Dick's Sweetheart*. Novel. New York: J.W. Lovell, 1885.

—. *In Durance Vile, and Other Stories*. Short stories. 3 vols. London: Ward & Downey, 1885. New York: Lovell, 1889.

—. *A Maiden All Forlorn, and Other Stories*. Short stories. 3 vols. London: Ward & Downey, 1885.

—. *Mildred Trevanion*. Novel. New York: G. Munro, 1885.

—. *Dolores; or, Green Pleasure and Grey Grief*. Novel. 3 vols. London: Smith & Elder, 1886.

—. *The Haunted Chamber*. Novel. New York: Lovell, 1886.

—. *Lady Branksmere*. Novel. 3 vols. London: Smith & Elder, 1886.

—. *Lady Valworth's Diamonds*. Novel. New York: Lovell, 1886.

—. *A Life's Remorse*. Novel. 3 vols. London: Ward & Downey, 1887. Philadelphia: Crawford, 1890.

—. *A Modern Circe*. Novel. 1887. London: Ward & Downey.

—. *The Duchess*. Novel. London: Hurst & Blackett, 1887. New York: Lovell, 1888.

—. *Marvel*. Novel. 3 vols. London: Ward & Downey, 1888.

—. *Undercurrents*. Novel. 3 vols. London: Smith & Elder, 1888.

—. *A Troublesome Girl*. Novel. London: n.p., 1889.

—. *April's Lady*. Novel. 3 vols. London: F.V. White, 1890. N.p.: Lovell, 1891.

—. *A Born Coquette*. Novel. 3 vols. London: Spencer Blackett, 1890.

—. *Her Last Throw*. Novel. London: F.V. White, 1890.

—. *A Little Rebel*. Novel. London: F.V. White, 1890. N.p.: Lovell, 1891.

—. *A Little Irish Girl, and Other Stories*. Short stories. London: Henry, 1891.

—. *Nor Wife, Nor Maid*. Novel. London: Heinemann, 1891. New York: Hovendon, 1892.

—. *A Conquering Heroine*. Novel. London: F.V. White, 1892.

—. *Lady Patty*. Novel. London: F.V. White, 1892.

—. *A Mental Struggle*. Novel. 3 vols. London: Chatto & Windus, 1892.

—. *The O'Connors of Ballynahinch*. Novel. London: Heinemann, 1892. New York: Hovendon, 1893.

—. *Nora Creina*. Novel. London: F.V. White, 1892. New York: Hovendon, 1893.

—. *The Hoyden*. Novel. 3 vols. London: Heinemann, 1893. Philadelphia: J.B. Lippincott, 1894.

—. *Lady Verner's Flight*. Novel. 2 vols. London: Chatto & Windus, 1893.

—. *The Red House Mystery*. Novel. 2 vols. [Titled *The Red House*] Chicago, New York: Rand, McNally, 1893. London: Chatto & Windus, 1894.

—. *A Mad Prank*. Novel. London: F.V. White, 1894.

—. *Peter's Wife*. Novel. 3 vols. London: F.V. White, 1894.

—. *An Unsatisfactory Lover*. Novel. 3 vols. London: F.V. White, 1894.

—. *Molly Darling, and Other Stories*. Short stories. London: Fisher Unwin, 1895.

—. *The Professor's Experiment*. Novel. 3 vols. London: Chatto & Windus, 1895.

—. *The Three Graces*. Novel. 2 vols. London: Chatto & Windus, 1895.

—. *A Tug of War*. Novel. London: F.V. White, 1895.

—. *A Lonely Maid*. Novel. Philadelphia: J.B. Lippincott, 1896. [Titled *A Lonely Girl*] London: Downey, 1896.

—. *Molly Bawn*. Novel. 3 vols. 1878. London: Smith & Elder, 1896.

—. *A Point of Conscience*. Novel. 3 vols. London: Chatto & Windus, 1896.

—. *Portia: or, By Passions Rocked*. Novel. 3 vols. 1878. Philadelphia: J.B. Lippincott, 1896.

—. *An Anxious Moment*. Short stories. London: Chatto & Windus, 1897.

—. *The Coming of Chloë*. Novel. London: F.V. White, 1897.

—. *Lovice*. Novel. London: Chatto & Windus, 1897.

—. *Mrs Geoffrey*. Novel. 3 vols. London: Smith & Elder, 1906.

Secondary sources
Black, Helen C. *Notable Women Authors of the Day*. Glasgow: Bryce, 1893.

Duffy, Mairéad Tuohy. Contemporary. Co. Kerry. Novel, autobiography, poetry.

A native Kerrywoman, she now lives in Dublin. She trained as a teacher and worked for several years before retiring to write on a full-time basis. Her first book (1992) recounts her life in Kerry, as a student and later as a teacher in Wicklow, Offaly and Dublin. Her second publication (1996) is a novel written as a first-person narrative.

She has also written short stories and poems, in English and Irish, which have been published in newspapers and magazines, especially in the Dublin publication of the Kerry Association. Three of her poems are included in *Bí ag Caint* (1993) published by Gill & Macmillan for the Junior Certificate examination course in secondary schools.

Select bibliography
Duffy, Mairéad Tuohy.

—. *From the Roughty to the Liffey: The Story of a Teacher*. Memoir. Dublin: Obelisk, 1992.

—. *Dublin Janine*. Novel. Dublin: Obelisk, 1996.

Dunne, [Mary] Chavelita. See Egerton, George.

Dunne, Miriam. Contemporary. Cork. Fiction.

Lives on Sherkin Island, Co. Cork. Her first novel, *Blessed Art Thou A Monk Swimming*, was published in 1997. She is currently working on her second novel.

Select bibliography
Dunne, Miriam.

—. *Blessed Art Thou A Monk Swimming*. Novel. London: Hodder Headline, 1997.

Egan, Patricia. 1931–2005. Cork city. Children's writing.

Born in the fishing village of Ballycotton in East Cork in 1931, she went to Drishane Convent School before taking up her first employment as a library assistant with Cork County Council. She has spent her life working in libraries in Cork and retired as Executive City Librarian for the city in 1993. She took a particular interest in nurturing a love of reading in children. She has published several stories for children and has translated a well-loved school text and a classic tale, *Jimeen* (1984). She has also been closely involved in adult education and older people's issues, and in 1983 was a member of the Commission for Adult Education: Lifelong Learning.

Select bibliography
Egan, Patricia.
—. *Nineteenth Century Cork Authors: A Bibliography*, 1978. (Unpub.) history. Notes: Held at Cork City Library Special Collection
—. *Rambling round Cork with Consonants*. Journalism. Cork: Co. Cork Vocational Educational Committee, 1980s.
—. *Jimeen: An Irish Comic Classic by Pádraig O Siochfhradha (An Seabhac – The Hawk)* [*Jimín Mháire Thaidhg*]. Children's writing. Dublin: O'Brien, 1984.
—. Pat Donlon, Eilís Dillon and Peter Fallon, eds. *The Lucky Bag: Classic Irish Children's Stories*. Dublin: O'Brien, 1984.
—. *St Patrick and the Snakes*. Children's writing. N.p.: n.p., 1991.
—. *St Brigid: The Girl Who Loved to Give*. Children's writing. Dublin: Veritas, 1994.
—. *St Brigid and the King of Leinster's Fox*. Children's writing. N.p.: n.p., n.d.

Secondary sources
O'Carroll, Máire. "All for the Love of Books." *Wise Women: A Portrait*. Cork: Bradshaw Books, 1994. 119–25.

Egerton, George [Mary Chavelita Dunne]. 1860–1945. Millstreet, Co. Cork. Short stories, plays, novel.

Born in Melbourne, Australia, the daughter of an Irish Catholic army captain, she travelled widely with her family before settling down in Dublin in 1868. Her mother's death in 1875 broke up the family and 'Chav', as she was known, was sent to Germany to work as a teaching assistant for two years. On her return she continued to care for her siblings, as she had done during her mother's illness. She emigrated to New York in 1833 but stayed for less than a year – her only novel, *The Wheel of God* (1898), was based on her experiences there. In 1887 she eloped with Henry Higginson, a bigamist, and the couple went to live in Norway. There she learned the Scandinavian languages, encountered the work of Ibsen and Hansson, and mixed with writers and artists, including the Nobel prize-winning Knut Hamsun, whose novel *Sult* (1896) she later translated.

Returning to London after Higginson's death in 1889, she met and married Newfoundlander George Egerton Clairmonte and, in an effort to live within their modest means, the two moved to Millstreet, Co. Cork. There, in an effort to make ends meet, she wrote her most celebrated short-story collection, *Keynotes* (1893). This collection, published by John Lane at

The Bodley Head, with a cover design and illustrations by Aubrey Beardsley, created one of the biggest sensations of the 1890s and is synonymous with the New Woman genre of fiction, which "told the truth about sexuality". Following the success of her second collection, *Discords* (1894), Egerton moved to London in 1895, where she became part of *fin de siècle* decadent circles. Her husband left for South Africa soon after the birth of her only child, and writing then became Egerton's sole source of income. Subsequent publications include the short-story collections *Discords* (1894) and *Symphonies* (1897), as well as contributions to *fin de siècle* journals such as *The Yellow Book*.

In the changed climate following the Wilde trials, and the subsequent backlash against decadent culture, Egerton found it much more difficult to publish her experimental fiction. She published a short-story collection, *Fantasias*, in 1898, and in 1901 she wrote an epistolary novel, *Rosa Amorosa: The Love Letters of a Woman*. That same year, her first husband having since died, she married Reginald Golding Bright, a dramatic agent many years her junior. Under his influence, she translated and wrote several plays including *Camilla States Her Case* (London, 1925) produced by G.B. Shaw, and *His Wife's Family* (New York, 1908). Following her marriage, her only publications apart from stage adaptations were *Flies in Amber* (1905), a collection of short stories, and her only novel, *The Wheel of God*. Golding Bright treated Egerton's son, George Clairmonte, as his own and the couple were devastated by his death as a young volunteer in the First World War. Unable to begin work on a long-promised autobiography, *Things I Meant to Tell You*, Egerton gave up writing in later life.

Select bibliography
Egerton, George.
—. *Keynotes*. Short stories. London: Elkin Mathews and John Lane, 1893.
—. *Discords*. Short stories. London: John Lane, 1894.
—. "A Lost Masterpiece." Short story. *The Yellow Book* 1 (1894): 189–96.
—. *Fantasias*. Short stories. London: John Lane, 1897.
—. *Symphonies*. Short stories. London: John Lane, 1897.
—. *The Wheel of God*. Novel. London: Grant Richards, 1898.
—. *Rosa Amorosa: The Love Letters of a Woman*. Letters. London: Grant Richards, 1901.
—. *Flies in Amber*. Short stories. London: Hutchinson, 1905.
—. "A Keynote to *Keynotes*." *Ten Contemporaries*. Autobiography. Ed. J. Gawsworth. London: Ernest Benn, 1932.

Secondary sources
de Vere White, Terence. *A Leaf from The Yellow Book*. London: Richards Press, 1958.
O'Toole, Tina. "*Keynotes* from Millstreet, Co. Cork." *Irish Women Novelists 1800–1940*. Special issue. *Colby Quarterly* 36.2 (2000): 145–56.
—. "Narrating the New Woman: The Feminist Fictions of George Egerton." *Irish Journal of Feminist Studies* 5.1&2 (2003).

Erde, Maureen. Contemporary. Co. Kerry. Autobiography.
Born in England in 1941, she trained as a nurse and moved to the USA, where she was Director of Nursing and later Hospital Administrator of a

regional medical centre. In 1989 she retired and moved to Co. Kerry, where she runs a guesthouse. She is a member of a local writers' group and her book, *Help! I'm an Irish Innkeeper* (1997), recounts how she came on holiday to Ireland, and ended up buying a huge derelict house, restoring it and running it as a guesthouse.

Select bibliography
Erde, Maureen.
—. *Help! I'm an Irish Innkeeper*. Autobiography. Dublin: Poolbeg, 1997.

Esmonde, Eily. *fl.*1914–32. Tipperary. Poetry.
She married Dr John Esmonde, MP for North Tipperary, in 1910. Her poetry appeared in the *Irish Monthly*, the *Freeman's Journal* and the *Westminster Gazette* between 1914 and 1932.

Evans, Martina. Contemporary. Co. Cork. Novels, poetry.
Born in Co. Cork in 1961, she trained as a radiographer in Dublin. She went to England in 1988, where she took a degree in English and Philosophy. She writes fiction as well as poetry; many of her poems have appeared in anthologies, magazines and newspapers. In 1999 she received an Arts Council of England Writer's Award. Her first novel was *Midnight Feast* (1996), which is set in a convent boarding school and touches on the contemporary problem of bulimia. It won a Betty Trask Award. Her next novel, *The Glass Mountain* (1997), is also a first-person narrative, set in a university.

Select bibliography
Evans, Martina.
—. *The Iniscara Bar and Cycle Rest*. Poetry. Ware, Herts.: Rockingham, 1996.
—. *Midnight Feast*. Novel. London: Sinclair-Stevenson, 1996.
—. *The Glass Mountain*. Novel. London: Sinclair-Stevenson, 1997.
—. *All Alcoholics Are Charmers*. Poetry. London: Anvil, 1998.
—. *No Drinking, No Dancing, No Doctors*. Novel. London: Bloomsbury, 2000.

Secondary sources
Cowman, Roz. "Rev. of *No Drinking, No Dancing, No Doctors*, by Martina Evans." *Southword* 3.1 (2001): 61–3.

Everett, Katherine, née Herbert. 1872–1951. Killarney, Co. Kerry. Memoir, short stories.
Born at Cahirnane, Killarney, Co. Kerry, she was the daughter of Henry Herbert, and her relatives owned the Muckross Estate. Her own background was not affluent, but she was educated at the Slade School, and went on to work as a nurse in Dublin *c.*1916, before setting off to travel. In her memoir *Bricks and Flowers* (1949) she describes a three-month voyage to Australia. She went on to live for some time in British Columbia, and then married Henry Everett, an artist, and the couple continued to travel together and live in many countries, including Italy and England, as well

as Ireland. *Walk with Me* (1951) contains short stories reflecting the customs and social history of the Muckross area in the early twentieth century. In these she depicts the decline of Anglo-Irish society, discusses relationships between landowners and their tenants, and illustrates her own interest in houses, gardens and furniture.

Select bibliography
Everett, Katherine.
—. *Bricks and Flowers.* Memoir. London: Constable, 1949.
—. *Walk with Me.* Short stories. London: Constable, 1951.

Feiritéar, Cáit [Ní Ghuithín / Feiritéar, Bab]. Comhaimseartha. Dún Chaoin, Corca Dhuibhne, Co. Chiarraí. Scéalaíocht agus seanchas / béaloideas.

Saolaíodh Bab Feiritéar i mBaile na hAbha, Dún Chaoin i 1916. Ba iad Seán Ó Guithín agus Eibhlín Ní Shé a tuismitheoirí. Cailleadh a máthair cúpla lá tar éis di teacht ar an saol. Bhí deirfiúr amháin aici, ach fuair sí bás agus í fós ina cailín óg. Phós Bab Séamus Feiritéar, agus bhí seachtar clainne acu, cúigear mac agus beirt iníoneacha. Is mar scéalaí is mó atá aithne ag pobal na Gaeilge ar Bhab, agus bhí an bua céanna ag cuid dá muintir ar an dá thaobh. Scéalaithe ab ea a seanaintín, Máire Ruiséal, a hathair críonna, Mícheál Ó Guithín, agus a máthair chríonna, Cáit Ruiséal.

Foilsíodh naoi scéal déag dá cuid agus tuairisc féinbheathaisnéise in *Ó Bhéal an Bhab: Cnuas-scéalta Bhab Feiritéar* (2002) agus téann dhá dhlúthdhiosca leis an saothar sin. Tá scéalta eile dá cuid i gcló in *Field Day Anthology 4.* Tá sí le clos ar dhiosca, freisin, agus í ag rá rannta agus scéalta do leanaí in *Rabhlaí Rabhlaí* (1998) agus *Scéilín ó Bhéilín* (2003). Bíonn sí ag caint ó am go chéile ar Raidió na Gaeltachta, ar TG4 agus ar RTÉ, agus tá "líon ollmhór taifeadtaí fuaimthéipe – na céadta uair an chloig, is dóichí-tógtha uaithi ag mórán institiúidí agus daoine aonaracha ó 1950 i leith...Tagann mic léinn agus scoláirí Gaeilge is béaloidis go Baile na hAbha ar a tuairisc ó chian is ó chóngar." (*Ó Bhéal an Bhab* 11). Tá sí tar éis páirt a ghlacadh i gcomórtais éagsúla, agus bhuaigh sí an chéad duais sa scéalaíocht ag Oireachtas na Gaeilge i dTrá Lí i 1988.

Select bibliography
Feiritéar, Cáit.
—. "Cuaird na Maighdine", "An Cóta Mór ar an nGa Gréine." *Field Day Anthology.* Scéalaíocht / béaloideas. Eag. Angela Bourke *et al.* Cork: Cork UP, 2002. 1416–19.
—. *Ó Bhéal an Bhab: Cnuas-scéalta Bhab Feiritéar.* Scéalaíocht / béaloideas, beathaisnéis. Eag. Bo Almqvist agus Roibeárd Ó Cathasaigh. Indreabhán: Cló Iar-Chonnachta, 2002.

Fitzgerald, Barbara, née Gregg. 1911–82. Cork. Novels.

Daughter of the Bishop of Ossory, she was born in Cork in 1911 but later moved to Dublin and Kilkenny. She was educated in England and then graduated from TCD. In 1935 she married a nephew of Edith Somerville,

Michael Fitzgerald Somerville, who worked with an oil company in West Africa, where the couple spent several years. She returned to England during the Second World War and worked in intelligence. While living in Armagh after 1944 with her children she wrote her first novel about the Anglo-Irish situation, *We Are Besieged* (1946). A second novel, *Footprints Upon Water*, written in 1955, was published posthumously in 1983. The couple retired to Ireland in 1968 but Barbara spent her last years in ill health.

Select bibliography
Fitzgerald, Barbara.
—. *We Are Besieged*. Novel. London: Peter Davies, 1946.
—. *Footprints Upon Water*. Novel. Belfast: Blackstaff, 1983.

Secondary sources
Frehner, Ruth. *The Colonizers' Daughters: Gender in the Anglo-Irish Big House*. Novel. Tubingen: Franacke, 1999.
O'Faoláin, Seán. "Rev. of *We Are Besieged*, by Barbara Fitzgerald." *The Bell* 12.2 (1946): 172–3.

Fitzgerald, Frances. Contemporary. Croom, Co. Limerick. Handbook.

Born 1950, Croom, Co. Limerick, she was educated at Sion Hill Convent, Co. Dublin. Fitzgerald was chairwoman of the Women's Political Association, 1987–9, chairwoman of the Council for the Status of Women, 1988–92 and a member of the Second Commission on the Status of Women, 1990–93. She was a Fine Gael TD, 1992–2002.

Select bibliography
Fitzgerald, Frances.
—. Maureen Gaffney, Andy Conway and Fr Paul Andrews. "Parenting – A Handbook for Parents." Handbook. Dublin: Town House, 1991.

Fitzgibbon, Theodora (nee Rosling). 1916–91. Clonlara, Co. Clare; Castleconnell, Co. Limerick. Autobiography, cookbooks, novel.

Born in London of Irish parents, she was educated in Tipperary and Clare, before going to England, Belgium and France. She later spent time in India, America, France, Italy and Ireland. Her reputation rests on her cookery books, about twenty-four in all, variously titled *Cosmopolitan Cookery*, *Weekend Cookery*, *The High Protein Diet and Cookery Book*, *Country House Cooking*, *The Young Cook's Book*, *Game Cooking*, *The Art of British Cooking*, *Eat Well and Live Longer*. She was also well known through her weekly column in the *Irish Times*, which she wrote for sixteen years. She wrote one novel, *Flight of the Kingfisher* (1967), which was dramatized for television. She recounted her life in two volumes of autobiography, *With Love* (1982) and *Loves Lies A Loss* (1985). She was a friend of Dylan and Caitlin Thomas (*q.v.*) while living in London and the first volume is dedicated to Caitlin and the memories of Dylan and Peter (Rose Pullman) with whom she was living during those years.

Select bibliography
Fitzgibbon, Theodora.
—. *Flight of the Kingfisher*. Novel. London: Dent, 1967.
—. *A Taste of Ireland: Irish Traditional Food*. Cookbook. London: Dent, 1968.
—. *A Taste of Rome: Traditional Food*. Cookbook. London: Dent, 1975.
—. *The Food of The Western World: An Encyclopaedia from Europe and North America*. Cookbook. London: Hutchinson, 1976.
—. comp. *The Pleasures of the Table*. Cookbook. Oxford: Oxford UP, 1981.
—. *With Love: 1938–1946*. Autobiography. London: Century, 1982.
—. *Irish Traditional Food*. Cookbook. Dublin: Gill & Macmillan, 1983.
—. *Love Lies A Loss: 1946–1959*. Autobiography. London: Century, 1985. London: Pan, 1985.
—. *Your Favourite Recipes*. Cookbook. Dublin: Gill & Macmillan, 1985.

Fitzpatrick, Geraldine. *fl.* **1948.** Cork. Plays, novels.

Born in South Wales, she was educated in Surrey and at Presentation Convent in Cork. She worked in the civil service in Dublin, married in 1950 and settled in Galway. In addition to her 1948 novel, she is said to have written several plays in Irish for children.

Select bibliography
Fitzpatrick, Geraldine.
—. *The Green Eagle*. Novel. London: Johnson, 1948.

Flannery, Sarah. Contemporary. Cork. Autobiography, science.

Born in Blarney in 1982, she ws educated at Scoil Mhuire Gan Smál, where she completed her Leaving Certificate in 2000. In 1999, Flannery was awarded the title "Irish Young Scientist of the Year" at the ESAT Telecom Young Scientist and Technology Exhibition for a project on cryptography. This award also included the honour of being the sole Irish representative at the 11th EU Contest for Young Scientists, where she was a first-place prizewinner. She was also chosen as Cork Person of the Month in October 1999. Following on from the success of her project, Flannery co-authored the Irish number-one bestseller *In Code: A Mathematical Journey* with her father, David Flannery. The book has since has been translated into Korean, Chinese and Japanese. Flannery is currently at Cambridge University, where she is reading for Honours in Computer Science.

Select bibliography
Flannery, Sarah.
—. and David Flannery. *In Code: A Mathematical Journey*. Autobiography. London: Profile Books, 2001.

Fleischmann, Ruth. Contemporary. Cork. Academic writing.

Born in Cork in 1942, she took her PhD at UCC. She is the daughter of Tilly and Aloys Fleischmann, the composer. She currently lectures in English at the University of Bielefeld, Germany.

Select bibliography
Fleischmann, Ruth.
—. *Catholic Nationalism in the Irish Revival: A Study of Canon Sheehan 1852–1913.*
Academic writing. Basingstoke: Macmillan, 1997.
—. *Joan Denise Moriarty: A Founder of Irish National Ballet: Material for a History of Dance in Ireland.* Biography. Dublin: Mercier, 1998.
—. *Aloys Fleischmann 1910–92.* Biography. Cork: Mercier, 2000.

Flitton, Sheila, née Ahern. Contemporary. Cork. Novels, plays.

Born in Cork in 1935, she was educated locally. After leaving school she worked in a factory and in 1952 emigrated to England, where she worked as a maid in an English household. Later she trained as a nurse, married and returned with her family to Ireland in 1960. Having previously taken up an acting career in England, she now combined it with her writing. One of her first acting awards was the Dublin Theatre Festival Award for Best Drama Student in 1972.

Her first play, *Harbour Nights* (1979), won a national competition and, with the author in the starring role, it was well received by the critics. Her first full-length play, *For Better or For Worse* (1982), won the Listowel Writers' Week Award in 1982. She won the Listowel Playwright Award for the following two years also. Other play titles are *Heavenly Visitation*, a one-act comedy, and *Beezie (A Ghost's Story)*, a one-woman show, co-authored with her son. She has appeared in many film and television productions, including *The Manions of America*, *The Irish R.M.*, *Black Beauty* and *The Country Girls*. Her novels, which have a strong autobiographical content, were published in the early 1990s, when she was living in Dublin.

Select bibliography
Flitton, Sheila.
—. *Notions.* Novel. Cork: Glencree, 1991.
—. *Whispers.* Novel. Cork: Emperor, 1992.
—. *More Notions.* Novel. Cork: Emperor, 1993.
—. *Harbour Nights.* (Unpub.) Play. N.d.
—. *For Better or for Worse.* (Unpub.) Play. N.d.
—. *Heavenly Visitation.* (Unpub.) Play. N.d.
—. *Beezie.* (Unpub.) Play. N.d.

Fogarty, Anne. Contemporary. Cork. Academic writing, literary criticism.

Anne Fogarty was born in Douglas, Cork, attending the Eglantine National School, Christ the King Secondary School and UCC, where she took a PhD. She is currently a lecturer in the Department of English, UCD. She is director of the annual James Joyce Summer School. Her research interests include Renaissance literature, colonial literature, feminist theory, and Irish women's writing.

Select bibliography
Fogarty, Anne.
—. "The Colonization of Language: Narrative Strategies in *A View of the Present State of Ireland* and *The Faerie Queene*, Book VI." *Spenser and Ireland: An Interdisciplinary*

Perspective. Literary criticism. Ed. Patricia Coughlan. Cork: Cork UP, 1989. 75–108.

—. "'The Business of Attachment': Romance and Desire in the Novels of Kate O'Brien." *Ordinary People Dancing: Essays on Kate O'Brien*. Literary criticism. Ed. Éibhear Walshe. 1993. Cork: Cork UP. 101–19.

—. "'The Influence of Absences': Eavan Boland and the Silenced History of Irish Women's Poetry." Literary criticism. *Colby Quarterly* 35 (1999): 256–74.

—. ed. *Irish Women Novelists 1800–1940*. Literary criticism. *Special Issue Colby Quarterly*. Vol. 36. 2000.

—. "'A Woman of the House': Gender and Nationalism in the Writings of Augusta Gregory." *Border Crossings: Irish Women Writers and National Identity*. Literary criticism. Ed. Kathryn Kirkpatrick. 2000. Tuscaloosa: Alabama UP. 100–102.

—. "'The Horror of the Unlived Life': Mother–Daughter Relationships in Contemporary Irish Women's Fiction." *Writing Mothers and Daughters: Renegotiating the Mother in Western European Narratives*. Literary criticism. Ed. Adalgisa Giorgio. New York: Berghahn, 2002. 71–98.

Forrest, Anne-Marie. Contemporary. Cork. Novels.

Raised in Blarney, Co. Cork, she took a degree in English and Geography at UCC, before moving to Dublin to do an MA in Urban and Regional Planning at UCD. She has published three novels since 2000 and now lives in Dublin.

Select bibliography

Forrest, Anne-Marie.

—. *Who Will Love Polly Odlum?* Novel. Dublin: Poolbeg, 2000.

—. *Dancing Days*. Novel. Dublin: Poolbeg, 2001.

—. *Something Sensational*. Novel. Dublin: Poolbeg, 2002.

Frost, Mary. Contemporary. Cork. Poetry.

Born in Cork in 1936, she was educated locally and graduated from UCC with a BA in English and History. She moved to Galway after her marriage but has also spent some years living in Thunder Bay, Canada. Two of her poems are included in the anthology *Pillars of the House* (1987).

Select bibliography

Frost, Mary.

—. "Hawthorn." *Pillars of the House: An Anthology of Verse by Irish Women from 1690 to the Present*. Poetry. Ed. and sel. A.A. Kelly. Dublin: Wolfhound, 1987, 1997. 126–7.

—. "Rain Shower." *Pillars of the House: An Anthology of Verse by Irish Women from 1690 to the Present*. Poetry. Ed. and sel. A.A. Kelly. Dublin: Woflhound, 1987, 1997. 127.

Gaffney, Maureen. Contemporary. Cork. Journalism.

Born in Cork in 1947, she was educated at UCC and the University of Chicago. She trained as a psychologist, lectured in TCD for a number of years and now works in a private practice in Dublin. From 1986 to 1996 she was a member of the Law Reform Commission, appointed by the Irish government, the only Irish and only non-legal member. She is currently a council member of the Economic and Social Research Institute, chair of the National Economic and Social Forum and director of the doctoral programme in Clinical Psychology at TCD. Gaffney is a well known broad-caster and journalist writing on social issues in Irish society.

Select bibliography
Gaffney, Maureen.
—. *Glass Slippers and Tough Bargains: Women, Men and Power*. Political writing. Dublin: Attic, 1991.
—. A. Conway, P. Andrews and F. Fitzgerald. *Parenting: A Handbook for Parents*. Handbook. Dublin: Town House, 1991. Notes: Published in association with the Gay Byrne [radio] Show.
—. *The Way We Live Now*. Sociology. Dublin: Gill & Macmillan, 1996.

Gallagher, Miriam. Contemporary. Waterford. Plays.

Born in Waterford in 1940, she was educated in Ireland, London and Austria. Her work consists mainly of short plays, many of which have been translated into Irish, Russian, Dutch and Finnish. She has also written a text on speech disorders in children, *Let's Help Our Children Talk* (1977). A number of her compositions, which she describes as theatrical/musical inter-ludes, are based on the lives of Irish composers and have been performed both in Ireland and abroad. She has received several awards for her televi-sion scripts and sceenplays and *Gypsies*, a short film that she wrote, produced and directed in 1994, has been shown in Ireland, New York and at major film festivals. She holds membership in the Society of Irish Play-wrights and has also been closely involved with Irish PEN, the writers' organization. The National Library in Dublin holds a collection of her playscripts and related materials for the period 1984–1990.

Select bibliography
Gallagher, Miriam.
—. *Let's Help Our Children Talk*. Handbook. Dublin: O'Brien, 1977.
—. *Fancy Footwork*. (Unpub.) Play 1983.
—. *Dreamkeeper*. (Unpub.) Play 1984.
—. *The Sealwoman and the Fisher*. (Unpub.) Play 1984.
—. *Labels*. (Unpub.) Play 1985.
—. *Lemon Soufflé*. (Unpub.) Play 1985.
—. *Omelettes*. (Unpub.) Play 1985.
—. *Carolan's Cap*. Radio play. Prod. William Styles. RTÉ Radio 1. 25 Dec. 1986.
—. *Carolan's Cap*. Play. 1986. Notes: Based on the life of Turlough Carolan.
—. *Dusty Bluebells*. (Unpub.) Play 1987.
—. *Nocturne*. Play. 1987. Notes: Based on the life of John Field.
—. *The Ring of Mont de Balison*. (Unpub.) Play 1988.
—. *Bohemians*. Play. 1989. Notes: Based on the lives of Michael William Balfe and William Vincent Wallace.
—. *Easter Eggs*. (Unpub.) Play 1990.
—. *Fancy Footwork: Selected Plays*. Plays. Dublin: Society of Irish Playwrights, 1991.
—. *Shyllag*. Radio play. Prod. Seán O Briain. RTÉ Radio 1. Nov. 1999.

Geoghegan, Mary. *fl.*1886–1930. Ennis, Co. Clare. Poetry.

Published poetry in *Cornhill*, *Macmillan's Magazine*, *The Woman's World*, *Time* and *Chambers' Journal* from 1886 on. She also published poetry, and some translations from the Irish language, in the *Irish Monthly*.

Select bibliography
Geoghegan, Mary.
—. "An Irish Thrush." Poetry. *Irish Monthly* 65.Dec. (1917): 810.
—. "The Song of Crede, Daughter of Guare." Poetry. *Irish Monthly* 66.Oct. (1918): 563–4.
—. "The Viking Terror." Poetry. *Irish Monthly* 66.Sept (1918): 532.
—. "Hospitality." Translation, poetry. *Irish Monthly* 67.July (1919): 368.
—. "Quatrains." Translation, poetry. *Irish Monthly* 67.Sept (1919): 445–8.
—. "The Scribe." Translation, poetry. *Irish Monthly* 67.May (1919): 250.
—. "Song of the Sea." Translation, poetry. *Irish Monthly* 67.Feb. (1919): 92–3.
—. "Colum Cille – The Scribe." Translation, poetry. *Irish Monthly* 68.Oct. (1920): 523.
—. "Dirge for Niall of the Nine Hostages." Poetry. *Irish Monthly* 53.Aug. (1925): 436–7.
—. "King and Hermit." Translation, poetry. *Irish Monthly* 68.Aug. (1930): 445–8.
Notes: From Kuno Meyer's *Ancient Irish Poetry.*

Ginnane, Sr Rose Anne. Contemporary. Clare. Autobiography.

Born on Coney Island, Co. Clare, in 1913. Her father was a farmer and her mother taught in the local school which Ginnane attended until the age of fifteen. She went to study at the Presentation Sisters' Technical School in Dundrum to prepare for the role of farmer's wife. Having completed her secondary education, she moved to Ennis and began to consider entering the religious life. A local priest informed her about the Bon Secours Sisters and the charitable work they did for the poor in Cork city. Ginnane was impressed by this and also by the fact that novices were sent to Paris during their training, as she had a desire to travel. Ginnane joined the Bon Secours Sisters in 1937. She spent time in German-occupied France during the Second World War, travelled to Rome and throughout the US, and was instrumental in establishing a mission in Peru. In 1989 she wrote her autobiography, donating all revenue from the sales of the book to the education of native Peruvian nuns.

Select bibliography
Ginnane, Sr Rose Anne.
—. *From Coney Island to Paris.* Autobiography. Cork: Self-published, 1989.

Girouard, Lady Blanche, née Beresford. 1898–1940. Curraghmore, Co. Waterford. Children's writing.

Daughter of the 6th Marquis of Waterford, she spent much of her life at the family home near Waterford. She married Richard Girouard in 1927. She published one novel, *The Story of Keth* (1928), and a collection of short stories, *The World is for the Young* (1935). She was killed in a car crash at the age of forty-two.

Select bibliography
Girouard, Lady Blanche.
—. *The Story of Keth.* Novel. London: Macmillan, 1928.
—. *The World is for the Young.* Short stories. London: n.p., 1935.

Glavanis-Grantham, Kathy. Contemporary. Cork. Academic writing, sociology.

Received a PhD in Sociology and Social Anthropology from the University in Hull in 1984. She is a lecturer in the Department of Sociology, UCC. Research interests include the sociology of underdevelopment, the sociology of the Middle East, feminism, gender and women's studies.

Select bibliography
Glavanis-Grantham, Kathy.
—. and Pandeli Glavanis. *The Rural Middle-East: Peasant Lives and Modes of Production*. Academic writing, sociology. London: Zed, 1989.
—. "The Women's Movement, Feminism and the National Struggle in Palestine: Unresolved Contradictions." *Women and Politics in the Third World*. Academic writing, sociology. Ed. Haleh Afshar. London and New York: Routledge, 1996. 171–85.

Gouk, Isabella J. [Isa Gouk]. *fl.***1884.** Cork. Poetry.

From Cork. Published poetry in the *Christian Treasury c.* 1884.

Goulding, June [Crotty]. Contemporary. Cork. History.

Lives in Kanturk, Co. Cork. Her book, *The Light in the Window*, details the plight of young women in a home for unmarried mothers in Cork during the 1950s. It was published in Ireland and Australia and formed the basis for the BBC television production *Sinners*.

Select bibliography
Goulding, June.
—. *The Light in the Window: Story of Bessboro Unmarried Mothers' Home*. History. Dublin: Poolbeg Press, 1998.

Graves, Clotilde Inez Mary [Richard Dehan]. 1864–1932. Buttevant, Co. Cork. Plays, novels.

Daughter of an Irish clergyman based in Buttevant, Co. Cork, she went to London to study art in Bloomsbury. She became a journalist, contributing to comic papers in London. A well known playwright, according to Cleeve she had sixteen of her plays produced in London and New York. These include *Nitocris* (Drury Lane 1887), *The Lovers' Battle* (1902), which was based on "Rape of the Lock", and a pantomime, *Puss in Boots* (Drury Lane 1898). She also wrote novels, the best known of which was *The Dop Doctor* (1911), written under the pseudonym Richard Dehan, and *Between Two Thieves* (1912).

Select bibliography
Graves, Clotilde Inez Mary.
—. *The Belle of Rock Harbour: A Tale*. London: n.p., 1887.
—. *Nicrotis, a Play in Verse*. (Unpub.) Play. 1887.
—. *Maids in a Market Garden*. London: Judy, 1889.
—. *The Pirate's Hand: A Romance of Heredity*. London: Judy, 1889.
—. *Seven Xmas Eves: Being a Romance of a Social Evolution*. Short story. 1896. London: Hutchinson. Notes: Graves is one of seven contributors.

—. *A Well-Meaning Woman*. London: Hutchinson, 1896.

—. *Puss in Boots*. (Unpub.) Play. 1898.

—. *The Lover's Battle; A Heroical Comedy in Rhyme; Founded upon Alexander Pope's "Rape of the Lock"*. Play. London: Grant Richards, 1902.

—. *A Mother of Three: An Original Farce in Three Acts*. Play. London: T.H. Lacy's Acting Edition of Plays, 1909.

—. *Between Two Thieves*. Novel. London: Heinemann, 1911.

—. *The Dop Doctor*. Novel. London: Heinemann, 1911.

—. *The Headquarter Recruit*. London: Heinemann, 1913.

—. *The Cost of Wings*. London: Heinemann, 1914.

—. *The Man of Iron*. Novel. London: Heinemann, 1915.

—. *Off Sandy Hook*. London: Heinemann, 1915.

—. *Dragon's Teeth*. Novel. London: n.p., 1916. London: Henry Hardingham, n.d.

—. *Earth to Earth*. Short stories. London: Heinemann, 1916.

—. *Gilded Vanity*. London: Heinemann, 1916.

—. *Under the Hermes*. London: Heinemann, 1917.

—. *That Which Hath Wings: A Novel of the Day*. Novel. London: Heinemann, 1918.

—. *A Sailor's Home*. London: Heinemann, 1919.

—. *The Eve of Pasqua and Other Stories*. Short stories. London: Heinemann, 1920.

—. *The Pipers of the Market-Place*. Novel. London: Thornton, Butterworth, 1920.

—. *The Villa of the Peacock and Other Stories*. Short stories. London: Heinemann, 1921.

—. *The Just Steward*. Novel. London: Heinemann, 1922.

—. *The General's Past*. Play. London: Stage Play Publishing Bureau, 1925.

—. *The Sower of the Wind*. Novel. London: Thornton, Butterworth, 1927.

—. *The Lovers of the Market-Place*. London: Thornton, Butterworth, 1928.

—. *Shallow Seas*. Novel. London: Thornton, Butterworth, 1930.

—. *The Man with the Mask*. London: Thornton, Butterworth, 1931.

—. *Dead Pearls*. London: John Long, 1932.

—. *The Third Graft*. London: John Long, 1933.

Gray, Breda Contemporary. Cork/Limerick. Academic writing, sociology.

Moved to Cork after completing her PhD at Lancaster University in September 1997. She lectured at the Department of Sociology, UCC, 1997–9, and coordinated research on migration and staying in Ireland at the Irish Centre for Migration Studies, UCC, 1999–2002. She has held the position of Senior Lecturer, Women's Studies, in the Department of Sociology, University of Limerick, since September 2002. Her research interests include: the gendered dynamics of emigration in twentieth-century Ireland; the relationships between diaspora and globalization; the ethics of multiculturalism(s); feminist theory; memory and life narratives. She is a member of the editorial board for *Migration Letters. An International Journal of Migration Studies*.

Select bibliography

Gray, Breda.

—. "The Irish Diaspora – Refiguring 'Home' and 'Away'". Sociology. *Irish Journal of Sociology* 11.2 (2002): 123–44.

—. "'Whitely Scripts': Irish Women's Racialised Belongings in London". Sociology. *European Journal of Cultural Studies* 5.2 (2002): 257–74.

—. "Global Modernities and the Gendered Epic of the Irish Empire". *Uprootings/Regroundings: Questions of Home and Migration*. Sociology, political

writing. Ed. Sara Ahmed, Claudia Castaneda, Anne-Marie Fortier and Mimi
Sheller. Oxford: Berg, 2003. 157–78

—. "'Too Close for Comfort": Re-membering the Forgotten Diaspora of Irish
Women in England". *Diaspora, Identity and Religion. New Directions in Theory and
Research.* Sociology, political writing. Ed. Waltraud Kokot, Khachig Tololyan and
Carolin Alfonso. London and New York: Routledge, 2004. 33–52.

—. *Women and the Irish Diaspora.* Sociology. London and New York: Routledge, 2004.

—. "Breaking the Silence: Emigration, Gender and the Making of Irish Cultural
Memory". *Modern Irish Autobiography: Self, Nation and Society.* Sociology. Ed.
Liam Harte. Basingstoke: Palgrave, 2005.

Greer, Sarah D., née Strongman [Mrs Greer]. 1806–91. Waterford. Fiction, history, autobiography.

Wife of John R. Greer of Waterford, she was a Quaker "for forty years", as
she tells us herself. However, in *Quakerism, or the Story of My Life* (1851)
she attempted to discredit the Society of Friends. Its publication was greeted
with a flurry of pamphlets, the best known of which was Standham Elly's
Ostentation. It seems that the Greers had been ejected from the Society of
Friends, prompting Mrs Greer to publish this account. In 1852 she
published a collection of poetry, *The Chained Bible, and Other Poems.* In the
Preface, dated 20 July 1852, she tells us that an earlier version of the title
poem was printed to "aid the cause of the Missions in the West of Ireland",
following the success of which she published this collection. Subscribers to
the book include the Bishop of Tuam. Greer is listed in Samuel Allibone's
1854 dictionary as "Mrs. J.R. Greer", the author of *Quakerism* and another
text, *The Society of Friends: A Domestic Narrative.*

Select bibliography
Greer, Sarah D.

—. *The Chained Bible, and Other Poems.* Poetry. Dublin: Herbert, 1851.

—. *Quakerism, or the Story of My Life.* History, autobiography, religious writing.
Dublin: Samuel B. Oldham, 1851.

—. *The Society of Friends, a Domestic Narrative Illustrating the Peculiar Doctrines
Held by the Disciples of George Fox.* Historical novel. 2 vols: Saunders & Otley,
1852.

Griffin, Amy. *fl.*1904. Co. Clare. Novel.

Clare author of one novel that we know of, in the early twentieth century.

Select bibliography
Griffin, Amy.

—. *His Share in the World: An Irish Story.* Novel. N.p.: n.p., 1904.

Grubb, Isabel. 1881–1972. Carrick-on-Suir, Co. Waterford. History, historical fiction.

A Quaker from Waterford, she took an MA, and went on to write historical
studies, some of which related to her own community, such as *Quakers in
Ireland 1654–1900* (1927).

Select bibliography
Grubb, Isabel.
—. *Quakers in Ireland 1654–1900*. History. London: Swarthmore Press, 1927.
—. *J. Ernest Grubb of Carrick-on-Suir*. Biography. Dublin: Talbot, 1928.
—. *Quakerism and Industry Before 1800*. History. London: Williams & Norgate, 1930.
—. *Quaker Homespuns 1655–1833*. Short stories. London: H.R. Allenson, 1932.

Gubbins, Beatrice Edith. 1878–1944. Glanmire, Co. Cork. Diaries, travel writing.

An artist who studied at the Crawford School of Art – some of her paintings still hang in the family home at Dunkathel and can be viewed by the public. The daughter of Thomas Wise Gubbins, who owned Wise's distillery in Cork, Beatrice Gubbins was born in Limerick but grew up at Dunkathel, Glanmire, Co. Cork. She was a keen motorist and travelled widely, sketching and taking photographs wherever she went. During the First World War she worked as a nurse both in Cork and Exeter. Throughout her life she kept a series of diaries, which recorded her travels, frequently illustrated with sketches of the countries she visited (Kelly, 1995, 169–73). Note: Her diaries are kept at Dunkathel, which is now owned by the Russell family.

Gyles, Althea. 1868–1949. Kilmurry, Co. Waterford. Poetry.

From a well known Anglo-Irish family in West Waterford, her parents were George Gyles and Alithea Emma Grey. She studied art in Dublin, where she joined the Theosophists. According to Colman, she was considered a disciple of AE during her early career (Colman, 104–5). In 1892 she went to study at the Slade School in London. There she became well known for her illustrations of volumes of poetry by W.B. Yeats and contributed designs to books by Wilde and Matthew Russell. She also published in London journals such as *Pall Mall*, *Saturday Review*, *Kensington* and others. Some of her poetry was included in the anthology *A Treasury of Irish Poetry in the English Tongue*, ed. Brooke and Rolleston (1900), with an introduction by Yeats. Some of her work was published under the pseudonym "John Meade".

Colman's account of Gyles's subsequent decline gives us an interesting insight into the vagaries of the marketplace, and the effect of social disapproval on a woman's career at the *fin de siècle*. Her brief affair with Leonard Smithers, a publisher of erotica, caused the end of her working relationship with Yeats – who had banned Smithers from his house. This, accompanied by health problems she suffered in the early 1900s, caused her to descend into penury. She refused financial assistance from her family, insisting on her need to live independently. Arthur Symons began to act as her literary agent in 1904, and several other of her friends assisted her during this period. In 1910 she left London and lived in Folkestone, Cornwall and, briefly, with an aunt in Ireland. Colman tells us that she began a church fresco in Cornwall, which was never finished, and that she made a small living from casting horoscopes in her later years (Colman, 104–6).

Select bibliography
Gyles, Althea.
—. *Dew-Time*. Poetry. London: self-published, 1894.
—. *Six Carols*. Poetry. N.p.: privately printed for the Order of the Holy Mount, 1910.

Hanafin, Joan. Contemporary. Munster. Academic writing.

A lecturer in the Department of Education, UCC, her research interests include gender, curriculum and assessment, Multiple Intelligences theory and teacher development.

Select bibliography
Hanafin, Joan.
—. ed. *Towards New Understandings: Assessment and the Theory of Multiple Intelligences*. Academic writing. Cork: Curriculum and Assessment Action Research Project, UCC, 1997.
—. M. Clarke, M. Kenny, R. Malone, and M. Shevlin, eds. *Background Paper on Education and Equality*. Academic writing. Dublin: Equality Authority, 2002.

Hanley, Mary, née Nealon. *fl.* 1977. Limerick.

Founder of the Yeats Kiltartan Society, she was also instrumental in the restoration of Lady Gregory's Coole Park. She wrote *Thoor Ballylee* (1965), which tells the story of Yeats's tower. She was a teacher and literary historian. She died in 1979.

Select bibliography
Hanley, Mary.
—. and Liam Miller. *Thoor Ballylee: Home of William Butler Yeats*. Dublin: Dolmen Press, 1965. Notes: Based on a lecture given by Mary Hanley to the Kiltartan Society in 1961, rearranged with additional material by Liam Miller.

Harnett, Penelope Mary [P.M.H., P.M. and D.L.]. *fl.*1870–85. Newcastle West, Co. Limerick. Poetry.

From Limerick, she was a contributor to *The Nation* and *Weekly News*. Her poems were published in the *Irish Monthly* 1874, and were anthologized in Sullivan, *Emerald Gems* (1885) (Colman, 108).

Harris, Anne, née O'Sullivan. Contemporary. Cork. Journalism.

Born in Cork in 1947, she was educated there. However, most of her life was spent in Dublin, where she has worked on the magazine *Hibernia*, as well as the *Irish Independent* and the *Sunday Independent*, where she is Assistant Editor. She has also worked as a presenter of radio and television programmes, and as Editor of *Image*, a women's fashion magazine.

Harrison, Cora. Contemporary. Cork. Children's writing.

Born in Cork in 1939, she was educated at Scoil Mhuire and at UCC, where she took a BA in French and German in 1960. She taught in primary schools in England for twenty-five years before returning to live on a farm in north-west Clare. Her series of children's stories, known as the "Drumshee

Timeline Series", is inspired by an Iron Age fort enclosing the remains of a small castle on the farm, and her books trace the survival of the ringfort through the centuries.

Select bibliography
Harrison, Cora.

—. *Nuala and Her Secret Wolf.* Children's writing. Dublin: Wolfhound, 1997.
—. *Secret of the Seven Crosses.* Children's writing. Dublin: Wolfhound, 1997.
—. *Famine Secret.* Children's writing. Dublin: Wolfhound, 1998.
—. *Secret of Drumshee Castle.* Children's writing. Dublin: Wolfhound, 1998.
—. *Secret of 1798.* Children's writing. Dublin: Wolfhound, 1998.
—. *Titanic: A Voyage from Drumshee.* Children's writing. Dublin: Wolfhound, 1998.
—. *The Drumshee Rebels.* Children's writing. Dublin: Wolfhound, 1999.
—. *millennium@drumshee.* Children's writing. Dublin: Wolfhound, 1999.
—. *Murder at Drumshee.* Children's writing. Dublin: Wolfhound, 2000.
—. *A Viking at Drumshee.* Children's writing. Dublin: Wolfhound, 2000.
—. *Dark Days at Drumshee.* Children's writing. Dublin: Wolfhound, 2001.
—. *World War II: Rescue at Drumshee.* Children's writing. Dublin: Wolfhound, 2001.

Harvey, Hannah L. *fl.*1896. Waterford. Poetry.

From Waterford, she was an ardent nationalist and ex-Quaker, who resigned her membership of the Society of Friends as a result of her political beliefs. Her poem "The Jungfrau" was anthologized in Armitage, *The Quaker Poets of Great Britain and Ireland* (1896).

Harvey, Margaret Boyle. 1786–1832. Cork. Diary, travel writing.

Author of a journal (ms. in Dublin Friends Historical Library) kept during a voyage to Cork from Philadelphia, 1809–12, in which she describes the landscape and society of Cork in the early 1800s. For example, here she discusses Passage West: "In the summer it is very gay, owing to the ladies that go from there for the benefit of the bathing as the water is quite salt; there is a new and commodious bathing house erected; there are assembly rooms in it, in which they hold balls and assemblies through the season" (42). Similarly, her first impressions of Cork give us a perspective of the city from the viewpoint of a society lady; she lists the plate in the house she attends for dinner, and describes the cultural life of the city thus: "There is a very fine theatre in the city, and as it happened to be play night, I had an opportunity of seeing a great many carriages, in which were fine looking women dressed with great taste and elegance" (46).

Select bibliography
Harvey, Margaret Boyle.

—. *Journal of a Voyage from Philadelphia to Cork in the year of Our Lord 1809, together with a Description of a Sojourn in Ireland.* Travel writing. Philadelphia: West Park, 1913. Notes: Her granddaughter, Dora Harvey Develin, contributed to this publication also.

Haslam, Anna, née Fisher. 1829–1922. Youghal, Co. Cork. Political writing.

Daughter of Abraham Fisher and Jane Moore, she came from a middle-class Quaker background in Youghal, Co. Cork, where Abraham ran a cornmill.

She was educated at Newtown School in Waterford, and Castlegate, York. She went on to teach at the well known Quaker school at Ackworth in Yorkshire. There, she met her husband, Thomas Haslam. They married in 1854, following which they lived in Clonmel for a time before moving to Dublin. They were a very united couple, and together they became involved in political activism at the turn of the century. Described by her contemporaries as "one of the giants of the women's cause" (Cullen, 161), Anna Haslam founded the Dublin Women's Suffrage Association in 1876. She was involved in every first-wave campaign for women's rights in Ireland and her work as an organizer and a leader within the feminist movement was widely recognized. Haslam also worked with many reform groups not directly connected with the feminist movement.

Although she was not a prolific writer, only publishing two pamplets in the 1890s, it is probable that her ideas and discussions with Thomas formed the basis of his many publications, which included *A Few Words on Prostitution and the Contagious Diseases Acts* (1870) and *The Rightful Claims of Women* (1906). Cullen tells us that, although Anna Haslam's political activism took place in the nineteenth century, she maintained links with the early-twentieth-century women's movement, and she inspired many younger women to continue the feminist struggle (162).

Haslam died in 1922 and is buried in the Friends' Burial Ground at Temple Hill, Blackrock, Co. Dublin. There is a memorial seat to the Haslams in St Stephen's Green in Dublin.

Select bibliography
Haslam, Anna.
—. "Irishwomen and the Local Government Act." *Englishwomen's Review*. Political writing. 15 October 1898.
—. *Suggestions for Intending Lady Guardians*. Handbook, political writing. Dublin: Dublin Women's Suffrage Association, 1898.
—. *Suggestions for Intending Women Workers Under the Local Government Act*. Handbook, political writing. Dublin: Dublin Women's Suffrage Association, n.d.

Secondary sources
Quinlan, Carmel. *Genteel Revolutionaries: Anne and Thomas Haslam, Pioneers of Irish Feminism*. Cork: Cork UP, 2002.

Hassett, Margaret. See Daly, Kathleen.

Haverty, Anne. Contemporary. Thurles, Co. Tipperary. Novels, biography, poetry, literary criticism.

Born in 1959 in Thurles, Co. Tipperary, she studied at TCD. Her first publication was a biography of Constance Markievicz in 1988, followed by a novel, *One Day as a Tiger* (1997), which won the Rooney prize that year. The novel was Ireland's entry in 1998 for the Aristeion Prize and was shortlisted for the Whitbread award. She was also one of the writers who contributed an unidentified chapter to a novel co-written with well known Irish women authors, *Ladies' Night at Finbar's Hotel* (1999). She became a member of Aosdána in 2000.

Select bibliography
Haverty, Anne.

—. *Constance Marckievicz: An Independent Life*. Biography. London: Pandora, 1988.

—. *Elegant Times: A Dublin Story*. History. Dublin: Sonas, 1995.

—. *One Day as a Tiger*. Novel. London: Chatto, 1997.

—. *The Beauty of the Moon*. Poetry. London: Chatto, 1999.

—. contributor. *Ladies' Night at Finbar's Hotel*. Fiction. Ed. Dermot Bolger. London: Picador, 1999.

—. *The Far Side of a Kiss*. Novel. London: Chatto, 2000.

—. "Ladies Waiting Room, Thurles Station." *Slow Time: 100 Poems to Take You There*. Poetry. Ed. Niall MacMonagle. Dublin: Marino, 2000. 92.

Hayes, Joanne. Contemporary. Tralee, Co. Kerry. Social history.

Born in 1959, she came to national attention in 1984 at the centre of what came to be known as the "Kerry Babies Case". That year she concealed the birth and death of her second child on the family farm near Tralee. At the same time the body of a baby was washed onshore at Cahirciveen. Nell McCafferty describes the way in which the investigation of this infanticide was carried out – the gardaí interrogating large numbers of women in the locality who were suspected of being sexually promiscuous (13). Hayes was an unmarried woman, and was having a relationship with a local married man, Jeremiah Locke, by whom she already had one child. Under interrogation, she confessed to the infanticide of the Cahirciveen baby, and members of her family confessed to conspiring to hide its body. Despite the fact that all the scientific evidence available at the time proved she could not have been its mother, when the charges against her were finally dropped, police continued to insist that she must have given birth to twins conceived by different men. The case had gained considerable public attention, and a journalist for the *Sunday Independent* published an investigative piece following the collapse of the case in court. Serious questions had been raised about garda methods during the investigation, questions were asked in the Dáil, and a tribunal was finally established to enquire into the episode in 1985.

However, during this tribunal, Joanne Hayes was effectively put on trial, as her medical, social and moral character were all opened up to public scrutiny. The police sought to vindicate their actions by calling a series of experts to testify against Hayes, in the full spotlight of media attention. Demonstrations were organized locally by the Tralee Women's Group to show support for Joanne Hayes and her family during the tribunal. Gradually, they were joined by a number of other women's groups from all over the country, and a protest march was held in Dublin. The slogan "who's on trial?" became central to these protests as feminist groups pointed up the way in which cross-examination was used, both in the initial arrest and the subsequent court hearings, to publicly parade Hayes' sexuality, and thus discredit her. Six months later, charges against her were finally dropped, and she returned to lead a quiet life on the farm in Abbeydorney. Two books were published about this case in 1985, McCafferty's *A Woman to Blame* and Hayes's own account of the case, *My Story*.

Select bibliography
Hayes, Joanne.
—. and John Barrett. *My Story*. Autobiography. Dingle: Brandon, 1985.

Secondary Sources
Nell McCafferty. *A Woman to Blame*. Dublin: Attic Press, 1985.

Healy, Isabel. Contemporary. Cork. Journalism.

While she was studying at UCC in 1967, her work was published in a feature on new Irish writing in the *Irish Press*. She later worked as a librarian before becoming a full-time journalist in 1978. She has researched, written and presented magazine programmes and documentaries for radio and television, and she has been art critic for the *Cork Examiner* and has had a regular column with that paper since 1988. She was born and lives in Cork.

Select bibliography
Healy, Isabel.
—. "A Cork Girlhood." *The Cork Anthology*. Memoir. Ed. Seán Dunne. Cork: Cork UP, 1993. 117–23.

Heath, Lady Mary [Sophie Mary Pierce-Evans]. 1896–1939. Newcastle West, Co. Limerick. Autobiography, handbook.

Born in Newcastle West, she was educated in Dublin. Her particular interest was athletics, and she was co-founder and later vice-president of the British Women's Amateur Athletic Association in 1922. She competed in several competititons at the World Championships in England in 1923, and also held an Irish record in the 100m hurdle event. She spoke at the Olympic Committee meeting in Prague in 1925 and, thanks to her efforts, women were allowed to participate in the 1928 Olympic Games. She wrote a coaching manual for women and girls, *Athletics for Women and Girls*.

Evans was also interested in flying and in 1925 she had the distinction of becoming the first woman to qualify for a British pilot's licence. From then on, flying became her main interest, and she became the first woman to fly solo from Cape Town in South Africa to Croydon in Surrey in 1928. The journey covered 10,000 miles and took 3½ months. In 1929 she wrote about the joys of flying in *Woman and Flying*. She spent some time demonstrating flying and lecturing in the United States until a serious accident ended her flying career. She returned to Ireland in 1931, lost her money on the purchase of an airline and ended her days in obscurity and ill-health in London, where she died in 1939.

Select bibliography
Heath, Lady Mary.
—. *Athletics for Women and Girls*. Manual. N.p.: n.p., n.d.
—. *Woman and Flying*. Autobiography. N.p.: n.p., 1929.

Hely Walshe, Elizabeth. 1835–68. Limerick. Historical novel.

A short biographical sketch of the author is provided by her sister in the introduction to *The Manuscript Man* (1869). The Hely Walshe family were based in Limerick, their father had an LLD from Trinity, and was a member of the Royal Irish Academy. Elizabeth taught in a Sunday school, and was a follower of Rev. H. Grattan Guinness. She contributed to *The Leisure Hour* and *Sunday at Home*, as well as writing publications for the Religious Tract Society. Her best-known work was *Golden Hills: or, A Story of the Irish Famine* (1865). She died of consumption while convalescing in the Isle of Wight in 1868.

Select bibliography
Hely Walshe, Elizabeth.
—. *Golden Hills: or, A Tale of the Irish Famine*. Historical novel. London: Religious Tract Society, 1865.
—. *The Foster-Brother of Doon: A Tale of the Irish Rebellion of 1798*. Historical novel. London: Religious Tract Society, 1866.
—. *The Manuscript Man: or, The Bible in Ireland*. Religious writing. London: Religious Tract Society, 1869.
—. *Cedar Creek: From the Shanty to the Settlement: A Tale of Canadian Life*. Historical novel. London: Religious Tract Society, n.d.

Henry, Hanora M., née Carroll. Contemporary. Dunmanway, Co. Cork, Cork. History.

Born in 1931 in Dunmanway, Co. Cork, she qualified as a nurse. After studying for a Tutor Fellowship at the Royal College of Surgeons in Dublin, she became a Nurse Tutor at Our Lady's Psychiatric Hospital in Cork in 1960. She played an active part in introducing changes in psychiatric care in Ireland during the latter part of the twentieth century, both at local and national level. Her first book was a history of Our Lady's psychiatric hospital at Sunday's Well in Cork, in which she examined the treatment of mental illness over the past two centuries.

Select bibliography
Henry, Hanora M.
—. *Our Lady's Hospital Cork: A History of the Mental Hospital in Cork Spanning 200 Years*. History. Cork: Haven, 1989.
—. *A History of the Irish Guild of Catholic Nurses: Seventy-five Years of Services 1922–1997*. History. Dublin: Irish Guild of Catholic Nurses, 1998.
—. and Richard Deady. *Mental Health Nursing in Ireland: An Overview of the Many Factors Both Directly and Indirectly Influencing the Shape of Psychiatric Nursing in Ireland Today*. History. Kilkenny: Red Lion, 2001.

Herbert, Dorothea. 1770–1829. Carrick-on-Suir, Co. Tipperary. Memoir.

Born *c.*1770 (she is not entirely honest about her age) in Carrick-on-Suir, Co. Tipperary, she was the daughter of a clergyman of very good circumstances. Her memoir/autobiography *Retrospections*, tells the story of her failed love affair and subsequent madness. Her work also gives a very detailed account of the day-to-day life of a country parsonage, and the friends and family who formed their circle. Her own title for the work was *Retrospections of an Outcast Or the Life of Dorothea Herbert Authress of The Orphan Plays and Various Poems and Novels In Four Volumes Written in Retirement Volume the Fourth Adorned with Cuts.* The original manuscript is held in TCD. This is her only extant work, published posthumously.

Select bibliography
Herbert, Dorothea.
—. *Retrospections of Dorothea Herbert.* Memoir. Dublin: Town House, 1988.

Herbert, Máire. Comhaimseartha. Cathair Chorcaí / An Baile Dubh, Co. Chiarraí. Scríbhneoireacht acadúil.

Is as An Baile Dubh í, Máire. Ba mhúinteoirí iad a tuismitheoirí. D'fhreastail sí ar Mheánscoil na Toirbhirte, Trá Lí. Bhain sí céim BA amach sa Ghaeilge agus sa Stair in Ollscoil na Gaillimhe, agus ghnóthaigh céim MA sa tSean agus sa Mheán-Ghaeilge san ollscoil chéanna. Bhain sí PhD amach i gCambridge agus chaith tréimhse mar chomhalta iardhochtúireachta in Institiúid Ard-léinn Bhaile Átha Cliath. Is Ollamh í i Roinn na Sean-Ghaeilge i gColáiste na hOllscoile, Corcaigh faoi láthair.

Máire Herbert is from Ballyduff. Her parents were both teachers. She attended secondary school in Tralee. She graduated from UCG with a BA in Irish and History and she went on to graduate with an MA in Old and Middle Irish from the same university. She has a PhD from Cambridge University and she spent some time as a postdoctoral fellow of the Dublin Institute for Advanced Studies. She is currently Professor of Old Irish in UCC.

Select bibliography
Herbert, Máire.
—. agus Pádraig de Brún. *Catalogue of Irish Manuscripts in Cambridge Libraries.* Scríbhneoireacht acadúil. Cambridge; New York: Cambridge UP, 1986.
—. *Betha Adamnáin: The Irish Life of Adamnán.* Scríbhneoireacht acadúil, eagarthóireacht. Eag. Máire Herbert agus Pádraig Ó Riain. ITS 54. London: ITS, 1988.
—. *Iona, Kells and Derry: the history and hagiography of the monastic familia of Columba.* Scríbhneoireacht acadúil, stair. Oxford: Clarendon, 1988. Baile Átha Cliath: Four Courts, 1996.
—. agus Martin Mc Namara, Eag. agus aist. *Irish biblical apocrypha: selected texts in translation.* Litríocht an Bhíobla. Edinburgh: Clark, 1989.
—. "Celtic Heroine? The Archaeology of the Deirdre Story." *Gender in Irish Writing.* Scríbhneoireacht acadúil. Eag. Toni O'Brien Johnson agus David Cairns. Milton Keynes: Open UP, 1991. 13–22.
—. "Goddess and King: The Sacred Marriage in Early Ireland." *Women and Sovereignty (Cosmos 7).* Scríbhneoireacht acadúil, léirmheastóireacht. Eag. Louise D. Fradenberg. Edinburgh: Edinburgh UP, 1992. 263–75.
—. "The Universe of Male and Female: A Reading of the Deirdre Story." *Celtic Languages and Celtic Peoples: Proceedings of the Second North American Congress of Celtic Studies.* Scríbhneoireacht acadúil, léirmheastóireacht. Eag. Cyril J. Byrne, Margaret Harry agus Pádraig Ó Siadhail. 1992. 53–64.

—. *Studies in Irish Hagiography*. Scríbhneoireacht acadúil. Eag. Máire Herbert, John Carey agus Pádraig Ó Riain. Baile Átha Cliath: Four Courts Press, 2001.

Hickson, Mary Agnes. 1825–99. Tralee. Local history.

Born in Tralee, Co. Kerry, in 1825, she was one of fourteen children of prominent local solicitor John James Hickson and his wife, Sarah, the daughter of the local rector. Sadly, ten of their children died of tuberculosis and the only surviving daughters were Mary and her sister Sarah. From an Irish-speaking nurse, she gained an interest in the Irish language, which was reflected in her writing on Kerry place-names in her later years. Mary was educated at a local school before going to boarding school. When her father died, when Mary was thirteen years old, she and her sister became wards of their brother James, who, having neglected his father's legal practice, ran into further financial difficulties when his tenants were unable to pay their rent due to the hardship wrought by the Famine. Fortunately for Mary and her other brother, John (her sister had died at the age of nine), her mother was able to survive on a small private income, but on her death in 1852 Mary was left virtually penniless. How she spent the following years is unclear, but she appears to have moved around to stay with different relatives.

She returned to Tralee in the late 1860s and began submitting articles on local history to the *Kerry Evening Post*. These were based on the old manuscripts she inherited from her father. She became a regular contributor, and with the money she earned she carried out further historical research in London and Dublin. This led to the publication of her two volumes of Old Kerry Records, published privately in 1872 and 1874. She then became interested in local antiquities, became a member of the Royal Society of Antiquaries of Ireland and wrote articles for its journal. She also carried out genealogical research on her own family, while continuing to write on a variety of topics. She ended her days in Mitchelstown, Co. Cork, and was buried in her native Tralee.

Select bibliography
Hickson, Mary Agnes.
—. *Selections from Old Kerry Records*. History. 1872, 2 vols. 1974.
—. *Ireland in the Seventeenth Century, or the Irish Massacres of 1641–2: Their Causes and Results I*. History. 2 vols. London: Longmans, 1884. Notes: Includes extracts from unpublished state papers, and unpublished mss. in the Bodleian Library

Secondary sources
Manning, Peter, comp. *Index of Persons to the 2 Volumes of Ireland in the Seventeenth Century, on the Massacres of 1641*. Kent: Rainham, 1990.
McMorran, Russell. "Mary Hickson: Forgotten Kerry Historian." *Kerry Magazine* 11 (2000): 34–7.

Hill, Judith. Contemporary. Limerick. History.

Born in London in 1959, she graduated with a degree in Art History in 1982. She subsequently qualified as an architect in 1989. She is currently living in Limerick city.

Select bibliography
Hill, Judith.
—. *The Building of Limerick*. History. Cork: Mercier, 1991.
—. *Irish Public Sculpture: A History*. History. Dublin: Four Courts, 1998.

Hoare, Mary Ann. c.1818–72. Monkstown, Co. Cork. Short stories.
Only child of John Pratt of Woburn Place, Cork, and Miss Hawkes of Bandon, she married William Barry Hoare, who was a solicitor from Monkstown, Co. Cork, in 1837. The couple had six children, three of whom died in infancy. In 1870 her son Edward, a captain in the Northumberland Fusiliers, committed suicide on board a ship leaving India. Her best known work, *Shamrock Leaves* (1851), was a collection of short stories published under the name "Mrs Hoare", with a Preface by the author written in Monkstown. *The Wellesley Index of Victorian Periodicals* attributes a short story, "The Mysterious Sketch", published in *Temple Bar* in 1872, to the same author, referring to a controversy relating to the authorship of previously published versions of the story.

Select bibliography
Hoare, Mary Ann.
—. *Shamrock Leaves: or, Tales and Sketches of Ireland*. Short stories. Dublin: J. McGlashan, 1851.
—. "The Mysterious Sketch." Short story. *Temple Bar* 34 (1872): 212–24.

Hogan, Ita Margaret. *fl.* 1966. Cork. Music history.
Born in Cork, she received her academic education at UCC. Her publication on Anglo-Irish music is an account of musical activities in Ireland with biographies and bibliographies of musicians, composers and visiting singers.

Select bibliography
Hogan, Ita Margaret.
—. *Anglo-Irish Music (1780–1830)*. History. Cork: Cork UP, 1966.

Hopkin, Alannah [Rachel Warren]. Contemporary. Cork. Fiction, travel writing, novels.
Born in Singapore in 1949, she is a graduate of the University of London and received an MA in the Sociology of Literature from the University of Essex in 1976. From 1977 to 1982 she was based in London working as a freelance writer contributing to the *Evening Standard*, *Time Out*, *Sunday Times Magazine*, *Over21*, *Ms London*, *Irish Times* and *Books and Bookmen*. From 1981 to 1982 she taught a creative-writing course in the City Lit, London, an adult-education institute. In 1982 she moved to Kinsale, Co. Cork, where her mother was born, and published her first novel, *A Joke Goes a Long Way in the Country*. She continued to write and publish during the 1980s and in 1991 published *Inside Cork*, a book-length visitor's guide to Co. Cork. Hopkin also continued to work in freelance journalism, and in 1996 was runner-up in the Campus Radio Fallen Leaves competition,

UCC. Her competition entry was recorded and broadcast on 17 Dec. 1996. During the 1990s she continued to publish fiction and travel writing, occasionally under the name Rachel Warren. She is currently art critic for the *Irish Examiner*, arts correspondent in the south-west region for the *Sunday Times* and contributing editor for *Circa* magazine. Hopkins writes book reviews for the *Irish Times* and the *Sunday Tribune*, is the area editor for *Fodor's Guide to Ireland* and writes travel pieces for *Ireland of the Welcomes* (the Irish Tourist Board Magazine) and the *Irish Times* magazine.

Select bibliography
Hopkin, Alannah.
—. *A Joke Goes a Long Way in the Country*. Novel. London: Hamish Hamilton, 1982.
—. *The Out-Haul*. London: Hamish Hamilton, 1985.
—. *The Living Legend of St Patrick*. London: Grafton Books, 1989.
—. *Inside Cork*. Travel writing. Cork: The Collins Press, 1991.
—. "The Dogs of Inishere." Short story. *Books Ireland* 107 (1996).
—. *Southwest Ireland*. Travel writing. N.p.: Insight Guides/Apa Publications, 1997.
—. "The Dogs of Inishere." Short story. *The Literary Review* (1998).
—. "You Can't Call It That." Short story. *The Cork Review* (1999).
—. *The West of Ireland*. Travel writing. N.p.: Insight Guides/Apa Publications, n.d.
—. *The Wild Geese Came Back*. (Unpub.).
—. *You Can't Call It That and Other Stories*. Short stories.

Humphreys O'Donoghue, Sighle. 1899–1994. Limerick. Letters.

From Limerick, she was the daugher of David Humphreys and Mary Ellen O'Rahilly. Her uncle, Michael Joseph "The O'Rahilly", was a Volunteer leader, and her brother, Dick, was in the GPO in Dublin in the 1916 Rising. Sighle herself was an active member of Cumann na mBan, and was imprisoned in the North Dublin Union, Kilmainham and Mountjoy. Her account of this period in her life was published in Mac Eoin, *Survivors* (1980). She married Dónal O'Donoghue, a Republican who was interned during the Civil War, in 1925. He went on to become editor of *An Phoblacht*, the Republican newspaper (*Field Day V*, 174).

Select bibliography
Humphreys O'Donoghue, Sighle.
Survivors. Ed. Uinseann Mac Eoin. Dublin: Argenta, 1980.

Hutchins, Ellen. 1785–1815. Bantry, Co. Cork. Science.

Daughter of Thomas Hutchins, a Protestant wine merchant who is known to have opposed the Penal Laws and who at one point insisted that a local priest be paid a fair price for a horse he was selling. She attended school in Dublin, where, as a result of her ill-health, she came under the care of a family friend, Whitley Stokes, a keen naturalist and Professor of Medicine at the Royal College of Physicians. He encouraged her to take up botany in order to give her a healthy outdoor hobby.

Because of her friendship with Stokes, Hutchins met many leading botanists of the day – such as James Townsend Mackay, curator of Trinity's first botanic garden in Ballsbridge. Mackay encouraged her growing interest in collecting and identifying specimens, and she became an expert on mosses, lichens, liverwort and particularly seaweed. Through Mackay, she was asked to contribute to Dawson Turner's publication on mosses and seaweeds, *Muscologiae Hibernicae Specilegium* (1804), the first book on the mosses of Ireland. She also contributed records, specimens and illustrations of seaweeds for his *Historia Fucorum* (1808–19), as well as to Lewis Dillwyn's *British Confervae*. Chesney comments that women were discouraged from publishing their own scientific findings during this period (33) and thus Hutchins's work was passed on to her male peers, although she is credited with having written many reports on particular species in their publications.

In 1805 Hutchins, now the only surviving daughter in her family, returned to Ballylickey House to care for her mother and invalid brother. There, she took up gardening, and some of her original plantings can still be found in the area called "Ellen's Garden". Some of her finest botanical work dates from this period, when she carried out research on the West Cork coast. Turner, Dillwyn and other celebrated botanists visited her to consult with her. Several species bear her name – such as the *Hutchinsia* alpine flowering plant. Even after her death the algae expert, William Henry Harvey, based some of his drawings in *Phycologia Britannica* (1846–61) on her work – and he credits her with finding and recording a number of new species. Hutchins battled with tuberculosis (it is known that in 1814 she was prescribed mercury for it) and she died in 1815 at the age of thirty.

Hutchins, Patricia. 1911–85. Co. Cork. Academic writing, children's writing.

Born in Ardnagashel, Bantry, in West Cork, her mother was a Londoner who married into an Anglo-Irish family and Patricia's childhood was spent in London and Co. Cork. She was educated at home due to ill-health, and later went to school in Scotland and various parts of England. She lived in Spain, France and Belgium at different times. She was interested in documentary films and wrote frequently for *Sight and Sound*, the journal of the British Film Institute. She also reviewed books for *The Bell* magazine. She married the Ulster poet and critic Robert Greacen in 1946, and they had a daughter, Arethusa. To further both of their careers they moved to London, and visited Bantry on holidays. They divorced in 1966. Some years later Patricia returned to Bantry with her daughter, and lived there until she died in 1985. In his autobiography Robert Greacen states that "in today's terms she was a feminist" and was intent on a career for herself.

Her first novel was written for children, *Ivan and His Wonderful Coat* (1945), and was illustrated by the celebrated Irish artist, Nano Reid. Her later works focused on James Joyce and Ezra Pound and in particular on the places associated with them. Her *James Joyce's World* (1957) is a comprehensive topographical review written with the assistance of many who knew Joyce. These included his brother Stanislaus, his son Giorgio, Eugene Jolas, Beckett, Sean O'Casey, Jung and George Yeats. Shortly before her death she was scheduled to give a talk on Ezra Pound at the Tate Gallery but illness prevented her. Her book on Ezra Pound had appeared in 1965. She was featured in an exhibition of Cork writers held in Cork city in 1957.

Select bibliography
Hutchins, Patricia.
—. "Pattern Day." Local history. *The Bell* 3.2 (1941): 132–9.
—. *Ivan and His Wonderful Coat and Other Stories*. Children's writing. Dublin: New Frontiers, 1945. Notes: Illus. Nano Reid.
—. "Cycling in West Cork." *Introducing Ireland*. Travel writing. Ed. Cyril Moore. London: n.p., 1947.
—. "The Man Who Ate His Wife." Short story. *The Bookman* 2 (1947): 5–8.
—. "The Boathouse." Short story. *Irish Writing* 6 (1948): 45–8.
—. "Joseph Hone – Biographer." Academic writing. *Irish Writing* 7 (1949): 71–6.
—. *James Joyce's Dublin*. History. London: Grey Walls, 1950.
—. "Rev. of *The Shelbourne*, by Elizabeth Bowen."*Irish Writing* 17 (1951): 67.
—. "Schoolmaster." Short story. *Blarney Annual of Fact & Fancy* 3 (1951): 73.
—. "Maria Edgeworth." Literary criticism. *Blarney Annual of Fact & Fancy* 4 (1952): 74–5.
—. "Rev. of *Exiles*, by James Joyce."*Irish Writing* 19 (1952): 56–7.
—. "Daniel Corkery: Poet of Weather and Place." Academic writing. *Irish Writing* 25 (1953): 42–9.
—. *James Joyce's World*. History. London: Methuen, 1957.
—. *Il mondo di James Joyce* [James Joyce's World]. History. Trans. Roberto Samesi and Cathy Berberian. Milan: Lerici, 1960.
—. *Ezra Pound's Kensington: An Exploration 1885–1913*. History. London: Faber & Faber, 1965.

Secondary sources
MacManus, Francis. "Rev. of *James Joyce's Dublin*, by Patricia Hutchins." *Irish Writing* 14 (1951): 61–2.

Hyland, Áine. Contemporary. Cork. Academic writing.

Born in Meath in 1942, she worked as Executive Officer with the Department of Education until her marriage in 1964, when she resigned under the requirements of the Civil Service marriage ban. She was awarded a PhD from TCD in 1983 and was appointed Professor of Education and Head of the Education Department, UCC, in 1993. In 1999 she became Vice-President of UCC. Hyland is a trustee of Monkstown Educate Together School, North Dublin National School Project and a patron of the Northern Ireland Council for Integrated Education. She has co-edited a three-volume collection of extracts from educational documents in Ireland from earliest times to 1990: *Irish Educational Documents Volumes 1, 2 and 3*.

Select bibliography
Hyland, Áine.
—. ed. *Irish Educational Documents*. Academic writing. Vols. 1–3. Dublin: Church of Ireland College of Education, 1985–95. Notes: A selection of extracts from official documents relating to Irish education from earliest times to 1990.
—. "Multi-Denominational Schools in the Republic of Ireland." *Education Together*

for a Change. Academic writing. Ed. Chris Moffatt. Belfast: Fortnight Educational Trust, 1993.

—. ed. *Irish Educational Studies.* Academic writing. Vols. 12, 13. 1995–6.

—. "Primary and Second-Level Education in the Early 21st Century." *Ireland in the Coming Times.* Academic writing. Ed. F. O'Muircheartaigh. Dublin: Institute of Public Administration, 1997.

—. "The Curriculum of Vocational Education." *Teachers' Union: The TUI and Its Forerunners, 1899–1994.* Academic writing. Ed. John Logan. Dublin: A. & A. Farmar, 1999.

—. "School Culture and Ethos – the Republic of Ireland Experience." *School Culture and Ethos.* Academic writing. Ed. Catherine Furlong and Luke Monahan. Dublin: Marino Institute of Education, 2000.

—. "Education in Post-Christian Ireland." Academic writing. *The Irish Review* (2001).

Iota [Kathleen Mannington Caffyn]. *fl.*1893–1900. Co. Tipperary. Novels.

Born at Waterloo House, Co. Tipperary, the daughter of William Hunt and Louisa Goring, she lived in Ireland until she was twenty-one. She trained as a nurse at St Thomas's Hospital and after a short nursing career married Dr Mannington Caffyn. The couple moved to Australia because of his health. In 1893 she returned to live in London, where she wrote her best-known work, *A Yellow Aster* (1893), an important feminist novel of the period, central to the New Woman literature of the 1890s. During her writing career she contributed to many magazines, and her other novels include *Children of Circumstances* (1894), *A Comedy in Spasms* (1895) and *The Minx* (1899).

Select bibliography
Iota.
—. *A Yellow Aster.* Novel. London: n.p., 1893.
—. *Children of Circumstance.* Novel. London: Hutchinson, n.d.
—. *A Comedy in Spasms.* Novel. London: Hutchinson, n.d.
—. *The Minx.* Novel. London: Hutchinson, 1900.
—. *Anne Mauleverer.* Novel. N.p.: n.p., n.d.
—. *Poor Max.* Novel. N.p.: n.p., n.d.
—. *A Quaker Grandmother.* Novel. N.p.: n.p., n.d.

Jacob, Rosamond. 1888–1960. Waterford. History, historical fiction, children's writing.

Of a Waterford Quaker background, she was educated at Newtown School in Waterford. She remained true to her Quaker origins in many ways; for example, she was a pacifist, and in her life and work she advocated freedom of religion and women's rights. She lived in Dublin from 1920 on, and continued her involvement with a number of organizations, working as a secretary to various feminist and Republican committees. Despite having written several critically acclaimed works, Jacob is best known as a political activist. She was a suffragette, as well as being a member of Cumann na mBan, and she was a close friend of Hanna Sheehy-Skeffington. Meaney points out that it was Jacob who proposed the successful motion for women's suffrage at the Sinn Féin convention of 1917. She was also involved with Louie Bennett and Maud Gonne in the women's peace committee, which attempted to broker a ceasefire at the outset of the Civil War (*Field Day V*, 1044).

Jacob had a deep interest in Irish history and mythology. Two of her works, *The Rise of the United Irishmen* (1937) and *The Rebel's Wife* (1957) – a fictional autobiography of the wife of Wolfe Tone – derive from her knowledge of Irish history. She was a historian, a novelist, and wrote fiction for children, such as *The Raven's Glen* (1960). Although she wrote throughout her life, many of her works remain out of print. She died in 1960.

Notes: Leann Lane's biography of Rosamond Jacob is forthcoming in the CUP Radical Lives series, and Gerardine Meaney is currently working on Jacob's diaries, which are held by the National Library.

Select bibliography
Jacob, Rosamond.
—. "Rosamund Jacob Papers". 1878–1960. (Unpub.) letters. Notes: Held in the National Library of Ireland Ms. Collection List 30.
—. *Callaghan*. Novel. Dublin: Lester, 1921.
—. *The Rise of the United Irishmen 1791–94*. History. London: Harrap, 1937.
—. *The Troubled House: A Novel of Dublin in the Twenties*. Historical novel. Dublin: Browne & Nolan, 1938.
—. *The Rebel's Wife*. Historical fiction. Tralee, Co. Kerry: *The Kerryman*, 1957.
—. *The Raven's Glen*. Children's Writing. Dublin: A. Figgis, 1960.

Secondary sources
Doyle, Damian. "Rosamond Jacob (1888–1960)." *Female Activists: Irish Women and Change 1900–1960*. Ed. Mary Cullen and Maria Luddy. Dublin: Woodfield Press, 2001.

Jenkins, Lee. Contemporary. Cork. Academic writing, literary criticism.

Born in the UK in 1966, she received a PhD in English from Cambridge University. From 1992 to 1994 she worked on a British Academy Postdoctoral Research Fellowship, and she has lectured at the English Department, UCC, since 1994. Her research interests include American and Irish modernist poetry and black American writing. She has published articles on Thomas MacGreevy, an Irish poet originally from Tarbert, Co. Kerry. Jenkins has carried out extensive research on the works of Frederick Douglass, who travelled to Ireland in 1845 for a speaking tour which brought him to Dublin, Belfast, Limerick and Cork.

Select bibliography
Jenkins, Lee.
—. "Beyond the Pale: Frederick Douglass in Cork." Academic writing. *The Irish Review* (1999).
—. "The Black O'Connell: Frederick Douglass and Ireland." Academic writing. *Nineteenth Century Studies* 13 (1999): 22–46.
—. "A Position Intermediate: The Modernism of Thomas MacGreevy." Academic writing. *Angel Exhaust* 17 (1999): 61–8.
—. *Wallace Stevens: Rage for Order*. Academic writing. Brighton: Sussex Academic Press, 1999.

Johnson, Joan C. Contemporary. Waterford. History.

Born in Dublin, she is a qualified physiotherapist. She has lived in Waterford since 1965, and is a member of the Religious Society of Friends. Johnson is a scholar of local history and Irish Quaker history. She is honorary archivist at Newtown School in Waterford and at the Waterford Friends' Meeting House. She contributed to *The Famine in Waterford* (1995) and was responsible for the republication of transactions of the Society of Friends during the Famine in Ireland (1995). She wrote an essay about the artist Hilda Roberts for her retrospective exhibition in 1998, and her most recent work was based on Waterford Quaker history.

Select bibliography
Johnson, Joan C.
—. "The Quaker Relief Effort in Waterford." *The Famine in Waterford 1845–1850: Teacht na bPrátaí.* Local history. Ed. Des Cowman and Donald Brady. Waterford: Geography/Waterford Co. Council, 1995. 215–38.
—. "Quaker Relief in Waterford during the Famine." Local history. *Decies* 51 (1995): 25–36.
—. "Early Quaker Burial Grounds in Waterford City 1689–1826." Local history. *Decies* 56 (2000): 69–80.
—. *James & Mary Ellis: Background on Quaker Famine Relief in Letterfrack.* Local history. N.p.: Historical Committee of the Religious Society of Friends in Ireland, 2000.
—. "Waterford Quakers: A Brief History 1650–1800." Local history. *Decies* 58 (2002).

Joy, Breda. Contemporary. Killarney, Co. Kerry. Journalism.

Educated in Dublin, she now lives in Killarney. She is an award-winning journalist, having been Provincial Journalist of the Year in 1997. In 1996 she wrote the biography of a person suffering from cancer, *Against the Odds.*

Select bibliography
Joy, Breda.
—. *Against the Odds.* Biography. Dingle, Co. Kerry: Brandon, 1996.

Joyce-Prendergast, K.M. *fl.* **1944–58.** Cork. Novels, religious writing.

Born in Cork, she was a writer of novels and religious texts in the 1940s and 1950s.

Select bibliography
Joyce-Prendergast, K.M.
—. *This – My Land.* Novel. Dublin: Gill, 1944.
—. *Vintage.* Novel. Dublin: Gill, 1945.
—. *Windyhill.* Novel. Cork: Mercier, 1946.
—. *The Opening Way.* Novel. Cork: J. Marian Pio, 1951.
—. *Janice Gray.* Novel. Cork: J. Marian Pio, 1953.
—. "Dear Little Prince." Religious writing. *The Fold* 6 (1958): 19.
—. "Dear Pontiff." Religious writing. *The Fold* 6 (1958): 9.

Kavanagh, Julia. 1824–77. Thurles, Co. Tipperary. Novels, biography.

Born in Thurles, Co. Tipperary, she moved with her family to France. Her father, Morgan Kavanagh, was a poet and philologist. The insight she gained into French life and character was faithfully portrayed in many of her works.

She moved to London in 1844 at the age of 20, where her writing career began with a series of essays for periodicals of the day. *Madeleine* (1848), the story of a peasant girl of Auvergne, established her reputation, later built on by her historical and biographical works, such as: *Women in France during the Eighteenth Century* (1850) and *French Women of Letters* (1862). Consisting of about twenty novels, her work had a wide circulation in the USA and England, as well as in France. Tynan says of her literary reputation: "All Miss Kavanagh's books have passed through several editions, and most of them have been published in America where she was a favourite". Her best-known works are *Nathalie* (1850), *Madeleine*, *Daisy Burns* (1853) and *Rachel Gray* (1856). In 1853, she toured the Continent, revisiting France and travelling through Switzerland and Italy, after which she wrote *A Summer and Winter in Two Sicilies* (1858). On the whole she led a quiet life, caring for her invalid mother. After the outbreak of the Franco-Prussian war she moved from Paris to Rouen, and then to Nice, where she died aged fifty-four. Her final collection of short stories, *Forget-Me-Nots* (1878), appeared posthumously.

Select bibliography
Kavanagh, Julia.
—. *The Three Paths: A Story for Young People*. Novel. London: n.p., 1847.
—. *Madeleine: A Tale of Auvergne*. Historical novel. 1848. London: Chapman & Hall, 1873.
—. *Nathalie: A Tale*. Fiction for girls. London: Hurst & Blackett, 1850.
—. *Women in France during the Eighteenth Century*. History. London: Smith & Elder, 1850.
—. *Women of Christianity: Exemplary for Acts of Piety and Charity*. Religious writing. London: n.p., 1852.
—. *Daisy Burns*. Novel. 3 vols. London: n.p., 1853.
—. *Grace Lee*. Novel. 3 vols. London: n.p., 1855.
—. *Rachel Gray*. Novel. London: n.p., 1855.
—. *Adèle*. Novel. 3 vols. London: n.p., 1858.
—. *A Summer and Winter in Two Sicilies*. Travel writing. N.p: n.p., 1858.
—. *French Women of Letters*. Literary criticism. London: n.p., 1862.
—. *Queen Mab*. Novel. 3 vols. London: n.p., 1863.
—. *Beatrice*. Novel. 2 vols. London: n.p., 1864.
—. *Sibyl's Second Love*. Novel. 3 vols. London: n.p., 1867.
—. *Dora*. Novel. London: n.p., 1868.
—. *Forget-Me-Nots*. Short stories. Leipzig: Bernhard Tauchnitz, 1878.
—. *English Women of Letters: Biographical Sketches*. Biography, literary criticism. London: Hurst & Blackett, n.d.

Kavanagh, Liz [Mary Coveney]. Contemporary. Cork. Journalism, memoir, biography.

Born in Cork in 1936, she was educated at Drishane Convent, Millstreet, and then spent a short time with the Medical Missionaries of Mary in Clonmel as a postulant. She left the order and married a farmer, taking an active interest in rural life and attending farmers' meetings. Kavanagh was an exception to the rule in this regard, as very few women attended such meetings, and as a result a number of documentaries were made about her family and farm-life. Having developed something of a media profile, Kavanagh sat on the Eurovision Jury in 1980 and appeared on *The Late Late Show*. During a national farmers' protest in Dublin Kavanagh attracted attention by leading the parade aboard a tractor. The national coverage this earned led to an invitation to write a weekly column for the *Irish Farmer's Journal*, which she did for twenty-eight years. She has also completed a BA in English and Sociology at UCC and published collections of her writing.

Select bibliography
Kavanagh, Liz.
—. *Country Living*. Memoir. Dublin: Wolfhound Press, 1997.
—. *Home to Roost*. Memoir. Dublin: Wolfhound Press, 1998.
—. *From the Horse's Mouth*. Memoir. Dublin: Wolfhound Press, 1999.

Keane, Mary Ronayne. Contemporary. Carrigtwohill, Co. Cork. Plays.

Lives in Carrigtwohill near Cork city and has been interested in music all her life. In recent years she researched, wrote and produced two musical plays, *Flight of the Earls* and *The Ghosts of Barryscourt Castle*, at Barryscourt Castle. She also teaches music on a part-time basis.

Select bibliography
Keane, Mary Ronayne.
—. *Flight of the Earls*. (Unpub.) play. 2000.
—. *The Ghosts of Barryscourt Castle*. (Unpub.) play. 2000.

Keane, Maryangela. Contemporary. Charleville, Co. Cork, Lisdoonvarna, Co. Clare. Local history.

Born in Charleville, Co. Cork, she now lives in Lisdoonvarna, Co. Clare, close to the Burren area, which is her area of interest. She has lectured widely on the history of the Burren, both at home and to academic institutions like the British Library and the New York Metropolitan Museum.

Select bibliography
Keane, Maryangela.
—. *The Burren, Co. Clare*. Local history. Dublin: Eason, 1986.

Keane, Molly, née Mary Nesta Skrine [Farrell, M.J.]. 1904–96. Ardmore, Co. Waterford. Novels, plays.

Born in Co. Kildare in 1904, into an Anglo-Irish family. Her mother, Moira O'Neill, was a poet and the author of "The Songs of the Glens of Antrim". Molly was educated at home until the age of fourteen, when she was sent to a boarding school in Bray, Co. Wicklow. Her childhood was unhappy, and on leaving school she went to live with family friends, the Perrys of Woodruff House in Co. Tipperary. It was here that she met her future husband, Bobby Keane, and also John Perry, who worked with her on several of her successful plays in London.

She wrote her first novel, *The Knight of Cheerful Countenance,* when she was seventeen in order to supplement her dress allowance. This was published in 1926 by Mills & Boon, then not exclusively the publishers of romances. She wrote steadily through the 1920s and 1930s under the pseudonym M.J. Farrell (which hid her identity as well as her gender), and also wrote plays, many of which were written in collaboration with John Perry and directed by John Gielgud. Her husband died in 1938, and after the failure of one of her plays, *Dazzling Prospect,* she returned to Ireland in 1961 to raise her two daughters. In 1981, after twenty years of silence, she wrote *Good Behaviour* and had it published under her own name. It was short-listed for the Booker Prize and also made into a television serial. She wrote two later novels, *Time After Time* (1983) and *Loving and Giving* (1988), as well as a cookery book called *Nursery Cooking* (1985). As a result of her second string of successes in later life, many of her earlier novels were reprinted by Virago. She spent almost forty years living in Ardmore, Co. Waterford, where she took an active interest in community affairs and was also instrumental in furthering the writing careers of Clare Boylan, Jennifer Johnson and Tom McCarthy. She was elected to Aosdána in 1981.

Select bibliography
Keane, Molly.

—. *The Knight of Cheerful Countenance.* Novel. London: Mills & Boon, 1926. London: Virago, 1993.

—. *Young Entry.* Novel. London: Mathews & Marrot, 1928. New York: Holt, 1929.

—. *Taking Chances.* Novel. London: Mathews & Marrot, 1929. London: Virago, 1987.

—. *Mad Puppetstown.* Novel. London: Collins, 1931. New York: Farrar & Rinehart, 1932.

—. *Conversation Piece.* Novel. London: Collins, 1932.

—. *Red Letter Days.* Memoirs. London: Collins, 1933. London: André Deutsch, 1987.

—. *Devoted Ladies.* Novel. London: Collins, 1934. London: Virago, 1984.

—. *Full House.* Novel. London: Collins, 1935.

—. *The Rising Tide.* Novel. London: Collins, 1937. New York: Macmillan, 1938.

—. and John Perry. *Spring Meeting.* Play. London: Collins, 1938.

—. *Two Days in Aragon.* Novel. London: Collins, 1941.

—. *Ducks and Drakes.* Play. London: Collins, 1942.

—. *Treasure Hunt.* Novel. London: Collins, 1949.

—. and John Perry. *Treasure Hunt.* Play. London: Collins, 1950.

—. *Loving Without Tears.* Novel. London: Collins, 1951.

—. *Dazzling Prospect.* Play. London: French, 1961.

—. *Good Behaviour.* Novel. London: André Deutsch, 1981. London: Abacus, 1982.

—. *Time After Time.* Novel. London: André Deutsch, 1983. London: Abacus-Sphere, 1984.

—. *Molly Keane's Nursery Cooking.* Cookbook. London: Macdonald, 1985.

—. *Loving and Giving.* Novel. London: André Deutsch, 1988.

—. "Elizabeth of Bowen's Court." *The Cork Anthology.* Memoir. Ed. Seán Dunne. Cork: Cork UP, 1993. 312–16.

—. and Sally Phipps, comps. *Molly Keane's Ireland: An Anthology.* Anthology. London: HarperCollins, 1993.

Secondary sources

Adams, Alice. "Coming Apart at the Seams: *Good Behaviour* as an Anti-Comedy of Manners." *Journal of Irish Literature* 20 (1991): 27–35.

Imhof, Rüdiger. "Molly Keane: *Good Behaviour, Time After Time and Loving and Giving.*" *Ancestral Voices: The Big House in Anglo-Irish Literature.* Ed. Otto Rauchbauer. Hildesheim: Georg Olms, 1992. 195–203.

Kreikamp, Vera. "The Persistent Pattern: Molly Keane's Recent Big House Fiction." *Massachusetts Review.* 28 (1987): 453–60.

O'Toole, Bridget. "Three Writers of the Big House: Elizabeth Bowen, Molly Keane, and Jennifer Johnston." *Across a Roaring Hill: The Protestant Imagination in Modern Ireland: Essays in Honour of John Hewitt.* Ed. Gerald Dawe and Edna Longley. Belfast: Blackstaff, 1985. 124–38.

Weekes, Ann Owens. "Molly Keane: Bildungsromane Quenelles." *Irish Women Writers: An Uncharted Tradition.* Kentucky: Kentucky UP, 1990. 155–73.

Kelleher, Margaret. Contemporary. Cork. Academic writing, literary criticism.

Born in Mallow, Co. Cork, in 1964, she was educated at St Mary's Secondary School, Mallow. She took a BA in English and History at UCC in 1984 and in 1992 took a PhD at Boston College. Kelleher lectured at the Mater Dei Institute of Education from 1991 to 1996. In 1996 she joined the English Department at NUI Maynooth, where she is now a Senior Lecturer in English. She was the Burns Visiting Scholar at Boston College for the academic year 2002–3 and is currently co-editing the *Cambridge History of Irish Literature* with Philip O'Leary. Her research interests include famine literature, nineteenth-century Irish writing and Irish women's writing. She is a contributing editor to the *Field Day Anthology of Irish Writing, V*, on Writing Irish Women's Literary History.

Select bibliography
Kelleher, Margaret.
—. *The Feminization of Famine: Expressions of the Inexpressible?* Literary criticism. Cork: Cork UP, 1997.
—. and James H. Murphy, eds. *Gender Perspectives in Nineteenth Century Ireland.* Literary criticism. Dublin: Irish Academic Press, 1997.
—. ed. *Making It New: Essays on the Revised Leaving Certificate Syllabus.* Literary criticism. Dublin: Lilliput Press, 2000.

Kelleher, Maria. Contemporary. Carrigtwohill, Co. Cork. Memoir, local history.

East Cork author whose first publication, *Over the Bridge* (1992), is a record of the author's early life on a small farm in rural Cork. *The Road Home* (1999) is a local history of life in Carrigtwohill 1955–99.

Select bibliography
Kelleher, Maria.
—. *Over the Bridge.* Memoir, local history. N.p.: self-published, 1992.
—. *The Road Home.* Memoir, local history. N.p.: self-published, 1999.

Kelly, Maeve [Maeve O'Brien Kelly]. Contemporary. Limerick. Short stories, poetry, novels, political writing.

Born in Limerick, she moved with her family to Co. Louth, where she was educated. She trained as a nurse in London and returned to Limerick in 1955. In 1956 she moved to Oxford to do a postgraduate theatre course. She returned to Ireland in 1957, married in 1958 and currently lives in Limerick. During the 1970s and 1980s Kelly was a campaigner for women's rights. She was a founding member of Limerick Adapt, and Limerick Federation of Women's Organisations and established the Federation of Refuges to coordinate Women's Refuges in Ireland. She initiated the first major piece of Irish research on violence against women, which was published in two volumes, *Breaking the Silence* and *Seeking a Refuge from Violence* (1992). In 1972 Kelly won the Hennessy Literary Award. In 1985 she was writer in residence at the College of Saint Elizabeth, New Jersey. Her short stories have been published in a number of European languages.

Select bibliography
Kelly, Maeve.
—. *A Life of Her Own.* Short stories. Dublin: Poolbeg Press, 1976.
—. *Resolution.* Poetry. Dublin: Blackstaff Press, 1986.
—. "Amnesty." *Territories of the Voice: Contemporary Stories by Irish Women Writers.* Short story. Ed. Louise DeSalvo. Boston: Beacon, 1989. Boston: Beacon, 1999. 114–22.
—. *Florrie's Girls.* Novel. London: Michael Joseph, 1989.
—. *Necessary Treasons.* Novel. London: Michael Joseph, 1989.
—. *Orange Horses.* Short stories. London: Michael Joseph, 1989.
—. *Alice in Thunderland: Feminist Fairy Tale.* Fiction. Dublin: Attic Press, 1993.

Secondary sources
Haberstroh, Pamela Boyle. "New Directions in Irish Poetry." *Women Creating Women: Contemporary Irish Women Poets.* Syracuse: Syracuse UP, 1996. 197–224.
St Peter, Christine. "Maeve Kelly's *Florries.*" *Changing Ireland: Strategies in Contemporary Women's Fiction.* London: Macmillan, 2000. 32–9.

Kennedy, Geraldine. Contemporary. Carrick-on-Suir, Co. Tipperary. Journalism.

Born in Carrick-on-Suir in South Tipperary in 1951, she was educated there, in Waterford and in Dublin, where she studied journalism. Her first job was as a junior reporter with the *Cork Examiner* (1970–73), then she moved to the *Irish Times.* She went on to become political correspondent with the *Sunday Tribune* in 1980, the first woman to be appointed a political correspondent in Ireland. She spent five years with the *Sunday Press,* until her election to the Dáil as political representative for the Progressive Democrat party in 1987. Following a change in government she returned to the *Irish Times,* where she was the political editor before being appointed editor of the newspaper in 2002.

Kennedy, Sr Stanislaus. Contemporary. Kerry. Religious writing.

Born Treasa Kennedy in the village of Lispole in Co. Kerry in 1940, even as a child she became aware of the widening gap between rich and poor in her community. She joined the Order of Charity at the age of nineteen, and worked at first with Irish emigrants in London and later with youth groups in Dublin. In the late 1960s she studied Social Science in UCD, followed by further study in Manchester. She graduated with an MA from UCD in 1980.

In 1974 she was appointed chairperson of the state-sponsored Combat Poverty Committee, and in 1979 was made director of the Social Services Centre in Kilkenny, which dealt primarily with older people, members of the travelling community and people with disabilities. She has become a recognized voice of the underprivileged in Ireland, has written widely on their needs and calls them "our silent majority". She was a founder member of Focus Point Ireland, an organization founded to highlight the extent of homelessness in Ireland, and to lobby for greater and more coordinated service provision in this area.

In 1983 she was appointed Senior Research Fellow at the Department of Social Science, UCD. In more recent years her writings have been of a more spiritual nature, focusing on spiritual reflections and relationships. She continues to maintain her activist focus in the area of social justice and is involved in several NGOs, most recently working to advocate the rights of asylum seekers and refugees in Ireland.

Select bibliography
Kennedy, Sr Stanislaus.
—. ed. *One Million Poor: The Challenge of Irish Inequality.* Political writing. Dublin: Turoe, 1981.
—. *Who Should Care? The Development of the Kilkenny Social Services 1963–1980.* Political writing. Dublin: Turoe, 1981.
—. *But Where Can I Go?* Political writing. Dublin: Arlen House, 1985.
—. ed. *Streetwise: Homelessness among Young People in Ireland and Abroad.* Political writing. Dublin: Glendale, 1987.
—. and John Blackwell, eds. *Focus on Homelessness: A New Look at Housing Policy.* Political writing. Dublin: Columba, 1988.
—. *Focus on Residential Child Care in Ireland: 25 Years since the Kennedy Report.* Political writing. Dublin: Focus Ireland, 1996.
—. ed. *Spiritual Journeys: An Anthology of Writings by People Living and Working with Those on the Margins.* Religious writing. Dublin: Veritas, 1997.
—. *At Whose Discretion: The Operation of the Supplementary Welfare Allowance Scheme.* Political writing. Dublin: Focus Point, 1998.
—. *Now is the Time: Spiritual Reflections.* Religious writing. Dublin: Town House, 1998.
—. *Reaching Out to Right Relationships.* Religious writing. Dublin: Veritas, 1998.
—. *A Bundle of Blessings.* Religious writing. Maynooth: St Paul's, 1999.
—. *Gardening the Soul: A Spiritual Daybook through the Seasons.* Religious writing. Town House: Dublin, 2001.

Kenny, Collette Nunan. Contemporary. Moyvane, Fenit, Co. Kerry. Poetry.

Born in Moyvane, she was educated in Co. Clare, Limerick, and at the London College of Music and Drama. She also took a diploma in Catechetics at UCC. She has published several collections of poetry and worked as a broadcaster on local radio for ten years. She has also produced several local journals about the Fenit-Spa area. She continues to write poetry, as her father and grandfather did before her.

Select bibliography
Kenny, Collette Nunan.
—. *A Box of Words*. Poetry. N.p.: n.p., n.d.
—. *Earth Woman*. Poetry. N.p.: n.p., n.d.
—. *Mule to Mercedes: Solo Moroccan Experiences*. Travel writing. N.p.: n.p., n.d.
—. ed. "Poets for Africa." Poetry. N.p.: n.p., n.d.

Keyes, Marian. Contemporary. Cork. Novels.

Born in 1963, she studied law at UCD, and on completing her degree she moved to London and worked first as a waitress and then in an accounts office. She began writing fiction in 1993. Her personal life was briefly affected by alcohol dependency, and she entered rehabilitation in 1994. She married in 1995 and settled down to a career as a full-time writer. Her first novel, *Watermelon*, was published in 1995, and since then she has published a number of bestsellers which have been widely admired for their humorous observations of contemporary life.

Select bibliography
Keyes, Marian.
—. *Watermelon*. Novel. Dublin: Poolbeg, 1995.
—. *Lucy Sullivan is Getting Married*. Novel. Dublin: Poolbeg, 1996.
—. *Rachel's Holiday*. Novel. Dublin: Poolbeg, 1998.
—. *Last Chance Saloon*. Novel. Dublin: Poolbeg, 1999.
—. *No Dress Rehearsal*. Novel. Dublin: New Island, 2000.
—. *Sushi for Beginners*. Novel. Dublin: Poolbeg, 2001.
—. *Under the Duvet*. Novel. London: Michael Joseph, 2001.
—. *Angels*. Novel. Dublin: Poolbeg, 2002.

Kiely, Elizabeth. Contemporary. Cork. Academic writing, political writing, sociology.

Born in 1969, she graduated from UCC with an MA in Social Science in 1992 and a PhD in 2003. She is a lecturer in Social Policy in the Department of Applied Social Studies, UCC. Her research interests include youth policy, gender and education, and she recently completed an HEA-funded oral history project, "Women and Work in Munster 1930–1960", in collaboration with Máire Leane. This project resulted in the collection of over forty oral-history interviews with women living in counties Cork, Limerick and Kerry, which provide rich ethnographic accounts of women's experiences of diverse kinds of waged work in the 1940s and the 1950s.

Select bibliography
Kiely, Elizabeth.
—. "A Critical Understanding of Social Policy and the Welfare State." *Social Policy: A Course Reader*. Academic writing. Cork: UCC Centre for Adult and Continuing Education, 1996.
—. "Theory and Values of Youth Work." *Youth and Community Work: A Course Reader*. Academic writing. Cork: UCC Centre for Continuing Education, 1996.

—. "Single Lone Motherhood – Reality Versus Rhetoric." *Women and Irish Society*. Academic writing. Ed. A. Byrne and M. Leonard. Belfast: Beyond the Pale Publications, 1997.

—. "Basic Education in the Community: Women's Experiences." *Women and Education in Ireland*. Academic writing. Ed. A. Ryan and B. Connolly. Vol. 1. Maynooth: MACE, 1999.

—. "Struggling with Lifelong Learning in the Irish Context: Progression After Youthreach." *Lifelong Learning in Europe: Differences and Divisions*. Academic writing. Ed. A. Walther and B. Stauber. Vol. 2. 1999.

King-Hall, Magdalen [Cleone Knox, Mrs P. Perceval Maxwell]. 1904–71. Waterford. History, novels, journalism.

Born in London, she spent her childhood in a variety of different countries, as her father was an admiral and was posted at various ports around the world including Cobh. She began a career in journalism in the 1920s. Her best known work, *The Diary of a Young Lady of Fashion in the Year 1764–1765* (1925), caused a literary sensation. Many critics assumed the fiction to be an original eighteenth-century diary by a young Irish heiress called Cleone Knox. King-Hall was nineteen herself when she wrote it, as a retreat from the boredom of an exclusive seaside resort where she was surrounded by elderly companions.

She married Perceval Maxwell in 1929, and the couple lived in the Sudan (where he worked for the Sudan Cotton Plantation Syndicate) and London, before moving to Northern Ireland. In 1952 they moved to Headborough House in Waterford. She maintained her interest in writing throughout her life, and many of her novels contain Irish characters or settings, such as *Tea at Crumbo Castle* (1949), which is set on the River Blackwater. *Maid of Honour* (1936) juxtaposes the Anglo-Irish Protestant with the "wild Irish native". The Maxwells are buried in Fountain Churchyard in Waterford.

Select bibliography
King-Hall, Magdalen.
—. *The Diary of a Young Lady of Fashion in the Year 1764–1765*. Novel. London: Thornton Butterworth, 1925. Notes: Purported to be a diary written by Cleone Knox, the eponymous "young lady of fashion", edited by "her kinsman, Alexander Blacker Kerr".
—. *I Think I Remember*. Novel. N.p.: N.I.S., 1927.
—. *Gay Crusaders*. Historical novel. London: Davies, 1934.
—. *Maid of Honour*. Historical novel. N.p.: N.I.S., 1936.
—. *Lady Sarah*. Historical novel. N.p.: N.I.S., 1939.
—. *Sturdy Rogue*. Historical novel. N.p.: N.I.S., 1941.
—. *Life and Death of the Wicked Lady Skelton*. Historical novel. London: Davies, 1944.
—. *How Small a Part of Time*. Historical novel. London: Peter Davies, 1945.
—. *Lady Shane's Daughter*. Novel. London: Davies, 1947.
—. *Tea at Crumbo Castle*. Novel. London: Davies, 1949.
—. *The Edifying Bishop*. Biography. London: Davies, 1951.
—. *Hag Khalida*. Novel. London: Davies, 1954.
—. *The Venetian Bride*. Novel. London: Davies, 1954.

—. *18th Century Story*. Historical novel. London: Davies, 1956.
—. *The Story of the Nursery*. History. London: Routledge & Kegan Paul, 1958.
—. *The Noble Savages*. Novel. London: Bles, 1962.
—. *Jehan of the Ready Fists*. N.p.: n.p., n.d.

Kirchhoffer, Julia Georgiana Mary. 1855–78. Cork. Poetry.

Colman notes that her work was anthologized in MacCarthy, *A Birthday Book of the Dead* (1886), and MacIlwaine, *Lyra Hibernica Sacra* (1878) (Colman, 133).

Knott, Mary John, née Abell. 1783–1853. Cork. Travel writing.

From a Quaker family, her parents were Richard and Elizabeth Abell from Cork. She married John Knott in 1809. She wrote the guidebook *Two Months at Kilkee* (1836).

Select bibliography
Knott, Mary John.
—. *Two Months at Kilkee*. Travel writing. Dublin: William Curry, 1836. Ennis: Clasp, 1997.

Kravis, Judy. Contemporary. Cork. Academic writing, poetry, fiction, film script.

A lecturer in the Department of French, UCC, her research interests include French literature and the writings of Samuel Beckett.

Select bibliography
Kravis, Judy.
—. *The Prose of Mallarmé*. Academic writing. Cambridge: Cambridge UP, 1976.
—. *Packed Lunch*. Film script. 1988.
—. *Rough Diamante Words*. Poetry. Cork: Road Books, 1992.
—. *Tea With Marcel Proust*. Fiction. Cork: Road Books, 1993.
—. *Teaching Literature: Writers and Teachers Talking*. Academic writing. Cork: Cork UP, 1995.
—. *Lives Less Ordinary: Thirty-Two Irish Portraits*. History. Dublin: Lilliput Press, 1999.
—. *Cloughjordan Now*. History. Cork: Road Books, 2000.
—. *When the Bells Go Down: A Portrait of the Cork City Fire Brigade*. Biography. Cork: Road Books, 2001.

Kühling, Carmen. Contemporary. Limerick. Academic writing, sociology.

Lecturer at the Department of Sociology, UL, where she also teaches on the Women's Studies programme. Her research interests include the impact of technology on women's personal and professional lives, representations of masculinity and femininity in the media, explanations for the relatively low number of women in the "hard" sciences, women's health, and sex segregation in the work force. She is currently working on a project entitled "Gender and the Information Society", which examines the language, social organization and culture of information technology in terms of its effectiveness in meeting the employment needs of women. She is also working on a book which examines a range of phenomena in Irish society such as shifting modes and perceptions of gender, information technology, consumption, crime and transportation in terms of how these phenomena illustrate a "crisis of community" and changing individual and collective self-perceptions in Irish society.

Select bibliography
Kühling, Carmen.
—. "The New Age Ethic and the Spirit of Postmodernity". Sociology. *Contested Boundaries/ Different Sociologies*. Ed. P. Anisef and I. Davies. Toronto: York UP, 1996.
—. "New Age Travellers on Cool Mountain". Soc. *Ireland Encounters Modernity*. Ed. M.Peillion and E. Slater. Dublin: Institute of Public Administration, 1998.
—. *The New Age Ethic and the Spirit of Postmodernity*. Soc. New Jersey: Hampton Press, 2004.
—. and Kieran Keohane. *Collision Culture: Transformations in Everyday Life in Ireland*. Soc. Dublin. Liffey Press, 2004.

Lambe, Miriam. Contemporary. Tipperary. Local history.

A native of Tipperary, she works as a librarian in Dublin.

Select bibliography
Lambe, Miriam.
—. *A Tipperary Estate: Castle Otway, Templederry 1750–1853*. Local History. Maynooth Studies in Local History 17. Dublin: Irish Academic Press, 1998.

Lambert, Dorothy. *fl.* 1929–34. Mallow, Co. Cork. Novels.

Born in Mallow in 1892, she wrote over twenty romance novels.

Select bibliography
Lambert, Dorothy.
—. *Elizabeth Who Wouldn't*. Novel. London: Mills & Boon, 1929.
—. *Redferne, M.F.H.: An Irish Stew*. Novel. London: Mills & Boon, 1929.
—. *Aunts in Arcady: An Irish Idyll*. Novel. London: Mills & Boon, 1930.
—. *Three Meet*. Novel. London: Mills & Boon, 1930.
—. *Moons and Magpies*. Novel. London: Hodder & Stoughton, 1931.
—. *Taken at the Flood*. Novel. London: Mills & Boon, 1931.
—. *Rescuing Anne*. Novel. London: Collins, 1933.
—. *Strange Lover*. Novel. London: Collins, 1933.
—. *Independence*. Novel. London: Collins, 1934.
—. *Invitation*. Novel. London: Collins, 1934.
—. *Nothing to Forgive*. Novel. London: Collins, 1935.
—. *A Present for Mary*. Novel. London: Collins, 1935.
—. *Travelling Light*. Novel. London: Collins, 1935.
—. *All I Desire: A Romance*. Novel. London: Collins, 1936.
—. *Scotch Mist*. Novel. London: Collins, 1936.
—. *Emergency Exit: A Romance*. Novel. London: Collins, 1937.
—. *Fish Out of Water*. Novel. London: Collins, 1937.
—. *Much Dithering: A Romance*. Novel. London: Collins, 1938.
—. *Golden Grove: A Romance*. Novel. London: Collins, 1939.
—. *Two Birds and a Stone*. Novel. London: Collins, 1939.
—. *The Stolen Days*. Novel. London: Collins, 1940.
—. *Staying Put*. Novel. London: Collins, 1941.

—. *Birds on the Wing.* Novel. London: Collins, 1943.
—. *Way Back to Happiness: A Romance.* Novel. London: Collins, 1948.
—. *Music While You Work.* Novel. London: Collins, 1949.
—. *Harvest Home.* Novel. London: Collins, 1950.
—. *Something in the Air: A Romance.* Novel. London: Collins, 1953.
—. *Invitation.* Novel. N.p.: n.p., n.d.
—. *Strange Lover.* Novel. N.p.: n.p., n.d.

Lane, Temple [Jean Herbert]. 1899–1978. Tipperary. Novels, poetry.
Born Mary Isabel Leslie in Dublin, she grew up in Tipperary – her father
was the Dean of Lismore, Co. Waterford. She was educated first in England,
and then at TCD, where she took a doctoral degree in literature, winning
the 1922 Gold Medal. She published poetry in magazines and journals, but
it is for her novels that she is best known, and she was very prolific. She used
the pseudonym "Temple Lane" (possibly because of her father's position in
the church), which was based on the name of a street near her publishers.
Her works include *Fisherman's Wake* (1940), *Curlews* (1946), *The Little Wood*
(1930), which won the Tailteann Gold Medal, and *Friday's Well* (1943),
which was adapted for the stage by Frank Carney. Callaghan notes that she
is remembered for her poem "The Fairy Tree", which was set to music by
Dr Vincent O'Brien (Hogan, 680).

She also published critical material on the work of other women writers,
such as Teresa Deevy (*q.v.*). She was a friend of both Lady Gregory and
Elizabeth Bowen (*q.v.*), and Austin Clarke encouraged her writing.
Callaghan describes her work as "female fiction before the Liberation",
pointing out that she also may have been the author of Mills & Boon novels
under the pseudonym "Jean Herbert" (Hogan, 680). She is buried at St
Cathage's Cathedral, Lismore.

Select bibliography
Lane, Temple.
—. *Burnt Bridges.* Novel. London: John Long, 1925.
—. *No Just Cause.* Novel. London: John Long, 1925.
—. *Defiance.* Novel. London: John Long, 1926.
—. *Second Sight.* Novel. London: John Long, 1926.
—. *Watch the Wall.* Novel. London: John Long, 1927.
—. *The Bands of Orion.* Novel. London: Jarrolds, 1928.
—. *The Little Wood.* Novel. London: Jarrolds, 1930.
—. *Blind Wedding.* Novel. London: Jarrolds, 1931.
—. *Full Tide.* Novel. London: J. Heritage, 1932.
—. *Sinner Anthony.* Novel. London: Jarrolds, 1933.
—. *The Trains Go South.* Novel. London: Jarrolds, 1938.
—. *Battle of the Warrior.* Novel. London: Jarrolds, 1940.
—. *Fisherman's Wake.* Poetry. Dublin: Talbot, 1940. London: Longmans, 1941.
    Notes: Contains "The Fairy Tree".
—. *House of My Pilgrimage.* Poetry. Dublin: Talbot, 1941.
—. *Friday's Well.* Novel. Dublin: Talbot, 1943.
—. *Come Back.* Novel. Dublin: Talbot, 1945.
—. *Curlews.* Novel. Dublin: n.p., 1946.

—. *My Bonny's Away*. Novel. Dublin: Talbot, 1947.
—. "Self-Interview No. 3: Temple Lane." Biography. *Poetry Ireland* 17 (1952): 3–9.
—. *Battle of the Warrior*. Novel. London: Jarrolds, n.d.

Langbridge, Rosamund. *fl.* 1902–32. Limerick. Novels, short stories, biography.

Born in 1880, she was the daughter of Rev. Frederick Langbridge, rector of St John's, Limerick. Her father was also a writer, having written a number of novels at the turn of the century which incorporated his religious beliefs. We know that Rosamund Langbridge grew up and was educated in Limerick, but we have few details about her later life. She was a journalist, contributing to the *Manchester Guardian*, among other newspapers. She also wrote a number of novels, including *The Stars Beyond* (1907), which compares Catholic and Protestant social teaching. One of her works, *The Green Banks of the Shannon* (1929), is set in Limerick.

Some of her correspondence, now held by the National Library, includes letters from the writer Ella Young, her publisher T. Fisher Unwin, Mrs Martin Harvey (wife of the well known actor) and the editor of *The Irish Homestead*, H.F. Norman, which suggests she may have written for that periodical.

Select bibliography
Langbridge, Rosamund.
—. *Land Forever Young*. London: SPCK, 1902.
—. *The Flame and the Flood*. Novel. London: T. Fisher Unwin, 1903.
—. *The Third Experiment*. Novel. London: T. Fisher Unwin, 1904.
—. *Ambush of Young Days*. Novel. London: Duckworth, 1906.
—. *The Stars Beyond*. Novel. London: Eveleigh Nash, 1907.
—. *Imperial Richenda*. Novel. London: Alston Rivers, 1908.
—. "The Backstairs of the Mind." *The Best British Stories of 1922*. Short story. Ed. Edward J. O'Brien and John Cournos. London: Small, Maynard, 1922.
—. *The Single Eye*. Novel. London: Hutchinson, 1924.
—. *The Golden Egg*. Novel. London: John Long, 1927.
—. *Charlotte Brontë: A Psychological Study*. Biography. London: Heinemann, 1929.
—. *The Green Banks of Shannon*. London: Collins, 1929.
—. "The Will of the Widow." *Irish Short Stories*. Short story. Ed. George A. Birmingham. London: Faber & Faber, 1932. 267–78.

Lankford, Siobhán, née Creedon. 1894–1986. Cork. Memoir.

Grew up on a small farm at Mourne Abbey, North Cork. She worked in Mallow as a telephonist and joined the Gaelic League. She joined the IRA following the 1916 Rising, where she was an intelligence officer, and she subsequently lost her job as a telephonist because of her political activism. She married in 1932, and later wrote a memoir of her life and times (*Field Day V*, 174).

Select bibliography
Lankford, Siobhán.
—. *The Hope and the Sadness: Personal Recollections of Troubled Times in Ireland*. Memoir. Cork: Tower Books, 1980.

Lantry, Margaret. Contemporary. Cork. Academic writing.

Graduated with an MA in Latin and an MA in Librarianship, she is a qualified secondary school teacher and a member of the Chartered Institute of Library and Information Professionals. In the past she has worked as Senior Research Associate for the University of Cambridge, the Royal Academy and UCC. She has also held posts as consultant for Cambridge UP, the Heritage Council and the Heritage Office, UCC. She is currently the project manager for the Centre for Neo-Latin Studies, maintains the Department of Ancient Classics web pages and is project manager for the "Documents of Ireland" project. Research interests include Richard Stanihurst's *De Rebus in Hibernia Gestis*, academic project management, the history of mathematics and the history of cinema in Ireland, in particular the cinemas of Cork city.

Select bibliography
Lantry, Margaret.
—. "Some Irish Neo-Latin Writers From Cork." Academic writing. *Journal of the Cork Historical and Archaeological Society.* 2005.

Lavelle, Patricia, née O'Mara. 1898–1963. Limerick. History, biography.

Born in London, she grew up there but lived in Limerick as a child, where her father had business interests. Her mother supported the suffragette movement and Patricia counted Hannah Sheehy Skeffington and her sisters among her childhood friends. Her family became interested in the nationalist cause while living in England. At the outbreak of the Second World War they returned to Dublin, where they stayed in Ely House, leased from Oliver St John Gogarty, and where they met many of the prominent literary and artistic figures of the city. Patricia studied science at UCG. She wrote two books, one a biographical account of her father's political activities; the other, *Crumbling Castle* (1949), recounts the fortunes of Co. Cork families in various stations of life. Her private papers have been given to the National Library in Dublin.

Select bibliography
Lavelle, Patricia.
—. *Crumbling Castle.* Novel. Dublin: Clonmore & Reynolds, 1949.
—. *James O'Mara: A Staunch Sinn Féiner 1873–1948.* Biography. Dublin: Clonmore & Reynolds, 1961.

Leach, Bernadette. Contemporary. Cork. Young adult fiction.

Born in Birmingham in 1948, she was educated at the University of Sussex. She came to live in Ireland in 1983. Her first book, written for young adults, was published in 1992; the last one in 1998. These six books were published as part of the Bright Sparks series by Attic Press. She lives near Cork city and now teaches writing to adults and children. She devised these courses, called "Making Words Work" and "Working with Words".

Select bibliography
Leach, Bernadette.

—. *I'm a Vegetarian*. Young adult fiction. Dublin: Attic, 1992.
—. *Summer Without Mum*. Young adult fiction. Dublin: Attic, 1993.
—. *Anna Who?* Young adult fiction. Dublin: Attic, 1994.
—. *Vanessa*. Young adult fiction. Dublin: Attic, 1994.
—. *A Place to Call Home*. Young adult fiction. Dublin: Attic, 1995.
—. *4Ever Friends*. Young adult fiction. Dublin: Attic, 1998.

Leahy, Ellen Maria. 1803–74. Cork. Local history.

A member of the Presentation Order at South Presentation Convent, Cork (the founding house of this order in Cork). Ellen was known as Mother di Pazzi, and she compiled the convent annals, a manuscript volume in her own hand, until 1853 (Luddy, *Field Day IV*, 535).

Leane, Máire. Contemporary. Cork. Academic writing, sociology.

Born in 1967, she graduated from UCC with a PhD in 1999. She currently lectures in the Department of Applied Social Studies and is a coordinator of postgraduate studies in the department. Her research interests include women's studies, sexuality, family policy, gender issues and oral history. Recently, she was the project leader of an oral history project based at UCC on "Women and Work in Munster 1930–1960" (www.ucc.ie/wisp) in collaboration with Elizabeth Kiely. This project, funded by the Irish government, resulted in the collection of over forty oral history interviews with women living in counties Cork, Limerick and Kerry, which provide rich ethnographic accounts of women's experiences of diverse kinds of waged work in the region throughout the period of the study.

Select bibliography
Leane, Máire.
—. "Single Lone Motherhood: Rhetoric Versus Reality." *Women and Irish Society: A Sociological Reader*. Academic writing. Ed. A. Byrne and M. Leonard. Belfast: Beyond the Pale, 1997. 296–311.
—. "Deinstitutionalisation in the Republic of Ireland: A Case for Redefinition?" *Mental Health Social Work in Ireland: Comparative Issues in Policy and Practice*. Academic writing. Ed. J. Campbell, and R. Manktelow. Aldershot: Ashgate, 1998. 85–101.
—. "Inclusive Practice in Mental Health: Issues for Social Work Education." *Personal Social Services in Northern Ireland, No. 57*. Academic writing. Belfast: Social Services Inspectorate, Department of Health and Social Services, 1998. 83–93.
—. "It's All Changed From Here: Women's Experiences of Community Education." *Woman and Education in Ireland*. Academic writing. Ed. B. Connolly and A.B. Ryan. Vol. 1. Maynooth: MACE, 1999. 131–53.
—. *Attrition in Sexual Assault Offence Cases in Ireland: A Qualitative Analysis*. Academic writing. Dublin: Government Publications, 2001. 166.
—. "Feminist Research Practice: Learning From Older Women." Academic writing. *Education and Ageing* 17.1 (2002): 35–53.

Lee, Grace Lawless. *fl.*1936. Cork.

Daughter of Philip George Lee, MD, of Cork, she was educated at TCD, and wrote a book on the Huguenots in Ireland.

Select bibliography
Lee, Grace Lawless.
—. *The Huguenot Settlements in Ireland*. History. London: Longmans, 1936.

Leland, Mary. Contemporary. Cork. Journalism, political writing, travel writing, short stories.

Born in Cork in 1941, she has worked with the *Cork Examiner* as a reporter in Dublin and Cork. Her story "Displaced Persons" won the Listowel Short Story Award in 1980. Leland has published novels, short-story collections and articles which have been published in the *Sunday Independent*, the *Irish Times* and the *Sunday Tribune*. Her writings have been published in a number of anthologies, and her work, *The Killeen*, has received much critical acclaim. She currently works as a freelance journalist in Cork.

Select bibliography
Leland, Mary.
—. "Displaced Persons". *The Cork Review*, 1981.
—. *The Killeen*. Novel. London: Hamish Hamilton, 1985.
—. *The Little Galloway Girls*. Short stories. London: Hamish Hamilton, 1985.
—. *Approaching Priests*. Novel. London: Sinclair-Stevenson, 1991.
—. *The Lie of the Land: Literary Journeys through Cork City and County*. Literary criticism. Cork: Cork UP, 1999.
—. *That Endless Adventure – A History of the Cork Harbour Commissioners*. History. Cork: Port of Cork, 2001.

Lendennie, Jessie. Contemporary. Co. Clare. Poetry, handbooks.

From the USA, she was educated at King's College London. She moved to Galway in 1981, and was a founder member of the Galway Writing Workshop that year. She was also a founding editor of *The Salmon International Literary Journal* (1982) and in 1985 co-founded Salmon Press, which is now based on the Cliffs of Moher on the west coast of Clare. She has been the editor and managing director of Salmon since 1986. Its particular interest is Irish and international poetry, and it has been instrumental in publishing first collections for women poets. She has been actively involved in literary organizations, festival and workshops, especially in the Galway area, and in 1990 she was nominated for a Bank of Ireland Arts Award for service to the arts in Ireland. She also returns to the US for readings and lectures. In 1988 she published her first collection of writings, *Daughter: A Prose Poem*, which was reprinted in 2001 as *Daughter and Other Poems*. Her writings have been anthologized in several Irish publications. She has also produced two guides to writing and publishing in Ireland.

Select bibliography
Lendennie, Jessie.
—. *Daughter: A Prose Poem*. Poetry. Galway: Salmon, 1988.
—. *The Salmon Guide to Poetry Publishing in Ireland*. Handbook. Galway: Salmon, 1990.
—. *The Salmon Guide to Creative Writing in Ireland*. Handbook. Galway: Salmon, 1992.
—. "Daughter." *Irish Poetry Now*. Poetry. Ed. Gabriel Fitzmaurice. Dublin: Wolfhound, 1993.

—. "Between Us." *The White Page / An Bhileog Bhán: Twentieth Century Irish Women Poets*. Poetry. Ed. Joan McBreen. Galway: Salmon, 1999. 127–8.
—. *Daughter and Other Poems*. Poetry. Cliffs of Moher, Co. Clare: Salmon, 2001.
—. "Holy Ground." *Irish Spirit: Pagan Celtic Christian Global*. Memoir. Ed. Patricia Monaghan. Dublin: Wolfhound, 2001. 70–4.

Secondary sources
Weekes, Anne Owens. *Unveiling Treasures: The Attic Guide to the Published Works of Irish Women Literary Writers: Drama, Fiction, Poetry*. Dublin: Attic, 1993. 188–9.

Leonard, Mae [Mae Clancy-Leonard]. Contemporary. Limerick. Poetry, short stories, children's writing, memoir.

Born in Limerick city. Her first writings appeared in the *Evening Press* in 1972 and continued to do so for over sixteen years. She has won several awards for both poetry and prose. She broadcasts regularly on radio and one of her books, *My Home is There* (1996), is a collection based on stories and articles from RTÉ radio programmes. Another publication, *Tarzan Clancy* (1983), is due to be reissued, and she is currently preparing a poetry collection called *I Shouldn't Be Telling You This* for publication. Some of her poems previously appeared in an anthology of six women poets, *Six for Gold* (1995), published in Wexford.

Select bibliography
Leonard, Mae.
—. *Tarzan Clancy*. Children's writing. N.p.: self-published, 1983.
—. *Six for Gold*. Poetry. Wexford: The Works, 1995.
—. *My Home is There*. Short stories. Limerick: Isle, 1996.
—. "Memories of Michael McNamara." *The Limerick Compendium*. Memoir. Ed. Jim Kemmy. Dublin: Gill & Macmillan, 1997. 145–6.

Lincoln, Siobhán. Contemporary. Ardmore, Co. Waterford. Local history.

Born in 1919 in Ardmore, Co. Waterford, where she was educated. She went to teacher-training college in Dublin, and spent most of her teaching career in the Ardmore area. She describes herself as "just a retired primary school teacher with a deep interest in the locality in which [she] was born and reared". She has published three texts, with the assistance of family members who collaborated in the research and design, and she is currently working on an account of St Declan's Road to Cashel.

Select bibliography
Lincoln, Siobhán.
—. *A Walk Around Ardmore*. Local history. N.p.: self-published, 1979.
—. *Declan of Ardmore*. Local History. N.p.: self-published, 1995.
—. *Ardmore: Memory and Story*. Local history. Ardmore: Ardmore Pottery Shop, 2000. Notes: Fwd. Fergal Keane.

Lindsay, Fanny E. [Fanny E. Fisher]. *fl.*1864. Limerick. Poetry.

Married a Dr Fisher from Limerick, and they lived in London for a time. The preface to her 1864 collection was written from Limerick (Colman, 144).

Select bibliography
Lindsay, Fanny E.
—. *Lonely Hours*. Poetry. Dublin: Hodges, Smith, 1864.
—. *Ainsworth's Heir, and Other Poems*. Poetry. London, 1866.
—. *Poems*. Poetry. London, 1889.
—. *Poems, Collected Edition*. Poetry. London, 1891.

Llywelyn, Morgan. Contemporary. Clare. Children's writing, historical writing. Born in NewYork City, she moved to Ireland in 1985. She began her writing career in America, publishing *The Wind from the Hastings* (1978) and *Lion of Ireland: The Legend of Brian Boru* (1980). *The Horse Goddess* earned her the Novel of the Year Award by the American League of Penwomen. She was a guest of Ronald Reagan's at the White House during his presidency – Reagan quoted from her writing in his inauguration speech. She has continued to write extensively since moving to Ireland. Llywelyn divides her time between Dublin and Co. Clare, where she lives while writing.

Select bibliography
Llywelyn, Morgan.
—. *The Wind from Hastings*. NewYork: Houghton Mifflin, 1978.
—. *Lion of Ireland*. Historical fiction. London: Bodley Head, 1980.
—. *The Horse Goddess*. Historical fiction. London: Macdonald, 1983.
—. *Brian Boru: Emperor of the Irish*. Children's fiction. Dublin: O'Brien, 1990.
—. *Druids*. Historical fiction. London: Heinemann, 1991.
—. *On Raven's Wing*. Historical writing. London: Mandarin, 1991.
—. *Strongbow: The Story of Richard and Aoife*. Children's fiction. Dublin: O'Brien, 1992.

Longfield, Ada K. [Mrs H.G. Leask]. Contemporary. Cloyne, Co. Cork. History.

Born near Cloyne in Co. Cork, she married Harold Leask, a recognized scholar and authority on Irish Romanesque and medieval Georgian church architecture. She shares his interests and has published on the subject. She has also written several historical works, including a full-length history of Irish lace.

Select bibliography
Longfield, Ada K.
—. *Anglo-Irish Trade in the Sixteenth Century*. History. London: George Routledge & Sons, 1929.
—. ed. *The Shapland Carew Papers*. History. Dublin: Stationery Office, 1946.
—. *Some Irish Churchyard Sculpture*. History. Ballycotton, Co. Cork: Gifford & Craven, 1974. Notes: Fwd. Sir John Betjeman.
—. *Irish Lace*. History. Irish Heritage 21. Dublin: Easons, 1978.
—. "Limerick Lace." *The Limerick Compendium*. Handcrafts. Ed. Jim Kemmy. Dublin: Gill & Macmillan, 1997. 69–70.
—. *Catalogue to the Collection of Lace: National Museum of Ireland*. History. Dublin: Stationery Office, n.d.
—. *Moor Abbey, Co. Tipperary: A Short Historical and Descriptive Account Reprinted from the 106th Annual Report of the Commissioners of Public Works*. History. Dublin: Stationery Office, n.d.

—. *St Patrick's Rock, Cashel*. History. Dublin: Stationery Office, n.d.

Longfield, Cynthia. 1896–1991. Cloyne, Co. Cork. Science.

Born in 1896 at the Castle Mary estate in Cloyne, Co. Cork, she was the daughter of Mountiford and Alice Longfield. Her maternal grandfather, James Mason, was a scientist who had made his fortune from copper mining in Portugal, and her mother had helped him write up his notes in her teens. Alice Mason was a well-educated woman, and maintained her interest in archaeology after her marriage, although her other intellectual pursuits were hampered by domestic and social duties. However, she nurtured her daughter's interest in the natural world, and in science, from an early age. The Longfields spent their summers in Cloyne and wintered in London, in common with others of their social class during that period. For Cynthia Longfield, summers meant Cloyne, and the opportunity to expand her natural history notebooks. She was also an enthusiastic member of the Girl Guides, formed in 1912. During the First World War, she joined the Royal Army Service Corps as a driver, and later went to work in an aeroplane factory. Her father continued to farm the estate at Cloyne, but Castle Mary was burned down during the Troubles in the 1920s and a smaller house was built within its walls.

Longfield travelled widely during the 1920s and 1930s, participating in many expeditions, where her sense of adventure and survival skills came to the fore. One of her trips was an expedition replicating Darwin's journey to the Pacific Ocean in 1924. During this expedition she fell in love with another member of the expedition, Cyril Collenette. When she returned to London she was an experienced field entomologist, and she went to work as an unpaid associate member of the British Museum, cataloguing the collection from the Pacific Islands. Mountiford Longfield died in 1929, and her inheritance enabled her to continue this work until her retirement in 1957. Her particular interest and area of knowledge was in dragonflies: she co-authored a book on dragonflies in 1937; this was revised and reprinted in 1945. She donated her collection of natural history books and offprints to the Royal Irish Academy in 1979.

Select bibliography
Longfield, Cynthia.
—. *The Dragonflies of the British Isles*. Science. London: F. Warne, 1937.
—. Philip S. Corbet and N.W. Moore. *The New Naturalist Dragonflies*. Science. London: Collins, 1960.

Secondary sources
Gambles, R.M. "Odonatological Bibliography of C.E. Longfield (1929–1974)." *Odonatologica* 4 (1975): 57–9.

Lordan, Nuala. Contemporary. Cork. Academic writing, sociology.

A member of the UCC staff since 1970, she is currently a director of the Higher Diploma in Social Science and European Coordinator for the Department of Applied Social Studies. Her research interests include social groupwork, residential care, community development and ageing.

Select bibliography
Lordan, Nuala.
—. "Issues of Empowerment: Anti-oppressive Groupwork by Disabled People in Ireland." Sociology. *Groupwork* 7.1 (1994): 189–202.
—. "Le Travail Social en Irlande." Sociology. *Vie Sociale* 4 (1995).
—. "The Use of Sculpt in the Social Groupwork Education." Sociology. *Groupwork* 9.1 (1996): 62–79.
—. "The Irish Model of Social Work." *Social Change, Social Policy and Social Work in the New Europe.* Sociology. Ed. Anna Kwak and Robert Gingwall. Aldershot: Ashgate, 1998. 183–97.
—. "Finding a Voice, Empowerment of Disabled People in Ireland." Sociology. *Journal of Progressive Human Services* 11.1 (2000).

Loudon, Margracia, née Margareta Ryves. c.1795–1857. Novels, political writing.

Born *c.*1795 at Ballyskiddane Castle (Castlejane), Limerick, she was the daughter of William and Frances Catherine Ryves. She wrote a number of books, including *First Love* (1830), *Philanthropic Economy* (1835) and *The Light of Mental Science* (1845). She married Charles Loudon in 1830 in Leamington Spa, Warwickshire. Little is known about her later life.

Select bibliography
Loudon, Margracia.
—. *First Love.* Novel. London: Saunders & Otley, 1830.
—. *Fortune-Hunting.* Novel. London: Colburn & Bentley, 1832.
—. *Dilemmas of Pride.* Novel. London: Bull & Churton, 1833.
—. *Philanthropic Economy, or the Philosophy of Happiness, Practically Applied to the Social, Political, and Commercial Relations of Great Britain.* Political writing. London: n.p., 1835.
—. *Corn Laws (Selections from Mrs Loudon's Philanthropic Economy).* Political writing. Manchester: National Anti-Corn Law League, 1842.
—. *The Light of Mental Science.* London: n.p., 1845.
—. *The Voices of Bulgaria.* N.p.: n.p., 1846.
—. *The Fortunes of a Woman.* Novel. N.p.: n.p., 1849.
—. *Maternal Love.* Novel. London: n.p., 1849.

Luby, Catherine. *fl.*1820s–1840s. Tipperary. Poetry.

A native of Tipperary, she was related to T.C. Luby, the Fenian (Colman, 146).

Select bibliography
Luby, Catherine.
—. *The Spirit of the Lakes, or Muckross Abbey: A Poem in Three Cantos with Notes.* Poetry. London: Longman, Hurst, Rees, Orme & Brown, 1822.
—. *Father Mathew, or Ireland as She Is: A National Poem.* Poetry. Dublin: S.J. Machen, 1845.

Luddy, Maria. Contemporary. Clonmel, Co. Tipperary. History, biography.

Born in 1958, she spent her childhood in Ballycullane, Co. Wexford, Westport, Co. Mayo, and Clonmel, Co. Tipperary. She was educated in the

Presentation convent, Clonmel, and at Mary Immaculate College in Limerick. She worked for a number of years as a primary school teacher in Dungarvan and Tipperary Town. She was awarded an MA in history in 1985 and a PhD in 1989 from UCC.

With Mary Cullen she established the Feminist History Forum in Dublin in 1987, which provided a space where scholars working on women's history could discuss their work. She was also a founder member in 1989 of the Women's History Association of Ireland (formerly Irish Association for Research in Women's History).

She has taught at Warwick University in Coventry, England, since 1991 and is currently a reader in the Department of History there. From 1997 to 2001 she was director of the Women's History Project, which was based in Dublin and funded by the Department of Arts, Heritage, Gaeltacht and the Islands (see www.nationalarchives.ie/wh). Her research interests include nineteenth- and twentieth-century Irish history, with a specific focus on Irish women's history. She is particularly interested in "outcast" women: prostitutes, vagrants, unmarried mothers and those destitute women who used the workhouses.

Select bibliography
Luddy, Maria.

—. "Women and Charitable Organisations in Nineteenth-Century Ireland." History. *Women's Studies International Forum* 11.4 (1988).

—. "Whiteboy Support in County Tipperary, 1761–1789." History. *Tipperary Historical Journal* 2 (1989): 66–89.

—."The Convents of Clonmel." History. *The Nationalist: Centenary Edition* (December 1990): 102–3.

—. "The Lives of the Poor in Fethard in 1821." History. *Tipperary Historical Journal* 3 (1990): 121–7.

—. "Prostitution and Rescue Work in Nineteenth-Century Ireland." *Women Surviving: Studies in Irish Women's History in the 19th and 20th Centuries*. History. Ed. Maria Luddy and Cliona Murphy. 1990. Dublin: Poolbeg. 51–84.

—. and Cliona Murphy, eds. *Women Surviving: Studies in Irish Women's History in the 19th and 20th Centuries*. History. Dublin: Poolbeg, 1990.

—. *The Diary of Mary Mathew*. History. Tipperary: Tipperary Historical Society, 1991.

—. "The Lives of the Poor in Cahir in 1821." History. *Tipperary Historical Journal* 4 (1991): 73–9.

—. "An Agenda for Irish Women's History, Part II, 1800–1900." History. *Irish Historical Studies* 28.109 (1992): 19–37.

—. "An Outcast Community: The Wrens of the Curragh." History. *Women's History Review* 1.3 (1992): 341–55.

—. "Presentation Convents in County Tipperary, 1813–1900." History. *Tipperary Historical Journal* 5 (1992): 84–95.

—. "Irish Women and the Contagious Diseases Acts." History. *History Ireland* 1.1 (1993): 32–4.

—. "Placing Women in Irish History." History. *Stair: Journal of the Irish History Teachers Association* (1993): 2–7.

—. "Women and Work in Clonmel: The Evidence of the 1881 Census." History. *Tipperary Historical Journal* 6 (1993): 95–101.

—. "Irish Association for Research in Women's History." History. *Irish Archives* (1994): 59–60.

—. *Hannah Sheehy Skeffington.* Biography. Dundalk: Irish Historical Association, 1995.

—. "Isabella M.S. Todd, 1836–1896." *Women, Power and Consciousness in 19th Century Ireland: Eight Biographical Studies.* History. Ed. Maria Luddy and Mary Cullen. Dublin: Attic Press, 1995. 197–230.

—. *Women and Philanthropy in 19th Century Ireland.* History. Cambridge: Cambridge UP, 1995.

—. *Women in Ireland 1800–1918: A Documentary History.* History. Cork: Cork UP, 1995.

—. and Mary Cullen, eds. *Women, Power and Consciousness in 19th Century Ireland: Eight Biographical Studies.* History. Dublin: Attic Press, 1995.

—. "A Women's Archive?" History. *Irish Archives* (1995): 12–15.

—. "District Nursing in Ireland." History. *Tipperary Historical Journal* 6.1 (1996): 23–30.

—. "Women and Philanthropy in Nineteenth-Century Ireland." History. *Volúntas* 7.4 (1996): 350–64.

—. "'Abandoned Women and Bad Characters': Prostitution in Nineteenth-Century Ireland." History. *Women's History Review* 6.4 (1997): 485–503.

—. "Religion, Philanthropy and the State in Late Eighteenth and Early Nineteenth Century Ireland." *Women in Nineteenth-Century Ireland.* History. Ed. Maryann Gialanella Valiulis and Mary O'Dowd. Dublin: Wolfhound, 1997. 89–108.

—. "The Women's History Project." History. *Irish Archives* Autumn (1997): 12–19.

—. gen. ed. *Irish Women's Writing 1830–1890.* History. 6 vols. London: Thoemmes/Routledge, 1998.

—. "William Drennan and Martha McTier: A 'Domestic' History." *The Drennan-McTier Letters 1776–1793.* History. Ed. Jean Agnew. Vol. 1. Dublin: Women's History Project/Irish Manuscripts Commission, 1998. 29–51.

—. "'Angels of Mercy': Nuns as Workhouse Nurses 1860–1898." *The Social History of Health, Medicine and Disease in Ireland, c. 1700–1950.* History. Ed. G. Jones and B. Malcolm. Cork: Cork UP, 1999. 102–16.

—. C. Cox, L. Lane, D. Urquhart, J. Agnew, R. Raughter and S. Costly, eds. *A Directory of Sources for Women's History in Ireland.* Anthology, history. Dublin: Women's History Project/Irish Manuscripts Commission, 1999. Notes: Available at www.nationalarchives.ie/wh.

—. "The Women's History Project: An Update." History. *Irish Archives* (1999): 11–15.

—. "Women and Work in Ireland in the Nineteenth and Early Twentieth Centuries." *Women and Work in Ireland.* History. Ed. B. Whelan. Dublin: Four Courts, 2000. 51–62.

—. "The Army and Prostitution in Nineteenth-Century Ireland: The Case of the 'Wrens' of the Curragh." History. *Bullán: An Irish Studies Journal* 6.1 (2001): 67–83.

—. and Mary Cullen, eds. *Female Activists: Irish Women and Change, 1900–1960.* History. Dublin: Woodfield, 2001.

—. "Moral Rescue and Unmarried Mothers in Ireland in the 1920s." History. *Women's Studies* 30.6 (2001): 797–817.

—. "Sources for the History of County Tipperary from the Women's History Project." History. *Tipperary Historical Journal* (2001): 33–42.

—. "Women, Philanthropy and Politics in Nineteenth-Century Ireland." *Women, Philanthropy and Civil Society.* History. Ed. D. McCarthy. Indiana: Indiana UP, 2001. 9–28.

—. Angela Bourke, *et al.*, eds. *Field Day Anthology of Irish Women's Writing, Vols. IV and V: Irish Women's Writings and Traditions*. Anthology. Cork: Cork UP, 2002.

Lynch, Patricia. 1891–1972. Cork. Children's writing, political writing.

Born *c.*1891 in Cork city, she was educated in Ireland, England and Belgium. From an early age she displayed a talent for telling and writing short stories. She began her literary career by contributing stories and articles to a variety of magazines and newspapers, and after moving to London she married the writer and historian R.M. Fox. At one time she was writing three short stories per week for English publications, and many appeared, unsigned, in children's annuals. She returned to Dublin in 1916, where she wrote the first eye-witness account of the 1916 Rising from an Irish point of view. This was published in the *Worker's Dreadnought*, Sylvia Pankhurst's weekly newspaper, considered by many to be the first eye-witness account of the rebellion.

Her career as a writer for children took off with the publication of *The Cobbler's Apprentice*, which appeared in 1930 and won the Tailteann Silver Medal for Literature that year. She wrote a total of 50 novels and 200 short stories. Her fame rests on her children's writings: her "Brogeen" series, beginning with *Brogeen of the Stepping Stones* (1948), was serialized by Irish radio, and a serial, *Turf Cutter's Children*, ran in the *Irish Press* every day for three years. This was the source of later books on the *Turf Cutter's Donkey*. In April 1949 the Junior Bookshelf issued a special "Patricia Lynch" number.

She was elected to membership of the Irish Academy of Letters in 1967 and was also active in the PEN organization for writers. Her works were translated into Irish, French, German, Swedish, Dutch, Spanish, Malay and Braille, and she also won many international and national literary awards. She died in Dublin in 1972.

Note: Some confusion surrounds her birth date but the date given here is in a short biography provided by her husband for the two-volume type-written bibliography compiled by Mary Collins for the Cork City Library in 1969.

Select bibliography
Lynch, Patricia.
—. *The Green Dragon*. Children's writing. London: Harrap, 1925.
—. *Turf Cutter's Daughter*. Children's writing. Dublin: Catholic Trust Society of Ireland (CTSI), 1929.
—. *The Cobbler's Apprentice*. Children's writing. London: Harold Shaplen, 1930. Dublin: Clonmore & Reynolds, 1948. Notes: Illus. Mildred R. Lamb.
—. *The Turf Cutter's Donkey: An Irish Story of Mystery and Adventure*. Children's writing. London: Dent, 1934. Notes: Illus. Jack B. Yeats.
—. *The Turf Cutter's Donkey Goes Visiting: The Story of a Holiday*. Children's writing. London: Dent, 1935. Notes: Illus. George Altendorf.
—. *King of the Tinkers*. Children's writing. London: Dent, 1938. Notes: Illus. Katherine Lloyd.
—. *The Grey Goose of Kilnevin*. Children's writing. London: Dent, 1939. Notes: Illus. John Keating.

—. *Fiddler's Quest.* Children's writing. London: Dent, 1941. Notes: Illus. Isobel
Morton-Sale.

—. *Long Ears: The Story of a Little Grey Donkey.* Children's writing. London: Dent,
1943. Notes: Illus. Joan Kiddell-Monroe.

—. *Knights of God: Tales and Legends of the Irish Saints.* Children's writing. 1945.
London: Hollis & Carter. Notes: Illus. Alfred Kerr.

—. Helen Staunton and Teresa Deevy. *Lisheen at the Valley Farm, and Other Stories.*
Dublin: Gayfield, 1945.

—. *Strangers at the Fair, and Other Stories.* Children's writing. Dublin: Browne &
Nolan, 1945. Notes: Illus. Eileen Coghlan.

—. *Reminiscences.* Memoir. Cork: Woodlands, 1946.

—. *Rí na dTincleoirí* [King of the Tinkers]. Children's writing. Trans. Maighread Nic
Mhaicin. Dublin: Oifig an tSoláthair, 1946.

—. *The Turf Cutter's Donkey Kicks up His Heels.* Children's writing. Dublin: Browne &
Nolan, 1946. Notes: Illus. Eileen Coghlan.

—. *A Storyteller's Childhood.* Autobiography. London: Dent, 1947. Notes: Illus. Harry
Kernoff.

—. *Brogeen of the Stepping Stones.* Children's writing. London: Kerr-Cross, 1947.

—. *The Mad O'Haras.* Children's writing. London: Dent, 1948. Notes: Illus. Elizabeth Rivers.

—. "The Rusty Spade." Short story. *Irish Writing* 12 (1950): 19–26.

—. *The Seventh Pig, and Other Irish Fairy Tales.* Children's writing. London: Dent,
1950. Notes: Illus. J. Sullivan.

—. *The Dark Sailor of Youghal.* Children's writing. London: Dent, 1951. Notes: Illus.
Jerome Sullivan.

—. *The Boy at the Swinging Lantern.* Children's writing. London: Dent, 1952. Notes:
Illus. Joan Kiddell-Monroe.

—. *Tales of Irish Enchantment.* Children's writing. Dublin: Clonmore & Reynolds,
1952. Cork: Mercier, 1989.

—. "The Fourth Man." Short story. *Irish Writing* 25 (1953): 5–9.

—. *Fiona Leaps the Bonfire.* Children's writing. London: Dent, 1957.

—. *The Old Black Sea Chest.* Children's writing. London: Dent, 1958. Notes: Illus.
Peggy Fortnum.

—. *The Black Goat of Slievemore.* Children's writing. London: Dent, 1959.

—. *Jinny the Changeling.* Children's writing. London: Dent, 1959.

—. *The Stone House at Kilgobbin.* Children's writing. Dublin: Burke, 1959.

—. *The Kerry Caravan.* Children's writing. London: Dent, 1967.

—. *The Grey Goose of Kilnevin.* Radio play. Prod. Kieran Sheedy. RTÉ Radio. 13 Apr.
1985.

—. *Sally from Cork.* Children's writing. N.p.: n.p., n.d.

Secondary sources
Anon. "Rev. of *A Cobbler's Apprentice*, by Patricia Lynch." *Dublin Magazine* new
series 6.1 (1931): 63–4.

Anon. "Rev. of *A Storyteller's Childhood*, by Patricia Lynch." *Dublin Magazine* new
series 23.1 (1948): 67.

Anon. "Rev. of *Orla of Burren*, by Patricia Lynch." *Dublin Magazine* new series 31.2
(1956): 52.

B.M. "Rev. of *A Storyteller's Childhood*, by Patricia Lynch." *Irish Writing* 4 (1948):
90–91.

Deevy, Teresa. "Patricia Lynch – A Study." *Irish Writing* 5 (1948): 76–82.

Dunbar, Robert, ed. *Secret Lands: The World of Patricia Lynch.* Dublin: O'Brien, 1998.

E.K. "Rev. of *Strangers at the Fair*, by Patricia Lynch." *Dublin Magazine* new series 25.2 (1950): 72.
N.H. "Rev. of *The Turf Cutter's Donkey Goes Visiting*, by Patricia Lynch." *Dublin Magazine* new series 11.3 (1936): 84.
Prone, Terry, interviewer. Interview with Patricia Lynch. *Here and Now*. Radio programme. RTÉ Radio 1. Apr. 1970.

Lynch, Patricia A. Contemporary. Limerick. Academic writing, literary criticism.

Born in Co. Roscommon, she moved to Douglas, Cork. She took four degrees, BA, MA, HDip in Education, and PhD at UCC, and subsequently did an MA in TEFL/Linguistics at York University. She is currently a lecturer in English Studies at the UL. She has been involved in the International Association for the Study of Irish Literature (IASIL) for many years, and was treasurer and officer of IASIL 2000–2003, convenor of the 1998 IASIL, and is currently a member of its executive. Her research interests include: Irish writing in English (all periods), literary stylistics, Hiberno-English and Irish folk medicine in the nineteenth century.

Select bibliography
Lynch, Patricia A.
—. "The Use of Placenames in the Poetry of John Montague and Seamus Heaney". *Poetry Now: Contemporary British and Irish Poetry in the Making*. Academic writing. Ed. S. Coelsch-Foisner, W. Görtschacher and H. Klein. Tübingen: Stauffen Verlag, 1999. 201–15.
—. "A Stylistic Approach to Irish Writing". Academic writing. *Irish University Review* 27.1 (1997): 33–54.
—. "Change and Continuity in Recent Irish Writing in English". *New Developments in English and American studies: Continuity and Change*. Academic writing. Ed. Z. Mazur and T. Bela. Proceedings of the Seventh International Conference in English and American Literature and Language. Kraków: Kraków Universitas, 1997. 257–71.
—. "Language and Literacy: Hiberno-English". *Encyclopedia of Irish History and Culture*. Academic writing. Ed. James S. Donnelly Jr. *et al.* New York: Macmillan, 2004.
—. Joachim Fischer and Brian Coates, eds. *Back to the Present, Forward to the Past: Irish Writing and History since 1798*. Academic writing. 2 vols. Amsterdam: Rodopi, 2005.
—. "The Stylistics of Time and Tense in 'Home Again' by John Montague". Academic writing. *Hungarian Journal of English and American Studies*. (2005).

Lynch, Rose. fl. 1922–8. Cork. Novels, short stories.

A Cork writer of the 1920s. One of her novels, *Call of the Orient* (n.d.), is dedicated to the "many friends I made in 1926 during a happy winter in North Africa" and is illustrated by John Power. A second publication, *Mary, Alanna* (1922), has illustrations from paintings by the author herself.

Select bibliography
Lynch, Rose.
—. *Mary, Alanna*. Novel. Dublin: Gill, 1922.
—. *The West a'Calling*. Novel. Dublin: Browne & Nolan, 1925.

—. *Life in Many Lands*. Short stories. London: Burns, Oates & Washbourne, 1928.
—. *Call of the Orient*. Novel. Dublin: Talbot, n.d.

Lytton, Rosina, Lady, née Wheeler. 1802–82. Ballywire, Co. Limerick. Novels.

Daughter of Anna Doyle Wheeler (*q.v.*) and Francis Massey-Wheeler, she was born in 1802, when her mother has seventeen, on her father's estate at Ballywire, on the Limerick–Tipperary border. Her parents' marriage was unhappy and violent and Anna Doyle Wheeler eventually fled from Ballywire, taking Rosina and her sister, Henrietta, with her, and they lived in Guernsey for several years. The Wheeler girls were educated in French and Italian there, and when in their teens were sent to school in Dublin and London, while their mother went to Caen to join the Saint-Simonian socialist group. Massey-Wheeler died in the 1820s, and in 1826 Henrietta died of a wasting disease. We know that Henrietta shared her mother's politics, but little is known about Rosina's views.

Shortly after her sister's death, Rosina married the writer and politician Edward Bulwer, Lord Lytton, against the wishes of his family. Rosina's mother was also unhappy with the match, remarking that Lytton treated her daughter like a playful doll (Dooley 1996, 86). The couple had two children, Emily and Edward, but their marriage quickly degenerated into bitterness and ended nine years later. Lytton figures as the villain in several of Rosina's novels, which she began to write following the breakup of her marriage. She is thought to have written twelve or more novels, the best known of which is *Chevely, or the Man of Honour* (1839). Lytton's public reputation, contacts and influence enabled him to attack his ex-wife in the popular press. However, in 1857, Rosina Lytton made public her side of the quarrel by issuing her *Appeal to the Justice and Charity of the English Public* (1857). Dooley tells us that this was timed to confront Bulwer Lytton just as he began his campaign to run for Parliament, and it set out the story of his abusive behaviour and philandering (Dooley, 87). In 1858 Rosina was kidnapped and illegally confined to an asylum by her ex-husband, in an effort to silence her. Although she was released after three weeks, incarceration in a nineteenth-century asylum must have had a lasting effect on her. Rosina Lytton died in 1882, and two years later her son Edward published a memoir which denigrated women's rights and defended his father's stance in the affair. Interestingly, Constance Lytton, Edward's daughter and Rosina Lytton's granddaughter, went on to become a prominent feminist and member of the Women's Social and Political Union.

Select bibliography
Lytton, Rosina, Lady.

—. *Chevely, or the Man of Honour*. Novel. Paris: Baudry's European Library, 1839.
—. *Lady Chevely, or the Woman of Honour: A New Version of Chevely, the Man of Honour*. Poetry. Paris: Baudry's European Library, 1839.
—. *The Budget of the Bubble Family*. Novel. 3 vols. London: Edward Bull, 1840.
—. *The Prince-Duke and the Page, a Historical Novel*. Novel. London: T. & W. Boone, 1841.

—. *Bianca Cappello: An Historical Romance*. Novel. 3 vols. London: Edward Bull, 1843.
—. *Memoirs of a Muscovite*. Novel. 3 vols. London: n.p., 1844.
—. *The Peer's Daughters*. Novel. 3 vols. London: T.C. Newby, 1849.
—. *Miriam Sedley; or, the Tares and the Wheat: A Tale of Real Life*. Novel. 3 vols. London: W. Shobert, 1851.
—. *The School for Husbands; or Molière's Life and Times*. Novel. 3 vols. London: C.J. Skeet, 1852.
—. *Behind the Scenes*. Novel. 3 vol. London: C.J. Skeet, 1854.
—. *Appeal to the Justice and Charity of the English Public*. Social history. London: n.p., 1857.
—. *The World and His Wife; or, a Person of Consequence: A Photographic Novel*. Novel. 3 vols. London: C.J. Skeet, 1858.
—. *Very Successful*. Novel. London: C.H. Clarke, 1859.
—. *The Household Fairy*. Novel. London: Hall, 1870.
—. *Shells from the Sands of Time*. Essays. London: Bickers, 1876.
—. *A Blighted Life: Rosina Bulwer Lytton*. Autobiography. Ed. Mary Mulvey. N.p.: n.p., 1880. Bristol: Thoemmes, 1994.
—. *Unpublished Letters of Lady Bulwer Lytton to A.E. Chalon, R.A.* London: Eveleigh Nash, 1914.

Secondary sources

Devey, Louisa. *Letters of the Late Edward Bulwer, Lord Lytton, to his Wife: With Extracts from her Ms. "Autobiography" and other Documents, Published in Vindication of her Memory*. London: Swan Sonnenschein, 1884.
Devey, Louisa. *Life of Rosina, Lady Lytton: With Numerous Extracts from her Ms. Autobiography and Other Original Documents*. London: Swan Sonnenschein, Lowrey, 1887.
Dooley, Dolores. *Equality in Community: Sexual Equality in the Works of William Thompson and Anna Doyle Wheeler*. Cork: Cork UP, 1996.
Mulock, Thomas Samuel. *British Lunatic Asylums: Public and Private with an Appendix Containing the Case of Doctor Peithman; and Special References to the Cases of Lady Lytton Bulwer, and Mrs Turner*. Stafford: n.p., 1858.
Sadleir, Michael. *Bulwer: A Panorama. Edward & Rosina, 1803–1836*. London: Constable, 1931.

Mac Curtain, Margaret. Contemporary. Cork. History, social history, political writing.

A historian, pioneer of Irish women's history and feminist activist, she has made a unique contribution to the fields of history and education both in and outside the academy in Ireland. Born in Cork in 1929, and educated at UCC, Mac Curtain joined the Dominicans in 1950, taking the name "Sr Benvenuta". Throughout her career she has worked at many levels within the Irish educational system – she was the prioress of Sion Hill Convent and chair of the board of governors of St Catherine's Home Economics College there. She was the founding principal of Ballyfermot Senior College, which established public education in Dublin. From 1964 to 1994 she lectured at the Irish History Department, UCD, where she was known to her students as "Sister Ben". From 1972 to 1989 she was Professor at the School of Irish Studies in Dublin. She held the Burns Chair of Irish Studies in Boston College, 1992–3, and more recently was the Baldwin Scholar in the College of Notre Dame of Maryland (Baltimore). Her many publications include *Women in Early Modern Ireland* (1991) and *From Dublin to New Orleans: Nora and Alice's Journey to America 1889* (1994) (see Nora Prendiville, q.v.).

Mac Curtain has been involved in a number of feminist and human rights campaigns, advocating the abolition of corporal punishment in schools and the rights of special needs children, among others. She has also been active in Irish feminist campaigns against domestic violence and for contraception and divorce. She was a member of the anti-apartheid movement and a delegate at the World Peace Conferences annual meetings.

She is renowned for her activism within the academy, particularly in the fields of women's history and women's studies, and has had an important role as mentor to a generation of Irish feminist scholars. A founder member of the Irish Association for Research in Women's History and the Women's Education Resource and Research Centre in UCD in 1993, Mac Curtain has been crucial to the development of women's history in Ireland as a legitimate subject of scholarly enquiry. In 1993 she won the Éire Society of Boston Gold Medal for her scholarship in the field of Irish women's history. She is currently chairperson of the National Archives Advisory Council and she was an editor of the *Field Day Anthology*, *IV and V* (2002).

Select bibliography
Mac Curtain, Margaret.
—. and Mark Tierney. *The Birth of Modern Ireland*. History. Dublin: Gill & Macmillan, 1969.
—. *Tudor and Stuart Ireland*. History. Dublin: Gill & Macmillan, 1972.
—. and Donnchadh Ó Corráin, eds. *Women in Irish Society: The Historical Dimension*. History. Thomas Davis Lecture ser. Dublin: Women's Press, 1978.
—. Mark Tierney, Tomás F. Mac Anna, agus Seán Mac Pháidín. *Éire sa nua-aois* [*The Birth of Modern Ireland*]. History. Baile Átha Cliath: Oifig an tSoláthair, 1979.
—. *Missing Pieces: Women in Irish History*. History. Dublin: Irish Feminist Information / Women's Community Press, 1983.
—. and Mary O'Dowd. *Women in Early Modern Ireland*. History. Edinburgh: Edinburgh UP, 1991.
—. and Suellen Hoy. *From Dublin to New Orleans: Nora and Alice's Journey to America 1889*. History. Dublin: Attic, 1994.
—. Angela Bourke, *et al.*, eds. *Field Day Anthology of Irish Women's Writing, Vols. IV and V: Irish Women's Writings and Traditions*. Anthology. Cork: Cork UP, 2002.

Secondary sources
Valiulis, Maryann Gialanella, and Mary O'Dowd, eds. *Women & Irish History: Essays in Honour of Margaret MacCurtain*. Dublin: Wolfhound, 1997.

MacCarthy, Bridget Gerard 1904–1993. Cork. Academic writing, plays.

Born in Cork in 1904, she attended UCC. She completed her PhD at Cambridge in 1940, and her thesis was the basis of her well known work *The Female Pen* (1944), a literary history of women writers and their works from the early 1600s to the early 1800s. While she rejected any notion of being a feminist, as the term was understood at that period, her critical work on earlier women authors was groundbreaking. In the introduction to the 1994 reissue of *The Female Pen* Janet Todd points out that B.G. MacCarthy's work remains valid today despite the changes in research that have developed since the 1940s. The fact that her work was out of print for so many years meant that scholars working on feminist projects in the intervening half-century did not have the benefit of her research.

Her teaching career took her to Edinburgh first, where she worked at the Craiglockhart RC Training College (Todd, xix). She was married, but the marriage was not a success, and she returned to UCC as a lecturer in the Department of Education. She went back home to live with her mother on her return to Cork, and then with her aunt, to whom the second part of *The Female Pen* was dedicated. She wrote a play entitled *The Whip Hand*, a comedy in three acts, which had twenty-four performances at the Abbey Theatre in 1942. MacCarthy was later appointed Professor of English Literature at UCC, a post she held until her retirement in 1966. In later life she became an ardent nationalist, and she edited a collection of poems by Terence MacSwiney. Another play, a historical drama in five scenes, was published in a *Studies* journal (1946). She wrote extensively on Irish and English novelists.

Select bibliography

MacCarthy, Bridget Gerard.

—. *The Psychology of Genius: Studies in Browning*. Literary criticism. London: London UP, 1936.

—. "Centenary of William Maginn 1794–1842." Literary criticism. *Studies* 32 (1943): 347–60.

—. "Thomas Crofton Croker 1798–1854." Academic writing. *Studies* 32 (1943): 539–56.

—. "The Cinema as a Social Factor." Social history. *Studies* 33 (1944): 45–67.

—. ed. *Despite Fools' Laughter: Poems by Terence MacSwiney*. Poetry. Dublin: Gill, 1944.

—. "Factors Which Influenced Early Women Writers of Fiction." Literary criticism. *Studies* 33 (1944): 349–59.

—. *The Female Pen 1621–1818*. Academic writing. Cork: Cork UP, 1944. Vols. 1 & 2. Cork: Cork UP, 1994. Notes: Intro. Janet Todd.

—. *The Whip Hand: A Comedy in Three Acts*. Play. Cork: Duffy, 1944.

—. *Women Writers: Their Contribution to the English Novel 1621–1744*. Academic writing. Vol. 1. Cork: Cork UP, 1944; repr. 1946.

—. "E.OE. Somerville and Martin Ross." Academic writing. *Studies* 34 (1945): 183–94.

—. ed. *Some Problems of Child Welfare*. Political writing. Cork: Cork UP, 1945.

—. "Irish Regional Novelists of the Early Nineteenth Century." Academic writing. *Dublin Magazine* 21.1 (1946): 26–32.

—. "Irish Regional Novelists of the Early Nineteenth Century." Academic writing. *Dublin Magazine* 21.3 (1946): 28–37.

—. "Jeremiah J. Callanan: His Life." Academic writing. *Studies* 35 (1946): 215–29; 387–9.

—. "Raven of Wicklow: An Historical Play in Five Scenes." Play. *Studies* 35 (1946): 481–512.

—. "James Boswell: A Problem." Academic writing. *Studies* 36 (1947): 319–25.

—. "The Riddle of Rose O'Toole." *Essays and Studies Presented to Professor Tadhg Us Donnchadha (Torna) on the Occasion of His Seventieth Birthday September 4th, 1944*. History. Ed. Séamus Pender. Cork: Cork UP, 1947. 171–82.
—. "Black Eagle of the North: The Story of Archdeacon John Murphy (1796–1883)." History. *Studies* 38 (1949): 46–56.
—. "Young Ireland Sets a Problem." Essay. *Irish Digest* 34 (1949): 1–3.
—. "Emily Brontë." Academic writing. *Studies* 39 (1950): 15–30.
—. "Thackeray in Ireland." Academic writing. *Studies* 40 (1951): 51–68.

MacCarthy, Catherine Phil. Contemporary. Crecora, Co. Limerick. Poetry.

Born in Crecora, Co. Limerick, in 1954, she was educated at UCC. She did postgraduate studies at the School of Drama in TCD and at the Central School of Speech and Drama in London. She now lives in Dublin, where she teaches part-time at the Drama Centre at UCD and continues to work at her own writing. She won literary competitions in the early 1990s, including the Sense of Place competition organized by Poetry Ireland, which she shared with Susan Connolly. Their winning entries were published jointly as *How High the Moon* (1991).

MacCarthy's first collection of poetry, *This Hour of the Tide*, appeared in 1994, and a further collection, *The Blue Globe*, in 1998. She received an Arts Council Bursary in 1994 and also served as Writer in Residence for the City of Dublin the same year.

Select bibliography
MacCarthy, Catherine Phil.
—. and Susan Connolly. "Sanctuary." *How High the Moon*. Poetry. Dublin: Poetry Ireland, 1991.
—. *This Hour of the Tide*. Poetry. Galway: Salmon, 1994.
—. *The Blue Globe*. Poetry. Belfast: Blackstaff, 1998.

MacIntosh, Sophie, née Donaclift *fl.*1902. Kinsale, Co. Cork. Short stories.

Born and lived in Kinsale, until she married Henry MacIntosh, who later became headmaster of the Methodist College, Belfast. Her short stories were noted for their descriptions of the people of her native town, as Katherine Tynan comments in her introduction to "Jim Walsh's Tin Box": "she resided [in Kinsale] in kindly intimacy with the fishing-folk and peasants. She has a delightful talent, particularly for describing the people of her native town" (*Cabinet of Irish Literature*). Some of her work was published in a collection titled *The Last Forward* (1902).

Select bibliography
MacIntosh, Sophie.
—. *The Last Forward and Other Stories*. Short stories. London: Brimley Johnson, 1902.
—. *Love's Conflict*. Short stories. London: Ward, Lock, 1906.

MacNamara, Rachel Swete. *fl.*1911–50. Cork. Novels.

Born in Ennis, Co. Clare, she was educated in Cork, where she lived for many years. She travelled extensively, and was a prolific writer of romances.

Select bibliography
MacNamara, Rachel Swete.
—. *Spinners in Silence*. Novel. London: Blackwood, 1911.
—. *White Witch*. Novel. London: Hurst & Blackett, 1934.
—. *The Awakening*. Novel. London: Hurst & Blackett, 1936.
—. *Fandango*. Novel. London: Hurst & Blackett, 1936.
—. *Let Them Say!* Novel. London: Hurst & Blackett, 1936.
—. *The Lovely Ghost*. Novel. London: Hurst & Blackett, 1936.
—. *Strange Encounter*. Novel. London: Hurst & Blackett, 1936.
—. *Gay by Name*. Novel. London: Hurst & Blackett, 1937.
—. *Kiss a Stranger*. Novel. London: Hurst & Blackett, 1937.
—. *Yesterday's April*. Novel. London: Hodder, 1939.
—. *Mirror for Josephine*. Novel. London: Hodder, 1940.
—. *Melissa*. Novel. London: Hodder, 1941.
—. *Alphabet for Ladies*. Novel. London: Hodder, 1942.
—. *My Face is My Fortune*. Novel. London: Hodder, 1943.
—. *The Door*. Novel. London: Hodder, 1944.
—. *Portrait in Ivory*. Novel. London: Hodder, 1944.
—. *Glass Walls*. Novel. London: Hurst & Blackett, 1947.
—. *Morning Joy*. Novel. London: Hurst & Blackett, 1947.
—. *Witchcraft in your Lips*. Novel. London: Hurst & Blackett, 1947.
—. *Cuckoo*. Novel. London: Hurst & Blackett, 1949.

Mac Néill, Máire. 1904–87. Co. Clare. Academic writing, folklore, translation, biography.

Born in Co. Dublin, she was the daughter of Agnes Moore and Eoin Mac Néill, who was a founder of the Gaelic League and of the Irish Volunteers. He later served as Minister for Education in the first Free State Government. She was educated in Dublin, and graduated from UCD with a degree in Celtic Studies in 1925. Her first job was with Cumann na nGael as secretary, business manager and journalist, editing its monthly publication and later sub-editing its weekly paper, *United Ireland*. She then obtained a position with the newly established Irish Folklore Commission, where she remained from 1935 to 1949. It was here that she began her research on the survival of the Celtic harvest festival, *The Festival of Lughnasa* (1962), for which she was awarded a DLitt by NUI in 1964. Following her marriage to John L. Sweeney, who was Curator of Harvard's Lamont Poetry Room, she went to America in 1949 and spent some years living in Boston. While there she was appointed Visiting Lecturer in Irish Folklore and was instrumental in promoting interest in that topic among American students.

Máire and her husband retired to Inchiquin in Co. Clare in 1967 but she continued her work, translating two texts, Seán S. Ó hEochaidh's *Siscéalta ó Thír Chonaill* (1977) and Séamus Ó Duilearga's *Leabhar Sheáin Í Chonaill* (1981), and developing a keen interest in the folklore of Co. Clare, especially that of the Burren. However, she took a particular interest in the seventeenth-century heroine, Máire Rua of Leamaneh. Having lectured publicly on this character, she wrote her story and this was published posthumously in 1990.

Select bibliography
Mac Néill, Máire.
—. *The Festival of Lughnasa*. Folklore. Oxford: Oxford UP, 1962. Dublin: Comhairle Bhéaloideas Éireann, 1983.
—. trans. *Fairy Legends from Donegal* [*Síscéalta ó Thír Chonaill*], originally collected by Seán S. Ó hEochaidh. Folklore. Dublin: Comhairle Bhéaloideas Éireann, 1977.
—. *Seán Ó Conaill's Book: Stories and Traditions from Iveragh* [*Leabhar Sheáin Í Chonaill*, recorded and ed. with foreword and notes by Séamus Ó Duilearga]. Folklore. Dublin: Comhairle Bhéaloideas Éireann, 1981.
—. *Máire Rua, Lady of Leamaneh*. Biography. Ed. Maureen Murphy. Whitegate, Co. Clare: Ballinakella, 1990.

Secondary sources
Breathnach, Diarmuid agus Máire Ní Mhurchú. "Mac Neill, Máire (1904–87)." *1983–2002 Beathaisnéis*. Baile Átha Cliath: An Clóchomhar, 2003.

MacSwiney, Mary [Ni Shuibhne, Máire]. 1872–1942. Cork. Political writing.

Moved from England to Cork while still a child. Her father left the family there and emigrated to Australia. As the eldest of seven children, Mary felt a keen sense of responsibility towards her siblings, especially her brother Terence. She was educated in Cork and trained as a teacher at Cambridge University. In 1892 she went to teach at a strict Catholic convent school in Kent, England, but when her mother died in 1904 she returned to Cork to care for her sisters and brothers.

In the early years of the twentieth century, her brother Terence began to take an interest in nationalist politics, while Mary joined the Gaelic League and Inghínidhe na hÉireann. She also joined the Munster Women's Franchise League, founded by Somerville and Ross, but her interests lay in the Irish independence movement. She continued to teach, but her support of the 1916 rebellion and subsequent imprisonment resulted in her dismissal from the school. She and her sister Annie then set up a school for girls, St Ita's, where all the subjects were taught in Irish. When Terence, then Lord Mayor of Cork, went on the hunger strike that resulted in his death she managed the publicity surrounding the event, and later toured the United States with his widow, Muriel, promoting the Republican cause.

She joined the Sinn Féin party and was elected to the Dáil in 1921. She supported de Valera during the Civil War, which led to two periods of imprisonment during which she went on hunger strike. Following her release she kept her seat in the General Election of 1923, but her refusal to join de Valera's Fianna Fáil party resulted in her losing her Dáil seat in 1927. However, she maintained her support for the old-guard Republicanism despite her declining health in later years and died in Cork in 1942. Notes: The National Library of Ireland holds several documents and letters relating to her public activities.

Select bibliography
MacSwiney, Mary.
—. *Ireland's Fight for IndePENdence* [Address of Miss Mary MacSwiney, sister of the

late Lord Mayor of Cork, delivered at the Olympic Theatre, Chicago]. Political writing. Chicago: All-American Bureau of Speakers for the Irish Republic, 1921.
—. *Poblacht na hÉireann: The Republic of Ireland*. Political writing. Cork: Lee, 1932.
—. *Address by Máire Nic Suibhne T.D.* [Leas-uachtarán to Árd Fheis Sinn Féin, 16 Deireadh Fomhair 1924]. Political writing. N.p.: n.p., n.d.
—. *The Background of the Irish Republic: The Testimony Given Before the American Commission on Conditions in Ireland*. Political writing. Chicago: Benjamin Franklin Bureau, n.d.

Secondary sources
Broderick, Marian. *Wild Irish Women: Extraordinary Lives from History*. Dublin: O'Brien, 2001. 182–6.
Ward, Margaret. *Unmanageable Revolutionaries: Women and Irish Nationalism*. London: Pluto, 1983, 1995.

Madden, Deirdre. Contemporary. Cork. Academic writing.

Born in Cork in 1967, she graduated from UCC with a PhD in 2000. She was called to the bar in 1989 and has lectured in the Law Department, UCC, since 1992. Her research interests include medical law, especially in the area of assisted human reproduction. She was appointed to the Commission on Assisted Human Reproduction in 2000 and is a member of the Expert Evaluation Panel on Bioethics for the European Commission. She is the medico–legal columnist for the *Irish Medical News*.

Select bibliography
Madden, Deirdre.
—. "Ireland." *Reproductive Medicine and Embryological Research – A European Handbook of Bioethical Legislation*. Academic writing. Edinburgh: European Bioethical Research, 1997. 17–18.
—. "Is There a Right to a Child of One's Own?" Academic writing. *Medico-Legal Journal of Ireland* (1999): 8–13.
—. "The Quest for Parenthood in Assisted Human Reproduction." Academic writing. *Dublin University Law Journal* 21 (1999): 1–39.
—. "Recent Developments in Assisted Human Reproduction: Legal and Ethical Issues." Academic writing. *Medico-Legal Journal of Ireland* 7.2 (2001): 53–62.
—. contributor. *The Ethics of New Reproductive Technologies: Cases and Questions*. Academic Writing. Oxford: Berghahn Books, 2002.
—. *Medicine, Law and Ethics in Ireland*, 2002. (Unpub.) academic writing.

Madden, Mabel S. *fl.* 1910. Cork. Short stories, novels.

Daughter of Samuel Owen Madden, Dean of Cork, sister of Rev. Owen Madden, rector of Castletownshend, she contributed to many periodicals and wrote a novel, *The Fitzgerald Family* (1910), about the family of an Irish clergyman.

Select bibliography
Madden, Mabel S.
—. *The Fitzgerald Family*. Novel. London: Religious Tract Society, 1910.

Maguire, Anita. Contemporary. Cork. Science.

Lecturer in the Department of Chemistry, UCC, she is also chairman of the European Cooperation in the Field of Scientific and Technical

Research management committee for action D12. Her research activities include asymmetric synthesis and the development of novel synthetic methodology.

Select bibliography
Maguire, Anita.
—. "Single Step Stereospecific Transformation of 2-Phenylthio Secondary Amides into (Z)-3-Chloro-2-Phenylthio Acrylamides." Science. *Tetrahedron Lett.* 36 (1995).
—. "Efficient Kinetic Resolution of 2-Benzenesulfonylcyclopentanone Derivatives." Science. *Journal of Molecular Catalysis B: Enzymatic* 1 (1996): 115–26.
—. "Excellent Stereocontrol in Intramolecular Buchner Cyclisations and Subsequent Cycloadditions: Stereospecific Construction of Polycyclic Systems." Science. *Chem. Commun* 2595 (1996).

Maguire, Muireann. Contemporary. Dingle, Co. Kerry. Short stories, poetry.

Born in West Kerry in 1979, she grew up there. She studied European Studies at TCD and began writing at an early age. She has won prizes for her short stories at Listowel Writers' Week (1995–98), and in 1996 she won the Windows Student Poetry Competition. The same year, eight of her poems were part of the third *Windows Authors and Artists Introduction*, and she has given readings of her work around the country. Her poems have been published in several anthologies, and in 1999 she was chosen as a Kerry Podium Poet. Her first collection of poetry was published in 2001.

Select bibliography
Maguire, Muireann.
—. *The Nightingale Seed.* Poetry. Belfast: Lapwing, 2001.

Mahony, Agnes [Agnes Hickson]. *fl.*1820–35. Dromore Castle, Co. Kerry. Poetry.

Daughter of Col. John Mahony (Irish Volunteer and delegate to the Dungannon Convention 1782), she married Conway Hickson of Fermoyle, Co. Kerry, in 1831. Her poetry appeared in the 1820s and 1830s (Colman, 155).

Mangan, Celine. Contemporary. Killorglin, Co. Kerry. Religious writing.

Born in Killorglin, 1939, she is a Dominican sister. She took an MA in semitic languages at UCD, and she has a Licentiate in sacred scripture from the Pontifical Commission in Rome. She lectures at the Milltown Institute of Philosophy and Theology in Dublin, and her field of enquiry involves the way in which scripture relates to women and ecology.

Select bibliography
Mangan, Celine.
—. *I Am with You: Biblical Experiences of God.* Religious writing. Dublin: Veritas, 1975.
—. *1 and 2 Chronicles, Ezra and Nehemiah.* Religious writing. Old Testament Message Ser. Wilmington: Glazier, 1982.
—. *Can We Still Call God Father?* Religious writing. Wilmington: Glazier, 1983.
—. *Women in the New Testament* [Study Programme for the Women's Study Group]. Religious writing. Dublin: Irish Commission of Justice and Peace, 1994.

Manning, Mrs R. *fl.*1880s. Clonmel. Poetry.

Lived and wrote in Clonmel in the 1880s.

Select bibliography
Manning, Mrs. R.
—. *In Memoriam. V. Rev. T.N. Burke, O.P.* Poetry. Clonmel: *Chronicle*, 1883.

Le Marquand Hartigan, Anne. Contemporary. Limerick. Poetry, plays.

Born in England in 1937. Having received a qualification in fine art she moved to her mother's family farm in Limerick in 1962. She continued to paint with some success but she gradually became more interested in writing. In 1975 her first poem was published in the *Irish Times*, and since then she has published four poetry collections. Hartigan's play *Beds* was performed at the Dublin Theatre Festival in 1982, followed by *La Corbiére* in 1990. Another play, *A Secret Game*, won the Mobil Prize for Irish Playwrights in 1995. She currently lives in Dublin.

Select bibliography
Le Marquand Hartigan, Anne.
—. *Beds*. 1982 (Unpub.) Play.
—. *Long Tongue*. Poetry. Dublin: Beaver Row Press, 1982.
—. *Now is a Moveable Feast*. Poetry. Galway: Salmon, 1991.
—. *Immortal Sins*. Poetry. Cliffs of Moher: Salmon, 1993 [includes script of La Corbiére].
—. *A Secret Game*. 1995. (Unpub.) Play.
—. *Clearing the Space*. Philosophy. Cliffs of Moher: Salmon Publishing, 1996.

Secondary sources
Haberstroh, Pamela Boyle. "New Directions in Irish Women's Poetry." *Women Creating Women: Contemporary Irish Women Poets*. Syracuse: Syracuse UP, 1996. 197–224.

Martin, Joy, née Green. Contemporary. Limerick; Whitegate, Co. Clare. Novels.

Born in Limerick in 1937. Financial constraints prevented her attending university so she trained as a journalist, first at a local newspaper and later at the *Evening Press* in Dublin. After marriage she moved to South Africa, where she continued her journalistic work, worked as assistant editor on *Femina* magazine and wrote two non-fiction books. One consisted of a series of interviews with twelve men and women from black townships near Johannesburg (*Twelve Shades of Black*), and the other (*Myth and Magic*) investigated the Shona people of Zimbabwe. She also spent time with the Zambia Broadcasting Corporation. She has broadcast on the BBC Home and External Services as well as in Ireland and South Africa. Her first novel, *A Wrong to Sweeten*, was published in 1987. Her novel *The Moon is Red in April* (1989) is set around the early days of the House of Hennessy Cognac in eighteenth-century Ireland and France.

Select bibliography
Martin, Joy.
—. *A Wrong to Sweeten*. Novel. London: Weidenfeld & Nicholson, 1987.

—. *The Moon is Red in April.* Novel. London: Grafton-Collins, 1989.
—. *Ulrick's Daughter.* Novel. London: Grafton, 1990.
—. *A Heritage of Wrong.* Novel. London: HarperCollins, 1991.
—. *Image of Laura.* Novel. London: HarperCollins, 1992.
—. *The House by the Shore.* Novel. London: Hodder-Headline, 1997.
—. *Harlequin's Daughter.* Novel. London: Hodder-Headline, 1999.

McCaffrey, Mary W. Contemporary. Cork. Academic writing, science.

Lecturer in the Department of Biochemistry, UCC, since 1991, she graduated from the University of London with a PhD in 1988. Her research interests include understanding the molecular events which control eukaryotic intracellular membrane trafficking and the role of Rab4 in endocytosis.

Select bibliography
McCaffrey, Mary W.
—. "Rab4 Affects Both Recycling and Degradative Endosomal Trafficking." Science. *FEBS Letters* 495 (2001): 21–30.
—. "The Small GTPase Rab4A Interacts with the Central Region of Cytoplasmic Dynein Light Intermediate Chain-1." Science. *BBRC* 281 (2001): 1141–53.
—. "The Novel Rab11 – FIP/Rip/RCP Family of Proteins Displays Extensive Homo- and Hetero-Interacting Abilities." Science. *Biochem Biophys Res Commun* 292 (2002): 909–15.
—. "Rab Coupling Protein (RCP), A Novel Rab4 and Rab11 Effector Protein." Science. *Journal of Biological Chemistry* 277 (2002): 12190–99.

McCarthy, Bairbre. Comhaimseartha. Co. an Chláir. Litríocht leanaí.

Is é atá in *Favourite Irish Legends: A Dual Language Book* ná leaganacha simplí dátheangacha de na scéalta "Balor Drochshúile", "Leanaí Lir" agus "Tóraíocht Etain". Saolaíodh Bairbre i gCo. an Chláir ach tá sí ag cur fúithi i Nua-Eabhrac faoi láthair.

Bairbre was born in Co. Clare but is currently living in New York. *Favourite Irish Legends: A Dual Language Book* (1997) contains simple bilingual versions of "Balor Drochshúile", "Leanaí Lir" and "Tóraíocht Etain".

Select bibliography
McCarthy, Bairbre.
—. *Favourite Irish Legends: A Dual Language Book.* Litríocht leanaí. Corcaigh: Mercier, 1997.
—. *Irish Leprechaun Stories.* Litríocht leanaí. Corcaigh: Mercier, 1998.
—. *The Adventures of Cúchulainn.* Litríocht leanaí. Corcaigh: Mercier, 2000.

McCarthy, Ely. 1828–48. Cork.

Born in Cork *c.*1828, she was the eldest daughter of a clerk to the city magistrates. Fluent in French and Italian, she was employed to teach languages to upper-class pupils in Cork. Her brother Justin McCarthy went on to become a prominent journalist, historian and politician, and, according to him, Ely translated a George Sand novel, which was published by a magazine of the period. She also translated poems by Petrarch and Alfieri, which were locally published. She died at the age of twenty, following a long illness (Colman, 147).

McCarthy, Geraldine. Contemporary. Cork. Academic writing.

Currently Professor of Nursing Studies and Head of the Department of Nursing Studies, UCC, she has been established in the department since 1994. McCarthy lectures on nursing research; her research interests include stress and coping with chronic illness, leadership and management of the Health Service and competency of nursing managers.

Select bibliography
McCarthy, Geraldine.
—. "Appraisal, Coping and Adaptation: A Study of Irish Women Diagnosed with Breast Cancer." *Nursing in Ireland – A Research Base.* Academic writing. Ed. P. Treacy and A. Hyde. N.p.: n.p., 1999. 152–68.
—. and C. Cronin. *An Investigation of Student Nurse Characteristics: Biographical, Educational, Motivational and Attitudes Held to Nursing as a Career.* Academic writing. Dublin: Department of Health and Children, 1999.
—. *Needs, Perceptions and Experiences of First Time Mothers.* Academic writing. Cork: UCC for Niche, 2000.
—. "Typical Students?" Academic writing. *The World of Irish Nursing* 8.2 (2000): 11–13.

McCarthy, Joan. Contemporary. Cork. Academic writing, philosophy.

Born in Killarney in 1959, she took an MA at UCC in 1983 and a PhD in 2001. She has also taken a Dilpoma in Life Development Skills from the College of Holistic Medicine. McCarthy is a lecturer in the Department of Philosophy, UCC. Her research interests include gender theory, feminist philosophies, nursing ethics, narrative theories of self, bioethics and lesbian studies.

Select bibliography
McCarthy, Joan.
—. "Identity, Existence and Passionate Politics." *Lesbian and Gay Visions of Ireland.* Academic writing. Ed. Ide O'Carroll and Eoin Collins. London and New York: Cassell, 1995. 99–109.
—. D. Dooley, T. Garanis-Papadatos and P. Dalla-Vorgia. *The Ethics of Reproductive Technologies.* Academic writing. Oxford: Berghahn Books, 2002.

McCarthy, Justine. Contemporary. Cork. Journalism.

Born in 1959 in Cork, she was educated there and at the College of Commerce in Rathmines, where she obtained a diploma in journalism. She worked as a journalist on various Irish magazines from 1979 till 1984, when she joined the staff of the *Irish Independent.* She has been the recipient of a number of A.T. Cross journalism awards and has contributed to international newspapers and journals, including the *Washington Post,* the *European,* the *Guardian* and the *Observer.* She has published an unauthorized biography of the current President of Ireland, Mary McAleese.

Select bibliography
McCarthy, Justine.
—. *Mary McAleese: The Outsider – An Unauthorised Biography.* Biography. Dublin: Blackwater, 1999.

McCarthy, May [Nicholson, Mary; McCann, M.]. 1921–99. Clonakilty, Co. Cork. Memoir.

Born in 1921, the fourth of ten children, she grew up on a farm in Casheliskey, near Clonakilty. She emigrated to London in 1939–40, where she was to spend the rest of her life, although she frequently returned to her native area on holiday. She married Duncan Nicholson, and they had four children. She took up creative writing in later life, having been an avid reader of all types of literature. Her memoir, *The Old House on the Hill*, was written under the pseudonym M. McCann and was published a few years before her death. It is an account of her childhood in West Cork, interspersed with descriptions of nature, the landscape and the changing seasons.

Select bibliography
McCarthy, May.
—. *The Old House on the Hill*. Memoir. London: Minerva Press, 1996.

McCarthy, Sr Philomena. Kenmare, Co. Kerry. Local history, religious writing.

A religious sister and a member of St Clare's convent in Kenmare, Co. Kerry, she has published a number of books about the history of Kenmare, its church and its religious history, as well as a pamphlet about Margaret Ann Cusack, the Nun of Kenmare, in 1989.

Select bibliography
McCarthy, Sr Philomena.
—. *The Nun of Kenmare: The True Facts*. History. Killarney: self-published, 1989.
—. *Poor Clare Convent, Kenmare: The Women Who did not Sit and Wait*. Local history. Killarney: self-published, 1999.
—. *Holy Cross Church, Kenmare*. Local history. Killarney: self-published, 2000.
—. *Kenmare and Its Storied Glen: From the Cursing Stones up to the Christian Chanticleer*. Local history. Killarney: self-published, n.d.

McCoole, Sinéad. Contemporary. Limerick. History, biography, political writing.

Born in New York in 1968, she moved to Limerick with her family in 1972. She is a historical researcher currently based in Dublin and is best known for her work in the field of women's history. In 1997 she published *Guns and Chiffon*, based on the political activism of women prisoners in Kilmainham Gaol during the War of Independence and the Civil War. The publication was accompanied by an exhibition of materials relating to the women's activism, which is now a permanent part of the heritage centre at Kilmainham. She has recently published a study of Irish women revolutionaries in the early twentieth century, *No Ordinary Women* (2003).

Select bibliography
McCoole, Sinéad.
—. *Hazel: A Life of Lady Lavery*. Biography. Dublin: Lilliput, 1996.
—. *Guns and Chiffon: Women Prisoners and Kilmainham Gaol 1916–1923*. History. Dublin: Stationery Office, 1997.

—. Patricia Butler and Carla Briggs. *Mary Herbert of Muckross House, 1817–1893.*
Biography. Killarney: Muckross House, 1999.
—. *Researcher's Handbook: Sources for Twentieth Century Irish History: Limerick City
Library Historian in Residence Millennium Project.* Handbook. Limerick: Limerick
Corporation, 2000.
—. *No Ordinary Women: Irish Female Activists in the Revolutionary Years 1900–1923.*
History. Dublin: O'Brien Press, 2003.

McCraith, Laura M. [L.M. McCraith]. *fl.* 1912–23. Tipperary. Local history.

Best known for her work *The Suir from Its Source to the Sea* (1912), she was an
early historian of her native Tipperary. She was born in 1870 at Loughloher
House, outside Cahir, where her ancestors had settled in the early eighteenth
century. The McCraiths were well known landowners and magistrates in that
part of the country, and her father was a captain in the Tipperary Artillery
(Walsh, 175). She travelled extensively, and in 1900 she married Dr John
Henry Blakeney. They moved to Cheltenham following his posting there in
1909, but frequently travelled back and forth between there and Cahir, and
maintained an active interest in her native place – she and her husband
donated a silver chalice to St Paul's Church in Cahir in 1915. At the outbreak
of the First World War, she became a member of the St John's Ambulance
Brigade and the superintendent of a nursing division. In 1915 she was
appointed Commandant of the St John's Voluntary Hospital for soldiers in
Cheltenham.

Walsh tells us that McCraith was friendly with Rev. William P. Burke, who
wrote his *History of Clonmel* while working as a curate in Cahir. The two
compared notes on their writing and shared sources on the history of the
area. In *Cashel of the Kings* (1923) she acknowledges Canon Burke's involvement in her research (176). In addition to her works of local history,
McCraith also contributed to periodicals such as the *New Ireland Review*, on
issues as diverse as suffrage, tourism and Irish music. Little is known about
her later years.

Select bibliography
McCraith, Laura M.
—. "In Old Gardens." Local history. *New Ireland Review* 4 (Nov 1895): 137–40.
—. "The Genius of Irish Music." History. *New Ireland Review* 6 (Sept. 1896): 45–52.
—. "Historic Houses." Local history. *New Ireland Review* 5 (July 1896): 293–9.
—. "Concerning Leinster House." *New Ireland Review* 11 (Aug. 1899): 368–72.
—. "A Forgotten Great Irishwoman." History. *New Ireland Review* 14 (Sept. 1900): 45–50.
—. "A Touch of the Wand." *New Ireland Review* 19 (July 1903): 285–9.
—. "Does Ireland Want Tourists?" Travel writing. *New Ireland Review* 29 (Aug. 1908): 350–53.
—. *The Green Tree.* Dublin: Sealy, Bryers & Walker, 1908.
—. "Irishwomen and Their Vote." Political writing. *New Ireland Review* 30 (Dec. 1908): 193–8.
—. "At Geoffrey Keating's Grave.""*New Ireland Review* 32 (Nov. 1909): 177–81.
—. "The Irish Novel." Literary criticism. *New Ireland Review* 31 (Mar. 1909): 33–40.

—. "Athassel Abbey and Its Patrons." Local history. *New Ireland Review* 34 (Dec. 1910): 214–20.

—. *The Suir from Its Source to the Sea.* Local history. Clonmel: *The Clonmel Chronicle*, 1912.

—. *The Romance of Irish Heroines.* History. Dublin: Longman, Green, 1913.

—. *Cashel of the Kings.* Local history. Clonmel: *The Clonmel Chronicle*, 1923.

McDonnell, Orla. Contemporary. Limerick. Academic writing.

Took a PhD at UCC and a Graduate Diploma in Women's Studies at UL, where she is currently a junior lecturer in sociology. Her research interests include health, medicine and science, bioethics and the sociology of the body.

Select bibliography
McDonnell, Orla.
—. "Shifting Paradigms: Discourse Analysis as an Evaluation Approach for Technology Assessment." Academic writing. *Evaluation: The International Journal of Theory, Research and Practice* 1.2 (1995): 217–35.
—. "Conversing on Class Activism: Claiming Our Space in Feminist Politics." Political writing. *Irish Journal of Feminist Studies* 2.1 (1997): 67–85.
—. "Ethical and Social Implications of Technology in Medicine: New Possibilities and New Dilemmas." *The Sociology of Health and Illness in Ireland.* Academic writing. Ed. A. Cleary and P. Treacy. Dublin: UCD Press, 1997.
—. "The Politics of New Reproductive Technologies in Ireland." *In from the Shadows.* Academic writing. Ed. C. Aniagolu. Limerick: Limerick UP, 1997.
—. "Shifting Debates on New Reproductive Technology: Implications for Public Discourse in Ireland." *Nature, Risk and Responsibility: Discourses of Biotechnology.* Academic writing. Ed. P. O'Mahony. London: Macmillan, 1999.

McIntosh Gillian, Contemporary. Cork. Academic writing, history.

Born in Cork city in 1968 like her three sisters before her, she attended Scoil Mhuire, from 1973 to 1986. She went on to UCC, where she did a BA in English and history and then an MA in Irish history. In 1993 she went to Belfast, where she took a PhD in modern history at QUB. She has since held three research fellowships at the Institute of Irish Studies there. Her research interests focus mainly on the culture, politics and literature of Northern Ireland in the twentieth century, and in 1999 she published *The Force of Culture: Unionist Identities in Twentieth-Century Ireland.* She is currently working on an Economic and Social Research Council (ESRC)-sponsored devolution project to explore attempts to represent or imagine the new political dispensation in Northern Ireland through rituals and symbols.

Select bibliography
McIntosh, Gillian.
—. *The Force of Culture: Unionist Identities in Twentieth-Century Ireland.* Cork: Cork UP, 2000.
—. "'Life is a Series of Oppositions': The Prose Work of W.R. Rodgers." History. *The Honest Ulsterman* 105 (Spring, 1998). Also in *Irish Studies Review* 8.2 (2000).
—. "Symbolic Mirrors: Commemorations of Edward Carson in the 1930s." History. *Irish Historical Studies* 32.125 (May 2000).

—. "CEMA and the National Anthem: The Arts and the State in Post-War Northern Ireland." History. *New Hibernia Review* 5.3 (2001).

—. "'Cultivating Their Own Garden': Broadcasting and Culture in Northern Ireland in the 1930s and 1940s." History. *Bullán* 6.1 (2001).

—. "A Performance of Consensus? The Coronation Visit of Elizabeth II to Northern Ireland, 1953." History. *Irish Studies Review* 10.3 (2002).

—. "More Than the Wife of the 'Nominated Bard': The Diaries of Roberta Hewitt." *Ireland (Ulster) Scotland: Concepts, Contexts, Comparisons.* History. Ed. Edna Longley, Eamonn Hughes and Des O'Rawe. Belfast Studies in Language, Culture and Politics ser. Belfast: QUB, 2003.

McElligott, Laura. Contemporary. Listowel, Co. Kerry. Poetry.

A pupil at Dromclough National School, Co. Kerry, she has contributed poems to a variety of collections and newspapers, including the *Kerryman*. She has won several awards for her work, including competitions at Listowel Writers' Week. Her great-grandfather was a North Kerry poet who published as "Bob Boland". She is currently preparing a collection for publication.

McMorran, Clare. Contemporary. Tralee, Co. Kerry. Travel writing, handbooks.

A travel writer based in Tralee, Co. Kerry, she has co-written and illustrated travel guides for the North Kerry area with Russell McMorran.

Select bibliography
McMorran, Clare.
—. *Castlegregory Guide.* Local history. Dingle: n.p., 1975.
—. and Russell McMorran. *Cloghane-Brandon Guide.* Local history. Dingle: n.p., 1976.
—. and Russell McMorran. *Dingle: A Guide Book.* Local history. Dingle: self-published, 1977.

McNamara, Sarah. Contemporary. Parteen, Co. Limerick. History, anthology.

Born in Co. Wexford, she has been a lifelong member of the Irish Country-women's Association, having served at local level and on the National Executive from December 1988 to May 1992. Her first book is a history of the early years of the Association, and her second is a collection of writings compiled from the Association's monthly journal.

Select bibliography
McNamara, Sarah.
—. *Those Intrepid United Irishwomen: Pioneers of the Irish Countrywomen's Association.* History. Parteen, Limerick: self-published, 1995.
—. ed. *Miscellany of Creative Writings.* Anthology. Parteen, Limerick: self-published, 1997.

Meade, L.T. [Elizabeth Thomasina Meade]. 1844–1915. Nohoval, Co. Cork. Novels, short stories.

Daughter of Rev. R.T. Meade and Sarah Lane, she was born *c.*1844 in Bandon, Co. Cork. The family moved to Nohoval in East Cork, where her father was rector, when she was quite young. She wrote her first book at seventeen and published her first novel, *Ashton-Morton*, anonymously, in 1866. By the end of her career she had published over 300 novels, making her, as Tynan noted, "perhaps the most voluminous of all living writers" (193). Following the death of her mother and her father's remarriage in 1874 she moved to London, where she initially lived with a doctor and his wife who encouraged her to continue with her writing. She married Alfred Toulmin Smith in 1877 and moved to Dulwich, where the couple had three children.

A book for young children, *Scamp and I* (1877), was the first of her books to achieve success, but she was primarily known as a writer of fiction for adolescent girls. Tynan comments: "Mrs Meade's lot must be counted happy. She is beloved of little girls, and some girls well on in their teens. She has an immense popularity, and she knows how to write of little girls with great charm and truth." Flint points out that, in a 1906 survey of reading habits among British, colonial and Indian girls, the latter two groups rated L.T. Meade as their fifth-favourite author (160–61). The theme of books such as *The Rebel of the School* (1902), about an Irish girl's adventures at an English boarding school, had clearly found favour with a group of girls who shared the experience of being sent overseas to boarding schools in Britain. *Polly: A New-Fashioned Girl* (1908), one of her most popular novels, was published by six New York houses and came out in three different editions. Many of her school novels depict passionate attachments between girls and women, which were acceptable to readers during the era when "romantic friendships" between women were common. Meade edited the girls' magazine *Atlanta* from 1887 to 1898, which H. Rider Haggard and R.L. Stevenson contributed to. Loeber has pointed out the importance of this magazine as a conduit for women's writing – the magazine ran writing competitions for young girls, posting winners' names in the magazine, and printed instructions on how to approach writing (Loeber 2001).

The fact that Meade's fame was as a writer for children and adolescent girls may be one of the reasons for her relative obscurity today. However, recent research shows that in fact she wrote over a wide range of genres such as social protest, science fiction, crime fiction (some of which which she co-authored with Edgar Beaumont) and fiction for young women, as well as her better-known schoolgirl fiction (Loeber and Stouthamer-Loeber 1999). For example, *Lettie's Last Home* (1875) and *Great St Benedict's: A Tale* (1876) discuss social problems of the day. Much of her fiction for children also addressed urban poverty, such as *Dot and Her Treasures* (1879), which depicts an orphaned girl who looks after her brothers and sisters in a London loft. The Loebers also tell us that Meade was a member of the feminist Pioneer Club in London, which suggests she was involved at some level with women's rights at the turn of the century. Her novel *The Cleverest Woman in England* (1898) addresses the difficulties of a feminist activist after her marriage to a conservative man (Loeber and Stouthamer-Loeber ms.).

Select bibliography

Meade, L.T.

Note: We list all of Meade's material held by the National Library of Ireland, below, along with some other titles held by other Irish libraries, such as the TCD Library. A full bibliography of L.T. Meade's works can be found in the British Library catalogue: http://blpc.bl.uk. Where the dates of individual works are unclear, we have used the British Library date.

—. *Ashton-Morton*. Novel. London: n.p., 1866.

—. *Lettie's Last Home*. Novel. London: n.p., 1875.

—. *Dorothy's Story, or, Great St Benedict's: A Tale*. Novel. London: John F. Shaw, 1876.

—. *A Knight of Today*. Novel. London: n.p., 1877. Notes: Illus. L.Taylor.

—. *Scamp and I: A Story of City By-ways*. Children's writing. London: Shaw, 1877.

—. *Bel Marjory*. Novel. London: Partridge, 1878.

—. *The Children's Kingdom: The Story of a Great Endeavour*. Children's writing. London: Shaw, 1878.

—. *Outcast Robin, or Your Brother and Mine: A Cry from the Great City*. Novel. London: Shaw, 1878.

—. *Dot and Her Treasures*. Novel. London: John F. Shaw, 1879.

—. *Andrew Harvey's Wife*. Novel. London: Ibister, 1880.

—. *A Dweller in Tents*. Novel. London: Ibister, 1880.

—. "Mou-Setsé: A Negro Hero." *Two Tales*. Short stories. 1880. London: W. Ibister, 1880. Notes: Published in the same volume as "The Orphan's Pilgrimage" by T. von Gumpert.

—. *The Children's Pilgrimage*. Novel. London: Nisbet, 1883.

—. *How It All Came Round*. Novel. London: Hodder & Stoughton, 1883.

—. *Water Gypsies: A Story of Canal Life in England (The Adventures of Tag, Rag and Bobtail)*. Children's writing. London n.p., 1883.

—. *The Autocrat of the Nursery*. Novel. London: Hodder & Stoughton, 1884. Notes: Illus. T. Pym.

—. *A Band of Three*. Novel. London: Ibister, 1884.

—. *The Angel of Love*. Novel. N.p.: n.p., 1885. London: Hodder & Stoughton, 1900.

—. *A World of Girls: The Story of a School*. Fiction for girls. London: Cassell, 1886, 1892 (Illus. M.E. Edwards).

—. *The O'Donnells of Inchfawn*. Novel. London: Hatchards, 1887.

—. *The Palace Beautiful: A Story for Girls*. Novel. London: Cassell, 1887.

—. *Sweet Nancy*. Novel. London: Partridge, 1887.

—. *Daddy's Boy*. Children's writing. London: n.p., 1888. London: Hatchards, 1907 (Illus. L. Tronbridge).

—. *Nobody's Neighbours*. Fiction for girls. London: Ibister, 1888.

—. *A Farthingful*. Novel. London: Chambers, 1889.

—. *The Lady of the Forest*. Novel. London: Partridge, 1889.

—. *The Little Princess of Tower Hill*. Novel. London: Partridge, 1889.

—. *Polly: A New-Fashioned Girl*. Novel. London, 1889. Notes: Illus. M.E. Edwards.

—. *The Beresford Prize*. Fiction for girls. London, 1890.

—. *Frances Kane's Fortune*. Fiction for girls. London: Warne, 1890.

—. *The Home of Silence*. Novel. London, 1890.

—. *Marigold*. Novel. London: Partridge, 1890.

—. *The Honourable Miss: A Story of an Old-Fashioned Town*. Novel. London: Methuen, 1891.

—. *A Sweet Girl Graduate*. London: Cassell, 1891. N.p.: n.p., 1910. Notes: Illus. H. Ludlow.

—. *Bashful Fifteen*. Novel. London: Cassell, 1892.

—. *Four on an Island: A Story of Adventure*. Children's Writing. London: Chambers, 1892.

—. *The Medicine Lady*. Fiction for girls. London: Cassell, 1892.

—. *A Ring of Rubies*. Novel. London: Ward, Lock, 1892. London: Innes, 1903.

—. *A Young Mutineer*. Novel. London: Wells, Gardner, Darton, 1893.

—. *In an Iron Grip*. Novel. London: Chatto & Windus, 1894.

—. and Clifford Halifax (pseud. Edgar Beaumont). *Stories from the Diary of a Doctor*. Short stories. Vols. 1 & 2. London: Newnes, 1894. London: Bliss, Sands, 1896.

—. *Betty: A Schoolgirl*. Fiction for girls. London: Chambers, 1895.

—. *Engaged to be Married: A Tale of To-day*. Novel. London: Griffith, Farran, 1895.

—. *A Little Silver Trumpet*. Novel. London: Hodder & Stoughton, 1895.

—. *A Princess of the Gutter*. Fiction for girls. London: Wells, Gardner, 1895.

—. *Catalina: Art Student*. Fiction for girls. London: Chambers, 1896.

—. and Clifford Halifax (pseud. Edgar Beaumont). *Dr Rumsey's Patient: A Very Strange Story*. Novel. London: Chatto & Windus, 1896.

—. *A Girl in Ten Thousand*. Fiction for girls. London: Oliphant, 1896.

—. *Girls, New and Old*. Fiction for girls. London: Chambers, 1896.

—. *A Little Mother to the Others*. Novel. London: F.V. White, 1896.

—. *Merry Girls of England*. Novel. London: Cassell, 1896.

—. *The Scamp Family*. Children's writing. London: Chambers, 1896. Notes: Illus. M.E. Edwards.

—. *A Son of Ishmael*. Novel. London: White, 1896. London: Chatto, 1918.

—. *Bad Little Hannah*. Short stories. London: F.V. White, 1897.

—. *A Handful of Silver*. Novel. Edinburgh: Oliphant, Anderson & Ferrier, 1897. Notes: Illus. Ida Lovering.

—. and Robert Kennaway Douglas, Keeper of Oriental Printed Books and Manuscripts, British Museum. *Under the Dragon Throne*. Short stories. London: Wells, Gardner, 1897.

—. *The Way of a Woman*. Novel. London: F.V. White, 1897.

—. *Wild Kitty*. Fiction for girls. London: Chambers, 1897.

—. *Cave Perilous*. Novel. London: Religious Tract Society, 1898.

—. *The Cleverest Woman in England*. Novel. London: Nisbet, 1898.

—. *Mary Gifford, M.B.* Novel, political writing. London, 1898.

—. and Robert Eustace (pseud. E. Rawlins). *A Master of Mysteries*. Novel. London: Ward, Lock, 1898.

—. *The Rebellion of Lil Carrington*. Novel. London: Cassell, 1898.

—. *The Siren: A Novel*. Novel. London: F.V. White, 1898.

—. and Robert Eustace (pseud. E. Rawlins). *The Brotherhood of the Seven Kings*. Short stories. London: Ward, Lock, 1899.

—. and Robert Eustace (pseud. E. Rawlins). *The Gold Star Line*. Short stories. London: Ward, Lock, 1899.

—. et al. *The Kingfisher's Egg and Other Stories*. Short stories. London: Nisbet, 1899.

—. *Light o' the Morning: The Story of an Irish Girl*. Fiction for girls. London: Chambers, 1899. Notes: Illus. W. Rainey.

—. *A Public School Boy*. Memoir. London: J. Nisbet, 1899. Notes: A memoir of H.S. Wristbridge. Pref. A.H. Gilkes.

—. and Clifford Halifax (pseud. Edgar Beaumont). *Where the Shoe Pinches: Fifty-Two Stirring Tales for Girls*. Fiction for girls. London: Hutchinson, 1899.

—. *The Beauforts*. Novel. N.p.: n.p., 1900. Oxford: Oxford UP, 1918.

—. and Robert Eustace (pseud. E. Rawlins). *The Sanctuary Club*. Novel. London: Ward, Lock, 1900. Notes: Illus. S. Paget.

—. *Seven Maids*. Novel. London: Chambers, 1900.

—. *Wages: A Novel*. Novel. London: Nisbet, 1900.

—. *Daddy's Girl*. Novel. London: Newnes, 1901. Notes: Illus. Gordon Browne.

—. *Girls of the True Blue*. Fiction for girls. London: Chambers, 1901.

—. *The New Mrs Lascelles*. Novel. London: James Clarke, 1901.

—. and Clifford Halifax (pseud. Edgar Beaumont). *A Race with the Sun*. Novel. Vols. 1 & 2. London: Ward, Locke, 1901.

—. *A Sister of the Red Cross: A Tale of the South African War*. Novel. London: Nelson, 1901.

—. and Clifford Halifax (pseud. Edgar Beaumont). *This Troublesome World*. Novel. London: Chatto & Windus, 1901.

—. *A Very Naughty Girl*. Fiction for girls. London: Chambers, 1901.

—. *Wheels of Iron*. Fiction for girls. London: Nisbet, 1901.

—. *Confessions of a Court Milliner*. Novel. London: John Long, 1902.

—. *Drift*. Novel. London: Methuen, 1902.

—. *The Girls of St Wodes*. Fiction for girls. London: Chambers, 1902.

—. *Girls of the Forest*. Fiction for girls. London: Chambers, 1902.

—. and Robert Eustace (pseud. E. Rawlins). *The Lost Square*. Novel. London: Ward, Lock, 1902.

—. *Margaret*. Novel. London: F.V. White, 1902.

—. *The Princess Who Gave It All Away*. Fiction for girls. London: Ernest Nister, 1902.

—. *Queen Rose*. Novel. London: Chambers, 1902.

—. *The Rebel of the School*. Fiction for girls. London: Chambers, 1902.

—. *The Squire's Little Girl*. Novel. London: Chambers, 1902.

—. *A Gay Charmer: A Story for Girls*. Fiction for girls. London: Chambers, 1903.

—. *The Manor School*. Fiction for girls. London: Chambers, 1903.

—. *Peter the Pilgrim*. Novel. London: Chambers, 1903.

—. *Resurgam*. Novel. London: Methuen, 1903.

—. *The Sorceress of the Strand*. Novel. London: Ward, Lock, 1903. Notes: Illus. Gordon Browne.

—. *Stories from the Old Old Bible*. Religious Writing. London: Newnes, 1903. Notes: Illus. T.H. Robinson.

—. *That Brilliant Peggy*. Fiction for girls. London: Hodder & Stoughton, 1903.

—. *The Witch-Maid*. Novel. London: Nisbet, 1903.

—. *The Girls of Mrs Pritchard's School*. Fiction for girls. London: Chambers, 1904.

—. *A Madcap*. Novel. London: Cassell, 1904.

—. *A Maid of Mystery*. Fiction for girls. London: F.V. White, 1904.

—. *A Modern Tomboy*. Novel. London: Chambers, 1904.

—. *Nurse Charlotte*. Novel. London: John Long, 1904.

—. *Playmates: A Story for Boys and Girls*. Children's writing. London: Chambers, 1904.

—. *Bess of Delany's*. Novel, political writing. London: Digby, Long, 1905.

—. *Dumps: A Plain Girl*. Fiction for girls. London: Chambers, 1905. Notes: Illus. R. Lillie.

—. *Little Wife Hester*. Novel. London: John Long, 1905.

—. *The Other Woman*. Novel. London: Walter Scott, 1905.

—. *Wilful Cousin Kate*. Fiction for girls. London: Chambers, 1905.

—. *From the Hand of the Hunter*. Novel. London: John Long, 1906.

—. *A Golden Shadow*. Novel. London: Ward, Lock, 1906.

—. *The Hill-Top Girl*. Fiction for girls. London: Chambers, 1906. Notes: Illus. L. Baumer.

—. *In the Flower of her Youth*. Novel. London: Nisbet, 1906.

—. *The Maid with the Goggles*. Fiction for girls. London: Digby, Long, 1906.

—. *Sue: The Story of a Little Heroine and Her Friend*. Novel. London: Chambers, 1906. Notes: Illus. C. Flower.

—. *A Girl from America*. Novel. London: Chambers, 1907.

—. *Little Josephine*. Novel. London: John Long, 1907.

—. *The Little School-Mothers*. Novel. London: Cassell, 1907.

—. *The Love of Susan Cardigan*. Novel. London: Digby, Long, 1907.

—. *The Red Cap of Liberty*. Novel. London: Nisbet, 1907.

—. *Three Girls from School*. Fiction for girls. London: Chambers, 1907.

—. *Betty of the Rectory*. Fiction for girls. London: Cassell, 1908.

—. *The Court-Harman Girls*. Fiction for girls. London: Chambers, 1908. Notes: Illus. W. Rainey.

—. *The School Favourite*. Novel. London: Chambers, 1908.

—. *The School Queens*. Fiction for girls. London: Chambers, 1908. Notes: Illus. W. Rainey.

—. *Betty Vivian: A Story of Haddo Court School*. Fiction for girls. London: Chambers, 1909. Notes: Illus. A.S. Boyd.

—. *A Bevy of Girls*. Fiction for girls. London: Chambers, 1909.

—. *Brother or Husband*. Novel. London: F.V. White, 1909.

—. *The Fountain of Beauty*. Novel. London: John Long, 1909.

—. *The Necklace of Parmona*. Fiction for girls. London: Ward, Lock, 1909.

—. *The Princess of the Revels*. Fiction for girls. London: Chambers, 1909.

—. *The Stormy Petrel*. Historical novel. London: Hurst & Blackett, 1909.

—. *Wild Heather*. Novel. London: Cassell, 1909.

—. *The A.B.C. Girl*. Novel. London: F.V. White, 1910.

—. *Belinda Treherne*. Novel. London: John Long, 1910.

—. *A Girl of To-day*. Fiction for girls. London: John Long, 1910.

—. *Lady Anne*. Novel. London: Nisbet, 1910.

—. *Micah Faraday: Adventurer*. Fiction for girls. London: Ward, Lock, 1910.

—. *Nancy Kennedy*. Novel. London: Partridge, 1910.

—. *The Voice of the Charmer*. Novel. London: Greening, 1910.

—. *A Wild Irish Girl*. Novel. London: Chambers, 1910. Notes: Illus. Lewis Baumer.

—. *The Doctor's Children*. Novel. London: Chambers, 1911. Notes: Illus. A.S. Boyd.

—. *The Girl and Her Fortune*. Fiction for girls. London: Digby, Long, 1911.

—. *The Girl from Spain*. Fiction for girls. London: Digby, Long, 1911.

—. *The Girls of Merton College*. Fiction for girls. New York: Hurst, 1911.

—. *Miss Gwendoline*. Fiction for girls. London: John Long, 1911.

—. *Twenty-Four Hours: A Novel of Today*. Novel. London: n.p., 1911.

—. *Corporal Violet*. Fiction for girls. London: Hodder & Stoughton, 1912.

—. *A Girl of the People*. Novel. London: Everett, 1912.

—. *Kitty O'Donovan*. Fiction for girls. London: Chambers, 1912.

—. *Lord and Lady Kitty*. Novel. London: F.V. White, 1912.

—. *Peggy from Kerry*. Fiction for girls. London: Chambers, 1912. Notes: Illus. A. Anderson.

—. *The Chesterton Girl Graduates*. Fiction for girls. New York: Hurst, 1913.

—. *The Girls of Abinger Close.* Fiction for girls. London: Chambers, 1913. Notes: Illus. Percy Tarrant.

—. *The Passion of Kathleen Duveen.* Novel. London: Stanley Paul, 1913.

—. *Elizabeth's Prisoner.* Novel. London: Stanley Paul, 1914. London: Federation Press, 1925.

—. *A Girl of High Adventure.* Fiction for girls. London: Chambers, 1914.

—. *The Wooing of Monica.* Novel. London: John Long, 1914.

—. *The Darling of the School.* Fiction for girls. London: Chambers, 1915. Notes: Illus. W.A. Cuthbertson.

—. *The Daughter of a Soldier.* Fiction for girls. New York: Hurst, 1915.

—. *Daughters of Today.* Novel. London: Henry Frowde, 1916. London: Hodder & Stoughton, 1917. Notes: Published earlier as *Engaged to be Married* (1890).

—. *The Maid Indomitable.* Fiction for girls. London: Ward, Lock, 1916.

—. *Mother Mary: A Story for Girls.* Fiction for girls. London: Chambers, 1916.

—. *Better Than Riches.* Novel. London: Chambers, 1917.

—. and Robert Eustace. "The Detections of Miss Cusack." *The Princess of the Revels.* Ed. Douglas G. Greene and Jack Adrian. Ontario: Battered Silicon Dispatch Box, 1998. Notes: With the original illustrations by Victor Venner, Ernest Prater and R.W. Wallace.

Secondary sources

Flint, Kate. *The Woman Reader, 1837–1914.* Oxford: Clarendon Press, 1993.

Loeber, Rolf. "Irish Women Novelists in the 19th Century". Ireland and the Novel in the 19th Century Conference. CEIR, Cardiff University, 14–16 Sept. 2001.

Mhac an tSaoi, Máire. [Mac Entee/ Cruise O'Brien, Máire]. Comhaimseartha.

Corca Dhuibhne, Co. Chiarraí. Filíocht, gearrscéalaíocht, scríbhneoireacht acadúil, aistriúchán, beathaisnéis.

Saolaíodh Máire i mBaile Átha Cliath i 1922 ach b'as Corca Dhuibhne a tháinig muintir a máthar. Triúr a bhí sa chlann, agus ba í Máire an duine ba shine. Polaiteoir ab ea a hathair, Seán Mac an tSaoi, a bhí ina Thánaiste i rialtas De Valera, agus múinteoir ab ea a máthair, Máiréad (*née* de Brún) Mhac an tSaoi. Fuair Máire a cuid scolaíochta in Alexandra College, i nDún Chaoin, agus i gClochar Loreto, Ráth Fearnáin. Tar éis di BA a bhaint amach sna Nuatheangacha agus sa Léann Ceilteach ó Choláiste na hOllscoile, Baile Átha Cliath, d'fhreastail sí ar Óstaí an Rí agus glaodh chun an bharra í sa bhliain 1944. Scríobh sí a tráchtas máistreachta ar an bhfile Duibhneach, Piaras Feirtéar. D'oibrigh sí i Scoil an Léinn Cheiltigh, Institiúid Ard-Léinn Bhaile Átha Cliath, agus ansin chuaigh sí chuig Páras na Fraince chun staidéar a dhéanamh ag an Institut des Hautes Études, Sorbonne. Thosaigh sí ag obair sa Roinn Gnóthaí Eachtracha i 1947 agus chaith sí tréimhsí i bPáras, i Maidrid agus sa Chongó. Bhí sí ar fhoireann an *English–Irish Dictionary* (Baile Átha Cliath: Oifig an tSoláthair, 1959), ach d'fhill sí ar an Roinn Gnóthaí Eachtracha ansin, mar a raibh cúraimí éagsúla uirthi: An Deasc Idirnáisiúnta um Ghnóthaí Eachtracha, Toscaireacht Éireannach ag an gComhdháil Ghinearálta dena NA, agus Ionadaí na hÉireann ag Comhairle na hEorpa, Strasbourg.

Phós sí Conor Cruise O'Brien i 1962, agus d'éirigh sí as a post. Tá beirt pháistí uchtaithe acu. Chónaigh sí san Afraic agus ansin i Nua-Eabhrac, mar ar thug sí léachtaí ar chúlra na Litríochta Angla-Éireannaí ag Queen's College. Chaith sí seal mar Aoi-léachtóir i Roinn an Bhéaloidis, University of Pennsylvania i 1989. Tá sí ag cur fúithi i mBinn Éadair lena fear céile faoi láthair. Is mar fhile atá clú agus cáil bainte amach ag Máire. Cuireadh cúig chnuasach filíochta léi i gcló idir 1956 agus 1999. "Téamaí a bhaineann le Corca Dhuibhne, le stair agus le seanlitríocht na tíre, agus le deora an tsaoil, a chleachtann sí" (Ó Góilidhe 1975, 135). Deineann sí a cuid filíochta a aithris ar na caiséidí *Ómós do Scoil Dhún Chaoin* (Claddagh Records, 1970) agus *Guth an Fhile* (Cló Iar-Chonnachta, 1992). Foilsíodh dánta léi i mórán díolamaí, mar shampla: *An Crann faoi Bhláth / The Flowering Tree* (1991), *Ireland's Women* (1994), *Modern Irish Writing* (1979), agus *Field Day Anthology of Irish Writing* (1991). Aistríodh a saothar go hEabhrais, go Seapáinis, go Fraincis, go Gearmáinis agus go Béarla. Bronnadh D.Litt Celt. honoris causa uirthi ó Ollscoil na hÉireann sa bhliain 1992 agus bhuaigh sí an O'Shaughnessy Poetry Award of The Irish American Cultural Institute i 1998.

Tá mórán oibre déanta ag Máire mar aistritheoir agus mar eagarthóir. Tá filíocht na Gaeilge clasaicí aistrithe go Béarla aici in *A Heart Full of Thought*, agus filíocht ón ré chéanna curtha in eagar aici in irisí acadúla. Tá filíocht Ghaeilge ón seachtú agus ón ochtú haois aistrithe aici freisin in *Trasládáil*. Sa leabhar *Dhá Sgéal Artúraíochta*, ba í a chum an leagan Gaeilge de na scéalta agus a chóirigh iad. D'aistrigh sí filíocht a huncail, an Mons. de Brún, ó Bhéarla go Gaeilge. Tá sí tar éis an iris, *Poetry Ireland Review*, a chur in eagar. Foilsíodh aistí léi in irisí éagsúla, mar shampla in *Studies*, *XXXXIV* (1955), *The Celtic Consciousness* (Celtic Arts of Canada, 1981), *Studia Hibernica* (1984–8), *Oghma 2*, *The Southern Review* (1995), agus sa leabhar *The Pleasures of Gaelic Poetry*. Foilsíodh a dírbheathaisnéis le déanaí, *The Same Age as the State* (2003).

Máire Mhac an tSaoi was born in Dublin in 1922, but her mother's people were from West Kerry. There were three in the family and she was the eldest. Her father, Seán Mac an tSaoi, was a politician, who was Tánaiste in de Valera's Government, and her mother, Mairéad (*née* de Brún), was a teacher. Máire received her schooling in Alexandra College, in Dunquin, Co. Kerry, and in Loreto Convent, Rathfarnham, Co. Dublin. After graduating with a degree in modern languages and Celtic studies from UCD she attended King's Inns and was called to the bar in 1944. She wrote her Master's thesis on a poet from West Kerry, Piaras Feirtéar. She worked in the School of Celtic Studies, Dublin Institute of Advanced Studies and she then went to Paris to study at the Institute of Higher Learning at the Sorbonne. She started working in the Department of Foreign Affairs in 1947 and she spent periods in Paris, Madrid and the Congo. She was on the staff of the *English–Irish Dictionary* (Baile Átha Cliath: Oifig an tSoláthair, 1959) but then returned to the Department of Foreign Affairs, where she held a number of positions: at the International Desk of Foreign Affairs, Irish Delegation at the General Assembly of the UN and as Irish representative at the European Council, Strasbourg.

She married Conor Cruise O'Brien in 1962, and gave up her job. They have two children. She lived in Africa and then in New York, where she gave lectures at Queen's College on the background of Anglo-Irish Literature. She spent a while as visiting lecturer in the Department of Folklore, University of Pennsylvania, in 1989. She is currently living in Howth with her husband. It is primarily as a poet that she is famous. Five collections of her poetry, were published between 1956 and 1999. West Kerry, the history and ancient literature of Ireland and life's sorrows are the themes that feature in her poetry according to Ó Góilidhe (1975, 135). She recites her poetry on the cassettes *Ómós do Scoil Dhún Chaoin* (Claddagh Records, 1970) and *Guth an Fhile* (Cló Iar-Chonnachta, 1992). Many of her poems were published in collections of poetry, for example: *The Flowering Tree* (1991), *Ireland's Women* (1994), *Modern Irish Writing* (1979), and *Field Day Anthology of Irish Writing* (1991). Her work has been translated into Hebrew, Japanese, French, German and English. She was awarded an honorary DLitt Celt by the NUI in 1992, and she won the O'Shaughnessy Poetry Award of the Irish American Cultural Institute in 1998.

She has done a lot of work as a translator and editor. She has translated poetry from classical Irish to English in *A Heart Full of Thought*, and she has edited poetry from the same era in academic journals. She has also translated poetry from the seventeenth and eighteenth centuries in *Trasládáil*. In *Dhá Sgéal Artúraíochta* she has written and edited the Irish version of the stories. She has translated the poetry of her uncle, Mons. de Brún, from English to Irish. She has edited the journal, *Poetry Ireland Review.* Her essays have been published in various journals, for example in *Studies, XXXXIV* (1955), and in the book *The Pleasures of Gaelic Poetry.* She recently published her autobiography, *The Same Age as the State* (2003).

Select bibliography

Mhac an tSaoi, Máire.
—. Eag. *Dhá Sgéal Artúraíochta.* Scríbhneoireacht acadúil, litríocht. N.p.: n.p., 1946. Baile Átha Cliath: Institiúid Ard-Léinn Bhaile Átha Cliath, 1984.
—. "Filíocht den tSeachtú Aois Déag." Scríbhneoireacht acadúil, léirmheastóireacht. *Celtica* 1.1 (1954): 141–57.
—. *Margadh na Saoire.* Filíocht. N.p.: n.p., 1956. Baile Átha Cliath: Sáirséal agus Dill, 1971.
—. aist. *A Heart Full of Thought.* Filíocht, aistriúchán. Dublin: Dolmen, 1959.
—. aist. *Miserere.* Filíocht, aistriúchán. Leis an Mons. de Brún. Baile Átha Cliath: Gill & Macmillan, 1971.
—. agus Conor Cruise O'Brien. *Concise History of Ireland.* Scríbhneoireacht acadúil, stair. London: Thames & Hudson, 1972.
—. *Coladh an Ghaiscígh agus véarsaí eile.* Filíocht. Baile Átha Cliath: Sáirséal agus Dill, 1973.
—. *An Galar Dubhach.* Filíocht. Baile Átha Cliath: Sáirséal agus Dill, 1980.
—. *An Cion go dtí Seo.* Filíocht. Baile Átha Cliath: Sáirséal – Ó Marcaigh, 1987.
—. aist. *Trasládáil.* Filíocht, aistriúchán. Belfast: Lagan Press, 1997.
—. *Shoa agus dánta eile.* Filíocht. Baile Átha Cliath: Sáirséal – Ó Marcaigh, 1999.

—. *A Bhean óg ón…* Úrscéalaíocht. Indreabhán: Cló Iar-Chonnachta, 2001.

—. *The Same Age as the State.* Autobiography. Dublin: O'Brien Press, 2003.

Secondary sources

Cleeve, Brian. "Mhac an tSaoi, Máire." *Dictionary of Irish Writers:Writers in the Irish Language.* Cork: Mercier, 1971.

O'Brien, Frank. "Máire Mhac an tSaoi." *Filíocht Ghaeilge na Linne Seo: Staidéar Criticiúil.* Leabhair Thaighde 17. N.p.: n.p., 1968. Baile Átha Cliath: An Clóchomhar, 1978. 163–202.

Ó Cearnaigh, Seán. "Mac an tSaoi, Máire Mhac an tSaoi." *Scríbhneoirí na Gaeilge 1945–1995.* Baile Átha Cliath: Comhar, 1995.

Ó Tuama, Seán. "Saothar Teann Tíorthúil." *Feasta* (Márta 1957).

Uí Nia, Gearóidín. eag. "Mhac an tSaoi, Máire." *Eolaire Chló Iar-Chonnachta de Scríbhneoirí Gaeilge.* Indreabhán: Cló Iar-Chonnachta, 1998.

Mhic Ghearailt, Caitlín. Comhaimseartha. Leataoibh Meánach agus Cill Chúile, Corca Dhuibhne, Co. Chiarraí. Beathaisnéis, seanchas, cuimhní cinn.

Saolaíodh Caitlín i Leataoibh Meánach agus chuaigh sí chun cónaithe go Cill Chúile sna 1940adaí nuair a phós sí. Blúirí gearra ar a hóige agus ar phríomhimeachtaí an phobail agus í ag fás aníos atá ina leabhar, a foilsíodh i 1992.

Select bibliography

Mhic Ghearailt, Caitlín.

—. *Nach Aon Saol mar a Thagann Sé.* Beathaisnéis, seanchas, cuimhní cinn. Baile Átha Cliath: Coiscéim, 1992.

Mhic Ghiolla Chuda, Clíodhna [Mhic Ghiolla Chuda, Clíona]. Comhaimseartha. Rinn Ó gCuanach, Na Déise, Co. Phort Láirge. Scríbhneoireacht acadúil, aistí.

Tá Clíodhna ag cur fúithi i gCnocán an Phaoraigh Uachtarach. Oibríonn sí le Meitheal Mara na Rinne (Ó Macháin agus Nic Dhonnchadha 1997, 95–6). Ina haiste in *An Linn Bhuí 1* (1997, 22–5) chuir sí síos ar fhorbairt thionscal na n-oisrí i nDún Garbhán, agus ar an tslí a bhfuil borradh an tionscail seo tar éis dul i bhfeidhm ar mhuintir na háite.

Select bibliography

Mhic Ghiolla Chuda, Clíodhna.

—. "Oisrí sa Chuan." *An Linn Bhuí: Iris Ghaeltacht na nDéise.* Scríbhneoireacht acadúil, aiste. Eag. Pádraig Ó Macháin agus Aoibheann Nic Dhonnchadha. Vol. 1. Baile Átha Cliath: Leabhair na Linne, 1997.

Mhic Mhurchú, Dóirín. Comhaimseartha. An Rinn, Na Déise, Co. Phort Láirge. Scríbhneoireacht acadúil / stair áitiúil.

Saolaíodh Dóirín i Learpholl, Sasana i 1930. Tógadh i gCill Chathlaigh í, Co. an Chabháin. Phós sí agus bhí cúigear páistí acu. D'oibrigh sí mar oide Spáinnise agus mar shaor-iriseoir. Chónaigh sí san Astráil ag tús na 1960adaí. Tá sí ag maireachtáil sa Rinn ó shin i leith.

Select bibliography
Mhic Mhurchú, Dóirín.
—. *Bealach na Bó Finne.* Scríbhneoireacht acadúil / stair, taisteal, creideamh. Baile
Átha Cliath: Coiscéim,1994.
—. "An Stór." *An Linn Bhuí: Iris Ghaeltacht na nDéise.* Aiste. Eag. Pádraig Ó
Macháin agus Aoibheann Nic Dhonnchadha.Vol. 4. Baile Átha Cliath: Leabhair
na Linne, 2000.
—. "An Chois." *An Linn Bhuí: Iris Ghaeltacht na nDéise.* Aiste. Eag. Pádraig Ó
Macháin agus Aoibheann Nic Dhonnchadha.Vol. 6. Baile Átha Cliath: Leabhair
na Linne, 2002.

Mhic Néill, Seosaimhín [Aherne, Seosaimhín]. 1895–1969. Mainistir Fhear Maí, Co. Chorcaí agus Durlas Éile, Co. Thiobraid Árann. Litríocht, aistriúchán.

Saolaíodh Seosaimhín i Mainistir Fhear Maí. Lucht gnó ab ea a muintir agus bhí cúigear muirear orthu. Bhí Gaeilge ag a tuismitheoirí de réir dealraimh. Fuair Seosaimhín a cuid meánscolaíochta i Scoil Loreto, agus ghnóthaigh sí BA sna Nuatheangacha ó Choláiste na hOllscoile, Baile Átha Cliath. Chaith sí tamall ag múineadh i gCo. Mhaigh Eo, agus ansin sa chlochar i nDurlas Éile, Co. Thiobraid Árann. Bhí sí páirteach i gConradh na Gaeilge agus i gCumann na mBan i mBaile Átha Cliath agus i nDurlas Éile.

Bhí sí geallta le Piaras Mac Cana, ach cailleadh é siúd sa bhliain 1919. Phós sí James Mac Néill cúig bliana níos déanaí, deartháir le hEoin Mac Néill, an scoláire mór a raibh baint aige le bunú Chonradh na Gaeilge. Chaith James cúig bliana ina Ard-Choimisinéir ag an Saorstát i Londain, agus ansin fuair sé post mar Phríomh-Ghobharnóir na hÉireann sa bhliain 1928. Bhí rialtas Fhianna Fáil, 1932–48, go mór i gcoinne oifig an Phríomh-Ghobharnóra, agus briseadh Mac Néill as a phost.

D'éirigh Seosaimhín gníomhach i gcúrsaí polaitíochta. Thug sí tacaíocht do Chlann na Poblachta agus chuaigh sí go dtí An Háig mar Aire na hÉireann sa bhliain 1950. Ba é an chéad uair a tugadh a leithéid de phost do bhean in Éirinn. Chuir sí suim sa cheol agus san ealaín agus bhí baint aici le Bantracht na Tuaithe. D'aistrigh sí *Finnsgéalta ó India* go Gaeilge; ba é an t-aon leabhar amháin léi a foilsíodh.

Select bibliography
Mhic Néill, Seosaimhín.
—. aist. *Finnsgéalta ó India.* Litríocht, aistriúchán. Baile Átha Cliath: Comhlucht
Oideachais na h-Éireann, 1932.

Secondary sources
Breathnach, Diarmuid agus Máire Ní Mhurchú. "Mac Néill, Seosaimhín (1895–1969)."
1882–1982 Beathaisnéis a Trí. Baile Átha Cliath: An Clóchomhar, 1992.
de Hae, Risteárd agus Brighid Ní Dhonnchadha, Eag. *Clár Litridheacht na Nua-Ghaedhilge 1850–1936.* Baile Átha Cliath: Oifig Dhíolta Foilseacháin Rialtais, 1938.

Michael, Christine. Contemporay. Cork. Poetry, short stories.

Known as Nottingham's Singing Poet, she trained initially as a teacher and in 1986 she took an MA in Anglo-Irish literature at UCC. She has been involved with many poetry and creative writing groups, was co-founder of the Cork Women's Poetry Circle with Máire Bradshaw and founded the Community Expansions in Literature festival. Michael has performed her poetry in venues across the UK, Ireland and Germany.

Select bibliography
Michael, Christine.
—. ed. *The Box Under the Bed: A Collection of Work by Women Writing in Cork.* Poetry. Cork: Bradshaw Books, 1986.

Miller, Áine. Contemporary. Poetry.

The 1992 winner of the Kavanagh Prize for an unpublished collection of poems entitled *Goldfish in a Baby Bath*. This has since been published (1994), and she followed it with *Touchwood* (2000).

Select bibliography
Miller, Áine.
—. *Goldfish in a Baby Bath*. Poetry. Dublin: Salmon, 1994.
—. *Touchwood*. Poetry. Cliffs of Moher, Co. Clare: Salmon, 2000.

Monkhouse, Elisabeth. Comhaimseartha. Ros Cré, Co. Thiobraid Árann / Melbourne, An Astráil. Beathaisnéis.

Saolaíodh Elisabeth i Melbourne i 1970, agus chaith sí formhór a hóige ag taisteal lena muintir. Bhain sí céim mhúinteoireachta amach agus thosaigh sí ag taisteal timpeall an domhain. Chaith sí tréimhsí ag taisteal i Meiriceá agus san Eoraip, stop sí in Éirinn i 1992, agus phós sí fear ó Ros Cré, mar a bhfuil sí ina cónaí fós. Chaith sí roinnt ama ag obair sa tSeapáin agus chuaigh sí thar n-ais go dtí an Astráil cúpla uair. Ghnóthaigh sí céim MA san Oideachas le déanaí. Foilsíodh leabhar amháin léi, beathaisnéis mhná ó Thiobraid Árann, Daisy Bates, a d'oibrigh i measc na ndaoine dúchasacha san Astráil, agus aistríodh an leabhar seo go Gaeilge.

Elisabeth Monkhouse was born in Melbourne in 1970, and spent most of her childhood travelling with her family. After taking a teaching degree she set off to see the world, and having travelled through America and Europe she stopped briefly in Ireland in 1992 and married a man from Roscrea, where she still lives. She has spent some time working in Japan and made several trips back to Australia. She has recently completed an MA in Education. Her only published work is a biography of a Tipperary woman, Daisy Bates, who worked among the Australian aboriginal peoples, which has been translated into Irish.

Select bibliography
Monkhouse, Elisabeth.
—. agus Emmet Arrigan. *Daisy Bates*. Beathaisnéis. aist. Ciardha Ní Mháirtín. Baile Átha Cliath: An Gúm, 1999.

Moore, Emma [E.M. Lauderdale]. *fl.*1880–90. Cork. Handbook, journalism, fiction.

Married to George F. Moore of Guys' Printing Works in Cork, she was the compiler of many of the *Guy's Directories* for the city and county, including *Guy's Illustrated Gossiping Guide to the South of Ireland* (1885). She also contributed to a number of periodicals, including *The Munster Journal* (1888–90), *Southern Industry* (1889) and *Shandon Bells* (1889). She published the novel *Tivoli* in 1886 under the pseudonym E.M. Lauderdale. Moore died in 1916.

Select bibliography
Moore, Emma.
—. *Tivoli*. Novel. Cork: Guy, 1886.
—. *Handbook to St Anne's Church, Shandon*. Handbook. Cork: Guy, n.d.
—. Francis Guy's *Illustrated Descriptive & Gossiping Guide to the South of Ireland: Describing also the Cork Exhibition of 1883*. Cork: Guy, n.d.

Morton, May [Morton, Mary Elizabeth]. 1876–1957. Co. Limerick. Poetry.

Born and raised in Co. Limerick, she moved to Belfast in her twenties. She was a founding member of the Young Ulster Society and was associated with the Quota Press in Belfast. She also became the vice-principal of the Girls' Model School, a post she held until 1934. She published volumes of poetry, as well as contributing poems to journals such as *Rann*, *Lagan* and *Poetry Ireland* in the 1940s and 1950s. She broadcast on the BBC and Radio Éireann and also played an active role in Belfast PEN, the writers' organization. One of her compositions, *Spindle and Shuttle*, won the Festival of Britain Northern Ireland poetry award and appeared in published form in 1951.

Select bibliography
Morton, May.
—. *Dawn and Afterglow*. Poetry. Belfast: Quota, 1936.
—. *Masque in Maytime*. Poetry. Lisburn: Lisnagarvey, 1948.
—. *Spindle and Shuttle*. Poetry. Belfast: HMSO, 1951.
—. *Sung to the Spinning Wheel*. Poetry. Belfast: Quota, 1952.

Secondary sources
W.P.M. "Rev. of *Masque in Maytime*, by May Morton." *Dublin Magazine* new series 25.4 (1950): 67–9.

Mould, Daphne D.C. Pochin. Contemporary. Co. Cork. History, religious writing.

Born in 1920 in Salisbury, and, living close to Stonehenge, she became interested in archaeology. She was also influenced by her mother's interest in photography. After graduating from Edinburgh University she came to Ireland in 1951 to research Celtic history and decided to settle in Aherla, near Cork city. Her other interest is flying, and aerial photographs feature in her publications. She has the distinction of being Ireland's first woman flying intructor. Her first book, *The Roads from the Isles*, describing the old cattle tracks in the Scottish Western Isles, was published in 1950, and she has continued to write steadily since then. She has a strong investment in religion, which is reflected in her writings. In 1993 she received an honorary doctorate from UCC, when she was described as "a scientist and a free spirit, a courageous pioneer and an outstanding woman warrior".

Select bibliography

Mould, Daphne D.C. Pochin.

—. *The Roads from the Isles: A Study of the North-West Highland Tracks.* Edinburgh: Oliver & Boyd, 1950.

—. *Scotland of the Saints.* Religious writing. London: Batsford, 1952.

—. *Ireland of the Saints.* Religious writing. London: Batsford, 1953.

—. *The Rock of Truth.* Religious writing. Dublin: Sheed & Ward, 1953.

—. *West-Over-Sea: An Account of Life in the Outer Hebrides Set against the Legendary and Historical Backgrounds.* Local history. Edinburgh: Oliver & Boyd, 1953.

—. *Irish Pilgrimage.* Religious writing. Dublin: Gill, 1955.

—. *The Mountains of Ireland.* Local history. London: Batsford, 1955.

—. *The Celtic Saints: Our Heritage.* Religious writing. Dublin: Clonmore & Reynolds, 1956.

—. *The Irish Dominicans: The Friar Preachers in the History of Catholic Ireland.* History. Dublin: Dominican, 1957.

—. *Peter's Boat: A Convert's Experience of Catholic Living.* Religious writing. Dublin: Clonmore & Reynolds, 1959.

—. *The Lord is Risen: The Liturgy of Paschal Time.* Religious writing. Dublin: Catholic Truth Society of Ireland, 1960.

—. *Irish Saints.* Religious writing. Dublin: Catholic Truth Society of Ireland, 1961.

—. *The Second Vatican Council.* Religious writing. Dublin: Catholic Truth Society of Ireland, 1963.

—. *The Irish Saints: Short Biographies of the Principal Irish Saints from the Time of St Patrick to that of St Laurence O'Toole.* Religious writing. Dublin: Clonmore & Reynolds, 1964.

—. *Saint Brigid.* Religious writing. Dublin: Clonmore & Reynolds, 1964.

—. *Saint Finbar of Cork.* Religious writing. Dublin: Catholic Truth Society of Ireland, 1965.

—. *The Aran Islands.* Local history. Newton Abbott: David & Charles, 1972.

—. *Ireland from the Air.* History. Newton Abbott: David & Charles, 1972.

—. *The Monasteries of Ireland: An Introduction.* History. London: Batsford, 1976.

—. *The Mountains of Ireland.* History. Dublin: Gill & Macmillan, 1976.

—. *Valentia: Portrait of an Island.* Local history. Dublin: Blackwater, 1978.

—. *Discovering Cork.* History, travel writing. Dingle, Co. Kerry: Brandon, 1991.

—. "Brother Gerard of Taizé." *Miscellany of Creative Writings.* Religious writing. Ed. Sarah McNamara. Parteen, Co. Limerick: n.p., 1997. 103–5.

Secondary sources

M.J. O'K. "Rev. of *Irish Pilgrimage*, by Daphne D.C. Pochin Mould." *Blarney Magazine* 10 (1956): 70–71.

Spray, Glenys. "A Magnificent Woman in her Flying Machine." *Wise Women: A Portrait.* Cork: Bradshaw Books, 1994. 129–37.

Mount Cashell, Lady Margaret [Margaret Jane King]. 1772–1835.
Kilworth. Children's writing, handbooks.

As a child, she was a pupil of Mary Wollestonecraft, who was then working as a governess to her family in Mitchelstown. This had a lasting effect on her politics, and she remained an independent-minded woman through-out her life, maintaining an interest in the Irish republican cause, much to the chagrin of her husband, Stephen, Earl Mount Cashell. In 1802, the Mount Cashells travelled with their small children and Katherine Wilmot (*q.v.*), a neighbour and family friend, to the Continent. Travel had been impossible since 1789 and, although the Peace of Amiens had recently been declared, Europe was still a turbulent place for a party of nine aristo-crats to travel. Lady Mount Cashell, then thirty and pregnant with her seventh child, smuggled a man into her suite on the cross-channel boat because he could not get a passport. In Paris they dined with Tallyrand and Napoleon, and Margaret gave birth to another son. However, their tour was interrupted by Napoleon's military manoeuvres. Four of the Mount Cashell children had been left behind at Nimes with their tutor, and they escaped to Geneva. The family was later reunited in Rome, where she gave birth to her eighth child.

Soon after this, she fell in love with George William Tighe and left her husband to live in Pisa with him under the name Mrs Mason (taken from a Mary Wollestonecraft story), where the couple had two daughters. Her story is said to have inspired Shelley's "The Sensitive Plant". She was a writer of children's fiction and handbooks. Her handbooks relate to child-rearing, focusing specifically on medical matters. It is thought that she was also the author of two unpublished novels, *Selene* and the historical novel *Chieftain of Erin, Romance of the Time of Queen Elizabeth*. There are also pamphlets attributed to her, although their authorship has not been proved.

Select bibliography
Mount Cashell, Lady Margaret.
—. *Stories of Old Daniel, or, Tales of Wonder and Delight: Containing Narratives of Foreign Countries and Manners, and Designed as an Introduction to the Study of Voyages, Travels, and History in General.* Travel writing. London: Printed for M.J. Godwin at the Juvenile Library, 1813.

Secondary sources
Todd, Janet. *Daughters of Ireland: The Rebellious Kingsborough Sisters and the Making of a Modern Nation.* New York: Ballantine Books, 2004.

Moxley, Gina. Contemporary. Cork. Plays.

Born in 1957, she is probably best known as an actress. She has written for several RTÉ productions, including *The Hidden Basement Comedy Show*, *Hidden Agenda* and *Sunday Miscellany*. She has also written plays, including *Danti-Dan* (Project Theatre Dublin, 1995), *The Dog House* (Cottesloe Theatre London, 1997), *Toupes and Snare Drums* (Peacock Theatre, 1998) and *Tea Set* (Fishamble Theatre, 2000).

Moynihan, Hannah. *fl.*1916–23. Co. Kerry. Diary.

A cousin of the Power sisters (see Cis and Jo Power, *q.v.*), she was a member of Cumann na mBan. Hannah was involved in the production of anti-Treaty propaganda during the Civil War, and wrote for the Tralee newspaper *The*

Invincible. She was interned in Kilmainham Gaol in 1923, where she kept a jail journal.

Select bibliography
Moynihan, Hannah.
—. *Diary* (Unpub.) diary. Notes: Part of Kilmainham Gaol Collection.

Mullally, Siobhan. Contemporary. Cork. Academic writing.

Born in London, she grew up in Michelstown, Co. Cork. She is a graduate of UCC and the University of London. Mullally lectured in international law at the University of Hull from 1990 to 1995 and in 1995 she began lecturing in the Department of Law, UCC. While working at the Faculty of Law in the Univeristy of Pakistan (1992–3, 1995) she participated in a human rights investigation in Kashmir on behalf of the Human Rights Commission of Pakistan, and she has also worked in Kosovo. Her research interests include human rights, gender and law, equality law and refugee law. She is currently completing a doctorate at the European University Institute, Florence.

Select bibliography
Mullally, Siobhan.
—. "Women's Rights and Human Rights." *New Directions in Women's Studies for the 1990s.* Academic writing. Ed. Stacey, Phoenix and Hinds. London: Falmer, 1992. 113–24.
—. "Equality Guarantees in Irish Constitutional Law." *Ireland's Evolving Constitution: 1937–1997.* Academic writing. Ed. T. Murphy and P. Twomey. Oxford: Hart Publishing, 1998.
—. "Searching for Foundations in Irish Constitutional Law." Academic writing. *Irish Jurist* (1998): 333–50.
—. "Ireland's Legal and Extra-Legal Responses to the EC's Recommendation and Code of Practice on Protecting the Dignity of Women and Men at Work." *Comparative European Law on the Dignity of Women and Men at Work.* Academic writing. Portugal: Universidad da Fernando Pessao Press, 2001.
—. "The Irish Supreme Court and the Illegal Immigrants (Trafficking) Bill, 1999." Academic writing. *International Journal of Refugee Law* 13 (2001).
—. "Mainstreaming Equality in Ireland: A Fair and Inclusive Accommodation for All?" Academic writing. *Legal Studies* (2001).

Murphy, Clíona. Contemporary. Cork. Academic writing.

Born in Cork in 1957, she graduated from UCC with an MA in History in 1982. She took a PhD at the State University of New York. She is Professor of modern Western European history at Bakersfield University, California. Murphy is on the editorial board of the *Women's History Review* and the *Women's Studies Review.* Her research focuses on the history of women in Ireland, and she has published on nationalism, feminism, the Irish Women's Suffrage Movement and on H.G. Wells.

Select bibliography
Murphy, Clíona.
—. "H.G. Wells and Votes for Women." History. *The Wellsian* (1987): 11–20.

—. *The Women's Suffrage Movement and Irish Sociey in the Early Twentieth Century.* History. Brighton: Harvester, 1989.

—. and Maria Luddy, eds. *Women Surviving: Studies on Irish Women in the Nineteenth and Twentieth Centuries.* History. Dublin: Poolbeg, 1990.

—. "H.G. Wells." *Biographical Dictionary of Literary Influences 1800–1914.* Biography. Ed. John Powell. Westport, Conn: Greenwood, 2000. 441–2.

—. "Hannah Sheehy Skeffington." *Women in World History: A Biographical Encyclopedia.* History. Ed. Anne Commire and Deborah Klezmer. Vol. 8. Waterford, Conn: Yonkin, 2000.

—. "The Destruction of the Protestant Church and Dismemberment of the Empire: Charlotte Elizabeth's Outlook on Religious Tensions in Pre-Famine Ireland." History. *Women's Studies: An Interdisciplinary Journal* 30.6 (2001): 741–62.

—. Introduction. Special Issue, *Women's Studies: An Interdisciplinary Journal on Women and Ireland: A Historical Perspective* 30.6 (2001): 737–40.

Murphy, Dervla. Contemporary. Lismore, Co. Waterford. Travel writing, autobiography, journalism.

Born in 1931 in Lismore, Co. Waterford, she still lives there. She was the daughter of the Waterford County Librarian and was educated locally and at the Ursuline Convent in Waterford. She left before finishing school to care for her invalid mother. She always dreamed of travelling and writing and after her mother's death in 1962 she took off for India on her bicycle and worked with Tibetan refugees before returning home to write her first two books. She reached immediate fame with her first book, *Full Tilt* (1965), which was selected as the Book Society Alternative Choice for Ireland that year. This was followed by *Tibetan Foothold* (1966). Since then she has travelled in the most remote areas of India, the Middle East, Africa and South America and has achieved international renown for her accounts of these trips. Her writing has been described by one reviewer, Sara Wheeler, as "solid, chatty, unadorned and utterly reliable".

Murphy has also addressed political issues such as the Northern Ireland situation in *A Place Apart* (1978), which received the second Christopher Ewart-Biggs Memorial Prize, and again in 1984 in *Changing the Problem: Post-Forum Reflections.* She also contributed to a collection of personal reflections from both sides of the border, edited by Paddy Logue (1999), which also included articles by fellow-writers Seamus Deane and Frank McGuinness, and the singer Christy Moore. *Woman's World* (1995), in the Travellers' Tales Guides series, also included her writing. In *Race to the Finish?* (1981) she wrote about the threat to mankind posed by the nuclear arms industry. She has also written an account of her childhood and earlier years in *Wheels within Wheels* (1979).

Murphy has received several awards, including the American Irish Foundation Literary Award in 1975 and the Irish-American Cultural Institute Literary Award in 1985. She has one daughter, Rachel, who has accompanied her on many of her trips, the first one when she was only five years old.

Select bibliography
Murphy, Dervla.

—. ed. *Down and Out in Paris and London.* Travel writing.

—. *Full Tilt: Ireland to India with a Bicycle.* Travel writing. London: John Murray, 1965.

—. *Tibetan Foothold.* Travel writing. London: John Murray, 1966.

—. *The Waiting Land: A Spell in Nepal.* Travel writing. London: John Murray, 1967.

—. *In Ethiopia with a Mule.* Travel writing. London: John Murray, 1968.

—. *On a Shoestring to Coorg: An Experience of South India.* Travel writing. London: John Murray, 1976.

—. *Where the Indus is Young: A Winter in Baltistan.* Travel writing. London: John Murray, 1977.

—. *A Place Apart: Northern Ireland.* Political writing. London: John Murray, 1978.

—. *Wheels within Wheels: Autobiography.* Autobiography. London: John Murray, 1979.

—. *Race to the Finish? The Nuclear Stakes.* Political writing. London: John Murray, 1981.

—. *Eight Feet in the Andes.* Travel writing. London: John Murray, 1983.

—. *Changing the Problem: Post-Forum Reflections.* Political writing. Mullingar, Co. Westmeath: Lilliput, 1984.

—. contributor. *Bell, Bike and Saddle.* Radio programme. Prod. Jim Lockhart. RTÉ Radio 1. 20 May 1985.

—. and Klaus D. Francke. *Ireland.* Travel writing. London: Orbis, 1985.

—. *Muddling Through in Madagascar.* Travel writing. London: John Murray, 1985.

—. *Tales from Two Cities: Travel of Another Sort.* Travel writing. London: John Murray, 1987.

—. *Cameroon with Egbert.* Travel writing. London: John Murray, 1989.

—. "Foreword." *Grandmother and Wolfe Tone.* History. By Hubert Butler. Mullingar, Co. Westmeath: Lilliput, 1990.

—. ed. *Images of India by Sophie Baker.* Travel writing. London: Hamlyn, 1990.

—. ed. *Embassy to Constantinople: The Travels of Lady Mary Wortley Montague.* London: John Murray, 1992.

—. *Transylvania and Beyond.* Travel writing. London: John Murray, 1992.

—. *The Ukimwi Road: From Kenya to Zimbabwe.* Travel writing. London: John Murray, 1993.

—. *South Africa.* Travel writing. London: John Murray, 1995.

—. *South from the Limpopo: Travels through South Africa.* Travel writing. London: Overlook, 1998.

—. *Visiting Rwanda.* Travel writing. Mullingar, Co. Westmeath: Lilliput, 1998.

—. *One Foot in Laos.* Travel writing. London: John Murray, 1999.

—. contributor. *The Border: Personal Reflections from Ireland North and South.* Ed. Paddy Logue. Dublin: Oak Tree Press, 1999.

—. and John Harrison. *Off the Map.* Travel writing. London: Summersdale, 2001.

—. Foreword. *The Spirit of Rural Ireland.* Travel writing. By Christopher Somerville. London: New Holland, 2001.

—. *Through the Embers of Chaos: Balkan Journeys.* Travel writing. London: John Murray, 2002.

Secondary sources
Burnett, Sandy, interviewer. Interview with Dervla Murphy. *Calling the Tune.* Radio programme. RTÉ Radio 1. 13 Nov. 1999.

Doyle, Ann, presenter. "Life and Times of Dervla Murphy." *Marian Finucane Show.* Radio programme. RTÉ Radio 1. 30 Apr. 2001.

Finucane, Marian, presenter. Interview with Dervla Murphy. *Women Today.* Radio programme. RTÉ Radio 1. 15 Oct. 1979.

Phelan, Mary, prod. Interview with Rachel Murphy about her childhood and her mother, Dervla Murphy. *Growing Up Different.* Radio programme. Radio programme. RTÉ Radio 1. 17 Aug. 1996.

Quinn, John, prod. Interview with Dervla Murphy. *Portrait of the Artist as a Young Girl.* RTÉ Radio 1. 16 Sept. 1985.

Murphy, Hazel. *fl.* 1932–34. Clonmel, Co. Tipperary. Novels.

Born in Clonmel, Co. Tipperary, in 1908, she was educated in Dublin and in England. She travelled extensively in Europe and lived in different parts of Munster (Tipperary, Waterford and Limerick) and in Kildare.

Select bibliography
Murphy, Hazel.
—. *Himself.* Novel. London: Methuen, 1932.
—. *The Travelling People.* Novel. London: Collins, 1934.

Murphy, Kate Mary [Brigid and Elizabeth Townsbridge]. 1840–85. Cork. Short stories, poetry.

Daughter of a coal merchant, whose family moved from Ballyhooley to Pope's Quay in Cork city, she herself opened a small coal store in Cork after her father's death in 1865, but found it difficult to make ends meet, and eventually her business failed. From then on, her only income came from her writing – she published in many Irish newspapers, contributing short stories and poems to the *Cork Examiner, The Boston Pilot, Young Ireland, The Nation* (as "Brigid") and others.

She had a series of health problems throughout her life, more than likely as a result of the poverty she struggled against. She eventually entered the South Infirmary hospital in 1884 where she died at the age of forty-five, possibly from cancer.

Select bibliography
Murphy, Kate Mary.
—. "How Tom Dillon Became a Zoave, or The Story of County Cork." *Cabinet of Irish Literature.* Short story. Ed. Katherine Tynan. Vol. 4. London: Gresham, 1905.
—. "Sentenced to Death." Poetry. *The Nation,* n.d.

Secondary sources
Russell, Matthew. "Our Poets, No. 14: Katharine Murphy (Brigid)." *Irish Monthly* 13 (1885): 433–40.
Sherlock, Thomas. "Kate Mary Murphy (Brigid)." *Young Ireland* 11 (1885): 320–21.

Murphy, Nancy. Contemporary. Limerick. Handbooks.

Born in Roscommon in 1945, she lives in Limerick, is a trained general nurse and midwife and manages a Well Woman Clinic in Newcastle West, Co. Limerick.

Select bibliography
Murphy, Nancy.
—. *Self-Preparation for Childbirth*. Handbook. Limerick: Tiernan Publications, 1993.
—. *Walkabout Nenagh*. Local history. Nenagh, Co. Tipperary: Relay, 1994.
—. *Guilty or Innocent? The Cormack Brothers – Trial, Execution and Exhumation*. History. Nenagh, Co. Tipperary: Relay, 1997.
—. and Fiona O'Brien, comp. *More of Nenagh's Yesterdays*. Local history. Nenagh, Co. Tipperary: Relay, 1997.
—. *A Trip Through Tipperary Lakeside*. Travel writing. Nenagh, Co. Tipperary: Relay, 1997.

Murphy, Orla. Contemporary. Cork. Short stories, plays, poetry, novels, fiction.

Born in Cork city to an artistic family, she is a granddaughter of Joseph Higgins, a painter and sculptor, daughter of Seamus Murphy, the sculptor and author of *Stone Mad*, and sister of Colm Murphy, a painter and musician. Her works have been included in anthologies, performed on stage and broadcast on radio.

Select bibliography
Murphy, Orla.
—. *The Sway of Winter*. Novel. Dublin: Lilliput, 2002.

Murray, Teri. Contemporary. Limerick city. Plays, short stories, poetry.

Born in England, she grew up in Dublin but now lives in Limerick. She won her first award for a children's play at the Wicklow Community Awards competition in 1987, and has since published short stories, poetry and magazine articles. Another play, *A Time Under Heaven*, centred on poverty in Limerick for several generations and was performed at the Belltable in 1996. She has published one collection of poetry with Limerick poet Liam Mulligan, *Coddle and Tripe* (1998). She has also edited an anthology entitled *Scratches on the Wall*.

Select bibliography
Murray, Teri.
—. ed. *Scratches on the Wall*. Limerick: Tholsol, 1995.
—. *A Time Under Heaven*. 1996 (Unpub.) Play.
—. and Liam Mulligan. *Coddle and Tripe*. Poetry. Ennis, Co. Clare: Stonebridge, 1998.

Neeson, Geraldine, née O'Sullivan. 1895–1980. Cork. Autobiography, journalism.

Born in Sunday's Well, Cork, to a large, affluent family. Her father was a tea, wine and spirit merchant in the city, her mother was a Fitzgerald, originally from Bandon. Throughout her life she was deeply involved in the artistic and cultural life of the city. She was constantly involved in theatre and counted Michael Mac Liammóir and Hilton Edwards among her closest friends. An accomplished piano player, she often gave recitals in the Imperial Hotel, Cork, a number of which were attended by Adele Astaire and her well known brother, Fred. Neeson's other great passion was politics and from an early age she adopted a decidedly Republican stance. Over time she became close friends with Mary (*q.v.*), Annie and Terence MacSwiney, teaching for a time in their school, St Ita's in Belgrave Place, Cork. Neeson was also friends with Muriel Murphy and attended her wedding to Terence MacSwiney. As a result of her close friendship with the MacSwineys, Neeson was often at the heart of Republican activism. She subsequently met her husband, Sean Neeson, through these mutual friends and they married in Mount Mellary, Co. Waterford, in 1925. In later years Sean was closely connected to the music department in UCC. Geraldine and Sean both worked for 6CK radio, which was based in the Women's Gaol, Cork, during the early 1920s. Although 6CK was a short-lived project, it was of great national importance, not least because it was the first radio station outside of Dublin. Geraldine also contributed to the *Cork Examiner* over many years. She died in Cork in 1980, and her autobiography was published posthumously.

Select bibliography
Neeson, Geraldine.
—. *In My Mind's Eye: The Cork I Knew and Loved*. Autobiography. N.p.: Prestige Books, n.d.
—. *Our Heritage – Cork*. History. Dublin: Bruce Spicer Ltd, 1971.

Neville, Grace. Contemporary. Cork. Academic writing.

Born in Cork city, she took a BA in French and Irish at UCC, followed by an MA in French. Her PhD is from the Université de Lille, where she then taught. She also taught at the Université de Metz before returning to UCC, where she is now a statutory lecturer in French. She has published on medieval French literature, the interface between French and Irish literature/culture from the medieval period onwards, and in the field of women's studies. She has given over 180 research presentations in France, Ireland and North America (including the French Senate, the Collège de France, the Sorbonne and Harvard). She is particularly interested in practitioners of "la nouvelle histoire", whose work she finds very useful.

Neville has recently begun to work in archives of previously unexplored material (in Ireland, England and France). Some of this work formed part of a 2004 RTÉ television documentary, *Not Fade Away*, which focused on the work of two young French women, Marguerite Mespoulet and Madelaine Mignon, amateur photographers who arrived in Ireland in 1913. They created seventy-five colour plates of Ireland, mostly of the West, and matched them with 160 pages of handwritten notes, all of which provide a fascinating photographic record and social history of the period. Her other publications include a jointly edited collection of essays on Franco-Irish relations from the early modern period onwards and a book on Continental European visitors to Cork (sixteenth century onwards), for publication in 2005, when Cork becomes European Capital of Culture. She is also working on a monograph on Irish emigration to North America.

Select bibliography
Neville, Grace.
—. "'She Never Then After That Forgot Him': Irishwomen and Emigration to the United States in Irish Folklore." Academic writing. *Mid-America: An Historical Review* 74.3 (1992): 271–89.
—. "Dark Lady of the Archives: Towards an Analysis of Women and Emigration of North America in Irish Folklore." *Chattel, Servant or Citizen: Women's Status in Church, State and Society.* Academic writing. Belfast: The Institute of Irish Studies /QUE, 1995. 200–214.
—. "L'Invention du mythe de Napoleon dans la mémoire irlandaise." Academic writing. *Revue de GRAAT Special Issue Irlande: Vision (s) / Revisions (s)* 19 (1998): 181–91.
—. "Cette Contrée Méconnue et si Souvent Outragée: Towards an Analysis of the Writings of J.J. Prevost, a Traveller in Mid-Nineteenth-Century Ireland." Academic writing. *Cucnos: Irlande – Exils* 15.2 (1999): 111–25.
—. historical consultant, translator. *Not Fade Away.* Television programme. Prod. Roy Esmonde. Townlands ser. RTÉ 1. 18 Aug. 2004.

Newsome, Phoebe. 1797–1851. Waterford, Limerick. Diaries.
A Quaker, she married William Newsome of Limerick in 1824. She wrote an unpublished journal, which in parts takes the form of a spiritual diary (Ms at the Dublin Friends Historical Library), between 1834 and 1851.

Select bibliography
Newsome, Phoebe.
—. *Journal,* 1834–51. (Unpub.). Notes: Held at Dublin Friends Historical Library.

Ní Ailpín, Treasa. 1894–1983. Garraí Eoin, Co. Luimnigh agus An Rinn, Na Déise, Co. Phort Láirge. Scríbhneoireacht acadúil, leabhar teagaisc.
Saolaíodh Treasa i nGarraí Eoin. Siúinéir ab ea a hathair, Joseph Halpin, agus Mary Ellen Moore an t-ainm a bhí ar a máthair. Bhí cúigear muirear orthu faoin mbliain 1901 agus ba í Treasa an tarna duine ba shine. Fuair sí a cuid oideachais ag Cnoc na Labhras, Luimneach. Sárcheoltóir, amhránaí agus rinceoir den scoth ab ea í agus bhuaigh sí mórán duaiseanna Oireachtais dá bharr. Mhúin sí ceol agus rince i Scoil na Leanbh, Coláiste na Rinne ar feadh na mblianta fada. Phós sí Seán Ó Cuirrín as Baile na nGall, An Rinn, Co. Phort Láirge sa bhliain 1923. Ghnóthaigh sé céim ó Choláiste na hOllscoile, Corcaigh, agus bhí sé ina mhúinteoir sa Rinn agus i gCnoc Mheilearaí. Eagarthóir, aistritheoir agus file ab ea é, leis. Scríobh Treasa agus Seán téacsleabhar ceoil don fhidil, *Teagascleabhar na Bheidhlíne* (1923).

Select bibliography
Ní Ailpín, Treasa.
—. agus Seán Ó Cuirrín. *Teagascleabhar na Bheidhlíne.* Scríbhneoireacht acadúil, leabhar teagaisc. 1923.

Secondary sources
Breathnach, Diarmuid agus Máire Ní Mhurchú. "Ó Cuirrín, Seán (1894–1980)." *1882–1982 Beathaisnéis a Cúig.* Leabhair Thaighde 81. Baile Átha Cliath: An Clóchomhar, 1997.

Ní Annagáin, Maighréad [Hannagan, Margaret / Ní Annagáin, Máiréad]. *fl.* 1914–27. An Seanphobal, Na Déise, Co. Phort Láirge agus Cloch na gCoillte, Co. Chorcaí. Filíocht, amhránaíocht / béaloideas.

Chuir Maighréad dhá chnuasach d'amhráin in eagar i gcomhar lena fear céile, Séamus de Chlanndiolúin, *An Lon Dubh* (1914), leabhar a raibh dhá amhrán déag ann, agus *Londubh an Chairn* (1927), ina raibh cúig amhrán déag is trí scór. Is é atá sa tarna leabhar ná amhráin a bhíodh á rá ag tuismitheoirí Mhaighréad, chomh maith le hamhráin a bhailigh sí ó dhaoine in áiteanna eile. Chum sí ceithre amhrán nua, agus dhein Séamus amhrán grinn amháin, atá i gcló sa leabhar seo i dteannta an ábhair a bhailigh siad. Bhí féith an cheoil agus na filíochta i muintir Mhaighréad ar an dá thaobh. Tháinig muintir Uí Annagáin go dtí na Déise ar dtús timpeall na bliana 1690 agus saolaíodh athair Mhaighréad i 1825. Is ó mhuintir Uí Fhoghlú, Áth-na-Croise, a shíolraigh a máthair agus bhí muileann acu san áit sin (Ní Annagáin agus de Chlanndiolúin 1927, vii).

Tá an chuma ar an scéal go raibh Maighréad agus a fear céile ag cur fúthu in Iarthar Chorcaí ar feadh tamaill. Deir sí an méid a leanas faoi amhrán amháin a bhailigh sí: "This beautiful air I took down from the singing of Fionán McColluim, when he visited our house in Darrara, Clonakilty, about fourteen years ago" (1927, 16). Ba sheoladh i mBaile Átha Cliath a tugadh ag deireadh na nótaí a ghabhann leis na hamhráin: "I nDrom-Chonrach dúinn.i. ag 17 Bóthar Droma Chuilinn" (1927, 36). Dar le Brenda Ní Ríordáin, bhí Maighréad agus a fear céile cairdiúil leis an scríbhneoir, Máire Ní Shíthe, gurb as Cloch na gCoillte di agus deir Ní Ríordáin gur "chaith Séamus ó 1905 go 1912 i Scoil na Talmhaíochta i nDairbhre, in aice le Cloch na gCoillte" (1993, 44).

Select bibliography
Ní Annagáin, Maighréad.
—. agus Séamus de Chlanndiolúin, eag. *An Lon Dubh*. Filíocht, amhránaíocht / béaloideas. Oxford: Oxford UP, 1914.
—. agus Séamus de Chlanndiolúin, eag. *Londubh an Chairn*. Filíocht, amhránaíocht / béaloideas. London: Oxford UP, 1927.

Secondary sources
Breathnach, Diarmuid, agus Máire Ní Mhurchú. "De Chlanndiolúin, Séamus (1878–1944)." *1882–1982 Beathaisnéis a hAon*. Leabhair Thaighde 49. Baile Átha Cliath: An Clóchomhar, 1986.
Ní Ríordáin, Brenda. "Cérbh í "Dul Amú"?" *Comhar* Lúnasa (1993): 40–44.

Ní Athairne, Cáit. Comhaimseartha. Baile Mhic Cairbre, Na Déise, Co. Phort Láirge. Scríbhneoireacht acadúil, stair.

I mBaile Mhic Cairbre a saolaíodh Cáit. Chaith sí dhá scór blianta i mBaile Átha Cliath, ag obair mar státseirbhíseach, mar mhúinteoir agus mar abhcóide (Ó Macháin agus Nic Dhonnchadha, 1999, 146–7). Ina haiste in *An Linn Bhuí 3* (1999, 32–7) chuir sí síos ar an taighde atá déanta aici ar eachtra a thit amach ina háit dhúchais in aimsir shuaite na bliana 1803, nuair a crochadh ceathrar fear. Tá aiste eile aici in uimhir a cúig den iris chéanna.

Select bibliography
Ní Athairne, Cáit.
—. "Bearna na Gaoithe." *An Linn Bhuí: Iris Ghaeltacht na nDéise.* Scríbhneoireacht
　acadúil, stair. Eag. Pádraig Ó Macháin agus Aoibheann Nic Dhonnchadha. Vol.
　3. Baile Átha Cliath: Leabhair na Linne, 1999. 32–7.
—. "Eachtra ar Mhóinchearta i nGleann Dá Lachan." *An Linn Bhuí: Iris Ghaeltacht
　na nDéise.* Scríbhneoireacht acadúil, stair. Eag. Pádraig Ó Macháin agus
　Aoibheann Nic Dhonnchadha. Vol. 5. Baile Átha Cliath: Leabhair na Linne,
　2001.

Ní Bhriain, Neilí [O'Brien, Ellen]. 1864–1925. Co. Luimnigh / Co. an
Chláir. Scríbhneoireacht acadúil, iriseoireacht.

Ba ghariníon le William Smith O'Brien í. Chónaigh sí lena haintín, Charlotte
Grace O'Brien i mBaile Átha Cliath tar éis di seal a chaitheamh ag déanamh
staidéir ar an ealaín i Londain. Bhunaigh sí scoil Ghaeilge i gCo. an Chláir i
1912, Coláiste Eoghain Uí Chomhraí. Bhí sí ina ball de Chonradh na
Gaeilge cé gur Phrotastúnach agus Dhílseoir ab ea í. Bhunaigh sí iris
dhátheangach Phrotastúnach, *An t-Eaglaiseach Gaedhalach* (1919–28).

Select bibliography
Ní Bhriain, Neilí.
—. Scríbhneoireacht acadúil, iriseoireacht. *An t-Eaglaiseach Gaedhalach / The Gaelic
　Churchman* 1–8 (1919–1928).

Secondary sources
Breathnach, Diarmuid agus Máire Ní Mhurchú. "Ó Briain, Neilí [Ní Bhriain]
　(1864–1925)." *1882–1982 Beathaisnéis a hAon.* Baile Átha Cliath: An
　Clóchomhar Tta, 1986.

Ní Bhruadair, Gobnait [Broderick, The Hon. Albinia]. 1861–1955. Doire
Fhionáin, West Cove, agus an tSnaidhm, Co. Chiarraí. Filíocht, aistí
polaitiúla, beathaisnéis.

Bhain Albina Broderick le teaghlach Angla-Éireannach rachmasach.
Saolaíodh i Londain í agus chaith a hóige i Sasana. Ba iad an tOchtú
Bíocunta Middleton agus Augusta Mary Freemantle a tuismitheoirí. Ba é a
deartháir an chéad Iarla Middleton, agus bhí sé ina cheannaire ar na
hAontachtóirí i ndeisceart na hÉireann. Bhí tuairimí polaitiúla Albina an-
éagsúil le cinn a dearthár áfach, agus nuair a d'fhiafraítí di ina dhiaidh sin an
raibh aon ghaol eatarthu, deireadh sí, "Ba é mo dheartháir é tráth dá raibh."
Tháinig sí go hÉirinn den chéad uair i 1897 chun cuairt a thabhairt ar
eastáit a hathar. Scríobh sí alt ar bhochtanas iarthair na hÉireann i 1903,
ach níl aon chóip de ar marthain anois. D'fhill Albina ar Éirinn timpeall an
ama sin agus oileadh í mar bhanaltra i mBaile Átha Cliath. Bhí sí ina ball de
Chonradh na Gaeilge i mBaile Átha Cliath, d'fhoghlaim sí Gaeilge, labhair
í le tuin Shasanach agus thug Gobnait Ní Bhruadair uirthi féin.
Nuair a cailleadh a hathair i 1910, fágadh í go maith as agus d'aistrigh sí

go dtí an tSnaidhm, Co. Chiarraí. D'íoc sí as ospidéal nua do na bochtáin sa bhliain 1912, "Baile an Chúnaimh", agus rith sí é ar feadh fiche bliain ina dhiaidh sin. Scríobh sí an t-eagarfhocal don *Catholic Bulletin* le linn na bliana 1916. Bhí sí ina ball de Chumann na mBan, agus thugadh sí fothain do phoblachtánaigh ar a gcoimeád le linn Chogadh na Saoirse. Toghadh í do Shinn Féin ar Chomhairle Chontae Chiarraí i 1920. Is mar gheall ar an mbaint a bhí aici leis an iris phoblachtánach, *Saoirse*, is mó atá cáil uirthi; rith sí í idir 1926–1937. Gabhadh í le linn Chogadh na mBráthar, agus d'eagraigh sí an iris *The NDU Invincible* le linn di bheith sa phríosún. Chuaigh sí ar stailc ocrais ar feadh seacht lá déag agus í ann. Thug sí tacaíocht do Chumann na mBan sna 1920adaí, cé go mbíodh sí ciapaithe cráite ag saighdiúirí an stáit. D'éirigh sí as i 1933, áfach, agus bhunaigh Mná na Poblachta i gcomhar le Mary McSwiney. Fuair Gobnait bás i 1955 agus cuireadh í sa tSnaidhm. Cailleadh a cuid cáipéisí i ndiaidh a báis, ach thángthas ar a dialann sa bhrablach i bhfothrach Bhaile an Chúnaimh. Tá an dialann i dtaisce i gcnuasach príobháideach i Sasana anois.

Albinia Broderick was a member of a wealthy Anglo-Irish family. She was born in London and spent her childhood in England. Her parents were the eighth Viscount of Middleton and Augusta Mary Freemantle. Her brother went on to become the first Earl of Midleton, and was the leader of the Unionists in the South of Ireland. Albinia's politics, however, were to take on a very different hue, and when later asked if they were related she would reply, "He used to be my brother." She paid her first visit to Ireland in 1897, to visit her father's estates, and in 1903 she wrote an article on poverty in the west of Ireland (there are no remaining copies of this piece). Broderick returned to Ireland about this time and trained as a nurse in Dublin. While in Dublin she joined the Gaelic League, learned to speak Irish (which she spoke with an Oxford accent) and changed her name to Gobnait Ní Bhruadair.

On her father's death in 1910 she was financially independent and moved to Sneem in Co. Kerry. In 1912 she financed the building of a hospital for the poor ("Baile an Chúnaimh" – "the household of help") and ran it for the next twenty years. During 1916 she wrote editorials for the *Catholic Bulletin*, and she joined Cumann na mBan in 1917, sheltering IRA men during the War of Independence. In 1920 she was elected to Kerry County Council as a Sinn Féin member. She is possibly best known for her involvement in the Republican journal, *Saoirse*, which she ran from 1926 to 1937. Arrested by the Free State Government during the Civil War, she organized the production of a jail journal, *The NDU Invincible*. She went on hunger strike for seventeen days while interned. Throughout the late 1920s she supported Cumann na mBan, despite ongoing harassment and raids by government troops. However, in 1933 she resigned, and along with Mary McSwiney (*q.v.*) founded the political group Mná na Poblachta ("Women of the Republic"). Ní Bhruadair died in 1955 and is buried in Sneem. Her papers were lost after her death, but in 1958 her journal was found in the rubble of the ruined Baile an Chúnaimh. The journal is now held in a private collection in England.

Select bibliography
Ní Bhruadair, Gobnait.
—. Filíocht, eagarthóireacht. *The Catholic Bulletin* Bealtaine-Meitheamh (1916).

Nic Craith, Máire. Comhaimseartha. Cnocán an Phaoraigh Uachtarach, Rinn Ó gCuanach, Na Déise, Co. Phort Láirge. Scríbhneoireacht acadúil, aistí.

I gCnocán an Phaoraigh Uachtarach a saolaíodh agus a tógadh Máire. Is aturnae í (Ó Macháin agus Nic Dhonnchadha 1997, 95–6). Míníonn sí don ghnáthdhuine cad is uacht ann ina haiste in *An Linn Bhuí 1* (1997, 48–51), agus molann sí do gach éinne uacht a dhéanamh chun bruíon agus argóintí a sheachaint. Tá aiste eile aici in uimhir a cúig den iris chéanna.

Select bibliography
Nic Craith, Máire.
—. "Fágaim le hUacht é." *An Linn Bhuí: Iris Ghaeltacht na nDéise.* Aiste. Eag. Pádraig Ó Macháin agus Aoibheann Nic Dhonnchadha. Vol. 1. Baile Átha Cliath: Leabhair na Linne, 1997.
—. "Tar isteach insna hÓglaigh." *An Linn Bhuí: Iris Ghaeltacht na nDéise.* Aiste. Eag. Pádraig Ó Macháin agus Aoibheann Nic Dhonnchadha. Vol. 5. Baile Átha Cliath: Leabhair na Linne, 2001.

Nic Craith, Máiréad. Comhaimseartha. Cathair Chorcaí. Scríbhneoireacht acadúil, stair shóisialta, teangeolaíocht agus filíocht.

Bhain Máiréad na céimeanna seo a leanas amach ó Choláiste na hOllscoile, Corcaigh: BA, An tArdteastas san Oideachas, MA agus PhD. Chaith sí seal ag obair mar léachtóir le Nua-Ghaeilge in Institiúid Léann na hÉireann in Ollscoil Learphoill. Tá sí ag obair anois san Acadamh don Staidéar ar Oidhreacht Chultúrtha Éireannach in Ollscoil Uladh, Campas Magee, Doire. Is é an chéad leabhar léi a foilsíodh ná *An tOileánach Léannta*, cuntas ar an tabhairt suas a bhí ag Tomás Ó Criomhthain sa Ghaeilge agus sa Bhéarla agus ar an gcaidreamh a bhí aige le scoláirí agus le cuairteoirí éagsúla a tháinig go dtí an t-oileán. D'eascair an leabhar *Malartú Teanga* as a tráchtas dochtúireachta. Déantar scagadh sa leabhar seo ar chúlú na Gaeilge ar fud chontae Chorcaí idir 1800–1900 agus ar na cúiseanna a bhí leis. Foilsíodh *The Politics of Identity [in divided societies]* sa bhliain 2001 (University of Liverpool). Pléann *Plural Identities-Singular Narratives* le teangacha agus cúrsaí ionannais i gCúige Uladh (2002). Cuireann Máiréad suim ar leith sna mionteangacha agus sna teangacha Ceilteacha in Éirinn agus san Eoraip.

Máiréad Nic Craith was awarded the following degrees from UCC: BA, HDip in Education, MA and PhD. She has worked as a lecturer of modern Irish in the Institute of Irish Studies in the University of Liverpool. Now she is working in the Academy for the Study of Irish Cultural Heritages at the University of Ulster, Magee Campus, Derry. Her first book to be published was *An tOileánach Léannta* (1988), an account of Tomás Ó Criomhthain's knowledge of literature in Irish and in English and his relationship with scholars and various visitors to the island. The book *Malartú Teanga* (1993) grew out of her doctoral thesis. This book is an examination of the ways in which Irish declined all over Co. Cork between 1800 and 1900, and of the reasons for this decline. *The Politics of Identity [in Divided Societies]* was published by the Liverpool UP in 2001. *Plural Identities–Singular Narratives* (2002) discusses language and identity in the province of Ulster. Máiréad is interested in minority languages and in Celtic languages in Ireland and in Europe.

Select bibliography
Nic Craith, Máiréad.

—. *An tOileánach Léannta: oiliúint Thomáis Uí Chriomhthain, a chairde, a chuid léitheoireachta agus a chuid scríbhinní.* Scríbhneoireacht acadúil, léirmheastóireacht. Baile Átha Cliath: Clóchomhar, 1988.
—. *Malartú Teanga: An Ghaeilge i gCorcaigh sa Naoú hAois Déag.* Scríbhneoireacht acadúil, teangeolaíocht. Bremen: Cumann Eorpach Léann na hÉireann, 1993.
—. eag. *Watching One's Tongue: Aspects of Romance and Celtic Languages.* Scríbhneoireacht acadúil, teangeolaíocht. Liverpool: Liverpool UP, 1996.
—. eag. *Watching One's Tongue: Issues in Language Planning.* Scríbhneoireacht acadúil, teangeolaíocht. Liverpool: Liverpool UP, 1996.
—. *Cultural Diversity in Northern Ireland and the Good Friday Agreement.* Scríbhneoireacht acadúil, stair shóisialta. IBIS Working Paper no. 7. Working Papers in British–Irish Studies 7. Baile Átha Cliath: Institute for British-Irish Studies, UCD, 2001.
—. *The Politics of Identity [in Divided Societies].* Scríbhneoireacht acadúil. Liverpool: Liverpool UP, 2001.
—. *Plural Identities–Singular Narratives: The Case of Northern Ireland.* Scríbhneoireacht acadúil. Oxford/New York: Berghahn Books, 2002.
—. *Culture and Identity Politics in Northern Ireland.* Scríbhneoireacht acadúil. New York: Palgrave Macmillan, 2003.

Nic Dhiarmada, Bríona. Comhaimseartha. Co. Phort Láirge. Scríbhneoireacht acadúil, taighde agus léirmheastóireacht.

Saolaíodh i bPort Láirge í i 1957 ach d'aistrigh sí go Loch Garman agus í fós ina leanbh. D'fhreastail sí ar TCD agus ar UCD agus fostaíodh í mar léachtóir in U.C.D. Tá a tráchtas dochtúireachta bunaithe ar fhilíocht Nuala Ní Dhomhnaill. Bhí sí ina ball de bhord eagarthóireachta *Innti* agus *Graph* agus ba chomhairleoir scripte agus teanga le Rannóg na gClár Gaeilge í in R.T.É. Tá roinnt aistí léi foilsithe in *Comhar*: "Ceist na Teanga – Dioscúrsa na Gaeilge", "An Fhilíocht agus Dioscúrsa na mBan" (1982), "Bláthú an Traidisiúin" (1987) agus "Léirmheas ar Cé hi sin Amuig" (1993) agus foilsíodh saothair eile léi in irisí éagsúla.

Chuir sí *Téacs agus Comhthéacs: Gnéithe de Chritic na Gaeilge* in eagar le Máiréad Ní Annracháin (1998). Is é atá ann ná cnuasach d'aistí scríofa ag criticeoirí liteartha ina bpléann siad an cónasc idir an chritic liteartha idirnáisiúnta agus litríocht na Gaeilge. Tá aiste ag Bríona sa leabhar sin faoi chúrsaí feimineachais.

Select bibliography
Nic Dhiarmada, Bríona.
—. "Ceist na Teanga – Dioscúrsa na Gaeilge", "An Fhilíocht agus Dioscúrsa na mBan." Scríbhneoireacht acadúil. *Comhar.* Bealtaine (1992): 160-67.

—. "Smulcairí, Fiosracht agus Eile: Cás na Critice sa Ghaeilge." *Léann na Gaeilge –*
Súil Siar, Súil Chun Cinn. Scríbhneoireacht acadúil. Eag. Ruairí Ó hUigínn.
Léachtaí Cholm Cille XXVI. Maigh Nuad: An Sagart, 1996.
—. agus Máiréad Ní Annracháin, eag. *Téacs agus Comhthéacs: Gnéithe de Chritic na*
Gaeilge. Scríbhneoireacht acadúil, léirmheastóireacht. Corcaigh: Cló Ollscoile
Chorcaí, 1998.

Nic Dhonnchadha, Aoibheann [Ní Dhonnchú, Aoibheann]. Comhaimseartha. Durlas Éile, Co. Thiobraid Árann agus Na Déise, Co. Phort Láirge. Scríbhneoireacht acadúil.

Saolaíodh Aoibheann i nDurlas Éile. Is ann a fuair sí a bunscolaíocht agus a
meánscolaíocht i gClochar na nUrsulach. D'fhreastail sí ar Scoil na Leanbh,
Coláiste na Rinne, Dún Garbhán, Co. Phort Láirge, 1961–2. Céimí de
chuid Choláiste na Tríonóide, 1975 (BA Mod), 1988 (PhD) is ea í. Bhí sí
ina léachtóir le Gaeilge i gColáiste Bhantiarna na Trócaire, An Charraig
Dhubh, Co. Bhaile Átha Cliath 1980–85 agus ina Cúntóir Taighde i Scoil an
Léinn Cheiltigh, Institiúid Ard-Léinn Bhaile Átha Cliath, 1985–1993. Tá sí
ina hOllamh Cúnta ann ó 1993 i leith. Is é a réimse taighde ná lámhscríbhinní agus téacsanna leighis na Gaeilge 1300–1650 (féach www.celt.dias.ie
agus www.isos.dcu.ie). Tá sí ina heagarthóir (leis an Dr Pádraig Ó Macháin)
ar an iris Dhéiseach *An Linn Bhuí* 1–7 (1997–2003). Tá seanchas agus
béaloideas bailithe aici i nDéise Mumhan agus tá míreanna as an
mbailiúchán san foilsithe in *An Linn Bhuí.*

Aoibheann Nic Dhonnchadha was born in Thurles. She received her
primary and secondary education in the Ursuline Convent, Thurles. She
attended Ring College, Dungarvan, Co. Waterford, from 1961 to 1962. She
is a graduate of Trinity College, Dublin, 1975 (BA Mod), 1988 (PhD). She
was a lecturer of Irish in the College of Our Lady of Mercy, Blackrock, Co.
Dublin, from 1980 to 1985 and she was a Research Assistant in the School
of Celtic Studies, Institute of Higher Learning, Dublin, from 1985 to 1993.
She has been an Assistant Professor in the same Institute since 1993. Her
area of research includes manuscripts and medical texts in Irish from 1300
to 1650 (see www.celt.dias.ie and www.isos.dcu.ie). She is editor (with Dr
Pádraig Ó Macháin) of the journal *An Linn Bhuí* 1–7 (1997–2003). She has
collected folklore in the Decies, Co. Waterford, and extracts from that collection have been published in *An Linn Bhuí.*

Select bibliography
Nic Dhonnchadha, Aoibheann.
—. "Early Modern Irish medical writings." Scríbhneoireacht acadúil. *Scéala Scoil an*
Léinn Cheiltigh: Newsletter of the School of Celtic Studies 4 (1990): 35–9.
—. "Irish medical manuscripts." Scríbhneoireacht acadúil. *Irish Pharmacy Journal*
69.5 (1991): 201–2.
—. "Irish Pharmaceutical Texts." Scríbhneoireacht acadúil. *Irish Pharmacy Journal*
69.7 (1991): 274–5.
—. agus Pádraig Ó Macháin, eag. *An Linn Bhuí: Iris Ghaeltacht na nDéise.*
Scríbhneoireacht acadúil, béaloideas. Vols. 1–7. Baile Átha Cliath: Leabhair na
Linne, 1997–2003.

—. "Leabharlann Choláiste na Rinne." *Féile Náisiúnta Drámaíochta 1999.* Scríbhneoireacht acadúil. Rinn Ó gCuanach: Camus, 1999. 53–8.

—. "Medical Writing in Irish 1400–1700." *Two Thousand Years of Irish Medicine.* Scríbhneoireacht acadúil. Eag. J.B. Lyons. Baile Átha Cliath: 1999.

—. "Medical Writing in Irish 1400–1700." Scríbhneoireacht acadúil. *Irish Journal of Medical Science* 169.3 (2000): 217–20.

—. "Eagarthóir, téacs agus lámhscríbhinní: Winifred Wulff agus an *Rosa Anglica.*" *Oidhreacht na Lámhscríbhinní.* Scríbhneoireacht acadúil. Eag. Ruairí Ó hUigínn. Léachtaí Cholm Cille 34. Maigh Nuad (2004): 105–47.

—. "Téacs ó scoil leighis Achaidh Mhic Airt." *Ossary, Laois and Leinster* (2004): 50–75.

Nic Einrí, Úna. Comhaimseartha. Co. Luimnigh. Scríbhneoireacht acadúil, filíocht.

Saolaíodh Úna i Luimneach i 1941. Is léachtóir sinsir í i gColáiste Mhuire gan Smál, Luimneach. I 1970 d'fhoilsigh sí *Stair Litríocht na Gaeilge* agus baineadh feidhm as mar leabhar teagaisc don Ardteistiméireacht ar feadh roinnt mhaith blianta. I 2001 foilsíodh leabhar Nic Einrí ar shaol an fhile ó Phort Láirge, Tadhg Gaelach.

Select bibliography
Nic Einrí, Úna.

—. *Stair Litríocht na Gaeilge.* Scríbhneoireacht acadúil. Baile Átha Cliath: Folens, 1970.

—. *An Cantaire Siúlach: Tadhg Gaelach.* Beathaisnéis, filíocht. An Daingean: An Sagart, 2001.

—. agus Pádraig Ó Cearbhaill. *Canfar an Dán: Uilliam English agus a chairde.* Scríbhneoireacht acadúil, filíocht. An Daingean: An Sagart, 2003.

Nic Eoin, Máirín. Comhaimseartha. Cathair Luimnigh. Scríbhneoireacht acadúil, léirmheastóireacht, agus beathaisnéis.

Saolaíodh Máirín i gcathair Luimnigh i 1958, ach tá cónaí uirthi le tamall fada i mBaile Átha Cliath. Fuair sí a cuid scolaíochta i gCnoc Síon, An Charraig Dhubh agus i gColáiste na hOllscoile, Baile Átha Cliath. Bronnadh céim sa Ghaeilge agus sa Tíreolaíocht uirthi, mar aon leis an Ardteastas san Oideachas agus MA sa Nua-Ghaeilge. Chaith sí seal ag obair mar mhúinteoir i Scoil Phobail Bhaile an tSaoir, agus is léachtóir le Gaeilge í i gColáiste Phádraig, Droim Conrach anois.

Is saothar critice é *An Litríocht Réigiúnach* ina ndéantar plé agus cíoradh ar scríbhneoirí Chorca Dhuibhne agus Thír Chonaill. Tá an-chuid taighde déanta ag Máirín, leis, ar Eoghan Ó Tuairisc, agus tá na torthaí ar fáil sna leabhair *Eoghan Ó Tuairisc: Beatha agus Saothar*, beathaisnéis, agus *Religio Poetae agus Aistí Eile*, eagrán d'aistí dá chuid. Mórshaothar léi is ea *B'ait leo bean*, ina bhféachtar ar ghnéithe den idé-eolaíocht inscne i dtraidisiún liteartha na Gaeilge, ó thréimhse na Sean-Ghaeilge agus na Meán-Ghaeilge anonn go dtí an lá inniu. Foilseofar leabhar eile léi go luath, *'Trén bhFearann Breac': An Díláithriú Cultúir i Nualitríocht na Gaeilge* (Cois Life). Tá ailt léi ar litríocht na Gaeilge foilsithe in irisí éagsúla, mar shampla: *Comhar, Léachtaí*

Cholm Cille, Irisleabhar Mhá Nuad, Oghma, Graf, Eighteenth Century Ireland
agus sna leabhair *Ceiliúradh an Bhlascaoid 2* (Máire Ní Chéilleachair, eag.)
agus *Gnéithe den Ghorta* (Cathal Póirtéir, eag.).

Select bibliography

Nic Eoin, Máirín.

—. "Éistear le mo Ghlór! Caithfear Éisteacht ..." Scríbhneoireacht acadúil. *Nua-Aois* (1981): 45–59.

—. *An Litríocht Réigiúnach.* Leabhair Thaighde 40. Baile Átha Cliath: An Clóchomhar Tta, 1982.

—. "Úrscéalaíocht na Gaeilge 1974–1984." Scríbhneoireacht acadúil, léirmheastóireacht. *Comhar* Lúnasa (1984): 15–21.

—. "Éirí Amach 1916 agus Litríocht na Gaeilge." Scríbhneoireacht acadúil. *Irisleabhar Mhá Nuad* (1985): 38–61.

—. "An Pholaitíocht Faoi Cheilt." Scríbhneoireacht acadúil. *Comhar* Nollaig (1986): 24–8.

—. eag. *Religio Poetae agus Aistí Eile.* Scríbhneoireacht acadúil. Le Eoghan Ó Tuairisc. Baile Átha Cliath: An Clóchomhar, 1987.

—. *Eoghan Ó Tuairisc: Beatha agus Saothar.* Scríbhneoireacht acadúil. Baile Átha Cliath: An Clóchomhar, 1988.

—. "Idir an Teoiric agus an Teagasc: Fadhbanna Téacs agus Comhthéacs i Múineadh na Litríochta Gaeilge." Scríbhneoireacht acadúil. *Oghma* (1989): 61–73.

—. "Gender's Agendas." Scríbhneoireacht acadúil. *Graph.* Samhradh / Fómhar (1992): 5–8.

—. "Léiriú na mBan sna Leabhair." *Leath na Spéire.* Scríbhneoireacht acadúil. eag. Eoghan Ó hAnluain. Baile Átha Cliath: An Clóchomhar, 1992. 13–41.

—. *An Ghaeilge i gCill Chainnigh.* Scríbhneoireacht acadúil, teangeolaíocht. Baile Átha Cliath: Comhar na Múinteoirí Gaeilge, 1993.

—. "Secrets and Disguises? Caitlín Ní Uallacháin and Other Female Personages in Eighteenth-Century Irish Political Poetry." Scríbhneoireacht acadúil. *Eighteenth Century Ireland* 11 (1996): 7–45.

—. agus Liam Mac Mathúna, eag. *Ar Thóir an Fhocail Chruinn.* Scríbhneoireacht acadúil. Baile Átha Cliath: Coiscéim, 1997.

—. *B'ait leo bean: Gnéithe den Idé-eolaíocht Inscne i dTraidisiún Liteartha na Gaeilge.* Baile Átha Cliath: An Clóchomhar Tta, 1998.

—. Liam Mac Mathúna agus Ciarán Mac Murchaidh, eag. *Teanga, pobal agus réigiún: aistí ar chultúr na Gaeltachta inniu.* Scríbhneoireacht acadúil. Baile Átha Cliath: Coiscéim, 2000.

—. eag. *Gaolta Gairide: rogha dánta comhaimseartha ar théamaí óige agus caidrimh teaghlaigh.* Filíocht. Baile Átha Cliath: Cois Life, 2001.

Secondary sources

Bairéad, Peadar. "Léirmheas ar *Pacáiste Eolais: An Ghaeilge i gCill Chainnigh.*" *An tUltach* (1995).

Ó Cearnaigh, Seán. "Mac Eoin, Máirín Nic Eoin." *Scríbhneoirí na Gaeilge 1945–1995.* Baile Átha Cliath: Comhar, 1995.

Titley, Alan. *An tÚrscéal Gaeilge.* Leabhair Thaighde 67. Baile Átha Cliath: An Clóchomhar, 1991.

Uí Nia, Gearóidín Eag. "Nic Eoin, Máirín." *Eolaire Chló Iar-Chonnachta de Scríbhneoirí Gaeilge.* Indreabhán: Cló Iar-Chonnachta, 1998.

Nic Ghearailt, Eibhlín. Comhaimseartha. Cathair Chorcaí. Scríbhneoireacht acadúil, taighde.

Ghnóthaigh Eibhlín máistreacht ó Choláiste na hOllscoile, Corcaigh. Foilsíodh leabhar léi bunaithe ar an tráchtas sin i 1988, *Seán Ó Ríordáin agus "An Striapach Allúrach"*.

Select bibliography
Nic Ghearailt, Eibhlín.
—. *Seán Ó Ríordáin agus "An Striapach Allúrach"*. Scríbhneoireacht acadúil. Baile Átha Cliath: Clóchomhar, 1988.

Nic Ghearailt, Máire Áine. Comhaimseartha. Baile an tSléibhe, Fionntrá, Co. Chiarraí. Filíocht.

Saolaíodh Máire Áine i mBaile an tSléibhe i 1946. Feirmeoirí ab ea a muintir. Tá tréimhsí ama caite aici i gCiarraí, i Luimneach, i gCorcaigh, agus i mBaile Átha Cliath. D'fhreastail sí ar Choláiste Íde, An Daingean agus ar Choláiste Mhuire gan Smál, Luimneach mar ar oileadh í mar mhúinteoir bunscoile. Dhein sí cúrsa san Oideachas Speisialta i gColáiste Phádraig, Droim Conrach agus bhí MA ar bun aici ansin i Maigh Nuad. Tá aistí agus dánta léi foilsithe in *Innti, Comhar, Feasta, Iris Chonradh na Gaeilge Nua Eabhrac, Nua-Fhilí III, The Kerryman, Iris na gColáistí Oiliúna, Anois* agus *Inniu*. Bhuaigh sí duaiseanna Oireachtais dá cuid filíochta idir na blianta 1966–71. Cuireadh cuid dá dánta ar shiollabas an Teastais Shóisearaigh.

Select bibliography
Nic Ghearailt, Máire Áine.
—. *Éiric Uachta*. Filíocht. Baile Átha Cliath: An Clóchomhar, 1971.
—. *Leaca Liombó*. Filíocht. Baile Átha Cliath: Coiscéim, 1990.
—. *An tUlchabhán agus Dánta eile*. Filíocht. Baile Átha Cliath: Coiscéim, 1990.
—. *Mo Chúis Bheith Beo*. Filíocht. Baile Átha Cliath: Coiscéim, 1991.
—. *Ó Ceileadh an Bhreasail*. Filíocht. Baile Átha Cliath: Coiscéim, 1992.

Secondary sources
Ó Cearnaigh, Seán. "Mac Gearailt, Máire Áine Nic Ghearailt." *Scríbhneoirí na Gaeilge 1945–1995*. Baile Átha Cliath: Comhar, 1995.

Ní Chadhla, Áine [Ní Chadhlaigh, Anna]. fl. 2000. Cill Rosantaigh, Co. Phort Láirge. Filíocht, caoineadh / béaloideas.

Bhí ceangal ag Áine le Cill Rosantaigh. Is é an saothar léi is mó cáil ná "Marbhchaoine an Athar Seán Ó Maonaigh" a thosaíonn leis an líne, "Mo chreach géar fada 's mo dheacair", atá curtha in eagar ag Breandán Ó Buachalla in aiste dar teideal céanna in *Saoi na hÉigse* (2000, 200).

Select bibliography
Ní Chadhla, Áine.
—. "Marbhchaoine an Athar Seán Ó Maonaigh." Eag. Breandán Ó Buachalla. *Saoi na hÉigse: Aistí in Ómós do Sheán Ó Tuama*. Filíocht / béaloideas. Eag. Pádraigín Riggs, Seán Ó Coileáin agus Breandán Ó Conchúir. Baile Átha Cliath: An Clóchomhar, 2000. 197–208.

Ní Chaoilte, Eibhlín [Quilty, Ellen]. *fl.*1831. Cathair Druinge, Co. Chorcaí. Filíocht / béaloideas.

Luann "Fiachra Éilgeach" (Risteárd Ó Foghludha) Eibhlín Ní Chaoilte ina aiste "Filí Chorcaighe" (*Saothar Suadha*, iml. 1, 1908). Deir sé: "Na - bain-fhilí féinidh ní rabhadar maol ... Níor mhór do dhuine iarracht fí leith chun teacht thórsa-san is thar a gcuid amhrán, agus sin rud ná fuil im chumas-sa den scríb seo" (39). Deir Hardiman gur chan Eibhlín Ní Chaoilte an dán, "Ionurbudh Sheaghuin Bhuidhe", ach cuireann sé an t-agús seo ann: "It is said to have been composed by Ellen Quilty, a fair Munster Lady, but this was probably a nom-de-guerre, assumed by some bard to avoid detection" (Hardiman 1831, 149).

Select bibliography
Ní Chaoilte, Eibhlín.
—. "Ionurbudh Sheaghuin Bhuidhe." *Irish Minstrelsy*. Filíocht / béaloideas. Bail. / eag. James Hardiman. London: Joseph Robins, 1831. 82–4.

Secondary sources
Éilgeach, Fiachra. "Filí Chorcaighe." *Saothar Suadha: Aistí do léigheadh os comhair Dáil na hÉigse, i gCorcaigh, Meadhon Foghmhair, 1907.* Vol. 1. Baile Átha Cliath: Muinntir an Ghoill, Teo., 1908.

Ní Chaoimh, Máire [Bray, Mary]. 1890–1973. Ceapach Choinn, Co. Phort Láirge. Filíocht agus seanchas / béaloideas.

Saolaíodh Máire i gCnoc na Faille, baile fearainn atá cúpla míle ó Chnoc Mheilearaí. Bhí beirt deartháireacha aici, Seán agus Séamus. Gaeilge a labhraítí sa tigh. "Chuaigh na deartháracha go Scoil na mBráthar ag Meilearaí, áit a bhfuaireadar oiliúint ar léamh agus den scríobh na Gaeilge. Chuaigh Máire ar Scoil na gCailíní áit nach raibh aon Ghaeilge á múineadh ag an am. Mar sin féin phioc sí suas cuid den léamh agus den scríobh óna deartháracha agus bhí sí ábalta litreacha a scríobh i nGaeilge i mblianta deireanacha a saoil" (Ó hAirt 1998, 50). Scríobh Séamus leabhar dar teideal *An Sléibhteánach* (Maigh Nuad 1989) agus bhíodh ailt ag Seán in irisí éagsúla; *An Claidheamh Solais, Ireland's Own* agus *An Sguab*, mar shampla.

Laistigh den traidisiún béil a d'oibrigh Máire. Bhí stór mór scéalta, filíochta agus amhrán aici agus dhein sí féin blúirí filíochta a chumadh ó am go chéile, leis. Thóg an tAthair Piaras de Hindeberg ábhar uaithi ar théip, mar a dhein an tAthair Uinseann Ó Maidín freisin. Tá na téipeanna i dtaisce i Leabharlann Choláiste na Rinne agus tá Diarmaid Ó hAirt tar éis cuid de dhánta Mháire a chur in eagar agus a fhoilsiú in *An Linn Bhuí 2* agus in *Waterford History and Society*.

Bhí Máire pósta le Liam Brae agus bhí triúr muirear orthu, mac agus beirt iníonacha.

Select bibliography
Ní Chaoimh, Máire.
—. Dánta léi in "Seanchas ó Chnoc na Faille." Diarmaid Ó hAirt. *Waterford History and Society: Interdisciplinary Essays on the History of an Irish County.* Filíocht / béaloideas. Eag. William Nolan *et al.* Dublin: Geography Publications, 1992.

—. Dánta léi in "Máire Ní Chaoimh, File agus Seanchaí." Diarmaid Ó hAirt. *An Linn Bhuí: Iris Ghaeltacht na nDéise*. Filíocht / béaloideas. Eag. Pádraig Ó Macháin agus Aoibheann Nic Dhonnchadha. Vol. 2. Baile Átha Cliath: Leabhair na Linne, 1998.

Ní Chatháin, Cáit Mhicí [Bean Uí Chonchubhair]. *fl.*1930. An Blascaod Mór [An tOileán Tiar], Co. Chiarraí. Scéalaíocht / béaloideas.

Saolaíodh Cáit sa bhliain 1859 ar an mBlascaod Mór. Deirfiúr le Rí an Oileáin ab ea í. Seán Ó Dubhda a bhailigh agus a d'fhoilsigh dhá bhlúire seanchais uaithi in *Béaloideas* (1930).

Select bibliography
Ní Chatháin, Cáit Mhicí.
—. scéalaí. "Sgéilíní ó Dhuibhneachaibh: "An t-Aodhaire a Bhí in Inis Mhicileáin". Seanchas / béaloideas. *Béaloideas* 2.4 (1930): 402.

Ní Chéadagáin, Máire. *fl.*1941, 1990. Oileán Chléire, Co. Chorcaí. Seanchas / béaloideas.

Bhí Máire ag maireachtáil ar Oileán Chléire. Saolaíodh í timpeall na bliana 1863. Bhailigh Seán Ó Conaill ábhar uaithi i 1935 nuair a bhí sí dhá bhliain déag is trí fichid. Tá an béaloideas seo i dtaisce i gcartlann Choimisiún Bhéaloideas Éireann (Iml. 174) agus foilsíodh cuid de in *Céad Fáilte go Cléire* (Gunn 1990). Bhailigh Donnchadh Ó Floinn scéalta uaithi chomh maith, agus d'fhoilsigh sé iad in *Béaloideas* 6.1 (1941).

Select bibliography
Ní Chéadagáin, Máire.
—. scéalaí. "Béaloideas Ó Chléire." Scéalaíocht / béaloideas. *Béaloideas* 6.1 (1941): 3–77.
—. seanchaí. "Seanchas léi." *Céad Fáilte go Cléire*. Seanchas / béaloideas. Eag. Marion Gunn. Baile Átha Cliath: An Clóchomhar, 1990. 42, 45–6, 176.

Ní Cheallacháin, Máire. Comhaimseartha. Cathair Chorcaí agus Mainistir Fhear Maí, Co. Chorcaí. Scríbhneoireacht acadúil, eagarthóireacht.

Chuir Máire eagar ar *Filíocht Phádraigín Haicéid* (1962). Ghnóthaigh sí MA ó Choláiste na hOllscoile, Corcaigh, i 1959. Ba é an tOllamh Risteárd A. Breathnach a stiúir an taighde. Chaith sí seal n Institiúid Ard-Léinn Bhaile Átha Cliath (1959–61).

Select bibliography
Ní Cheallacháin, Máire.
—. eag. *Filíocht Phádraigín Haicéid*. Scríbhneoireacht acadúil. Baile Átha Cliath: An Clóchomhar, 1962.

Ní Cheallaigh, Máire [Ní Cheallaigh, Polly]. 1905–98. Ceann an Bhathala, An Móta agus Baile na nGall, An Rinn, Na Déise, Co. Phort Láirge. Beathaisnéis / béaloideas.

I gCeann an Bhathala a saolaíodh agus a tógadh Polly. Bhí ochtar muirear ar a tuismitheoirí, agus cailleadh a máthair nuair a bhí Polly sna déaga. Bhíodh a hathair ag gabháilt don fheirmeoireacht agus don iascach. Thug sí blianta ag obair i mBaile Átha Cliath, d'fhill ar an mbaile agus chaith seal ag maireachtáil lena deartháir, Liam. Phós sí Pádraig Ó Faoileáin sa bhliain 1964 agus chuaigh chun cónaithe go dtí an Móta. D'aistríodar go Baile na nGall ina dhiaidh sin. Nuair a cailleadh a fear céile tháinig deirfiúr léi chun a bheith in aontíos léi. Thug sí cuntas gairid ar a saol do Nioclás Mac Craith agus foilsíodh é in *An Linn Bhuí* 3.

Select bibliography
Ní Cheallaigh, Máire.
—. "Polly." Nioclás Mac Craith. *An Linn Bhuí: Iris Ghaeltacht na nDéise*. Cuntas beathaisnéise / béaloideas. Eag. Pádraig Ó Macháin agus Aoibheann Nic Dhonnchadha. Vol. 3. Baile Átha Cliath: Leabhair na Linne, 1999: 123–9.

Ní Chearnaigh, Máire. *fl.*1935. An Clochán Dubh, Baile na nGall, Co. Chiarraí. Seanchas / béaloideas, paidreacha.

Bhí Máire ina cónaí ar an gClochán Dubh i 1923 nuair a bhailigh an Bráthair Lúcás paidreacha uaithi. D'fhoilsigh sé iad in *Béaloideas* 5.2 (1935).

Select bibliography
Ní Chearnaigh, Máire.
—. Seanchaí. "Sean-phaidreacha: 'Seacht n-Athchuinghí na Seachtmhaine', "Paidir na h-Oidhche" agus 'Paidir an Trom-Luighe'." Seanchas / béaloideas, paidreacha. *Béaloideas* 5.2 (1935): 216–18.

Ní Chéileachair, Síle. 1924–85. Cúil Aodha, Múscraí, Co. Chorcaí agus Co. Luimnigh. Gearrscéalaíocht.

D'fhás Síle aníos ar fheirm i mBreac-Ghaeltacht Chúil Aodha i gCo. Chorcaí. Siobhán Ní Mhulláin agus Dónall Bán Ó Céileachair ab ea a tuismitheoirí agus bhí seisear muirear orthu. File ab ea deartháir a máthar agus fear mór seanchais ab ea a hathair. Foilsíodh *Scéal mo Bheatha* le Dónall Bán i 1940. D'fhreastail Síle ar an gcoláiste ullmhúcháin, Coláiste Bhríde, An Fál Carrach agus ar Choláiste Mhuire gan Smál i Luimneach. D'oibrigh sí mar oide bunscoile i gCrois Araild agus i gCroimghlinn. Phós sí Dónall Ó Cochláin i 1953 agus bhí seisear clainne orthu.

Scríobh Síle agus a deartháir, Donncha, na gearrscéalta atá sa chnuasach *Bullaí Mhártain* a foilsíodh i 1955. Naoi ngearrscéal le Síle atá ann agus cúig cinn déag le Donncha. Bhuaigh Síle duais Oireachtais i 1950 do ghearrscéal dá cuid. Bhí baint aici agus ag Donncha le Cumann na Scríbhneoirí i mBaile Átha Cliath. Tá ábhar foilsithe ag deartháir eile leo, freisin, an tAthair Dáithí.

Select bibliography
Ní Chéileachair, Síle.
—. agus Donncha Ó Céileachair. *Bullaí Mhártain*. Gearrscéalaíocht. Baile Átha Cliath: Sáirséal agus Dill, 1955.

Secondary sources
Breathnach, Diarmuid, agus Máire Ní Mhurchú. "Ó Céileachair, Donncha (1918–60)." *1882–1982 Beathaisnéis a Ceathair*. Baile Átha Cliath: An Clóchomhar, 1994.

Cleeve, Brian. "Ní Chéileachair, Síle." *Dictionary of Irish Writers: Writers in the Irish Language*. Cork: Mercier, 1971.

Ní Chéilleachair, Máire. Comhaimseartha. Corca Dhuibhne, Co. Chiarraí / Cathair Luimnigh / Cathair Chorcaí. Scríbhneoireacht acadúil, leabhar teagaisc.

Is as Corca Dhuibhne do Mháire, agus is craoltóir le Raidió na Gaeltachta í. Tá sí tar éis na cláir "An Saol ó Dheas" agus "Cois Laoi" a léiriú. Is léachtóir í ar an gcúrsa "An Teastas i dTeagasc na Gaeilge", agus chaith sí seal ina léachtóir le Gaeilge i gColáiste Oideachais Thuamhumhan (mar a thugtaí air), Luimneach.

Select bibliography
Ní Chéilleachair, Máire.
—. "Mná i Litríocht an Bhlascaoid." *Oidhreacht an Bhlascaoid*. Scríbhneoireacht acadúil, aiste. Eag. Aogán Ó Muircheartaigh. Baile Átha Cliath: Coiscéim, 1989. 321–33.
—. *Bí ag Caint*. Scríbhneoireacht acadúil, leabhar teagaisc. Baile Átha Cliath: Gill & Macmillan, 1993.
—. *Eolas na Slí: Gaeilge Duitse*. Scríbhneoireacht acadúil, leabhar teagaisc agus caiséad. Baile Átha Cliath: Gill agus Macmillan, 1994.
—. *Sprioc*. Scríbhneoireacht acadúil, leabhar teagaisc agus caiséad. Indreabhán: Cló Iar-Chonnachta, 1996.
—. eag. *Tomás Ó Criomhthain 1855–1937*. Scríbhneoireacht acadúil. Ceiliúradh an Bhlascaoid 11. An Daingean: An Sagart, 1998.
—. eag. *Peig Sayers Scéalaí 1873–1958*. Scríbhneoireacht acadúil. Ceiliúradh an Bhlascaoid 111. Baile Átha Cliath: Coiscéim, 1999.
—. eag. *Muiris Ó Súilleabháin 1904–1950*. Scríbhneoireacht acadúil. Ceiliúradh an Bhlascaoid V. Baile Átha Cliath: Coiscéim, 2000.
—. eag. *Seoirse Mac Tomáis 1903–1987*. Scríbhneoireacht acadúil. Ceiliúradh an Bhlascaoid IV. Baile Átha Cliath: Coiscéim, 2000.

Ní Chinnéide, Gobnait. *fl.*1929. An Blascaod Mór [An tOileán Tiar] agus Na Gorta Dubha, Baile an Fheirtéaraigh, Co. Chiarraí. Scéalaíocht / béaloideas.

Saolaíodh ar an mBlascaod Mór, Co. Chiarraí i 1888 í. Is ann a bhí sí ina cónaí i 1928 nuair a bhailigh Robin Flower scéalta uaithi. D'fhoilsigh Flower na scéalta sin in *Béaloideas* 2 (1929). Deineann sé tagairt di, leis, ina leabhar *The Western Island* (1944).

Select bibliography
Ní Chinnéide, Gobnait.
—. scéalaí. "Sgéalta ón mBlascaod: "Sean 's an Bás" agus "Purty Deas Squary". Scéalaíocht / béaloideas. *Béaloideas* 2.1 (1929): 102–8.
—. scéalaí. "Sgéalta ón mBlascaod: "Bean an Tuirmisg" agus "Deasa Meallta na mBan". Scéalaíocht / béaloideas. *Béaloideas* 2.2 (1929): 206–8.

Secondary sources
Flower, Robin. *The Western Island or The Great Blasket*. Oxford: Clarendon Press, 1944.

Ní Chinnéide, Máire. 1878–1967. Corca Dhuibhne, Co. Chiarraí.
Drámaíocht, aistriúchán, agus scríbhneoireacht acadúil /
eagarthóireacht.

Saolaíodh Máire i mBaile Átha Cliath agus tógadh i mBaile an Bhóthair í.
B' as Co. Thiobraid Árann a hathair agus as Co. an Chláir a máthair.
Seisear a bhí sa chlann. D'fhreastail sí ar mheánscoil na nDoiminiceach i
gCnoc Síon, An Charraig Dhubh, Baile Átha Cliath agus ghnóthaigh sí
céim sa Nua-Litríocht ón Ollscoil Ríoga. I gcoláiste i gCearnóg Mhuirfean
a d'fhreastail sí ar na ranganna toisc go raibh cosc ar mhná a bheith i láthair
ag léachtaí i gColáiste Bhaile Átha Cliath ag an tráth sin. Bhuaigh sí
scoláireacht trí bliana sa Léann Ceilteach agus ceapadh í mar Ollamh le
Gaeilge in Ardscoil Mhuire, Domhnach Broc, Baile Átha Cliath. Ghlac sí
páirt ghníomhach in imeachtaí Gaelacha de gach saghas. Dhein sí an-chuid
oibre ar fud Bhaile Átha Cliath, idir mhúinteoireacht agus riarachán. Bhí
baint aici le bunú Chumann na Scríbhneoirí i 1921. Bhí ról aici sa dráma
Casadh an tSúgáin a léiríodh sa Gaiety sa bhliain 1901. Bhuaigh sí
duaiseanna Oireachtais dá haistí sna blianta 1902 agus 1908 – tá an tarna
haiste i gcló in *Irisleabhar na Gaeilge* (1909).

Chuir sí cumann camógaíochta ar bun do chailíní i mBaile Átha Cliath.
Phós sí Seán Mac Gearailt, státseirbhíseach ó Bhaile Deasumhan, Co.
Chiarraí sa bhliain 1906 agus bhí iníon amháin acu, Niamh, a chuaigh le
haisteoireacht nuair a d'fhás sí aníos. Chaith Máire agus a fear céile na
blianta ag maireachtaí i nDeilginis, Baile Átha Cliath. Cailleadh í sa bhliain
1967. Scríobh sí seacht ndráma, ceann amháin acu, *Cois Abhann Araglainn*, a
léiríodh i 1911 ach nár foilsíodh. Cuireadh aistí, léirmheasanna agus
aistriúcháin léi i gcló idir 1903–35 sna hirisí *An Claidheamh Soluis, Banba, An
Branar, Misneach, The Irish Rosary, St. Stephen's* agus *Ar Aghaidh*. D'aistrigh sí
Scéalta Ó Ghrimm go Gaeilge agus an dá dhráma ón bhFraincis go Gaeilge:
Dúbhairt sé Dábhairt sé agus *Nuair is Cruaidh do'n Chailligh*. Léiríodh na
drámaí sin i 1916. Thug sí spreagadh do Pheig Sayers scéal a beatha a insint,
agus chuir sí eagrán de *Peig* agus *Machnamh seana-mhná* in eagar.

Select bibliography
Ní Chinnéide, Máire.
—. *Gleann na Sidheóg*. Drámaíocht. Baile Átha Cliath: Muintir na Leabhar
   Gaedhilge, 1905.
—. *An Dúthchas: dráma éin-ghníomha*. Drámaíocht. Baile Átha Cliath: Conradh na
   Gaeilge, 1908.
—. *Gleann na Sidheóg [Dráma éin-ghníomha]*. Drámaíocht. Baile Átha Cliath:
   Connradh na Gaedhilge, 1908. Sreath Drámaí i nGaedhilg don Aos Óg. Baile
   Átha Cliath: Comhlucht Oideachais na hÉireann, 1935.
—. "Seanlitríocht na nGael agus nualitríocht na hEorpa curtha i gcóimheas lena
   chéile féachaint cé acu is fearr mar cheap agus mar sholaoid nualitríochta do
   scríbhneoirí na Gaeilge." Scríbhneoireacht acadúil. *Irisleabhar na Gaeilge*
   Eanáir, 1909.
—. aist. *Sgéalta ó Ghrimm*. Litríocht leanaí, aistriúchán. Le Jacob L.C. Grimm. Baile
   Átha Cliath: Connradh na Gaedhilge, 1923.
—. *Sidheóga na mBláth: dráma i gcomhair leanbhaí*. Drámaíocht. Baile Átha Cliath:

Connradh na Gaedhilge. Sreath Drámaí i nGaedhilg don Aos Óg. Baile Átha Cliath: Comhlucht Oideachais na hÉireann, 1935.

—. eag. *Peig.i. a scéal féin*. Scríbhneoireacht acadúil, eagarthóireacht. Le Peig Sayers. Baile Átha Cliath: Clólucht an Talbóidigh, 1936.

—. *Cáit Ní Dhuibhir*. Drámaíocht. 1938.

—. *An Cochall draoidheachta*. Drámaíocht. 1938.

—. eag. *Machnamh seana-mhná*. Scríbhneoireacht acadúil, eagarthóireacht. 1939. Scéalaí, Peig Sayers. Baile Átha Cliath: Oifig an tSoláthair, 1980.

—. *Peig: tuairisc do scríobh Peig Sayers ar imeachtaí a beatha féin, Máire Ní Chinnéide a d'ullmhaigh an chéad eagrán*. Scríbhneoireacht acadúil, eagarthóireacht. Baile Átha Cliath: Co. Oideachais na hÉireann, 1950.

—. *Scéal an Tí*. Drámaíocht. Baile Átha Cliath: Oifig an tSoláthair, 1952.

Secondary sources
Breathnach, Diarmuid, agus Máire Ní Mhurchú. "Ó Cinnéide, Máire [Ní Chinnéide] (1878–1967)." *1882–1982 Beathaisnéis a Dó*. Baile Átha Cliath: An Clóchomhar, 1990.

Ní Chinnéide, Nóra. 1859–1936. An Carn, Ráth na mBiríneach, An Rinn, Co. Phort Láirge. Seanchas agus scéalaíocht / béaloideas,

Bhí cónaí ar Nóra ar an gCarn. Ba é an tArdeaspag Ó Síothcháin a bhreac síos an scéal uaithi atá i gcló in *An Linn Bhuí 1* agus foilsíodh an scéal céanna in *Cnó Coilleadh Craobhaighe* (1907) ar dtúis. Bhailigh Eibhlín de Priondargás scéalta uaithi agus d'fhoilsigh sí iad in *Béaloideas 1* (1928) agus 2 (1929). Bhreac Áine Ní Chróinín paidreacha síos uaithi agus chuir sí in eagar iad in *Béaloideas 3.4* (1932). D'fhoilsigh Mícheál Ó hAodha seanchas a bhailigh sé uaithi, "Seanchas ós na Déisibh" in *Béaloideas 14* (1944).

Select bibliography
Ní Chinnéide, Nóra.
—. scéalaí. *Cnó Coilleadh Craobhaighe*. Scéalaíocht / béaloideas. Bail. agus eag. P. Ó Síothcháin. 1910. Dublin: Gill, 1917.
—. scéalaí. "Triúr Mac Feirmeóra a Chuaidh ag Foghluim Béarla." Scéalaíocht / béaloideas. *Béaloideas* 1.3 (1928): 298–300.
—. scéalaí. "'Fág Fé Dia an Dioghaltas agus Ná Bain an tSlat as a Láimh' agus 'Mallacht na Máthar'." Scéalaíocht / béaloideas. *Béaloideas* 1.4 (1928): 64.
—. scéalaí. "Na Trí Ceisteanna." Scéalaíocht / béaloideas. *Béaloideas* 2.2 (1929): 196–8.
—. scéalaí. "Orthaí agus Paidreacha ón Rinn." Seanchas / béaloideas, paidreacha. *Béaloideas* 3.4 (1932): 427–31.
—. seanchaí. "Seanchas ós na Déisibh." Seanchas / béaloideas. *Béaloideas* 14 (1944): 77–8.
—. scéalaí. "An tSeanchailleach sa Chófra." *An Linn Bhuí: Iris Ghaeltacht na nDéise*. Scéalaíocht / béaloideas. Eag. Pádraig Ó Macháin agus Aoibheann Nic Dhonnchadha. Vol. 1. Baile Átha Cliath: Leabhair na Linne, 1997.

Ní Chinnéide, Síle. 1900–1980. An Trá Mhór agus Cathair Phort Láirge / Cathair Chorcaí. Scríbhneoireacht acadúil, stair.

Saolaíodh Síle i gcathair Phort Láirge. Dochtúir ab ea a hathair. Deichniúr a bhí sa chlann, ach cailleadh beirt agus iad ina bpáistí. Bhí an teaghlach ag cur fúthu sa chathair ar dtús ach d'aistrigh siad go dtí An Trá Mhór ansin. Ghnóthaigh Síle BA, MA agus an tArdteastas san Oideachas ó Choláiste na hOllscoile, Corcaigh. Bhuaigh sí scoláireacht taistil agus chaith sí tréimhse thar lear agus tamall ag obair mar theagascóir. Fuair sí post mar léachtóir le Stair i gColáiste na hOllscoile, Gaillimh sa bhliain 1927. Ceapadh í mar Chomh-Ollamh agus mar Ollamh Gradaim níos déanaí ina saol. Dhein sí obair cheannródaíoch i dteagasc trí Ghaeilge ag an tríú leibhéal. Scríobh sí an téacsleabhar *An tSean Eoraip* (1947). Ba é cuspóir an leabhair ná "an stair a mhúineadh, gluaiseacht ar ghluaiseacht, gan bacaint le mionstaidéar ar chúrsaí speisialta, go dtí go mbeidh eolas réasúnta cruinn ag lucht foghlumtha ar chnámharlach scéil na hEorpa" (Ní Chinnéide 1947, réamhrá). Bhí baint aici le bunú na hirise *Galvia* agus d'fheidhmigh sí mar chomheagarthóir na hirise sin ar feadh tamall fada. Scríobhadh sí do thréimhseacháin staire agus seandálaíochta chomh maith.

Select bibliography
Ní Chinnéide, Síle.
—. *An tSean Eoraip*. Scríbhneoireacht acadúil, leabhar teagaisc. Baile Átha Cliath: An Gúm, 1947.
—. *Napper Tandy and the European Crisis of 1798–1803: O'Donnell Lecture delivered at University College Galway, June 1962*. Scríbhneoireacht acadúil, léacht. Dublin: NUI, 1962.

Secondary sources
Breathnach, Diarmuid agus Máire Ní Mhurchú. "Ó Cinnéide, Síle (1900–1980) [Ní Chinnéide]." *1882–1982 Beathaisnéis a Cúig*. Baile Átha Cliath: An Clóchomhar, 1997.
Ó Tuathaigh, Gearóid. "Obituary: An tOllamh Síle Ní Chinnéide, M.A. (1900–1980)." *North Munster Antiquarian Journal* XXII (1980): 79.

Ní Chnáimhín, Áine [Ní Chnáimhín / Bowman, Stáis]. 1908–2001.
Luimneach. Scríbhneoireacht acadúil, aistriúchán, drámaíocht, litríocht leanaí.

I gCo. Uíbh Fhailí a saolaíodh Áine. Ba iad Thomas Nevin agus Alice Higginson a tuismitheoirí agus bhí cúigear deartháireacha aici. Chuaigh an teaghlach chun cónaithe go cathair Chill Chainnigh, mar a ndeachaigh Áine ar scoil ar dtúis agus chuadar go cathair Luimnigh ina dhiaidh sin, áit a bhfuair sí meánscolaíocht. D'fhreastail sí ar Choláiste Mhuire gan Smál agus d'oibrigh mar mhúinteoir i gcathair Luimnigh ar feadh tamall fada ina dhiaidh sin. Bhí sí pósta le Séamus Bowman ó Phailís Ghréine, Co. Luimnigh. Ní raibh aon mhuirear orthu.

Thosaigh sí ag aistriú drámaí don Ghúm ón mbliain 1931 amach. Scríobh sí ceithre dhráma dá cuid féin, a foilsíodh sna 1940adaí, chomh maith leis an saothar *Pádraig Ó Conaire*, a tháinig amach i 1947. Bronnadh duais Oireachtais agus Duais an Chraoibhín uirthi dá leabhar ar an gConarach.

Select bibliography
Ní Chnáimhín, Áine.
—. aist. *Gogaile Gó* [*Goose Chase* le Mabel Constanduros agus Howard Agg]. Drámaíocht. Baile Átha Cliath: Oifig an tSoláthair, 1944.

—. aist. *Breacóg: mion-dráma i gcomhair cailíní scoile [Freckles* le Violet M. Methley]. Drámaíocht. Baile Átha Cliath: Oifig an tSoláthair, 1945.

—. aist. *Rathmhartach agus Casann: dráma beag i gcomhair malrach [Fortunatus and Cassandra* le Githa Sowerby]. Drámaíocht. Baile Átha Cliath: Oifig an tSoláthair, 1945.

—. *Tar éis a tuigtear: dráma dhá radharc i gcomhair cailíní.* Drámaíocht. Baile Átha Cliath: Oifig an tSoláthair, 1945.

—. *Agus annsan—? dráma aoin-ghnímh i gcomhair cailíní.* Drámaíocht. Baile Átha Cliath: Oifig an tSoláthair, 1946.

—. *An Bhrionglóid: dráma aoin-ghnímh i gcomhair cailíní.* Drámaíocht. Baile Átha Cliath: Oifig an tSoláthair, 1946.

—. *Meascán mearaidhe: dráma dhá ghníomh i gcomhair cailíní scoile.* Drámaíocht. Baile Átha Cliath: Oifig an tSoláthair, 1946.

—. aist. *An tOthar: dráma aoin-ghnímh do cheathrar cailíní [The Injured* le Violet M. Methley]. Drámaíocht. Baile Átha Cliath: Oifig an tSoláthair, 1946.

—. aist. *Lá Deiridh an Téarma: dráma aoin-ghnímh d'ochtar cailíní [The Last Day of Term* le H.M. Paull]. Drámaíocht. Baile Átha Cliath: Oifig an tSoláthair, 1947.

—. *Pádraig Ó Conaire.* Scríbhneoireacht acadúil. Baile Átha Cliath: Oifig an tSoláthair, 1947.

Secondary sources
Breathnach, Diarmuid, agus Máire Ní Mhurchú. "Ó Cnáimhín, Áine [Stáis Ní Chnáimhín / Bowman] (1908–2001)." *1983–2002 Beathaisnéis.* Baile Átha Claith: An Clóchomhar, 2003.

Ní Chonaill, Eibhlín Dubh. 1743–1800. Doire Fhionáin agus Na Foidhrí, Co. Chiarraí / Maigh Chromtha agus Carraig an Ime, Co. Chorcaí. Filíocht, caoineadh / béaloideas.

Saolaíodh Eibhlín i nDoire Fhionáin. Ba nia léi an polaiteoir mór le rá, Domhnall Ó Conaill. Ba iad Domhnall Mór Ó Conaill agus Máire Ní Dhonnabháin Dubh tuismitheoirí Eibhlín agus deirtear go raibh bua na filíochta ag Máire. Bhí rachmas nach beag acu agus mhaireadar go compordach, sócúlach. Saolaíodh beirt pháistí agus fiche dóibh, ach cailleadh deichniúr acu agus iad ina bpáistí. Deineadh cleamhnas d'Eibhlín agus í sna déaga le seanfhear ó na Foidhrí, ach cailleadh é siúd laistigh de leathbhliain. Chaoin Eibhlín é agus mhair an fhilíocht ar bhéal na ndaoine áitiúla go ceann tamaill. Thit sí i ngrá le hArt Ó Laoghaire nuair a bhí cuairt á tabhairt aici ar thigh a deirféar. Fear gustalach as ceantar Mhaigh Chromtha ab ea é, agus bhí seal tugtha aige in arm na hOstaire. Phósadar i 1767, cé nach raibh aon mheas ag muintir Eibhlín air.

Thit Art agus an giúistís, Abraham Morris, amach lena chéile. Bhí sé beartaithe ag Art, a deirtear, go maródh sé Morris ach a mhalairt a tharla. Maraíodh Art ag Carraig an Ime i 1773. Is ar an ócáid sin a chum Eibhlín an caoineadh agus chuir deirfiúr Airt agus athair Airt rann nó dhó an duine leis. Chuaigh Morris saor ó phíonós. Dhein deartháir Airt ionsaí air ina dhiaidh sin agus cé nár maraíodh é, ní raibh an tsláinte go maith aige as sin amach. Bhí beirt mhac ag Eibhlín, Fear agus Conchubhar, agus bhí sí ag súil leis an tríú leanbh nuair a maraíodh Art. Tá cur síos Chonchubhair ar bhás Airt i lámhscríbhinní John Windele in Acadamh Ríoga na hÉireann.

Foilsíodh an caoineadh den chéad uair mar aguisín in *The Last Colonel of the Irish Brigade* (1892). Chuir an scoláire Seán Ó Cuív eagrán den chaoineadh ar fáil a foilsíodh i 1908 agus chuir Seán Ó Tuama eagrán eile amach sa bhliain 1961. Tá saothar an Tuamaigh bunaithe ar dhá leagan den chaoineadh ó bhéalaithris Nóra Ní Shíndhle, a breacadh síos timpeall na bliana 1800 agus arís in 1850. Deineann an Tuamach pearsanra, leaganacha agus comhthéacs an chaointe a chíoradh. Ar na leaganacha scríofa atá ar fáil inniu, foilsíodh ceann suimiúil in *An Músgraigheach 6* (1944), a cumadh, de réir an tseanchais, d'fhonn clú Airt a chosaint toisc gur cuireadh ina leith é go mbuaileadh sé Eibhlín. Deir Eibhlín sa leagan seo nár chaith sé go dona léi ach amháin nuair a bhíodh sé i bhfeirg agus gur uirthi féin an locht ar na hócáidí sin. Foilsíodh an caoineadh go forleathan i ndíolamaí sa chéad leath den fhichiú haois: *Féithe Fódla. Gill's Irish reciter* (O'Kelly 1907), *An cúigeadh Leabhar* (Laoide 1914), *Fíon na Filidheachta* (Breathnach 1931), *Caiseal* (Ua Duinnín 1935), *150 de Dhuanta Gaedhilge* (Ó Súilleabháin 1936), agus ina lán cnuasach eile, nach, iad ó shin i leith. Ina theannta sin, aistríodh go Béarla agus go teangacha eile é.

Select bibliography
Ní Chonaill, Eibhlín Dubh.
—. *Cuíne Airt Í Laere*. Filíocht/ béaloideas. Dublin: The Irish Book Company, 1908. Eag. Seán Ó Cuív. Baile Átha Cliath: Brún agus Ó Nualláin, 1923.
—. "Caoine Airt Uí Laoghaire." Filíocht / béaloideas. *An Músgraigheach 6* Fóghmhar (1944): 3–6.
—. *Caoineadh Airt Uí Laoghaire*. Eag. Seán Ó Tuama. Filíocht / béaloideas. Baile Átha Cliath: An Clóchomhar, 1961.
—. "The Lament for Art O'Leary." *Kings, Lords and Commons: an anthology from the Irish*. Filíocht / béaloideas. Aist. Frank O'Connor. California: Ford & Bailie, 1961. London: Macmillan, 1989. 109–19.
—. "Caoineadh Airt Uí Laoghaire / The Lament for Art O'Leary." *An Duanaire: Poems of the Dispossessed 1600–1900*. Filíocht / béaloideas. Eag. Seán Ó Tuama. Aist. Thomas Kinsella. Portlaoise: Dolmen, 1981. 200–220.
—. *Klagesang for Art Ó Laoghaire*. Filíocht / béaloideas. Aist. P. Mc Manus. Copenhagen: Brøndums Forlag, 1995.

Secondary sources
Bourke, Angela. "The Irish Traditional Lament and the Grieving Process." *Women's Studies International Forum* 11.4 (1988): 287–91.
Bourke, Angela. "Performing – Not Writing." *Graph: Irish Literary Review* 11 (1991–2): 28–31.
Boylan, Henry. "Ní Chonaill, Eibhlín Dhubh." *A Dictionary of Irish Biography*. 3rd ed. Dublin: Gill & Macmillan, 1998. 294.
Bromwich, Rachel. "The Keen for Art O'Leary, Its Background and its Place in the Tradition of Gaelic Keening." *Éigse* V (1948): 236–52.
Cleeve, Brian. "Ní Chonaill, Eibhlín Dubh." *Dictionary of Irish Writers: Writers in the Irish Language*. Cork: Mercier, 1971.

Cullen, L.M. "Caoineadh Airt Uí Laoghaire: The Contemporary Political Context." *History Ireland* 1.4 (1993).
Cullen, L.M. "The Contemporary and Later Politics of Caoineadh Airt Uí Laoire." *Eighteenth-Century Ireland* (1993).
Kennelly, Brendan. "Poetry and Violence." *History and Violence in Anglo-Irish Literature.* Ed. Joris Duytschaever and Geert Lernout. Amsterdam: Rodopi, 1988. 5–27.
Ó Buachalla, Breandán. *An Caoine agus an Chaointeoireacht.* Baile Átha Cliath: Cois Life, 1998.
Ó Tuama, Seán. "The Lament for Art O'Leary." *Repossessions: Selected Essays on the Irish Literary Heritage.* Cork: Cork UP, 1995. 78–100.

Ní Chonaill, Nóra (1). *fl.*1912. Baile an Sceilg, Uíbh Ráthach, Co. Chiarraí. Scéalaíocht / béaloideas.

Saolaíodh i mBaile an Sceilg í. Chuir sí scéal go dtí an *An Lóchrann* agus foilsíodh é i 1912. Tá leagan den scéal céanna a tógadh óna hathair, Seán Ó Conaill, ag Séamas Ó Duilearga in *Béaloideas* 2.2 (1929). D'fhoilsigh an Duileargach mórchnuasach Sheáin ina dhiaidh sin. Chuaigh Nóra go dtí na Stáit Aontaithe agus í ina cailín óg.

Select bibliography
Ní Chonaill, Nóra (1).
—. Scéalaí. "Diarmuid na Feasóige." Scéalaíocht / béaloideas. *An Lóchrann.* Iúil – Meán Fómhair (1912).

Secondary sources
Ó Duilearga, Séamas. *Leabhar Sheáin Í Chonaill: Sgéalta agus Seanchas ó Íbh Ráthach.* Baile Átha Cliath: Cumann le Béaloideas Éireann, 1948.

Ní Chonaill, Nóra (2) [Uí Uidhir, Bean]. *fl.*1937. Na hUllánaibh, Baile Bhuirne, Co. Chorcaí. Filíocht / béaloideas, amhránaíocht.

Saolaíodh Nóra i 1857. Bhí an-chuid amhrán aici a fuair sí ón lucht siúil a thugadh cuairt ar thigh thuismitheoirí a máthar ar an Ráth Dúbháin, Co. Chorcaí. Chaith sí tréimhsí sa tigh sin le linn a hóige. Fuair sí roinnt amhrán eile ó chéile a haintín, Peadí Ó Mulláin i Sráid an Mhuilinn. Fuair sí an chuid is mó de na hamhráin a bhí aici óna muintir féin agus óna cuid comharsan sna hUllánaibh. Chaith sí tréimhse ar an gClaon-Rath in Uíbh Laoghaire nuair a phós sí Diarmuid Ó hUidhir ach d'fhág sí an áit nuair a cailleadh é timpeall na bliana 1897. Chaith sí seal i gCrois Thuath na nDromann i gCill na Martra. D'aistrigh sí go Cúil an Bhuacaigh i 1936 agus bhí sí fós ann i 1937 nuair a bhailigh Proinséas Ó Ceallaigh amhráin uaithi. Foilsíodh iad sin in *Béaloideas* 7 (1937). Scríobh sé síos 125 amhrán ar fad uaithi. Bhuaigh sí a lán duaiseanna ag na feiseanna i mBaile Bhuirne, i mBéal Átha an Ghaorthaidh, i Maigh Chromtha agus ar na Tuaimeacha.

Select bibliography
Ní Chonaill, Nóra (2).
—. amhránaí. "Amhráin Ó Mhúscraighe: 'B'fhearr Leogaint D'ól', 'Raithineach, a Bhean Bheag', 'Greadadh agus Cás Ort', 'Fallaing a Bhacaigh', 'An Spailpín Fánach' agus amhráin éagsúla eile." Amhránaíocht agus filíocht. *Béaloideas* 7.1 (1937): 19–44.

Ní Chríodáin, Nóra ["Nóra an tSleasa"]. fl.1944, 1982. Béal Átha an Ghaorthaidh agus na Millíní, Muscraí, Co. Chorcaí. Filíocht / béaloideas.

Luaigh Seán Ua Cróinín "Nóra an tSleasa Ní Chríodáin" ar liosta d'fhilí Mhúscraí sa tréimhseachán *An Músgraigheach 2* (1943, 10). Mhair sí le linn aimsir Pheaid Bhuí Í Luínse. Saolaíodh i mBéal Átha an Ghaorthaidh í agus phós sí Amhlaoibh Óg ón Slios. Ní raibh an tsláinte go maith aici tar éis pósta di. Bhí cúigear muirear uirthi, agus ba í an iníon ba shine a fuair an fheirm. Chum sí go leor véarsaí beaga deisbhéalacha agus í i mbun cainte leis na comharsana, go mórmhór nuair a bheadh fonn uirthi iad a cháineadh. Tá cuid de na rannta sin i gcló in *An Músgraigheach 4*, faoi mar a chuala Nóra Ní Scanail iad ó bhéalaithris sheanóirí na háite (1944, 16–17). Bhí amhrán amháin dá cuid ag Pádraig Ó Crualaoi, is é sin "Amhrán na gCearc" (Ó Crualaoi 1982, 147).

Select bibliography
Ní Chríodáin, Nóra.
—. file. "Nóra an tSleasa." Filíocht / béaloideas. *An Músgraigheach* 4. Earrach (1944): 16–17.

Secondary sources
Ó Crualaoi, Pádraig. *Seanachas Phádraig Í Chrualaoi.* Eag. Donncha Ó Cróinín. Baile Átha Cliath: Comhairle Bhéaloideas Éireann, 1982.
Ua Cróinín, Seán. "Filí agus Filíocht Mhúsgraighe, 2." *An Músgraigheach 2* Fóghmhar (1943): 10–13.

Ní Chróinín, Áine [Ní Chróinín / Uí Shúilleabháin, Neans]. 1910–84. An Ráth agus Oileán Chléire, Co. Chorcaí. Scríbhneoireacht acadúil, eagarthóireacht.

Ba é An Ráth, Co. Chorcaí áit dhúchais Áine. Ba é Patrick Cronin a hathair agus ba í Kate Moran a máthair. Bhain sí BA amach sa Léann Ceilteach i gColáiste na hOllscoile, Baile Átha Cliath i 1931. Bhailigh sí béaloideas ina ceantar dúchais a cuireadh amach in *Béaloideas* sna blianta 1930, 1932 agus 1932. Ghnóthaigh sí MA i 1933 agus foilsíodh codanna de san iris *Éigse* i 1945 agus i 1946. Chaith sí tréimhsí ag staidéar sa Chríoch Lochlann agus i bPáras, agus bhí spéis aici i réimsí éagsúla den léann, sa litríocht agus sa teangeolaíocht ach go háirithe. Bhí labhairt na Breatnaise agus na Gaeilge aici, agus théadh sí go rialta go hOileán Chléire.

Bhí sí ina heagarthóir cúnta ar an tsraith *Leabhair ó Láimhsgríbhnibh* ó 1939 go 1942. Chuir sí dhá shaothar eile in eagar a tháinig amach i 1952 agus bhí baint aici leis an eagrán de *Duanaire Finn 111* a foilsíodh i 1953. D'oibrigh sí in Acadamh Ríoga na hÉireann mar eagarthóir ar *Dictionary of the Irish Language* ar feadh breis is fiche bliain. Bhí sí ina léachtóir cuairte sa Mhoch-Ghaeilge in Ollscoil Londain agus ina scrúdaitheoir sa Cheiltis ann ar feadh tamaill. D'oibrigh sí i Scoil an Léinn Cheiltigh ó 1967 amach, áit ar chabhraigh sí le Daniel Binchy *Corpus Iuris Hibernici* a ullmhú. Chuir sí eagar ar an imleabhar déanach de *The Book of Leinster formerly Lebor na Nuachongbála* (1983) agus bhí *Poems on Marcher Lords* á ullmhú aici nuair a cailleadh í; ba é Pádraig Ó Riain a chuir críoch leis agus foilsíodh é i 1987.

Bhíodh aistí agus léirmheasanna aici in irisí léannta éagsúla. Tá leabharliosta iomlán ar fáil in *Studia Celtica* (1987–88).

Bhí sí pósta le William O' Sullivan, a bhí ina choimeádaí ar lámhscríbhinní i gColáiste na Tríonóide. Bhí suim acu beirt in obair Edward Lhuyd. Scríobh siad an réamhrá leis an eagrán de *Archaeologia Britannica* a foilsíodh in 1971, chomh maith le haiste ar bhailiúchán lámhscríbhinní de chuid Lhuyd.

Select bibliography
Ní Chróinín, Áine.
—. bail. 'Some Co. Cork Folk Tales.' *Béaloideas*. Scríbhneoireacht acadúil. Vol. 2, no. 4. Baile Átha Cliath: An Cumann le Béaloideas Éireann, 1930.
—. 'The Sources of Keating's *History of Ireland.*' *Éigse*. Scríbhneoireacht acadúil. Vol. 4, no. 4. Geimhreadh 1944 [1945] *et seq.*
—. eag. *Beatha Chríost*. Scríbhneoireacht acadúil. Leabhair ó Láimhsgríbhnibh XVII. Baile Átha Cliath: Oifig an tSoláthair, 1952.
—. eag. *Eachtra Ridire na Leomhan*. Scríbhneoireacht acadúil. Leabhair ó Láimhsgríbhnibh XVIII. Baile Átha Cliath: Oifig an tSoláthair, 1952.
—. *The Book of Leinster formerly Lebor na Nuachongbála*. Scríbhneoireacht acadúil. Vol. 6. Baile Átha Cliath: DIAS, 1983.

Secondary sources
Breathnach, Diarmuid agus Máire Ní Mhurchú. "Ó Cróinín, Áine [Neans Ní Chróinín / Uí Shúilleabháin] (1910–1984)." *1983–2002 Beathaisnéis*. Baile Átha Cliath: An Clóchomhar, 2003.

Ní Chrualaíoch, Peig. *fl.* **1982.** Baile Bhuirne, Múscraí, Co. Chorcaí. Filíocht / béaloideas.

B' as Baile Bhuirne do Pheig. Deirtear go raibh an chumhacht aici francaigh a ruaigeadh as an teach le filíocht (Ó hÓgáin 1982, 381).

Secondary sources
Ó hÓgáin, Daithí. *An File: Staidéar ar Osnádúrthacht na Filíochta sa Traidisiún Gaelach*. Baile Átha Cliath: Oifig an tSoláthair, 1982.

Ní Chrualaoich, Máire [Sappho na Mumhan]. Átha Chonna, Cill na Martra, Co. Chorcaí. Filíocht / béaloideas.

Saolaíodh Máire in Átha Chonna. Is duine í a raibh a hainm in airde mar fhile, cé nár tháinig aon ní slán dár chum sí (Ó Cróinín 1943, 19). Dar le Pádraig Ó Crualaoi, ba bhandia na filíochta í Sappho, agus ba é sin an fáth go dtugtaí "Sappho na Mumhan" ar Mháire. Chum an file Seán na Ráithíneach (Ó Murachú) caoineadh ar ócáid a báis agus tá blúire de in *Seanachas Phádraig Í Chrualaoi* (1982, 143). Ina theannta sin, luann "Fiachra Éilgeach" (Risteárd Ó Foghludha) Máire Ní Chruadhlaoich ina aiste "Filí Chorcaighe" (1908). Deir Máirín Nic Eoin gur leasiníon Mhíchíl Óig Uí Longáin ab ea Máire agus gurbh é Mícheál a scríobh an caoineadh nuair a cailleadh í ar 2 Aibreán 1821 (1998, 167).

Secondary sources
Éilgeach, Fiachra. "Filí Chorcaighe." *Saothar Suadha: Aistí do léigheadh os comhair Dáil na hÉigse, i gCorcaigh, Meadhon Foghmhair, 1907*. Vol. 1. Baile Átha Cliath: Muinntir an Ghoill, Teo., 1908.

Nic Eoin, Máirín. *B'ait leo bean: Gnéithe den Idé-eolaíocht Inscne i dTraidisiún Liteartha na Gaeilge.* Baile Átha Cliath: An Clóchomhar Tta, 1998.

Ó Cróinín, Donnchadh. "Filí agus Filíocht Mhúsgraighe." *An Músgraigheach* 1. Meitheamh (1943): 15–20.

Ó Crualaoi, Pádraig. *Seanachas Phádraig Í Chrualaoi.* Eag. Donncha Ó Cróinín. Baile Átha Cliath: Comhairle Bhéaloideas Éireann, 1982.

Ní Chuilleanáin, Eiléan. Contemporary. Cork. Poetry, literary criticism, academic writing.

Born in Cork in 1942, she is the daughter of writer Eilís Dillon (*q.v.*) and Cormac Ó Cuilleanáin, Professor of Irish at UCC. Descended on both sides from nationalist families, she was raised in Cork city, living as a child on the campus of UCC, where her father was warden of the Honan Hostel. Educated at UCC and at Oxford, she became a lecturer in medieval and Renaissance literature at TCD, and is now a Fellow of the college. She is married to poet Macdara Woods, with whom (and others) she founded and co-edits the literary review, *Cyphers*. Though she has played an important role for many years in enabling the work of others in Dublin literary circles, Ní Chuilleanáin has only relatively recently begun to be widely appreciated for her own work. Principally known for her prize-winning poetry, she has also published able critical essays on several topics in her area of academic interest, especially on the work of Edmund Spenser and his connections with Munster as a sixteenth-century planter in north Co. Cork. The use of Munster rural landscapes and of those of Cork city as settings is a prominent feature of her work. Her own Munster background, woven as it is into the cultural nationalism of her milieu as a child, is an important regional characteristic, necessary to the understanding of her vision as it has developed since the 1970s. Italian locations also begin to feature prominently in her later work as it flowers from the late 1980s on. The material for these derives from her family's possession of a house in Northern Italy and her regular periods of residence there, but their presence in her poetry also fulfils an important thematic function.

Ní Chuilleanáin has published seven collections of poetry from 1972 to 2002. Her work is, to some extent, *sui generis.* It combines a subtle and understated poetic style with a characteristic and even idiosyncratic range of subject matter; its consistent qualities and slow-growing excellence have only in very recent years begun to be recognized. The territory she chooses to explore is markedly Catholic: convent life, the experience of nuns, the tales of saints' lives, cults, relics, shrines, ceremonies and Catholic ritual, are all prominent material in her work. Yet her imagination and characteristic tone are sometimes delightedly comic, sometimes even sardonic. The interpretation of her work as quasi-mystical which has begun to be constructed, especially within the North American reception of her work, may be somewhat misguided. These emphases may perhaps be better understood in two quite other ways. They seem to be part, in the first place, of a broadly nationalist resistance to British cultural hegemony, in both its empiricist and imperialist aspects. In the second place, they gradually reveal a feminist position vis-à-vis the patriarchal and masculinist character both of Irish nationalism and of literary culture and historiography in general. The Robust invocations of the violent suppressions of the Irish colonial past co-exist, in her earlier and middle work, with a gentle attention to the victims of physical force and to the "nightmare" of history (from which Stephen Dedalus also was trying to awake).

Her deployment of Irish and Italian locations is linked with her intellectual and academic interests in the culture and sensibilities of pre-modern Europe; these form a kind of other way out of the prevalent Irish–British binary. Furthermore, her reading of these sensibilities as offering at least a haven, and often lively potential channels of development, for women's lives, thoughts and experiences is made increasingly evident in her later work. These highly original aspects of her vision afford links with the Irish past, both distant and more recent, which mark her work out among that of her contemporaries, both male and female. Her 1995 "*Cailleach* Writes about the Renaissance" essay touches on these topics, but it is the poetry itself which provides a detailed, challenging and ultimately feminist working out of their implications. Altogether, her original poetic voice and vision constitute an indispensable imaginative resource for Ireland in its struggle into the postmodernist era and one still largely waiting to be tapped. Well beyond the best-known anthology pieces ("The Lady in the Tower", "Swineherd", "*J'ai mal à nos dents*" and others), Ní Chuilleanáin's work as a whole is a formidable aesthetical and visionary achievement.

Select bibliography
Ní Chuilleanáin, Eiléan.

—. *Acts and Monuments*. Poetry. Oldcastle, Co. Meath: Gallery Press, 1972.
—. "Gaelic Ireland Rediscovered, Courtly and Country Poetry." *Irish Poets in English*. Literary criticism. Ed Seán Lucy. Cork: Mercier Press, 1972. 44–59.
—. *Site of Ambush*. Poetry. Oldcastle, Co. Meath: Gallery Press, 1975.
—. *Cork*. Poetry. Dublin: Gallery Press, 1977. Notes: Illus. Brian Lawlor.
—. *The Second Voyage*. Poetry. Oldcastle, Co. Meath: Gallery Press, 1977.
—. *The Rose Geranium*. Poetry. Oldcastle, Co. Meath: Gallery Press, 1981.
—. ed. *Irish Women: Image and Achievement*. Political writing. Dublin: Arlen House, 1985.
—. "Women as Writers: Dánta Grá to Maria Edgeworth." *Irish Women: Image and Achievement*. Literary criticism. Ed. Eiléan Ní Chuilleanáin. 1985. Dublin: Arlen House. 111–27.
—. "Poetry in Translation." Poetry. *Irish Translators' Association Newsletter* 1.1 (1987): 5.
—. *The Magdalene Sermon*. Poetry. Oldcastle, Co. Meath: Gallery Press, 1989.
—. trans. *Pharoah's Daughter*. Poetry. By Nuala Ní Dhomhnaill. Oldcastle, Co. Meath: Gallery Press, 1990.
—. *The Brazen Serpent*. Poetry. Oldcastle, Co. Meath: Gallery Press, 1994.
—. "Acts and Monuments of an Unelected Nation: The *Cailleach* Writes about the Renaissance." *The Southern Review* 31.3 (1995): 570–80.
—. "Borderlands of Irish Poetry." *Contemporary Irish Poetry: A Collection of Critical Essays*. Literary criticism. Ed Elmer Andrews. London: Macmillan, 1996. 25–40.

Secondary Sources
Conboy, Sheila C. "What You Have Seen is Beyond Speech: Female Journeys in the Poetry of Eavan Boland and Eiléan Ní Chuilleanáin." *Canadian Journal of Irish Studies* 16.1 (1990): 65–72.

Emmit, Helen. "The One Free Foot Kicking under the White Sheet of History: Eiléan Ní Chuilleanáin's Uncanny Landscapes." *Women's Studies* 29.4 (2000): 477–94.

Haberstroh, Patricia Boyle. "A Conversation with Eiléan Ní Chuilleanáin." *Four Quarters* 3.2 (1989): 15–19.

Haberstroh, Patricia Boyle. "An Interview with Eiléan Ní Chuilleanáin." *Canadian Journal of Irish Studies* 20.2 (1994): 63–94.

Johnston, Dillon. "Our Bodies' Eyes and Writing Hands: Secrecy and Sensuality in Ní Chuilleanáin's Baroque Art." *Gender and Sexuality in Modern Ireland*. Ed. Bradley, Anthony and Maryann Gialanella Valiulis. Amherst: Massachusetts UP, 1997.

Kerrigan, John. "Hidden Ireland: Eiléan Ní Chuilleanáin and Munster Poetry." *Critical Quarterly* 40.4 (1998): 76–100.

Praga, Ines. "Eiléan Ní Chuilleanáin." *Ireland in Writing: Interviews with Writers and Academics*. Ed. Jacqueline Hurtley *et al*. Amsterdam: Rodopi, 1998.

Ray, Kevin. "Interview with Eiléan Ní Chuilleanáin." *Éire/Ireland* 31.1 & 2 (1999): 62–73.

Ray, Kevin. "Sites of Ambush: Eiléan Ní Chuilleanáin's Bordered Silences." *Contemporary Irish Women Poets: Some Male Perspectives*. Ed. Alexander Gonzalez, Westport, CT: Greenwood, 1999.

Stanfield, Paul Scott. "How She Looks in that Company: Eiléan Ní Chuilleanáin as Feminist Poet." *Contemporary Irish Women Poets: Some Male Perspectives*. Ed. Alexander Gonzalez. Westport, CT: Greenwood, 1999.

Williams, Leslie. "The Stone Recalls Its Quarry: An Interview with Eiléan Ní Chuilleanáin." *Representing Ireland: Gender, Class, Nationality*. Ed. Susan Shaw Sailer. Florida: Florida UP, 1997.

Nic Pháidín, Caoilfhionn. Comhaimseartha. Corca Dhuibhne, Co. Chiarraí. Scríbhneoireacht acadúil, eagarthóireacht.

Saolaíodh i mBaile Átha Cliath í agus tá sí pósta leis an scríbhneoir Liam Ó Muirthile. Chaitheadh sí tamall go minic i gCiarraí nuair a bhí a tráchtais ollscoile ar siúl aici agus caitheann sí tréimhsí ann fós. Tá staidéar déanta aici ar chanúintí Chorca Dhuibhne, Uíbh Ráthaigh agus Chléire. Is é an saothar canúna is mó léi ná *Cnuasach Focal ó Uíbh Ráthach* (1987). Tá sí ina sraitheagarthóir ar *Lúb ar Phár* agus tá sí ina Stiúrthóir ar FIONTAR i DCU faoi láthair. Chaith sí tréimhsí i mbun taighde, foilsitheoireachta, agus eagarthóireachta in Acadamh Ríoga na hÉireann, *The Irish Times, Comhar* agus An Gúm. Chomhbhunaigh sí an comhlacht foilsitheoireachta Cois Life Teo i 1995. Bhí sí ina ball de Choimisiún na Gaeltachta, 2000–2002.

Chuir sí leabhar le Tomás Ó Criomhthain *Dinnseanchas na mBlascaodaí* in eagar. "Tá an t-eagrán bunaithe ar lámhscríbhinn an údair féin agus é curtha in eagar go tuisceanach ag Caoilfhionn Nic Pháidín" (Mícheál de Mórdha, *Foinse* Lúnasa 1999). Scríobh sí leabhar faoi *Fáinne an Lae* chomh maith: "an anáil a bhí ag an nuachtán *Fáinne an Lae* ar shaothrú na Gaeilge ó thús céad bliain ó shin go díreach. Cíortar staid na teanga agus staid na litearthachta go mion ag an am, agus pléitear an iriseoireacht agus an pobal maidir le bunú agus fás na nua-litríochta féin" (Books Ireland, Samhain 1998). Tá leagan de *Séadna* le Peadar Ó Laoghaire athchóirithe aici do leanaí agus d'fhoghlaimeoirí fásta agus tá dlúthdhiosca den scéal, á léamh ag Liam Ó Muirthile, le fáil leis an leabhar.

Select bibliography
Nic Pháidín, Caoilfhionn.
—. eag. *Dinnseanchas na mBlascaodaí.* Seanchas / béaloideas. Baile Átha Cliath: An Gúm, 1935. Le Tomás Ó Criomhthain. 2 Ed. Baile Átha Cliath: Cois Life, 1999.
—. "Irisleabhar na Gaeilge 1882–1909." *Comhar* 41. Samhain (1982): 4–16.
—. eag. *Cnuasach Focal ó Uíbh Ráthach.* Scríbhneoireacht acadúil, foclóireacht. Baile Átha Cliath: ARÉ, 1987.
—. a chóirigh. *Séanna.* Litríocht leanaí. Le Peadar Ó Laoghaire. Baile Átha Cliath: Cois Life, 1996.
—. *Fáinne an Lae agus an Athbheochan 1898–1900.* Scríbhneoireacht acadúil, léirmheastóireacht. Baile Átha Cliath: Cois Life, 1998.
Secondary sources
De Mórdha, Mícheál. "Léirmheas ar *Dinnseanchas na mBlascaodaí.*" *Foinse.* Lúnasa (1999).

Ní Dhabhoireann, Máire. c.1910–90. Co. an Chláir. Aistriúchán, drámaíocht.

I gCill Fhionnúrach, Co. an Chláir a saolaíodh Máire. Ghnóthaigh sí BA agus an tArdteastas san Oideachas agus chaith tamall mar mheánmhúinteoir. Fuair sí post mar eagarthóir cúnta leis an nGúm ansin, áit ar chaith sí an chuid eile dá saol oibre. D'aistrigh sí dráma de chuid Molière. Tá sí adhlactha ina háit dhúchais.

Select bibliography
Ní Dhabhoireann, Máire.
—. aist. *Fear na Sainnte* [le Molière]. Drámaíocht. Baile Átha Cliath: Oifig an tSoláthair, 1937.
Secondary sources
Breathnach, Diarmuid, agus Máire Ní Mhurchú. "Ó Dabhoireann, Máire [Ní Dh.] (*c.* 1910–1990)." *1983–2002 Beathaisnéis.* Baile Átha Claith: An Clóchomhar, 2003.

Ní Dhomhnaill, Nuala. Comhaimseartha. Corca Dhuibhne, Co. Chiarraí agus Co. Thiobraid Árann. Filíocht, gearrscéalaíocht, drámaíocht, aistriúchán agus scríbhneoireacht acadúil.

Saolaíodh Nuala i Lancashire i 1952. D'fhás sí aníos i nGaeltacht Chorca Dhuibhne agus in Aonach Urmhumhan, Co. Thiobraid Árann. Máinlia ab ea a hathair, a bhí gníomhach i gConradh na Gaeilge. Dochtúir ab ea a máthair, as Fionn Trá. Bronnadh BA sa Ghaeilge agus sa Bhéarla ar Nuala i gColáiste na hOllscoile, Corcaigh (1972) agus dhein sí an tArd-Teastas san Oideachas san Ollscoil chéanna. Bhí baint mhór aici leis an iris *Innti* agus í ina mac léinn. D'oibrigh sí mar mhúinteoir; phós sí an geolaí Dogan Leflef, agus chaith tamall sa Tuirc agus san Ollainn. Ar fhilleadh di ar Éirinn, chónaigh sí i nGaeltacht Chorca Dhuibhne sna hochtóidí luatha, agus ansin shocraigh sí síos i mBaile Átha Cliath lena fear céile agus a gcuid páistí. Bronnadh D.Phil. *honoris causa* uirthi ó Ollscoil Chathair Bhaile Átha Cliath i 1995.

Tá seacht gcnuasach filíochta léi i gcló, agus ina theannta sin, foilsíodh dánta dá cuid i mórán díolamaí. I nGaeilge amháin a chumann sí féin, ach tá a cuid filíochta aistrithe go Béarla, lena cabhair, ag roinnt de mhór-fhilí

Éireannacha na haoise (agus go mórán teangacha eile). Is minic a dheineann sí a cuid filíochta a reic go poiblí, agus cuireadh amach *Spíonáin is Róiseanna* i bhfoirm téipe. Scríobh sí trí drámaí do pháistí idir 1987 and 1993, agus chum an libretto *The Wooing of Éadaoin* (National Chamber Choir 1994); chuir sí an bailiúchán *Jumping Off Shadows: Selected Contemporary Irish Poets* (Cork University Press, 1995) in eagar i gcomhar le Greg Delanty. Foilsíodh dánta dá cuid in iliomad irisí, agus aistí, ailt agus agallaimh in irisí agus leabhair éagsúla.

Born in Lancashire, 1952, daughter of a veterinary surgeon and a doctor, Nuala grew up in the West Kerry Gaeltacht, her mother's birthplace, and in Nenagh, Co. Tipperary. While studying for a BA in Irish and English (UCC, 1972) and a H.Dip. in Education (1973), she published poetry in the journal *Innti*. She married geologist Dogan Leflef, with whom she lived in Holland and Turkey for some years. In the early 1980s she lived in West Kerry, then settled in Dublin with her husband and children. Dublin City University awarded her an Honorary D.Phil. (1995).

One of the best-known poets of the period, she published seven collections of poetry from 1981 onwards. Her work also appears in many journals and anthologies, and has been translated into English and several other languages: writing only in Irish, she has however actively assisted a succession of translators who include several distinguished contemporary Irish poets. She enjoys a wide international reputation which far exceeds that of most Irish-language writers. A gifted oral presenter of her work, she has given bilingual readings far and wide. She has also written children's plays and a libretto, and essays and articles – including the important: "What Foremothers?" (1992) and "Why I Write in Irish" (1995) – given published interviews, and co-edited the anthology *Jumping Off Shadows: Selected Contemporary Irish Poets* (Cork University Press, 1995).

From the 1980s Ní Dhomhnaill emerged as a figure of increasing cultural importance. Rooted linguistically and imaginatively in ancient traditions of literature and folklore, her poetry nevertheless decisively inhabits Irish postmodernity. It combines a vigorously feminist character with sexual openness, and also conducts a continuing dialogue with Jungian visions of selfhood. Engaging in a dialectical, interrogative relationship with gender roles in Irish traditional ideology, it sets inherited images - such as the *murúch* or mermaid figure – against a sceptical urban milieu, and explores women's desire as an emphatic force. Darkly depressive, humorously bawdy, often delicately lyrical, the poems draw brilliantly upon the extensive body of Irish oral traditions; Ní Dhomhnaill added systematic study of this material to her own experience of Gaeltacht cultural life. Both in her work, and in her cultural impact as a figure of compelling charm and formidable imaginative energy, Ní Dhomhnaill makes vital links for post-modern Ireland between past and future. Her vision of possible femininities is original in renegotiating the binaries which have sometimes confined Irish women poets of her generation and before. In its playful grace, intense feeling, and depth of reach into tradition, her poetry is an inimitable contribution both to women's writing and to Irish literature in general.

Select bibliography:

Ní Dhomhnaill, Nuala.

—. *An Dealg Droighin*. Filíocht. Baile Átha Cliath: Mercier, 1981.

—. ""Dán do Mhelissa", "An Bhábóg Bhriste", "Iascach Oíche" agus "Aubade"." Filíocht. *Comhar* Eanáir (1984): 22.

—. *Selected Poems: Rogha Dánta*. Filíocht. 1986. Aist. Nuala Ní Dhomhnaill agus Michael Hartnett, 1988, 1990. Dublin: New Island (Raven Arts) , 2000.

—. "An Fhilíocht á Cumadh: Ceardlann Filíochta." Filíocht. *Léachtaí Cholm Cille* 17 (1986): 147-79.

—. *Selected Poems*. Filíocht. Aist. Michael Hartnett. Baile Átha Cliath: Raven Arts, 1986.

—. "Making the Millennium". *Graph* 1 (1986).

—. *Féar Suaithinseach*. Filíocht. 1984. Maigh Nuad: An Sagart, 1988.

—. Interview. *Sleeping with Monsters: Conversations with Scottish and Irish Women Poets*, ed. Gillian Somerville-Arjat and Rebecca Wilson. Dublin: Wolfhound, 1990.

—. *Pharoah's Daughter: New and Selected Poems in Irish with Translations into English*. Filíocht. An Mhí: Gallery, 1990.

—. *Feis*. Filíocht. Indreabhán: Cló Iar-Chonnachta. Maigh Nuad: An Sagart, 1991.

—. *The Astrakhan Cloak* . Filíocht. Indreabhán: Cló Iar-Chonnachta, 1991. Aist. Paul Muldoon. Baile Átha Cliath: Gallery, 1992.

—. "What Foremothers?" Scríbhneoireacht acadúil. *Poetry Ireland Review* 36 Autumn (1992): 18-31.

—. *Spíonáin is Róiseanna: compánach don chaiséad CIC L21*. Filíocht. Indreabhán: Cló Iar-Chonnachta, 1993.

—. "Why I Write in Irish: The Corpse that Sits up and Talks Back". *New York Times*, 8 January 1995.

—, Eag. *Jumping Off Shadows: Selected Contemporary Irish Poets*. Filíocht. Eag. Nuala Ní Dhomhnaill agus Greg Delanty. Corcaigh: Cork UP, 1995.

—. *Cead Aighnis*. Filíocht. An Daingean: An Sagart, 1998.

—. *The Water Horse: poems in Irish with translations into English by Medbh McGuckian and Eiléan Ní Chuilleanáin*. Filíocht. An Mhí: Gallery, 1999.

Secondary sources:

Bourke, Angela. "Bean an Leasa". *Leath na Spéire*, eag. Eoghan Ó hAnluain. Baile Átha Cliath: An Clóchomhar, 1992.

de Paor, Pádraig. *Tionscnamh Filíochta Nuala Ní Dhomhnaill*. Leabhair Thaighde 82. Baile Átha Cliath: An Clóchomhar, 1997.

Gonzalez, Alexander G. *Contemporary Irish Women Poets: Some Male Perspectives*. Westport/London: Greenwood, 1999.

Haberstroh, Patricia Boyle. *Women Creating Women: Contemporary Irish Women Poets*. Baile Átha Cliath: Attic, 1996.

MacWilliams Consalvo, Deborah. "The Linguistic Ideal in the Poetry of Nuala Ní Dhomhnaill". *Éire/Ireland* (Summer 1995).

Nic Dhiarmada, Bríona. "Bláthú and Traidisiúin". *Comhar* (Bealtaine 1987).

—. "Immram sa tSícé: Filíocht Nuala Ní Dhomhnaill agus Próiséas an Indibhidithe". *Oghma* 5 (1991).

Ó Cearnaigh, Seán. "Ó Domhnaill, Nuala Ní Dhomhnaill." *Scríbhneoirí na Gaeilge 1945-1995*. Baile Átha Cliath: Comhar, 1995.

O'Connor, Mary. "Lashings of Mother Tongue: Nuala Ní Dhomhnaill's Anarchic

Laughter ." *The Comic Tradition in Irish Women Writers*. Ed. Theresa O'Connor. Florida: Florida UP, 1996. 149-70.

O'Donoghue, Bernard. Review, *Cead Aighnis*. *Irish Times* 17 April 1999.

Ó Tuama, Seán. "The Living and Terrible Mother in the Early Poetry of Nuala Ní Dhomhnaill." *Repossessions: Selected Essays on the Irish Literary Heritage*. Cork: Cork UP, 1995.

Sewell, Frank. *Modern Irish Poetry: A New Alhambra*. Oxford: Oxford UP, 2001.

Uí Nia, Gearóidín. "Ní Dhomhnaill, Nuala." *Eolaire Chló Iar-Chonnachta de Scríbhneoirí Gaeilge*. Indreabhán: Cló Iar-Chonnachta, 1998.

Ní Dhonnchadha, Máirín [Ní Dhonnchú, Máirín]. Comhaimseartha. Co. Chorcaí. Scríbhneoireacht acadúil, eagarthóireacht, aistriúchán.

Saolaíodh Máirín i gCorcaigh. Is Ollamh hÉireann, Gaillimh i Scoil na Gaeilge, Ollscoil na í. D'oibrigh sí mar thaighdeoir ag an Institiúid Ard-Léinn Bhaile Átha Cliath, 1984–6. Cuireann sí suim ar leith sna hábhair a leanas: litríocht na meánaoiseanna, dlíthe na mbreithiún, eagarthóireacht théacsúil agus filíocht an ochtú haois déag. Tá sí tar éis an tsaothair *Gnéithe de Chultúr, Stair agus Polaitíocht na hÉireann c.1600–1900* a chur in eagar; deich n-aiste atá ann atá bunaithe ar léachtaí a tugadh ag Coláiste Merriman i gCill Chainnigh sna blianta 1994/1995. Ba chomheagarthóir í ar *Celtica 22* (1991) agus ar an *Field Day Anthology of Irish Writing IV,V* (2002). Tá trí scéal ón Sean-Ghaeilge aistrithe aici sa cheathrú heagrán de *The Celtic Heroic Age* (2003).

Select bibliography

Ní Dhonnchadha, Máirín.

—. "An Address to a Student of Law." *Sages, Saints and Storytellers*. Scríbhneoireacht acadúil. Eag. Donnchadh Ó Corráin, Liam Breathnach agus Kim McCone. Maigh Nuad: An Sagart, 1989. 159–77.

—. "*Inailt* 'Foster-sister, Fosterling'." Scríbhneoireacht acadúil. *Celtica* 18 (1990): 185–92.

—. eag. *Revising the Rising*. Scríbhneoireacht acadúil, stair. Comheagarthóir Theo Dorgan. Doire: Field Day, 1991.

—. "Reading the So-Called *Caillech Bérri* Poem." Scríbhneoireacht acadúil. *Scéala Scoil an Léinn Cheiltigh* 6ú Bealtaine (1993): 15.

—. "Two Female Lovers." Scríbhneoireacht acadúil. *Ériu* 45 (1994): 113–19.

—. "*Caillech* and Other Terms for Veiled Women in Medieval Irish Texts." Scríbhneoireacht acadúil. *Éigse* 28 (1995): 71–96.

—. "The *Lex Innocentium*: Adomnán's Law for Women, Clerics and Youth, 697 AD." *Chattel, Servant or Citizen: Women's Status in Church, State and Society*. Scríbhneoireacht acadúil. Eag. Mary O'Dowd agus Sabina Wichert. Belfast: Institute of Irish Studies, 1995. 58–69.

—. eag. *Gnéithe de Chultúr, Stair agus Polaitíocht na hÉireann c.1600–1900*. Scríbhneoireacht acadúil. Baile Átha Cliath: An Clóchomhar, 1996.

Ní Dhonnchú, Síle. *fl.* 1990. Oileán Chléire, Co. Chorcaí. Seanchas / béaloideas.

Saolaíodh Síle timpeall na bliana 1856. Bhí sí ag maireachtáil ar Oileán Chléire, Co. Chorcaí. Bhailigh Seán Ó Conaill ábhar uaithi i 1935 agus í naoi mbliana déag is trí fichid. "Pinsinéir" a tugadh uirthi. Tá an béaloideas seo i dtaisce i gCartlann Roinn Bhéaloideas Éireann (Iml. 174) agus foil-síodh cuid de in *Céad Fáilte go Cléire*.

Select bibliography
Ní Dhonnchú, Síle.
—. "Seanchas uaithi." *Céad Fáilte go Cléire*. Seanchas / béaloideas. Eag. Marion Gunn. Baile Átha Cliath: An Clóchomhar, 1990. 40, 175.

Ní Dhonnagáin, Máire [Ní Dhonogáin / Ní Dhonnabháin, Máire "Máire an Bhata"]. *fl.* 1760. Sliabh gCua, Na Déise, Co. Phort Láirge. Filíocht, caoineadh / béaloideas.

Bhí sí ina cónaí i gCarraig a' Chodlata i Sliabh gCua. Deir Tadhg Ó Donnchadha ina leabhar "Seán na Raithíneach" (272) gur "fhile líofa" ab ea í. Ar a shon sin, ní mór iad na dánta dá cuid atá tagtha anuas chugainn: 'An Peacach', atá foilsithe sa *Field Day Anthology* (Iml. 4, 'Courts and Coteries 2') agus caoineadh a dhein sí ar bhás a dearthár. Bhí cáil uirthi mar bhean a raibh teanga ghéar aici, más fíor don seanchas faoi chomhrá a bhí idir í agus sagart (Ó hÓgáin 1982, 35). Tá rannta léi agus seanchas fúithi in eagar ag Pádraig Ó Milléadha in *Béaloideas* 6 (1936).

Select bibliography
Ní Dhonnagáin, Máire.
—. "Rannta léi i 'Seanchas Sliabh gCua'." Eag. Pádraig Ó Milléadha. Filíocht / béaloideas. *Béaloideas* 6 (1936): 192–4.
—. "An Peacach." *Field Day Anthology of Irish Writing IV*. Eag. Angela Bourke, *et al.* Filíocht / béaloideas. Cork: Cork UP, 2002.

Secondary sources
Breathnach, Diarmuid, agus Máire Ní Mhurchú. "Ó Donnagáin, Máire [Ní Dh.] (*fl.* 1760)." *1983–2002 Beathaisnéis*. Baile Átha Claith: An Clóchomhar, 2003.
Ó Súilleabháin, Seán. *Caitheamh Aimsire ar Thórraimh*. Baile Átha Cliath: An Clóchomhar, 1961.
Pléimeann, Seán. "Máire Ní Dhonogáin." *The Gaelic Journal* 3 (1889): 105.
Pléimeann, Seán. "Máire Ní Dhonogáin." *The Gaelic Journal* 4 (1890): 29.

Ní Dhroma, Máiréad [Ní Dhroma, Máire]. *fl.* 1978. Rinn Ó gCuanach, Na Déise, Co. Phort Láirge. Filíocht / béaloideas.

Bhí cáil ar Mháiréad Ní Dhroma de thoradh amhráin áirithe a chum sí agus bhí an t-amhrán sin ina iomlán ag Seán Ó Meachair. B' as Baile na nGall na Rinne é agus fear mór amhrán agus seanchais ab ea é. Bhreac Nioclás Tóibín "Na Prátaí Dubha" síos uaidh agus tá sé i gcló anois in *Duanaire Déiseach* (1978, 19–21). Tá an t-amhrán céanna i gcló in *Croí Cine* (de Fréine 1990, 258). Bhíodh leisce ar mhuintir na háite an fhilíocht seo a rá toisc go raibh blúire ann a d'fhéadfadh olc a chur ar an gcléir:

Ní hé Dia a cheap riamh an obair seo,
Daoine bochta a chur le fuacht is le fán.

"Deirtear gurb iad sin na línte a chrosann an t-amhrán, mar gurb é toil Dé nó ceadú Dé gach aon rud, bíodh sé olc nó maith" (Tóibín 1978, 17). Ba í Máiréad Ní Dhroma, a bhíodh ag cur fúithi i mBaile na nGall, a chum an t-amhrán. Ní raibh aon oideachas foirmeálta ar Mháiréad, ach muna raibh "is ann [.i. san amhrán] atá an cheapadóireacht agus fós é ag fiuchadh le diagacht agus fealsúnacht" (Tóibín, 17).

Select bibliography
Ní Dhroma, Máiréad.
—. "Na Prátaí Dubha." *Duanaire Déiseach*. Filíocht / béaloideas. Eag. Nioclás Tóibín. Baile Átha Cliath: Sáirséal agus Dill, 1978. 19–21.
—. "Na Prátaí Dubha." *Croí Cine*. Filíocht / béaloideas. Eag. Seán de Fréine. Baile Átha Cliath: An Clóchomhar, 1990. 258.

Ní Dhuibh, Máire [Ní Dhonnchadha, Máire]. 1702–95. Deisceart Chiarraí. Filíocht / béaloideas.

Ba mháthair Eibhlín Dubh Ní Chonaill í Máire; ba í Eibhlín a chum 'Caoineadh Airt Uí Laoghaire'. Ba sheanmháthair Dhónaill Uí Chonaill í agus bhí cáil uirthi mar fhile. Deirtear in *Leabhar Sheáin Í Chonaill*, "Bhíodh an Consailéir agus Seán Segerson i gcoinnibh a chéile i gcúrsaí dlí, agus deireadh Seán leis nach le léann a bhí Dónall ró-mhaith dhó ach le filíocht a bhí aige ó chailleach de sheana-mháthair dó" (1948, 281). Tá cuid de rannta Mháire foilsithe in alt a scríobh Ríonach Uí Ógáin uirthi i *Sinsear*.

Select bibliography
Ní Dhuibh, Máire.
—. Rannta léi in "Máire Ní Dhuibh." Le Ríonach Uí Ógáin. Filíocht / béaloideas. *Sinsear* (1981): 101–7.

Secondary sources
Ó Duilearga, Séamas. *Leabhar Sheáin Í Chonaill: Sgéalta agus Seanchas ó Íbh Ráthach*. Baile Átha Cliath: Cumann le Béaloideas Éireann, 1948.
Ó hÓgáin, Daithí. *An File: Staidéar ar Ósnádúrthacht na Filíochta sa Traidisiún Gaelach*. Baile Átha Cliath: Oifig an tSoláthair, 1982.

Ní Dhuibhir, Máire. Comhaimseartha. Leacht Uí Chonchúir, Co. an Chláir. Filíocht.

Saolaíodh Máire i Leacht Uí Chonchúir. D'oibrigh sí mar mhúinteoir, mar ollamh i gColáiste Laighean, agus mar chigire ciondargairdín don Roinn Oideachais. Phós sí Pádraig Ó Discín, léachtóir i gColáiste na hOllscoile, Gaillimh. Foilsíodh dhá dhán léi, "Iníon an tSaoil" agus "Don Pháiste Éislinneach" in *Nua-Fhilí 2*.

Select bibliography
Ní Dhuibhir, Máire.
—. "'Iníon an tSaoil' agus 'Don Pháiste Éislinneach'." *Nua-Fhilí 2 (1953–1963)*. Filíocht. Eag. Séamas Ó Céileachair. Baile Átha Cliath: Oifig an tSoláthair, 1968: 183–5.
—. *Tús*. Filíocht. Baile Átha Cliath: Foilseacháin Ábhair Spioradálta, 1989.

Ní Dhuinneacha, Áine [Bean Dubh an Ghleanna, Carraigín na mBláth,

and An tSiúr M.C.] 1886–1975. Béal Átha an Ghaorthaidh, Múscraí, Co. Chorcaí agus Co. Thiobraid Árann. Drámaíocht, scríbhneoireacht acadúil, leabhar teagaisc, aistí.

Saolaíodh Áine i nGarrán na gCapall, Béal Átha an Ghaorthaidh. Ba iad Cornelius Dennehy agus Mary Hallissey a tuismitheoirí agus bhí seachtar muirear orthu. Táilliúir ab ea Cornelius. Tugadh an chraobh d'Áine i gcomórtais éagsúla amhránaíochta ag feiseanna áitiúla. Bhí sí ag dul lena haintíní, Máiréad agus Síle Ní Ailgheasa, a raibh cáil orthu cheana mar amhránaithe. D'oibrigh Áine mar mhúinteoir i mBealach (idir Crois an Ghúlaigh agus Dún Droma, Co. Thiobraid Árann) agus i gCnoc an Bhile timpeall na bliana 1906, agus bhí an teist uirthi gurbh oide díograiseach í. Chuaigh sí isteach sna mná rialta am éigin idir 1910–1914. Is i mBéal Átha Ragad agus i gCallainn, Co. Chill Chainnigh a bhí sí lonnaithe agus í mar bhall de Shiúracha na Trócaire agus bhí sí ina huachtarán ar an dá chlochar ar feadh tréimhsí áirithe.

D'ullmhaigh sí téacsleabhar do ranganna a cúig agus a sé, *Leabhar Ghobnatan*, a foilsíodh den chéad uair i 1930. Scríobh sí roinnt drámaí ar éirigh go maith leo i gcomórtais an Oireachtais, mar shampla *Bean Sí agus Bean Tí*, agus *Coisc na Mná Feasa* (1941). Bhuaigh sí duais Oireachtais eile sa bhliain 1946 ar scéal do dhaoine óga. Meastar go mbíodh drámaí dá cuid á gcraoladh ar Raidió Éireann. Bhí úrscéal tosaithe aici sular cailleadh í.

Select bibliography
Ní Dhuinneacha, Áine.
—. *Leabhar Ghobnatan: An tSiúr M.C. do scríobh*. Scríbhneoireacht acadúil, leabhar teagaisc. 1930. Baile Átha Cliath: Comhlucht Oideachais na hÉireann, 1946.
—. *Coisc na Mná Feasa: "Carraigín na mBláth" do cheap*. Drámaíocht. Sreath Drámaí i nGaedhilg don Aos Óg. Baile Átha Cliath: Comhlucht Oideachais na h-Éireann, 1941.

Secondary sources
Breathnach, Diarmuid, agus Máire Ní Mhurchú. "Ó Duinneacha, Áine (1886–1975) [Ní Dhuinneacha]." *1882–1982 Beathaisnéis a Cúig*. Baile Átha Cliath: An Clóchomhar, 1997.

Ní Dhuinnshléibhe, Máire. fl. 1982. Dún Chaoin, Corca Dhuibhne, Co. Chiarraí. Filíocht, seanchas / béaloideas.

B'iníon leis an bhfile Seán Ó Duinnshléibhe í. Ní rabhthas róshásta go raibh féith na filíochta inti mar ceapadh go mbeadh deireadh leis an bhfilíocht i sliocht Uí Dhuinnshléibhe as sin amach (*Na hAird ó Thuaidh*). Foilsíodh véarsa léi agus deineadh tagairt di in *An File: Staidéar ar Ósnádúrthacht na Filíochta sa Traidisiún Gaelach* le Daithí Ó hÓgáin.

Secondary sources
Ó hÓgáin, Daithí. *An File: Staidéar ar Osnádúrthacht na Filíochta sa Traidisiún Gaelach*. Baile Átha Cliath: Oifig an tSoláthair, 1982: 46, 157.
Ó Maoileoin, Pádraig. *Na hAird Ó Thuaidh*. Baile Átha Cliath: Sáirséal agus Dill, 1960: 87–8.

Ní Dhuinnshléibhe, Máirín. Comhaimseartha. An Blascaod Mór, Corca Dhuibhne, Co. Chiarraí. Scríbhneoireacht acadúil, aiste.

Saolaíodh Máirín ar an mBlascaod Mór. Tá a haiste "Saol na mBan" foilsithe in *Oidhreacht an Bhlascaoid* (1989).

Select bibliography
Ní Dhuinnshléibhe, Máirín.
—. "Saol na mBan." *Oidhreacht an Bhlascaoid*. Aiste. Eag. Aogán Ó Muircheartaigh. Baile Átha Cliath: Coiscéim, 1989. 334–45.

Ní Drisceoil, Cáit. *fl.* 1990. Ceathrúna, Oileán Chléire, Co. Chorcaí. Seanchas / béaloideas.

Saolaíodh Cáit timpeall na bliana 1816. Bhí sí ag maireachtáil ar Oileán Chléire. Bhailigh Ciarán Ó Síocháin ábhar ó Chonchúr Ó Drisceoil i 1938. Bhí an méid a d'aithris Conchúr cloiste aige ó Cháit Ní Drisceoil timpeall na bliana 1896. Tá an béaloideas seo i dtaisce i gCartlann Roinn Bhéaloideas Éireann (Iml. 558 agus 609) agus foilsíodh cuid de in *Céad Fáilte go Cléire* (43–5, 56–7, 80–2, 102–4, 176–7, 181). Tá leagan de "Caoineadh Airt Uí Laoghaire" a bhí ag Cáit i gcló i leabhar Gunn leis.

Select bibliography
Ní Drisceoil, Cáit.
—. "Seanchas uaithi." *Céad Fáilte go Cléire*. Eag. Marion Gunn. Seanchas / béaloideas. Baile Átha Cliath: An Clóchomhar Tta, 1990.

Ní Eachtigheirnn, Eibhlín. *fl.* 1908. Co. Chorcaí. Filíocht / béaloideas.

Luann "Fiachra Éilgeach" (Risteárd Ó Foghludha) Eibhlín Ní Eachtigheirnn agus filí eile ina aiste "Filí Chorcaighe" (1908). Deir sé "na bain-fhilí féinidh ní rabhadar maol ... Níor mhór do dhuine iarracht fí leith chun teacht thórsa-san is thar a gcuid amhrán, agus sin rud ná fuil im chumas-sa den scríb seo" (1908, 39).

Secondary sources
Éilgeach, Fiachra. "Filí Chorcaighe." *Saothar Suadha: Aistí do léigheadh os comhair Dáil na hÉigse, i gCorcaigh, Meadhon Foghmhair, 1907.* Vol. 1. Baile Átha Cliath: Muinntir an Ghoill, Teo., 1908.

Ní Fhaoláin, Máire. *fl.* 1936. Na Sceithíní, Béal na Molt, Co. Phort Láirge. Scéalaíocht agus seanchas / béaloideas.

Saolaíodh Máire i 1852. Bhí sí ina cónaí sna Sceithíní i 1936 nuair a bhailigh Pádraig Ó Milléadha scéalta agus seanchas uaithi. Bhí sí ceithre bliana is ceithre fichid ag an am sin. Foilsíodh an seanchas sin in *Béaloideas* 6.2 (1936).

Select bibliography
Ní Fhaoláin, Máire.
—. scéalaí. "Seanchas Sliabh gCua: 'Amhrán' uimh. 41 agus 'Scéal' uimh. 111. Scéalaíocht agus amhránaíocht / béaloideas. *Béaloideas* 6.2 (1936): 169–256.

Ní Fhearuíola, Máiréad. 1845–1932. Baile Mhic Chairbre, Co. Phort Láirge. Scéalaíocht / béaloideas.

Saolaíodh Máiréad i mBaile Mhic Cairbre agus bhí cáil uirthi mar scéalaí i bPort Láirge. Scríobh a garnia, Pádraig Ó Fianúsa, a cuid scéalta síos uaithi. D'fhoilsigh sé na scéalta sin in *Béaloideas* 3.3 (1932).

Select bibliography
Ní Fhearuíola, Máiréad.
—. scéalaí. "Measgra Dhéiseach." Scéalaíocht / béaloideas. *Béaloideas* 3.3 (1932): 283–9.

Ní Fhiannúsa, Áine. Comhaimseartha. Cathair Phort Láirge agus Ceapach Choinn, Co. Phort Láirge. Scríbhneoireacht acadúil, aistí.

Saolaíodh Áine i gCeapach Choinn agus tá cónaí uirthi i gcathair Phort Láirge anois. Cuireann sí suim i gcúrsaí ceoil agus cultúir. Is comheagarthóir í ar imeachtaí chomhdháil Mhuintir. Pléann sí buntáistí agus míbhuntáistí na ríomhairí agus na teicneolaíochta ina haiste in *An Linn Bhuí 3*.

Select bibliography
Ní Fhiannúsa, Áine.
—. "Saol na Ríomhairí." *An Linn Bhuí: Iris Ghaeltacht na nDéise*. Scríbhneoireacht acadúil, aiste. Eag. Pádraig Ó Macháin agus Aoibheann Nic Dhonnchadha. Vol. 3. Baile Átha Cliath: Leabhair na Linne, 1999.

Ní Fhoghludha, Áine [Uí Néill, Áine Bean / Ní Fhoghlú, Áine]. 1880–1932. An Móta, An Rinn, Na Déise, Co. Phort Láirge agus Cathair Saidhbhín, Co. Chiarraí. Filíocht, aistriúchán, litríocht leanaí.

Saolaíodh Áine sa Mhóta sa bhliain 1880. Múinteoirí bunscoile ab ea a tuismitheoirí agus bhí ceathrar clainne orthu. Bhí an teist ar a hathair gur shármhúinteoir Gaeilge é. Chuaigh Áine go dtí Clochar na Trócaire, Dún Garbhán agus go dtí Coláiste na hOllscoile, Corcaigh mar ar bhain sí BA amach sa Ghaeilge. Chuir sí suim sa cheol agus san ealaín. Mhúin sí i gClochar na Trócaire, Dún Garbhán, agus i ndá bhunscoil áitiúla, ach briseadh as a post í ar chúiseanna polaitiúla. Bhí ag teip uirthi post eile a fháil agus é beartaithe aici dul ar imirce nuair a bhuail sí le Séamus Ó Néill. Phósadar i 1917, agus chuaigh siad chun cónaithe go dtí Caiseal, Co. Thiobraid Árann. Ní raibh aon pháistí orthu. Oileadh Séamus mar mhúinteoir, ach chaill sé a phost tar éis imeachtaí 1916, agus chaith sé tamall i bpríosúin éagsúla. D'oibrigh Áine mar mhúinteoir i dTiobraid Árann ag an am, agus bhí baint mhór aici le Cumann na mBan. Chuaigh a fear céile isteach sna Gardaí Síochána tar éis bhunú an stáit nua, agus chaith an lánúin tréimhsí ag cur fúthu i mBaile Átha Cliath, i gCuan Bhaile na Cúirte agus i gCathair Saidhbhín, Co. Chiarraí. Ní raibh Áine ar fónamh ar feadh na mblianta sular cailleadh í. I gCathair Saidhbhín a d'éag sí agus is sa Rinn a adhlacadh í.

Foilsíodh cnuasach filíochta amháin léi, *Idir na Fleadhanna* i 1922 agus ba í "an banfhile Gaeilge í ba mhó ar a raibh aird an phobail roimh 1940" dar le Breathnach agus Ní Mhurchú (1990, 105). Deir Ó Droighneáin gurb é is brí le na "fleadhanna" ná "gach buadh a fuair na Gaedhil ar a náimhdibh ó 1916 go dtí 1921" (1937, 89). Bhíodh dán dá cuid ar chúrsa na hArdteiste,.i. 'An Chraobh Chrom' agus ceann eile ar chúrsa na meánteiste, 'Dréachtín'. Cuireadh an dán léi dar líne tosaigh "Om luascadh, 'om luascadh' i gcló i ndíolamaí difriúla: *Fíon na Filidheachta*, *An Bhláithfhleasc Bheag*, agus *150 de Dhuanta Gaedhilge*.

Chomh maith leis an bhfilíocht, scríobh sí cnuasach scéalta do leanaí, *Brosna* (1925) agus d'aistrigh sí ceithre dhráma leis an Athair Gaffney go Gaeilge.

Select bibliography
Ní Fhoghludha, Áine.
—. *Idir na Fleadhanna*. Filíocht. Baile Átha Cliath: An Gaedheal Comhlucht, 1922. Baile Átha Cliath: Oifig Dhíolta Foilseacháin Rialtais, 1930.
—. *Brosna*. Litríocht leanaí. 1925.
—. aist. *Breacadh an Lae*. Drámaíocht, aistriúchán. Le Rev. Michael Gaffney. Baile Átha Cliath: Oifig Dhíolta Foilseacháin Rialtais, 1934.
—. aist. *Bréig-riocht Apollo agus Cúiteamh.i. dhá dhráma i gcóir na ngasóg*. Drámaíocht, aistriúchán. Le Rev. Michael Gaffney. Baile Átha Cliath: Oifig Dhíolta Foilseacháin Rialtais, 1934.
—. aist. *Díthreabhach an Tobair agus San Tomás Acuin*. Drámaíocht, aistriúchán. Le Rev. Michael Gaffney. Baile Átha Cliath: Oifig Dhíolta Foilseacháin Rialtais, 1934.
—. aist. *Róis Dhearga agus Buadhann Críost*. Drámaíocht, aistriúchán. Le Rev. Michael Gaffney. Baile Átha Cliath: Oifig Dhíolta Foilseacháin Rialtais, 1934.
Secondary sources
Breathnach, Diarmuid agus Máire Ní Mhurchú. "Ó Foghludha, Áine [Ní Fhoghludha] (1880–1932)." *1882–1982 Beathaisnéis a Dó*. Baile Átha Cliath: An Clóchomhar, 1990.
de Hae, Risteárd agus Brighid Ní Dhonnchadha, eag. "Clár Litridheacht na Nua-Ghaedhilge 1850–1936." Vol. 1. Baile Átha Cliath: Oifig Dhíolta Foilseacháin Rialtais, 1938: 85, 103, 193.
Ó Droighneáin, Muiris. *Taighde i gComhair Stair Litridheachta na Nua-Ghaedhilge ó 1882 anuas*. 1936. Baile Átha Cliath: Oifig Dhíolta Foilseacháin Rialtais, 1937.
Ó Góilidhe, Caoimhghin, eag. *Ardteistiméireacht Díolaim Filíochta: Eagrán Oifigiúil*. Baile Átha Cliath: Folens, 1974.

Ní Ghallchobhair, Méadhbh [Ní Ghallchóir, Méabh]. Comhaimseartha. Co. Chiarraí. Gearrscéalaíocht.

D'oibrigh Méadhbh mar Oifigeach Leighis i Sasana, sa Bhreatain Bheag, i gCiarraí agus i mBaile Átha Cliath. Foilsíodh scéalta léi in irisí míosúla ó 1964 i leith ach ba é *An Gúna agus Scéalta Eile* an chéad chnuasach gearrscéalta léi.

Select bibliography
Ní Ghallchobhair, Méadhbh.
—. *An Gúna agus Scéalta Eile*. Litríocht leanaí. Baile Átha Cliath: Coiscéim, 1995.

Ní Ghaoithín, Máire [Ní Ghuithín / Uí Chíobháin, Máire]. 1909–88. An Blascaod Mór [An tOileán Tiar], Corca Dhuibhne, Co. Chiarraí. Beathaisnéis.

Saolaíodh Máire ar an mBlascaod Mór, Co. Chiarraí i 1909. Ba iad Maidhc Léan Ó Gaoithín agus Máire Pheats Mhicí Ní Chatháin a tuismitheoirí. Ba é Pádraig Ó Catháin a hathair críonna, ar a dtugtaí 'Rí an Oileáin.' Chabhraíodh Máire lena tuismitheoirí nuair a thagadh cuairteoirí go dtí an tOileán ag foghlaim Gaeilge; i dtigh an Rí a d'fhanadh Robin Flower. Deir Breathnach agus Ní Mhurchú gur éirigh sí "taithíoch ar nótaí a scríobh faoi chúrsaí san oileán" timpeall an ama san. D'oibrigh sí ar feadh tamaill i gColáiste Moibhí i nGlas Naíon. Phós sí Labhrás John Larry Ó Cíobháin agus bhí beirt iníonacha acu. Cailleadh i 1988 í. Cur síos ar shaol agus ar sheanchas an Bhlascaoid – agus ar chúraimí na mban ach go háirithe – atá sa dá leabhar a scríobh sí.

Select bibliography
Ní Ghaoithín, Máire.
—. *An tOileán a Bhí*. Beathaisnéis. Baile Átha Cliath: Clóchomhar, 1978.
—. *Bean An Oileáin*. Beathaisnéis. Baile Átha Cliath: Coiscéim, 1986.

Secondary sources
Breathnach, Diarmuid, agus Máire Ní Mhurchú. "Ó Guithín, Máire [Ní Ghuithín / Uí Chíobháin] (1909–1988)." *1983–2002 Beathaisnéis*. Baile Átha Cliath: An Clóchomhar, 2003.

Ní Ghlinn, Áine. Comhaimseartha. Durlas Éile, Co. Thiobraid Árann. Filíocht, litríocht leanaí, drámaíocht agus scríbhneoireacht acadúil, léirmheastóireacht.

Saolaíodh Áine i gCo. Thiobraid Árann i 1955, agus bunmhúinteoirí ab ea a tuismitheoirí. Cúigear a bhí sa chlann, agus ba í Áine an duine ab óige. Fuair sí a cuid meánscolaíochta i gClochar na Toirbhirt, Durlas Éile agus bhain sí BA amach ó Choláiste na hOllscoile, Baile Átha Cliath. Dhein sí an tArdteastas san Oideachas agus mhúin sí Gaeilge agus Béarla ar feadh beagnach deich mbliana. Fuair sí cáilíocht san iriseoireacht ansin. D'oibrigh sí ar an raidió agus ar an teilifís in Éirinn, agus scríobh sí d'irisí agus do nuachtáin in Éirinn agus i Sasana.

Bhí an oiread éilimh ar a céad leabhar filíochta, *An Chéim Bhriste*, gur cuireadh athchló air. Foilsíodh teidealdán an leabhair seo go forleathan i gcnuasaigh filíochta éagsúla, in *Pillars of the House* (Kelly 1997, 162–163) mar shampla. Tá dhá leabhar filíochta eile scríofa aici, *Gairdín Pharthais* agus *Deora Nár Caoineadh /Unshed Tears*. Tá filíocht dá cuid aistrithe go Gearmáinis agus go Béarla. Bhuaigh sí duaiseanna Oireachtais sna blianta 1985 agus 1989 agus ghnóthaigh sí Duais Bhord na Gaeilge, Seachtain na Scríbhneoirí, Lios Tuathail sa bhliain 1987. Tá dhá leabhar scríofa aici do dhéagóirí chomh maith, *Mná as an nGnáth* agus *Daoine agus Déithe* agus dhá leabhar do leanaí óga, *Daifni Dineasar* agus *Moncaí Dána*.

Select bibliography
Ní Ghlinn, Áine.
—. *An Chéim Bhriste*. Filíocht. Baile Átha Cliath: Coiscéim, 1984.
—. *Gairdín Pharthais*. Filíocht. Baile Átha Cliath: Coiscéim, 1988.
—. *Mná as an nGnáth*. Litríocht leanaí. Baile Átha Cliath: An Gúm, 1990.

—. *Daoine agus Déithe.* Litríocht leanaí. Baile Átha Cliath: An Gúm, 1995.
—. *Deora Nár Caoineadh / Unshed Tears.* Filíocht. Aist. Pádraig Ó Snodaigh. Baile Átha Cliath: Dedalus, 1996.
—. *Daifní Dineasar.* Litríocht leanaí. Baile Átha Cliath: O'Brien Press, 2001.
—. *Moncaí Dána.* Litríocht leanaí. Baile Átha Cliath: O'Brien Press, 2002.

Secondary sources

Kelly, A. A., ed. *Pillars of the House: An Anthology of verse by Irish Women from 1690 to the Present.* N.p.: n.p., 1987. Dublin: Wolfhound, 1997.
Kelly, Rita. "Léirmheas ar *Deora Nár Caoineadh / Unshed Tears.*" *Comhar* (Lúnasa 1997).
Ní Annracháin, Máire. "Dearbhú Beatha." *Comhar* (Lúnasa 1984): 55–8.
Ó Cearnaigh, Seán. "Ó Glinn, Áine [Ní Ghlinn]." *Scríbhneoirí na Gaeilge 1945–1995.* Baile Átha Cliath: Comhar, 1995.
Uí Nia, Gearóidín eag. "Ní Ghlinn, Áine." *Eolaire Chló Iar-Chonnachta de Scríbhneoirí Gaeilge.* Indreabhán: Cló Iar-Chonnachta, 1998.

Ní Ghráda, Máiréad. 1896–1971. Cill Mháille, Inis, Co. an Chláir.

Drámaíocht, aistriúchán, gearrscéalaíocht, filíocht, litríocht leanaí, scríbhneoireacht acadúil, leabhar teagaisc.

Saolaíodh Máiréad i gCill Mháille. Feirmeoirí ab ea a muintir. Chuaigh sí ar scoil go dtí Clochar na Trócaire, Inis agus bronnadh scoláireacht uirthi chun freastal ar Choláiste na hOllscoile, Baile Átha Cliath. Ghnóthaigh sí BA sa Ghaeilge, san Fhraincis agus sa Bhéarla, chomh maith le MA sa Ghaeilge. Bhí sí páirteach i gCumann na mBan agus i gConradh na Gaeilge. Phós sí státseirbhíseach dárbh ainm Risteárd Ó Cíosáin i 1923 agus bhí beirt mhuirear orthu. D'oibrigh sí mar mhúinteoir ar feadh tréimhsí éagsúla, mar thimire, agus mar rúnaí d'Earnán de Blaghd. D'oibrigh sí sa stáisiún raidió 2RN ag ullmhú clár do mhná agus do pháistí agus mar bholscaire raidió ina dhiaidh sin. Ba í an chéad bholscaire mná in Éirinn í. Chuaigh sí i mbun obair eagarthóireachta leis na foilsitheoirí Brún agus Ó Nualláin ansin. Is mar dhrámadóir a tharraing sí clú uirthi féin. Ba é *An Uacht* an chéad dráma a scríobh sí agus léiríodh é in Amharclann an Gheata. Léiríonn grúpaí amaitéaracha a cuid drámaí ann fós sa lá atá inniu ann agus *An Uacht* ina measc.

Is iad *An Triail* (1964) agus *Breithiúnas* (1968) a saothar is mó cáil. Léiríodh *An Triail* ar dtús in amharclann an Damer i 1964 i mBaile Átha Cliath agus ar an teilifís an bhliain chéanna. Cuireadh leagan Béarla de ar an stáitse an bhliain dár gcionn. Scríobh sí go leor drámaí eile freisin a léiríodh, mar shampla *Giolla an tSolais* (1945), *Lá Buí Bealtaine* (1953), *Úll glas Oíche Shamhna* (1955), *Súgán Sneachta* (1959), *Stailc Ocrais* (1960), agus *Mac Uí Rudaí* (1961). Ghnóthaigh *Stailc Ocrais* Duais na Comhairle Ealaíon 1960. Chleacht Máiréad *genres* eile scríbhneoireachta leis, mar shampla d'aistrigh sí *Peter Pan* go Gaeilge – *Tír na Deo* an teideal a bhí air – agus scríobh sí cnuasach gearrscéalta. Ina theannta sin, d'ullmhaigh sí téacsleabhair Ghaeilge. Ba chara le Peig Sayers í. Bhí sí ina heagarthóir ar *Teacher's Work* ar feadh tamall fada. Scríobh sí scéalta do pháistí *An Bheirt Dearbhráthar agus Scéalta Eile*, chomh maith le húrscéal ficsin eolaíochta, *Mannán*. Bhí sí gníomhach sa Chomhairle Náisiúnta Drámaíochta agus i gCumann na

Scríbhneoirí. Bhíodh dréachtaí filíochta á scríobh aici agus foilsíodh dán amháin léi "D'Fhile nach Maireann G.M.H" i *Nua-Fhilí 2*.

Select bibliography

Ní Ghráda, Máiréad.

—. aist. *Tír na Deo* [Peter Pan]. Litríocht leanaí, aistriúchán. Le J.M. Barrie. Baile Átha Cliath: Oifig Dhíolta Foilseacháin Rialtais, 1938.

—. *An Bheirt Dearbhráthar agus Scéalta Eile*. Gearrscéalaíocht. Baile Átha Cliath: Oifig an tSoláthair, 1939.

—. *Mannán*. Litríocht. Baile Átha Cliath: Oifig an tSoláthair, 1940.

—. bail. *Foclóir Gaeilge Béarla: an litriú caighdeánach*. Scríbhneoireacht acadúil, foclóireacht. Baile Átha Cliath: Brún agus Ó Nualláin, 1949.

—. *Giolla an tSolais: duais-dráma trí mhír*. Drámaíocht. Baile Átha Cliath: Oifig an tSoláthair, 1954.

—. *Lá Buí Bealtaine*. Drámaíocht. Baile Átha Cliath: Oifig an tSoláthair, 1955.

—. *Úll glas Oíche Shamhna*. Drámaíocht. 1955. Baile Átha Cliath: Oifig an tSoláthair, 1960.

—. *Súgán Sneachta*. Drámaíocht. 1959. Baile Átha Cliath: Oifig an tSoláthair, 1962.

—. *Stailc Ocrais*. Drámaíocht. 1960. Baile Átha Cliath: Oifig an tSoláthair, 1966.

—. *Mac Uí Rudaí*. Drámaíocht. 1961. Baile Átha Cliath: Oifig an tSoláthair, 1963.

—. *An Tóirse: Cúrsa Leanúna sa Ghaeilge*. Scríbhneoireacht acadúil, leabhar teagaisc. Baile Átha Cliath: Brún agus Ó Nualláin, 1966.

—. aist. *On Trial* [An Triail]. Drámaíocht, aistriúchán. Baile Átha Cliath: James Duffy, 1966.

—. *Ar Aghaidh Leat: bunaithe ar an ábhar sa dara leath den chúrsa comhrá Hóra, a Pháid*. Scríbhneoireacht acadúil, leabhar teagaisc. Baile Átha Cliath: Brún agus Ó Nualláin, 1968.

—. *Féach Leat: bunaithe ar an ábhar sa gcéad leath den chúrsa comhrá Dúisigh, a Bhríd*. Scríbhneoireacht acadúil, leabhar teagaisc. Baile Átha Cliath: Brún agus Ó Nualláin, 1968.

—. *Léigh Leat: bunaithe ar an ábhar sa chúrsa comhrá Colm agus Nuala*. Scríbhneoireacht acadúil, leabhar teagaisc. Baile Átha Cliath: Brún agus Ó Nualláin, 1968.

—. *Breithiúnas: Dráma Dhá Ghníomh*. Drámaíocht. Baile Átha Cliath: Oifig an tSoláthair, 1978. Baile Átha Cliath: An Gúm, 1996.

—. *An Triail*. Drámaíocht. Baile Átha Cliath: Oifig an tSoláthair, 1978. Baile Átha Cliath: An Gúm, 1995.

—. *Cúrsaí an Lae: cur síos ar gach éinní a bhaineann le saol an scoláire*. Scríbhneoireacht acadúil. Baile Átha Cliath: Brún agus Ó Nualláin, g.d.

—. *Progress in Irish: A Graded Course for Beginners and Revision*. Scríbhneoireacht acadúil, leabhar teagaisc. Dublin: Longman / Browne and Nolan Ltd., g.d.

Secondary sources

Breathnach, Diarmuid, agus Máire Ní Mhurchú. "Ó Gráda, Máiréad [Ní Ghráda] (1896–1971)." *1882–1982 Beathaisnéis a hAon*. Baile Átha Cliath: An Clóchomhar, 1986.

Cleeve, Brian. "Ní Ghráda, Máiréad." *Dictionary of Irish Writers: Writers in the Irish Language*. Vol. 3. Cork: Mercier, 1971.

Ní Bhrádaigh, Siobhán. *Máiréad Ní Ghráda Ceannródaí Drámaíochta*. Indreabhán: Cló Iar-Chonnachta, 1996.

Ó Cearnaigh, Seán. "Ó Gráda, Máiréad Ní Ghráda." *Scríbhneoirí na Gaeilge 1945–1995*. Baile Átha Cliath: Comhar, 1995.

Ó Céileachair, Séamas, eag. *Nua-Fhilí 2 (1953–1963)*. Baile Átha Cliath: Oifig an tSoláthair, 1968.

Ó Cíosáin, Éamon. "Máiréad Ní Ghráda agus a Saothar Liteartha." *An Triail, Breithiúnas*. Baile Átha Cliath: Oifig an tSoláthair, 1978.

Ní Iarlaithe, Siobhán [Ní Iarlaithe, Síle]. *fl.*1982. Uíbh Ráthach, Co. Chiarraí. Filíocht, seanchas / béaloideas.

"Nuair a chuala an tAthair Seoirse Ó Súilleabháin Ó Chill Orglan, go raibh Síle Ní Iarlaithe ina file d'fhiafraigh sé dhi: 'An tusa an duine a bhíonn ag moladh na ndaoine?' 'Is mé, a Athair,' ar sise, 'agus molfaidh mé tusa, leis, más maith leat é.' 'Na mol is ná cáin mé, ach fág mar atá mé!'". (Ó hÓgáin 1982, 296)

Secondary sources
Ó hÓgáin, Daithí. *An File: Staidéar ar Osnádúrthacht na Filíochta sa Traidisiún Gaelach*. Baile Átha Cliath: Oifig an tSoláthair, 1982.

Ní Laeire, Máire [Ní Laoire, Máire]. *fl.*1982. Baile Bhuirne agus Maigh Chromtha, Co. Chorcaí. Filíocht, caoineadh / béaloideas.

Chuala Pádraig Ó Crualaoi – a saolaíodh i mBaile Bhuirne agus a chuaigh chun cónaithe go Maigh Chromtha – trácht ar an mbean seo, agus dar leis gur bhean chaointe logánta í. Bhí blúire de chaoineadh a chum sí ar bhás an Róistigh Mhóir aici. Nuair a bhí an caoineadh á rá ag Máire anallód i dtigh an tórraimh chum seanduine a bhí i láthair an tarna véarsa. D'fhreagair Máire láithreach é le véarsa eile dá déantús féin (Ó Crualaoi 1982, 55–6).

Secondary sources
Ó Crualaoi, Pádraig, seanchaí. *Seanachas Phádraig Í Chrualaoi*. Eag. Donncha Ó Cróinín. Baile Átha Cliath: Comhairle Bhéaloideas Éireann, 1982.

Ní Laoghaire, Máire Bhuidhe [Ní Laoire, Máire Bhuí]. 1774–1848. Muscraí, Co. Chorcaí. Filíocht / béaloideas.

Saolaíodh Máire Bhuí i dTúirín na nÉan, Béal Átha an Ghaorthaidh. Phós sí Búrcach i gCéim an Fhia. Duine an-deisbhéalach a bhí inti. Ba iad Siobhán agus Diarmuid Ó Laoghaire a tuismitheoirí agus bhí ochtar muirear orthu. Phós sí Séamus de Búrca ón Sciobairín timpeall na bliana 1792. Bhí talamh acu ar Oileán Aibhneach Beag, Béal Átha an Ghaorthaidh agus sna hInsí, cóngarach do Chéim an Fhia. Deichniúr páistí a bhí acu. Bhíodar go maith as ag an tús, ach tharla dhá rud a chuir i gcruachás iad. Ar an gcéad dul síos, d'ardaigh tiarna talún nua an cíos orthu. Ar an dara dul síos, bhí ar a gcuid mac teitheadh tar éis Chath Chéim an Fhia, rud a d'fhág gan chabhair ar an bhfeirm iad. Cuireadh amach as an tigh iad timpeall 1847, agus thug duine de na mic fothain dóibh. D'éag Máire Bhuí go luath ina dhiaidh sin agus adhlacadh í in Inse Geimhleach.

Ní raibh léamh ná scríobh ag Máire Bhuí, cé go ndeir Máirín Nic Eoin go bhfuil tionchar na litríochta clasaicí le brath ar a cuid filíochta. Is é "Cath Chéim an Fhia" an t-amhrán is mó cáil a chum sí agus cuireadh i gcló é i mórán díolamaí filíochta. Giománaigh agus Buachaillí Bána in aghaidh a chéile sa bhliain 1822 a spreag an dán. Bhí deartháir léi, Diarmuid, ina fhile chomh maith. Chum Máire véarsaí mar gheall ar an achrann idir a muintir féin, an Chlann Bhuí, agus muintir Uí Shúilleabháin, an Chlann Dhíomhaoin. Chum sí véarsaí freisin chun freagra a thabhairt ar rannta a dhein filí áitiúla eile, mar shampla Donnacha Bán Ó Luínse agus Diarmaid 'ac Séamuis Ó Crothúir.

Bhunaigh an tAthair Donncha Ó Donnchú leabhar *Filíocht Mháire Bhuidhe Ní Laoghaire* ar fhoinsí scríofa agus ar chuntais ó bhéal. Bhain sé leas as lámhscríbhinn d'amhráin Mháire Bhuí ar bhailigh Domhnall Ó Luasa agus Crochúr A Coitir agus as béalaithris mhuintir Mhúscraí a raibh filíocht Mháire ina gceann fós acu (Ní Laoghaire 1931, 36). I réamhrá an leabhair, tá cur síos ar fáil ar ghinealach Mháire, ar a clann, ar chomhthéacs stairiúil agus polaitiúil na ndánta, agus ar an sórt filíochta a chum sí. Chleacht sí an aisling go minic, mar shampla "Cath Chéim an Fhia" agus "Ar Leacain na Gréine", ach ina theannta sin dhein sí "aistí crábhaidh agus caointe, amhráin grádha agus grinn, ceathrúna caointe agus strangcáin óil agus suilt agus ragairne" (33).

Select bibliography
Ní Laoghaire, Máire Bhuidhe.
—. *Filíocht Mháire Bhuidhe Ní Laoghaire.* Filíocht / béaloideas. Eag. An tAthair Donncha Ó Donnchú. Baile Átha Cliath: Oifig Dhíolta Foilseacháin Rialtais, 1931.

Secondary sources
Breathnach, Diarmuid, agus Máire Ní Mhurchú. "Ó Laoghaire, Máire 'Bhuí' (1774–c.1848) [Ní Laoghaire]." *1782–1881 Beathaisnéis.* Baile Átha Cliath: An Clóchomhar, 1999.
Cleeve, Brian. "Ní Laoghaire, Máire Bhuidhe." *Dictionary of Irish Writers: Writers in the Irish Language.* Vol. 3. Cork: Mercier, 1971.
Nic Eoin, Máirín. *B'ait leo bean: Gnéithe den Idé-eolaíocht Inscne i dTraidisiún Liteartha na Gaeilge.* Baile Átha Cliath: An Clóchomhar, 1998.
Ó Cróinín, Donnchadh. "Filí agus Filíocht Mhúsgraighe." *An Músgraigheach 1.* Meitheamh (1943): 15–20.
Ó Crualaoi, Pádraig. *Seanachas Phádraig Í Chrualaoi.* Eag. Donncha Ó Cróinín. Baile Átha Cliath: Comhairle Bhéaloideas Éireann, 1982: 109–16, 124–5.
Ó Góilidhe, Caoimhghin, eag. *Duanaire na Meánteistiméireachta.* Baile Átha Cliath: Folens, 1975.
Ó Muirthile, Diarmaid. *Cois an Ghaorthaidh, filíocht ó Mhúscraí 1700–1840.* Baile Átha Cliath: An Clóchomhar, 1987.

Ní Laoghaire, Nell ["Nell Ghaolach" / Ní Laoire, Nell]. 1842–1940. Béal Átha an Ghaorthaidh, Múscraí, Co. Chorcaí. Beathaisnéis agus seanchas / béaloideas.

Beartaíodh go n-inseodh Nell scéal a beatha agus go scríobhfadh a gariníon síos é. Bhí sí críonna go leor ag an tráth sin áfach, agus cailleadh í sula raibh an deis aici an obair a chur i gcrích. Foilsíodh an méid a bhí inste aici in *An Músgraigheach 8* (1945, 15–22). Saolaíodh Nell in 1842 i nGort an Phludaigh. Bhí cuimhne aici ar an nGorta Mór agus ar na prátaí a bheith lofa. Cailleadh a hathair nuair nach raibh sí ach sé bliana déag d'aois agus bhí a máthair ag súil le leanbh ag an am. Deichniúr ar fad a bhí sa chlann. Bhí triúr deirfiúracha agus seisear deartháireacha ag Nell. Ba í siúd an ceathrú duine ab óige. Ba bheag scolaíochta a fuair sí, ach bhíodh sí ag obair go cruai sa bhaile ag plé le bainne, le him agus le móin. Chomh maith le saol na hoibre, cuireann sí síos ar na caithimh aimsire a bhíodh ag an bpobal lena linn, ar na tithe a bhíodh acu, agus ar an mbia a bhíodh á chaitheamh acu.

Select bibliography
Ní Laoghaire, Nell.
—. "An Seana-Shaoghal." Beathaisnéis agus seanchas / béaloideas. *An Músgraigheach* 8. Samhradh (1945): 15–22.

Ní Loingsigh, Máiréad. Comhaimseartha. An Bhlárna, Co Chorcaí. Scríbhneoireacht acadúil, eagarthóireacht.

Is Corcaíoch í Máiréad Ní Loingsigh. Fuair sí a cuid scolaíochta sa Bhlárna agus bhain sí an BA agus an MPhil amach i gColáiste na hOllscoile, Corcaigh mar a bhfuil sí ina Múinteoir Teangan anois i Roinn na Nua-Ghaeilge. Dhein sí eagarthóireacht ar lámhscríbhinn *Cín Lae Eibhlín Ní Shúilleabháin* mar ábhar tráchtais MPhil agus foilsíodh an téacs úd sa bhliain 2000. Tá suim ar leith aici i gcúrsaí eagarthóireachta agus aistriúcháin agus in úsáid na litríochta i múineadh na teangan.

Select bibliography
Ní Loingsigh, Máiréad.
—. eag. *Cín Lae Eibhlín Ní Shúilleabháin*. Eagarthóireacht. Baile Átha Cliath: Coiscéim, 2000.

Ní Loinsigh, Eibhlín. *fl.*1944. Múscraí, Co. Chorcaí. Scríbhneoireacht acadúil, aiste.

B'as Múscraí í Eibhlín. Scríobh sí an aiste "Na hOlltaigh" a cuireadh i gcló in *An Músgraigheach 6* ina bpléann sí tagairtí do mhuintir Uladh i seanchas Mhúscraí le dhá chéad bliain anuas.

Select bibliography
Ní Loinsigh, Eibhlín.
—. "Na hOlltaigh." Aiste. *An Músgraigheach* 6. Fóghmhar (1944): 6–11.

Ní Luínse, Siobhán [Ní Loinsigh, Siobhán]. Múscraí, Co. Chorcaí. Filíocht / béaloideas.

B'as Múscraí do Shiobhán. Iníon le Diarmaid a' Scrithin Ó Luínse ab ea í. Phós sí fear de mhuintir Luasa. "D'fhéatadh sí véarsa a dhéanamh go maith" (Ó Crualaoi 1982, 157). Cé go raibh a hainm in airde mar fhile, ní mhaireann aon ní inniu dar chum sí.

Secondary sources
Ó Crualaoi, Pádraig. *Seanachas Phádraig Í Chrualaoi*. Eag. Donncha Ó Cróinín. Baile Átha Cliath: Comhairle Bhéaloideas Éireann, 1982.

Ní Mhainnín, Máire. Comhaimseartha. Corca Dhuibhne, Co. Chiarraí. Scríbhneoireacht acadúil, eagarthóireacht.

Chuir Máire eagrán nua de *Peig* (1998) ar fáil i gcomhar le Liam P. Ó

Murchú nuair a bhí sí ina hiníon léinn iarchéime i gColáiste na hOllscoile, Corcaigh. "Ainneoin go bhféachtar le neamhréireachtaí litrithe ón mbuneagrán a choigeartú, fágtar na leaganacha canúnacha slán" (litríocht.com). Í ag obair ina ceantar dúchais, Corca Dhuibhne, anois.

Select bibliography
Ní Mhainnín, Máire.
—. agus Liam P. Ó Murchú, eag. *Peig: A Scéal Féin*. Le Peig Sayers. An Daingean: An Sagart, 1998.

Ní Mhiléadha, Máire. *fl*. 1936. Na Sceithíní, Sliabh gCua, Co. Phort Láirge. Filíocht, caoineadh / béaloideas.

Bhí Máire ina cónaí sna Sceithíní agus bhí cáil uirthi mar fhile. Tá caoineadh léi a chum sí ar bhás a cait in eagar ag Pádraig Ó Milléadha in *Béaloideas* 6 (1936).

Select bibliography
Ní Mhiléadha, Máire.
—. File béaloidi. "Caoineadh léi i "Seanchas Sliabh gCua"." Filíocht, caoineadh / béaloideas. *Béaloideas* 6 (1936): 195–6.

Ní Mhionacháin, Máiréad [Minihane, Peig]. 1861–1957. Béarra, Co. Chorcaí. Scéalaíocht agus seanchas / béaloideas.

Saolaíodh Máiréad i gCill Chaitiairn. Ba iad Tadhg Ó Mionacháin agus Nóra Ní Rathaile a tuismitheoirí. Bhí naonúr muirear orthu, agus ba í Máiréad an ceathrú duine ab óige. Fuair sí a cuid oideachais sa scoil áitiúil, agus bhí idir léamh agus scríobh an Bhéarla aici. Nuair a bhí sí scór blianta, deineadh cleamhnas di le Seán D. Ó Súilleabháin, An Goirtín, Dhá Dhrom Amuigh, fear a bhí i bhfad níos sine ná í. Pósadh iad i 1882, agus bhí 13 páistí acu. Chuaigh a bhformhór go Meiriceá ar imirce, cailleadh cuid eile acu go hóg, agus shocraigh a mac, Mícheál, síos ar an bhfeirm i dteannta a mhná céile. Bhíodh Mícheál as baile go minic de bharr a chuid oibre agus chabhraigh Máiréad go mór lena bhean chéile an t-ál óg a thógáil. Scríobh bailitheoir lánaimseartha le Coimisiún Bhéaloideas Éireann, Tadhg Ó Murchú, seanchas agus scéalta ó Mháiréad idir 1950–1952 (Ní Mhionacháin 1999, 21–43). Is é Máirtín Verling a chuir an t-ábhar seo in eagar, agus a chuir cúlra agus comhthéacs ar fáil sa leabhar *Béarrach Mná ag Caint* (1999). Aistríodh an saothar seo go Béarla le déanaí, *Beara Woman Talking* (2003).

Select bibliography
Ní Mhionacháin, Máiréad.
—. seanchaí. *Béarrach Mná ag Caint: Seanchas Mháiréad Ní Mhionacháin*. Seanchas / béaloideas. Tadhg Ó Murchú a bhailigh. Máirtín Verling a chuir in eagar agus a chóirigh. Indreabhán: Cló Iar Chonnachta, 1999.
—. *Beara Woman Talking: The Lore of Peig Minihane. Folklore from the Beara Peninsula, Co. Cork*. Seanchas / béaloideas. Collected by Tadhg Ó Murchú. Ed., arr. and trans. by Martin Verling. Cork: Mercier, 2003.

Ní Mhóra, Máiréad. *fl*.1980. Múscraí, Co. Chorcaí. Filíocht / béaloideas.
Chum sí paidir tar éis béile, ach ní beannacht a bhí inti ach maslú na

gcomharsan i Múscraí ó thús deiridh! Cuireadh an t-altú i gcló in *Seanachas Amhlaoibh Í Luínse* (1980, 294) agus in *Béaloideas 3* (1932, 463).

Secondary sources

Ó Luínse, Amhlaoibh, seanchaí. *Seanachas Amhlaoibh Í Luínse*. Eag. Donncha Ó Cróinín. Baile Átha Cliath: Comhairle Bhéaloideas Éireann, 1980.

Ní Mhóráin, Brighid [Ní Mhóráin, Bríd]. Comhaimseartha. Corca Dhuibhne agus Trá Lí, Co. Chiarraí. Filíocht, gearrscéalaíocht agus scríbhneoireacht acadúil.

Saolaíodh Brighid in Áth Trasna, Co. Chorcaí, ach d'aistrigh go Duibhneach nuair a bhí sí cúig bliana d'aois. Bhí cúigear sa chlann agus bhí Brighid i lár baill. Fuair sí a cuid oideachais i scoil Thobar Mhuí Doire, Trá Lí, Co. Chiarraí. Bhain sí BA amach sa Ghaeilge, sa Bhéarla agus san Fhraincis ó Choláiste na hOllscoile, Corcaigh, áit ar dhein sí an tArdteastas san Oideachas freisin. Bhí sí ag múineadh teangacha i dTrá Lí ó 1976 go dtí 2001. Fuair sí dioplóma sa Teangeolaíocht Fheidhmeach agus M.Litt. ó Choláiste na Tríonóide.

Foilsíodh an cnuasach filíochta *Ceiliúradh Cré* i 1992 agus *Fé Bhrat Bhríde* in 2002. Cuireadh dánta léi i gcló ina lán irisí, mar shampla *Comhar*, *Innti* agus *Feasta*. Foilsíodh dhá ghearrscéal léi in *Imeachtaí na Ceardlainne* (Coiscéim, 1985.) Craoladh a lán dá saothar ar Raidió na Gaeltachta, go mórmhór ar na cláir *Siosmaid* agus *Peann agus Pár*. Bhuaigh sí duaiseanna Oireachtais sa bhliain 1988 d'fhilíocht, i 1989 do dhán fada agus i 1992 do shaothar próis. Bhronn An Chomhairle Ealaíon sparántacht uirthi i 2000.

Is é atá sa saothar toirtiúil *Thiar sa Mhainistir atá an Ghaolainn Bhreá* (1997) ná a tráchtas M.Litt. ar an athrú a tháinig ar líon na gcainteoirí dúchais Gaeilge in Uíbh Ráthach, ó os cionn 80% den daonra sa bhliain 1851 go dornán beag sa lá atá inniu ann.

Select bibliography

Ní Mhóráin, Brighid.

—. *Ceiliúradh Cré*. Filíocht. Baile Átha Cliath: Coiscéim, 1992.

—. *Thiar sa Mhainistir atá an Ghaolainn Bhreá: Meath na Gaeilge in Uíbh Ráthach*. Scríbhneoireacht acadúil. An Daingean: An Sagart, 1997.

—. "Dánta – le Bríd Ní Mhóráin." *Feasta* 54.9 (2001): 6.

—. *Fé Bhrat Bhríde*. Filíocht. An Daingean: An Sagart, 2002.

Secondary sources

Mac Fhearghusa, Pádraig. "Blúiríní." *Feasta* 54.9 (2001): 26.

Ó Cearnaigh, Seán. "Ó Móráin, Brighid [Ní Mhóráin]." *Scríbhneoirí na Gaeilge 1945–1995*. Baile Átha Cliath: Comhar, 1995.

Ruiséal, Pól. "Léirmheas ar *Thiar sa Mhainistir atá an Ghaolainn Bhreá*." *Comhar* 11ú Bealtaine (1997).

Uí Nia, Gearóidín, eag. "Ní Mhóráin, Brighid." *Eolaire Chló Iar-Chonnachta de Scríbhneoirí Gaeilge*. Indreabhán: Cló Iar-Chonnnachta, 1998.

Ní Mhuláin, Siubhán [Ní Mhuláin, Síle]. *fl.*1931. Cúil Aodha, Múscraí, Co. Chorcaí. Seanchas / béaloideas, paidreacha.

Saolaíodh agus tógadh i gCúil Aodha í agus bhí sí ina cailín óg nuair a bhailigh

Gearóid Ó Murchadha paidir uaithi a foilsíodh in *Béaloideas* 3 (1931).

Select bibliography
Ní Mhuláin, Siubhán.
—. seanchaí. "Véursaí agus Paidreacha ó Iarthar Chorcaighe: 'Aisling Mhuire'."
Seanchas / béaloideas, paidreacha. *Béaloideas* 3.2 (1931): 237.

Ní Mhurchadha, Máire [Ní Mhurchú, Máire]. *fl.*1908. Co. Chorcaí.
Filíocht / béaloideas.
Luann "Fiachra Éilgeach" (Risteárd Ó Foghludha) Máire Ní Mhurchadha
agus filí eile ina aiste "Filí Chorcaighe" (1908).

Secondary sources
Éilgeach, Fiachra. "Filí Chorcaighe." *Saothar Suadha: Aistí do léigheadh os comhair*
Dáil na hÉigse, i gCorcaigh, Meadhon Foghmhair, 1907. Vol. 1. Baile Átha Cliath:
Muinntir an Ghoill, 1908. 26–41.

Ní Mhurchú, Eibhlín [Ní Mhurchú, Nell]. Comhaimseartha. Baile Loisce,
Corca Dhuibhne, Co. Chiarraí. Litríocht, taisteal, beathaisnéis /
scríbheoireacht acadúil, aistí.

Ón mBaile Loisce, Corca Dhuibhne is ea Eibhlín ó dhúchas ach maireann sí
i mBaile Átha Cliath anois. Foilsíodh leabhar amháin léi, *Siúlach Scéalach*
(1968). Is é atá sa leabhar seo ná "cnuasach aistí faoina cuid taistil, ag tosú
le turas a rinne sí go hAlbain ar mhí na meala" (Nic Eoin 1982, 67). Ina
theannta sin, tá sí tar éis roinnt aistí a scríobh ar sheanchas agus ar stair
shóisialta Chorca Dhuibhne.

Select bibliography
Ní Mhurchú, Eibhlín.
—. *Siúlach Scéalach.* Litríocht, taisteal, beathaisnéis. Baile Átha Cliath: Cló
Grianréime, 1968.
—. "An tIascach a Bhí." *Céad Bliain 1871–1971.* Aiste, seanchas áitiúil. Eag. Mícheál
Ó Ciosáin. Baile an Fheirtéaraigh: Muintir Phiarais, 1973. 194—212.
—. "Peig Sayers." *Oidhreacht an Bhlascaoid.* Aiste, seanchas áitiúil. Eag. Aogán Ó
Muircheartaigh. Baile Átha Cliath: Coiscéim, 1989. 238–52.
—. "Ceol agus Rince mo Cheantar Dúchais 1800–1880." *An Canónach Séamas*
Goodman. Aiste, seanchas áitiúil. Eag. Pádraig Ó Fiannachta. Iris na hOidhreachta
2. Baile an Fheirtéaraigh: Oidhreacht Chorca Dhuibhne, 1990. 99–120.
—. "Mícheál Ó Sé: Maidhc Sé. File, Rinceoir agus Ceardaí." *Ár bhFilí.* Aiste,
seanchas áitiúil. Eag. Pádraig Ó Fiannachta. Iris na hOidhreachta 3. Baile an
Fheirtéaraigh: Oidhreacht Chorca Dhuibhne, 1991.
—. "Kruger." *Is Cuimhin Linn Kruger: Kruger Remembered.* Aiste, seanchas áitiúil.
Eag. Tadhg Ó Dúshláine. Maigh Nuad: An Sagart, 1994. 86–8.

Secondary sources
Nic Eoin, Máirín. *An Litríocht Réigiúnach.* Leabhair Thaighde 40. Baile Átha Cliath:
An Clóchomhar, 1982.

Ní Mhurchú, Maria. Comhaimseartha. Baile an Fheirtéaraigh agus An
Daingean, Co Chiarraí. Drámaíocht.

Saolaíodh Maria ar an mBaile Íochtarach agus ghnóthaigh sí BA le
honóracha ó Choláiste na hOllscoile, Gaillimh. Tá baint aici leis an

gcomhlacht físeán, "Dovinia", i mBaile an Fheirtéaraigh. Sa bhliain 1995 a chuaigh sí i mbun pinn den chéad uair. Léirigh "Dovinia" a dráma teilifíse *An Turas* i 1996, scannán a mhaireann 30 nóiméad. Is scriptscríbhneoir í ar an sobalchlár *Ros na Rún* a bhíonn á léiriú ar TG4. Tá cáilíocht aici i Smidiú don Teilifís agus don Stáitse, agus is í an tOifigeach Scannaíochta le Féile na Bealtaine a bhíonn ar siúl sa Daingean gach bliain. Is é *Tomás na bPúcaí* an chéad dráma le Maria a cuireadh i gcló. Scríobh sí é i 1997 agus foilsíodh é i 1999. D'éirigh go maith leis i gcomórtas a bhí eagraithe ag Oifig Ealaíona Chontae Phort Láirge i gcomhar le hÚdarás na Gaeltachta agus leis an gComhlachas Náisiúnta Drámaíochta. Cuireadh síol an dráma seo in intinn Mharia agus í ag éisteacht le scéalta a máthar críonna, Nóra, a saolaíodh in Imleá. Carachtar is ea Tomás a mhaireann fós i gcuimhne na ndaoine agus sa seanchas áitiúil.

Select bibliography
Ní Mhurchú, Maria.
—. *Tomás na bPúcaí*. Drámaíocht. Binn Éadair, Baile Átha Cliath agus An Charraig, Corca Dhuibhne: Coiscéim, 1999.

Ní Mhurchú, Nell [Ní Mhurchú, Neillí]. *fl.*1937. Baile Bhuirne, Múscraí, Co. Chorcaí. Filíocht / béaloideas.

Chaith an file seo an chuid ba mhó dá saol san áit a saolaíodh agus a tógadh í, ar an Leacan, Gort na Tiobratan. Meastar gur mhair sí sa tréimhse chéanna, a bheag nó a mhór, le Máire Bhuidhe Ní Laoghaire. Bhíodh sí ag obair i dtithe feirmeoirí sa cheantar. Phós sí agus bhí iníon amháin aici, Peig. Ó bhéalaithris Dhiarmuid Uí Dhuinnín a tháinig amhráin Nell anuas chugainn agus ba é Seán Ua Cróinín a chuir i gcló iad in *An Músgraigheach 3* (1943, 9–13). Is iad ainmneacha na n-amhrán ná: "Amhrán an Aoiligh", "Amhrán na gCearc", "Amhrán na nGabhar", agus "Muc an Chúil Ruaidh". Chuir Proinseas Ó Ceallaigh cuid de na hamhráin seo i gcló freisin in *Béaloideas* 7.1 (1931) agus bhí roinnt acu ar eolas ag Pádraig Ó Crualaoi. Deirfiúr ab ea Nell le seanathair Phádraig Uí Chrualaoi.

Select bibliography
Ní Mhurchú, Nell.
—. "Amhráin Ó Mhúscraighe." Filíocht, amhránaíocht. *Béaloideas* 7.1 (1937): 32–3.

Secondary sources
Ó Crualaoi, Pádraig. *Seanachas Phádraig Í Chrualaoi*. Eag. Donncha Ó Cróinín. Baile Átha Cliath: Comhairle Bhéaloideas Éireann, 1982.
Ó hÓgáin, Daithí. *An File: Staidéar ar Osnádúrthacht na Filíochta sa Traidisiún Gaelach*. Baile Átha Cliath: Oifig an tSoláthair, 1982.
Ua Cróinín, Seán. "Neil Ní Mhurchadha: Ban-Fhile." *An Músgraigheach 3*. Nodlaig (1943): 9–13.

Ní Néill, Maighréad [Ní Néill, Máiréad]. *fl.*1900. An Rinn, Na Déise, Co. Phort Láirge. Filíocht / béaloideas.

Chum Maighréad "An Cat Fireann Buí" timpeall na bliana 1900. B'as na Corráin, An Rinn í. Bean shingil ab ea í, a bhí ag maireachtáil in aontíos lena deartháir, a raibh muirear mór air. Bhíodh drogall ar dhaoine an t-amhrán seo a aithris mar bhí blas an-logánta air agus ainmníodh cuid de mhuintir na háite ann (Tóibín 1968, 61). Bhreac Nioclás Breathnach an t-amhrán síos ó dhuine sa Seanphobal agus thug sé do Nioclás Tóibín é. Foilsíodh ansin é in *Duanaire Déiseach* (65–6).

Select bibliography
Ní Néill, Maighréad.
—. "An Cat Fireann Buí." *Duanaire Déiseach*. Filíocht / béaloideas. Eag. Nioclás Tóibín. Baile Átha Cliath: Sáirséal agus Dill, 1978.

Ní Nuadháin, Nóirín. Comhaimseartha. Cathair Luimnigh. Scríbhneoireacht acadúil, eagarthóireacht, leabhar teagaisc.

Saolaíodh Nóirín i mBealach an Doirín i 1947, Co. Ros Comáin agus tá sí tar éis tamall a chaitheamh i Luimneach ina léachtóir i gColáiste Mhuire gan Smál. Múinteoirí ab ea a tuismitheoirí. Fuair sí a cuid scolaíochta i Meánscoil Naomh Lughaidh, Coillte Mach, Co. Mhaigh Eo. Bhí an tSíceolaíocht, an Ghaeilge agus an Stair mar ábhair aici i gColáiste na hOllscoile, Baile Átha Cliath. Tá cáilíochtaí aici chomh maith sa diagacht agus i modhanna múinte teangacha.

Tá dhá leabhar scríofa aici agus dhá leabhar curtha in eagar. Feidhmíonn na leabhair seo mar áiseanna teagaisc i múineadh na Gaeilge do pháistí. I gcomhar le G. Mac Ionrachtaigh, scríobh sí trí chnuas-scéal do pháistí óga, diosca don ríomhaire agus leabhrán don mhúinteoir: *Gaelsoft* (Ionad Forbartha Curaclaim, Coláiste Mhuire gan Smál 1993). Is é atá i "Cluichí Teanga sa Seomra Ranga" (Ionad na Múinteoirí, An Charraig Dhubh, Baile Átha Cliath, 1988) ná físeán do mhúinteoirí agus script.

Select bibliography
Ní Nuadháin, Nóirín.
—. *Aimsigh na Difríochtaí*. Scríbhneoireacht acadúil, leabhar teagaisc. Baile Átha Cliath: Ionad na Múinteoirí, An Charraig Dhubh, 1986.
—. eag. *33 Drámaí do Ghasúir Scoile*. Drámaíocht. Indreabhán: Cló Iar-Chonnachta, 1989.
—. eag. (ar an tarna cló de) *An Táin: ceann de mhórscéalta na tíre seo agus an domhain, curtha in oiriúint do leanaí 8–11 bliana*. Litríocht leanaí. Le Liam Mac Uistín. Indreabhán: Cló Iar-Chonnachta, 1991.
—. eag. *Buail ar an Doras*. Scríbhneoireacht acadúil, leabhar teagaisc. Indreabhán: Cló Iar-Chonnachta, 1992.
—. *Cluichí Teanga do na Bunranganna*. Scríbhneoireacht acadúil, leabhar teagaisc. Luimneach: Ionad Forbartha Curaclaim, Coláiste Mhuire gan Smál, 1992.

Secondary sources
Ní Ríordáin, Michelle. "Léirmheas ar *33 Drámaí do Ghasúir Scoile*." *Comhar* Márta (1990).
Ó Cearnaigh, Seán. "Ó Nuadháin, Nóirín Ní Nuadháin." *Scríbhneoirí na Gaeilge 1945–1995*. Baile Átha Cliath: Comhar, 1995.
Uí Nia, Gearóidín, eag. "Ní Nuadháin, Nóirín." *Eolaire Chló Iar-Chonnachta de Scríbhneoirí Gaeilge*. Indreabhán: Cló Iar-Chonnachta, 1998.

Ní Rathaille, Sisile [O'Rahilly, Cecile]. 1894–1980. Lios Tuathail, Co. Chiarraí. Scríbhneoireacht acadúil, aistriúchán, taighde, fileolaíocht, stair.

Bhain Sisile cáil idirnáisiúnta amach sa Léann Ceilteach mar scoláire Gaeilge agus Breatnaise. Saolaíodh í i Lios Tuathail, Co. Chiarraí. Bhí 15 leanaí sa chlann, ach cailleadh beirt acu go hóg. Fuair Sisile a cuid meánscolaíochta i Scoil Chlochar na nDoiminiceach, Sráid Eccles, Baile Átha Cliath agus bhain sí céim amach le céad onóracha sa Léann Ceilteach ó Choláiste na hOllscoile, Baile Átha Cliath. Chuaigh sí ar scoláireacht taistil go dtí an Bhreatain Bheag agus ghnóthaigh MA. D'eascair a leabhar *Ireland and Wales* as duais-aiste a scríobh sí i 1920 ar chúrsaí idir an Bhreatain Bheag agus Éirinn sna meánaoiseanna. Chaith sí suas le fiche bliain ag múineadh i gCardiff mar ar bhain sí ardchaighdeán amach sa Bhreatnais sular fhill sí ar Éirinn.

Fuair sí post mar Ollamh i Scoil an Léinn Cheiltigh san Institiúid Ard-Léinn Bhaile Átha Cliath agus chuir trí leabhar in eagar idir na blianta 1946–1955. Ba é an Táin an t-ábhar staidéir ab ansa léi féin, agus dhein sí mórán taighde sa ghort seo, saothar a foilsíodh idir 1961 agus 1976. Dhein sí sár-obair ar an ábhar seo, obair a mhaireann fós mar gheall ar a fheabhas is atá sí. Ní raibh cúrsaí sláinte go rómhaith aici, agus thugadh a cara, Myfanwy Williams, aire di. Ach duine an-lách a bhí inti, a raibh lé aici leis an múinteoireacht. Deartháireacha léi ab ea Tomás, scoláire Gaeilge a d'fhoilsigh scata leabhar, *Irish Dialects Past and Present* (1932) ina measc, agus Alfred, a bhí ina Uachtarán ar Choláiste na hOllscoile, Corcaigh. Chuaigh sé dian uirthi cáil a bhaint amach di féin agus a deartháir, Tomás, ag obair sa réimse céanna den léann, ach d'éirigh go geal léi é seo a dhéanamh ar deireadh.

Cecile O'Rahilly gained an international reputation in Celtic Studies as a scholar both of Irish and of Welsh. She was born in Listowel, Co. Kerry. There were fifteen children in the family, but two of them died at a young age. Cecile received her secondary schooling in the Dominican Convent, Eccles Street, Dublin, and she was awarded a first-class honours degree in Celtic Studies from UCD. She went on a travelling scholarship to Wales and received an MA. Her book *Ireland and Wales* (1924) emanated from an award-winning essay she wrote in 1920 on relations between Ireland and Wales in medieval times. She spent up to twenty years teaching in Cardiff, where she became highly proficient in Welsh before returning to Ireland.

She was appointed to a Professorship in the School of Celtic Studies at the Dublin Institute for Advanced Studies, and she edited three books between 1946 and 1955. The *Táin Bó Cuailnge* was her preferred area of study; between 1961 and 1976 she published extensive research in this field, and her work on this subject is still acknowledged as excellent. Her health was poor, and her friend Myfanwy Williams took care of her. Her teaching benefited from her warm and kind personality. Tomás, one of her brothers, was an Irish scholar who published many books, including *Irish Dialects Past and Present* (1932). It was difficult for her to forge a reputation for herself when her brother was working in the same field, but she succeeded in doing this in the end. Alfred, another brother, became President of UCC.

Select bibliography
Ní Rathaille, Sisile.

—. *Ireland and Wales: Their Historical and Literary Relations.* Scríbhneoireacht acadúil. London: Longmans, Green, 1924.

—. eag. agus aist. *Tóruigheacht Gruaidhe Ghriansholus.* Scríbhneoireacht acadúil, litríocht. Irish Texts Society 74. London / Baile Átha Cliath: Simpkin, Marshall / Irish Texts Society, 1924.

—. eag. *Five seventeenth-century political poems.* Scríbhneoireacht acadúil, léirmheastóireacht. N.p.: n.p., 1946. Dublin: DIAS, 1952.

—. eag. *Eachtra Uilliam edited, with English translation, by Cecile O'Rahilly* [Guillaume de Parlerne, leagan Gaeilge de William of Parlerne]. Scríbhneoireacht acadúil. Dublin: DIAS, 1949.

—. eag. *Trompa na bhFlaitheas* [La Trompette du ciel]. Scríbhneoireacht acadúil. Le Antoine Yvan. Baile Átha Cliath: DIAS, 1955.

—. "Copgha, ga cop, ga cró." Scríbhneoireacht acadúil, fileolaíocht. *Éigse* 9 (1958–61): 181–6.

—. eag. *The Stowe version of Táin Bó Cuailgne.* Scríbhneoireacht acadúil, litríocht. N.p.: n.p,. 1961. Baile Átha Cliath: DIAS, 1978.

—. eag. *Cath Finntrágha: Edited from MS. Rawlinson B 487.* Scríbhneoireacht acadúil. 1962. Scríobhaí Lámhscríbhinne Finnlaech Ó Cathasaigh. Medieval and Modern Irish series. Baile Átha Cliath: DIAS, 1975.

—. "Tecosc." Scríbhneoireacht acadúil, fileolaíocht. *Éigse* 11.3 (1965–6): 214–15.

—. "*Marcach* = 'messenger'?" Scríbhneoireacht acadúil, fileolaíocht. *Celtica* 7 (1966): 32.

—. "On a Passage in *Cath Ruis na Ríg.*" Scríbhneoireacht acadúil. *Celtica* 7 (1966): 46–7.

—. eag. *Táin Bó Cuailgne from the Book of Leinster.* Scríbhneoireacht acadúil, litríocht. Irish Texts Society 49. Baile Átha Cliath: DIAS, 1967.

—. "Words Descriptive of Hair in Irish." Scríbhneoireacht acadúil, fileolaíocht. *Éigse* 13 (1969–70): 177–80.

—. eag. agus aist. *Táin Bó Cuailgne Recension 1.* Scríbhneoireacht acadúil, eagarthóireacht. Baile Átha Cliath: DIAS, 1976.

Secondary sources
Breathnach, Diarmuid, agus Máire Ní Mhurchú. "Ó Rathaille, Sisile [Ní Rathaille] (1894–1980)." *1882–1982 Beathaisnéis a Dó.* Baile Átha Cliath: An Clóchomhar, 1990.

Ní Réagáin, Neans. Comhaimseartha. An tSeanchill, Rinn Ó gCuanach, Na Déise, Co. Phort Láirge. Scríbhneoireacht acadúil, stair shóisialta.

Is sa tSeanchill, Rinn Ó gCuanach, na Déise, Co. Phort Láirge a saolaíodh Neans, agus tá sí ina cónaí fós ann. Is cigire scoile san eacnamaíocht bhaile í agus múinteoir i meánscoil San Nioclás (Ó Macháin agus Nic Dhonnchadha 1997, 95–6). San aiste a scríobh sí in *An Linn Bhuí 1* (1997,

212 Munster Women Writers 1800–2000

3–12) cuireann sí síos ar an saghas bia a bhíodh ag muintir na nDéise sa seansaol, conas an bia a ullmhú, agus an leas a bhaintí as bia agus as luibheanna áirithe chun tinneas a leigheas. Tá cuntas aici ar a máthair, Peig Turraoin (Uí Réagáin), a bhí ina hardchainteoir Gaeilge, in *An Linn Bhuí* 4.

Select bibliography

Ní Réagáin, Neans.

—. "Fulacht Folláin ár nÓige." *An Linn Bhuí: Iris Ghaeltacht na nDéise.* Aiste, stair shóisialta. Eag. Pádraig Ó Macháin agus Aoibheann Nic Dhonnchadha. Vol. 1. Baile Átha Cliath: Leabhair na Linne, 1997. 3–12.

—. "Ár Máthair Peig." *An Linn Bhuí: Iris Ghaeltacht na nDéise.* Aiste, stair shóisialta. Eag. Pádraig Ó Macháin agus Aoibheann Nic Dhonnchadha. Vol. 4. Baile Átha Cliath: Leabhair na Linne, 2000. 3–15.

Ní Riain, Nóirín. Contemporary. Caherconlish, Co. Limerick. Handbooks.

Born in Co. Limerick, she studied music at UCC, graduating in 1972. She is a well known musician and singer who is particularly associated with sacred music and plainchant. Ní Riain has also carried out scholarly research on Irish music, and took an MA for a thesis on "Traditional Irish Song in Irish". She performs worldwide, has sung with the American composer John Cage and has represented Ireland at many international festivals. One of her best-known recordings, *Vox de Nube* (1989), was recorded with the monks of Glenstal Abbey.

Select bibliography

Ní Riain, Nóirín.

—. *Gregorian Chant Experience: Sing and Meditate with Nóirín Ní Riain.* Handbook. Dublin: O'Brien, 1997.

O'Riordan, Michelle [Ní Ríordáin, Michelle]. Comhaimseartha. Cathair Chorcaí. Scríbhneoireacht acadúil, taighde, aistí.

Is as Cathair Chorcaí do Mhichelle. Bhain sí céim amach sa Stair agus sa Ghaeilge in Ollscoil Chorcaí. D'fhoilsigh Cló Ollscoile Chorcaí leabhar léi, *The Gaelic Mind and the Collapse of the Gaelic World* (1990). Litríocht na Gaeilge mar fhoinse don staraí is ábhar don leabhar seo agus tá sé bunaithe ar chéim dhochtúireachta a bhí ar siúl aici in Ollscoil Chorcaí idir 1981 agus 1985. Tá dhá aiste léi san iris *Comhar* (Bealtaine agus Meitheamh 1990) agus tá ceann léi in *Feasta* (Meán Fómhair 2001).

Select bibliography

O'Riordan, Michelle.

—. *The Gaelic Mind and the Collapse of the Gaelic World: A Study of the Motifs of Bardic Poetry.* Scríbhneoireacht acadúil, stair. Cork: Cork UP, 1990.

—. "Na Speuclairean Dubha 'le Iain Mac A' Ghobhainn." Scríbhneoireacht acadúil, léirmheas. *Comhar* Meitheamh (1990).

—. "Rubble na Mickies." Scríbhneoireacht acadúil, aiste. *Comhar* (Bealtaine 1990): 28–9.

—. "Comhréir agus Gramadach Ghaeilge Uladh i 1600." Scríbhneoireacht acadúil. *Feasta* 54.9 (2001): 10.

Ní Scanail, Nóra. *fl.***1944.** Múscraí, Co. Chorcaí. Scríbhneoireacht acadúil, aistí.

Scríobh sí aiste san iris *An Músgraigheach 4* (1944) faoin bhfile "Nóra an tSleasa" (Ní Chríodáin). Scríobh sí síos an scéal "Sgeilmis" ó bhéalaithris Mháire Aodha de Róiste agus foilsíodh é in *An Músgraigheach 7* (1944).

Select bibliography
Ní Scanail, Nóra.
—. "Nóra an tSleasa." Aiste. *An Músgraigheach* 4 Earrach (1944): 16–17.
—. bail. agus eag. "Sgeilimis." Aiste. *An Músgraigheach* 7 Nodlaig (1944): 4–6.

Ní Shéaghdha, Máire [Ní Shé, Máire]. *fl.* **1922.** Co. Chiarraí. Beathaisnéis.

Cuireadh dhá eagrán den chín lae *Laethanta Geala* i gcló. Luaitear Máire Ní Shéaghdha agus Brighid Ní Shíothcháin leis an gceann a foilsíodh i 1922. Níl ach ainm Mháire le heagrán 1916 áfach, go bhfuil cóipde á choimeád i leabharlann Acadamh Ríoga na hÉireann (de Hae agus Ní Dhonnchadha 1938, 40–41). Deir an leas-leabharlannaí, Bernadette Cunningham, gur dialann do mhí an Mhárta 1916 atá ann, agus go bhfuil 16 leathanach ar fad ann. Deir sí go dtugtar "leanbh scoile" ar an údar ar an gcéad leathanach, agus "cailín scoile i gCiarraighe" uirthi ar an gclúdach (nóta ríomhphoist, 3 Meán Fómhair 2001).

Select bibliography
Ní Shéaghdha, Máire.
—. agus Brighid Ní Shíothcháin. *Laethanta Geala. Cunntasaí cinn lae do scríobh beirt chailín sgoile [.i. M. Ní Shéaghdha agus Brighid Ní Shíothcháin].* Beathaisnéis. Eag. Finghin na Leamhna. Baile Átha Cliath: Brún agus Ó Nualláin, 1922.

Secondary sources
De Hae, Risteárd agus Brighid Ní Dhonnchadha, eag. *Clár Litridheacht na Nua-Ghaedhilge 1850–1936*. Vol. 1. Baile Átha Cliath: Oifig Dhíolta Foilseacháin Rialtais, 1938.

Ní Shéaghdha, Nóra [Ní Shé, Nóra]. **1905–75.** Corca Dhuibhne, Co. Chiarraí. Litríocht, úrscéalaíocht, drámaíocht, scríbhneoireacht acadúil, stair shóisialta agus aistriúchán.

Saolaíodh Nóra i mBaile an Mhórdhaigh, Paróiste an Fheirtéaraigh. D'fhreastail sí ar bhunscoil Chill Chuain agus is i dTrá Lí a fuair sí a cuid meánscolaíochta. Chuaigh sí ar aghaidh ansin chuig Coláiste Mhuire gan Smál, Luimneach le traenáil mar mhúinteoir bunscoile. Chaith sí seacht mbliana ag múineadh ar an mBlascaod Mór, a chuir inspioráid ar fáil don chéad leabhar léi *Thar Bealach Isteach: Leabhar Eile ón mBlascaod* (1940). D'fhill sí ar an míntír agus phós sí Dónall Ó Héalaí, a bhí ag obair ar an bhFeothanach. Bhí triúr muirear orthu, mac agus beirt iníon. Tá a mac, Pádraig Ó Héalaí, ina scoláire Gaeilge agus béaloidis.

Is é a húrscéal *Peats na Baintreabhaighe* – scéal éadrom, rómánsúil – a saothar is mó cáil. Is rí-annamh a luaitear úrscéal Gaeilge le bean. As an liosta atá curtha le chéile ag Alan Titley d'úrscéalta Gaeilge do dhaoine fásta a foilsíodh idir 1901–90, níl ach beirt bhan ó Chúige Mumhan: Nóra Ní Shéaghdha, a scríobh *Peats na Baintreabhaighe* agus Siobhán Ní Shúilleabháin, a scríobh *Ospidéal* (feic *An tÚrscéal Gaeilge* 1991, 613–7).

Scríobh Nóra an dráma *Dún an Óir*, a craoladh ar Raidió Éireann sa bhliain 1960. D'aistrigh sí mórán drámaí ó Bhéarla chun go bhféadfaí iad a léiriú ar an stáitse, agus bhí an-shuim aici i gcúrsaí drámaíochta i gCorca Dhuibhne. Scríobh sí ailt faoi ghnéithe éagsúla de shaol an oileáin i mí Mhárta, Aibreáin, na Bealtaine, agus Iúil den iris *Inniu* (1974). Bhíodh sí ag caint ar Raidió na Gaeltachta ó am go chéile agus tá agallamh a dhein sí le Pádraig Tyers i gcló in *Leoithne Aniar* (1982). Chuir sí Gaeilge ar go leor leabhar Béarla don fhoilsitheoir An Gúm, leis.

Select bibliography
Ní Shéaghdha, Nóra.
—. *Thar Bealach Isteach: Leabhar Eile ón mBlascaod.* Litríocht. Baile Átha Cliath: Oifig an tSoláthair, 1940.
—. *Peats na Baintreabhaighe.* Úrscéalaíocht. Baile Átha Cliath: Oifig an tSoláthair, 1945.
—. "Póstaí agus cleamhnaistí." *Céad Bliain 1871–1971.* Scríbhneoireacht acadúil, stair shóisialta. Eag. Mícheál Ó Cíosáin. Baile an Fheirtéaraigh: Muintir Phiarais, 1973.

Secondary sources
Breathnach, Diarmuid, agus Máire Ní Mhurchú. "Ó Shéaghdha, Nóra [Ní Shéaghdha] (1905–1975)." *1882–1982 Beathaisnéis a Dó.* Baile Átha Cliath: An Clóchomhar, 1990.
Nic Eoin, Máirín. *An Litríocht Réigiúnach.* Leabhair Thaighde 40. Baile Átha Cliath: An Clóchomhar Tta, 1982. 223.
Ó Cearnaigh, Seán. "Ó Shéaghda, Nóra Ní Shéaghdha." *Scríbhneoirí na Gaeilge 1945–1995.* Baile Átha Cliath: Comhar, 1995.
Tyers, Pádraig, eag. *Leoithne Aniar.* Baile an Fheirtéaraigh: Cló Dhuibhne, 1982.

Ní Shíndhile, Nóra [Singleton, Norry]. 1773–1873. Sráid an Mhuilinn, Co. Chorcaí. Filíocht, caoineadh / béaloideas.

Bhí Nóra ag cur fúithi ar an mBuaile Mór, ceithre mhíle soir ó Shráid an Mhuilinn, Co. Chorcaí. Tógadh dhá leagan de "Caoineadh Airt Uí Laoghaire" uaithi. Scríobh Éamoinn de Bhál an chéad leagan síos timpeall na bliana 1800. Tá sé i gcló in aguisín an leabhair *The Last Colonel of the Irish Brigade* (1892, Iml. 2, 327). Ceaptar gur bhreac Domhnall Mac Cába an tarna ceann ó bhéalaithris Nóra agus í dulta in aois. Tá cóip den leagan seo ar fáil i bhfoirm lámhscríbhinne i gColáiste na hOllscoile, Baile Átha Cliath, *Ferriter 1* (298–305). Tá cóiriú Sheáin Uí Thuama, *Caoineadh Airt Uí Laoghaire* (1961, 48–50), bunaithe don chuid is mó ar an méid a thug Nóra uaithi. De réir Uí Thuama, "tá brí an dáin le tuiscint go hiomlán, geall leis, as na leaganacha a thug sí dúinn; agus is deimhniú láidir é ar bhuaine a cuimhne an dá leagan a aithris sí a bheith ag teacht chomh mór sin le chéile, bíodh go mb'fhéidir go raibh leathchéad bliain d'achar aimsire idir an tráth a tógadh an chéad leagan uaithi agus an tráth a tógadh an dara leagan" (1961, 50).

Secondary sources
Breathnach, Diarmuid, agus Máire Ní Mhurchú. "Ó Conaill, Eibhlín Dubh
(*c*.1743–1800) [Ní Chonaill]." *1782–1891 Beathaisnéis*. Baile Átha Cliath: An
Clóchomhar, 1999.
Ní Chonaill, Eibhlín Dubh. "Caoineadh ar mharú Airt Uí Laoghaire." *The Last
Colonel of the Irish Brigade: Count O'Connell and Old Irish Life at Home and Abroad
1745–1883*. Mrs M.J. O'Connell. Vol. 2. London: Kegan Paul, 1892.
Ní Chonaill, Eibhlín Dubh. *Caoineadh Airt Uí Laoghaire*. 1961. Eag. Seán Ó Tuama.
Baile Átha Cliath: An Clóchomhar, 1963.

Ní Shíocháin, Bríd (Cléire) [Mhic Choitir, Bríd Bean]. Oileán Chléire, Co. Chorcaí. Filíocht / béaloideas.

Bhí Bríd ag cur fúithi i gCrathach ar Oileán Chléire. Ba dheirfiúr í le Ciarán
Ó Síocháin, a bhí ina scéalaí agus ina bhailitheoir béaloidis. "Ciarán's sister,
Bríd Bean Mhic Chotir, Crathach, penned some pleasant verses in Irish, a
few of which have been published elsewhere" (Lankford 1999, 117).

Secondary Sources
Lankford, Éamonn. *Cape Clear Island: Its People and Landscape*. Jonathan Cape Clear
Museum, Co. Cork, 1999.

Ní Shíocháin, Cáit. 1882–1962. Oileán Chléire, Co. Chorcaí. Filíocht, scéalaíocht agus seanchas / béaloideas.

Saolaíodh Cáit ar Oileán Chléire, Co. Chorcaí. Foilsíodh dhá dhán léi i
Nua-Fhilí 2, "An Geimhreadh" agus "An Dreoilín" (Ó Céilleachair 1968,
81–2). Foilsíodh sraith de chúig alt dar teideal "Ó Chléire" le Cáit Ní
Shíocháin san iris *An Lóchrann* i 1931. Ba iad Peadar Ó Síocháin agus Cáit
Ní Dhrisceoil a tuismitheoirí. Bhí ochtar muirear orthu, seisear mac agus
beirt iníon. Cuireadh ailt i gcló lena dhearthráir, Conchúr, in *An Lóchrann*
freisin. Fear mór seanchais agus béaloidis ab ea é, agus dheachtaigh sé
leabhar inar thug sé cuntas cuimsitheach ar chúrsaí farraige, iascaigh agus
bádóireachta, *Seanchas Chléire*.

Select bibliography
Ní Shíocháin, Cáit.
—. "Litreacha ó Chléire." Seanchas / béaloideas. *An Lóchrann* (Feabhra 1931).
—. "Ó Chléire." Seanchas / béaloideas. *An Lóchrann* (Márta 1931).
—. "Béaloideas Ó Chléire." Seanchas / béaloideas. *Béaloideas* 5.1 (1935): 137.
—. Seanchaí. "Sean-nós." Seanchas / béaloideas. *Béaloideas* 5.2 (1935): 136.
—. "An t-Asal Cliste." Scéalaíocht / béaloideas. *An tÉireannach* 7ú Nollaig (1935).
—. Scéalaí. "Béaloideas Ó Chléire." Scéalaíocht / béaloideas. *Béaloideas* 6.1 (1941):
3–77.
—. "Cáit Ní Shíocháin." *Nua-Fhilí 2 (1953–1963)*. Filíocht. Eag. Séamas Ó
Céileachair. Baile Átha Cliath: Oifig an tSoláthair, 1968.

Secondary sources
Gunn, Marion, eag. *Céad Fáilte go Cléire*. Baile Átha Cliath: An Clóchomhar,
1990.
Ó Síocháin, Conchúr, a dheachtaigh. *Seanchas Chléire*. Ciarán Ó Síocháin agus Mícheál
Ó Síocháin a chuir i scríbhinn. Baile Átha Cliath: Oifig an tSoláthair, 1940.

Ní Shíocháin, Máire [McDonogh O'Mahony, Mrs]. 1886–1936. Cathair Saidhbhín, Co. Chiarraí. Drámaíocht, aistriúchán.

Saolaíodh Máire i gCathair Saidhbhín. Táilliúir ab ea a hathair. Trí dhuine dhéag a bhí sa chlann, agus ba í Máire an duine ba shine. Bhí Gaeilge acu ag baile. Chuaigh Máire go dtí Clochar na Trócaire i gCathair Saidhbhín, áit a raibh sármhúinteoir Gaeilge aici, an tSiúr Máire Treasa. Phós sí Tomás Mac Donncha Ó Mathúna sa bliain 1908 agus d'aistríodar go dtí Baile Átha Cliath. Níor éirigh leis an bpósadh, agus scaradar lena chéile seacht mbliana níos déanaí gan aon mhuirear orthu.

Bhí Máire páirteach i gConradh na Gaeilge i gCiarraí agus bhí sí an-ghníomhach i gcúrsaí drámaíochta i gCraobh Uíbh Ráthaigh. Bhí clú agus cáil uirthi mar aisteoir ag an Oireachtas idir na blianta 1906–1911. Sa bhliain 1916 ghlac sí an phríomhpháirt sa dráma *Oidhreacht*, a bhí aistrithe aici féin go Gaeilge agus a foilsíodh ag tús na dtríochaidaí. Deir Breathnach agus Ní Mhurchú go mb'fhéidir "gur aistrigh sí drámaí eile mar tagraíonn Máire Nic Shiubhlaigh [*q.v.*] in *The Splendid Years* do 'some fine Irish translations by Mrs McDonogh O'Mahony'." Bhí sí ina ball de na hAisteoirí – grúpa a d'eascair ó Chonradh na Gaeilge – agus den Chomhar Drámaíochta i mBaile Átha Cliath. Cé gurbh é saol na hamharclainne ab ansa léi, bhí a hainm in airde mar oide chomh maith. Is cosúil gur mhúin sí i gCathair Saidhbhín sular phós sí agus mhúin sí Gaeilge i gColáiste Laighean agus i gColáiste Chonnacht níos déanaí ina saol.

Select bibliography
Ní Shíocháin, Máire.
—. aist. *Oidhreacht* [Birthright]. Drámaíocht. Le Tomás C. Ó Muireadha. Baile Átha Cliath: Oifig Dhíolta Foilseacháin Rialtais, 1931.

Secondary sources
Breathnach, Diarmuid, agus Máire Ní Mhurchú. "Ó Síocháin, Máire (1886–1936)." *1882–1982 Beathaisnéis a Ceathair*. Baile Átha Cliath: An Clóchomhar, 1994.
Kenny, Edward. *The Splendid Years: Recollections of Máire Nic Shiubhlaigh, As Told to Edward Kenny*. Dublin: Duffy, 1955.

Ní Shíocháin, Máire (Cléire). *fl.*1990. Oileán Chléire, Co. Chorcaí. Seanchas / béaloideas.

Saolaíodh Máire i 1860 agus bhí sí ag maireachtáil i gCill Leice Fórabháin ar Oileán Chléire. Bhailigh Ciarán Ó Síocháin ábhar uaithi i 1938. Bhí sí ocht mbliana déag agus trí fichid ag an am. Tá an béaloideas seo i dtaisce i gCartlann Roinn Bhéaloideas Éireann (Iml. 609) agus foilsíodh cuid de in *Céad Fáilte go Cléire* (Gunn 1990, 124–5, 182).

Select bibliography
Ní Shíocháin, Máire (Cléire).
—. "Béaloideas uaithi." *Céad Fáilte go Cléire*. Seanchas / béaloideas. Eag. Marion Gunn. Baile Átha Cliath: An Clóchomhar, 1990.

Ní Shíocháin, Peig. *fl.*1941–90. Oileán Chléire, Co. Chorcaí. Scéalaíocht agus seanchas / béaloideas.

Saolaíodh Peig timpeall na bliana 1860. Bhí sí ag maireachtáil i Lios Ó Móine ar Oileán Chléire. Bhailigh Seán Ó Conaill béaloideas uaithi sa bhliain 1934 (RBÉ iml. 52) agus 1935 (RBÉ iml. 174). Bhailigh Seán Stundún ábhar uaithi i 1933 (RBÉ iml. 49). Foilsíodh cuid dá stór in *Céad Fáilte go Cléire* (Gunn 1990, 23, 29–30, 37–9, 41, 49–55, 65–75, 126–7, 173–5). Bean tí agus bean feirmeora ab ea í. Bhailigh Donnchadh Ó Floinn béaloideas uaithi nuair a bhí sí 75 bliain d'aois agus d'fhoilsigh sé é in *Béaloideas* 6.1 (1941).

Select bibliography
Ní Shíocháin, Peig.
—. scéalaí. "Béaloideas Ó Chléire." Scéalaíocht / béaloideas. *Béaloideas* 6.1 (1941).
—. "Béaloideas uaithi." *Céad Fáilte go Cléire.* Seanchas agus scéalaíocht / béaloideas. Eag. Marion Gunn. Baile Átha Cliath: An Clóchomhar, 1990.

Ní Shíothcháin, Brighid (Ciarraí) [Ní Shíocháin, Bríd]. *fl.*1922. Co. Chiarraí. Beathaisnéis.

Cuireadh dhá eagrán den chín lae *Laethanta Geala* i gcló. Luaitear Máire Ní Shéaghdha agus Brighid Ní Shíothcháin leis an gceann a foilsíodh i 1922. Níl ach ainm Mháire amháin le heagrán 1916 áfach, go bhfuil cóip de á choimeád i leabharlann Acadamh Ríoga na hÉireann (de Hae agus Ní Dhonnchadha 1938, 40–41).

Select bibliography
Ní Shíothcháin, Brighid (Ciarraí).
—. agus M. Ní Shéaghdha. *Laethanta Geala. Cunntasaí cinn lae do scríobh beirt chailín sgoile [.i. M. Ní Shéaghdha agus Brighid Ní Shíothcháin].* Beathaisnéis. Eag. Finghin na Leamhna. Baile Átha Cliath: Brún agus Ó Nualláin, 1922.

Secondary sources
De Hae, Risteárd, agus Brighid Ní Dhonnchadha, eag. *Clár Litridheacht na Nua-Ghaedhilge 1850–1936.* Vol. 1. Baile Átha Cliath: Oifig Dhíolta Foilseacháin Rialtais, 1938.
Ní Shéaghdha, Máire. *Laethanta Geala. Cailín scoile i gCiarraighe [.i. M. Ní Shéaghdha] do scríobh.* Corcaigh: Oifig "An Lóchrainn", g.d.

Ní Shíthe, Máire [Ní Shíthigh, Máire / "Dul Amudha" / "Dul Amú"]. 1867–1955. Iarthar Chorcaí. Drámaíocht, aistriúchán, scríbhneoireacht acadúil, iriseoireacht.

Saolaíodh Máire in aice le Cloch na gCoillte. Feirmeoir ab ea a hathair agus bhí Gaeilge ón gcliabhán ag a máthair. D'fhreastail sí ar bhunscoil Dhairbhre agus ar Chlochar na Trócaire, Cloch na gCoillte mar ar oibrigh sí mar mhonatóir. Phós sí Donncha Ó Laoghaire sa bhliain 1915, agus bhí cónaí orthu i dTigh Molaige ar dtús agus i gCúirt Mhic Shéafraidh ansin.

Scríobhadh sí aistí sna hirisí Gaeilge idir na blianta 1899–1924, mar shampla *Fáinne an Lae, An Claidheamh Soluis, An Lóchrann, Banba* agus *The Father Matthew Record Book.* Bhain sí úsáid as an ainm cleite "Dul Amudha".

Ghnóthaigh aiste, a bhí scríofa aici le Pádraig Ó Séaghdha, an tarna duais ag Feis na Mumhan. Ba í an t-eagarthóir Gaeilge í ar an nuachtán *The Cork Sun* sa bhliain 1903. Is mó duais Oireachtais a bhuaigh sí, mar shampla, don dráma *Suipéar Dhiarmuda Mhic Pháidín* a bhí bunaithe ar scéal le Séamus Mac Maghnuis. Scríobh sí an dráma *Beart Nótaí* i gcomhar le hEilís Ní Mhurchadha. Léiríodh é i mBéal Feirste sa bhliain 1902 agus bhí páirt ag Máire ann. Léiríodh é don tarna huair i 1913 i mBaile Átha Cliath; tá léirmheas ar fáil in *An Claidheamh Soluis*, Aibreán 1918. Bhí cur amach aici ar an bhFraincis agus ar an nGearmáinis agus d'aistrigh sí mórán scéalta, a foilsíodh i dtréimhseacháin éagsúla. Léiríodh *An Geocach Duine Uasal*, a bhí aistrithe aici ó Fhraincis a bhí in úsáid ag Molière, i mBaile Átha Cliath timpeall na bliana 1930, agus léiríodh arís é sa bhliain 1958.

Bhí Máire sáite i saol na Gaeilge. Tá comhfhreagras idir Máire agus Conraitheoirí éagsúla, Pádraig Mac Piarais ina measc, i dtaisce i gClochar na Trócaire, Cloch na gCoillte. Ina theannta sin, mhúin sí Gaeilge ar chúrsaí samhraidh do mhúinteoirí sna blianta 1923, 1924 agus 1925.

Select bibliography
Ní Shíthe, Máire.
—. aist. "Kittie." *Irish Independent*. Scríbhneoireacht acadúil, iriseoireacht. Le Máire de Buitléir. Meitheamh agus Iúil. 1902.
—. "Beart Nótaí." Drámaíocht. *Banba* Nollaig (1903).
—. "Suipéar Dhiarmuda Mhic Pháidín." *Imtheachta an Oireachtais 1901*. Drámaíocht. Eag. Tadhg Ó Donnchadha. Vol. 1. Baile Átha Cliath, 1903.
—. agus Eilís Ní Mhurchadha. *Beart Nótaí: dráma suilt. Iar n-a chur amach ag Cuideachta Bhanba*. Drámaíocht. Leabhráin Bhanba 1. Baile Átha Cliath: Brún agus Ó Nualláin, 1904.
—. "Beart Nótaí." Drámaíocht. *Banba* Meitheamh (1906).
—. aist. "'Aal mit teufel-sauce' le Síle Beuren Hahn (Eascú agus anlann diabhail)." Scríbhneoireacht acadúil, iriseoireacht. *An Claidheamh Soluis* Aibreán (1907).
—. aist. "Eachtra an Bhosga." *An Claidheamh Soluis*. Scríbhneoireacht acadúil, iriseoireacht. Bealtaine. 1907.
—. aist. "Peata an Ríogh." *Irisleabhar na Gaeilge*. Scríbhneoireacht acadúil, iriseoireacht. Bealtaine / Meitheamh. 1909.
—. aist. *An geocach duine uasail; dráma cúig ngníomh* [*Le bourgeois gentilhomme*]. Drámaíocht. Le Jean B.P. de Molière. Baile Átha Cliath: Oifig an tSoláthair, 1930.

Secondary sources
Breathnach, Diarmuid, agus Máire Ní Mhurchú. "Ó Síthe, Máire (1867–1955)." *1882–1982 Beathaisnéis a Ceathair*. Baile Átha Cliath: An Clóchomhar, 1994.
E.O.N. "Na hAisteoirí." *An Claidheamh Soluis* 8. 19ú Aibreán (1913).
Ní Ríordáin, Brenda. "Cérbh í 'Dul amú'? Máire Ní Shíthe, 1968–1955, Drámadóir, Aistritheoir, Conraitheoir." *Comhar* Lúnasa (1993): 39–44.
Ó Siadhail, Pádraig. *Stair Dhrámaíocht na Gaeilge 1900–1970*. Indreabhán: Cló Iar-Chonnachta, 1993: 45–6.

Ní Shíthigh, Caitlín [O'Grady, Fand /Cruise O'Brien, Kathleen]. 1886–1938. An Teampall Mór, Co. Thiobraid Árann. Litríocht leanaí, drámaíocht, aistriúchán.

Saolaíodh Caitlín i Luachma. Muilleoir ab ea a hathair, David Sheehy, a bhí ina bhall parlaiminte idir na blianta 1885–1918. Seisear a bhí sa chlann agus ba í Caitlín an duine ab óige. Cainteoir Gaeilge ó Cho. Luimnigh ab ea a seanathair, a bhí in aontíos leo. D'aistrigh an teaghlach go Baile Átha Cliath, áit ar fhreastail Caitlín ar Scoil na nDoiminiceach, Sráid Eccles agus ar ranganna do mhná i gColáiste Loreto, Faiche Stiabhna chun céim a bhaint amach sa nualitríocht ón Ollscoil Ríoga. Ghnóthaigh sí máistreacht chomh maith.

Chuir sí suim in imeachtaí éagsúla Gaeilge. Bhíodh sí istigh ar chomórtais an Oireachtais san aithriseoireacht agus théadh sí ar laethanta saoire go dtí hÁrainn. Thug sí tacaíocht do ghluaiseacht na mban, mar a dhein a deirfiúracha, Mary agus Hanna. Phós a deirfiúr, Hanna, Francis Sheehy-Skeffington [feic, leis, an iontráil as Béarla ar Hanna Sheehy-Skeffington (*q.v.*)]. Phós Caitlín Francis Cruise O'Brien sa bhliain 1912, rud nár thaitin rómhór lena muintir. Is mac léi Conor Cruise O'Brien. Scríobh sí dhá leabhar do pháistí agus an dráma *Apartments* mar Fand O'Grady. Léiríodh é in Amharclann na Mainistreach cúpla uair agus d'aistrigh Séamus Ó Cuinn go Gaeilge é i 1936 faoin teideal *Na Lóisdéirí*.

Select bibliography
Ní Shíthigh, Caitlín.
—. *A First Irish Book. By Mrs Cruise O'Brien.* Litríocht leanaí. London: Dent, 1924.
—. *Na Trí Muca: Sgéalta greannmhara i gcóir na bpáistí.* Litríocht leanaí. 1925.
—. *Na Lóisdéirí: Cluiche Grinn.* Drámaíocht. Aist. Aindrias Ó Cuinn. Baile Átha Cliath: Oifig Dhíolta Foilseacháin Rialtais, 1936.
—. aist. *Gregg Shorthand: Adapted to Irish by Kathleen Cruise O' Brien.* Scríbhneoireacht acadúil, aistriúchán. London: Gregg, g.d.

Secondary sources
Breathnach, Diarmuid, agus Máire Ní Mhurchú. "Ó Síthigh, Caitlín (1886–1938) [Ní Shíthigh]." *1882–1982 Beathaisnéis a Ceathair.* Baile Átha Cliath: An Clóchomhar, 1994.
Cruise O'Brien, Conor. *States of Ireland.* London: Hutchinson, 1972.
Levenson, Leah, and Jerry H. Natterstad. *Hanna Sheehy-Skeffington, Irish Feminist.* Syracuse: Syracuse University Press, 1986.

Ní Shíthigh, Siobhán. Comhaimseartha. Corca Dhuibhne, Co. Chiarraí.
Saolaíodh Siobhán i mBaile Eaglaise, Corca Dhuibhne agus tá sí ag cur fúithi i gCeatharlach le tamall maith de bhlianta. Tháinig a cnuasach filíochta *Briathar an Tráthnóna* amach sa bhliain 2000 agus foilsíodh cuid de na dánta roimhe sin in *Samhlaíocht Chiarraí, Ceramics Ireland, Feasta* agus *Irisleabhar Mhá Nuad.* Deirfiúr is ea í le Domhnall Mac an tSíthigh, ar foilsíodh a shaothar *Fan Inti: Naomhóga ó Chorca Dhuibhne go Cábán tSíle* (Coiscéim, 2004) le déanaí.

Select bibliography
Ní Shíthigh, Siobhán.
—. *Briathar an Tráthnóna.* Baile Átha Cliath: Coiscéim, 2000.

Ní Shúilleabháin, Eibhlín [Ní Shúilleabháin, Neilí Sheáin Lís]. 1900–1949. An Blascaod Mór (an tOileán Tiar), Corca Dhuibhne, Co. Chiarraí / Springfield, Massachusetts, Meiriceá. Beathaisnéis.

Saolaíodh Eibhlín ar an mBlascaod Mór ag tús na haoise seo caite. Cúigear ar fad a bhí sa chlann – triúr mac agus beirt iníon. Cailleadh a máthair agus iad go hóg. Ní raibh an leathbhliain féin slánaithe ag an duine ab óige, Muiris, nuair a cuireadh don Daingean é go dtí go raibh sé in aois scoile (Ní Shúilleabháin 2000, 11). "Dialann is ábhar don leabhar, *Cín Lae Eibhlín Ní Shúilleabháin*, a bhí á choimeád aici idir Bealtaine agus Samhain na bliana 1923. Is dealraitheach gurbh é Brian Ó Ceallaigh a spreag í chun dul i mbun scríbhneoireachta. Thángthas ar an lámhscríbhinn sa Leabharlann Náisiúnta, Baile Átha Cliath. Ag feidhmiú mar bhean an tí a bhí Eibhlín i 1923. A hathair agus a deartháir, Muiris, a bhí in aontíos léi ag an am. Chuaigh sí ar imirce go Springfield, Massachusetts go luath ina dhiaidh sin, áit a raibh a deirfiúr, Máire, ag maireachtáil ann cheana." (Réamhrá le heagrán Mháiréad Ní Loinsigh.). Cur síos ar an oileán trí shúile an duine óig atá sa leabhar seo. Tá atmaisféar gealgháireach le brath tríd síos ann. Tugtar léargas maith ar shaol na mban, idir chúirtéireacht, chúraimí tí agus chaitheamh aimsire. Ba dheirfiúr í Eibhlín le Muiris Ó Súilleabháin, údar an leabhair *Fiche Blian ag Fás*. I gcaitheamh na tréimhse 1929–32 a scríobh Muiris an dírbheathaisnéis seo agus é i gConamara, agus dealraíonn sé, mar sin, gurb í Eibhlín ba thúisce a chuaigh i mbun pinn.

Thángthas ar a thuilleadh iontrálacha den chín lae a bhaineann le tús na bliana 1923, a foilsíodh i dtús báire sa nuachtán *The Echo and South Leinster Advertiser*, agus a cuireadh i gcló arís san iris *Feasta* (Bealtaine, Meitheamh, Iúil agus Lúnasa 2004).

Select bibliography
Ní Shúilleabháin, Eibhlín.
—. *Cín Lae Eibhlín Ní Shúilleabháin*. Beathaisnéis. Eag. Máiréad Ní Loinsigh. Baile Átha Cliath: Coiscéim, 2000.

Secondary sources
Breathnach, Diarmuid, agus Máire Ní Mhurchú. "Ó Súilleabháin, Eibhlín [Ní Sh. (1900–1949)." *1983–2002 Beathaisnéis*. Baile Átha Claith: An Clóchomhar, 2003.
Mac Congáil, Nollaig. "The Echo agus Cín Lae Eibhlín Ní Shúilleabháin." *Feasta: Móreagrán na Bealtaine 2004*. Vol. 57, No. 5 *et seq.*
Ó Súilleabháin, Muiris. *Fiche Blian ag Fás*. Eag. Pádraig Ó Fiannachta. 4ú eagrán Maigh Nuad: An Sagart, 1995.

Ní Shúilleabháin, Eibhlís [Uí Chriomhthain, Lís]. 1911–71. An Blascaod Mór (An tOileán Tiar) agus an Mhuiríoch, Corca Dhuibhne, Co. Chiarraí. Litreacha.

Saolaíodh Eibhlís ar an mBlascaod Mór i 1911. Foilsíodh leabhar amháin léi, a bhí bunaithe ar chuid de na litreacha a scríobh sí i mBéarla chuig George Chambers i Londain, a bhí tar éis cuairt a thabhairt ar an oileán i 1931. D'fhill Chambers ar an oileán i 1938 agus bhí sí pósta faoin am sin le Seán Ó

Criomhthain, mac Thomáis Uí Chriomhthain, a scríobh *An tOileánach*. D'fhág sí an t-oileán lena fear céile agus lena hiníon i 1942 agus chuaigh siad "ar deoraíocht" go dtí an Mhuiríoch ar an mórthír. Scríobh sí na litreacha in imeacht fiche bliain idir 1931 agus 1951 agus rangaíodh sa leabhar iad de réir ábhair. Léiríonn siad slí bheatha shimplí, an aimsir, an obair, na nósanna sóisialta agus creideamh láidir na n-oileánach. Chomh maith leis sin, cuireann sí síos ar an gcaoi ar thug sí aire d'athair a céile roimh a bhás i 1937.

Eibhlís Ní Shúilleabháin was born on the Blasket Island of the west coast of Kerry in 1911. Her sole publication is based on a selection of letters written mainly by her to George Chambers, who had visited the Blasket Island in 1931, in London. He returned to the island in 1938, by which time she was married to Seán Ó Criomhthain, son of Tomás Ó Criomhthain, author of *The Islandman*. She left the island with her husband and daughter in 1942 to go and live "in exile" in Muiríoch nearby on the mainland. The letters were written over a twenty-year period between 1931 and 1951 and are grouped by subject in the book. They highlight the simple lifestyle, the weather, the work, the social customs and strong religious faith of the islanders. She also describes how she cared for her father-in-law before his death in 1937.

Select bibliography
Ní Shúilleabháin, Eibhlís.
—. *Letters from the Great Blasket*. Litreacha, stair shóisialta. Eag. Seán Ó Coileáin. Corcaigh: Mercier, 1978.

Secondary sources
Breathnach, Diarmuid, agus Máire Ní Mhurchú. "Ó Criomhthain, Seán (1898–1975)." *1882–1982 Beathaisnéis a Cúig*. Baile Átha Cliath: An Clóchomhar, 1997.

Ní Shúilleabháin, Muirn. *fl.*1998. Na hAoraí, Béarra, Co. Chorcaí. Filíocht / béaloideas.

Ba mháthair altrama Mhurtaí Óig Uí Shúilleabháin í Muirn. Bhagair an maor cánach, John Puxley, uirthi agus chuir sé a tigh trí thine faoi dheireadh. Mharaigh Murtaí Puxley agus maraíodh Murtaí ina dhiaidh sin. Bhí teanga ghéar aici agus chuir sí mallacht – i bhfoirm véarsa – ar an gconstábla, Tadhg Ó Scólaí. Chum sí marbhna, leis, ar bhás Mhurtaí, "Osna go cruaidh le guais na scéal so ag rith." Tá seanchas fúithi, chomh maith leis an véarsa mallachtach sin léi, in eagar ag Máirín Nic Eoin in *B'ait Leo Bean* (1998, 260).

Select bibliography
Ní Shúilleabháin, Muirn.
—. "Véarsa." *B'ait Leo Bean*. Filíocht / béaloideas. Eag. Máirín Nic Eoin. Baile Átha Cliath: An Clóchomhar, 1998.

Secondary sources
Breathnach, Pádraig A. "Muircheartach Óg Ó Súilleabháin (+1734): Stair, Traidisiún, agus Marbhnaí." *Téamaí Taighde Nua-Ghaeilge*. Eag. Pádraig A. Breathnach. Maigh Nuad: An Sagart, 1997. 178–95.

Nic Eoin, Máirín. *B'ait Leo Bean*. Baile Átha Cliath: An Clóchomhar, 1998.

O'Mahony, John. "Morty Oge O'Sullivan, Captain of the Wild Geese." *Journal of the Cork Historical and Archaeological Society* 1 (1892): 24.

Ní Shúilleabháin, Nell. *fl.* 1933. Cois Mainge, Corca Dhuibhne, Co. Chiarraí. Filíocht / béaloideas.

Cumadh "Amhrán an Athar Eoghan Ó Súilleabháin" uair éigin idir 1849 agus 1856. Bhí sé ina shagart paróiste sa Daingean agus é go mór i gcoinne "lucht an tsúip", rud a chuir olc orthu siúd. "Do thairgeadar breab do mhnaoi de mhuinntir Shúilleabháin, driofúr do Mhícheál Ó Súilleabháin (Micí na gCloch), ach aor do cheapadh dho. Sé rud a dhein sí ná é mholadh go hárd" (Ó Dubhda 1933, 91). Foilsíodh an t-amhrán in *Duanaire Duibhneach* (9–13).

Select bibliography
Ní Shúilleabháin, Nell.
—. "Amhrán an Athar Eoghan Ó Súilleabháin." *Duanaire Duibhneach: bailiú d'amhránaibh agus de phíosaibh eile filidheachta a ceapadh le tuairim céad bliain i gCorca Dhuibhne, agus atá fós i gcuimhne agus i mbéaloideas na ndaoine ann.* Filíocht / béaloideas. Eag. Seán Ó Dubhda. 1933. Baile Átha Cliath: Oifig Dhíolta Foilseacháin Rialtais, 1969.

Ní Shúilleabháin, Nóra. *fl.* 1982. Uíbh Ráthach, Co. Chiarraí. Filíocht/ béaloideas.

Ba dheirfiúr í le hEoghan Rua Ó Súilleabháin agus ní raibh Eoghan Rua sásta go raibh filíocht aici in aon chor (Ó hÓgáin 1982, 159).

Secondary sources
Ó hÓgáin, Daithí. *An File: Staidéar ar Osnádúrthacht na Filíochta sa Traidisiún Gaelach.* Baile Átha Cliath: Oifig an tSoláthair, 1982.

Ní Shúilleabháin, Siobhán. Comhaimseartha. Baile an Fheirtéaraigh, Corca Dhuibhne, Co. Chiarraí. Gearrscéalaíocht, úrscéalaíocht, litríocht leanaí agus drámaíocht.

Saolaíodh Siobhán ar an Imleá i 1928. Bhí feirm ag a tuismitheoirí agus bhí seisear muirear orthu. Is é a deartháir Mícheál Ó Súilleabháin a scríobh *An Fear Aduaidh* (1978). Chuaigh Siobhán go dtí Coláiste Íde sa Daingean agus go dtí Coláiste Dhún Chéirigh ina dhiaidh sin. Cháiligh sí mar bhunmhúinteoir agus d'oibrigh sí sa Scoil Náisiúnta, i gCabrach, mBaile Átha Cliath. Bhí sí ar fhoireann an fhoclóra Béarla-Gaeilge freisin a bhí á chur in eagar ag Tomás de Bhaldraithe (Baile Átha Cliath: Oifig an tSoláthair, 1959). Tar éis pósta di, chónaigh sí i mBaile Átha Cliath, i mBéal Feirste, i gConamara agus sa Ghaillimh.

Scríobh sí an t-úrscéal *Ospidéal*, an dráma *Cití*, agus ocht leabhar do dhéagóirí. Craoladh an scéal "Méinín" go seachtainiúil ar Raidió na Gaeltachta 1972–9. Tá ocht ndráma scríofa aici do chumainn amaitéaracha agus tá na scripteanna á gcoimeád in Áras an Chomhlachais i gCamus. Léiríodh trí dhráma léi ar Raidió Teilifís Éireann agus ocht ndráma ar Raidió

Éireann. Cuireadh sliocht as *Mise Mé Féin* ar chúrsa na hArdteiste (1993). Is é an t-úrscéal is déanaí ó pheann Shiobhán ná *Aistriú* (2004); baineann an scéal le haistriú samhailteach líon tí ó Chorca Dhuibhne go Contae na Mí sna tríochadaí, faoi mar a fheictear é trí shúile cailín ocht mbliana d'aois.

Is mó duais atá buaite aici le himeacht na mblianta: an duais drámaíochta *Irish Life* 1974 dá dráma *Cití*, duaiseanna an Oireachtais don drámaíocht, d'úrscéal, do ghearrscéal agus do leabhar do dhéagóirí, duaiseanna do ghearrscéal in *Comhar* agus in *An tUltach*, agus duais Sheachtain na Scríbhneoirí i Lios Tuathail. Is scriptscríbhneoir í a hiníon, Tina Nic Enri, agus tá dhá úrscéal léi, *An Coimhthíoch Caol Dubh* (1994) agus *Tuige Mise?* (2001) foilsithe ag Coiscéim.

Select bibliography

Ní Shúilleabháin, Siobhán.

—. *Triúr Againn*. Litríocht leanaí. Baile Átha Cliath: Sáirséal agus Dill, 1955.

—. *Cúrsaí Randolf*. Litríocht leanaí. Baile Átha Cliath: Sáirséal agus Dill, 1957.

—. *Dúinne an Samhradh*. Litríocht leanaí. Baile Átha Cliath: An Comhlacht Oideachais, An Preas Talbóideach, 1957.

—. *Cití: dráma trí ghníomh*. Drámaíocht. 1975. Baile Átha Cliath: Sáirséal agus Dill, 1986.

—. *Mé Féin agus Síle*. Litríocht leanaí. Baile Átha Cliath: An Gúm, 1978.

—. *Ospidéal*. Úrscéalaíocht. Baile Átha Cliath: F.N.T., 1980.

—. *Mise Mé Féin*. Úrscéalaíocht. Indreabhán: Cló Iar-Chonnachta, 1987.

—. *Eoghan*. Úrscéalaíocht. Indreabhán: Cló Iar-Chonnachta, 1992.

—. *Máirtín*. Litríocht leanaí. Indreabhán: Cló Iar-Chonnachta, 1994.

—. *Rósanna sa Ghairdín*. Litríocht leanaí. Baile Átha Cliath: Coiscéim, 1994.

—. "Ceaite." *An Aimsir Óg*. Úrscéalaíocht. Eag. Mícheál Ó Cearúil. Baile Átha Cliath: Coiscéim, 1999. 82–6.

—. *Í Siúd*. Gearrscéalaíocht. Indreabhán: Cló Iar-Chonnachta, 1999.

—. *Cnuasach Trá*. Filíocht. Baile Átha Cliath: Coiscéim, 2000.

—. *Aistriú*. Úrscéalaíocht. Indreabhán: Cló Iar-Chonnachta, 2004.

Secondary sources

Ó Cearnaigh, Seán. "Ó Súilleabháin, Siobhán Ní Shúilleabháin." *Scríbhneoirí na Gaeilge 1945–1995*. Baile Átha Cliath: Comhar, 1995.

Ó Dúill, Eoghan. "Léirmheas ar *Máirtín*." *Anois* 10–11ú Meán Fómhair (1994).

Uí Nia, Gearóidín. "Ní Shúilleabháin, Siobhán." *Eolaire Chló Iar-Chonnachta de Scríbhneoirí Gaeilge*. Indreabhán: Cló Iar-Chonnachta, 1998.

Ní Úrdail, Méidhbhín [Ní Úrdail, Méibhín]. Comhaimseartha. Cathair Chorcaí. Scríbhneoireacht acadúil.

Céimí de chuid Choláiste na hOllscoile, Corcaigh is ea Meidhbhín Ní Úrdail. Bronnadh céim onóracha sa Ghaeilge agus sa Bhéarla uirthi sa bhliain 1987. Chríochnaigh sí an tArdteastas san Oideachas an bhliain dár gcionn agus thosnaigh sí ar chéim mháistreachta faoi stiúir an Ollaimh Seán Ó Coileáin sa bhliain 1989. Is ar thraidisiún liteartha Dhál gCais sa tréimhse iarchlasaiceach a bhunaigh sí a cuid taighde. Fuair sí scoláireacht ó rialtas na Gearmáine sa bhliain 1989 agus chaith sí bliain mar mhac léinn i Roinn an Léinn Cheiltigh, Albert-Ludwigs-Universität, Freiburg i.

Beisgau. Bronnadh céim MA uirthi sa bhliain 1991 do thráchtas dar teideal "Litríocht Dhál gCais: An Fráma Ginearálta". Fuair sí post mar chúntóir taighde in Ollscoil Freiburg sa bhliain 1991 mara raibh sí ag obair ar thionscnamh dar teideal "Übergänge und Spannungsfelder zwischen Mündlichkeit und Schriftlichkeit" (The Oral and the Written in Tension and Transmission).

Thosaigh sí ar thráchtas dochtúireachta i Freiburg sa bhliain 1993 faoi stiúir an Ollaimh Hildegard Tristram agus bronnadh céim dhochtúireachta uirthi sa bhliain 1996. Is ar an scríobhaí agus ar thraidisiún na lámhscríbhinní Gaeilge san ochtú agus sa naoú céad déag a bhunaigh sí a cuid taighde. D'fhoilsigh sí leabhar le déanaí dar teideal *The Scribe in Eighteenth Century and Nineteenth Century Ireland: Motivations and Milieu* (Münster 2000).

Sna blianta idir 1996 agus 1998, bhí post aici mar Léachtóir Coláiste sna Ranna Gaeilge, Coláiste na hOllscoile, Corcaigh. Chaith sí bliain ag léachtóireacht sa Choláiste Ollscoile, Baile Átha Cliath (1998–99). Bronnadh Comhaltacht Iar dhochtúra i Léann na Gaeilge/An Léann Ceilteach uirthi sa bhliain 1999, agus chaith sí dhá bhliain mar Chomhalta i Roinn na Nua-Ghaeilge, An Coláiste Ollscoile, Baile Átha Cliath. Chaith sí tamall leis ag obair mar scoláire i Scoil an Léinn Cheiltigh, Institiúid Ard-Léinn Bhaile Átha Cliath.

Select bibliography
Ní Úrdail, Méidhbhín.
—. "Cath Chluana Tarbh." *Aktes Des Ersten Symposiums Deutschsprachiger Keltologen (Gosen bei Berlin, 8–10, April 1992).* Scríbhneoireacht acadúil. Eag. M. Rockel agus S. Zimmer. Tubingen, 1993. 183–98.
—. "The Literary Tradition of the O'Mahonys: Irish and European Connections." Scríbhneoireacht acadúil. *Irisleabhar Uí Mhathúna* 17 (1994): 3–9.
—. "Oralisierung: der Fall der Handschrift RIA 12 Q 13." *Oralisierung.* Scríbhneoireacht acadúil. Eag. H.L.C. Tristram. Tubingen, 1996. 263–82.
—. "On the Colophons, Correspondence and Notes of the Ó Longáin Manuscripts." *Medieval Insular Literature Between the Oral and the Written II.* Scríbhneoireacht acadúil. Eag. H.L.C. Tristram. Tubingen, 1997. 221–47.
—. "Das Lyrische Werk von Seán Ó Ríordáin." *Kindlers Literatur Lexikon 22.* Scríbhneoireacht acadúil. Munchen, 1998. 238–40.
—. "'An Geal do Chur 'na Duibhe'", achoimre ar pháipéar a léadh ag an 10ú Comhdháil Idirnáisiúnta den Léann Cheilteach." *Celtic Connections.* Scríbhneoireacht acadúil. Eag. R. Black, W. Gillies agus R. Ó Maolalaigh. Linton, 1999. 534–5.
—. "An Scríobhaí agus a Chuid Aistriúcháin i Lámhscríbhinní Déanacha na hÉireann." *Ubersetzung und Akkulturation in Insularen Mittelalter.* Scríbhneoireacht acadúil. Eag. E. Poppe agus H.L.C. Tristram. Münster, Germany, 1999. 319–36.
—. *The Scribe in Eighteenth Century and Nineteenth Century Ireland: Motivations and Milieu.* Scríbhneoireacht acadúil. Münster, Germany, 2000.
—. "Máire Bhuí Ní Laoghaire: File an "rilleadh cainte"." Scríbhneoireacht acadúil. *Eighteenth-Century Ireland, Iris an Dá Chultúr* 17. (2000): 146–65.
—. "Two poems attributed to Muireadhach Albanach Ó Dálaigh." Scríbhneoireacht acadúil. *Ériú* 53 (2003): 19–52.

—. "Seachadadh *Cath Cluana Tarbh* sna lámhscríbhinní." Scríbhneoireacht acadúil. *Léachtaí Cholm Cille* 34 (2004): 179–215.

—. Iontrálacha éagsúla. *Encyclopaedia of Ireland*. Scríbhneoireacht acadúil. Ed. B. Lalor. Dublin, 2003.

Secondary Sources

Breathnach, Diarmuid, agus Máire Ní Mhurchú. "Ó Bruadair, Gobnait [Ní Bhruadair] (1863–1955)." *1882–1982 Beathaisnéis a hAon*. Baile Átha Cliath: An Clóchomhar, 1986.

Ó Céirín, Kit agus Cyril. *Women of Ireland*. Gaillimh: Tíreolas, 1996.

Ó Loinsigh, Pádraig. *Gobnait Ní Bhruadair: Beathaisnéis* [The Hon. Albinia Lucy Broderick]. Aist. Pádraig Mac Fhearghusa. Baile Átha Cliath: Coiscéim, 1997.

Nunan, Betty, née Barry. Contemporary. Cork. Short stories.

Born in Cork city in the 1930s, she is a cousin of the playwright Sebastian Barry. She pursued her studies at UCD, where she received a BA in Arabic and Islamic civilization in 1989, followed by an MA in semitic languages in 1991. She is also a Fellow of Trinity College of Music in London. She has had her writings published in newspapers and magazines and her short stories have been read on national radio. She wrote, produced and presented a programme called *Arabic Writers in Translation* on radio Riyadh in Saudia Arabia for over two years. She has also won a number of awards for her writings. Her most recent publication was a book of memoirs, *On the Edge of the Map* (2001), based on her experiences living in Iraq, Saudi Arabia, Zimbabwe, Bhutan and Albania. Her current project is a portrait of the Cork writer Frank O'Connor.

Select bibliography

Nunan, Betty.

—. "Adventures in Heatherside", "Children", "Dad's Bicycle", "The Dream" and "Rocky Bay". *Sailing Bread: An Anthology of Poetry and Prose*. Poetry. Ed. Grainne Farren. Dublin: Blackrock Writers, 2001. 40–45.

—. *On the Edge of the Map*. Memoir. Blackrock, Co. Dublin: Primrose, 2001.

O'Brien, Attie. 1840–83. Clare. Short stories, poetry, diaries.

After her mother died, when she was a young child, her father remarried and emigrated to New York with his second wife, taking the older children with them but leaving Attie and her younger brother Mahon to live with their grandmother in Tulla, Co. Clare. Mahon followed his siblings to the USA in his late teens, where he later fought in the American Civil War. Attie, alone of her family, spent her life in Co. Clare, living at her aunt's house at Kildysart, West Clare, where she moved with her grandmother when still a child. The family were reasonably well-off landowners, and Attie herself had a small personal income. However, this income dried up during the Land War period, and she contemplated applying to a fund established for "Ladies who are badly off on account of the Land War", a proposal that was vetoed by her aunt. She suffered from asthma all her life, and was considered too delicate to be sent to school, and so was self-educated: "Her own habit of thoughtful reading was a good substitute for a systematic education" (*Irish Monthly* 11 (1883), 279–80). In her journals she discusses a wide range of reading material in her ken, which includes Newman and Milton, her favourite writer. Tynan says of her: "we get beautiful glimpses of a delicate, warm-hearted personality with intellectual and imaginative gifts which, but for her constant weakness of health, would have carried her far" (vol. 4, 212).

She began her writing career by publishing poetry in a local newspaper in Ennis, going on to contribute poems and short stories to various Dublin periodicals, such as the *Irish Monthly*, the *Nation* and *Tinsley's Magazine*. Her earlier work was signed "A. O'B". Much of her work was published by the *Irish Monthly*, alongside other Catholic upper-middle-class writers like Rosa Mulholland, M.E. Francis, Katherine Roche and M.E. Connolly. Murphy tells us that these writers "wished to demonstrate that the Irish could be as respectable as the English and often chose the genre of the romantic comedy to make their point" and thus their work "conform[ed] closely to the social conventions of English Victorian society" (60). As her correspondence with editors and publishers attests, she struggled continuously to have her writings published, with limited success. At one point, T.D. Sullivan, editor of *Young Ireland*, turned down one of her stories because the hero was a British officer. Despite her best efforts, she could not get published in English magazines at all. In a letter to her from Lady Georgina Fullerton she was advised that "Catholic literature does not take with Protestant editors".

Her neighbour Mary Ann O'Connell (*q.v.*) published *Glimpses of a Hidden Life* about her after her death, which discusses some of her difficulties with the world of publishing. Discussing O'Brien's encounters with Rev. Matthew Russell, the editor of the *Irish Monthly*, O'Connell gives us some insight into the kinds of debates surrounding the direction taken by Catholic literature in this period. According to her, Attie O'Brien attempted to address the wider problems of life in her fiction, which Russell found incompatible with Catholic literature: "[He] was thinking of his own safe and sure little public, of schools and quiet families and clergy, and how the Reverend Mothers would not have their dovecotes fluttered by precocious notions of billing and cooing."

She died at the age of forty-three, and following her death the *Irish Monthly* published some of her serial stories, including "The Cardassan Family"(1888). She is buried in the churchyard at Kildysart.

Select bibliography
O'Brien, Attie.
—. "Come Up Hither." Poetry. *Irish Monthly* 6 Sept. (1878): 504–5.
—. "Gethsemane." Poetry. *Irish Monthly* 6 May (1878): 251–3.
—. "Going to Play." Poetry. *Irish Monthly* 6 Oct. (1878): 543–4.
—. "Lost in the Moonlight." Poetry. *Irish Monthly* 6 Dec. (1878): 668–81.
—. "One Summer by the Sea." Poetry. *Irish Monthly* 6 Aug.–Sept. (1878): 451–7; 473–86.
—. "A Passion Flower." Poetry. *Irish Monthly* 6 Nov. (1878): 602.
—. "The Stilling of the Tempest." Poetry. *Irish Monthly* 6 Mar. (1878): 168–9.
—. "Thine Eyes are Doves." Poetry. *Irish Monthly* 6 Feb. (1878): 79.

—. "Mary! Rabboni." Poetry. *Irish Monthly* 7 July (1879): 379–80.
—. "On the Doorstep." Poetry. *Irish Monthly* 7 Sept. (1879): 462–3.
—. "A Pillar Saint." Poetry. *Irish Monthly* 7 Dec. (1879): 635–8.
—. "Stone the Woman; Let the Man Go Free." Poetry. *Irish Monthly* 7 June (1879): 291–5.
—. "A Hot Day." Poetry. *Irish Monthly* 8 July (1880): 376–7.
—. "A Rosary of Sonnets." Poetry. *Irish Monthly* 8 Feb.–Apr. (1880): 88–9; 147–8; 219–20.
—. "The Old Man's Angelus." Poetry. *Irish Monthly* 9 Feb. (1881): 99–100.
—. "St Cecilia." Poetry. *Irish Monthly* 9 July (1881): 351.
—. "A Vision of Earth." Poetry. *Irish Monthly* 9 Sept. (1881): 463–9.
—. "The Monk's Prophecy." Fiction series. *Irish Monthly* 10–11 Jan. 1882–Mar. 1883.
—. "An Old Man's Reverie." Poetry. *Irish Monthly* 14 June (1886): 314–15.
—. "The Caradassan Family." Fiction series. *Irish Monthly* 16 Jan.–Dec. (1888).
—. "Won by Worth." Fiction series. *Irish Monthly* 19 April 1891–July 1892.
—. *The Cardassan Family*. Novel. New York: Sadleir, 1897.
—. "Through the Dark Night." Fiction series. *Irish Monthly* 25–26 Jan. 1897–Dec.1898.
—. "A Belgian School Exhibition." *New Ireland Review* 18–19 Nov. 1902–Jan. 1903.
—. "Mrs Glynn on Marriage." *Cabinet of Irish Literature*. Ed. Katherine Tynan. Vol. 4. London: Gresham, 1903. 212.
—. "From Dark to Dawn." Short story. *Weekly Freeman* 4.
—. *The Monk's Prophecy*. Novel. N.p.: n.p., n.d.

Secondary sources

Anon. "Rev. of *Glimpses of a Hidden Life*, by Mary Anne O'Connell." *Irish Monthly* 15 (1887): 112.
Anon. "Attie O'Brien: A Hidden Life." *Molua* (1943): 15–23.
O'Connell, Mary Anne. *Glimpses of a Hidden Life: Memories of Attie O'Brien*. Dublin: Gill, 1887.
Fairbairn, Margaret. "Some Literary Remains of Attie O'Brien of Kildysart." *Molua* (1944): 9–22.
Murphy, James H. "'Things Which Seem to You Unfeminine': Gender and Nationalism in the Fiction of Some Upper Middle Class Catholic Women Novelists, 1889–1910." *Border Crossings: Irish Women Writers and National Identities*. Ed. Kathryn Kirkpatrick. Vol. 15. Dublin: Wolfhound, 2000. 58–78.
Russell, Matthew. "Attie O'Brien: In Memoriam." *Irish Monthly* 11 (1883): 279–81.
Russell, Matthew. "Attie O'Brien." *Irish Monthly* 15 (1887): 406–15.
Dawson, Charles. "Attie O'Brien." *Irish Monthly* 40 (1912): 633–40.

O'Brien, Breda. Contemporary. Dungarvan, Co. Waterford. Journalism.

Born 1963 in Waterford, she was educated at the Convent of Mercy there, and at Mater Dei Institute of Education, Dublin. She has worked as a video producer and a researcher for RTÉ, and now teaches at Muckross Park College, Dublin. She was a columnist for the *Sunday Business Post* (1997–2000), and since then has written for the *Irish Times* (*Field Day V*, 319). A frequent contributor to media discussions on religion and current affairs, she is an advocate of family values.

Select bibliography
O'Brien, Breda.
—. "Empty Rhetoric: A Feminist Enquiry into Abortion Advocacy and the "Choice" Ethic." *Swimming Against the Tide: Feminist Discussions on the Issue of Abortion.* Political writing. Ed Angela Kennedy. 1997. Dublin: Open Air. 28–37.
—. "Outpourings of a Spiritual Pygmy." *The Splintered Heart: Conversations with a Church in Crisis.* Religious writing. Ed. Eamonn Conway and Colm Kilcoyne. 1998. Dublin: Veritas. 107–17.

O'Brien, Bridie, née Carroll. Contemporary. Nenagh, Co. Tipperary. Local history.

Born in Kilbarron, North Tipperary, she was educated locally and attended UCD. She spent her working life in England teaching English and French until she retired in 1976, when she returned to her native townland. While living in England she started to write articles, based on her remembrances of old traditions and stories, for a magazine in North Tipperary, *Cois Deirge*. She is a founder member of local writers' and historical groups and contributes to their publications. She has a keen interest in local history and her book, *How We Were* (1998), is a detailed account of the lives of local personalities.

Select bibliography
O'Brien, Bridie.
—. *How We Were – In the Parish of Kilbarron-Terryglass, Co. Tipperary.* Local history. Nenagh, Co. Tipperary: Relay, 1998.

O'Brien, Charlotte Grace. 1845–1909. Limerick, Cork. Novels, poetry, political writing.

Known as Grace, she was the daughter of Lucy O'Brien (née Gabbett) (*q.v.*) of High Park, Co. Limerick, and the politician and patriot William Smith O'Brien. Her family combined the wealth of their Protestant Ascendancy background with a genealogy stretching back to the Gaelic aristocracy. Tynan refers to her as "the heiress of [her father's] philanthropy and his patriotism" (vol. 4, 274). On Smith O'Brien's return from penal servitude in Tasmania in 1854 the family moved to live with him in Brussels until 1856, when they were allowed to return to Cahirmoyle. Like many girls of the day, Grace received no formal education, unlike her brothers. Still in her teens when her mother died in 1861, she moved with her father to Killiney, and stayed with him until his death in Bangor in 1864. She then spent sixteen years living at Cahirmoyle, first as a housekeeper to her brothers and later to her brother Edward and his wife, Mary, helping to raise their three children following Mary's death in 1868. She built her own home in Foynes, Co. Limerick, in 1870, moving in when Edward remarried in 1880. It was then that her career as a writer began. In 1878 she published her first novel, *Light and Shade*, based on the Fenian rising of 1867, which was critically well received and highly popular. The *Guardian* review commented: "If 'Castle Daly' should stand as *the* historical novel of the famine, 'Light and

Shade' deserves a place beside it, as an illustration of the Fenian times." She followed this with the play *A Tale of Venice* in 1880, meanwhile contributing political articles to periodicals such as *Nineteenth Century* and *The Pall Mall Gazette*.

When emigration rose again in the 1880s O'Brien's attention turned to women emigrants, as her article in *Pall Mall* of 6 May 1881 attests. Her later poetry collection, *Lyrics* (1886), also refers to the experiences of emigrant women, many of whom were forced to beg or turn to sex-work in port towns in order to pay for short-term lodgings in advance of their departure, in an era when ships were frequently delayed by sea conditions. She established a refuge in Cork to provide accommodation for such women. These lodgings could cater for over a hundred women at a time, and approximately 3,000 people stayed there annually. She also set up a meeting service so that women arriving in American ports would have somewhere to go and, through her work, the conditions on emigrant ships were vastly improved. Commenting on her ability to combine philanthropy with literary endeavour, Tynan comments: "Her great work on behalf of the female emigrants to America will not soon be forgotten. Any woman, indeed, might be content to rest on such laurels. She has, however, found time for something of a literary life as well" (4, 274).

She continued to write articles for *The Nation, United Ireland* and the *Limerick Field Club Journal*, as well as contributing poems to *Irish Monthly*. Retiring from her work as a social reformer in 1886, she settled in Foynes once more, and began to study and write about the plant life of the Shannon area, contributing several articles to the *Irish Naturalist* on this subject. In a letter to Standish O'Grady, she writes: "Anything you do print of mine, put my name to it. I have always my father's word in mind – 'I will never beget that which I dare not father'" (*Selections*, 218). She converted to Catholicism before her death in 1909. Her nephew Stephen Gwynn wrote a memoir of her, and edited her posthumous collections.

Select bibliography
O'Brien, Charlotte Grace.
—. *Dominick's Trials: An Irish Story*. Novel. N.p.: Gall & Inglis, 1870.
—. *Light and Shade*. Novel. London: Kegan Paul, 1878.
—. *A Tale of Venice: Drama and Lyrics*. Play, poetry. Dublin: Gill, 1880.
—. "The Shannon." Poetry. *Dublin University Review* 1.10 (1885).
—. "An Essay on Birds." Essay. *Dublin University Review* 2.5 (1886).
—. *Lyrics*. Poetry. London: Kegan Paul, Trench, 1886.
—. "A Spring Morning on the Golden Height." *Dublin University Review* 2.8 (1886).
—. "Two Sonnets." Poetry. *Irish Monthly* 15 Nov. (1887): 664.
—. *Cahirmoyle; or, The Old Home*. Poetry. Limerick: Guy, 1888.
—. "Charles Murrough O'Brien." Poetry. *Irish Monthly* 16 Jan. (1888): 9–10.
—. "Girlhood." Poetry. *Irish Monthly* 16 Aug. (1888): 487.
—. "A Girl's Picture." Poetry. *Irish Monthly* 19 Sept. (1891): 493.
—. "Response to D.P. Moran 'Is the Irish Nation Dying?'." Letter. *New Ireland Review* Feb. (1899): 343–4.

—. "Bog Cotton on the Red Bog." *Cabinet of Irish Literature*. Short story. Ed Katherine Tynan. Vol. 4. London: Gresham, 1903.

—. *Charlotte Grace O'Brien: Selections from Her Writings and Correspondence, with Memoir by Stephen Gwynn*. Essays, letters. Ed. Stephen Gwynn. Dublin: Maunsel, 1909.

Secondary sources

Anon. "Rev. of *Selections from the Writings of Charlotte Smith O'Brien*, by Stephen Gwynn." *Irish Book Lover* 1 (1910): 89–90.

Coleman, James. "From South and West (On the Death of Miss Charlotte Grace O'Brien)." *Irish Book Lover* 1 Sept. (1909): 21–2.

Gwynn, Stephen. *Charlotte Grace O'Brien: Selections from Her Writings and Correspondence, with Memoir by Stephen Gwynn*. Dublin: Maunsel, 1909.

Keogh, M.C. "Charlotte Grace O'Brien." *Irish Monthly* 38 (1910): 241–5.

O'Connell, Anne. "Charlotte Grace O'Brien." *Women, Power and Consciousness in Nineteenth Century Ireland*. Ed. Mary Cullen and Maria Luddy. Dublin: Attic Press, 1995. 231–62.

O'Kennedy, Richard. "With the Emigrant." *Irish Monthly* 38 (1910): 661–72.

Russell, Matthew. "Our Poets, No. 20: Charlotte Grace O'Brien." *Irish Monthly* 16 (1888): 728–33.

O'Brien, Edna. Contemporary. Co. Clare. Novels, short stories, plays, essays, literary criticism.

Born in 1931 in Tuamgraney, Co. Clare, on the family farm, she was educated at Scarriff national school and at Mercy Convent secondary school in Loughrea, and as a pharmacist in Dublin. O'Brien's early interest was in writing poetry, then fiction, inspired by reading Joyce. In 1951 she married Ernest Gébler, a writer, with whom she had two sons; they divorced in 1964. She migrated to London in 1959, where she settled. She is the author of many novels, several collections of short stories and one play, and also of the illustrated essay *Mother Ireland* (1976), the anthology *Some Irish Loving*, and a short study of James Joyce (2000).

As a young writer O'Brien was already the subject simultaneously of excoriation in Ireland and adulation in Britain. From the appearance of her first novel, *The Country Girls* (1960), intermittently up to the present, her work has elicited shocked and angry reactions from conservative elements in Irish society, including actual censorship, indignant public responses and, during the 1960s, barracking at public meetings and readings. Such reactions were occasioned by the perceived transgressive sexual content of her writing and by its evident resistance to the then-dominant ideology.

O'Brien's work is important both aesthetically and ideologically. Her three autobiographical novels, now seen as a trilogy, published between 1960 and 1964, inaugurated the fictional representation of modern Ireland. Earthy and sexually explicit, they construct a radical critique of Irish Catholic ideology. In a literature dominated by masculine reputations, their fresh and vividly persuasive construction of specifically feminine viewpoints is even more innovative and effective. A particular strength of the trilogy is the pairing of the depressive heroine, Kate, with her pragmatic, devil-may-care friend Baba.

Using this doubling, O'Brien elaborates a sharply questioning account of Irish social formation, which is nevertheless richly humorous. Her writing on the body and sexuality is also noteworthy, and in its searching melancholy and frequent despair of gender inter-relations has given rise to well-justified comparisons with other women writers of sexual misery, such as Jean Rhys.

In subsequent novels, and in many highly effective short stories, O'Brien continued to develop her critique of Irish society. Her focus on the repressions, cruelties and silences of Irish rural life, in particular, is bleak and often merciless, but she is also a migrant writer, and several of her works which use London settings are valuable contributions to the literature of the diaspora. In some of her middle and later work O'Brien experiments with stream-of-consciousness techniques: the 1972 novel *Night* is a notably successful example. In the novel form, O'Brien's style is sometimes uneven and can tend to a kind of loose meditation, but her short stories are firmly controlled and beautifully executed.

In her fiction of the 1990s O'Brien has interested herself in themes from actual social scandal, history and politics, including militant Republicanism (*House of Splendid Isolation*, 1994) and child sexual abuse (*Down by the River*). Her 2002 novel *In the Forest* examined the terrible consequences, in a triple murder, of social neglect and brutality towards an orphaned child, drawing upon recent actual occurrences in O'Brien's home county of Clare. Opinions are currently divided on the aesthetic effectiveness of these very direct graftings of fiction onto actual historical material. Some prominent critics have attacked it, others have admired the painful and vivid compassion shown in the writing. For all the unevenness and occasional instances of a failure of literary or intellectual judgement in her work, O'Brien remains a figure of the greatest importance to Irish literature in the later twentieth century, and for contemporary women's writing she is a particularly significant forerunner.

Select bibliography
O'Brien, Edna.
—. *The Country Girls*. Novel. London: Hutchinson, 1960.
—. *The Lonely Girl*. Novel. London: Jonathan Cape, 1962. Note: Also published as *The Girl with Green Eyes*. London: Harmondsworth, Penguin, 1964.
—. *Girls in their Married Bliss*. Novel. London: Jonathan Cape, 1964.
—. *August is a Wicked Month*. Novel. London: Jonathan Cape, 1965.
—. *Casualties of Peace*. Novel. London: Jonathan Cape, 1966.
—. *The Love Object*. Short stories. London: Jonathan Cape, 1968.
—. *A Pagan Place*. Novel. Harmondsworth: Penguin, 1970.
—. *Zee & Co*. Novel. London: Weidenfeld and Nicholson, 1971.
—. *Night*. Novel. London: Weidenfeld and Nicholson, 1972.
—. *A Scandalous Woman and Other Stories*. Short Stories. 1972.
—. *Johnny I Hardly Knew You*. Novel. London: Weidenfeld and Nicholson, 1977.
—. *Mother Ireland*. Essay. London: Weidenfeld and Nicholson, 1976.
—. *A Rose in the Heart: Love Stories*. Short stories. London: Weidenfeld and Nicholson, 1978. Note: Also published as *Mrs. Reinhardt and Other Stories*.
—. ed. *Some Irish Loving: A Selection*. London: Weidenfeld and Nicholson, 1979.

—. *The Dazzle*. Children's fiction. London: Hodder and Stoughton, 1981.

—. *James and Nora: A Portrait of Joyce's Marriage*. Biography. 1981.

—. *A Christmas Treat*. Children's fiction. London: Hodder and Stoughton, 1982.

—. *Returning*. Short stories. London: Weidenfeld and Nicholson, 1982.

. *The Rescue*. Novel. London: Hodder and Stoughton, 1983.

—. *A Fanatic Heart: Selected Stories*. Short stories. London: Weidenfeld and Nicholson, 1985.

—. *Virginia: A Play*. Play. San Diego: Harcourt Brace Jovanovich, 1985.

—. *The Country Girls Trilogy and Epilogue*. Novel. London: Penguin, 1986.

—. ed. *Tales for the Telling: Irish Folk and Fairy Stories*. London: Pavilion, 1986.

—. *On the Bone*. Poetry. London: Greville, 1989.

—. *Far from the Land*. Novel. 1989.

—. *Lantern Slides*. Short stories. London: Weidenfeld and Nicholson, 1990.

—. *Time and Tide*. Novel. London: Viking, 1992.

—. *The House of Splendid Isolation*. Novel. London: Weidenfeld and Nicholson, 1994.

—. contributor. *What Future for Rural Ireland?* RTÉ Radio 1. 23 Dec. 1994.

—. *Down by the River*. Novel. London: Weidenfeld and Nicholson, 1996.

—. contributor. *Off the Shelf*. RTÉ Radio 1. 24 Aug. 1996.

—. *Wild Decembers*. Novel. London : Weidenfeld and Nicholson, 1999.

—. contributor. *Giant at My Shoulder*. RTÉ Radio 1. 26 Feb. 1999.

—. contributor. *Mrs. Reinhardt*. RTÉ Radio 1. 5 July 1999.

—. contributor. *Radio Review*. RTÉ Radio 1. 6 July 1999.

—. *James Joyce*. Biography. London: Phoenix, 2000.

—. *In the Forest*. Novel. London: Weidenfeld and Nicholson, 2002.

Secondary sources

Baird, Jean Lorraine. "Edna O'Brien: Annotated Check-List Bibliography and Biography." N.p.: McMaster University, 1993.

Cahalan, James. "Female and Male Perspectives on Growing Up Irish in Edna O'Brien, John McGahern, and Brian Moore". *Double Visions: Women and Men in Contemporary and Modern Irish Fiction*. Syracuse: U Syracuse P, 1999.

Eckle, Grace. Rev. of *Night*. *Éire-Ireland* 1.2 (1973): 151–3.

Friedlander, Adrienne L. *Edna O'Brien: An Annotated Secondary Bibliography (1980-1995)*. Florida: Fort Lauderdale, 1997.

Graham, Amanda. "'The Lovely Substance of Mother': Food, Gender and Nation in the Work of Edna O'Brien." *Irish Studies Review* 15 (1996): 16–20.

Greenwood, Amanda. *Representations of Femininity in the Novels of Edna O'Brien 1960-1996*. Hull: U of Hull P, 1999.

Hosey, Seamus, prod. Content regarding Edna O'Brien. *Off the Shelf: Frankfurt Bookfair*. Radio Programme. RTÉ Radio 1. 10 Oct. 1996.

Kenny, Pat, presenter. Content regarding Edna O'Brien. *Pat Kenny Show*. Radio Programme. RTÉ Radio 1. 8 June 1988.

Murphy, Mike, presenter. Content regarding Edna O'Brien. *The Arts Show*. Radio Programme. RTÉ Radio 1. 22 Aug. 1990.

Murphy, Mike, presenter. Content regarding Edna O'Brien. *Reading the Future*. Radio Programme. RTÉ Radio 1. 3 Feb. 2001.

Ní Bhrian, Doireann, presenter. Content regarding Edna O'Brien. *The Arts Show Hot Press Awards*. Radio Programme. RTÉ Radio 1. 3 Feb. 1993.

Ní Bhrian, Doireann, presenter. Content regarding Edna O'Brien. *The Arts Show: International Writers Week*. Radio Programme. RTÉ Radio 1. 28 Sept. 1993.

Pelan, Rebecca. "Edna O'Brien's 'Stage-Irish' Persona: An 'Act' of Resistance." *Canadian Journal of Irish Studies* 19.1 (1993): 67–78.

Quinn, John, presenter. Documentary on Edna O'Brien. *Portrait of the Artist as a Young Girl*. Radio Programme. RTÉ Radio 1. 2 Sept. 1985.

O'Brien, Grania R. Contemporary. Dromoland Castle, Whitegate, Co. Clare. History.

Raised in Dromoland Castle, the home of her forebears, in Co. Clare, she was educated in Canada and has since travelled extensively in Europe, the Far East and South America. She also worked in diplomatic missions in Spain, Japan, England and Peru. She is now co-director of Ballinakella Press with her husband, Hugh W.L. Weir, who is a well known historian and writer. Grania's own researches in Ireland and England enabled her to write the history of the O'Brien family, which was published in 1991.

Select bibliography
O'Brien, Grania R.
—. *These My Friends and Forebears: The O'Briens of Dromoland*. History. Whitegate, Co. Clare: Ballinakella, 1991.

O'Brien, Kate. 1897–1974. Limerick. Novels, plays, travel writing and journalism.

Born in Limerick, educated at the convent school Laurel Hill from the age of five, following the death of her mother, and later at UCD as a scholarship student. *The Land of Spices* (1941) is a fictionalized account of her school-days. She migrated to England, where she became a freelance journalist and later foreign-language translator for the *Manchester Guardian*. In 1921 she travelled to the USA with her brother-in-law Stephen O'Mara, who was the coordinator of de Valera's Bonds Drive. In 1922–3 she worked as a governess in the north of Spain, which formed the beginning of her enduring love for Spanish culture, reflected in novels such as *Mary Lavelle* (1936) and *That Lady* (1946), and the travel book *Farewell Spain* (1937).

Back in London in 1923 she married (briefly) the Dutch journalist Gustaaf Reiner, but her subsequent relationships were with women. When her marriage ended she returned to journalism, first editing a newspaper for the Sunlight League, but her creative writing career began with the sucess of her first play, *Distinguished Villa*, in 1926. She soon established herself as a prominent and prolific literary critic in both Britain and Ireland, and in 1938 was one of the first to comment favourably on Beckett's work.

Her own literary reputation was established by her first novel, *Without my Cloak* (1931), which won several prizes and became a bestseller. Other novels include its sequel *The Ante Room* (1934), *Pray for the Wanderer* (1938), *The Last of Summer* (1943), *The Flower of May* (1953) and *As Music and Spendour* (1958). Her works have been translated into French, German, Czech and Swedish. Her writing style owes much to Balzac and the Realists, and her admiration for George Eliot's work is evident in her own writing. However, it is the political and social aspects of her writing which have drawn modern critics to her work. In novels such as *Mary Lavelle* and *The Land of Spices*, O'Brien depicts the lives of Irish women in the early years of the Free State. She juxtaposes the bonds of family loyalty and religion with the struggles of individual women for autonomy in a patriarchal society. One of the distinguishing features of *The Land of Spices* is that one of the central figures, Anna Murphy, is enabled to see an artistic future for herself at the end of the novel, in a similar way to Stephen Dedalus in Joyce's *Portrait of the Artist as a Young Man*.

The two aforementioned novels were banned for alleged obscenity by the Irish Censorship Board, which illustrates the impact of her material on the body politic at the time, and the perceived threat of her radical themes of empowerment for Irish women. The censorship of these novels had a lasting effect on her work, and on her politics – in that she became a fierce critic of efforts to stifle radical ideas in life and literature. Because of her outspoken criticism of the regime of Franco in *Farewell Spain*, she was barred from Spain until 1957. Later novels, although not officially on the banned list, were often difficult to get in Ireland, and she retained the stigma of the banned author throughout much of her later career. Her last two novels, *The Flower of May*, a fairy tale of romantic friendship, and *As Music and Splendour*, a lesbian realist text, are currently out of print. Despite this, recent critical attention has focused on her lesbianism in terms of its impact on her writing (Donoghue 1995; Fogarty 1997).

The Last of Summer was produced as a play in 1944, directed by John Gielgud, and *That Lady*, a historical novel, was filmed in 1955. O'Brien bought a house in Roundstone, Co. Galway, with the royalties from these productions, where she lived between 1950 and 1960. But in 1960, bankrupt, she was forced to sell the house and she returned to Britain, where she had spent much of her adult life. In 1962, she published the travelogue *My Ireland*, and her final work in 1963 was the memoir *Presentation Parlour*. Critically neglected, she spent her last fourteen years in England, and she died in Canterbury in 1974. She was working on a novel, *Constancy*, at the time of her death in 1947, but it remains unfinished. Her gravestone bears the inscription "pray for the wanderer".

Select bibliography

O'Brien, Kate.

—. presenter. *Thought for the Day*. Radio programme. Radio Programme. RTÉ Radio 1. 22 Nov. 1922.

—. *Distinguished Villa*. Play. London: Ernest Benn, 1926.

—. *The Bridge*. (Unpub.) Play. 1927.

—. *Without My Cloak*. Novel. London: Heinemann, 1931. London: Virago, 1986.

—. *The Ante Room*. Novel. London: Heinemann, 1934. Dublin: Arlen House, 1980.

—. "Overheard." *Time and Tide* 2 (Mar. 1935).

—. *Mary Lavelle*. Novel. London: Heinemann, 1936. London: Virago, 1984.

—. *Farewell Spain*. Travel writing. London: Heinemann, 1937. London: Virago, 1985.

—. *Pray for the Wanderer*. Novel. London: Heinemann, 1938.

—. *The Land of Spices*. Novel. London: Heinemann, 1941. London: Virago, 1988.

—. *English Diaries and Journals*. Literary criticism. London: Collins, 1943.

—. *The Last of Summer* [US edition: *For One Sweet Grape*]. Novel. London: Heinemann, 1943. Dublin: Arlen House, 1982.

—. *That Lady*. Historical novel. London: Heinemann, 1946. London: Virago, 1988.

—. *Teresa of Avila*. Biography, religious writing. London: Parrish, 1951.

—. "A Fit of Laughing." *The Bell* 18.4 (1952): 220–71.

—. *The Flower of May*. Novel. London: Heinemann, 1953.

—. "A Bus from Tivoli." Travel writing. *Threshold* 1.2 (1957).

—. *As Music and Splendour*. Novel. London: Heinemann, 1958.

—. *My Ireland*. Travel writing. London: Batsford, 1962.

—. *Presentation Parlour*. Memoir. London: Heinemann, 1963.

—. contributor. *My Kind of Poetry*. Radio programme. Radio Programme. RTÉ Radio 1. 6 Jan. 1972.

—. "Work in Progress." *Winter's Tales from Ireland*. Short story. Ed. Casey. Dublin: Gill & Macmillan, 1972.

—. presenter. *Older and Wiser*. Radio Programme. RTÉ Radio 1. 29 Sept. 1973.

—. contributor. *Rich and Strange*. Radio Programme. RTÉ Radio 1. 3 June 1973.

—. "Memories of a Catholic Childhood." Memoir. *The Tablet* 4 (Dec. 1976).

—. *The Last of Summer*. Radio play. Prod. Frank Lawlor. Radio Programme. RTÉ Radio 1. 22 May 1979.

—. *The Ante Room*. Radio play. Prod. Kate Minogue. Radio Programme. RTÉ Radio 1. 1 Apr. 1997.

—. "A View from Toledo." Travel writing. *Argosy*, n.d.

Secondary sources

Boland, Eavan, speaker. Thomas Davis Lecture on Kate O'Brien. *Kate O'Brien: The Living Writer*. Lecture. Radio Programme. RTÉ Radio 1. 10 Nov. 1997.

Clune, Ann, speaker. Thomas Davis Lecture on Kate O'Brien. *The Novels of Kate O'Brien*. Lecture. RTÉ Radio 1. 13 Oct. 1997.

Cronin, John. "Kate O'Brien, *The Ante-Room*." *The Anglo-Irish Novel*. Vol. 2. Belfast: Appletree, 1990. 138–47.

Cullen Owens, Rosemary, interviewer. Interview with Lorna Reynolds about Kate O'Brien. *Moments in Time*. Radio programme. RTÉ. Oct. 29 1990.

Dalsimer, Adele. "A Not So Simple Saga: Kate O'Brien's *Without My Cloak*." *Éire-Ireland* 3.21 (1986): 55–72.

—. *Kate O'Brien: A Critical Study*. Dublin: Gill & Macmillan, 1990.

De Butler Foley, Maria Isabel, speaker. Thomas Davis Lecture on Kate O'Brien. *Kate O'Brien and Spain*. Lecture. RTÉ Radio 1. 27 Oct. 1997.

Donoghue, Emma. "Out of Order: Kate O'Brien's Lesbian Fictions." *Ordinary People Dancing*. Ed. Walshe, Éibhear. Cork: Cork UP, 1997.

Fogarty, Anne. "The Ear of the Other: Dissident Voices in Kate O'Brien's *As Music and Splendour* and Marcy Dorcey's *A Noise from the Woodshed*." *Ordinary People Dancing*. Ed. Éibhear Walshe. Cork: Cork UP, 1997. 170–201.

Hosey, Séamus, prod. *The Land of Spices* by Kate O'Brien. *Book on One*. Radio Programme. RTÉ Radio 1. 1–5 May 1999.

Jordan, John. "Kate O'Brien: A Note on Her Themes, Being a Consideration of *The Flower of May*." *The Bell* 19.7 (1954): 53–9.

—. contributor. *Provincial News Round-Up: Féile Luimní*. Radio Programme. RTÉ Radio 1. 9 May 1958.

—. "Kate O'Brien: A Passionate Talent." *Hibernia* 19 Aug 1974.

—. ed. *Kate O'Brien*. Spec. issue of *The Stony Thursday Book* 7 (1981).

Kiely, Benedict, prod. Kate O'Brien. *Appraisal Novels of Kate O'Brien*. Radio Programme. RTÉ. 12 Nov. 1974.

—. "Love, Pain and Parting: The Novels of Kate O'Brien." *The Hollins Critic* 29.2 (1992): 1–11.

Lehane, Tim, prod. *Moments from a Life*. Radio Programme. RTÉ Radio 1. 20 June 1991.

Lynch, John, prod. Interview with Kate O'Brien. *My Kind of Poetry*. Radio Programme. RTÉ Radio 1. 6 Jan. 1972.

McCarthy, Nodlaig. Interview with Kate O'Brien. *Hometown Limerick*. Radio Programme. RTÉ Radio 1. 5 May 1969.

Murphy, Russell, interviewer. Interview with Kate O'Brien. *Personal Choice*. Radio programme. RTÉ Radio 1. 5 May 1966.

O'Brien, John, speaker. Thomas Davis Lecture on Kate O'Brien. *My Aunt Kate O'Brien*. Lecture. RTÉ Radio 1. 22 Sept. 1997.

O'Connor, Kevin, prod. *That Lady*. Radio Programme. RTÉ Radio 1. 23 Jan. 1997.

Reynolds, Lorna, presenter. Content regarding Kate O'Brien. *Women Today*. Radio programme. RTÉ Radio 1. 1 Nov. 1984.

Reynolds, Lorna. "The Image of Spain in the Novels of Kate O'Brien." *Literary Interrelations: Ireland, England and the World*. Ed. Wolfgang Zach and Heinz Kosok. Vol. 3. National Images and Stereotypes ser. Tübingen: Guntar Narr Verlag, 1987. 181–7.

Reynolds, Lorna. *Kate O'Brien: A Literary Portrait*. Gerrards Cross, Bucks.: Colin Smythe, 1987.

Reynolds, Lorna, speaker. Thomas Davis Lecture on Kate O'Brien. *The Woman and the Writer*. Lecture. Radio Programme. RTÉ Radio 1. 29 Sept. 1997.

Rose Quiello. "Disturbed Desires: The Hysteric in Kate O'Brien's *Mary Lavelle*." *Éire-Ireland* 25.3 (1990): 46–57.

Smyth, Ailbhe, speaker. Thomas Davis Lecture on Kate O'Brien. *Kate O'Brien: Legend in her Own Time*. Lecture. RTÉ Radio 1. 3 Nov. 1997.

Walshe, Éibhear, ed. *Ordinary People Dancing: Essays on Kate O'Brien*. Cork: Cork UP, 1993.

—. speaker. Thomas Davis Lecture on Kate O'Brien. *Turning the Tables*. Lecture. RTÉ Radio 1. 1997.

O'Brien, Lucy, née Gabbett. 1811–61. Co. Limerick. Letters.

Born at High Park, Co. Limerick, she was the daughter of Joseph Gabbett, Conservative mayor of Limerick 1819–20. She married William Smith O'Brien in 1832, and the couple had six children. When Smith O'Brien was sentenced to penal servitude and deported to Tasmania following the 1848 rebellion, Lucy stayed behind in Limerick with their children. Her letters to her husband, which date mostly from this time, are in the National Library. In 1854, on Smith O'Brien's return to Europe, she moved to Brussels with their children and moved back to Cahirmoyle when he was finally permitted to live in Ireland again in 1856. She died in 1861. Her daughter Charlotte Grace O'Brien (*q.v.*) became a well known writer and social activist.

O'Brien, Margaret, née Cahill [Nan Cahill, Marguerite O'Brien]. 1908–90. Cork. Biography, autobiography, poetry.

Born in Cork city in 1908, she was educated in Cork and Vienna, where she was a teacher from 1927 to 1932. She returned to Cork, but much of her later life was spent in Co. Wicklow, where her husband worked. She built a studio there, and was known as a landscape artist, exhibiting in Europe and the United States. She published a collection of poetry, *Winds of Mount Helicon*, in 1938, as well as a biography of Sr Maria Fortunata Viti (1943) and an autobiography, *As the Crow Flies* (1967). She published under the names Nan Cahill and Marguerite O'Brien. She died in 1990.

Select bibliography
O'Brien, Margaret.
—. *Winds of Mount Helicon*. Poetry. London: Stockwell, 1938.
—. *A Modern Wonder Worker*. Biography. Monaghan: n.p., 1943.
—. *As the Crow Flies*. Autobiography. London: n.p., 1967.

O'Brien, Sr Pius. Contemporary. History.

Has written three texts recounting the achievements of the congregation of Sisters of Mercy in towns in Co. Clare and Co. Tipperary.

Select bibliography
O'Brien, Sr Pius.
—. *The Sisters of Mercy of Birr and Nenagh*. History. Ennis: Congregation of the Sisters of Mercy, 1994.
—. *The Sisters of Mercy of Kilrush and Kilkee*. History. Ennis: Congregation of the Sisters of Mercy, 1997.
—. *The Sisters of Mercy of Ennis*. History. Ennis: Congregation of the Sisters of Mercy, n.d.

O'Carroll, Harriet. Contemporary. Askeaton, Co. Limerick. Plays, short stories, poetry.

Born in Co. Kilkenny in 1941, she trained as a physiotherapist in Dublin in 1963. She has lived in various parts of Ireland, in England and in Denmark, and is now resident in Askeaton, Co. Limerick. She started writing in 1979 and had a winning short story published in an anthology, *The Wall Reader* (1979). Many of her short stories have been published in anthologies, magazines, the *Irish Times* and on BBC Radio 4 and RTÉ Radio. She started writing for television in 1988, and has written episodes for *Fair City*, *Glenroe* and *Monarch of the Glen*. She also was a story-line associate on the *Glenroe* series for about eight years. One of her significant scripts was a six-part adaptation of Stella Tillyard's biography, *Aristocrats*, for BBC television. It ran for six hours and followed the story of four aristocratic sisters over a period of fifty years. It was broadcast worldwide in 1999 and received an IFTA nomination. She has also written two other screenplays, one a period drama based on the writer Richard Brinsley Sheridan; the other has a more contemporary theme. She is currently working on a legal series, *King's Inns*, which has been commissioned by RTÉ television.

Three of her plays have been performed by a Limerick theatre company, *Bottle of Smoke* (1998), *The Trickster* (2000), an adaptation of Molière's *Les Fourberies de Scapin*, and *A Place in the World* (2001), based on the story of the Palatine migration to West Limerick in 1709. Titles of the plays broadcast on radio in Ireland and England are: *The Leaving is All*, *The Image of*

Her Mother (1988), *Minuet* (1999; nominated for the Prix Italia), *The World of the Walking Wounded, Passion Flowers, The Words Game, The Friendship of Migrants* and *Black and White* (1994).

Select bibliography

O'Carroll, Harriet.

—. "The Words Game." *The Adultery, and other Stories and Poems*. Short story. Dublin: Arlen House, 1982. 39–48.

—. *Image of Her Mother*. Radio play. Prod. John Penrose. RTÉ. Dublin. 4 Nov. 1988.

—. "A Pleasant Christmas for the Children." *The Blackstaff Book of Irish Short Stories*. Short story. Belfast: Blackstaff, 1988.

—. Bottle of Smoke 1988. (Unpub.) Play.

—. "Trust." *The Belfast Book of Short Stories*. Short story. Belfast: Blackstaff, 1988.

—. "The Day of the Christening." *Territories of the Voice: Contemporary Stories by Irish Women Writers*. Short story. Ed. Louise DeSalvo *et al*. Boston: Beacon, 1989, 1999. 53–61.

—. *Black and White*. Radio play. Prod. Scott Fredericks. RTÉ Radio 1. Dublin. 2 Feb. 1994.

—. *Minuet*. Radio play. Prod. Daniel Reardon. RTÉ Radio 1. Dublin. 9 Feb. 1999.

—. The Trickster 2000. (Unpub.) Play.

—. A Place in the World 2001. (Unpub.) Play.

Ó Céirín, Kit, née Foley. Contemporary. Lisdoonvarna, Co. Clare. Biography, translations, social history.

Trained as a nurse, she worked in South Africa in the early 1960s, where she met her hustand, Cyril. They returned to live in Ireland where he taught for several years before turning to full-time writing in 1988. Prior to that, however, they had collaborated on two publications, *Wild and Free* (1978), about the wild harvest, and *Séadna* (1989), a translation of the popular classic tale written by An tAthair Peadar Ó Laoire. This translation was originally published by Cyril in 1970 and the preface acknowledges Kit as "reader, editor, advisor and inspirer". The 1989 edition, however, puts her name on the title page. Their more recent collaboration, a biographical dictionary of Irish women, was published in 1996. Cyril died in 1999.

Select bibliography

Ó Céirín, Kit.

—. and Cyril Ó Céirín. *Wild and Free*. Social history. Dublin: O'Brien, 1978.

—. and Cyril Ó Céirín. *Séadna* (eds. and trans.). Translation. An tAthair Peadar Ó Laoire. N.p.: self-published, 1970. Dublin: Glendale, 1989.

—. and Cyril Ó Céirín. *Women of Ireland: A Biographic Dictionary*. Biography. Kinvara, Co. Galway: Tír Eolas, 1996.

—. A Place Called Doolin. Local history. N.p.: n.p., n.d.

Ó Cléirigh, Nellie. Contemporary. Valentia Island, Co. Kerry. Handcrafts.

Born in Clonmel, Co. Tipperary, she was educated at UCD. She attended embroidery classes at the Dublin School of Art, and this stimulated her interest in the craft of lace-making and its history. She has a collection of old Irish lace which has been exhibited in Ireland and abroad, and is well known for her knowledge of Irish lace, on which she has lectured, broadcast and written. She worked in the civil service in Dublin, where she opened a handcraft outlet. She now divides her time between Dublin and Valentia Island, where she runs a craft and curio shop. She has also written a history of Valentia Island.

Select bibliography
Ó Cléirigh, Nellie.
—. *Carrickmacross Lace: Irish Embroidered Net Lace, a Survey and Manual with Full Size Patterns.* Handcrafts. Mountrath: Dolmen, 1985. Gerrards Cross, Bucks.: Smythe, 1990.
—. *Valentia: A Different Irish Island.* Local history. Dublin: Portobello, 1992.
—. and Veronica Rowe. *Limerick Lace: A Social History and a Maker's Manual.* Handcrafts. Gerrards Cross, Bucks.: Smythe, 1995.

O'Connell, Mary Anne, née Bianconi. *fl.* 1896–1968. Caherdaniel, Co. Kerry. Essays, biography.

Mary Anne O'Connell's published works include a biography of her father, Charles Bianconi, and a memoir of Attie O'Brien (*q.v.*), *Glimpses of a Hidden Life*. In the latter, she refers to herself as a "landowner, daughter, widow, and mother of landowners" (1887, 149). She was married to Morgan John O'Connell, Daniel O'Connell's nephew, and lived at Caherdaniel, Co. Kerry. The O'Connells kept a shooting-lodge near Attie O'Brien's home in Clare, which is how the two became friends. O'Connell also contributed to the *Irish Monthly*.

[Her daughter-in-law, Arabella O'Connell Bianconi (née Hayes), was a folklorist who collected material from local people, particularly those living in the workhouses at Kildysart and Kilrush.]

Select bibliography
O'Connell, Mary Anne.
—. *Glimpses of a Hidden Life: Memories of Attie O'Brien.* Biography. Dublin: Gill, 1887.
—. and James G. Barry. *For Faith and Fatherland: Father Dominic of the Rosary.* Dublin: M. H. Gill & Son, 1888.
—. *Bianconi: King of the Irish Roads.* Biography. Dublin: Figgis, 1962.

O'Connor, Clairr. Contemporary. Limerick. Poetry, novels, plays, short stories.

Born in Croom, Co. Limerick, in 1951, she lived in Listowel, Co. Kerry, for a few years and was educated at UCC. She taught in London from 1972 to 1977, and returned to Ireland in 1978. She has worked as a secondary school teacher in London, Dublin and in Leixlip, Co. Kildare. O'Connor has written plays, poetry, short stories and novels. Her earlier writings included radio plays, *Getting Ahead* (BBC 1987) and *Costing the Coffins* (RTÉ 1990). Another play, *Alma*, about Alma Mahler, was translated into Polish and broadcast on Radio Warsaw in 1995. Her most recent play, *Bodies*, was given readings in Dublin and New York in 1991 and performed in Cork in 1992.

Her poetry has appeared in a variety of newspapers and periodicals, including *Poetry Ireland Review, New Irish Writing,* the *Irish Times, Spare Rib,* and *Writing Women* (Newcastle on Tyne). Her work has been included in anthologies such as *Under Bridgid's Cloak* (1994), *Other Voices* (1992), *On the Counterscarp* (1991) and *Pillars of the House* (1987). Her first collection of poetry, *When You Need Them,* was published by Salmon in 1989. Her first novel, *Belonging* (1991), was nominated for an the *Irish Times*/Aer Lingus award that year. Her second novel, *Love in Another Room* (1995), was short-listed for the Book of the Year Award at Listowel Writers' Week the following year.

She was chairwoman of the Irish Writers' Centre from 1994 to 1996, and she is one of the writers included in the *Great Book of Ireland,* (1991) the unique vellum manuscript of the work of poets and artists assembled to represent the best in contemporary Irish cultural life. Two of her poems have been set to music and recorded by the America composer Diana Segara on *Songs for Poems of the Spirit* (1997). Recent work has appeared in *Stony Thursday* (winter 2001), and she is also included in *The Field Day Anthology* (2002). She is currently working on her third novel.

Select bibliography
O'Connor, Clairr.
—. *Getting Ahead.* Radio play. BBC London. 1987.
—. *When You Need Them.* Poetry. Galway: Salmon, 1989.
—. *Costing the Coffins.* Radio play. RTÉ Radio 1. Dublin. 1990.
—. *Belonging.* Novel. Dublin: Attic, 1991.
—. *Alma.* Radio play. Radio Warsaw, Poland, Warsaw 1995. Bodies: 1991. (Unpub.) Play.
—. *Artemisia.* Radio play. RTÉ Radio. Dublin. 1995.
—. *Love in Another Room.* Novel. Dublin: Marino, 1995.

Secondary sources
Haberstroh, Patricia Boyle. "New Directions in Irish Poetry." *Women Creating Women: Contemporary Irish Women Poets.* Syracuse: Syracuse UP, 1996. 197–224.
St Peter, Christine. "Clairr O'Connor's *Belonging.*" *Changing Ireland: Strategies in Contemporary Women's Fiction.* London: Macmillan, 2000. 26–32.

O'Connor, Cynthia. 1918–99. Glenville, Co. Waterford. History, fiction.

Spent her early years in Ireland and England before settling in Glenville, Co. Waterford. An art dealer, she opened a shop and later a gallery in Dublin, specializing in old Irish paintings. She published articles in the *Bulletin of the Irish Georgian Society, Irish Arts Review* and the *Journal of the Society of Antiquaries of London.* She also contributed to *Burlington Magazine* and *A Dictionary of British and Irish Travellers in Italy 1701–1800.* In 1997 she wrote an account of Lord Charlemont's travels through the Mediterranean countries and how they influenced his architectural activities on his return to Ireland. Her daughter, Annabel Davis-Goff (*q.v.*), is also a writer.

Select bibliography
O'Connor, Cynthia.
—. *The Pleasing Hours: James Caulfield First Earl of Charlemont 1728–99, Traveller, Connoisseur and Patron of the Arts in Ireland.* History. Cork: Collins, 1999.

O'Connor, Kathleen. Contemporary. Cork. Novels.

Born in Cork city, she joined the religious order of the Irish Sisters of Charity at the age of seventeen. She taught in a Dublin school, but left the convent in 1958. She later married and ran a successful business with her husband. However, when ill-health and business failure occurred in 1985, she turned to writing, "as a release from tension and a therapy", and her novels are based on her personal experiences.

Select bibliography
O'Connor, Kathleen.
—. *A Question for Heaven*. Novel. Waterford: Glencree, 1989. Cork: Emperor, 1990.
—. *Stepping Stones*. Novel. Cork: Emperor, 1990.
—. *Mags*. Novel. Cork: Emperor, 1991.
—. *The Red Telephone*. Novel. Cork: Emperor, 1993.
—. *A Truly Irish Story Omnibus Featuring the Two Best-Selling Books*. Novels. Cork: Emperor, 1993.

O'Connor, Kathleen Sheehan. Contemporary. Waterford. Journalism, novels.

Born in Waterford in the 1930s, she pursued a career in print and radio journalism before becoming a novelist in the early 1990s. In a preface to one of her novels, *By Shannon's Way* (1999), she pays tribute to "her friends in the writing game", whom she names as June Considine, Margaret Dolan, Sheila Flitton, Nesta Tuomey and Nuala Campion. She lives in Dublin and is a member of PEN.

Select bibliography
O'Connor, Kathleen Sheehan.
—. *Silver Harvest*. Novel. Cork: Emperor, 1992.
—. *Hold Back the Tide*. Novel. 1994.
—. *The Son of a Nobody*. Novel. Dublin: Attic, 1995.
—. *By Shannon's Way*. Novel. Dingle, Co. Kerry: Mount Eagle, 1999.
—. *Different Kinds of Loving*. Novel. Dingle, Co. Kerry: Mount Eagle, 2000.

O'Connor, Pat. Contemporary. Limerick. Academic writing.

Pat O'Connor is Professor of Sociology and Social Policy and Dean of Humanities at UL. She has been a teacher and researcher for thirty years, at the Economic and Social Research Institute (ESRI) in Dublin, at the University of London, at National Institute for Social Work (NISW) London and at WIT. For many years, she was the director of the MA in Women's studies at UL. Her 1998 *Emerging Voices: Women in Contemporary Irish Society* is a key study for the understanding of gender, changes in family roles, and state and institutional constructions of identity in contemporary Ireland. Her research interests include the sociology of contemporary Irish society, gendered borders within organizations and society, identity, masculinities, children and childhood, friendship and informal support, the state/family interface.

Select bibliography
O'Connor, Pat.

—. et al. *Bridging Two Worlds* (with) United Kingdom: (Avebury, 1989.

—. *Friendships Between Women: A Critical Review.* Hemel Hempstead: Harvester Wheatsheaf; New York: Guildford, 1992.

—. "Tourism and Development: Women's Business?" Academic writing. *Economic and Social Review* 26.4 (1995): 368–401.

—. "Understanding Continuities and Changes in Marriage and Family Life: Putting Women Centre Stage." Academic writing. *Journal of the Sociological Association of Ireland* 5 (1995): 135–63.

—. *Barriers to Women's Promotion in the Midlands and Mid-Western Health Boards.* Academic writing. Limerick: Mid-Western Health Board, 1996.

—. *Invisible Players: Women, Tourism and Development in Ballyhoura.* Academic writing. Limerick: Limerick UP, 1996.

—. "Organisational Culture as a Barrier to Women's Promotion." Academic writing. *Economic and Social Review* 3 (1996): 187–216.

—. *Emerging Voices: Women in Contemporary Irish Society.* Academic writing. Dublin: Institute of Public Administration, 1998.

—. "A Society in Transition: Socially Created Problems and Solutions Irish Style." Academic writing. *Sociologica problemas é práticas* 27 (1998): 79–96.

—. "Women's Friendships in a Post-Modern World." *Placing Friendship in Context.* Academic writing. Ed. R.G. Adams and G.A. Allan. Cambridge: Cambridge UP, 1998.

—. "Does the Border Make the Difference?" *Ireland: North and South Perspectives from Social Science.* Academic writing. Ed. R. Breen, A. Heath and C.T. Whelan. Oxford: Oxford UP, 1999.

—. "Women in the Academy: A Problematic Issue?" *Women and Education.* Academic writing. Ed. A. Ryan and B. Connolly. Maynooth: Maynooth UP, 1999.

—. "Ireland: A Man's World?" *The Economic and Social Review* 31.1 (2000): 81–102.

—. "Structure, Culture and Passivity: A Case Study of Women in a Semi-State Organisation". *Public Administration and Development* 20 (2000): 265–75.

—. "Supporting Mothers: Issues in a Community Mother's Programme". *Community, Work and Family* 4.1 (2001): 63–85.

—. "A Bird's Eye View . . . Resistance in Academia." *Irish Journal of Sociology* 10.2 (2001): 86–104.

—. "Dealing with Organisational Nuts and Bolts: The Relevance of Organisational Practices to Women's Promotion". *Irish Journal of Feminist Studies* 4.1 (2001): 1–16.

O'Connor, Yvonne. Contemporary. Cork. Poetry, children's writing.

Born in Birr, Co. Offaly, she was educated in Thurles, Co. Tipperary and married a Corkman. She has lived in Cork for many years and raised her family there. Her writing has appeared in magazines. She has published two books of poetry and a collection of children's stories, based on the stories she heard from her father.

Select bibliography
O'Connor, Yvonne.

—. *Happy Endings.* Children's writing. Cork: Mt Pleasant, 1994.

—. *Gypsy Child.* Poetry. N.p.: self-published, n.d.

—. *Poems of the Golden Years.* Poetry. N.p.: Self-published, n.d.

O'Donnell, Katherine. Contemporary. Cork. Academic writing, short stories.

Born in Cork in 1966, she attended UCC and the University of California and was recently awarded a PhD from NUI. She coordinated the certificate in Women's Studies, UCC, and is currently a lecturer at the Women's Education, Research and Resource Centre, UCD. Her research interests include eighteenth-century studies, Irish literature, the history of sexuality and postcolonial and cultural theory.

Select bibliography
O'Donnell, Katherine.
—. "Emotionally Involved." *Phoenix Collection of Irish Short Stories 1998.* Short story. Ed. David Marcus. London: Phoenix, 1998.
—. and Michael O'Rourke, eds. *Love, Sex, Intimacy and Friendship Between Men 1550–1800.* Academic writing. London & New York: Palgrave MacMillan, 2002.

O'Donoghue, Jo. Contemporary. Killarney, Co. Kerry. Literary criticism.

Born in Killarney, Co. Kerry, in 1956, she was educated in UCC and TCD, where she was awarded an MLitt in 1988. She taught English for a short time in Cork city before becoming a publisher. From 1988 to 1993 she worked with Poolbeg Press and since 1994 has been with Mercier Press/ Marino Books. She has written a critical study of the Canadian writer Brian Moore, and in 1992 she edited with Seán McMahon a collection of Irish poems with translations in English. She currently lives in Dublin.

Select bibliography
O'Donoghue, Jo.
—. *Brian Moore: A Critical Study.* Literary criticism. Dublin: Gill & Macmillan, 1990.
—. and Seán McMahon, eds. *Taisce Duan: A Treasury of Irish Poems with Translations in English.* Poetry. Dublin: Poolbeg, 1992.
—. and Seán McMahon, eds. *Tales Out of School.* Short stories. Dublin: Poolbeg, 1993.
—. ed. *Golden Apples: Irish Poems for Children.* Poetry. Cork: Mercier, 1955.
—. and Seán McMahon, eds. *The Mercier Companion to Irish Literature.* Literary criticism. Cork: Mercier, 1998.

O'Donoghue, Mary. Contemporary. Tubber, Co. Clare. Poetry, short stories, academic writing.

Born in 1975 in Tubber, Co. Clare, she attended local schools. She took an MPhil in Irish Studies at UCG, and taught there for some years. She received the Seán Dunne Young Writer Award in 2000, and the following year she was awarded the inaugural Salmon Poetry Publication Prize. Salmon subsequently published the winning collection, entitled *Tulle.* She was also awarded the overall prize for her short story "The Byre" (2001), in the Hennessy Awards of 2001. She has published critical articles in *Review of Postgraduate Studies, Bloomsday Magazine* and the *Sunday Business Post.* Her poems have appeared in *The Cuirt Journal, The Burning Bush, Books Ireland, The Shop, Stinging Fly,* the *Tuam Herald, Markings and Ropes* and also in the anthology *A Moment's Grace*. In 2001 she was living and teaching in Massachusetts.

Select bibliography
O'Donoghue, Mary.
—. *Tulle*. Poetry. Galway: Salmon, 2001.

O'Donoghue, Sr Helena. Contemporary. Nenagh, Co. Tipperary. Religious writing.

Born in Nenagh, Co. Tipperary, in 1940, she entered the Mercy Order of nuns in 1958. She attended UCD, where she took the HDip in Education (1966). She was a teacher and later principal of the girls' secondary school run by her order in Nenagh. She left teaching in 1976 to work in a lay community in Dublin, then moved to Shannon before being appointed Superior General of the Mercy Sisters in Killaloe in 1985. She was also President of the Conference of Major Religious Superiors in Ireland from 1989 onwards. She has written for religious journals and published *Sisters in Transition* (1985). She is viewed by many as a progressive voice in Irish church life today.

Select bibliography
O'Donoghue, Sr Helena.
—. *Sisters in Transition*. Religious writing. Dublin: Veritas, 1985.

O'Donovan Rossa, Mary Jane, née Irwin [M.J.I., Cliadhna]. 1845–1916. Cork. Poetry.

From Clonakilty in Co. Cork, she married Jerry O'Donovan Rossa, the Fenian who founded the *United Irishman*. Their first child was born while O'Donovan Rossa was in prison, following which the family emigrated to New York. There, Mary Jane raised her husband's six children from previous marriages alongside the twelve children she bore herself. She contributed to American newspapers, such as *The Emerald*, and her poetry was published in the *Catholic Bulletin* of October 1916 (Colman, 121). She published one collection, *Irish Lyrical Poems* (1868), and her work is anthologized in Sparling's *Irish Minstrelsy* (1887). She returned to Ireland only once, following her husband's death in 1915, when she brought his body back for burial. She published a series of articles following this, "The Death and Funeral of O'Donovan Rossa", in the *Gaelic American*, Sept. 1915–Jan. 1916. She herself died in New York in 1916.

Select bibliography
O'Donovan Rossa, Mary Jane.
—. *Irish Lyrical Poems*. Poetry. New York, 1868.

Secondary sources
O'Kelly, Seamus G. *Sweethearts of the Irish Rebels*. Dublin: A1 Books, 1968.

O'Driscoll, Kathleen. Contemporary. Cork. Poetry, short stories.

Born in Cork in 1941, she graduated with a degree in languages from UCG. She has been a full-time writer since 1977 and has published in magazines and newspapers in Ireland, as well as broadcasting on RTÉ radio. Her first collection of poetry, *Goodbye Joe*, appeared in 1980, followed by her first book of short stories, *Ether*, in 1981. Two of her poems were included in A.A. Kelly's anthology, *Pillars of the House* (1987). In recent years she has turned to film production, and one of her films, *Berlin Blues*, which she wrote, shot and directed in Galway and Berlin, won first prize at the Cork Film Festival. She continues to write poetry and produce films.

Select bibliography

O'Driscoll, Kathleen.

—. *Goodbye Joe: A Collection of Poems*. Poetry. Dublin: Caledon, 1980.

—. *Esther: A Collection of Short Stories*. Short stories. Dublin: Caledon, 1981.

—. "Motherland" and "Theocrats." *Pillars of the House: An Anthology of Verse by Irish Women from 1690 to the Present*. Poetry. Ed. A.A. Kelly. Dublin: Wolfhound, 1987. 132–3.

—. *Berlin Blues*. Film 1993. Prod. David Power.

O'Faoláin, Eileen, née Gould. 1901–88. Cork. Children's writing.

Born in Cork city in 1901, she received her education locally and at UCC. She then taught in secondary schools in Ballinasloe, Co. Galway, and in Naas, Co. Kildare. She met the writer Seán O'Faoláin through their mutual interest in the Irish language, and she went with him to the United States, where they married. She spent one year teaching at an experimental progressive school in Boston, and three years in Middlesex in England. She was a distinguished writer of children's stories, many of which were translated into several languages.

Select bibliography

O'Faoláin, Eileen.

—. *The Little Black Hen: An Irish Fairy Story*. Children's writing. London: Oxford UP, 1940. Notes: Illus. Trefor Jones.

—. "Galway Hats." Journalism. *The Bell* 1.4 (1941): 68–74.

—. *The King of the Cats*. Children's writing. Dublin: Talbot, 1941. Notes: Illus. Nano Reid.

—. *Miss Pennyfeather and the Pooka*. Children's writing. Dublin: Browne & Nolan, 1942. Notes: Illus. Nora McGuinness.

—. "Stockings for Christmas." Journalism. *The Bell* 7.3 (1943): 249–54.

—. *The Children of Crooked Castle*. Children's writing. Dublin: Browne & Nolan, 1945. Notes: Illus. Edythe West.

—. *The Fairy Hen*. Children's writing. Dublin: Parkside, 1945.

—. *May Eve in Fairyland*. Children's writing. Dublin: Parkside, 1945.

—. *Miss Pennyfeather in the Springtime*. Children's writing. Dublin: Browne & Nolan, 1946. Notes: Illus. Muriel Brandt.

—. *Rí na gCat* [The King of the Cats]. Children's writing. Trans. Brighid Ní Loingsigh. Dublin: Oifig an tSoláthair, 1948.

—. *The Shadowy Man*. Children's writing. London: Longmans, 1949.

—. *The White Rabbit's Road*. Children's writing. London: Longmans, 1950. Notes: Illus. Phoebe Llewellyn Smith.

—. *Irish Sagas and Folk Tales*. Children's writing. Oxford: Oxford UP, 1954. Notes: Illus. Joan Kiddell-Munroe.

—. *Púca Bán Chorcaighe* [Miss Pennyfeather and the Pooka]. Children's writing. Trans. Brighid Ní Loingsigh. Dublin: Oifig an tSoláthair, 1955.

—. *High Sang the Sword*. Children's writing. London: Oxford UP, 1959.

—. *Children of the Salmon and Other Irish Folktales: Selections and Translations*. Children's writing. London: Longmans, 1965.

—. contributor. *I Stand the Self-Doomed, Unafraid*. Radio programme (documentary about James Joyce). Prod. Proinsias O Conluain. RTÉ Radio 1. 5 June 1982.

Secondary sources
E. MacC. "Rev. of *The King of the Cats*, by Eileen O'Faolain." *Dublin Magazine* new series 17.2 (1942): 70.

O'Flaherty, Kathleen. 1916–1984. Cork. Academic writing.

Born in Co. Wexford, she was educated at the Ursuline Convent, Waterford, Lille University in France, and UCC. She won the French Government Gold Medal in 1938, and in 1941 received a travelling scholarship in modern languages. She was assistant to the President of UCC from 1944 to 1952, while also lecturing in the French Department. She was appointed Professor of French in 1970. Her area of specialized interest was Chateaubriand. She also received the Chevalier de l'Ordre National du Mérite from the French Government for her contribution to French teaching. She retired in 1981. With her department colleague, Dr Yvonne Servais (*q.v.*), she published a selection of French poems for the Intermediate Certificate examination in the 1950s and 1960s.

Select bibliography
O'Flaherty, Kathleen.
—. "The Teaching of Modern Languages." Academic writing. *Cork University Record* 2 (1944): 41–3.
—. *Voltaire: Myth and Reality*. Literary criticism. Cork: Cork UP, 1945.
—. "The New Philosophy of Despair." Religious writing. *Irish Rosary* (1946): 158–61.
—. "Random Notes on QCC in the Fifties." History. *Cork University Record* 10 (1947).
—. *Paul Claudel and "The Tidings Brought to Mary"*. Literary criticism. 1948. Cork: Cork UP. Notes: Preface by Paul Claudel.
—. "Politics in QCC." History. *Cork University Record* 22 (1951).
—. and Yvonne Servais., ed. *L'explication française*. Cork: Cork UP, 1964.
—. "Monsignor Alfred O'Rahilly." History. *UCC Record* 45 (1970).
—. *The Novel in France 1945–1965: A General Survey*. Literary criticism. Cork: Cork UP, 1973.
—. "Rev. of *Somerville et Ross: Témoins d'Irlande d'hier*, by Guy Fehlmann." Literary criticism. *Irish University Review* 3.1 (1973): 111–13.
—. *Pessimisme de Chateaubriand: Resonances et limites*. Literary criticism. Paris: Académie Européenne du Livre, 1989.
—. and Yvonne Servais. *Choix de Poèmes avec notices biographiques, notes sur le vocabulaire, explications littéraires et questions*. Academic writing. Dublin: Educational Company of Ireland, n.d.
—. and Yvonne Servais, eds. *Intermediate Certificate Prescribed French Poems for 1970–1971: Annotated French Poetry*. Academic writing. Dublin: Educational Co. of Ireland, n.d.

Secondary sources
Clarke, Austin. "Rev. of *Voltaire: Myth and Reality*, by Kathleen O'Flaherty." *Dublin Magazine* new series 15.3 (1945): 45–7.

O'Gorman, Mary, née Flynn. Contemporary. Killarney, Co. Kerry, Clonmel, Co. Tipperary. Poetry.

Raised in Killarney and now living in Clonmel, she has received several awards for her poetry and was shortlisted for the Hennessy Emerging Poetry Award and the Strokestown Poetry Prize in 2000. Her work has also been broadcast on RTÉ radio.

Select bibliography
O'Gorman, Mary.
—. *Barking at Blackbirds*. Poetry. Cork: Bradshaw Books, 2001.

O'Higgins, Mai, née Carew. Contemporary. Dungarvan, Co. Waterford. Poetry, songs.

Born in Dungarvan, Co. Waterford, she was educated locally before joining the Irish Civil Service. She has written music and lyrics for two well known songs based on her native Waterford: "Dungarvan: My Home Town" (1959) and "Evening on Mount Melleray" (1960). She has composed other songs based on other places: "My Dublin Bay" (1954), "Sweet Youghal Bay", "Beautiful Bundoran" and "Moonlight on the Shannon River". She has travelled widely as a singer and her life story was written by Tom Keith in 1997.

Secondary sources
Keith, Tom. *Mai O'Higgins: All for a Song*. Dublin: Glenanna, 1997.

O'Kelly, Claire. *fl.* 1967. Cork. Academic writing.

An archaeoloist, and wife of former Professor of Archaeology at UCC Michael O'Kelly. Together they excavated and studied archaeological sites at Lough Gur and Newgrange, among others.

Select bibliography
O'Kelly, Claire.
—. *An Illustrated Guide to Newgrange*. Academic writing. Wexford: John English, 1967.

O'Leary, Ellen. 1831–89. Tipperary. Poetry, political writing.

Sister of John O'Leary, the Fenian, she herself was active in revolutionary politics. She began her writing and political career working for *The Irish People*, a Fenian paper run by her brother. She went on to contribute poetry to *The Nation*, the *Irish Monthly*, and other periodicals in Ireland and the USA. Colman recounts the conflicting stories surrounding her romance with Edward Duffy, a Fenian and close friend of her brother's: different accounts state that it was variously Ellen or her half-sister Mary who was engaged to Duffy (Colman, 177). In 1867 Duffy was arrested and died in solitary confinement in Millbank prison.

During her brother's exile in the early 1880s Ellen lived in Tipperary, working with the poor, through the Society of St Vincent de Paul, and with the Ladies' Land League. She was also a member of the Sacred Heart

Society, according to Colman (178). When John O'Leary came home in 1885, they lived together quietly in Rathmines, Co. Dublin. Soon after his return she was diagnosed with cancer, and she died in Cork, on a final visit to family members in 1889. A volume of her poetry was published posthumously, and her work was included in various anthologies.

Select bibliography
O'Leary, Ellen.
—. "Home to Carriglea." "My Old Home." "To God and Ireland True." *Cabinet of Irish Literature*. Poetry. Ed. Katherine Tynan. Vol. 4. London: Gresham, 1903.
—. *Lays of Country, Home, and Friends*. Poetry. Ed. T.W. Rolleston. Dublin: Sealy, Bryers and Walker, 1891. Notes: With an intro. and memoir by Charles Gavan Duffy.

Secondary sources
Anon. Obituary. *Cork Examiner* (16 Oct. 1889).
Mulholland, Rosa. "Some Recollections of Ellen O'Leary." *Irish Monthly* 39 (1911): 456–62.
Tynan, Katherine. Obituary. *Boston Pilot* (9 Nov 1889).
Yeats, W.B. "Ellen O'Leary: 1831–1889." *Poets and Poetry of the Century*. Ed. Alfred Miles. London: Hutchinson, 1892.

O'Leary, Margaret. *fl.* **1929–45.** West Cork. Short stories, novels, plays.
Born in West Cork, she was educated there, and took an MA at UCC. She was associated with Connradh na Gaeilge in Cork for many years. She taught at second-level schools for several years before retiring in 1927. She then travelled to France and, following her return to Ireland, she began to write stories for periodicals and plays. While living in Co. Clare in 1936 she was awarded the Harmsworth Prize for her first novel, *The House I Made* (1935). In a review of nine books in the *Dublin Magazine* in 1935, Norah Hoult asserts that *The House I Made* is "the most interesting book on my list for the reason that it is one of the few Irish novels to give an authentic picture of the life of the peasant farmer and his problems ... But she shows a capacity for clear-sighted observation, and a lack of squeamishness in portrayal which should make her next book definitely important." During the Second World War she took up teaching again in Scotland and continued to write.

O'Leary is perhaps best known for her plays, two of which, *The Woman* (1929) and *The Coloured Balloon* (1944), were staged at the Abbey Theatre. The former drama, produced by fellow Corkonian Lennox Robinson, came to the Cork Opera House for four performances in 1929 before returning to the Abbey for a further week. We know that the novel *Lightning Flash* (1929) is derived from this play because of a letter from W.B. Yeats to Lennox Robinson, published as the preface to the novel. Referring to the play, he declares O'Leary to be the "best realistic peasant dramatist who has yet appeared". Yeats suggested changing the end of the original draft of the play so that the heroine dies, instead of leaving her to walk the roads on her own;

he writes: "[her death] leaves her dominant over all, all there are answered and confounded. The act becomes strong and passionate instead of being as it is sentimental [...]. Her passion has to die as the sanctity of the saint has to die" (9). It is unrecorded whether or not O'Leary took his advice.

Select bibliography

O'Leary, Margaret.

—. "Mated." *The Best Short Stories of 1929*. Short stories. Ed. Edward J. O'Brien. London: Jonathan Cape, 1929. 252–62.

—. *The Woman*. Play. Prod. Lennox Robinson. Abbey Theatre, Dublin. 10 Sept. 1929.

—. *The House I Made*. Novel. London: Jonathan Cape, 1935.

—. *Lightning Flash*. Novel. London: Jonathan Cape, 1939.

—. "Beween Two Bridges." Short story. *The Bell* 2.3 (1941): 21–7.

—. "Seaside Landlady." Short story. *Irish Digest* 5.11 (1941): 41–4.

—. "The Woman from Leamlara." Short story. *Dublin Magazine* 16.3 (1941): 39–50.

—. "Bellows to Mend." Short story. *Irish Digest* 5.13 (1942): 30–33.

—. *The Coloured Balloon*. Play. Prod. Frank Dermody. Abbey Theatre, Dublin. 8 May 1943.

—. "Holiday in October." Short story. *Dublin Magazine* 20.3 (1945): 30–38.

Secondary sources

Hoult, Norah. "Rev. of *The House I Made*, by Margaret O'Leary." *Dublin Magazine* new series 10.3 (1935): 88.

Ó Murchú, Helen. Comhaimseartha. Co. Luimnigh. Scríbhneoireacht acadúil, teangeolaíocht, sochtheangeolaíocht agus litríocht leanaí.

Saolaíodh i gContae Luimnigh í. Bhí sí ina stiúrthóir ar an eagras Comhar na Múinteoirí Gaeilge.

Select bibliography

Ó Murchú, Helen.

—. le David Little agus David Singleton. *A Functional-Notional Syllabus for Adult Learners of Irish*. Scríbhneoireacht acadúil. Dublin: Centre for Language and Communications Studies, TCD, 1985.

—. le David Little agus David Singleton. *Towards a Communicative Curriculum for Irish*. Scríbhneoireacht acadúil. Dublin: Centre for Language and Communications Studies, TCD, 1985.

—. agus Mícheál W. Ó Murchú, eag. *Aspects of Bilingual Education: The Italian and Irish Experience*. Scríbhneoireacht acadúil. Baile Átha Cliath: Bord na Gaeilge, 1988.

—. "Aiste." *Náisiún na hÉireann Mar a Bhí agus Mar Atá*. Scríbhneoireacht acadúil, stair shóisialta. Eag. Diarmuid Ó Laoghaire. Baile Átha Cliath: Foilseacháin Ábhair Spioradálta, 1993.

—. *Aibítir na Gaeilge*. Scríbhneoireacht acadúil, litríocht leanaí. Baile Átha Cliath: Comhar na Múinteoirí Gaeilge, 1995.

—. agus Máirtín Ó Murchú. *Irish: Facing the Future [An Ghaeilge: a haghaidh roimpi]*. Scríbhneoireacht acadúil, teangeolaíocht. Dublin: Irish Committee for the European Bureau for Lesser Used Languages, 1999.

—. agus Muiris Ó Laoire. *Teagasc na Gaeilge*. Scríbhneoireacht acadúil. Vol. 7. Baile Átha Cliath: Comhar na Múinteoirí Gaeilge, 2000.

—. *Limistéar na Síbhialtachta: Dúshlán agus Treo d'Eagraíochtaí na Gaeilge.* Scríbhneoireacht acadúil. An Aimsir Óg, Paimfléad 2. Baile Átha Cliath: Coiscéim, 2003.

O'Reilly, Dolly. Contemporary. Cork. Local history.

Born and educated on Sherkin Island, Co. Cork, she completed her education at a boarding school in Rosscarbery before travelling. She visited France and Italy, and in 1987 sailed down the east coast of the USA before returning to Sherkin Island, where she currently lives.

Select bibliography
O'Reilly, Dolly.
—. *Sherkin Island.* Local history. 1994. Notes: There are no publication details available but the book can be purchased online at emara.com.

O'Shea, Mary. Contemporary. Waterford. Poetry, fiction, local history.

Born in Piltown, Co. Waterford, in 1962, she attended secondary school in Carrick-on Suir and since completing her Leaving Certificate in 1981 she has worked on the family farm. In 1984 she won the Allingham Prize for poetry and has been highly commended in many other poetry competitions, including the Boyle Arts Festival (2002) and the Austin Clarke Memorial Competition (1996). Her writings have also been published in anthologies and journals, including *Poetry Ireland Review*, *Ireland's Eye* and *Stroan*.

Select bibliography
O'Shea, Mary.
—. *The Marrying of Brigit and Christ in the Parish of Templeorum.* Local history. Kilkenny: Self-published, 1999.
—. *Parish of Templeorum: A Historical Miscellany.* Local history. Kilkenny: self-published, 1999.
—. *One Hundred Years of Piltown Co-operative and Its Branches.* Local history. Kilkenny: Piltown Co-operative Society, 2001.

O'Sullivan, Leanne. Contemporary. West Cork. Poetry.

O'Sullivan was born in 1983, and is from the Beara peninsula of West Cork. A student of English at UCC, she has been writing since her early teens and has won many poetry awards, including the Seacat, the RTÉ Rattlebag Poetry Slam and the Davoren Hanna Award for Young Emerging Irish Poet. Her work has been published in several poetry magazines and anthologies. She has read in Ireland and abroad, and broadcast on RTÉ radio. O'Sullivan's work treats painful subject-matter – a thematic focus of her first collection is bulimia – and her poems repeatedly stage intense conflict within the lyric self between destructive and nurturing impulses, but at its best her work achieves remarkable formal poise, and despite evidence of influences from Plath and Boland, O'Sullivan has developed a distinctive voice.

Select bibliography
—. *Waiting for My Clothes.* Tarset: Bloodaxe, 2004.
Guinness, Selina, ed. *The New Irish Poets.* Tarset: Bloodaxe, 2004.

O'Sullivan, Valerie. Contemporary. Cork. Journalism.

Born in Cork, she has worked as a photographer for news agencies in southern Ireland. Her publications combine photographic work and text based on the thoughts of well known, and lesser-known, women and men in Ireland. She has also caught instances of religious life and customs in Ireland in her *Sacred Moments* (1998). She worked with the Kerry Travellers' Association on their book entitled *Towards Inclusion*.

Select bibliography
O'Sullivan, Valerie.
—. *Towards Inclusion*. Ed. A. Parnell. Tralee: Kerry Travellers Development Project, 1996.
—. *Sacred Moments*. Journalism. Dublin: Veritas, 1998.
—. *Inner Thoughts: Reflections of Contemporary Irish Women*. Journalism. Dublin: Veritas, 1999.
—. *Reflections of Contemporary Irish Men*. Journalism. Dublin: Veritas, 2000.

O'Toole, Tina. Contemporary. Cork. Limerick Academic writing, literary criticism.

A native of Co. Wicklow, she has lived in Cork since 1994. Her MA was on the work of Kate O'Brien, and her PhD at NUI Cork focused on the literature and activism of the New Woman project of the 1890s. Her research interests include nineteenth- and twentieth-century literature in Ireland and Britain, *fin de siècle* culture and society, feminist and postcolonial theory, and the history of sexuality. She has recently co-authored, with Linda Connolly, an archival study of second-wave feminist activism in Ireland. She is a lecturer at the Department of Languages and Cultural Studies, UL.

Select bibliography
—. "*Keynotes* from Millstreet, Co. Cork: George Egerton's Transgressive Fictions." *Irish Women Novelists 1800–1940*. Ed. Anne Fogarty. Spec. issue *Colby Quarterly* 2 (June 2000) 145–56.
—. "'Hermaphrodite by Force of Circumstances': The New Woman Project of the 1890s." *Irish Journal of Feminist Studies*. 5.1 & 2 (2003).
—. "Moving into the Spaces Cleared by our Sisters: Lesbian Community Activism in Ireland and Canada." *Out of the Ivory Tower: Feminist Research for Social Change*. Toronto: Sumack P., 2003.
—. "The New Woman and the Boy in *fin de siècle* Irish Fiction." *New Voices in Irish Criticism* 5. Ed. Ann Coughlan. Dublin: Four Courts Press, 2005.
—. and Linda Connolly. *Documenting Irish Feminisms*. Dublin: Woodfield Press, 2005.

Okasha, Elisabeth. Contemporary. Cork. Academic writing.

Born in 1942, she took an MA at the University of St Andrews in 1963 and a PhD at the University of Cambridge in 1967. Okasha taught in various colleges in Aberdeen, Dundee, East Anglia, and Assiut, before being appointed to the Department of English, UCC, in 1977. Her research interests include Anglo-Saxon and Celtic epigraphy, Old English, Medieval English, applied linguistics and children's literature.

Select bibliography
Okasha, Elisabeth.
—. *Hand-List of Anglo-Saxon Non-Runic Inscriptions.* Academic writing. Cambridge: Cambridge UP, 1971.
—. "A Rediscovered Medieval Inscribed Ring." Academic writing. *Anglo-Saxon England* 2 (1973): 167–71.
—. "The Early Christian Inscribed and Carved Stones of Tullylease, Cork." Academic writing. *Cambridge Medieval Celtic Studies* 24 (1992): 1–36.
—. *Corpus of Early Christian Inscribed Stones of South-West Britain.* Academic writing. London: Leicester UP, 1993.
—. "The Inscribed Knife." *Late Viking Age and Medieval Waterford Excavations 1986–1992.* Academic writing. Ed. M.F. Hurley *et al.* Waterford: n.p., 1997. 524–8.
—. *Early Christian Inscriptions of Munster: A Corpus of the Inscribed Stones (excluding Ogham).* Academic writing. Cork: Cork UP, 2001.

Owen, Elizabeth. *fl.* **1826.** Cheekpoint, Co. Waterford. Poetry.

From Cheekpoint, Co. Waterford, she was author of *Poetical Recollections* (1826).

Select bibliography
Owen, Elizabeth.
—. *Poetical Recollections.* Poetry. Waterford: John Bull, 1826.

Palmer, Patricia. Contemporary. Kerry. Academic writing, literary criticism.

Born in Tralee in 1957, she graduated with an MA from UCC in 1980. She taught Communications at Dundalk IT (1983–7), after which she taught in UL (1987–2001). She was awarded a DPhil from Oxford University in 2000. She has been a member of the staff at the University of York since 2001. Her research interests include sixteenth-century and Renaissance writing.

Select bibliography
Palmer, Patricia.
—. *Language and Conquest in Early Modern Ireland: English Renaissance Literature and Elizabethan Imperial Expansion.* Literary criticism. Cambridge: Cambridge UP, 2001.

Paor, Máire. *fl.* **1936.** Béal na Molt, Co. Phort Láirge. Scéalaíocht agus seanchas / béaloideas.

Saolaíodh Máire i 1866. Bhí sí ina cónaí sa Chnoc Buidhe, Béal na Molt nuair a bhailigh Pádraig Ó Milléadha scéalta agus seanchas uaithi. Foilsíodh an t-ábhar sin in *Béaloideas* 6 (1936).

Select bibliography
Paor, Máire.
—. scéalaí. "Seanchas Sliabh gCua: Scéalta 26, 39, 65, 71, 83, 105, 110 agus 133." Scéalaíocht agus seanchas / béaloideas. *Béaloideas* 6.2 (1936): 169–256.

Penrose, Ethel, née Coghill. 1857–1938. Lismore, Co. Waterford. Children's writing.

A daughter of Sir Jocelyn Coghill of Glen Barrahane, Castletownshend, Co. Cork, she was a cousin of Edith Somerville. In 1880 she married James Penrose, and they had a large family. She wrote fiction for children, and contributed short stories to magazines such as *Argosy*. Her only extant full-length publication is *Clear as the Noon Day* (1893), in which the flyleaf notes that she was "the author of *The Fairy Cobbler's Gold* and others". The illustrations in *Clear as the Noon Day* are by Edith Somerville.

Select bibliography
Penrose, Ethel.
—. *Clear as the Noon Day*. Children's writing. London: Jarrold, 1893. Notes: Illus. E.OE. Somerville

Penrose, H.H., née Lewis. *fl.* 1911–14. Kinsale, Co. Cork. Short stories.

Born in Kinsale, she was educated at boarding school in Cork, and at TCD. She contributed short stories to magazines and published some novels. She went on to live in Surrey.

Select bibliography
Penrose, H.H.
—. *Denis Trench*. Novel. London: Rivers, 1911.
—. *A Faery Land Forlorn*. Novel. London: Rivers, 1912.
—. *Burnt Flax*. Novel. London: Mills & Boon, 1914.

Peters, Anne, née Condon. Contemporary. Puckane, Co. Tipperary. Poetry.

Born in Youghal in East Cork, she went to live after her marriage in 1939 in Oklahoma and Texas, USA. During the war, while her husband was in France and Germany, she experienced a twenty-eight-day crossing of the Atlantic in a convoy to England, and worked in an aeroplane-manufacturing plant and as a director of an Allied Forces Centre. In 1946 she and her husband returned to live in New York city where, she studied at New York University, before moving to Connecticut. In the early 1980s she divided her time between Oxford and Puckane, a village in North Tipperary. Her work has appeared in *Poets of Today*, *Poetry Ireland Review*, *The Gardener's Book of Verse*, *The Irish Press* and *Manifold Spirit America*.

Select bibliography
Peters, Anne.
—. *Rings of Green*. Poetry. Gerrards Cross, Bucks.: Smythe, 1982.
—. "Solace." Poetry. *Poetry Ireland Review* 11 (1984): 52.

Secondary sources
Ryan, Angela. "Les Poèmes d'Anne Peters." *Cahiers d'études irlandaises* (1983): 116–19.

Phelan, Angela, née Jones. Contemporary. Cork. Journalism, biography.

Born in 1946, she took a degree in applied psychology at UCC. She continued her studies in social psychology and communications at Foothill College in Santa Clara, California, and at Stanford University in California.

She began her journalistic career with Cork local radio, and also worked on radio programmes in California. She has worked as a journalist with Irish newspapers and has broadcast on RTÉ television and on Channel 21 in New York. She is described in *Who's Who in Ireland* as a hard-working, widely read columnist noted for a worldwide network of contacts. She has written a biography of the Irish politican Brian Lenihan.

Select bibliography
Phelan, Angela.
—. and Ann Lenihan. *No Problem: To Mayo and Back*. Biography. Dublin: Blackwater, 1990.

Pisco, Cristina. Contemporary. Clonakilty, Co. Cork. Novels, poetry, short stories.

Of Hispanic-Philipino-American origin, she has lived and reared her family in Clonakilty in West Cork. Both of her published novels, *Only a Paper Moon* (1998) and *Catch the Magpie* (1999), are set in that area.

Select bibliography
Pisco, Cristina.
—. *Only a Paper Moon*. Novel. Dublin: Poolbeg, 1998.
—. *Catch the Magpie*. Novel. Dublin: Poolbeg, 1999.

Polland, Madeleine. Contemporary. Co. Cork. Children's stories, novels.

Born in Co. Cork, she moved to live in Hertfordshire, England. She had planned to pursue a painting careeer but she turned to writing while employed as a librarian. During the Second World War she spent four years in the WAAF. She published her first children's book in 1960, which was chosen as an "Honor Book" in the *New York Herald Tribune* Spring List Festival. She has also published several historical novels for children, as well as books for adults.

Select bibliography
Polland, Madeleine.
—. *Children of the Red King*. Children's story. London: Hutchinson, 1960.
—. *Beorn the Proud*. Children's writing. London: Constable, 1961.
—. *Fingal's Quest*. Children's writing. New York: Doubleday, 1961.
—. *The Town Across the Water*. Novel. London: Constable, 1961.
—. *Mission to Cathay*. Novel. London: World's Work, 1962.
—. *The White Twilight*. Novel. N.p.: n.p., 1962. London: Constable, 1964.
—. *The Queen's Blessing*. Novel. London: Constable, 1963.
—. *City of the Golden House*. Novel. London: World's Work, 1964.
—. *Flame Over Tara*. Novel. Surrey: Chaucer Press, 1965.
—. *Deirdre*. Novel. London: World's Work, 1967.
—. *The Little Spot of Bother*. Novel. London: Hutchinson, 1967.
—. *Thicker Than Water*. Novel. London: Hutchinson, 1967.
—. *To Tell My People*. Novel. London: Hutchinson, 1968.
—. *Random Army*. Novel. London: Hutchinson, 1969.
—. *To Kill a King*. Novel. London: Hutchinson, 1970.
—. *Package to Spain*. Novel. London: Hutchinson, 1971.

—. *Sabrina*. Novel. New York: Delacorte, 1979. Leicester: Ulverstoft, 1981.
—. *All Their Kingdoms*. Novel. London: Collins, 1981.
—. *No Price Too High*. Novel. London: Piatkus, 1985.
—. *As It Was in the Beginning*. Novel. London: Sphere, 1989.
—. *Rich Man's Flowers*. Novel. London: Piatkus, 1990.
—. *The Pomegranate House*. Novel. London: Piatkus, 1992.

Power, Cis and Jo. *fl.* **1916–1925.** Kerry. Political writing, memoir.

Daughters of Catherine and Patrick Power from Rock Street, Tralee, Cis and Jo were political activists and members of the Kerry branch of Cumann na mBan. The sisters carried on a family tradition of political activism. Their uncle, Mick Power, was a well known Fenian and Land Leaguer, and their father was involved in the Land League, as well as being a close friend of Charles Stewart Parnell. Patrick Power was also a founder member of the Gaelic Athletic Association in Tralee and the local president of Sinn Féin. Cis and Jo joined Cumann na mBan and also worked for the Prisoners' Dependants Fund. Following the War of Independence they actively opposed the Treaty, and co-edited a typewritten Republican newsletter, *The Invincible* (all copies of which seem to have been lost in the intervening years). As a result of their activities they were arrested in March 1923, following the interception of a message they were sending to the Dublin branch of Cumann na mBan. They were interned first in Tralee Barracks and later in Kilmainham Jail and the North Dublin Union, along with their cousin Han Moynihan (*q.v.*), who had also been involved in the production of *The Invincible*. Cis described their arrival in Dublin in her jail journal: "Our mode of transportation to Kilmainham was an open lorry, and as night had fallen on our arrival there, we had no idea what the outside of our new abode looked like. When we got inside, the interior looked grim and foreboding, and our spirits by now were sinking to zero." During their imprisonment they became known as "the Invincibles". Cis was released in October 1923, but there are no records as to the release dates of the other two.

There are graduation photographs of the Power sisters, but it is unclear whether they attended university before or after their internment. Jo became a school teacher, and later took an MA and went on to become a National School Inspector in Kerry. The sisters lived out their years together in Rock Street, where they looked after their parents – Patrick Power died in his eighties in 1938. Jo outlived Cis, who died in Tralee in February 1968. Sinéad McCoole (*q.v.*) has recently carried out further research on the Powers as part of her study of the women of Cumann na mBan.

Select bibliography
Power, Cis and Jo.
—. "Blaze Away With Your Little Gun: A Memoir of Three Jails, Tralee, Kilmainham and the North Dublin Union." (Unpub.) memoir [This may be a revised draft of "If Winter Comes"]. N.d.
—. "If Winter Comes: Memories of Kilmainham and the North Dublin Union." (Unpub.) memoir. N.d.

Secondary sources
McCoole, Sinéad. *No Ordinary Women: Irish Female Activists in the Revolutionary Years 1900–1923*. Dublin: O'Brien Press, 2003.
Han Moynihan. (Unpub.) diary. N.d.

Power, Marguerite, Countess of Blessington. 1789–1849. Knockbrit, Co. Tipperary. Novels.

Daughter of a small landowner from Clonmel, she had an interesting and varied career. Her childhood was dismal, due to her father's violent temper and his local reputation – he was regarded as a traitor to the Catholic cause as a result of his efforts to put down the '98 rising in the area. Forced by him to marry at the age of fifteen, she fled from her violent husband, Captain Farmer, after three months, returning to live with her parents. Farmer's military career ended when he drew a sword on his commanding officer in a quarrel – he was allowed to resign, and friends shipped him to the East Indies. He returned to England in 1816, and died after a fall from a windowledge at Fleet Prison during a drunken party. By that time his widow had left Ireland for London, residing first in the fashionable Manchester Square and later at St James's Square, where she soon earned a reputation as a famous hostess. Her biographer asserts that her conduct after the separation was beyond reproach, which suggests that there were rumours of indiscretions.

In 1818, a few months after Farmer's death, Marguerite married Charles John Gardiner, Earl of Blessington. Their shared tastes were extravagant and his estates heavily in debt. They went abroad in 1822, visited Byron in Genoa, and lived on the Continent until Blessington's death in 1829. The Count d'Orsay travelled with them, first as a friend, and then as the new husband of the Earl's daughter. Rumours suggested that d'Orsay was variously having affairs with both the Earl and Lady Blessington. Following the Earl's death the d'Orsays' marriage broke up, and the Count set up home next door to Lady Blessington in London, their relationship causing scandal for many years.

After her husband's death she supplemented her considerably reduced income by writing novels and contributing to various publications as author or editor. The "Idler" books were popular for their gossip, anecdote and sentiment. Her novels seem to have mainly consisted of fictionalized accounts of the lives of the aristocracy, as Tynan points out: "Lady Blessington introduces to her readers the leading representatives of art, literature and politics, whom she has received as friends or met in society." She also edited *The Keepsake* and *The Book of Beauty* for several years, as well as contributing sketches and articles to other periodicals of the day. Despite her large earnings, she went bankrupt and fled to Paris in 1849, where she died of apoplexy.

Select bibliography
Power, Marguerite, Countess of Blessington.
—. *The Magic Lantern, or, Sketches of Scenes in the Metropolis*. Short stories. London: Longman, Hurst, Rees, Orme & Brown, 1822.

—. *Sketches and Fragments.* 1822.
—. "Conversations with Lord Byron." Memoir. *Colburn's New Monthly Magazine* (1832).
—. *Grace Cassidy, or The Repealers.* Novel. N.p.: n.p., 1833.
—. *Meredyth.* Novel. N.p.: n.p., 1843.
—. *The Two Friends.* Novel. London: Saunders & Otley, 1835.
—. *The Confessions of an Elderly Gentleman.* Novel. London: Longman, Rees, Orme, Brown, Green, & Longman, 1836.
—. *The Victims of Society.* Novel. Paris: A. & W. Galignan, 1837.
—. *The Governess.* Novel. N.p.: n.p., 1839.
—. *The Idler in Italy.* Travel writing. London: Henry Colburn, 1839.
—. *The Idler in France.* Travel writing. Paris: Baudry's European Library, 1841.
—. *Memoirs of a Femme de Chambre.* Novel. Leipzig: Bernhard Tauchnitz, 1846.
—. *Marmaduke Herbert, or, The Fatal Error.* Novel. Leipzig: Bernhard Tauchnitz, 1847.
—. *Country Quarters.* Novel. Leipzig: Bernhard Tauchnitz, 1850.
—. *The Confessions of an Elderly Lady and of an Elderly Gentleman.* Novel. London: Simms & McIntyre, 1853.
—. *The Belle of a Season.* Poem. London: Longman, Rees, Orme, Brown, Green & Longman, n.d.
—. *The Confessions of an Elderly Lady.* Novel. N.p.: n.p., n.d.
—. *The Lottery of Life.* Novel. N.p.: n.p., n.d.
—. *Tour Through the Netherlands to Paris.* Travel writing. N.p.: n.p., n.d.

Secondary sources
Madden, R.R., ed. "The Literary Life and Correspondence of the Countess of Blessington." London: T.C. Newby, 1855.
Sadleir, Michael. *Blessington-D'Orsay: A Masquerade.* London: Constable, 1933.

Power, Maud. *fl.* **1907.** Faithlegg, Co. Waterford. Travel writing.

Wrote and illustrated the book *Wayside India* (1907), based on her travels there 1901–46.

Select bibliography
Power, Maud.
—. *Wayside India.* Travel writing. Waterford: Downey, 1907. Notes: Illus. the author.

Poyntz, Sarah H.J. Contemporary. The Burren, Co. Clare. Diaries.

Born in 1926 in New Ross, Co. Wexford, she received her secondary education in Gorey, Co. Wexford, before going to UCD. She was a student there of Lorna Reynolds, whose guidance she has acknowledged publicly. In the 1950s she worked as a teacher in London, Cornwall and Cambridge. In 1971 she was awarded a fellowship to study for a term at Girton College, while continuing to teach English at Perse School for Girls in Cambridge. Ill-health forced her to take early retirement, but she continued to teach on a part-time basis both at her old school and at Girton College. With her life-long friend Professor Mary Ann Radzinowicz she spent several years in New York, where Radzinowicz was Professor of English at Cornell University. They spent their summer holidays in Ireland before finally retiring to Bally-vaughan in Co. Clare. Poyntz has lived there since 1986, and she writes, builds model ships and gardens. Since 1900 she has been writing a "Country Diary" for the *Guardian* newspaper in North Tipperary. These writings formed the basis of *A Burren Journal*, published in 2000.

Select bibliography
Poyntz, Sarah.
—. *A Burren Journal*. Diaries. Kinvara, Co. Galway: Tír Eolas, 2000. Notes: Illus. Gordon D'Arcy and Anne Korff.

Prendiville, Nora. 1868–1907. Castleisland, Co. Kerry. Diaries.

A Dominican missionary nun, she left Ireland for the USA in 1899, with her compatriot Alice Nolan, never to return. The nuns taught in New Orleans for the rest of their lives. They kept diaries of their journey from Dublin to New Orleans, which were edited by Margaret Mac Curtain (*q.v.*) and Suellen Hoy, and published in 1994.

Select bibliography
Prendiville, Nora.
—. *From Dublin to New Orleans: The Journey of Nora and Alice*. Diary. Ed. Suellen Hoy and Margaret Mac Curtain. Dublin: Attic, 1994.

Price, K. Arnold. 1893–1989. Co. Limerick. Novels, short stories, poetry.

Born in Co. Mayo, she spent her childhood in Co. Limerick. Her mother was a descendant of Thomas Arnold of Rugby and her father was a teacher. Kathleen was educated privately, and in 1917 graduated with a BA in English and French from TCD. She carried out further study in London and at the University of Lyons. She travelled widely in England and France and her poetry and short stories were published in Irish and British papers and periodicals, such as *Dublin Magazine, Irish Writing, Envoy* and the *Irish Press*. She wrote one novel, *The New Perspective* (1980), published when she was eighty-seven years of age, and a collection of short stories, *The Captains's Paramour* (1985). William Trevor described the novel as "deceptively quiet, its elegant exterior disguising an explosion that echoes and reverberates long after the novel has been read". The latter years of her life were spent in Wicklow and in Dublin city. She always signed her work with the gender-neutral "K. Arnold Price".

Select bibliography
Price, K. Arnold.
—. "Death at Tea-Time." Poem. *Dublin Magazine* new series 18.4 (1943): 7.
—. "The Glencree River." Poem. *Dublin Magazine* new series 19.3 (1944): 8–9.
—. "Swans Coming into Killough Harbour." Poetry. *Dublin Magazine* new series 20.2 (1945): 4–5.
—. "February 1947." Poem. *Dublin Magazine* new series 22.4 (1947): 3.
—. "Jug-Jug." Poem. *Dublin Magazine* new series 22.1 (1947): 4.
—. "Will You Ask Me to Your Party?" Short story. *Dublin Magazine* new series 24.1 (1949): 32–7.
—. "For Tammuz." Poetry. *Dublin Magazine* new series 27.1 (1952): 4.

—. "Matt the Drum." Short story. *Irish Writing* new series 27 (1954): 27–33.
—. *The New Perspective*. Novel. Swords, Co. Dublin: Poolbeg, 1980.
—. *The Captain's Paramour*. Short stories. London: Hamish Hamilton, 1985.

Pyne-Clarke, Olga. Contemporary. Dungarvan, Co. Waterford. Autobiography, social history.

Born in Dungarvan, Co. Waterford, in 1915, she is author of *She Came of Decent People* (1985) and *A Horse in My Kit Bag* (1988), which deal with her life in Ireland in the period 1920–50.

Select bibliography
Pyne-Clarke, Olga.
—. *She Came of Decent People*. Autobiography, social history. London: Pelham, 1985.
—. *A Horse in My Kit-Bag*. Autobiography, social history. London: Methuen, 1988.

Quarton, Marjorie, née Smithwick. Contemporary. Nenagh, Co. Tipperary. Novels, children's writing, memoirs, journalism.

Born in Nenagh, Co. Tipperary, in 1930, she was educated in Dublin. She is a farmer but has given considerable time to her writing career, which has included many varying interests: novels, memoirs, books on dogs, humorous books, children's writing, antiques and editorial work. Her first novel, *Corporal Jack* (1987), was serialized on BBC Radio 4. Her humorous writings (three published works) are based on dogs and a fourth one is currently appearing in serial form bi-monthly in WSN magazine in the UK. She wrote regularly over ten years for the *Farmers' Journal* and contributed a column to the *Irish Field* for six years as well as writing for local papers, the national press, and magazines in the UK. She teaches creative writing, gives lectures and is a member of PEN and the Writers' Union. Her current project is a collection of 300-year-old recipes handed down by one of her foremothers, which she plans to publish with some of her own material.

Select bibliography
Quarton, Marjorie.
—. *The Farm Dog*. Handbook. N.p.: n.p., 1981.
—. *One Dog and His Man*. Novel. Belfast: Blackstaff, 1984.
—. *All About the Working Border Collie*. Handbook. London: Pelham, 1986.
—. *One Dog and His Trials*. Novel. Belfast: Blackstaff, 1986.
—. *Corporal Jack*. Novel. London: Collins, 1987.
—. *No Harp Like My Own*. Novel. London: Collins, 1988.
—. *Breakfast the Night Before: Recollections of an Irish Horse Dealer*. Memoirs. London: André Deutsch, 1989.
—. *The Cow Watched the Battle*. Children's writing. Dublin: Poolbeg, 1990.
—. *The Other Side of the Island*. Children's writing. Dublin: Poolbeg, 1991.
—. *Renegade*. Novel. London: André Deutsch, 1991.
—. *One Dog, His Man and His Trials*. Novel. Dublin: Farming, 1993. Notes: Ed. version of two earlier books.
—. *Saturday's Child*. Memoirs. London: André Deutsch, 1993.

Quinlan, Carmel. Contemporary. Cork. Academic writing, history.

Born in Tipperary, she has lived in Munster all her life. She is the Mature Student Officer at UCC, and lectures in nineteenth-century social history in the Department of History. She was coordinator of the MA in Women's Studies in UCC for a number of years. Her research interests include the Irish famine, land agitation in nineteenth-century Ireland and Irish women's history.

Select bibliography
Quinlan, Carmel.
—. "Punishment from God: The Famine Questionnaire." History. *Irish Review* (1996).
—. *Genteel Revolutionaries: Anna and Thomas Haslam, Pioneers of Irish Feminism.* Academic writing. Cork: Cork UP, 2002.

Rani Sarma, Ursula. Contemporary. Clare. Plays, poetry, children's writing, film script.

Born in 1978 in Lahinch, Co. Clare, she began to write short stories from a young age. When she began her third-level studies at UCC, she became interested in writing for the stage. She wrote and directed *Like Sugar on Skin*, which was produced in 1999. The play was chosen to represent the university at the Irish Student Drama Awards that year, where it won five nominations and two awards. Following her graduation with a BA in English and history her play *... touched...* was presented at the Edinburgh Fringe Festival in 1999, where it received an award. She was commissioned to write *Blue* for the Cork Midsummer Festival in 2000, which earned Sarma a nomination for the Stuart Parker Award and the *Irish Times*/ESB Theatre Award Bursary. In 2000 she also co-founded Djinn Theatre Company with producer Kate Neville. In 2001 she wrote and directed *Gift* for the Unfringed Festival, and was commissioned by the BBC to write *Car Four*, which was aired on Radio 3 in December 2001. She was commissioned by RTÉ to write *The Fisherman*, which was aired in September 2003. She also wrote *Orpheus Road*, which was read in the Young Vic Theatre as part of Paines Plough's Wild Lunch series in 2003.

To date, she has been commissioned by a number of theatre companies worldwide, including the National Theatre London, the Traverse Theatre Edinburgh, the Abbey Theatre Dublin, and the Stephan Joseph Theatre in Scarborough under the directorship of Alan Ayckbourn. Her work has been translated into German, Swedish, Finnish, Danish, French, Spanish, Romanian, Italian and Irish to date. Her play *Blue* won the Audience Appreciation Award at the Heidelberg Festival in 2004. She herself has been commissioned by the National Theatre in London to translate an Italian play by the playwright Luca de Bei for publication in 2005. She has been Writer in Residence for The National Theatre and Paines Plough's Theatre Companies of London and is currently Writer in Residence for Galway's County and City Councils and Galway library service. Outside of her work for the stage, in 2005 she intends to publish her first children's book, *Kiran the Bear*, and a collection of poetry. She is also developing *Blue* for the screen.

Select bibliography
Rani Sarma, Ursula.
—. *Like Sugar on Skin.* (Unpub.) play. 1999.
—. *...touched...* Play. 1999. London: Oberon Books, 2002.
—. *Wanderings.* (Unpub.) play. 1999.
—. *Blue.* Play. 2000. London: Oberon Books, 2002.
—. *Gift.* (Unpub.) play. 2001.
—. *Car Four.* (Unpub.) radio play. 2001.
—. *Kiran the Bear.* (Unpub.) children's writing. 2002.
—. *The Fisherman.* (Unpub.) radio play. 2003.
—. *Orpheus Road.* (Unpub.) play. 2003.

Relihan, Nora. Contemporary. Kerry. Travel writing.

A native Kerry woman, she was commissioned to travel through the county, talk to the people there and broadcast her reports on radio. These reports subsequently appeared in published form. She trained as a nurse and also worked as a social worker with the National Council for the Blind. She is the founding chairman of St John's Theatre and Arts Centre in Listowel, and was also a founder of the renowned Writers' Week annual literary festival in that town. She has also won awards as actor and director, and has toured with her one-woman show in Ireland, London and New York.

Select bibliography
Relihan, Nora.
—. *Signposts to Kerry.* Travel writing. Cork: Mercier, 2001.

Richard, Mrs Victor, née Moore. fl. 1915–50. Cork. Novels, historical novel.

Born in Mitchelstown, Co. Cork, she was the daughter of a clergyman. She married Colonel Rickard, who was killed at Rue du Bois in May 1915. One of her novels, *The Story of the Munsters at Etreux, Fesubert, and Rue du Bois* (1915), was based on this battle. She was a prolific novelist and a resident of Cork, according to a catalogue on Cork writers of the twentieth century published in Cork in 1957.

Select bibliography
Richard, Mrs Victor.
—. *The Story of the Munsters at Etreux, Fesubert, and Rue du Bois.* Historical novel. Dublin: New Ireland, 1915. London: Hodder & Stoughton, 1918.
—. *Sorel's Second Husband.* Novel. London: Jarrolds, 1936.
—. *White Satin.* Novel. London: Jarrolds, 1945.
—. *Shandon Hall.* Novel. London: Jarrolds, 1950.

Richards, Maura, née O'Dea. Contemporary. Mitchelstown, Co. Cork. Novels, political writing.

Born in 1939 in Mitchelstown, Co. Cork. Having moved to Dublin in 1968, Richards had a daughter in 1970, and later wrote a fictionalized account of single motherhood in Ireland in the 1970s, *Two to Tango* (1981). She was involved in setting up Cherish, a group for single mothers, in the 1970s, and she later wrote *Single Issue* (1998), which also addresses single parenthood. Her second novel, *Interlude* (1982), is a lesbian novel.

Select bibliography
Richards, Maura.
—. *Two to Tango*. Novel. Dublin: Ward River Press, 1981.
—. *Interlude*. Novel. 1982.
—. *Single Issue*. Social history. Dublin: Poolbeg, 1998.

Richardson, Ita. Contemporary. Limerick. Academic writing.

Completed a PhD in 1999 and is currently Senior Lecturer in computer engineering at UL. She has been living in Limerick since 1979.

Select bibliography
Richardson, Ita.
—. "Software Process Matrix: A Small Company SPI Model." Academic writing. *Software Process: Improvement and Practice* 6.3 (2001).
—. "Development of a Generic Quality Function Deployment Matrix." Academic writing. *Quality Management Journal* 9.2 (2002).
—. "Software Processes in Very Small Companies." Academic writing. *Software Quality Professional* 4.2 (2002).

Riggs, Pádraigín. Comhaimseartha. Baile Thiobraid Árann, Co. Thiobraid Árann agus Cathair Chorcaí. Scríbhneoireacht acadúil.

Saolaíodh i 1949 í. Is as Baile Thiobraid Árann í. Chuaigh sí ar scoil i dTiobraid Árann agus i nDún Bleisce. Bhain sí dochtúireacht amach i gColáiste na hOllscoile, Corcaigh. Is Léachtóir Sinsearach í anois i Roinn na Nua-Ghaeilge san Ollscoil sin.

Select bibliography
Riggs, Pádraigín.
—. *Bua an tSeanchaí: tráchtaireacht agus treoir don leabhar 'Bullaí Mhártain' le Síle agus Donncha Ó Céileachair*. Scríbhneoireacht acadúil. Corcaigh: Cló Mercier, 1974.
—. eag. *An Chéad Chloch: Pádraic Ó Conaire*. Scríbhneoireacht acadúil. Le Pádraig Ó Conaire. Baile Átha Cliath: Mercier, 1978.
—. *Donncha Ó Céileachair: Anailís Stíleach*. Scríbhneoireacht acadúil. Baile Átha Cliath: An Gúm, 1978.
—. "An Deoraíocht i Saothar Phádraic Uí Chonaire." *Léachtaí Cuimhneacháin*. Scríbhneoireacht acadúil. Eag. Gearóid Denvir. Conamara, 1983. 19–29.
—. "Gnéithe de Theicníocht Reacaireachta Uí Chonaire." *Irisleabhar Mhá Nuad*. Scríbhneoireacht acadúil. Eag. Pádraig Ó Fiannachta. Má Nuad, 1984. 21–8.
—. "Ón bhFoirmiúlachas go dtí an Struchtúrachas." Scríbhneoireacht acadúil. *Comhar* Nollaig (1984): 25–8.
—. "File Eibhlín." Scríbhneoireacht acadúil. *Comhar* 4 (1986): 14–16.
—. "Nóra Uí Chonaire." Scríbhneoireacht acadúil. *Oghma* (1989): 35–42.
—. *Pádraic Ó Conaire: Deoraí*. Scríbhneoireacht acadúil. Baile Átha Cliath: An Clóchomhar, 1994.
—. "Imaginary Heroes: A New Look at the Representation of the Heroic in Two Stories by the Gaelic Writer Donncha Ó Céileachair." Scríbhneoireacht acadúil.

L'Irlande: Imagination et Representation, ouvrage publié avec le concours du Centre d'Etudes et de Recherche irlandaise de Lille III (C.E.R.U.L.) de la Societé Francaise d'Etudes Irlandaises (1997): 135–142.

—. "The Beginnings of the Society." *Irish Texts Society: The First Hundred Years.* Scríbhneoireacht acadúil. Eag. Pádraig Ó Riain. London: Irish Texts Society, 1998. 2–35.

—. "Adhlacadh mo Mháthar." *Saoi na hÉigse: Aistí in Ómós do Sheán Ó Tuama.* Scríbhneoireacht acadúil. Eag. Pádraigín Riggs, Seán Ó Coileáin agus Breandán Ó Conchúir. Baile Átha Cliath: An Clóchomhar, 2000. 327–37.

—. le Seán Ó Coileáin agus Breandán Ó Conchúir, eag. *Saoi na hÉigse: Aistí in Ómós do Sheán Ó Tuama.* Scríbhneoireacht acadúil. Baile Átha Cliath: An Clóchomhar, 2000.

—. "Caint na nDaoine: an Chaint agus na Daoine." *Aimsir Óg.* Scríbhneoireacht acadúil. Eag. Mícheál Ó Cearúil. 2001.

—. eag. *Dáibhí Ó Bruadair: His Historical and Literary Context.* Scríbhneoireacht acadúil. Irish Texts Society subsidiary series 11. London: Irish Texts Society, 2001.

—. "Pádraic Ó Conaire agus an Páipéar Buí." Scríbneoireacht acadúil. *Feasta* V (2003): 67–70.

"Deoraíocht." *Encyclopaedia of Ireland.* Scríbhneoireacht acadúil. Ed. B. Lalor. Dublin: n.p., 2003.

Secondary sources
Ó Muirí, Pól. "Léirmheas ar *Pádraic Ó Conaire: Deoraí.*" *Anois* Samhain (1995).
Uí Nia, Gearóidín, eag. "Riggs, Pádraigín." *Eolaire Chló Iar-Chonnachta de Scríbhneoirí Gaeilge.* Indreabhán: Chló Iar-Chonnachta, 1998.

Roche, Adi. Contemporary. Cork city. Political writing.

Born in Clonmel in 1955, Adi (Adrienne) was educated locally and in Dublin. She worked for Aer Lingus from 1975 to 1983, and then took voluntary redundancy to work as a full-time volunteer with the Irish Compaign for Nuclear Disarmament. She is now executive director of the Chernobyl Children's Project, which assists children suffering from the radioactive fall-out which followed the Chernobyl reactor explosion in 1986. She has written an account of this disaster and its aftermath and has also appeared in television documentaries on RTÉ and BBC. She has received several humanitarian awards, and in 1997 she was an unsuccessful candidate in the Irish presidential election.

Select bibliography
Roche, Adi.
—. *Children of Chernobyl: The Human Cost of the World's Worst Nuclear Disaster.* Political writing. London: Fount, 1996.

Roche, Regina Maria, née Dalton. 1764–1845. Waterford. Novels.

Born in Waterford, the daughter of Captain Blundell Dalton, she moved with her family to Dublin as a child. She married Ambrose Roche *c.*1794, and they moved to England. Her first two novels, written before she married, were ascribed to her father, as, she said, they were written: "at so early a period that those not acquainted with my dear father ascribed [them] to him". Read today as a minor Gothic and sentimental novelist, her third and best-known novel, *The Children of the Abbey* (1796), rivalled the popularity of Ann Radcliffe's *The Mysteries of Udolpho* (1794) during the period. Read well into the nineteenth century, both *Children of the Abbey* and *Clermont* (1798) went through several editions, and were translated into both French and Spanish.

Roche did not publish between 1800 and 1807, which is thought to be a result of financial difficulties caused by an unscrupulous solicitor. She resumed her writing career thanks to aid she received from the Royal Literary Fund, continuing to publish until 1834. She moved back to Ireland in the 1820s, and her later works have regional Irish settings. Her husband died in 1829, and she refers to her own ill-health in the preface to *Contrast* (1828), describing "long nights of sickness and privation". Jane Austen refers disparagingly to Roche's work on two separate occasions: *The Children of the Abbey* was one of Harriet Smith's favourite novels in *Emma* (1816), and *Clermont* was one of the "horrid novels" in *Northanger Abbey* (1818). However, Roche's popularity as a writer did not last, and when she died, in Waterford at the age of 81, her literary success was long forgotten. Her obituary in the July 1845 issue of *The Gentleman's Magazine* describes her as a "distinguished writer [who] had retired from the world and the world had forgotten her".

London Tales: or Reflective Portraits, 2 vols.(1814); *Plain Tales by Mrs Roche*, 2 vols. (1814); and *Anna, or Edinburgh: A Novel*, 2 vols. (1815), have also been attributed to Roche, but according to Connolly "were almost certainly written by another author, styling herself as Mrs Roche" (*Cambridge Bibliography of English Literature*, 990).

Select bibliography

Roche, Regina Maria.
—. *The Vicar of Landsdown: or, Country Quarters*. Baltimore: n.p., 1789. N.p.: n.p., 1802. [Trans. French 1789, German 1790.]
—. *The Maid of the Hamlet: A Tale*. 2 vols. N.p.: n.p., 1793. [Trans. French 1801.]
—. *The Children of the Abbey*. Novel. 2 vols. Cork: n.p., 1796 (2nd ed. 1798). [Trans. French 1797.]
—. *Clermont: A Tale*. Novel. 4 vols. 1798. [Trans. French 1798.] Notes: 1968 reprint ed. D.R. Varma.
—. *Nocturnal Visit: A Tale*. Novel. 4 vols. N.p.: n.p., 1800. [Trans. French, German 1801.]
—. *Alvondown Vicarage: A Novel*. Novel. N.p.: n.p., 1807. Notes: Published anonymously.
—. *The Discarded Son, or the Haunt of the Banditti: A Tale*. Novel. 5 vols. N.p.: n.p., 1807. [Trans. French 1820.]
—. *The Houses of Osma and Almeria: or, The Convent of St Ildefonso; A Tale*. Novel. 1 vol. Philadelphia: n.p., 1810.
—. *The Monastery of St Columb: or, The Atonement; A Novel*. Novel. 2 vols. New York and Philadelphia: n.p., 1812.
—. *Trecothick Bower: or The Lady of the West Country*. Novel. 3 vols. Philadelphia and Boston: n.p., 1814.
—. *The Munster Cottage Boy: A Tale*. Novel. 4 vols. N.p.: n.p., 1819.
—. *Bridal of Dunamore, and Lost and Won: Two Tales*. Short stories. 3 vols. N.p.: n.p., 1823. [Trans. French 1824.]

—. *The Tradition of the Castle: or, Scenes in the Emerald Isle.* Novel. N.p.: n.p., "1824" [1823.]. [Trans. French 1824.]
—. *The Castle Chapel: A Romantic Tale.* Novel. 3 vols. N.p.: n.p., 1825. [Trans. French 1825.]
—. *Contrast.* Novel. 2 vols. N.p.: n.p., 1828.
—. *The Nun's Picture.* Novel. 3 vols. N.p.: n.p., 1836. N.p.: n.p., 1843.

Rohan, Dorine, née Reihill. *fl.* **1969–74.** Midleton, Co. Cork. Social history, novel, journalism.

Born in Co. Cork in 1942, she was educated at home and in Killiney, Co. Dublin. She studied French at the Sorbonne, and also went to Spain to learn Spanish. She wrote freelance articles for Irish newspapers, magazines and journals in the late 1960s, and also wrote at least one novel, *Barriers Within* (1974). Her other full-length publication, *Marriage Irish-Style* (1969), was a sociological analysis of sexuality and marriage in an Irish context and the impact of the Catholic church on Irish social life. There is an extract of the latter in *Field Day IV*.

Select bibliography
Rohan, Dorine.
—. *Marriage Irish-Style.* Social history. Cork: Mercier, 1969.
—. *Barriers Within.* Novel. Dublin: Mercier, 1974.

Ronayne, Sr Mary Christina [S.M. Christina, Cape Yland]. *fl.* **1905–14.** Cork. Fiction

A member of the community of the Loreto Convent, Fermoy, Co. Cork, she published only one volume of short stories but contributed many series to periodicals, particularly Catholic magazines of the day. According to Brown, she was "an enthusiast for a literature which, while genuinely Irish, should also be Catholic in spirit" (620). She wrote serial stories for both English and French periodicals. Of these, "Kilvara", "The Forbidden Flame", "A Modern Cinderella", "Sir Rupert's Wife" and "A Steel King" were all Irish in subject. Her themes involve secret marriages, lost papers, lost and found heirs, as well as conversion to Catholicism. She also published short stories in French, which include "Une gerbe de lis" and "Mis à l'épreuve". She died in 1917.

Select bibliography
Ronayne, Sr Mary Christina.
—. *Lord Clandonnell.* Novel. London: Washborne, 1914.

Secondary sources
Anon. "Obituary." *Irish Book Lover* 8–10 (1917): 120.

Rose, Catherine. Contemporary. Cork. Political writing.

Born in Cork in 1944, she was educated there. She founded Arlen House in 1975 in Galway, Ireland's first feminist publishing house. In 1975 Rose also published her own feminist work, *The Female Experience.* She went on to work as a freelance writer and broadcaster, and joined RTÉ Radio as a features and current affairs producer. She is the CEO of Age and Opportunity, a national organization which promotes active participation by the elderly in society.

Select bibliography
Rose, Catherine.
—. *The Female Experience: The Story of the Woman Movement in Ireland.* Political writing. Galway: Arlen House, 1975.

Rowe, Veronica, née Hardy. Contemporary. Crusheen, Co. Clare. Handcrafts.

Spent her childhood in Crusheen, Co. Clare, near the home of her maternal grandmother, Florence Vere O'Brien, who was prominent in the Limerick lace industry. Veronica Rowe pursued her studies in textile design in Scotland, and later worked in the weaving business in Ireland. She won an Arts Council bursary to study in France and Italy, and obtained a diploma in the history of European painting. She has played a significant role in the crafts industry of Ireland and has organized exhibitions of lace in Dublin, Co. Clare and Co. Down. Apart from the text on Limerick lace, co-authored with Nellie Ó Cléirigh (*q.v.*), she has written several articles on the subject.

Select bibliography
Rowe, Veronica.
—. *Clare Embroidery.* Handcrafts. N.p.: n.p., 1985.
—. and Nellie Ó Cléirigh. *Limerick Lace: A Social History and a Maker's Manual.* Handcrafts. Gerrards Cross, Bucks.: Colin Smythe, 1995.

Ruiséal, Máire [Bean Uí Luing / Uí Lúbhaing, "Máire an Tobair"]. 1856–1946. Corca Dhuibhne, Co. Chiarraí. Scéalaíocht / béaloideas.

In Arda Mór a saolaíodh Máire, agus tar éis di cúpla babhta a chaitheamh in aimsir phós sí Seán Ó Luing, Dún Chaoin. I dtigh in aice le Tobar an Chéirín a mhaireadar. Bhí muirear mór orthu agus chuaigh a bhformhór go Meiriceá. Óna hathair a fuair Máire na seanscéalta agus bhí scéalta agus paidreacha ag a deirfiúr, Cáit Ruiséal, leis. Seanaintín leis an scéalaí Bab Feiritéar ab ea í.

Bhailigh Heinrich Wagner scéalta uaithi agus foilsíodh iad in *Oral Literature from Dunquin, Co. Kerry.* Ba iad Peig Sayers, Séamus Ó Lúbhaing agus Tomás Ó Lúbhaing na faisnéiseoirí eile. Bhailigh Proinsias Ó Raghalla scéalta uaithi, "Scéal an Bhullaí Mhóir Bháin" i 1928 agus "Poll Connor" agus "An Tórramh Bréagach" i 1929 agus foilsíodh iad in *Béaloideas* 1 (1928) agus in *Béaloideas* 2 (1929). Cuireadh scéal léi i gcló sa *Field Day Anthology*, Iml. 4 freisin.

Select bibliography
Ruiséal, Máire.
—. scéalaí. "Scéal an Bhullaí Mhóir Bháin." Scéalaíocht / béaloideas. *Béaloideas* 1.3 (1928): 286–9.
—. scéalaí. "Dhá Sgéal Ó Dhún Chaoin, Co. Chiarraighe: 'Poll Connor' agus 'An Tórramh Bréagach'." Scéalaíocht / béaloideas. *Béaloideas* 2.1 (1929): 52–5.

—. "Scéalta léi." *Oral Literature from Dunquin, Co. Kerry: Gaelic Texts with Phonetic Transcription, English Summaries and Folkloristic Notes by H. Wagner and N. Mac Congail.* Scéalaíocht / béaloideas. Eag. Heinrich Wagner agus Niall Mac Congail. Béal Feirste: IIS, 1983.
—. scéalaí. "An Tórramh Bréagach." *Field Day Anthology IV.* Scéalaíocht / béaloideas. Eag. Angela Bourke *et al.* Cork: Cork UP, 2002.

Secondary sources
Almqvist, Bo, agus Roibeárd Ó Cathasaigh, eag. *Ó Bhéal an Bhab: Cnuas-scéalta Bhab Feiritéar.* Scéalaíocht / béaloideas, beathaisnéis. Indreabhán: Cló Iar-Chonnachta, 2002: 15–19.

Ryan, Angela. Contemporary. Cork. Academic writing, literary criticism.

Born in Dublin in 1953, she received a Doctorat ès-lettres from the Université de Bordeaux in 1981. In 1983 she obtained eighth place in France in the post-doctoral Agrégation. She was appointed to the Université de Rennes II in 1981 and to UCC in 1988. In 2001 she was awarded the French Embassy's translation prize, "Prix de l'Ambassade", jointly with Dr Martin Munro. She is currently the convenor of the French Department research seminar. Her research interests include French and comparative literature and thought, myth and subjectivity, traductology, women and the media, and the rhetoric of the body.

Select bibliography
Ryan, Angela.
—. "Kathleen Ni Houlihan and her Discontents: The Heroine in Anglo-Irish Drama." Academic writing. *Alizés* 4 (1992): 21–46.
—. "Translation and Language Courses for Non-Specialist Students: The Implications for University Language Departments." *The Vital Link.* Academic writing. Ed. Angela Chambers and Jean Conaher. Limerick: Limerick UP, 1992. 78–95.
—. *Active Language Teaching Methods for Adult and Third Level Students.* Academic writing. Cork: School of Languages and Literature, NUI Cork, 1994.
—. *A Bibliography of Translation Studies.* Academic writing. Ed. Dr Lynne Bowker. Dublin: St Jerome Publishing, Dublin City University, 1999.

Ryan, Geraldine A. Contemporary. Cork. Academic writing.

Graduated from UCC with an MA in Economics in 1997 and has lectured in the Department of Economics, UCC, since 1998. Her research interests include game theory, business economics, financial economics and applied econometrics.

Select bibliography
Ryan, Geraldine A.
—. "Why Supermarkets Say 'No' to a Price War." *Irish Case Studies: Supplement for Principles of Economics.* Academic writing. Ed. David Begg. 5th ed. London: McGraw-Hill, 1998.
—. *The Effectiveness of Bord Fáilte Advertising: A Special Model Of Advertising 1975–1996.* Academic writing. Working Paper Series. Cork: Dept. of Economics, UCC, 2002.
—. *Irish Stock Returns and Inflation: A Long Horizon Perspective.* Academic writing. Working Paper Series. Cork: Dept. of Economics, UCC, 2002.

Ryan, Margaret Mary [Alice Esmonde, A.E., M.M.R., M.My.R.]. *fl.* **1885–1915.** Ballingarry, Co. Tipperary. Poetry.

Born in Tipperary, she was a most prolific contributor to the *Irish Monthly*, frequently using the name "Alice Esmonde". She published one volume of poems, *Songs of Remembrance* (1889). Tynan compares her work to that of Christina Rossetti (233).

Select bibliography
Ryan, Margaret Mary.
—. *Songs of Remembrance*. Poetry. Dublin: Gill, 1889.

Ryan, Marie. *fl.* **1991.** Millstreet, Co. Cork. Poetry.

Born in 1936, she published a poetry collection, *The Millstream*, in 1991.

Select bibliography
Ryan, Marie.
—. *The Millstream*. Poetry. Millstreet, Co. Cork: Millstream Press, 1991.

Ryan, Mary. *fl.* **1913–55.** Cork. Academic writing, religious writing.

Born in Rochestown, Cork, in 1873, she was educated in Cork, Berlin and in Neuilly-sur-Seine in France, and she joined the staff of UCC as a lecturer in German in 1909. She and her colleague Dr Lucy Smith became the first women officers of residence at the university the same year. The following year Ryan was appointed Professor of Romance Languages, the first woman to hold a chair in Ireland and the United Kingdom. She held this post until 1938. In 1935 the French Government, in recognition of her services in the cause of French culture, conferred on her the Order of the Légion d'Honneur.

Select bibliography
Ryan, Mary.
—. "A German Nun at the Reformation." Academic writing. *Studies* 2 (1913): 384–401.
—. "A Dante Discovery." Academic writing. *Studies* 10 (1921): 425.
—. "René Bazin 1953–1932." Academic writing. *Studies* 21 (1932): 627–34.
—. "The Catholic University of the Sacred Heart (Milan) and Its Founder." Academic writing. *Studies* 23 (1934): 634–48.
—. "Ludovico Necchi." Academic writing. *Studies* 24 (1935): 642–53.
—. *Alfred Noyes on Voltaire*. Academic writing. Dublin: Browne & Nolan, 1938.
—. "Alfred Noyes on Voltaire." Academic writing. *Studies* 28 (1939): 85–97.
—. "Some Impressions of Albania." Memoir. *Studies* 28 (1939): 293–302.
—. "A Topical Book." Religious writing. *Irish Rosary* 44 (1940): 666–71.
—. "In Defence of Paschal." Religious writing. *Irish Rosary* 45 (1941): 17–30.
—. "The Mother of a Saint." Religious writing. *Irish Rosary* 45 (1941): 934–42.
—. *Our Lady's Hours: An Introduction to the Little Office of Our Lady*. Religious writing. Cork: Forum, 1941.
—. *Out of the Depths: Notes on the Office of the Dead*. Religious writing. Cork: Forum, 1942.
—. "Random Recollections." Memoir. *Cork University Record* 5 (1945): 15–19.
—. trans. *The Intellectual Life: Its Spirit, Conditions, Methods by A. D. Sertillanges O.P.* Academic writing. Cork: Mercier, 1946.

—. "Doctrine and Life." Religious writing. *Irish Rosary* 53 (1949): 103–8, 166–71.
—. *Introduction to Paul Claudel.* Academic writing. Cork: Cork UP, 1951.
—. "Claudel, Poet of Love." Academic writing. *Studies* 42 (1953): 440–45.
—. "Man of Vision." Religious writing. *Irish Rosary* 58 (1954): 135–9.
—. "Paul Claudel." Academic writing. *Studies* 44 (1955): 143–50.

Ryan, Meda. Contemporary. Bandon, Co. Cork; Ennis, Co. Clare. Biography, history, journalism.

Born into a political family, she grew up knowing many of the participants in the Irish independence movement. In the mid-1970s and early 1980s she wrote a weekly column for the *Clare Champion.* She was also a freelance education correspondent to the *Cork Examiner* around that time and contributed articles to numerous magazines and journals. She delivered a lecture at the Celtic Women's International Conference in 1989 and again in 2001 and has been made an honorary member of Celtic Women International. Her published writings include biographies of three political figures from Irish history, Michael Collins, Tom Barry and Liam Lynch, and she has also written a biography of Biddy Early. Her recently published biography of Tom Barry, which is based on his private papers, will, she believes, clarify some of the controversies that have arisen since his death.

Select bibliography
Ryan, Meda.
—. *Biddy Early: The Wise Woman of Clare.* Biography. Cork: Mercier, 1978.
—. *The Real Chief: The Story of Liam Lynch.* Biography. Cork: Mercier, 1986.
—. *The Day Michael Collins Was Shot.* History. Dublin: Poolbeg, 1989.
—. *Michael Collins and the Women in His Life.* Biography. Cork: Mercier, 1996.
—. *Tom Barry: Column Commander and IRA Freedom Fighter.* Cork: Mercier, 2003.

Ryves, Francis Catherine, née Harding. *fl.* 1812. Limerick. Poetry.
Wife of William Ryves of Ryves Castle (Castlejane), Ballyskiddane, Limerick. She was a poet and author of *Cumbrian Legends; or, Tales of Other Times* (1812), which she wrote following a visit to the Lake District in the early 1800s. It was published by subscription in Edinburgh.

Select bibliography
Ryves, Francis Catherine.
—. *Cumbrian Legends; or, Tales of Other Times.* Poetry. Edinburgh: n.p., 1812.

Saors, Joan. *fl.* 1935. Baile na nGall, Co. Chiarraí. Seanchas / béaloideas, paidreacha.

Bhí sí ina cónaí ar an mBóthar Buidhe, Baile na nGall i 1923 nuair a bhailigh an Bráthair Lúcás paidreacha uaithi. Foilsíodh iad in *Béaloideas* 5 (1935).

Select bibliography
Saors, Joan.
—. seanchaí. "Sean-phaidreacha: 'Na Seacht nDóláig' agus 'Ortha na Fiacaile'." Seanchas / béaloideas, paidreacha. *Béaloideas* 5.2 (1935): 215.

Sargent, Maud Elizabeth. *fl.* **1908.** New Ross, Co. Waterford.
Lived in New Ross, and published one volume of poetry (Colman, 198).
Select bibliography
Sargent, Maud Elizabeth.
—. *Shamrocks and Roses.* Poetry. London, 1908.

Sayers, Peig [Uí Ghuithín / Uí Ghaoithín, Peig]. **1873–1958.** Corca
Dhuibhne, Co. Chiarraí. Beathaisnéis, scéalaíocht agus seanchas /
béaloideas.

Saolaíodh Peig i mBaile Bhiocáire, Dún Chaoin. Ba é Tomás Sayers a
hathair agus ba í Peig Ní Bhrosnacháin a máthair. Bhí 13 leanaí acu, cé nár
mhair ach ceathrar. D'fhreastail Peig ar bhunscoil Dhún Chaoin agus
chuaigh sí in aimsir ansin go dtí an Daingean. D'fhan sí ann ag obair ar
feadh ceithre bliana, ach theip an tsláinte uirthi agus b'éigean di filleadh ar
thigh a muintire. Chuaigh sí in aimsir don tarna huair ach ní raibh na
coinníollacha oibre rómhaith an uair sin. Deineadh cleamhnas di le Peatsaí
"Flint" Ó Guithín ón mBlascaod Mór. Phósadar sa bhliain 1892 agus is ar
an oileán a bhíodar ina gcónaí. Bhí muintir a céile in aontíos leo, agus bhí
deichniúr leanaí ag Peig, cé gur cailleadh ceathrar acu go hóg. Ní raibh
cúrsaí sláinte go maith ag Peatsaí agus d'éag sé tamall de bhlianta roimh
bhás Pheig. Thit mac amháin léi, Tomás, le haill go tubaisteach. Chuaigh a
páistí eile ar imirce go Meiriceá, ach d'fhill a mac, Micheal, ar Éirinn tar éis
tamaill. Chuaigh Peig agus Mícheál, nó "Maidhc File" mar ab fhearr aithne
air, chun cónaithe go dtí an mhíntír sa bhliain 1942. Cailleadh Peig in
ospidéal an Daingin agus tá sí curtha i nDún Chaoin.

Chuir cuairteoirí chun an oileáin aithne ar Pheig agus bhíodar tógtha léi
mar chainteoir Gaeilge, mar scéalaí agus mar sheanchaí. Cuireann an
scoláire Robin Flower síos uirthi ina leabhar *The Western Island or the Great
Blasket* (1944). Ba iad Máire Ní Chinnéide agus Léan Ní Chonalláin a
spreag Peig chun a scéal féin a aithris. Chuaigh a mac, Maidhc, i mbun
pinn chun deachtú Pheig a thaifeadadh. Ba í Máire Ní Chinnéide a chuir
an leabhar in eagar. Bhuaigh *Peig* duais an Chraoibhín i 1937. Bhí sé ar
shiollabas na hArdteiste ar feadh na mblianta agus d'aistrigh Bryan Mac
Mahon go Béarla é i 1974. Deineadh giorrú agus cinsireacht áirithe ar an
saothar seo nuair a d'eagraigh Máire Ní Chinnéide é le haghaidh siollabas
na meánscoile. Is ceist shuimiúil í an mó smachta a bhí ag Peig ar a téacs
féin. Tá na scoláirí a leanas tar éis tionchar Mhaidhc ar an leabhar a phlé:
Muiris Mac Conghail, Pádraig Ó Fiannachta agus Patricia Coughlan in
Oidhreacht an Bhlascaoid (1989).

Tháinig *Machnamh Seanamhná* amach don chéad uair i 1939, agus bhí
Máire Ní Chinnéide i mbun eagarthóireachta arís. D'aistrigh Séamus Ennis
go Béarla é. Béaloideas agus dinnseanchas atá sa leabhar seo. Thug bailitheoirí
éagsúla béaloidis cuairt ar Pheig: Kenneth Jackson, Robin Flower agus
Seosamh Ó Dálaigh ina measc. Cuireadh a cuid cainte ar cheirnín freisin le
craoladh ar Raidió Éireann. Deineadh an taifeadadh seo i mBaile Bhiocáire

agus in ospidéal an Daingin. Maidir le saibhreas agus líofacht teangan, deirtear go raibh foclóir de thríocha míle focal aici ina ceann. Dhein Muiris Mac Conghail físeán ar Pheig "Oileán Eile – Another Island" do RTÉ (Baile Átha Cliath,1984). Dhein Breandán Feiritéar clár faisnéise ar Pheig, "The Voices of the Generations – the Story of Peig Sayers", a craoladh ar an 8 Nollaig, 1998 agus clár dráma-faisnéise don teilifís "Slán an Scéalaí" i 1998. Tá 160 scéal neamhfhoilsithe ó Pheig, a bhailigh Seosamh Ó Dálaigh, i dtaisce i gCartlann Choimisiún Bhéaloideas Éireann.

Select bibliography
Sayers, Peig.
—. scéalaí. "Scéalta ón mBlascaod." Scéalaíocht / béaloideas. *Béaloideas* 2.1 (1929): 97–101.
—. scéalaí. "Sgéalta ón mBlascaod: 'Buile Luath an Luain agus Buile Déanach an tSathairn', 'Seathrún Céitinn' agus 'An Dá Chrann'." Scéalaíocht / béaloideas. *Béaloideas* 2.2 (1929): 199–206.
—. scéalaí. "Sgéalta ón mBlascaod: 'Conas Mar Fuair Seán Ó Briain Bean', 'An Bhean Leighis' agus 'An Bheirt Driféar'." Scéalaíocht / béaloideas. *Béaloideas* 2.4 (1930): 373–80.
—. scéalaí. "Dhá Scéal ón mBlascaod: 'An Tarbh Druíochta' agus 'An Pailitíneach agus an Buachaill Aimsire'." Scéalaíocht / béaloideas. *Béaloideas* 4.3 (1934): 299–311.
—. scéalaí. *Peig .i. a scéal féin do scríobh Peig Sayers.* Beathaisnéis. Eag. Máire Ní Chinnéide. Baile Átha Cliath: Clólucht an Talbóidigh, 1936.
—. scéalaí. *Peig: tuairisc a thug Peig Sayers ar imeachtaí a beatha féin.* Beathaisnéis. 1936. Eag. Máire Ní Chinnéide. Baile Átha Cliath: Comhlucht Oideachais na hÉireann, 1950.
—. scéalaí. *Scéalta ón mBlascaod.* Scéalaíocht / béaloideas. 1938. Scríofa síos ag Kenneth Jackson. Baile Átha Cliath: Cumann le Béaloideas Éireann, 1998.
—. scéalaí. *Machnamh seanamhná.* Beathaisnéis. 1939. Eag. Máire Ní Chinnéide. Baile Átha Cliath: Oifig an tSoláthair, 1980.
—. scéalaí. *Peig: The Autobiography of Peig Sayers of the Great Blasket Island.* Beathaisnéis. 1974. Aist. Bryan Mac Mahon. Baile Átha Cliath: Talbot, 1983.
—. *An Old Woman's Reflections.* Beathaisnéis. Aist. Séamus Ennis. Oxford: Oxford UP, 1978.
—. scéalaí. *Machnamh Seanmhná.* Beathaisnéis. Eag. Pádraig Ua Maoileoin. Baile Átha Cliath: Oifig an tSoláthair, 1980.
—. *So irisch wie ich: Eine Fischersfrau erzählt ihr Leben.* Scéalaíocht / béaloideas. Aist. Göttingen: Lamuv Verlag, 1996.
—. scéalaí. *Peig: a scéal féin.* Beathaisnéis. Eag. Máire Ní Mhainnín agus Liam P. Ó Murchú. An Daingean: An Sagart, 1998.
—. *Peig: autobiographie d'une grande conteuse d'Irlande; traduit de l'anglais par Joëlle Gac.* Beathaisnéis. Aist. J. Gac. Releg-Kerhuon: An Here, 1999.

Secondary sources
Boylan, Henry. "Sayers, Peig." *A Dictionary of Irish Biography.* 3rd. ed. Dublin: Gill & Macmillan, 1998. 391–2.
Breathnach, Diarmuid, agus Máire Ní Mhurchú. "Sayers, Peig (1873–1958)." *1882–1982 Beathaisnéis a Cúig.* Baile Átha Cliath: An Clóchomhar, 1997.
Coughlan, Patricia. "An Cur Síos ar Shaol na mBan i dTéacsanna Dírbheathaisnéise Pheig Sayers." *Oidhreacht an Bhlascaoid.* Eag. Aogán Ó Muircheartaigh. Baile Átha Cliath: Coiscéim, 1989.

Cleeve, Brian. "Sayers, Peig." *Dictionary of Irish Writers:Writers in the Irish Language.* Vol. 3. Cork: Mercier, 1971.

Mac Conghail, Muiris. *The Blaskets: People and Literature [The Blaskets: A Kerry Island].* Baile Átha Cliath: Country House, 1987. 2 ed., 1994.

Mac Mahon, Bryan. "Peig Sayers and the Vernacular of the Story Teller." *Literature and Folk Culture.* Eag. Alison Feder agus Bernice Schrank. St John's: Memorial University of Newfoundland, 1977. 83–109.

Ní Chéilleachair, Máire, eag. *Peig Sayers Scéalaí 1973–1958.* Ceiliúradh an Bhlascaoid. Baile Átha Cliath: Coiscéim, 1999. 111.

Ó Dálaigh, Seosamh. "Cuntas ar ar bhailigh Flower ó Pheig." *Oidhreacht an Bhlascaoid.* Eag. Aogán Ó Muircheartaigh. Baile Átha Cliath: Coiscéim, 1989.

Ó Fiannachta, Pádraig. "Aiste ar Pheig Sayers." *Oidhreacht an Bhlascaoid.* Eag. Aogán Ó Muircheartaigh. Baile Átha Cliath: Coiscéim, 1989.

Ó Gadhra, Seán. *Dúchas Pheig Mhóir: tráchtaireacht agus treoir don leabhar "Peig" le Peig Sayers.* Corcaigh: Mercier, 1972.

Ó Gaoithín, Mícheál. *Beatha Pheig Sayers.* Baile Átha Cliath: Foilseacháin Náisiúnta, 1970.

Wagner, Heinrich, agus Niall Mac Congail, eag. *Oral Literature from Dunquin, Co. Kerry: Gaelic Texts with Phonetic Transcription, English Summaries and Folkloristic Notes by H.Wagner and N. Mac Congail.* Béal Feirste: IIS, 1983.

Scannell, Yvonne. Contemporary. Kerry. Academic writing.

Born in Tralee in 1948, she has been Associate Professor of Law at TCD since 1998 and has won many distinctions for her work on environmental issues. Among these are the Spirit of Columbus Award for Contribution to the Environment (1994), and the Prix Michel Sepax awarded by the European Council for Environmental Law (2000). Scannell was named as Ireland's Leading Environmental Lawyer in 1997. Formerly chairwoman of the Environment Awareness Bureau and the Women's Political Association, Scannell is currently a member of the Boards of Directors of Forfás and the International and European Councils for Environmental Law. Her writings have been included in various anthologies, including *Ireland's Women – Writings Past and Present* (1994).

Select bibliography
Scannell, Yvonne.
—. *The Law and Practice Relating to Pollution Control in Ireland.* Academic writing. London: Graham & Trotman, 1974.
—. *The World Charter for Nature.* Academic writing. Berlin: Erich Schmidt Verlag, 1986.
—. "The Constitution and the Role of Women." *De Valera's Constitution and Ours.* Academic writing. Ed. Brian Farrell. Dublin: Gill & Macmillan, 1988. 123–36.
—. "Ireland." *International Encyclopedia of Laws.* Academic writing. The Hague: Kluwer, 1994.
—. *Environmental and Planning Law.* Academic writing. Dublin: Round Hall Press, 1995.

Servais, Yvonne. fl. 1953–78. Cork. Academic writing.

From Belgium, she came to UCC as a lectrice in the early 1930s and stayed in Cork for the rest of her life. She obtained her PhD at UCC in

1953 and remained on the staff of the French Department until her retirement. With her colleague Kathleen O'Flaherty (*q.v.*) she edited French poetry school texts for the Intermediate Examination for a number of years.

Select bibliography
Servais, Yvonne.
—. *Charles Péguy: The Pursuit of Salvation*. Academic writing. Cork: Cork UP, 1953.
—. *La dissertation française*. Academic writing. Cork: Cork UP, 1953.
—. *Julien Green: violence, détresse et apaisement*. Academic writing. Paris: Académie Européenne du Livre, 1957.
—. and Kathleen O'Flaherty. *L'explication française*. Academic writing. Cork: Cork UP, 1964.
—. *Péguy sur le chemin des "mystères"*. Academic writing. Cork: Cork UP, 1978.
—. and Kathleen O'Flaherty. *Choix de poèmes avec notices biographiques, notes sur le vocabulaire, explications littéraires et questions*. Academic writing. Dublin: Educational Company of Ireland, n.d.
—. and Kathleen O'Flaherty, eds. *Intermediate Certificate Prescribed French Poems: Annotated French Poetry*. Academic writing. Dublin: Educational Company of Ireland, n.d.

Sexton, Regina. Contemporary. Cork. Cookbooks, academic writing.

Born in 1967, she took a BA in English and History at UCC. Following her graduation she lived in Paris for a year before returning to Ireland. She established a tea house and craft shop in Barryscourt, Cork, and returned to UCC to pursue a postdoctorate degree in food history. Sexton is a food historian and food writer in Cork, and writes a weekly column for the *Irish Examiner*. She presented a successful television series on RTÉ, *A Little History of Irish Food*, and has published a book of the same name.

Select bibliography
Sexton, Regina.
—. and C. Cowan. *Ireland's Traditional Foods: An Exploration of Irish Local and Typical Foods and Drinks*. History. Dublin: Teagasc, 1997.
—. "Gruels and Breads: The Cereal Foodstuffs of Early Historic Ireland." *The Archaeology of Medieval Munster*. History. Ed. Mick A. Monk and John Sheehan. Cork: Cork UP, 1998.
—. "Food and Drink at Irish Weddings and Wakes." *Food and Rites of Passage*. History. Ed. Laura Mason. Devon: Prospect, 2002.
—. *A Little History of Irish Food*. Social history, cookbook. Dublin: Gill & Macmillan, 2002.

Shanahan, Kate. Contemporary. Limerick. Journalism.

Born in 1957 in Limerick, she was educated at UL and at TCD. She worked as a journalist and columnist for the *Irish Press* and *Hot Press*. She is now a current affairs producer in RTÉ.

Select bibliography
Shanahan, Kate.
—. *Crimes Worse Than Death*. Social history. Dublin: Attic, 1994.

Shaw, Charlotte Frances. 1857–1943. Rosscarbery, Co. Cork. Letters.

Born Charlotte Payne Townshend at Derry, a large Georgian house near Rosscarbery in Cork. Her father, Horace Townshend, was descended from a long line of Anglican clergyman. He wrote the *Statistical Survey of the County of Cork* (1810). Her mother thought the social life in West Cork too limited, and constantly urged her husband to move to London, which he refused to do. Leland thus describes Charlotte as being "caught between a socially ambitious and disappointed mother, and a docile, country-loving father", which made for an unhappy childhood at the Big House (114). Charlotte herself finally moved to London in 1877, and was heiress to a considerable estate when her father died while travelling on the Continent in 1885. Her friendship with Beatrice and Sidney Webb brought her into contact with G.B. Shaw, whom she married in 1898. Shaw later wrote *Major Barbara* at Derry in 1905. Charlotte Shaw's letters give us an insight into literary London in the early twentieth century.

Secondary sources
Dunbar, Janet. *Mrs G.B.S. A Biographical Portrait of Charlotte Shaw*. London: Harrap, 1963.

Sheehan, Mary. *fl.* 1931. Cúil Aodha, Co. Chorcaí. Seanchas / béaloideas.

Saolaíodh agus tógadh Mary i gCúil Aodha agus chaith sí tréimhse i Meiriceá. Bhailigh Gearóid Ó Murchadha seanchas uaithi agus d'fhoilsigh sé é in *Béaloideas* 3 (1931).

Select bibliography
Sheehan, Mary.
—. seanchaí. "Véursaí agus Paidreacha ó Iarthar Chorcaighe: 'Sasanach a Dhin an Aoine'." Seanchas / béaloideas. *Béaloideas* 3.2 (1931): 231–2.

Sheehy Skeffington, Hanna. 1877–1946. Templemore, Co. Tipperary. Politics, biography.

Born in Cork in 1877, she was a feminist and pacifist, the daughter of David Sheehy and Bessie McCoy. She grew up in Co. Tipperary, where her father was a mill-owner near Templemore. Her earliest memories were "the sound of the mill-wheel and of the waters of the Suir, the smell of fresh bread from the adjoining bakery" (quoted in Levenson and Nattersad, 5). Her grandfather, a native Irish speaker from Co. Limerick, lived with the family and influenced her youngest sister, Kathleen (Caitlín Ní Shíthigh (*q.v.*)), who later wrote in Irish. When Hanna was in her teens David Sheehy went into politics as an MP for South Meath, and the family moved to Dublin, which is the place more usually associated with her life and work. Hanna studied English literature at TCD, where she took a BA and an MA. Her social life centred on her family and home, where the Sheehys entertained a wide variety of guests, from her father's political colleagues to her university peers. Guests at the "Sunday evenings" in the Sheehy household included Tom Kettle, Cruise O'Brien, James Joyce, and the pacifist and feminist Francis Skeffington, with whom Hanna fell in love. She agreed to marry him in 1903, despite her serious misgivings about the institution of marriage. As a symbol of their commitment to feminist principles, the couple took each other's names on their marriage.

In 1901 she had first met Anna Haslam (*q.v.*), then secretary of the Irish Women's Suffrage and Local Government Association, an important influence in her life. She became involved in the campaign for co-education for women and men, which led to her involvement in the suffrage movement in Dublin, at Haslam's invitation (interestingly, her name had been suggested to Haslam by Ester Roper, the Manchester-based trade-union activist and partner of Eva Gore-Booth). After their marriage the Sheehy-Skeffingtons continued the tradition of "at homes" established in the Sheehy household, and their home became a forum for much radical discussion and networking during the period. Despite her shyness, Hanna Sheehy-Skeffington was much in demand as a public speaker, and she became known as a radical thinker, well versed in international as well as national affairs. Her involvement at a variety of levels in political activism contributed to her growing militancy. She became disenchanted with the Haslams' more liberal organization, and she resigned on political grounds in 1906. In 1908 she and Francis formed the Irish Women's Franchise League with Margaret and James Cousins. Hanna started the IWFL's journal *The Irish Citizen*, which she edited until its demise in 1920. The IWFL was to be a militant feminist group, one of the key organizations which campaigned to include votes for women in the Home Rule Bill. In 1913 Hanna was arrested for protesting at Dublin Castle and imprisoned for three months, where she went on hunger strike and was force-fed under the "Cat and Mouse" Act. On her release, she was dismissed from her job as a teacher.

In 1916, in one of the most famous incidents following the Easter Rising, Francis Sheehy-Skeffington was shot dead in the street by an English army officer, Captain Bowen-Colthurst. He had been trying to stop the looting following the uprising, and was shot because of his highly publicized anti-military stance. Despite her loss, and the fact that she was left to bring up her son alone, Hanna continued with her political activism. She fought the cover-up of her husband's death for years, refusing monetary compensation from the British Government. She published *British Militarism as I Have Known It* in 1917, but it was banned in Ireland and Britain until after the First World War. She travelled to the USA in 1919 to publicize the book, and was arrested and imprisoned in Holloway Gaol on her return.

Following the foundation of the Free State she was firmly Anti-Treaty. During the 1930s she was the assistant editor of the Sinn Féin newspaper *An Phoblacht*, and was imprisoned in Armagh Gaol for breaking a Northern Ireland Exclusion Order (she defied a ban on entering the six counties, put in place because of her political record). In 1943 she stood for election to the Dáil as an Independent candidate – in standing she encouraged other Republicans to do the same. Her platform called for equal pay for equal work, equal opportunities for women, the removal of the marriage ban and the restoration of jury rights, among other demands. The parallels between this agenda and that of the second-wave feminist movement in Ireland in the 1970s illustrates her understanding of the impact of such anti-feminist measures. However, by 1946 a lifetime of struggle and political activism had taken its toll on her body. Until her death that year she continued to work on her memoirs, and took a vital interest in the ongoing strike by the Irish National Teachers Organization.

Select bibliography
Sheehy-Skeffington, Hanna.
—. "Women and the University Question." Political writing. *New Ireland Review* 17.May–Aug. (1902): 148–51.
—. "Irish Secondary Teachers." Academic writing. *Irish Review*. Oct. (1912): 393–8.
—. "The Women's Movement – Ireland." Political writing. *Irish Review*. July (1912): 225–7.
—. "Irish Militants and the War." Political writing. *Irish Citizen* 1 (1915): 391.
—. *British Militarism as I Have Known It*. Political writing. New York: Donnelly Press, 1917.
—. *Impressions of Sinn Féin in America*. Political writing. Dublin: Davis, 1919.
—. "We Did Not Fight." *An Irish Pacifist*. Political writing. Ed. J. Bell. London: Cobden-Sanderson, 1935. 339–53.
—. "Biographical Notice." *Dark and Evil Days*. Biography. Ed. F. Sheehy-Skeffington. Dublin: James Duffy, 1936.
—. "Women in Politics." Political writing. *The Bell* 7 (1943): 143–8.
—. "A Pacifist Dies." *Dublin 1916*. Biography. Ed. R. McHugh. New York: Hawthorne Books, 1966. 276–88.
—. "Reminiscences of an Irish Suffragette." *Votes for Women: Irish Women's Struggle for the Vote*. Political writing. Ed. Andrée D. Sheehy-Skeffington and Rosemary Owens. Dublin: Attic, 1975. 12–26.
—. *Ireland – Present and Future*. Political writing. New York: Donnelly, n.d.

Secondary sources
Levenson, Leah, and Jerry H. Natterstad. *Hanna Sheehy-Skeffington: Irish Feminist*. New York: Syracuse UP, 1986.
Luddy, Maria. *Hannah Sheehy-Skeffington*. Dundalk: Irish Historical Association, 1995.
Ward, Margaret. *Hanna Sheehy-Skeffington: A Life*. Dublin: Attic, 1997.

Shoosmith, Terri. Contemporary. Clare. Novels.

Born in Brighton in 1955, she moved to Ireland in 1989 and lives in Co. Clare.

Select bibliography
Shoosmith, Terri.
—. *Blowin' in the Wind*. Novel. Dublin: Poolbeg, 2000.

Shortland, Gaye. Contemporary. Bandon; Knocknagree, Co. Cork. Novels.

Born in Cork, Gaye (Gabrielle) grew up in Bantry and Bandon in Co. Cork, graduated with an MA in English from UCC and taught at the University of Leeds. She lived in the Niger Republic for sixteen years before returning to Cork. She has written five novels since 1995 and one of them, *Mind That 'tis My Brother* (1995), was performed by the Meridian Theatre in Cork in 2002. She has been an editor with Poolbeg Press since 1998.

Select bibliography
Shortland, Gaye.
—. *Mind That 'tis My Brother*. Novel. Dublin: Poolbeg, 1995.
—. *Turtles All the Way Down*. Novel. Dublin: Poolbeg, 1997.
—. *Polygamy*. Novel. Dublin: Poolbeg, 1998.
—. *Harmattan*. Novel. Dublin: Poolbeg, 1999.
—. "Ned on the Inselberg." Novel extract. *Southword* 3.1 (2001): 33–8.
—. *Rough Rides in Dry Places*. Novel. Dublin: Poolbeg, 2001.

Sigerson, Hester, née Varian. 1828–98. Cork. Poetry.

Sister of Ralph Varian (see Elizabeth Varian (*q.v.*)), she married Dr George Sigerson and they had four children, one of whom died while still a boy. The family lived in Dublin, where Hester was a contributor to many newspapers and periodicals of the day, including the *Harp, Cork Examiner, Irish Fireside, The Gael, Young Ireland* and the *Irish Monthly* (Colman, 229). Her work is also included in Katherine Tynan's edition of *The Cabinet of Irish Literature*. Her two daughters, Dora (later Sigerson-Shorter) and Hester, grew up to become well known writers and artists, and both espoused nationalist politics.

Select bibliography
Sigerson, Hester.
—. *A Ruined Race; or, the Last Macmanus of Drumroosk*. Poetry. London: Ward & Downey, 1889.
—. "A Night in Fortmanus Villas." *Cabinet of Irish Literature*. Poetry. Ed. Katherine Tynan. Vol. 4. London: Gresham, 1903. 33.

Sinclair, Snoo. Contemporary. Kerry. Novels.

Born in Derry in 1931, she wrote murder mysteries in the 1960s, which were published by Hammond but which are now out of print. At that time she also edited trade papers and a woman's page and broadcast various pieces. She was proprietor of a riding school in Derry for twenty years and retired to south-west Kerry after her husband's death. Her most recent work, *Nott* (1998), is a fictional biography of a local figure of legend.

Select bibliography
Sinclair, Snoo.
—. *Nott*. Novel. London: Citrus, 1998.
—. "Alien." *Breacadh: An Anthology of Kerry Voices*. Poetry. Ed. Rosemary Canavan. Tralee: Kerry Co. Council, 2001. 44.

Sjoestedt-Jonval, Marie-Louise [Sjoestedt-Jonval / Sjoestedt, Marie-Louise agus "Máire Fhrancach"]. 1900–1940. Dún Chaoin agus An Blascaod Mór, Corca Dhuibhne, Co. Chiarraí. Scríbhneoireacht acadúil, taighde, teangeolaíocht.

Bhí post ag athair Marie-Louise in ambasáid na Sualainne i bPáras na Fraince agus scríbhneoir ab ea a máthair. Ceaptar go raibh triúr páistí acu. Ghnóthaigh Marie-Louise céim sa Léann Clasaiceach, agus bhí Rúisis agus Seicis ar a toil aici. Dhírigh sí ansin ar an Léann Ceilteach agus foilsíodh aistí léi in *Études Celtiques*. Ceapadh í ina léachtóir i gColáiste na Tríonóide,

Baile Átha Cliath agus chaith sí tréimhsí ama i nDún Chaoin agus ar an mBlascaod Mór chun taighde teangeolaíoch a dhéanamh ar chanúint Chorca Dhuibhne. Bhaist muintir na háite "Máire Fhrancach" uirthi. D'fhoilsigh sí dhá leabhar, *Phonétique d'un Parleur irlandais de Kerry* agus *Déscription d'un Parleur irlandais de Kerry*, chomh maith le dhá aiste mar thoradh ar an staidéar a dhein sí ann. Tháinig leabhar eile uaithi sa bhliain 1940, a d'aistrigh Myles Dillon ón bhFraincis, *Gods and Heroes of the Celts* (1949). Chaith sí bliain ag taisteal ar fud na Rúise lena fear céile, Michel Jonval, a phós sí i 1932. Cailleadh é trí bliana níos déanaí. Chaith sí tréimhse sa Bhreatain Bheag chomh maith. Tá an dealramh air gur chuir sí lámh ina bás féin nuair a bhí sí thar n-ais i bPáras ag obair.

Marie-Louise Sjoestedt's father had a job in the Swedish embassy in Paris, France, and her mother was a writer. It is thought that they had three children. Marie-Louise did a degree in the Classics, and she was also able to speak Russian and Czech. She focused then on Celtic studies, and her essays were published in *Études Celtiques*. She was appointed lecturer in TCD and she spent periods of time in Dunquin and on the Blaskets to conduct linguistic research on the dialect of West Kerry. She became known locally as "Máire Fhrancach". She published two books, *Phonétique d'un parler irlandais de Kerry* (1931) and *Déscription d'un parler irlandais de Kerry* (1938), as well as two essays, as a result of the study she did there. She published another book in 1940, which Myles Dillon translated from the French, *Gods and Heroes of the Celts* (1949). She spent a year travelling around Russia with her husband, Michel Jonval, whom she married in 1932. He died three years later. She spent a period of time in Wales as well. It appears that she committed suicide after she had returned to work in Paris.

Select bibliography
Sjoestedt-Jonval, Marie-Louise.
—. "L'influence de la langue anglaise sur un parleur local irlandais de Kerry." *Etrennes de linguistiques offertes a Emile Benveniste.* Scríbhneoireacht acadúil, teangeolaíocht. 1928.
—. "L'irlande d'aujourd'hui: Gens de la terre et de la côte." Scríbhneoireacht acadúil. *Revue des Deux Mondes* (15 juin 1930): 839–64.
—. *Phonétique d'un parleur irlandais de Kerry.* Scríbhneoireacht acadúil, teangeolaíocht. Paris: Leroux, 1931.
—. "Deux contes en dialecte de l'Ile Blasket." Scríbhneoireacht acadúil, teangeolaíocht. *Revue Celtique* XLIX (1932).
—. *Déscription d'un parleur irlandais de Kerry.* Scríbhneoireacht acadúil, teangeolaíocht. Paris: Librairie Ancienne Honoré Champion, 1938.
—. *Dieux et héros des Celtes.* Scríbhneoireacht acadúil. Paris, 1940.
—. *Gods and Heroes of the Celts* [*Dieux et héros des Celtes*]. Scríbhneoireacht acadúil, léirmheastóireacht. 1940. Aist. Myles Dillon. London: Methuen, 1949.

Secondary sources
Breathnach, Diarmuid, agus Máire Ní Mhurchú. "Sjoestedt-Jonval, Marie-Louise (1900–40)." *1882–1982 Beathaisnéis a Ceathair.* Baile Átha Cliath: An Clóchomhar, 1994.

Ó Lúing, Seán. " Marie-Louise Sjoestedt, Celtic Scholar, 1900–1940." *Journal of the Kerry Archaeological and Historical Society* 20 (1987): 79–83.

Skiddy, Ellen Mary [E.M.S.]. *fl.*1860s. Cork. Poetry.

A contributor to the Cork *Southern Reporter,* she co-authored a volume of poetry with her daughter, Mary Angela Skiddy (*q.v.*).

Select bibliography
Skiddy, Ellen Mary.
—. and Mary Angela Skiddy. *Miscellaneous Poems.* Poetry. Cork: Henry & Coghlan, 1866.

Skiddy, Mary Angela. *fl.*1840s–1860s. Cork.

Daughter of Ellen Mary Skiddy (*q.v.*), she also contributed to the Southern *Reporter* and the *Cork Examiner.* Colman suggests that she is the Miss M. Skiddy whose work is in the anthology *Echoes from Parnassus,* a collection of poetry from the Cork area published in 1849 (Colman, 206). The name Minna Skiddy is also associated with this collection, so this may or may not be the case.

Select bibliography
Skiddy, Mary Angela.
—. contributor. *Echoes from Parnassus: Selected from the Original Poetry of the Southern Reporter.* Cork: *Southern Reporter,* 1849.
—. and Ellen Mary Skiddy. *Miscellaneous Poems.* Poetry. Cork: Henry & Coghlan, 1866.

Slade, Jo. Contemporary. Limerick. Poetry.

A poet and painter, she was born in England in 1952. She was educated in Limerick and pursued third-level studies at the Limerick College of Art and Design, the National College of Art and Design (NCAD), TCD and at Mary Immaculate College, Limerick. She currently lives in Limerick. She was co-editor of *On the Counterscarp: Limerick Writing 1961–1991* (1991) and has published three collections of poetry. Her work also appears in anthologies and has been translated into French and Spanish.

Select bibliography
Slade, Jo.
—. *In Fields I Hear Them Sing.* Poetry. Galway: Salmon Publishing, 1989.
—. *et al.,* eds. *On the Counterscarp: Limerick Writing 1961–1991.* Anthology. Galway: Salmon, 1991.
—. *The Vigilant One.* Poetry. Dublin: Poolbeg, 1994.
—. *Certain Octobers / Parfois en octobre.* Poetry. Galway: Salmon, 1997.

Somerville and Ross [Edith Somerville: "Geilles Herring"; Violet Martin: "Martin Ross"]. 1858–1949; 1862–1915. Castletownshend, Co. Cork. Novels, short stories, biography.

Born in Corfu, in 1858, Edith Oenone Somerville was a member of the Somerville family of Drishane House in Castletownshend, Co. Cork, and she spent most of her life there, moving to the nearby Tally Ho House in

1946 when Desmond Somerville married and settled at Drishane. Her cousin, Violet Martin, belonged to the Martin family of Ross House, in Oughterard, Co. Galway. Their mothers were first cousins, two of seventy grandchildren of Charles Kendal Bushe and Nancy Crampton. While the cousins in Castletownshend comprised a varied and large social group, the Martins had no such extended family at Ross, and Violet's upbringing had been a somewhat quieter existence. Edith was educated privately at home before studying art in London and Paris. She and her sister Ethel spent one term at Alexandra College in Dublin, where Violet Martin had also been educated. Despite their having spent time at the same school, Somerville and Ross did not meet until January 1886, in Castletownshend, but following that first meeting they began a relationship and writing partnership that would last for thirty years. Indeed, even after Violet's death in 1915 Edith continued to publish under both their names, reasoning that her partner remained present to her through automatic writings.

In 1889, they published *An Irish Cousin*, under the pseudonyms "Geilles Herring" and "Martin Ross" (Violet continued to use this pseudonym throughout her life, and was known as Martin to her friends and family). This was popular, and secured them commissions to write travel articles, for which Violet wrote the text and Edith provided the illustrations. Their most famous creation was *Some Experiences of an Irish R[esident]M[agistrate]* (1890). In this, and the series that followed, they "sketched with cruel accuracy an Irish district such as West Cork at the end of the nineteenth century, sparing neither their own class of arrogantly decaying landowners, nor any other" (Cleeve, 118). Violet Martin's sense of humour is evident throughout the work they produced together. *The Real Charlotte* (1894) is one of the finest Irish nineteenth-century novels, with a dark, rather determinist, vision of the world. It drew much critical acclaim, and has been compared with *Middlemarch* (1871–2) and *Cousin Bette* (1847–8) (Hogan, 1133). Material published by Edith following Violet's death, such as *The Big House of Inver* (1925), tends to be more serious in tone.

Edith Somerville's deep connection with her home in West Cork is vividly depicted in her memoirs, *Irish Memories* (1917). Other material written by Somerville and Ross – such as *Some Irish Yesterdays* (1906); the short story "As I was Going to Bandon Fair" in *All on the Irish Shore* (1903); the memoir *Wheel Tracks* (1923); essays in *The Smile and the Tear* (1933); and the memoir *Happy Days!* (1946) – also attest to this. Their prolific writing career together was honoured in 1932, when TCD conferred an Honorary DLitt on Edith, which was posthumously awarded to Violet. The women are buried side by side in the graveyard of St Barrahane's Church, Castletownshend.

Select bibliography

Somerville and Ross.

—. *An Irish Cousin*. Novel. 1889. 2 vols. London: Richard Bentley, 1889. Notes: Somerville used the pseudonym "Geilles Herring".

—. *Some Experiences of an Irish R.M.* Short Stories. London: Longman's Green, 1895.

—. *Naboth's Vineyard*. Novel. London: Spencer Blackett, 1891.
—. *Through Connemara in a Governess Cart*. Travel writing, memoir. London: W.H. Allen, 1892. London: Virago, 1990.
—. *In the Vine Country*. Memoir, travel writing. London: W.H. Allen, 1893.
—. *The Real Charlotte*. Novel. London: Ward & Downey, 1894. Dublin: Farmar, 1999.
—. *Beggars on Horseback*. Travel writing. Edinburgh & London: William Blackwood, 1895.
—. *The Silver Fox*. Novel. London: Lawrence & Bullen, 1898.
—. *A Patrick's Day Hunt*. Short stories. Westminster: Constable, 1902.
—. *All on the Irish Shore*. Short stories. London: Longmans, Green, 1903.
—. *Some Irish Yesterdays*. Memoir. London: Longmans, Green, 1906.
—. *Dan Russell the Fox*. Novel. London: Methuen, 1911.
—. *In Mr Knox's Country*. Short stories. London: Longmans, Green, 1915.
—. *Mount Music*. Novel. London: Longmans, Green, 1919.
—. *Stray Aways*. Essays. London: Longmans, Green, 1920.
—. *Wheel-Tracks*. Memoir. London: Longmans, Green, 1923.
—. *The Big House of Inver*. Novel. London: Heinemann, 1925. Dublin: Farmar, 1999.
—. *French Leave*. Short stories. London: William Heinemann, 1928.
—. *An Incorruptible Irishman: Being an Account of Chief Justice Charles Kendal Bushe (1767–1843), and of his wife, Nancy Crampton*. Biography. London: Nicholson & Watson, 1932.
—. *The Smile and the Tear*. Memoir. London: Methuen, 1933.
—. *Sarah's Youth*. Novel. London: Longmans, Green, 1938.
—. *Notions in Garrison*. Memoir. London: Methuen, 1941.
—. *Happy Days!* Memoir. London: Longmans, Green, 1946.
—. *Maria and Some Other Dogs*. Short stories. London: Methuen, 1949.
—. *Further Experiences of an Irish R.M.* [republished as *The Irish R.M.*]. Short stories. London: Longmans, Green, 1989. London: Abacus, 1908.

Select bibliography
Somerville, Edith.
—. *The Mark Twain Birthday Book*. London: Remington, 1885.
—. *Slipper's ABC of Fox Hunting*. Anthology. London: Longmans, 1903.
—. *The Story of the Discontented Little Elephant*. Children's writing. London: Longmans, Green, 1912.
—. *Irish Memories*. Memoir. London: Longmans, Green, 1917.
—. *An Enthusiast*. Novel. London: Longmans, Green, 1921.
—. *The States Through Irish Eyes*. Boston & New York: Mifflin, 1930.
—. *Notes of the Horn: Hunting Verse, Old and New*. Poetry. London: Peter Davies, 1934.
—. *Records of the Somerville Family of Castle-haven and Drishane from 1174 to 1940*. Cork: Guy, 1940.

Secondary sources
Barlow, J.E.M. "A Memory of Martin Ross". *Country Life* 39.29 (1916): 136.
Cahalan, James M. "Humour with a Gender: Somerville and Ross and *The Irish R.M.*". *Éire-Ireland* 28.3 (1993): 87–102.
Coghill, Sir Patrick. "Somerville and Ross." *Hermathena* 79 (1952): 47–60.
Collis, Maurice. *Somerville and Ross: A Biography*. London: Faber & Faber, 1968.
Cowman, Roz. "The Smell and Taste of Castle T." *Sex, Nation and Dissent in Irish Writing*. Ed. Éibhear Walshe. Cork: Cork UP, 1997. 87–102.
Cronin, John. *Somerville and Ross*. Lewisburg, Pa.: Bucknell U, 1972.

—. "Somerville and Ross: The Real Charlotte." *The Anglo-Irish Novel: The Nineteenth Century*. Vol. 1. Belfast: Appletree, 1980. 135–52.

—. "An Ideal of Art: The Assertion of Realities in the Fiction of Somerville and Ross." *Canadian Journal of Irish Studies* 11.1 (1985): 3–19.

Cummins, Geraldine. *Dr E. OE. Somerville: A Biography*. London: Andrew Dakers, 1952.

Diez Fabre, Silvia. "El mundo de la Ascendancy y *The Real Charlotte*." University of Burgos, Spain, 2000.

Fehlmann, Guy. *Somerville et Ross: Témoins de l'Irlande d'Hier*. Caen: Publications de la Faculté de Lettres et Sciences Humaines de l'Université de Caen, 1970.

Hudson, Elizabeth. *A Bibliography of the First Editions of the works of E. OE. Somerville and Martin Ross*. New York: Sporting Gallery and Bookshop, 1942.

Hughes, Clair. "Hound Voices: The Big House in Three Novels by Anglo-Irish Women Writers." *International Aspects of Irish Literature*. Ed. Toshi Furomoto *et al*. Vol. 1. Gerrard's Cross, Bucks.: Colin Smythe, 1996. 349–55.

Lewis, Gifford, ed. *Somerville and Ross: A Critical Appreciation*. Dublin: Gill & Macmillan, 1980.

—. *Somerville and Ross: The World of the Irish R.M.* London: Penguin, 1987.

—. ed. *The Selected Letters of Somerville and Ross*. London: Faber & Faber, 1989.

—. *Edith Somerville: A Biography*. Dublin: Four Courts Press, 2004.

Lowell, Amy. "To Two Unknown Ladies." *North American Review* (1919): 263.

MacCarthy, B.G. "E.OE. Somerville and Martin Ross." *Studies* 24 (1945): 183–94.

Powell, Violet. *The Irish Cousins: The Books and Background of Somerville and Ross*. London: Heinemann, 1970.

Tynan, Katherine. "Violet Martin (Martin Ross) and E.OE. Somerville." *The Bookman* 50 (1916): 65–66.

Watson, Cresap. "The Collaboration of Edith Somerville and Violet Martin." Trinity College, 1953.

Sparling, Maureen, née Ryan. Contemporary. Limerick. Poetry, memoirs.

Born in Limerick, beside the house where the poet Gerald Griffin was born in the 18th century. She was educated locally and later wrote for the local paper, *The Limerick Leader*. Her writings are closely based on the area where she grew up and from them came the appellation "The Poet Laureate of King's Island". She has written four collections of poetry and two books of short stories. She is also a part-time teacher.

Select bibliography
Sparling, Maureen.
—. *Reflections of Life*. Poetry. N.p.: self-published, 1993.
—. *Tales from King's Island Cottage*. Folklore. Cork: Emperor, 1995.
—. *Ripples in the Sand*. Poetry. N.p.: self-published, 1997.
—. *The Gold Nugget*. Short stories. Limerick: Insignia, 2000.
—. *Echoes of Old Limerick*. Poetry. N.p.: self-published, n.d.
—. *Happy Moments*. Poetry. N.p.: self-published, n.d.

St Leger, Alicia. Contemporary. Cork. History.

Graduated from UCC with an MA in History, and took a PhD in Modern History at the University of Saskatchewan, Canada, in 1989. On her return to Cork in 1990 she began work as a freelance researcher in Irish history.

Select bibliography
St Leger, Alicia.
—. *MacCarthy People and Places*. History. Whitegate, Co. Clare: Ballinakella, 1990.

Stac, An tSiúr de Lourdes. fl. 1975–87. Corca Dhuibhne agus Cathair Saidhbhín, Co. Chiarraí. Beathaisnéis.

"Is dócha gurbh é an leabhar cáiliúil *I Leaped over the Wall* le Monica Baldwin, bean rialta a thréig an saol rialta, a spreag teideal an leabhair ón tSiúr de Lourdes" (Ó hOibicín, 143). D'fhan an tSiúr de Lourdes dílis dá hord, áfach. Is é atá sa leabhar *Thar Balla Isteach* ná cuntas an údair ar a saol mar nóibhíseach agus mar mhúinteoir bunscoile i gCathair Saidhbhín. Ba é an tAthair Pádraig Ó Fiannachta a spreag í chun dul i mbun scríbhneoireachta. Bhí sé mar léachtóir aici nuair a dhein sí cúrsa sa Diagacht i gColáiste Phádraig, Maigh Nuad.

Select bibliography
Stac, An tSiúr de Lourdes.
—. *As We Lived It*. Beathaisnéis. Tralee: *Kerryman*, 1980, g.d.
—. *Thar Balla Isteach*. Beathaisnéis. 1975. Maigh Nuad: An Sagart, 1982.
—. *Ard na Caithnia: Súil Siar*. Scríbhneoireacht acadúil, stair shóisialta. Baile Átha Cliath: Teangscéal, 1987.

Secondary sources
Ó hOibicín, Mícheál, eag. *Réaltra: Filíocht agus Prós don Ardteistiméireacht, Gnáthleibhéal*. Baile Átha Cliath: An Cló Ceilteach.

Stac, Brighid [Stac, Bríd]. fl. 1917–18. Corca Dhuibhne, Co. Chiarraí. Beathaisnéis.

Ba as Corca Dhuibhne do Bhrighid ó dhúchas. "Is í an dírbheathaisnéis an cineál litríochta is raidhsiúla a tháinig chughainn ón gceantar. Leabhrán beag le Brighid Stac, *Mí dem' shaoghal* (1918), an chéad saothar den chineál seo a foilsíodh. Cuntas ar shaol laethúil cailín óig atá anseo agus é scríofa i bhfoirm chín lae" (Nic Eoin 1982, 63).

Select bibliography
Stac, Brighid.
—. *Cúntas Cinn Lae*. Beathaisnéis. Leabhair Bheaga Bhlasda na Gaedhilge 5. Corcaigh: Oifig "An Lóchrainn", 1917.
—. *Mí dem' Shaoghal*. Beathaisnéis. Corcaigh: An Lóchrann. Baile Átha Cliath: Brún agus Ó Nualláin, 1918.

Secondary sources
Nic Eoin, Máirín. *An Litríocht Réigiúnach*. Leabhair Thaighde 40. Baile Átha Cliath: An Clóchomhar Tta, 1982.

Stacpoole Kenny, Louise M., née Dunne. 1885–1933. Limerick. Novels, biography.

Daughter of James K. Dunne and Mary Stackpoole of Moymore House, Killaspuglonane, Co. Clare, she married Thomas Hugh Kenny of Limerick.

Known as a popular novelist before the First World War, she also wrote biographies. Her best-known works include *Carrow of Carrowduff* (1911), and *Our Own Country* (1913). She was also concerned with and wrote articles on the subject of industrial development in Ireland. She died in Bray, Co. Wicklow, in 1933.

Select bibliography
Stacpoole Kenny, Louise M.
—. *The Red-Haired Woman – Her Autobiography.* Novel. London: John Murray, 1905.
—. *Love is Life.* Novel. London: Greening, 1910.
—. *At the Court of Il Moro.* Novel. London: Long, 1911.
—. *Carrow of Carrowduff.* Novel. London: Greening, 1911.
—. *St Charles Borromeo: A Sketch of the Reforming Cardinal.* Religious writing. London: Burns, Oates, 1911.
—. *The King's Kiss: An Historical Romance.* Historical novel. London: Digby, Long, 1912.
—. *Daffodil's Love Affairs.* Novel. London: Holden and Hardingham, 1913.
—. *Our Own Country – A Novel.* Novel. London: James Duffy, 1913.
—. *Mary: A Romance of West County.* Novel. London: Washbourne, 1915.
—. *Heart of the Scarlet Five – A Novel.* Novel. London: Heath, Cranton, 1916.
—. *Blessed John Bosco: The Story of a Modern Beatus.* Religious writing. Dublin: Catholic Truth Society of Ireland, 1930.
—. *Pope Pius X.* Biography. Dublin: Irish Messenger Office, 1951.
—. *Jacquetta: The Story of Co. Clare.* Novel. London: Burns, Oates, n.d.
—. *A Knight of the Green Shield.* Historical novel. London: Washbourne, n.d.
—. *Story of St Martin of Tonis.* Religious writing. N.p.: n.p., n.d.
—. *St Francis de Sales: A Biography of the Gentle Saint (1567–1622).* Religious writing. London: Burns, Oates, n.d.

Strong, Eithne [Ní Chonaill, Eithne]. 1923–99. Gleann na Searbh Úll, Ardacha, Co. Luimnigh agus Inis, Co. an Chláir. Gearrscéalaíocht, úrscéalaíocht, filíocht, aistriúchán agus léirmheastóireacht.

Saolaíodh Eithne i nGleann na Searbh Úll, Ardacha i 1923 ach chónaigh sí i mBaile Átha Cliath ón mbliain 1942 i leith. Oidí scoile ab ea a hathair agus a máthair. D'fhreastail sí ar scoil lánghaelach, Scoil Mhuire, Inis, Co. an Chláir. D'oibrigh sí mar státseirbhíseach ar feadh tamaill agus phós sí an Sasanach, Rupert Strong, a bhí ina shícanailísí agus ina fhile. Cailleadh é siúd i 1984. Bhí naonúr clainne orthu. Bhain sí BA amach sa Ghaeilge agus sa Bhéarla i gColáiste na Tríonóide, Baile Átha Cliath, mar ar dhein sí an tArdteastas san Oideachas chomh maith. D'oibrigh sí mar mhúinteoir meánscoile ar feadh roinnt blianta agus ansin chuaigh sí le hiriseoireacht. Mhúin sí scríbhneoireacht chruthaitheach i scoileanna éagsúla agus thug léachtaí ar fud na Stát Aontaithe.

Ba é *Songs of Living* (1960) an chéad chnuasach filíochta léi a foilsíodh. Scríobhadh sí sa Bhéarla agus sa Ghaeilge. Tá ceithre leabhar filíochta Gaeilge léi i gcló. Tá aistriúchán Gearmáinise dá dán "A Chéile na dTríocha mBliain" foilsithe in *Und suchte meine zunge ab nach* (Worten Edition Druckhaus Nevnzehn, 1996). Tá dánta agus ailt léi foilsithe in irisí éagsúla, mar shampla *An Glór, Comhar, An Peann Ceilteach* agus *Scéala Éireann/The Irish Press.* Is é an cnuasach filíochta léi is mó cáil sa Bhéarla ná *Spatial Nosing: New and Selected Poems* (Baile Átha Cliath: Salmon-Poolbeg, 1993). Tá deich leabhar Bhéarla foilsithe aici idir fhilíocht, ghearrscéalta agus úrscéalta. Foilsíodh a cuid saothair in irisí éagsúla, in *Aquarius 12* agus *North Dakota Quarterly* (geimhreadh 1989) mar shampla. Tá agallaimh le hEithne i gcló in: *Sleeping with Monsters* (1990), *Irish Literary Supplement* (Earrach 1994), *Women Creating Women* (1996), *Irish Times* (13 Samh. 1993), *Sunday Independent* (12 Samh. 1993). Is é atá in *Aoife faoi ghlas* (1990) ná cíoradh fileata ar fhadhb na ndrugaí, ar an gcóras dlí agus cirt agus, thar aon ní eile, ar an ngaol idir an t-aonarán agus *diktat* an phobail. Scríobh Eithne go leor léirmheasanna chomh maith ar leabhair agus ar léirithe amharclainne. Cailleadh sa bhliain 1999 í.

Eithne Strong was born in Ardagh, Co. Limerick, in 1923 but lived in Dublin from 1942 onwards. Her parents were both school teachers. She attended the All-Irish school, Scoil Mhuire, Ennis, Co. Clare. She worked as a civil servant for a time, and then married the Englishman Rupert Strong, who was both a psychoanalyst and a poet. He died in 1984. They had nine children. She graduated with a degree in Irish and in English from TCD, where she also did a Higher Diploma in Education. She worked as a secondary school teacher for a number of years and then she became a journalist. She also taught creative writing in a variety of schools, and she gave lectures throughout the United States.

The publication of *Songs of Living* (1961) first brought public attention to her poetry. She wrote in English and in Irish. She had four books of poetry published in Irish, and her poems in Irish have been published in a variety of journals, e.g., *An Glór, Comhar, An Peann Ceilteach* and *Scéala Éireann/The Irish Press.* Her most famous collection of poetry in English is *Spatial Nosing: New and Selected Poems* (1993). She had ten books published in English – poetry, short stories and novels. Her work in English has been published in a variety of journals, eg. *Aquarius 12* and *North Dakota Quarterly* (Winter 1989). A German translation of her poem "A Chéile na dTríocha mBliain" was published in *Und suchte meine zunge ab nach* (Worten Edition Druckhaus Nevnzehn, 1996). Interviews with Eithne were published in *Sleeping with Monsters* (1990), *Irish Literary Supplement* (Spring 1994), *Women Creating Women* (1996), *Irish Times* (13 Nov. 1993) and *Sunday Independent* (12 Nov. 1993). The subject of *Aoife faoi Ghlas* (1990) is a poetic exploration of the problem of drugs, of the justice system and, more than anything else, of the relationship between the individual and the *diktat* of the community. Eithne also wrote a lot of critiques on books and on theatrical performances. She died in 1999.

Select bibliography
Strong, Eithne.
—. *Poetry Quartos.* Poetry. Dublin: Runa, 1943–5.
—. "Poems." *Tidings.* Filíocht. Eag. Jonathan Hanaghan. Dublin: Dolmen, 1958.
—. *Songs of Living.* Filíocht. Baile Átha Cliath: Runa, 1961.

—. "Red Jelly." *Winter's Tales from Ireland 2.* Short story. Ed. Kevin Casey. Dublin: Gill & Macmillan, 1972. 95–110.
—. *Sarah, in Passing.* Filíocht. Dublin: Runa, 1974.
—. "Ages." *New Irish Writing.* Short story. Ed. David Marcus. London: Quartet, 1976. 139–47.
—. *Degrees of Kindred.* Úrscéalaíocht. Baile Átha Cliath: Tansy Books, 1979.
—. *Cirt Oibre.* Filíocht. Baile Átha Cliath: Coiscéim, 1980.
—. *Flesh – The Greatest Sin.* Filíocht. Dublin: Runa, 1980. Dublin: Attic Press, 1993.
—. *Patterns.* Gearrscéalaíocht. Baile Átha Cliath: Poolbeg, 1981.
—. "Buaire." Filíocht. *Comhar* (Iúil 1983): 23.
—. "Ceart Urraime." Filíocht. *Comhar* (Lúnasa 1983): 32.
—. *Fuil agus Fallaí.* Filíocht. Baile Átha Cliath: Coiscéim, 1983.
—. *My Darling Neighbour.* Filíocht. Belfast: Beaver Row, 1985.
—. "The Bride of Christ." *Territories of the Voice: Contemporary Stories by Irish Women Writers.* Short story. Ed. Louise DeSalvo *et al.* Boston: Beacon, 1989, 1999. 41–5.
—. *Aoife faoi Ghlas.* Filíocht. Baile Átha Cliath: Coiscéim, 1990.
—. *Let Live.* Filíocht. Galway: Salmon, 1990.
—. *An Sagart Pinc.* Filíocht. Baile Átha Cliath: Coiscéim, 1990.
—. *The Love Riddle.* Úrscéalaíocht. Baile Átha Cliath: Attic, 1993.
—. *Spatial Nosing: New and Selected Poems.* Poetry. Swords, Co. Dublin: Salmon, 1993.
—. "A Chéile na dTríocha Bliain." *Und suchte meine zunge ab nach.* Filíocht. Aist. Gearmáinis ag Andrea Nic Thaidhg. Worten Edition Druckhaus Nevnzehn, 1996.
—. *Nobel.* Filíocht. Baile Átha Cliath: Coiscéim, 1999.

Secondary sources
Haberstroh, Patricia Boyle. "Eithne Strong." *Women Creating Women: Contemporary Irish Women Poets.* Syracuse: Syracuse UP, 1996. 28–57.
McWilliam Consalvo, Deborah. "Review of 'The Love Riddle'." *Irish Studies Review* (Eanair 1996): 52–3.
Ó Cearnaigh, Seán. "Eithne Strong." *Scríbhneoirí na Gaeilge 1945–1995.* Baile Átha Cliath: Comhar, 1995.
Riggs, Pádraigín. "Léirmheas ar *Aoife faoi Ghlas.*" *Anois* 26–27ú Bealtaine (1990).
Ryan, Angela, trans. "Poems by Eithne Strong Translated into French." Ed. Denis Rigal. Paris: Sud domaine étranger, 1987. 83–107.
Strong, Eithne. "Eithne Strong." *Sleeping with Monsters: Conversations with Scottish and Irish Women Poets.* Interviewer Wilson, Rebecca E. Wilson. Dublin: Wolfhound, 1990. 109–19.
Uí Nia, Gearóidín, eag. "Strong, Eithne." *Eolaire Chló Iar-Chonnachta de Scríbhneoirí Gaeilge.* Indreabhán: Cló Iar-Chonnachta, 1998.
Wright, Nancy Means, and Hannan Dennis. "An Interview with Eithne Strong." *Irish Literary Supplement* 13 (Spring 1994): 13–15.

Swanton, Daisy, née Kingston. Contemporary. Cobh, Co. Cork. Diaries.
Daughter of Lucy O. Kingston, a Cork Quaker, feminist and pacifist, she is the author of *Emerging from the Shadow* (1994), based on the diaries her mother kept from 1913 to 1968, and those of her grandmother from the

1880s to 1926. Swanton describes the diaries thus: "Both sets of diaries cover domestic details of women's lives over that period in Co. Wicklow and in Dublin, and [...] graphic descriptions of the disturbed life in Dublin from 1913 up to late 1920s." This memoir of the three Lawrenson women takes in the concerns of her Victorian grandmother, her mother's involvement with the Women's Social and Progressive League and the Irish Housewives Association, and her aunt's life in Seattle, where she founded and ran an art gallery.

Daisy herself worked as a legal secretary, married William Swanton in 1949 and raised a family. She returned to work in 1972 and retired in 1988 to collate the diaries. She has been actively involved in environmental issues all her life. She lives in Cobh, Co. Cork.

Select bibliography
Swanton, Daisy.
—. ed. *Emerging from the Shadow: The Lives of Sarah Anne Lawrenson and Lucy Olive Kingston, Based on Personal Diaries 1883–1969*. Diaries. Dublin: Attic, 1994.

Secondary sources
O'Shea, Suzanne. "Behind History." *Wise Women: A Portrait*. Cork: Bradshaw, 1994. 113–15.

Swinfen, Averil, née Humphreys. Contemporary. Midleton, Co. Clare. History.

Born in Midleton in East Cork, she was a childhood friend of the horse trainer Vincent O'Brien, who wrote the preface to her history of the Irish donkey. She spent several years in England, where she worked in the prison service and as an interior designer. Having travelled widely, she returned to Ireland when her children had grown up and spent twenty years (1964–84) caring for donkeys in three villages in Co. Clare. She also took a keen interest in ancient churches in the county and wrote two books on the subject. She already had connections with Co. Clare, as her great grand-uncle, Rev. Robert Humphreys, served as rector and later dean in several parishes.

Select bibliography
Swinfen, Averil.
—. *The Irish Donkey*. History. Cork: Mercier, 1969. Notes: Preface by Vincent O'Brien.
—. *Donkeys Galore*. History. N.p.: n.p., 1976.
—. *The Ass in Bible Times*. Religious writing. 1986.
—. *Kilfenora Cathedral: A Short History*. Local history. 1986.
—. *Forgotten Stones: Ancient Church Sites of the Burren and Environs*. History. Dublin: Lilliput, 1992. Notes: Fwd. Peter Harbison.

Tanguay, Mary. Contemporary. Tralee, Co. Kerry. Novels, play, short story.

Born in Co. Tyrone, she was educated locally before going to TCD, where she took a BA in French and English, followed by a PhD from UCD in 1978 for her thesis on the work of Samuel Beckett. Following her marriage to a

Canadian she moved to Canada, and worked for Canadian International Development in the West Indies, Algeria, Nigeria and Turkey. She spent fifteen years travelling overseas and then returned to Canada, where she researched and wrote up the material on six forestry projects in Honduras. She then taught English at the University of Ottawa and has now retired from teaching to write full-time. She divides her time between Ottawa and Tralee. She has written novels as well as a play, *Return to Grosse Ile*, which was performed at Siamsa Tíre in Tralee, Co. Kerry. Some of her novels have Irish historical backgrounds and a short story, "A Woman's Liberation", was broadcast on BBC radio. Three novels are still in manuscript form. She received an Arts Council Award for one of them, *The Asphodels*, which deals with civil war in Algeria, where the author lived for six years.

Select bibliography
Tanguay, Mary.
—. *The Accident*. Novel. Ottawa: Coram, 1983.
—. *Be at the Windmill*. Historical novel. Ottawa: Coram, 1994.
—. *Kyask*. Novel. Ottawa: Penumbra, n.d.
—. *No Small Woman*. Novel. N.p.: n.p., n.d.
—. *Run with the Hare*. Young adult fiction. N.p.: n.p., n.d.

Taylor, Alice. Contemporary. Innishannon, Co. Cork. Memoirs, poetry, children's writing, religious writing.

Born on a farm in Co. Cork in 1938, she attended the local secondary school and worked at various jobs until her marriage to Gabriel Murphy, when she moved to Innishannon. Here she ran a guest-house, then a supermarket and a post office. She published her first book of memoirs, *To School Through the Fields*, in 1988. Based on anecdotes from her country childhood, it was an immediate popular success. The four sequels, *Quench the Lamp* (1990), *The Village* (1992), *Country Days* (1993) and *The Night Before Christmas* (1994), were also successful. These books of memoirs have been translated and sold internationally. More recently she has written two novels, as well as two books of poetry, a children's book and a book of religious writing. A video-recording of her first memoir was made by RTÉ in 1989.

Select bibliography
Taylor, Alice.
—. *The Way We Are*. Poetry. N.p.: n.p., 1983.
—. *An Irish Country Diary*. Diary. Dingle: Brandon, 1988.
—. *To School Through the Fields: An Irish Country Childhood*. Memoirs. Dingle: Brandon, 1988. New York: St Martin's, 1990.
—. *Close to the Earth: Poems of Country Life*. Poetry. Dingle: Brandon, 1989. Notes: Illus. Brian Lalor.
—. *Quench the Lamp*. Memoirs. Dingle: Brandon, 1990. New York: St Martin's, 1991.
—. *Secrets of the Oak*. Children's writing. Dingle, Co. Kerry: Brandon, 1992.
—. *The Village*. Memoirs. Dingle: Brandon, 1992.
—. *Country Days*. Memoirs. Dingle: Brandon, 1993.
—. *The Night Before Christmas*. Memoirs. Dingle: Brandon, 1994.

—. *The Winding Road to God: Thoughts from the Catechism of the Catholic Church*. Religious writing. Dublin: Veritas, 1995.
—. *The Woman of the House*. Novel. Dingle: Mount Eagle, 1997.
—. *A Country Miscellany*. Essays. Dingle: Mount Eagle, 1998.
—. *Going to the Well*. Poetry. Dingle: Mount Eagle, 1998.
—. *Across the River*. Novel. Dingle: Brandon, 2001.
—. Introduction. *Green Fields: A Journal of Irish Country Life*. By Stephen Rynne. Dingle, Co. Kerry: Brandon, n.d.

Taylor, Jessica. Contemporary. Listowel, Co. Kerry. Autobiography.

From Listowel, Co. Kerry, she emigrated to Toronto in Canada in 1967. Tragedy struck in 1969, when she fell and sustained multiple injuries, including brain damage. Her book, *The Journey Back* (1992), recounts her recovery, which has made both medical and legal history. She is now fully recovered, has returned to live in Kerry and spends her time writing and working on behalf of brain-injured patients.

Select bibliography
Taylor, Jessica.
—. *The Journey Back*. Autobiography. Dublin: New Leaf, 1992.

Thomas, Caitlin, née MacNamara. 1913–94. Ennistymon, Co. Clare. Autobiography.

Daughter of Francis MacNamara of Ennistymon House, Co. Clare, she was born and brought up in London. The MacNamaras were neighbours of the artists Augustus and Gwen John, and they remained close all their lives. She returned to Ennistymon in the 1930s and lived there with her father, who had converted his family house into the Falls Hotel. Caitlin's sister, Nicolette Devas (*q.v.*), has described their childhood and early years in her autobiography, *Two Flamboyant Fathers* (1966).

In 1937 Caitlin married the Welsh poet, Dylan Thomas, but financial hardship, infidelity, alcoholism and the poet's long absences ensured that the marriage was not a happy one. In 1957 Caitlin published the controversial *Leftover Life to Kill*, based on her life with Dylan Thomas. She wrote a second book in 1963, *Not Quite Posthumous Letter to My Daughter*. There are current plans to publish a book of her poetry. In 1957 Caitlin went to live in Italy with a Sicilian, Giuseppe Forzia, who worked in films. She died in Sicily in 1994 and is buried beside her husband in a Welsh churchyard.

Select bibliography
Thomas, Caitlin.
—. *Leftover Life to Kill*. Autobiography. London: Putnam, 1957.
—. *Not Quite Posthumous Letter to My Daughter*. Autobiography. London: Putnam, 1963.
—. with George Tremlett. *Caitlin: Life with Dylan Thomas*. Autobiography. London: Secker & Warburg, 1986.

Secondary Sources
Ferris, Paul. *The Life of Caitlin Thomas*. London: Hutchinson, 1993.

Thompson, Kate. Contemporary. Co. Clare. Children's writing, poetry, novels.

Born in Yorkshire in 1956, she has travelled and worked around the world. She trained racehorses in England and the USA, then studied law in London before taking off on an extensive tour of India. She also worked a smallholding in Co. Clare for ten years and was a member of the North Clare Writers' Workshop. Her writings have appeared in several anthologies and in literary magazines. *Switchers* (1994) was her first novel for young people. She continues to write novels, poetry and screenplays, but her renown rests on her children's writing, particularly the Switchers trilogy.

Select bibliog raphy
Thompson, Kate.
—. *Sugarbird: A Story About the Derains*. Children's writing. London: Harrap, 1963.
—. *Richard's War: A Story About the Derains*. Children's writing. London: Harrap, 1965.
—. *The Painted Caves: A Story About the Derains*. Children's writing. London: Harrap, 1968.
—. *It Means Mischief*. Children's writing. Dublin: New Island, 1988.
—. *There Is Something*. Poetry. Galway: Salmon, 1992.
—. *Switchers*. Young adult fiction. Wicklow: Aran, 1994. London: Bodley Head, 1997.
—. *Midnight's Choice [Switchers 2]*. Young adult fiction. London: Bodley Head, 1998. London: Red Fox, 1999.
—. *More Mischief*. Children's writing. Dublin: New Island, 1999.
—. *Thin Air*. Novel. London: Sceptre, 1999. London: Hodder & Stoughton, 2000.
—. *Wild Blood [Switchers 3]*. Young Adult Fiction. London: Bodley Head, 1999. London: Red Fox, 2001.
—. *The Missing Link*. Young adult fiction. London: Bodley Head, 2000.
—. *The Beguilers*. Children's writing. London: Bodley Head, 2001.

Thurston, Katherine Cecil, née Madden. 1875–1911. Cork; Ardmore, Co. Waterford. Novels.

Born in Cork, 1875, she was the only child of Paul Madden, friend of Parnell and nationalist mayor of Cork, and Catherine Barry. With the 1903 publication of *John Chilcote M.P.* she became a hugely popular novelist. She successfully defended herself from charges of plagiarism regarding the novel, and it was a hit both at home and in the USA (titled *The Masquerader*), where it was later filmed (Samuel Goldwyn, dir. Richard Wallace, 1933). She married Ernest Temple Thurston, another writer, in 1901, and the couple moved to Ardmore, Co. Waterford. However, their marriage was not a success, and during the divorce case Temple Thurston was alleged to have "deserted" his wife because her career was more successful than his own and she was earning more from her books than he was. Her later novels include *The Gambler* (1905), and *The Fly on the Wheel* (1908). A well known figure and popular public speaker, Thurston was rarely out of the limelight. Her sudden death, probably as the result of an epileptic fit, in a Cork hotel a month before she was due to remarry in 1911 caused much press attention and speculation that she had been murdered or had committed suicide.

Select bibliography
Thurston, Katherine Cecil.
—. *The Circle.* Novel. Edinburgh and London: Blackwood, 1903.
—. *John Chilcote M.P.* Novel. Edinburgh and London: Blackwood, 1903.
—. *The Gambler.* Novel. New York and London: Hutchinson, 1905.
—. *The Mystics.* Novel. Edinburgh and London: Blackwood, 1907.
—. *Max.* Novel. London: Hutchinson, 1910. Notes: Illus. Frank Craig.
—. *The Fly on the Wheel.* Novel. Edinburgh and London: Blackwood, 1908. London: Virago, 1987.

Secondary sources
Meaney, Gerardine. "Decadence, Degeneration, and Revolting Aesthetics: The Fiction of Emily Lawless and Katherine Cecil Thurston." *Colby Quarterly* 36.2 (2000): 157–76.

Tobin, Catherine. fl. 1855. Cork. Travel writing.

Daughter of Thomas Tobin, who was an officer at Ballincollig Barracks, Co. Cork, she wrote *Shadows of the East* (1855), a travel book about the eastern Mediterranean.

Select bibliography
Tobin, Catherine.
—. *Shadows of the East; or, Slight Sketches of Scenery, Persons and Customs, from Observations During a Tour in 1853 and 1854, in Egypt, Palestine, Syria, Turkey, and Greece.* Travel writing. London: n.p., 1855.

Tóibín, Cáit. fl. 1978. An Rinn, Na Déise, Co. Phort Láirge. Amhrán / béaloideas.

Thug Cáit amhrán darbh ainm "Cailíní Sheáin Uí Chuileannáin" do Nioclás Tóibín agus foilsíodh é in *Duanaire Déiseach* (1978, 92–3).

Select bibliography
Tóibín, Cáit.
—. "Cailíní Sheáin Uí Chuileannáin." *Duanaire Déiseach.* Amhrán / béaloideas. Eag. Nioclás Tóibín. Baile Átha Cliath: Sáirséal agus Dill, 1978.

Tóibín, Caitlín. Comhaimseartha. An Seanphobal, Na Déise, Co. Phort Láirge. Aiste / seanchas.

Sa Seanphobal a saolaíodh agus a tógadh Caitlín agus tá suim mhór aici i seanchas na háite sin.

Select bibliography
Tóibín, Caitlín.
—. "Oifig an Phoist an tSean-Phobail." *An Linn Bhuí: Iris Ghaeltacht na nDéise.* Aiste / seanchas. Eag. Pádraig Ó Macháin agus Aoibheann Nic Dhonnchadha. Vol. 5. Baile Átha Cliath: Leabhair na Linne, 2001.

Tóibín, Siubhán [Ní Sheáin, Siobhán]. fl. 1978. Co. Phort Láirge. Filíocht, amhránaíocht / béaloideas.

I.R.B. Jennings ab ea a hathair a d'oibrigh mar Chigire Contae ar an R.I.C. i gCo. Phort Láirge. "Bean éirimiúil, thréitheach a bhí i Siubhán, a bhí gníomhach in imeachtaí Chonradh na Gaeilge i mBaile Átha Cliath agus a raibh caidreamh aici le lucht na gluaiseachta náisiúnta agus le haois ealaíne agus litríochta na hardchathrach" (Tóibín 1978, clúdach). Phós sí Nioclás Tóibín i 1922, an bhliain chéanna a fuair sé post mar mhúinteoir Gaeilge i gCeatharlach. Bhí beirt muirear orthu, Naoise a cailleadh i 1974, agus Deirdre. Bhíodar ag cur fúthu i mBaile na Manach, Baile Átha Cliath ag deireadh a saoil. Saolaíodh Nioclás i mBaile na nGall, An Rinn i 1890. Scríobh sé úrscéalta, gearrscéalta, aistriúcháin agus aistí agus bhí suim mhór aige sa bhéaloideas agus sa cheol. Cailleadh é i 1966, agus d'fhág an-chuid amhrán i lámhscríbhinní agus in irisí. "Chuir a bhean, Siubhán, roimpi iad seo a bhailiú agus a chur in eagar 'do bhuanchoimeád a chuimhne beo'" (Tóibín 1978, clúdach). Cailleadh Siubhán i 1977. Foilsíodh *Duanaire Déiseach* tar éis a báis.

Select bibliography
Tóibín, Siubhán.
—. eag. *Duanaire Déiseach*. Filíocht, amhránaíocht / béaloideas. Tóibín, Nioclás. Baile
    Átha Cliath: Sáirséal agus Dill, 1978.

Tottenham, Luise. *fl.* 1952. Kildorrery, Co. Cork. Novels.

Born in Co. Cork in 1897, she was educated locally, in Surrey and at Reading University. One of her novels, *The New Woman* (1952), centres on a hillside farm on the Cork–Limerick border in pre-war days.

Select bibliography
Tottenham, Luise.
—. *The New Woman*. Novel. London: Victor Gollancz, 1952.

Townshend, (Laetitia Jane) Dorothea. *fl.* 1892–1930. Castletownshend, Co. Cork. Family history, biography, children's writing.

Daughter of the Rev. Ralph Bourne Baker, Rector of Hilderstone, she married Richard Baxter Townshend from Castletownshend, Co. Cork. Dorothea Townshend co-wrote family histories of the Townshend family with her husband, such as a biography of his ancestor, Col. Richard Townshend (*Burke's Irish Family Records*). She was also the biographer of Endymion Porter and of other historical figures. Her work includes fiction for children, such as *The Children of Nugentstown and Their Dealings with the Sidhe* (1911).

Select bibliography
Townshend, (Laetitia Jane) Dorothea.
—. and Richard Baxter Townshend, comp. and ed. "An Officer of the Long Parlia-
    ment and His Descendants: Being Some Account of the Life and Times of
    Colonel Richard Townshend of Castletown, and a Chronicle of His Family."
    Family history. London: Froude, 1892.
—. *Strange Adventures of a Young Lady of Quality*. Short stories. London: Digby, 1893.
—. *Willie Weston's Wonderful Sixpence*. Children's writing. London: E. Stock, 1895.
—. *The Life and Letters of Endymion Porter*. Biography. London: Fisher Unwin, 1897.
—. *Captain Chimney Sweep: A Story of the Great War*. Children's writing. London:
    Nelson, 1900.

—. *The Faery of Lisbawn*. London: Nelson, 1900.

—. *Ivy and Oak, and Other Stories for Girls*. Fiction for girls. London: Nelson, 1901.

—. *A Lost Leader: A Tale of Restoration Days*. Religious writing. London: Christian Knowledge Society, 1902.

—. *The Life and Letters of the Great Earl of Cork*. Biography. London: Duckworth, 1904.

—. *A Saint George of King Charles' Days*. Religious writing. London: Christian Knowledge Society, 1906.

—. *The Children of Nugentstown and Their Dealings with the Sidhe*. Children's writing. London: David Nutt, 1911.

—. *A Lion, a Mouse, and a Motor Car: A Fantasia*. Children's writing. London: Simpkin, Marshall, Hamilton, Kent, 1915.

—. *Whither? The Story of a Flight*. London: SPCK, 1918.

—. *George Digby, Second Earl of Bristol*. Biography. London: Fisher Unwin, 1924.

—. *What Happened at Garry-Eustace*. London: T.C. & E.C. Jack, 1927.

—. *Broken Lights, and Other Poems*. Poetry. London: John Lane, 1932.

Trant, Clarissa. 1800–44. Myrtleville, Co. Cork. Diary.

Her father, Nicholas, was born in Co. Cork but became one of the Wild Geese who, in the climate of the Penal Laws, left Ireland for France to attend a military school and then become a member of the Irish Brigade, and later the English army. Nicholas converted to Protestantism, and married an English woman. Clara, their first child, was born in Lisbon in 1800. Following her mother's death in 1805, Clara and her brother were sent to England, then returned to live in Portugal with their father, now Governor of Oporto, in 1810. The Trants left Oporto in 1815 to travel back to England, but their trip was interrupted by Napoleon's flight from Elba and the resurgence of fighting. Their father sent his children on to England, and joined the nearest English army unit in Marseilles. By the summer of 1815 the Trants were settled in England, and paid a visit to Cork. As a child, Nicholas had lived with Protestant cousins in Dunkettle, Co. Cork, and when in 1815 he took took his daughter Clarissa to Ireland for the first time, it was there they went. Clara recorded in her diary: "We entered Cork by the beautiful Glanmire road. My father showed me the woods of Dunkettle, formerly the property of Dominick Trant, where he had passed the first years of his infancy – it has long since passed into the hands of strangers and so far has shared the same fate with all that belonged to us both in Cork and Kerry (Clayton)."

This would be the first of many visits to the south of Ireland, but the pattern of travelling was maintained during Clara's youth. In 1816 she and her father returned to France, leaving her brother, Tom, at school in England. By this stage Clara was fluent in six languages, and her father's position meant that she met many well known people of the period, including Daniel O'Connell, whom she describes somewhat disparagingly in her journal as having "a most desperate Irish brogue". In 1822 Clara's uncle gave her father a piece of land at Baile an Chuainín, where they built Myrtleville Cottage. This became the Trants' summer home, and enabled Clara's entry into Cork society. While in Myrtleville, Clara became involved in philanthropy, and many entries in her diary record the living conditions of local people at the time, such as: "A wretched family who are actually living in a hole made between the angles of a hedge and covered with straw – the poor woman within three weeks of her confinement, her sick child stretched at her side." In an ironic twist, Tom Trant, who had followed in his father's footsteps by joining the English army, was billeted in 1831 to the west of Ireland to fight, as Clara says, "against our own poor savage, but in those parts, really rebellious countrymen" (Clayton). In 1832 Clara married the Rev. John Bramston, and moved to Great Baddow in Essex. They had three children, and their married life together was a happy one. Her diary was edited in 1925 by her granddaughter C.G. Luard, and was published by John Lane.

Select bibliography
Trant, Clarissa.
—. *The Journal of Clarissa Trant 1800–1832*. Diary. Ed. C.G. Luard. London: John Lane, 1925.

Troy, Shevaun [Gabriel Vand]. 1923–93. Clonmel, Co. Tipperary; Cork.

Sister of Una Troy (*q.v.*), she began to write poetry in 1974, when she joined the Lantern Theatre writers' group in Dublin. She published several poems in broadsheets produced by this group. She then moved to Cork, and her poems were published by *New Poetry*, *Tuesday Magazine* and *The Examiner*, sometimes under the pseudonym "Gabriel Vand". Shevaun Troy won first and second prize at the Doneraile Writers' Weekend in 1981, and the Jameson Prize at the Listowel Writers' Week in 1982. She published one volume of poetry, *Only by the Heron's Flight*.

Select bibliography
Troy, Shevaun.
—. *Only by the Heron's Flight*. Poetry. Cork: Cló Duanaire, n.d. Notes: Preface by Tom McCarthy.

Troy, Una [Elizabeth Connor]. 1918–93. Clonmel, Co. Tipperary; Bonmahon, Co. Waterford. Novels, plays, short stories.

Born in Fermoy, Co. Cork, she moved to Clonmel when her father was appointed District Justice in 1922. She was educated in Dublin. The family spent their summers in Bonmahon, Co. Waterford, where Una met Joseph C. Walsh, a medical doctor. They married in 1931, living in Bonmahon briefly before moving to Clonmel. They had one daughter. Having written poetry in her teens, Una began her career as a published author in 1936, using the pseudonym "Elizabeth Connor". Her first novel, *Mount Prospect*, was published in England but was banned in Ireland. By 1947 she had written her second novel, two short stories and four plays for the Abbey, all under the same pseudonym. Her plays were possibly better known than her other writing during this period. She shared the Abbey prize competition for new playwrights with a play also entitled *Mount Prospect*, a three-act tragedy. This was produced by Frank Dermody with the stage setting designed by Anne Yeats. It ran for twelve performances at the Abbey and had a week's run at the Cork Opera House.

Una Troy ceased to publish for a period from 1947 to 1955, when she resumed her career with *We Are Seven*, this time using the name "Una Troy". She wrote fifteen more novels and a short story, and co-wrote a film script (with T. J. Morrison), *She Didn't Say No*, based on her 1955 novel *We Are Seven*. The film starred Hilton Edwards and Ray McNally and was banned on its release in 1958. Her novels, set in rural Waterford, were very popular during the 1950s and 1960s. Published in England and the USA, her novels were also translated and some were serialized (the *Irish Independent* serialized *The Brimstone Halo* in 1965). Her short stories were published in *The Bell*, *Ireland Today* and the *Kilkenny Magazine*. When her husband died in 1969 Una moved to the summer house in Bonmahon, where she resided until her death in 1993.

Two of Una Troy's sisters were also involved in the arts. Her youngest sister, Shevaun (*q.v.*), was a poet, and their sister Gráinne, who taught at the Sedgely Park Training School in Manchester, published some musical compositions in the 1930s.

Note: Ann Butler has compiled a detailed bibliography of Troy's work, which is held by the National Library of Ireland.

Select bibliography

Troy, Una.
—. *Mount Prospect*. Novel. London: Methuen, 1936. New York: D. Appleton-Century, 1937. Notes: Republished as *No House of Peace*. U.S.: n.p., 1937.
—. "The White Glove." Short story. *Ireland Today* 2.9 (1937): 49–55.
—. *Dead Star's Light*. Novel. London: Methuen, 1938.
—. *Mount Prospect*. Play. Prod. Frank Dermody. Abbey Theatre. 22 Apr. 1940.
—. *Swans and Geese*. Play. Prod. Frank Dermody. Abbey Theatre. 22 Sept. 1941.
—. "The Apple." Short story. *The Bell* 5.1 (1942): 35–41.
—. *An Apple a Day*. Play. Prod. Frank Dermody. Abbey Theatre. 7 Sept. 1942.
—. *The Dark Road*. Play. Prod. Michael J. Dolan. Abbey Theatre. 12 May 1947.
—. *We Are Seven*. Novel. London: Heinemann, 1955. New York: Dutton, 1957.
—. *Maggie*. Novel. London: Heinemann, 1958. New York: Dutton, 1958. Notes: Republished as *Miss Maggie and the Doctor*. U.S.: n.p., n.d.
—. and T. J. Morrison. *She Didn't Say No*. Film script. Dir. Cynthia Frankel. Warner Bros. 1958.
—. *The Workhouse Graces*. Novel. London: Heinemann, 1959. New York: Dutton, 1960. Notes: Republished as *The Graces of Ballykeen*. U.S.: n.p., n.d.
—. *The Other End of the Bridge*. Novel. London: Heinemann, 1960. New York: Dutton, 1961.
—. *Esmond*. Novel. London: Hodder & Stoughton, 1962. New York: Dutton, 1962.
—. *Meine drei Ehemanner: Ein heiterer Roman aus Irland...* [*Esmond*]. Novel. Munich: Goldman, 1964.
—. *The Brimstone Halo*. Novel. London: Hodder & Stoughton, 1965. New York: Dutton, 1965. Notes: Republished as *The Prodigal Father*. U.S.: n.p., n.d.
—. "The Best Butter." Short story. *Kilkenny Magazine* 14 (1966): 48–61.
—. *The Benefactors*. Novel. London: Hale, 1969.
—. *The Castle that Nobody Wanted*. Novel. London: Hale, 1970.
—. *Tiger Puss*. Novel. London: Hale, 1970.
—. *Stop Press!* Novel. London: Hale, 1971.

—. *Doctor, Go Home!* Novel. London: Hale, 1973.

—. *Out of the Everywhere.* Novel. London: Hale, 1976.

—. *Caught in the Furze.* Novel. London: Hale, 1977.

—. *A Sack of Gold.* Novel. London: Hale, 1979.

—. *So True a Fool.* Novel. London: Hale, 1981.

—. "The Apple." *Woman's Part: An Anthology of Short Fiction by and about Irishwomen 1890–1960.* Short story. Sel. and introd. Janet Madden-Simpson. Dublin: Arlen, 1984. 161–7.

—. *Better to Burn.* (Unpub.) novel. Notes: Held in NLI Collection List no. 56. Mss. 35. 683–99.

Secondary sources
G.C. "Rev. of *Mount Prospect*, by Una Troy." *Dublin Magazine* new series 12.3 (1937): 90–91.
S. "Rev. of *The Other End of the Bridge*, by Una Troy." *Kilkenny Magazine* 4 (1961): 55.
T. de V.W. "Rev. of *Dead Star's Light*, by Una Troy." *Dublin Magazine* ns 13.2 (1938): 93–4.

Tuckey, Mary B. *fl.* **1840s.** Ferney, Co. Cork. Poetry, essays.

Born in Cork, she contributed to the *Dublin Literary Journal* from 1843 to 1845, as well as publishing several volumes of poetry.

Select bibliography
Tuckey, Mary B.
—. *The Wrongs of Africa: A Tribute to the Anti-Slavery Cause.* Political writing. Glasgow: n.p., 1838.
—. *The Great Exemplar: Religious Poetry.* Poetry. Dublin: Religious Tract and Book Society for Ireland, 1839.
—. *The Christian's Economy of Human Life.* Poetry. N.p.: n.p., 1845.
—. *Creation, or a Morning Walk.* Poetry. Dublin: n.p., 1845.
—. *Old James the Irish Pedlar; a Tale of the Famine.* Dublin: n.p., 1852.
—. *Harry and Willie.* Poetry. N.p.: n.p., n.d.

Turraoin, Peig [Uí Réagáin, Peig]. 1905–99. Baile na nGall, An Rinn, Na Déise, Co. Phort Láirge. Seanchas / béaloideas.

Saolaíodh Peig i mBaile na nGall agus bhí baint aici le Cumann na mBan agus le Cogadh na Saoirse. Chaith sí seal i Meiriceá agus d'fhill ar a háit dhúchais ansin. Phós sí Déaglán Ó Réagáin as ceantar na nDéise. Bhí sí gníomhach in eagraíochtaí éagsúla, idir Chonradh na Gaeilge agus an Cumann Lúthchleas Gael. Bhí stair Bhaile na nGall á scríobh aici i gcomhar le Nioclás Mac Craith don iris *An Linn Bhuí 4* (2000). Tá an óráid a thug Nioclás Mac Craith os comhair a huaighe i gcló in *An Linn Bhuí 3* (Ó Macháin agus Nic Dhonnchadha 1999, 135–6). Foilsíodh agallamh a chuir an Dr Seán Ua Súilleabháin uirthi in imleabhar a ceathair den iris chéanna, mar aon le cur síos uirthi óna hiníon Neans. Bhíodh sí le clos go rialta ar Raidió na Gaeltachta ó na 1970adaí i leith.

Secondary sources
Breathnach, Diarmuid, agus Máire Ní Mhurchú. "Ó Réagáin, Peig [Uí Réagáin] (1905–99)." *1983–2002 Beathaisnéis.* Baile Átha Claith: An Clóchomhar, 2003.

Mac Craith, Nioclás. "PeigTurraoin, Bean Uí Réagáin, 1905–1999." *An Linn Bhuí: Iris Ghaeltacht na nDéise.* Eag. Pádraig Ó Macháin agus Aoibheann Nic Dhonnchadha.Vol. 3. Baile Átha Cliath: Leabhair na Linne, 1999. 135–6.
Ua Súilleabháin, Seán. "Peig Bean Uí Réagáin, 1905–1999." *An Linn Bhuí: Iris Ghaeltacht na nDéise.* Eag. Pádraig Ó Macháin agus Aoibheann Nic Dhonnchadha.Vol. 4. Baile Átha Cliath: Leabhair na Linne, 2000.

Twohig, Elizabeth. Contemporary. Cork. Academic writing.

Born in Tipperary in 1946, she graduated from UCC with an MA in 1968. She has been a lecturer in the Department of Archaeology, UCC, since 1971 and was awarded a PhD in 1974. Her research interests include the megalithic and rock art of Ireland and megalithic tombs.

Select bibliography
Twohig, Elizabeth.
—. *The Megalithic Art of Western Europe.* Academic writing. Oxford: Oxford UP, 1981.
—. *Irish Megalithic Tombs.* Academic writing. Princes Risborough: Shire Archaeology, 1990.
—. "Megalithic Art in a Settlement Context: Skara Brae and Related Sites in the Orkney Islands." Academic writing. *Brigantium* 10 (1997): 377–89.
—. "Frameworks for the Megalithic Art of the Boyne Valley." *New Agendas in Irish Prehistory: Papers in commemoration of Liz Anderson.* Academic writing. Ed. A. Desmond, G. Jonson, M. McCarthy, J. Sheehan and E. Shee Twohig. Dublin: Wordwell, 2000. 89–106.

Uí Aimhirgín, Nuala. Comhaimseartha. Corca Dhuibhne, Co. Chiarraí. Scríbhneoireacht acadúil, eagarthóireacht.

Is as Corca Dhuibhne ó dhúchas do Nuala. Tá sí ag obair mar Fheidhmeannach Teanga in Oifig na Gaeilge Labhartha, Coláiste na hOllscoile, Gaillimh.

Select bibliography
Uí Aimhirgín, Nuala.
—. *Muiris Ó Súilleabháin: Saol agus Saothar.* Scríbhneoireacht acadúil. Maigh Nuad: An Sagart, 1983.
—. "Scríbhinní Mhuiris Uí Shúilleabháin." *Oidhreacht an Bhlascaoid.* Scríbhneoireacht acadúil, aiste. Eag. Aogán Ó Muircheartaigh. Baile Átha Cliath: Coiscéim, 1989: 222–37.
—. "Muiris Ó Súilleabháin ar an gCeathrú Rua." *Muiris Ó Súilleabháin: 1904–1950.* Scríbhneoireacht acadúil, aiste. Eag. Máire Ní Chéilleachair. Ceiliúradh an Bhlascaoid 5. Baile Átha Cliath: Coiscéim, 2000.
—. eag. *Ó Oileán go Cuilleán: ó Pheann Mhuiris Uí Shúilleabháin.* Scríbhneoireacht acadúil. Baile Átha Cliath: Coiscéim, 2000.

Uí Bheaglaoich, Neilí. Comhaimseartha. An Baile Loisce agus An Charraig, Corca Dhuibhne, Co. Chiarraí. Beathaisnéis.

Ba iad Tomás Ó Séaghdha agus Neilí Ní Shúilleabháin a tuismitheoirí. Bhíodar ag cur fúthu ar an mBaile Loisce le muintirThomáis. Saolaíodh triúr leanaí dóibh ann. D'aistríodar go dtí An Charraig, mar ar thug athairThomáis talamh dóibh. Saolaíodh cúigear leanaí eile dóibh ansin agus Neilí ina measc. Nuair a bhí sí an-óg cuireadh thar n-ais go Baile Loisce í go tigh a muintire, ach ní raibh sí ar a suaimhneas ann ceal comluadair leanaí óga agus d'fhill sí ar thigh a tuismitheoirí féin arís (Uí Bheaglaoich 1989, 5–6). Beathaisnéis atá ina leabhar *Carraig a' Dúin* "Réimeas fada cuimhní cinn atá anseo – ó sheanlaetha a hóige i gCorca Dhuibhne do bheith 'ar aimsir' i Meiriceá, go seanchas a linne théis filleadh ar a fód dúchais" (Uí Bheaglaoich 1989, clúdach).

Select bibliography
Uí Bheaglaoich, Neilí.
—. *Carraig a' Dúin*. Beathaisnéis. Baile Átha Cliath: Coiscéim, 1989.

Uí Chéadagáin, Eibhlín [Uí Chéadagáin, Bean Sheáin Mhóir]. *fl.* 1990. Oileán Chléire, Co. Chorcaí. Scéalta agus seanchas / béaloideas.

Bhí Eibhlín ag cur fúithi ar an mBaile Iarthach ar Oileán Chléire. Saolaíodh í uair éigin idir 1863 agus 1868. Bhailigh Seán Stundún béaloideas uaithi sa bhliain 1933. Tá an béaloideas sin le fáil i Roinn Bhéaloideas Éireann (CBÉ 49) anois. Foilsíodh cuid dá stór in *Céad Fáilte go Cléire* (Gunn 1990, 13, 25, 34, 172, 174–5). Feirmeoir ab ea í.

Select bibliography
Uí Chéadagáin, Eibhlín.
—. "Scéalta agus seanchas léi." *Céad Fáilte go Cléire*. Scéalaíocht agus seanchas / béaloideas. Eag. Marion Gunn. Baile Átha Cliath: An Clóchomhar, 1990.

Uí Cheárna, Bean [Uí Cheárnaigh, Bean]. *fl.* 1944. Múscraí, Co. Chorcaí. Filíocht, caoineadh / béaloideas.

Bhí Bean Uí Cheárna ina cónaí i Múscraí agus bhí blúire den chaoineadh a chum sí ar bhás a fir ag Amhlaoibh Ó Loinsigh. Foilsíodh é in *An Músgraigheach* 4 (1944, 20).

Select bibliography
Uí Cheárna, Bean.
—. "Caoineadh léi in 'Diosgán Eile ó Chúil Aodha'." Filíocht, caoineadh / béaloideas. *An Músgraigheach* 4. Earrach (1944): 19–21.

Uí Chiabháin, Bean (An Charraig). *fl.* 1931–3. An Charraig, Cill Maoilchéadair, Corca Dhuibhne, Co. Chiarraí. Seanchas / béaloideas.

Saolaíodh Bean Uí Chiabháin i 1850 agus bhí sí ag cur fúithi ar An gCarraig. Bhí leagan de "Céad slán chun na hÉireann" aici, a chum Liam Buidhe Ó Loinsigh ón Drom sa Leitriúch. Foilsíodh é in *Duanaire Duibhneach* (Ó Dubhda 1933, 136). Bhailigh an Seabhac scéalta uaithi agus foilsíodh iad in *Béaloideas* 3 (1931).

Select bibliography
Uí Chiabháin, Bean (An Charraig).
—. scéalaí. "Scéalta Creidimh agus Crábhaidh: 'Éadach an Mhairbh len' Anam' (a) agus (b)." Scéalaíocht / béaloideas. *Béaloideas* 3.1 (1931): 3–30.

Secondary sources
Ó Dubhda, Seán, eag. *Duanaire Duibhneach: bailiú d'amhránaibh agus de phíosaibh eile filidheachta a ceapadh le tuairim céad bliain i gCorca Dhuibhne, agus atá fós i gcuimhne agus i mbéaloideas na ndaoine ann.* 1933. Baile Átha Cliath: Oifig Dhíolta Foilseacháin Rialtais, 1969.

Uí Chiabháin, Bean (An Mhuirbheach). *fl.* 1933. Corca Dhuibhne, Co. Chiarraí. Seanchas / béaloideas.

Bhí Bean Uí Chiabháin ag cur fúithi ar an Muiríoch agus cailleadh í uair éigi idir 1907 agus 1932. Thug sí leagan de "Beauty Deas an Oileáin" agus de "Caoine na Luasach" do Sheán Ó Dubhda. Chum an file Seán Ó Duinnshléibhe an dá amhrán seo, agus foilsíodh iad in *Duanaire Duibhneach* (1933, 76–80, 82–3).

Secondary sources
Ó Dubhda, Seán, eag. *Duanaire Duibhneach: bailiú d'amhránaibh agus de phíosaibh eile filidheachta a ceapadh le tuairim céad bliain i gCorca Dhuibhne, agus atá fós i gcuimhne agus i mbéaloideas na ndaoine ann.* 1933. Baile Átha Cliath: Oifig Dhíolta Foilseacháin Rialtais, 1969.

Uí Choinghealla, Áine. *fl.* 1936. An Tuairín, Baile Mhic Cairbre, Co. Phort Láirge. Seanchas / béaloideas.

Saolaíodh Áine i 1848 agus bhí sí ina cónaí sa Tuairín. Thug sí an-chuid scéalta do Phádraig Ó Milléadha agus tá siad in eagar aige in *Béaloideas* 6 (1936). "Seo ceann des na scéalaidhthe is cruinne dár bhuail liom. Ní raibh scéalta fada aici; ach bhí an-chuid de scéilíní gairide aici, agus iad go cruinn, baileach aici. Rud eile, thug sí dhom go fonnmhar iad." (Ó Milléadha 1936, 254).

Select bibliography
Uí Choinghealla, Áine.
—. scéalaí. "Seanchas Sliabh gCua: Scéalta 10, 12, 18, 30, 42–8, 55, 60, 61, 64, 72, 73, 78, 87–91, 120, 123, 129, 130, 139, 147, 152–4, 160, 161 agus 163." Scéalaíocht agus seanchas / béaloideas. *Béaloideas* 6.2 (1936): 169–256.

Uí Chonaill, Bean Sheáin. *fl.*1926. Cill Rialaigh, Baile 'n Sgeilg, Co. Chiarraí. Scéalaíocht / béaloideas.

Bhí Bean Sheáin Uí Chonaill ina cónaí i gCill Rialaigh nuair a bailíodh scéalta uaithi i Mí na Nollag 1926 agus foilsíodh iad in *Béaloideas* 1 (1927).

Select bibliography
Uí Chonaill, Bean Sheáin.
—. "An Cailín gur Buaileadh Poc Uirri." Scéalaíocht / béaloideas. *Béaloideas* 1.2 (1927): 181.
—. "An tSochraid Sidhe." Scéalaíocht / béaloideas. *Béaloideas* 1.2 (1927): 187.

Uí Chonchubhair, Máirín [Uí Chonchúir, Máirín]. Comhaimseartha. Dún Chaoin agus Trá Lí, Co. Chiarraí. Scríbhneoireacht acadúil, taighde.

Saolaíodh Máirín i 1944. Is as Dún Chaoin í ach is i mBaile Átha Cliath atá sí ag cur fúithi anois. Cuireadh ar scoil go Trá Lí í sa bhliain 1956. Phós sí sa Róimh i 1969. Chaith sí tamall i gCeanada lena fear céile tar éis a bpósta. Foilsíodh *Flóra Chorca Dhuibhne* i 1995. D'aistrigh sí leabhar le hEleanor Lawrence agus le Sue Harniess go Gaeilge, *Sliogáin* (An Gúm, 1997).

Select bibliography
Uí Chonchubhair, Máirín.
—. "Kruger." *Is Cuimhin Linn Kruger: Kruger Remembered.* Scríbhneoireacht acadúil. Eag. Tadhg Ó Dúshláine. Maigh Nuad: An Sagart, 1994. 96–100.
—. *Flóra Chorca Dhuibhne: aspects of the Flora of Corca Dhuibhne.* Scríbhneoireacht acadúil. Baile an Fheirtéaraigh: Oidhreacht Chorca Dhuibhne, 1995.
—. aist. *Sliogáin.* Litríocht, aistriúchán. Le hEleanor Lawrence agus Sue Harniess. Baile Átha Cliath: An Gúm, 1997.

Secondary sources
"Léirmheas ar *Flóra Chorca Dhuibhne.*" *Anois* (30–31ú Nollaig 1995).
Uí Nia, Gearóidín. "Uí Chonchubhair, Máirín." *Eolaire Chló Iar-Chonnachta de Scríbhneoirí Gaeilge.* Indreabhán: Cló Iar-Chonnachta, 1998.

Uí Chróinín, Eibhlís [Cronin, Bess]. 1879–1956. Múscraí, Co. Chorcaí. Scéalaíocht agus amhránaíocht / béaloideas.

Saolaíodh Eibhlís sa Ráth, Ré na nDoirí agus ba é Seán Máistir Ó hIarlaithe a hathair, a mhúin i Scoil Chúil Aodha agus i Scoil Bharr D'Ínse. Ba í Máiréad Ní Thuama a máthair. Bhí ceathrar deirfiúracha agus dearthair amháin aici, chomh maith le beirt leasdeartháireacha. Phós sí Seán Ó Cróinín, agus bhíodar ag cur fúthu i gCarraig an Adhmaid, Baile Mhic Íre. Bhí cúigear clainne orthu. Tá clú agus cáil ar bheirt dá mac i saol an bhéaloidis, Seán, a bhí ina bhailitheoir agus Donncha, a bhí ina eagarthóir. Bhíodh an saol agus a mháthair ag tarraingt ar an tigh chun Gaeilge agus amhráin a fhoghlaim ó Eibhlís, dhá rud a bhí aici go fairsing. Cailleadh í in ospidéal Mhaigh Chromtha agus tá sí curtha i mBaile Bhuirne.

Is mar amhránaí atá clú uirthi, ach cuireadh ceithre scéal léi i gcló freisin. Foilsíodh ceann amháin acu in *Éigse* XVII, (1977) ar scríobh a mac, Donncha, síos é. Cuireadh dhá scéal eile ó bhéalaithris Eibhlís i gcló in *An Músgraigheach 5*, ceann amháin acu mar gheall ar iarlaisí, agus an tarna ceann faoi sprid a bhíodh le feiceáil timpeall na háite. Foilsíodh scéal eile uaithi in *An Músgraigheach 8*.

Tá garmhac le hEibhlís, Dáibhí Ó Cróinín, tar éis na hamhráin ar fad a bhí aici ina stór a bhailiú agus a chur in eagar. Tá sé ar intinn aige, leis, leabhar eile a chur amach bunaithe ar scéalta agus seanchas a deireadh Eibhlís. Dar le Dáibhí, bhí a cuid Gaeilge thar a bheith saibhir, agus bhí sí ar fhaisnéiseoirí Bhriain Uí Chuív dá leabhar *Cnósach focal ó Bhaile Bhúirne.* Nuair a bhí sí sna déaga, cuireadh ag obair í chuig feirm a huncail, Tomás Ó hIarfhlaithe, agus a bhean chéile (deirfiúr le máthair Eibhlíse), lánúin nach raibh aon mhuirear orthu. I dtigh a tuismitheoirí féin agus i dtigh a haintín a d'fhoghlaim sí formhór na n-amhrán a bhí aici.

Select bibliography
Uí Chróinín, Eibhlís.
—. "Seanchaidheacht." Scéalaíocht / béaloideas. *An Músgraigheach 5.* Samhradh (1944): 13–15.
—. "Micí MacHugh agus an Fear Siubhail." Scéalaíocht / béaloideas. *An Músgraigheach 8.* Samhradh (1945): 10–11.
—. "Tobairín na Leamhnachta." Scéalaíocht / béaloideas. *Éigse* XVII.Geimhreadh (1977).

Secondary sources
Breathnach, Diarmuid, agus Máire Ní Mhurchú. "Ó Cróinín, Eibhlís (1879–1956) [Uí Chróinín] [Bess Cronin]." *1882–1982 Beathaisnéis a Cúig.* Baile Átha Cliath: An Clóchomhar, 1997.
Ó Cróinín, Dáibhí, eag. *The Songs of Elizabeth Cronin, Irish Traditional Singer: The Complete Song Collection.* Baile Átha Cliath: Four Courts, 2000.
Ó Cróinín, Donncha. *Béaloideas 32* (1964).
Ó Cuív, Brian. *Cnósach focal ó Bhaile Bhúirne.* Baile Átha Cliath: n.p., 1947.

Uí Chuilleanáin, Brighid. *fl.* 1936. Cnoc an Bhainne, Baile Mhic Cairbre, Co. Phort Láirge. Scéalaíocht / béaloideas.

Saolaíodh Brighid i 1874 agus bhí sí ina cónaí i gCnoc an Bhainne i 1936 nuair a bhailigh Pádraig Ó Milléadha scéalta uaithi. Bhí sí dhá bhliain is trí scór ag an am sin. D'fhoilsigh Ó Milléadha na scéalta sin in *Béaloideas 6* (1936).

Select bibliography
Uí Chuilleanáin, Brighid.
—. scéalaí. "Seanchas Sliabh gCua: Sceálta uimh.13, 106, 117, 125 agus 134." Scéalaíocht / béaloideas. *Béaloideas* 6.2 (1936): 169–256.

Uí Dhálaigh, Máirín [Nic Dhiarmada / O Daly, Máirín]. c.1909–94. Trá Lí agus An tSnaidhm, Co. Chiarraí. Scríbhneoireacht acadúil, eagarthóireacht.

San India a saolaíodh Máirín, mar a raibh a hathair ag obair mar mhúinteoir. Cuireadh go hÉirinn í agus í dhá bhliain déag agus chaith sí tamall lena haintín i dTrá Lí. Ba i mBaile Átha Cliath a fuair sí a cuid meánoideachais. Ghnóthaigh sí BA sa Laidin agus sa Ghaeilge sa Choláiste Ollscoile, Baile Átha Cliath agus MA sa tSean-Ghaeilge. Phós sí Cearbhall Ó Dálaigh i 1934, a bhí ina uachtarán ar Éirinn blianta ina dhiaidh sin.

Ceapadh Máirín mar chúntóir i Roinn na Sean-Ghaeilge. Bhí sí ina ball de Bhord Scoil an Léinn Cheiltigh agus chaith sí tamall fada ag obair ar Fhoclóir an Acadaimh. Chuir sí gluais ar fáil do *Beatha Aodha Ruaidh Uí Dhomhnaill 2* (Cumann na Scríbheann nGaedhilge, 1957) agus chuir sí eagar ar *Cath Maige Mucrama*. Scríobhadh sí aistí d'irisí éagsúla léannta. Bhronn Ollscoil na hÉireann D.Litt.Celt uirthi agus ar a fear céile agus bhronn Ollscoil Bhaile Átha Cliath dochtúireacht uirthi. Tá sí curtha sa thSnaidhm, Co. Chiarraí. Bhronn Pádraig Ó Fiannachta leabharlann Mháirín ar Ionad an Bhlascaoid, Dún Chaoin.

Select bibliography
Uí Dhálaigh, Máirín.
—. 'Togail Bruidne Da Derga.' *Irish Sagas.* Scríbhneoireacht acadúil. Eag. Miles
   Dillon. Baile Átha Cliath: Oifig an tSoláthair, 1959.
—. 'The Metrical Dindshenchas.' *Early Irish Poetry.* Scríbhneoireacht acadúil. Eag.
   James Carney. Cork: Mercier, 1965.
—. 'Úar in Lathe do Lum Laine.' *Celtic Studies: Essays in Memory of Angus Matheson
   1912–1962.* Scríbhneoireacht acadúil. Eag. James Carney agus David Green.
   London: Routledge & Kegan Paul, 1968.
—. eag. *Cath Maige Mucrama:The battle of Mag Mucrama.* Scríbhneoireacht acadúil.
   Vol. 50. Baile Átha Cliath: Cumann na Scríbheann nGaedhilge,1975.

Secondary sources
Breathnach, Diarmuid, agus Máire Ní Mhurchú. "Ó Dálaigh, Máirín [Uí Dh. / Nic
   Dhiarmada] (*c.*1909–94)." *1983–2002 Beathaisnéis.* Baile Átha Claith: An
   Clóchomhar, 2003.

Uí Fhloinn, Máire. Comhaimseartha. Na Déise, Co. Phort Láirge.
Scríbhneoireacht acadúil, aistí.

I nDún na Mainistreach a saolaíodh Máire agus d'fhás sí aníos sa Ghleann
Beag. Is staraí áitiúil í. Cuireann sí síos go fileata ar Abha na Brice, idir
dhúlra, dhinnseanchas agus chuimhní a hóige féin san aiste a scríobh sí in
An Linn Bhuí 1.

Select bibliography
Uí Fhloinn, Máire.
—. "Cois Abha na Brice." *An Linn Bhuí: Iris Ghaeltacht na nDéise.* Scríbhneoireacht
   acadúil. Aiste. Ó Macháin, Pádraig agus Aoibheann Nic Dhonnchadha. Vol. 1.
   Baile Átha Cliath: Leabhair na Linne, 1997. 52–5.

Uí Fhoghlú, Áine. Comhaimseartha. Baile na nGall, An Rinn, Na Déise,
Co. Phort Láirge. Filíocht, aistí ar chúrsaí béaloidis.

Saolaíodh Áine i mBaile na nGall. Ba bhainisteoir ar Chomharchumann na
Rinne é a hathair, Éamonn Mac Murchú. D'fhreastail sí ar Choláiste na
hOllscoile, Corcaigh mar ar dhein sí staidéar ar an nGaeilge agus ar an
mBéaloideas. Is oide meánscoile í agus d'oibrigh sí ar Raidió na Gaeltachta
mar chraoltóir. File is ea í, leis, agus tá a céad chnuasach filíochta foilsithe ag
Coiscéim. Cuireann sí suim sa bhéaloideas, sa stair áitiúil, agus sa
tseandálaíocht. Chuir sí togra ar bun sa Rinn chun seanchas na háite a
chaomhnú ag tús na 1990adaí. D'éirigh léi cabhair airgid a fháil, agus thug sí
cuairt ar sheanóirí na paróiste chun seanchas, amhráin agus ceol a thaifeadadh
ar híseán. Úsáidtear an bailiúchán anois sa mheánscoil áitiúil mar áis teagaisc.
   Is an t-athrú atá tagtha ar shaol na tuaithe, ar an gCríostaíocht agus ar an
nGaeltacht féin na téamaí comhaimseartha atá in uachtar in *Aistear Aonair.*
Foilsíodh an dán "Do: E.J.M. 1918" in *Feasta* (Meitheamh, 2001), dán a
fuair an chéad duais do dhánta i nGaeilge i gComórtas Filíochta Bhéal Átha
na mBuillí, Co. Ros Comáin i 2001. Cuireadh "Fuascailt" i gcló san iris den
dáta céanna, dán go bhfuil an chéad duais buaite aige i gComórtas
Idirnáisiúnta Filíochta Dhún Laoghaire / Ráth an Dúin 1997.

Select bibliography
Uí Fhoghlú, Áine.
—. *Aistear Aonair*. Filíocht. Baile Átha Cliath: Coiscéim, 1999.
—. "Seanchas Déiseach." *An Linn Bhuí: Iris Ghaeltacht na nDéise*. Aiste. Eag. Pádraig Ó Macháin agus Aoibheann Nic Dhonnchadha. Vol. 3. Baile Átha Cliath: Leabhair na Linne, 1999. 103–7.
—. "Peig an Chroí Mhóir." *An Linn Bhuí: Iris Ghaeltacht na nDéise*. Filíocht. Eag. Pádraig Ó Macháin agus Aoibheann Nic Dhonnchadha. Vol. 4. Baile Átha Cliath: Leabhair na Linne, 2000.
—. "Mar Bhuíochas d'Úna." *An Linn Bhuí: Iris Ghaeltacht na nDéise*. Aiste. Eag. Pádraig Ó Macháin agus Aoibheann Nic Dhonnchadha. Vol. 4. Baile Átha Cliath: Leabhair na Linne, 2000.
—. "Duaisdhánta le hÁine Ní [sic] Fhoghlú." Filíocht. *Feasta* 54. Meitheamh (2001): 6.
Strokestown Poetry Competition. Web page. URL: http://www.strokestownpoetryprize.com/ (2002).

Uí Mhaoileoin, Máire [Méin "Máire an Ghabha" / Uí Mhilleóin, Bean Phádraig]. *fl.* 1931–48. An Clochán Dubh, Cill Maoilchéadair, Corca Dhuibhne, Co. Chiarraí. Seanchas / béaloideas.

Saolaíodh Máire i 1854 agus bhí sí ag maireachtáil ar an gClochán Dubh. Thug sí leagan de "Secstrum Saindí" do Sheán Ó Dubhda. Foilsíodh é in *Duanaire Duibhneach* (1933, 107). D'fhoilsigh Seán Ó Dubhda béaloideas uaithi in *Béaloideas* 1 (1928) agus 2 (1929). Bhailigh An Seabhac scéalta uaithi agus d'fhoilsigh sé iad in *Béaloideas* 2 (1929), 3 (1931) agus 16 (1948).

Select bibliography
Uí Mhaoileoin, Máire.
—. scéalaí. "Bean an Ghalair agus Iasacht Léine." Scéalaíocht / béaloideas. *Béaloideas* 1.3 (1928): 266.
—. scéalaí. "Scéalaidheacht Chorca Dhuibhne: "Seomra na h-Aithne". Scéalaíocht / béaloideas. *Béaloideas* 2.2 (1929): 213–15.
—. scéalaí. "Sgéalta Sidhe: 'Júile 'n Leasa' agus 'Airgead an Áirseóra'." Scéalaíocht / béaloideas. *Béaloideas* 2.1 (1929): 71–3.
—. scéalaí. "Ó Chorca Dhuibhne: 'Rí na Gréine agus Bannríon na Gaoithe' agus "Inghean Rí Ná Pósfadh". Scéalaíocht / béaloideas. *Béaloideas* 2.3 (1930): 274–81.
—. scéalaí. "Sgéilíní Andeas: 'An Chinniúint'." Scéalaíocht / béaloideas. *Béaloideas* 2.3 (1930): 286.
—. scéalaí. "Ó Uíbh Ráthach agus Corca Dhuibhne: 'An Roinnt a Thug Áibhis ar an bPraisigh'." Scéalaíocht / béaloideas. *Béaloideas* 3.2 (1931): 261 agus 271–2.
—. scéalaí. "Scéalta Creidimh agus Crábhaidh: 'An t-Árthach a Bádh mar Gheall ar Aenne "Mháin"', 'Mar Tháinig an tSainnt san Eaglais', 'Fear a' Dá Thrumpa', 'An Bhean a Chuaidh go hOfrann' agus 'Triúr Naomh Ghallaruis'." Scéalaíocht / béaloideas. *Béaloideas* 3.1 (1931): 3–30.
—. "Secstrum Sandi." *Duanaire Duibhneach: bailiú d'amhránaibh agus de phíosaibh eile filidheachta a ceapadh le tuairim céad bliain i gCorca Dhuibhne, agus atá fós i gcuimhne agus i mbéaloideas na ndaoine ann.* Filíocht / béaloideas. Eag. Seán Ó Dubhda. 1933. Baile Átha Cliath: Oifig Dhíolta Foilseacháin Rialtais, 1969. 107.
—. scéalaí. "Ó Dhuibhneachaibh." Seanchas, scéalaíocht agus filíocht / béaloideas. *Béaloideas* 16 (1948): 105–8.

Uí Mhuláin, Betty [Mullins / Ní Argáin, Betty]. *fl.* **1931.** Cúil Aodha, Co. Chorcaí. Seanchas / béaloideas.

Bhí Betty ina cónaí i gCúil Aodha i 1931 nuair a bhailigh Gearóid Ó Murchadha seanchas uaithi. D'fhoilsigh sé an seanchas sin in *Béaloideas* 3 (1931). Cheap sé go raibh Gaolainn mhaith aici agus ba i gCúil Aodha a tógadh í. Tá sí luaite arís ag Brian Ó Cuív in *Cnósach Focal ó Bhaile Bhúirne* (1947, 281). Mar atá luaite ag Seán Ó Súilleabháin in *Éigse* 33, lch 177, nóta 33, Beití Ní Argáin a bhí uirthi sular phós sí, agus bhí cónaí uirthi féin agus ar a fear, Tadhg, ar an Múirneach Beag. Luann Donncha Ua Buachalla, leis, í ina fhoclóir.

Select bibliography
Uí Mhuláin, Betty.
—. seanchaí. "Eachtraí, Véursaí agus Paidreacha ó Iarthar Chorcaighe: 'Dómhnall Ó Conaill', 'Coigilim an Teine seo' agus 'An Sgiath-Lúireach Bheannuighthe'." Seanchas / béaloideas. *Béaloideas* 3.2 (1931): 227–8, 234, 237.

Secondary sources
Ó Cuív, Brian. *Cnósach focal ó Bhaile Bhúirne.* Baile Átha Cliath: n.p., 1947.

Uí Mhurchadha, Bean [Iníon an Ruiséalaigh]. *fl.* **1933.** An Baile Loisce, Corca Dhuibhne, Co. Chiarraí. Seanchas / béaloideas.

Bhí Bean Uí Mhurchadha ag cur fúithi i mBaile Loisce. File ab ea a hathair, an Ruiséalach. Thug sí leagan de "Faoistine Cheallacháin" agus de "Má's Buairt Rómhór" do Sheán Ó Dubhda. Foilsíodh iad in *Duanaire Duibhneach.*

Select bibliography
Uí Mhurchadha, Bean.
—. "Faoistine Cheallacháin" agus "Má's Buairt Rómhór." *Duanaire Duibhneach: bailiú d'amhránaibh agus de phíosaibh eile filidheachta a ceapadh le tuairim céad bliain i gCorca Dhuibhne, agus atá fós i gcuimhne agus i mbéaloideas na ndaoine ann.* Filíocht / béaloideas. Eag. Seán Ó Dubhda. 1933. Baile Átha Cliath: Oifig Dhíolta Foilseacháin Rialtais, 1969. 100–102, 105.

Uí Nuanáin, Máire. Comhaimseartha. Trá Lí, Co. Chiarraí. Filíocht agus scríbhneoireacht acadúil, ailt.

Saolaíodh Máire in Árainn i 1929 ach tá cónaí uirthi i dTrá Lí, Co. Chiarraí anois. Tá ailt léi foilsithe i dtréimhseacháin éagsúla. Tá cainteanna tugtha aici ar an gclár "Peann agus Pár" ar Raidió na Gaeltachta. Tá BA sa Léann Ceilteach aici.

Select bibliography
Uí Nuanáin, Máire.
—. "Aiste." Scríbhneoireacht acadúil. *Samhlaíocht Chiarraí* (Nollaig 1995).
—. "Aiste." Scríbhneoireacht acadúil, ailt. *Feasta* (Lúnasa 1997).
—. *Tuirne Mháire: Óige in Árainn.* Filíocht. Baile Átha Cliath: Coiscéim, 1998.

Secondary sources
Uí Nia, Gearóidín, eag. "Uí Nuanáin, Máire." *Eolaire Chló Iar-Chonnachta de Scríbhneoirí Gaeilge.* Indreabhán: Cló Iar-Chonnachta, 1998.

Uí Ógáin, Ríonach. Comhaimseartha. Tíorabháin, Baile an Fheirtéaraigh, Co. Chiarraí. Scríbhneoireacht acadúil, léirmheastóireacht, stair shóisialta agus eagarthóireacht ar chaiséid agus ar dhlúthdhiosca.

Caitheann Ríonach go leor ama i dTíorabháin, gar do Bhaile an Fheirtéaraigh i gCorca Dhuibhne. Tá roinnt foilsithe aici a bhfuil baint aige leis an gceantar seo agus áiteanna eile i gCúige Mumhan. Tá sí ina cónaí i mBaile Átha Cliath.

Select bibliography
Uí Ógáin, Ríonach.
—. "Aifreann na Gine Aifreann is Fiche." Scríbhneoireacht acadúil, stair shóisialta. *Comhar* Nollaig (1983): 28–31.
—. "Ceol, Rince agus Amhráin." *Oidhreacht an Bhlascaoid*. Scríbhneoireacht acadúil, stair shóisialta. Eag. Aogán Ó Muircheartaigh. Baile Átha Cliath: Coiscéim, 1989. 109–28.
—. eag. *Beauty an Oileáin: Music and Song of the Blasket Islands*. Ceol. Baile Átha Cliath: Ceirníní Cladaigh, 1992.

Uí Shé, Máire Bean. Comhaimseartha. Co. Chiarraí. Beathaisnéis / seanchas.

Foilsíodh leabhar le Máire i 1991, *An Ghlaise Ghlé*. Is é atá ann ná bailiúchán mionseanchais as Ciarraí Theas le múinteoir a chaith a saol san áit.

Select bibliography
Uí Shé, Máire Bean.
—. *An Ghlaise Ghlé*. Beathaisnéis / seanchas. Bean Uí Shé "Cumann Bhríde"/ Féinfhoilsiú, 1991.

Uí Shíthigh, Máire. Comhaimseartha. Corca Dhuibhne, Co. Chiarraí. Scríbhneoireacht acadúil, taighde.

Tá Máire i gceannas ar Oidhreacht Chorca Dhuibhne, Baile an Fheirtéaraigh. Saolaíodh i mBÁC í ach Gaeilge na Mumhan atá aici agus tá cónaí uirthi i gCorca Dhuibhne leis na blianta.

Select bibliography
Uí Shíthigh, Máire.
—. agus Isobel Bennett, eag. *Clocha Oghaim Chorca Dhuibhne, Ogham Stones of the Dingle Peninsula*. Scríbhneoireacht acadúil, taighde. Baile an Fheirtéaraigh: Oidhreacht Chorca Dhuibhne, 1995.

Varian, Elizabeth Willoughby [Finola, Eilís Ní Chraoibhín]. 1830–96. Cork. Poetry.

Born in Co. Antrim *c.* 1830, she married Ralph Varian, a Cork poet and editor who was imprisoned in Sunday's Well Gaol in 1848 following demonstrations in support of William Smith O'Brien. He composed many well known ballads, such as "The Harp of Erin" and "The Spinning Wheel". Elizabeth Varian probably moved to Cork following her marriage, where she still lived – according to Colman – near the end of her life (Colman, 217). She contributed patriotic poetry to *the Nation* and The *Irish Monthly* mostly in the 1850s and 1860s, and also published several poetry collections. Her nickname was "Lizzie Twigg", and Leland tells us that one of her later collections was published under the name "Eilís Ní Chraoibhín" (Leland, 198). Hester Sigerson (*q.v.*) was her sister-in-law.

Select bibliography
Varian, Elizabeth Willoughby.
—. *Poems by Finola*. Poetry. Belfast: John Henderson, 1851.
—. *Never Forsake the Ship, and Other Poems*. Poetry: n.p. Dublin, 1874.
—. *The Political and National Poems of Finola*. Poetry. Dublin: n.p., 1877.
—. "A Plea for the Poor." Poetry. *Irish Monthly* 11.July (1883): 365–6.

Vassal, Michèle. Contemporary. Kenmare, Co. Kerry. Poetry.

From Barcelonnette in the Alpes de Haute-Provence, she came to live in Dublin in the late 1970s. By 2000, when her first collection of poetry, *Sandgames*, was published, she was living in Kenmare in Co. Kerry. Although French is her first language, she prefers to write in English and her poems have been published in anthologies and journals in Ireland and the USA. In 1999 she was awarded the Listowel Writers' Week Poetry prize.

Select bibliography
Vassal, Michèle.
—. *Sandgames*. Poetry. Cliffs of Moher, Co. Clare: Salmon, 2000.

Verschoyle, Moira. *fl.* 1960–63. Co. Limerick. Novels.

Born in Co. Limerick in 1904, she was educated privately. Her mother, Hilda, was raised in Italy, but moved to Castle Troy following her marriage to Frederick Verschoyle. Moira was the youngest of their children. She was particularly close to her mother, to whom she dedicated her autobiography, *So Long to Wait*, published in 1960.

Select bibliography
Verschoyle, Moira.
—. *So Long to Wait: An Irish Childhood*. Autobiography. London: Geoffrey Bles, 1960.
—. *Children in Love*. Novel. London: Hodder & Stoughton, 1961.
—. *Daughters of the General*. Novel. London: Hodder & Stoughton, 1963.

Voynich, E.L., née Boole. 1864–1960. Cork. Novels.

Born in 1864 in Cork, she was the daughter of the mathematician George Boole and Mary Everest Boole (*q.v.*), a scientist and philosopher. Ethel was educated in Cork and in Berlin, and while travelling in Russia she met a Polish patriot, whom she married in 1891. He changed his name to Wilfred Voynich and became well known as a bibliographer and antiquarian bookseller in London. The couple moved to New York in 1916, where the author stayed until her death in 1960.

She wrote many novels but none of them attained the success achieved by her first, *The Gadfly* (1897), based on the exploits of Garibaldi. A bestseller, it was particularly successful in Russia and Eastern Europe, was translated into over thirty languages and sold over five million copies worldwide over a sixty-year period. It was dramatized by George Bernard Shaw, and made into a film in Russia with a musical score by Shostakovich. Voynich spent the second half of her life in the USA. Her later novels, increasingly sombre in tone, were less successful. The best known of these were *An Interrupted Friendship* (1910), also set in Italy, *Olive Latham* (1904), set in revolutionary Poland, and *Jack Raymond* (1901). In addition to writing, Voynich also composed religious music, including an oratorio, *Babylon*, and five cantatas. She died in New York in 1960. In her later years she provided encouragement for younger English writers.

Select bibliography

Voynich, E.L.

—. trans. *Stories from Garshin*. London: Unwin, 1893.

—. *The Gadfly*. Novel. London: Heinemann, 1897. Moscow: Cooperative Publishing Society, 1936.

—. *Jack Raymond*. Novel. London: Heinemann, 1901.

—. *Olive Latham*. Novel. London: Heinemann, 1904.

—. *An Interrupted Friendship*. Novel. London: Hutchinson, 1910.

—. trans. "Chopin's Letters Collected by Henryk Opienski." Letters. London: Harmsworth, 1932. Notes: Trans. from the original Polish and French, with a preface and editorial notes.

—. *Put Off Thy Shoes*. Autobiography. New York: Macmillan, 1945. London: Heinemann, 1946.

Secondary sources

Kettle, Arnold. "E.L. Voynich: Forgotten English Novelist." *Essays in Criticism* 7 (1957).

Lockhart, Robin N. Bruce. *Ace of Spies*. London: Hodder & Stoughton, 1967.

Walsh, Anne. Contemporary. Cork. Academic writing.

A lecturer in the Department of Hispanic Studies, UCC, since 1995, she took a PhD in Spanish at NUI in 1997. Her research interests include the myth of Don Juan, the writings of Gonzalo Torrente Ballester, and the modern and post-civil-war Spanish novel. Walsh has published essays in a number of academic journals and anthologies. An essay exploring Spanish detective fiction is forthcoming in a collection entitled *National and Cultural Identities: Detective Fiction*.

Select bibliography

Walsh, Anne.

—. "Belief and Disbelief as Part of Narrative: Gonzalo Torrente Ballester's *Don Juan, A Road Less Travelled*." Academic writing. *Bulletin of Hispanic Studies* LXXVI (1999): 349–58.

—. "Gonzalo Torrente Ballester's *Don Juan*: A Novel Both Before and After Its Time?" *Selected Interdisciplinary Essays on the Representation of the Don Juan Archetype in Myth and Culture*. Academic writing. Ed. Andrew Ginger, John Hobbs and Huw Lewis. USA: Edwin Mellen, 2000. 215–35.

Walsh, Catherine. Contemporary. Limerick. Poetry.

Born in Dublin in 1964, she grew up in the inner-city district of Rialto. She also spent part of her childhood at her grandmother's farm in Wexford. She had a passion for reading and writing from an early age, and sought out poetry workshops and meetings in a bid to make contacts and meet like-minded people. As a result she met fellow poet and future husband Billy Mills and the couple moved to Barcelona in 1986, where she spent three years teaching English. She then moved to Eastbourne in England, where she spent six years, before returning to Dublin in 1995. Four years later she moved with her family to Limerick, where she now lives. With her husband she runs the small press, hardPressed Poetry, which has published four of her nine works to date. All of her writings have been issued through independent small presses due to the experimental nature of her work, which is quite resistant to a mainstream view of poetry as a closed lyric poem. Her poetry makes use of the entire space of the page and does not conform to structured stanza form, a practice that is relatively rare in terms of the Irish literary tradition.

Select bibliography
Walsh, Catherine.
—. *The Ca Pater Pillar Thing and More Besides*. Poetry. Dublin: hardPressed Poetry, 1986.
—. *Macula*. Poetry. Dublin: Red Wheelbarrow, 1986.
—. *Making Tents*. Poetry. Dublin: hardPressed Poetry, 1987.
—. *Short Stories*. Poetry. Twickenham: North and South, 1989.
—. *Prospect into Breath: Interviews with North and South Writers*. Interview. Ed. Peterjon Skelt. Twickenham: North and South, 1991. 171–89.
—. *From Pitch*. Poetry. London: Form, 1993.
—. *Pitch*. Poetry. Durham: Pig, 1994.
—. *Idir Eatortha and Making Tents*. Poetry. London: Invisible, 1996.
—. *City West*. Poetry. Limerick: hardPressed Poetry, 2000.
—. *Pompleat*. Poetry. Limerick: hardPressed Poetry, 2002.

Secondary sources
Caddel, Richard, and Peter Quatermain, eds. *Other: British and Irish Poetry since 1970*. Hanover: New England UP, 1999.
Davis, Alex. *A Broken Line: Denis Devlin and Irish Poetic Modernism*. Dublin: UCD, 2000.
Gilonis, Harry. *For the Birds: Proceedings of the First Cork Conference on New and Experimental Irish Poetry*. Surrey: Mainstream Poetry, 1998.
Goodby, John. *Irish Poetry since 1950: From Stillness into History*. Manchester: Manchester UP, 2000.
Tarlo, Harriet. "Provisional Pleasures: The Challenge of Contemporary Experimental Women Poets." *Feminist Review* 62 (1999): 94–112.
Tuma, Keith. "Pig Press." *Sulfur* 37 (1995): 204–9.
—. ed. *Anthology of Twentieth-Century British and Irish Poetry*. Oxford: Oxford UP, 2001.

Ward, Maisie. Contemporary. Limerick. Autobiography.

Born in 1911, she was the eldest of thirteen children and spent much of her childhood caring for her younger siblings. She was educated locally and in 1927 she met her future husband, Wilhelm, and went to live in Germany. Her autobiography describes her experiences during the war years. In 1946 she returned to live in Limerick

Select bibliography
Ward, Maisie.
—. *Always Look Forward.* Autobiography. Limerick: n.p., n.d.

Warnock, Gabrielle. Contemporary. West Cork. Novels, short stories.
Born in West Cork in 1947 she grew up in Cork city and Kilkenny. She studied at TCD and UCD. She won a Hennessy Literary Award in 1981.

Select bibliography
Warnock, Gabrielle.
—. *Fly in a Web.* Novel. Dublin: Poolbeg, 1984.
—. "Für Elise." *The Irish Eros: Irish Short Stories and Poems on Sexual Themes.* Short story. Ed. David Marcus. Dublin: Gill & Macmillan, 1996. 204–9.
—. *The Silk Weaver.* Novel. London: Trident, 1998.
—. and Jeff O'Connell. *Face to Face.* Novel. Clifden, Co. Galway: Trident, 2001.

Wassell, Elizabeth. Contemporary. West Cork. Novels.
Born in Manhattan, she has travelled extensively throughout Europe and now lives in West Cork. She has published three novels.

Select bibliography
Wassell, Elizabeth.
—. *The Honey Plain.* Novel. Dublin: Wolfhound, 1997.
—. *Sleight of Hand.* Novel. Dublin: Wolfhound, 1999.
—. *The Thing He Loves.* Novel. Dingle: Brandon, 2001.

Wells, Grace. Contemporary. Tipperary. Fiction.
Born in 1968 in London, she worked there as a television and video producer until 1991, when she moved to Ireland to work with Kerry-based artist Lily van Oost. This project completed, she settled in Tipperary and began work in a number of areas, including organic agriculture, working with people with special needs, as well as facilitating biography and poetry workshops. Her writing career began to take shape in 2002 when she was appointed literature officer at the South Tipperary Art Centre. The same year saw the publication of her first novel, *Gyrfalcon*, and she was also selected as an upcoming poet for Poetry Ireland's *Introductions Series 2002*. She has lived on the side of the Sliabh na mBan hills in Co. Tipperary for the past eleven years.

Select bibliography
Wells, Grace.
—. *Gyrfalcon.* Novel. Dublin: O'Brien, 2002.

Wheeler, Anna Doyle [Vlasta]. 1785–1849. Co. Tipperary. Political writing, sociology, philosophy.
Daughter of Anna Dunbar and Nicholas Milley Doyle, a Church of Ireland clergyman in Co. Tipperary. Her father died when Anna was two years old. Her interest in nationalism came from her godfather, Henry Grattan, and her uncle, Gen. Sir John Doyle, who travelled extensively in France. Following her father's death her family was not particularly well-off, which may

have been the reason for her marriage to Francis Massey-Wheeler when she was just fifteen years old. The couple lived on his Ballywire estate, on the Limerick–Tipperary border, and their married life was characterized by Massey-Wheeler's alcoholism and violence. She finally ran away from the marriage, taking her two children with her, and went to live with her uncle, the Governor of Guernsey. There, she received an education in French and Italian, alongside her daughters, and participated in the lively social world of the Governor's household.

Sending her teenage daughters to school in Dublin and London in 1816, Wheeler went to live in Caen, where she joined the Saint-Simonians, a group of socialists and free thinkers. At this point, Dooley tells us, "Wheeler began to construct her identity as a nineteenth-century salonnière" (63). In the 1820s, following the death of Massey-Wheeler, she divided her time between Dublin and London, and got to know members of the cooperative movement, as well as the utilitarians. One of her closest friends was Jeremy Bentham, the utilitarian leader. Dooley describes her at this stage in her life as: "a translator, a collaborator between French and English co-operators, a liaison person facilitating introductions to both Owen and Fourier, and a diplomatic ombudswoman among highly competitive men" (71).

Today, she is probably best known for her collaboration with William Thompson on the first socialist feminist manifesto, *Appeal of One-Half the Human Race, Women, Against the Pretensions of the Other Half, Men, to Retain Them in Political and thence in Civil and Domestic Slavery* (1825). Although her name is not recorded as co-author of this work, Thompson explains in the introduction, a "Letter to Mrs Wheeler", that the project was a joint effort: "our joint property, I being your interpreter and the scribe of your sentiments" (xxiii). This explanation of the kind of project undertaken by Thompson and Wheeler acknowledges Wheeler's part in it, and delineates her intellectual contribution to the finished work. We know that she actually did write some sections of the *Appeal*, but it seems clear that Thompson wrote much of it. However, Wheeler's arguments and ideas were well known to those in the cooperative movement in the period, and would have been recognizable to those familiar with her work, even in the sections penned by Thompson.

In 1826, one of Wheeler's daughters, Henrietta, died of a wasting disease. Henrietta shared her mother's radicalism, and had been involved, for example, in the political mobilization of Europeans to help the Greek national struggle (Dooley, 8). We know that following Henrietta's death Anna Wheeler was once again living in Ireland. Her other daughter, Rosina (*q.v.*), married the novelist and politician Bulwer Lytton, although their marriage was a turbulent one and ended after nine years. Interestingly, Constance Lytton, Anna Wheeler's great-granddaughter, was a prominent feminist and member of the Women's Social and Political Union.

It is by her political legacy that Wheeler is remembered today. In addition to the *Appeal*, her writing includes public lectures, correspondence and translations of feminist materials from French journals, which she published in the Owenite journal *The Crisis*, often under the pseudonym "Vlasta". A radical feminist who identified the subordinate position of women as one deliberately constructed through the institutions of marriage, education and religion, Wheeler participated in many debates on these issues with other women in *The Crisis*. Her investment in a community of political radicals and intellectuals remained with her throughout her life. For example, she maintained strong friendships with other Saint-Simonian women, such as Flora Tristan and Desirée Veret, whose writing and political activism contributed to the construction of early feminist principles. Her correspondence facilitated a nexus of exchanges between French and English philosophers and political activists throughout her lifetime. She was actively communicating with friends in France before the upheavals of 1848, and always yearned to return to live in France but was prevented by illness from travelling. It is thought that Wheeler died between 1848 and 1851, though we are not sure of the exact date.

Note: A full list of Wheeler's correspondence is provided in Dooley, (1996).

Select bibliography
Wheeler, Anna Doyle.
—. with William Thompson. *Appeal of One-Half the Human Race, Women, Against the Pretensions of the Other Half, Men, to Retain Them in Political and thence in Civil and Domestic Slavery*. Political writing. London: Longman, Hurst, Rees, Orme, Brown & Green, 1825. Cork: Cork UP, 1997.
—. "Rights of Women." Political writing. *The British Co-Operator* 1 (April 1830): 12–15.
—. "Rights of Women, Part 2." Political writing. *The British Co-Operator* 2 (May 1830): 33–6.
—. trans. "Appeal aux Femmes." Political writing. *La Femme Libre* 1.1–3 (1832).
—. "To the Editor of *The Crisis*." Letter, political writing. *The Crisis* 2 August (1833): 277–9.

Secondary sources
Dooley, Dolores. *Equality in Community: Sexual Equality in the Writings of William Thompson and Anna Doyle Wheeler*. Cork: Cork UP, 1996.
Mander, W. J., and A.P.F. Sell. *Dictionary of Nineteenth Century British Philosophers*. Bristol: Thoemmes Press, 2002.

Whelan, Bernadette. Contemporary. Limerick. Academic writing.

A lecturer in History at UL, she took an MA and PhD at NUI. Her research interests include American/Irish relations in the twentieth century, Irish foreign policy 1900–1960 and women in Ireland 1900–1960.

Select bibliography
Whelan, Bernadette.
—. Michael Holmes and Nicholas Rees. *The Poor Relation: Irish Foreign Policy and the Third World*. Academic writing. Dublin: Gill & Macmillan/ Trócaire, 1993.
—. ed. *The Last of the Great Wars: Essays on the War of the Three Kings in Ireland, 1688–91*. Academic writing. Limerick: Limerick UP, 1995.
—. ed. *Clio's Daughters: Essays on Irish Women's History 1845 to 1939*. Academic writing. Limerick: Limerick UP, 1997.
—. "Integration or Isolation: Ireland and the Invitation to Join the Marshall Plan."

Essays on Irish Foreign Policy in the Twentieth Century. Academic writing. Ed. Michael Kennedy and Joseph Skelly. Dublin: Four Courts, 2000.

—. *Ireland and the Marshall Plan, 1947–57.* Academic writing. Dublin: Four Courts, 2000.

—. ed. *Women and Paid Work in Ireland, 1500 to 1930.* Academic writing. Dublin: Four Courts, 2000.

—. "Non-Combatants and the Moral Context of Warfare in Seventeenth Century Ireland." *Conquest and Resistance History of Warfare 3: War In Seventeenth Century Ireland.* Academic writing. Ed. P. Lenihan. Leiden: Brill, 2001.

Willows, Liz. Contemporary. Cork city. Poetry, plays.

Born in Lancashire in 1960, she left school at sixteen to get married. She now lives in Cork city, and until recently was the literature officer at Tigh Filí (House of Poets). She published her first collection, *If This is Armageddon – It's Very Pretty*, in 2000. She describes herself as a Northern, working-class writer, a lesbian and a single parent. Recurring themes in her writings are love, life, sex, death and social exclusion.

Select bibliography
Willows, Liz.
—. *If This is Armageddon – It's Very Pretty.* Poetry. Cork: Bradshaw, 2000.

Wilmot, Katherine. 1774–1824. Cork. Diaries, letters, travel writing.

Daughter of Capt. Edward Wilmot, a Derbyshire man, and Miss Moore from Lota in Cork, she was the eldest in a family of nine. She grew up in Glanmire, and in 1802 inherited a fortune from her grandmother. In the same year she accompanied Lady Mount Cashell (*q.v.*) and her husband on their Grand Tour of the Continent. Katherine's letters and journals from this trip were edited and published by Thomas Sadleir, *An Irish Peer on the Continent* (1924). Dining with Napoleon and Talleyrand in Paris, and taking tours throughout France and Italy, where they had a private audience with the Pope, was a far cry from the quiet life of the Wilmot family at home in Glanmire.

On her return to Cork in 1803 Katherine remained at home for some months before she set off travelling again – this time to Russia, where her sister Martha Wilmot (*q.v.*) had been staying with the Princess Daschkaw for some time. Again, she wrote letters and journals about her travels, some of them with her sister Martha (see also Eleanor Cavanagh (*q.v.*)). These were later published as *The Russian Journals of Martha and Katherine Wilmot, 1803–1808* (1934). Some of the journals detail their association with Princess Daschkaw, then an elderly woman, and they provide an interesting portrait of her, as well as of Russia during the period. Katherine left Russia in 1807, sailing through Copenhagen the day before the bombardment by Lord Gambier.

On her return from Russia Katherine developed asthma, and she was advised not to live in Ireland because of the weather. Thus she migrated to Moulins, where she lived for four years. However, her chest problems continued, and she moved to Paris for medical treatment, where she died of tuberculosis several months later in 1824.

Note: Her original diaries and letters are in the library of the Royal Irish Academy.

Select bibliography
Wilmot, Katherine.
—. *An Irish Peer on the Continent 1801–1803.* Travel writing. Ed. Thomas U. Sadleir. London: Williams & Norgate, 1924.
—. and Martha Wilmot. *The Russian Journals of Martha and Katherine Wilmot, Being an Account by Two Irish Ladies of their Adventures in Russia as Guests of the Celebrated Princess Daskaw, Containing Vivid Descriptions of Contemporary Court Life and Society, and Lively Anecdotes of many Interesting Historical Characters. 1803–1808.* Travel writing, letters. Ed. the Marchioness of Londonderry and Montgomery Hyde. London: Macmillan, 1934.

Wilmot, Martha. 1775–1873. Glanmire, Co. Cork. Diaries, letters, travel writing.

Sister of Katherine Wilmot, she was also a remarkable traveller. On a visit to England in 1776 her father, Edward Wilmot, met the Princess Daschkaw, whom he invited to visit Cork. Three years later, on a visit to Ireland, she visited the Wilmots, and Martha made her acquaintance. In 1802 Martha's favourite brother, a promising young naval officer, died of yellow fever in the West Indies, and Martha suffered from serious depression following his death. In an attempt to lift her spirits, her friends encouraged her to travel, and accordingly, on the invitation of Princess Daschkaw, she set out for Russia in 1803, travelling by Dublin, London and Yarmouth to St Petersburg (see also Eleanor Cavanagh (*q.v.*)).

According to Sadleir, the Princess doted on Martha, and he suggests that there was a romantic friendship between the two (Katherine Wilmot, xi). Martha encouraged her to write her autobiography, which she did, on condition that the manuscript would not be published until after her death. When Katherine Wilmot visited Russia she intended to bring her sister home, but Martha could not part with Princess Daschkaw, and Katherine returned to Ireland alone. However, Martha's parents finally insisted on her return, and she travelled back across Europe in 1808, laden with presents from her Russian friend. One of these parcels contained £13,000 and a note which read: "I beseech you not to open this Pacquet, but after my death, and then accept the contents from a friend, a mother who taught (*sic*) herself under a great obligation to you, and who loved you most tenderly" (Wlilmot, xii). Shortly after Martha's departure the Princess became seriously ill and died. Martha's journals and letters concerning her European travels were later published.

Four years later, in 1812, Martha married William Bradford, chaplain to the British Embassy in Vienna, a city then at the centre of Europe. Some of her letters from this period were later published as *More Letters from Martha Wilmot, Vienna 1819–29* (1935). Following this the Bradfords moved to Sussex. Martha had a long life, and spent her final years living with her daughter at Taney House, Dundrum, Co. Dublin.

314 Munster Women Writers 1800–2000

Select bibliography
Wilmot, Martha.

—. *The Russian Journals of Martha and Katherine Wilmot, Being an Account by Two Irish Ladies of their Adventures in Russia as Guests of the Celebrated Princess Daskaw, Containing Vivid Descriptions of Contemporary Court Life and Society, and Lively Anecdotes of many Interesting Historical Characters. 1803–1808*. Travel writing. Ed. The Marchioness of Londonderry and Montgomery Hyde. London: Macmillan, 1934.
—. *More Letters from Martha Wilmot, Vienna 1819–29*. Ed. the Marchioness of Londonderry and Montgomery Hyde. N.p.: n.p., 1935.

Secondary Sources
Wilmot, Katherine. *An Irish Peer on the Continent 1801–1803*. Ed. Thomas U. Sadleir. London: Williams & Norgate, 1924.

Yasin, Brenda, née Meredith. 1921–80. Glengarriff, Co. Cork. Poetry.

Born in Dublin in 1921. Her father was a philosopher, an author of several literary works and a judge who served both Ireland and the League of Nations. Her mother, a well known patron of the arts, had studied under Paul Cézanne in Paris. Brenda was educated in Dublin, York and Lausanne, took a degree in philosophy and psychology at TCD, graduated in 1945 and later received an MA. She did voluntary work in Pakistan for some time. A lifelong Quaker and pacifist, she founded, joined and supported a number of organizations promoting peace, reconciliation, civil rights and human freedoms. She participated in campaigns for the Irish Pacifist Movement, for nuclear disarmament and against the Vietnam War. She represented Ireland as part of a delegation which travelled to Rome to meet Pope John XXIII following publication of the encyclical *Pacem in Terris*. She also worked on behalf of the Traveller community.

During the 1970s she made an extensive study of Allama Iqbal, Pakistan's national poet, and won a Commemorative Gold Medal for her research at a conference in Pakistan in 1977 commemorating Iqbal's centenary. Her last public address was at a gathering to honour Patrick Pearse's centenary at Dublin's United Arts Club in early 1979. She spoke on Pearse and his contemporaries. A posthumous collection of her poems was published by her husband and daughter in 1986. One of these poems was published in the official organ of the Irish Transport and General Workers' Union.

Select bibliography
Yasin, Brenda.

—. *Pilgrim Spirit: A Selection of Verse*. Poetry. Dublin: Elo, 1986.

Appendix 1:
Genre List

Categories used for English Entries

Academic writing
Anthology
Autobiography
Biography
Children's writing
Cookbooks
Diaries
Documentary
Education
Essays
Family history
Fiction
Fiction for girls
Film script
Folklore
Handbook / manual
Handcrafts
Historical novels

History
Interview
Journalism
Lecture
Letters
Literary criticism
Local history
Memoir
Novels
Papers
Philosophy
Play
Poetry
Political writing [inc. feminism]
Radio play
Radio programme
Reading

Religious writing
Reviews
Science
Short stories
Social history
Sociology
Songs
Spiritualism
Television drama
Translations
Travel writing
Web page
Young adult fiction

Categories used for Irish Entries

Ailt
Aistí
Aistriúcháin
Amhránaíocht
Beathaisnéis
Caoineadh/béaloideas
Drámaíocht
Eagarthóireacht
Filíocht
Filíocht/béaloideas

Filíocht/caoineadh
Gearrscéalaíocht
Gramadach
Iriseoireacht
Leabhair teagaisc
Léirmheastóireacht
Litreacha
Litríocht leanaí
Paidreacha
Scéalaíocht/béaloideas

Scríbhneoireacht acadúil
Seanchas/béaloideas
Stair
Stair shóisialta
Taighde
Taisteal
Teangeolaíocht
Úrscéalaíocht

Appendix 2: Library, Archival and Other Resouces

Attic Press / Róisín Conroy Collection at the Boole Library, UCC.

The archives of Attic Press, the Irish Feminist publishing house, were generated and collected by Róisín Conroy, co-founder and publisher of Attic Press and an activist in the Irish women's movement. They were deposited in the Boole Library by Conroy in 1997, and are now open for researchers to consult. The collection reflects the various facets of Conroy's career as a librarian and information officer, publisher, disseminator of information and campaigner for women's rights. The archive covers the years 1963–1991 and contains 133 boxes plus ephemera. There is a wide range of materials, including primary sources relating to Irish feminist activism, as well as the archives of the Press. There is an excellent catalogue, available to consult in the Special Collection section of the Library. Those interested in using the archive should contact Carol Quinn, the library archivist, or see http://booleweb.ucc.ie/search/subject/archives/atticpress.htm for further information.

Local Studies Sections in the Regional Library Network

Local studies sections are now central to the Irish library network, and were key to our research, as it was regional. Ennis Library is possibly the flagship for local studies in this part of the country, and we found a wealth of information on Clare writers in the collection there (see http://www.clarelibrary.ie/eolas/library/local-studies/locstudi1.htm). Similarly, local studies sections at the Kerry (http://www.kerrycolib.ie) and Waterford libraries (http://www.waterfordcity.ie/library.htm) proved useful to us during the research process, and Limerick city library's Local History Librarian, Mike Maguire, was extremely helpful (http://www.limerickcorp.ie). Tipperary local studies section (http://www.iol.ie/~tipplibs/Local.htm#Local) is augmented by the presence of the *Tipperary Historical Journal*, which was a useful resource. The Cork Collection at Cork City Library provides an important resource to local literary and historical researchers (http://www.corkcorp.ie/facilities/facilities_library.html), which is not to underestimate the importance of smaller libraries across the region, where local knowledge contributed greatly to our information on various writers.

The National Library of Ireland at Kildare St., Dublin 2 (http://www.nli.ie)

The National Library's mission is to collect, preserve and make available books, manuscripts and illustrative material of Irish interest. The Library contains the world's largest collection of Irish documentary material: books, manuscripts, newspapers, periodicals, drawings, photographs, maps, etc. It is open, free of charge, to all who want and need to use it. A Reader's Ticket is necessary in order to consult most categories of material. The Library does not lend books and reading is done in the various reading rooms. There is also a copying service and it is possible to get photocopies, photographs, slides or microfilm of most items in the collections.

The National Women's Library / Fawcett Library at London Guildhall University (http://www.lgu.ac.uk/fawcett/main.htm)

The National Women's Library exists to document the changing role of women in society, in the past, now and in the future. It seeks to collect materials relating to the changing role of women in society and to make these available to personal and to remote users, however they make contact.

RTÉ Sound Archive

The RTÉ Sound Archive holds a selection of news, sports, arts, traditional music, documentaries and drama recordings that relate to Irish women. Historical recordings are available on reel-to-reel ¼-inch tape from 1926. More comprehensive holdings date from $c.1947$. From 1996 on, live daytime RTE Radio 1 programmes, 2FM and flagship news programmes transmitted on a daily or weekly basis have been recorded. Due to funding limitations, the archive is not open to the public. However, researchers and academics may be able to gain access, in order to consult materials unavailable elsewhere, with prior agreement of the Librarian. Contact: Malachy Moran, Manager, Audio Services and Archives, via email (malachy.moran@rte.ie).

Appendix 3:
Select Online Sources

Munster Women Writers Online

A unique aspect of the project is the availability of this primary research to a very wide audience, not just by the publication of this dictionary, but also by the publication of an online searchable database. This database, available at www.ucc.ie/munsterwomen, will make the material of the dictionary available to anyone who has internet access. Those using the online dictionary will also be able to search the listings under the categories of place, genre and decade, but electronic users will probably not be able to gain such a vivid impression of the range and variety of writers all marshalled here as this volume provides. In the field of Irish studies, there are currently only a few other research projects of this kind available online, some of which are listed below.

Related Irish Online Sources

Directory of Sources for Women's History in Ireland (www.nationalarchives.ie/wh), the result of a survey undertaken by the Women's History Project, contains information and descriptions of over 14,000 collections of historical documents and sources in the Republic of Ireland and in Northern Ireland.

Electronic Irish Records Dataset (PGIL-Eirdata) (www.pgil-eirdata.com) is hosted by the Princess Grace Irish Library (Monaco) and has made available an impressive range of sources relating to Irish literary history and scholarship. It contains material relating to 4,500 Irish writers, and includes some extracts from their works.

Women in Irish Society Project (www.ucc.ie/wisp/iwm) provides resources relating to second-wave Irish feminist activism (1970s–present) in Ireland, on the website of the Irish Women's Movement Project, based at UCC.

International Online Projects

There are a number of ongoing literary projects internationally that are making resources for further research and reading available online.

A Celebration of Women Writers (www.digital.library.upenn.edu/women) provides a comprehensive listing of links to biographical and bibliographical information about women writers, and complete published books written by women.

Corvey Women Writers on the Web: An Electronic Guide to Literature 1796–1834 (www.shu.ac.uk/corvey/CW3) is based on the holdings of the Corvey Library and includes biographies, bibliographies, contemporary reviews and memoirs, images, synopses and keyword descriptions of texts, as well as new criticism and contextual material.

The Orlando Project (www.ualberta.ca/ORLANDO) at the University of Alberta is developing an online history of British women's writing.

The Perdita Project (www.human.ntu.ac.uk/perdita/PERDITA.HTM) is producing a database guide to approximately 400 sixteenth- and seventeenth-century manuscript archives compiled by women in the British Isles.

The Women Writers Project (www.wwp.brown.edu) at Brown University is developing an electronic textbase of women's writing in English before 1830, aiming to make the work of pre-Victorian women writers accessible to a wide audience.

The Victorian Women Writers Project (www.indiana.edu/~letrs/vwwp) is producing transcriptions of literary works by nineteenth-century British women writers. The works will include anthologies, novels, political pamphlets, religious tracts, children's books, and volumes of poetry and verse drama. Considerable attention will be given to the accuracy and completeness of the texts, and to accurate bibliographical descriptions of them.

Appendix 4:
Project Questionnaire

We used this questionnaire to try to follow up on initial information received about individual writers – these were distributed widely through the project website, library network and through the network of scholars established as the project developed.

The Munster Women Writers Project, Department of English, NUI Cork HEA Women in Irish Society Project (www.ucc.ie/wisp)

The remit of this project is to compile a database and biographical dictionary on Women's Writing from the Munster region in both English and Irish, 1800 to the present, and to make that material available to researchers in hardcover and via a website. We will include all kinds of writing – i.e. political and creative writing, letters, diaries and ephemera. The following is a questionnaire designed for circulation among writers, scholars working in this area, or readers who may have information relevant to the project. It has been designed to ensure that as many women writers as possible are included in the final bibliography. We would greatly appreciate it if you could fill this out and return it to us at the address given, and if possible, if you could also forward it to others who might have information on this area. Any information at all would be useful to our study, so please include writers even if you have very little detailed information about them – we may be able to piece an account together from a variety of contributors.

General Questions:
1. Can you suggest any Munster women writer/s who could be included in this project?
2. Could you give a brief indication as to your/their connections with Munster, e.g. place of birth, or what we call "place of association" where a writer may have lived/worked for a substantial period?
3. Can you suggest any useful critical, historical or biographical sources relating to this material, or other scholars working more generally in this field, who may have further information?

Individual Writers: please use a copy of this section for each writer you include
4. Writer's name, including pseudonym(s):
5. Dates:
6. Place(s) associated with:
7. Genre(s)/ kinds of writing:
8. Best-known works:

9. What are the other known or likely works of the writer(s)?

10.   Do you know where we might find copies of their works?

11. Are they in manuscript, typescript, or published form?

12. Can you indicate the location, public or private, of any archives or background information relating to this work/writer?

13. Are there any ongoing research projects, websites, or existing published work, which might be particularly useful in exploring these writings?

14. Do you have any biographical information about the writer(s) in question? (please attach a separate page where necessary) Can you give us any information about their literary estate, literary executor or relatives?

Bibliography: English entries

Allibone, Samuel, *A Critical Dictionary of English Literature and British and American Authors, Living and Deceased*, 3 vols. (London: N. Trubner, 1854–71).

Barry, Ann, "A Select Biographical and Bibliographical Index of Clare Writers in Print". Unpublished bibiography. (Ennis: Ennis Library, April 1972).

Blain, Virginia, Patricia Clements and Isabel Grundy (eds.), *The Feminist Companion to Literature in English: Women Writers from the Middle Ages to the Present* (London: Batsford, 1990).

Boada-Montagut, Irene, *Women Write Back: Contemporary Irish and Catalan Short Stories* (Dublin: Irish Academic Press, 2002).

Boland, Eavan, *Object Lessons: The Life of the Woman and the Poet in Our Time* (London: Vintage, 1996).

Brodhead, Richard H., *Cultures of Letters: Scenes of Reading and Writing in Nineteenth-Century America* (Chicago: University of Chicago Press, 1994).

Brown, Stephen J., *Guide to Books in Ireland* (Dublin: Hodges, Figgis, 1912).

— (ed.), *Catalogue of Novels and Tales by Catholic Writers*, 3rd ed. (Dublin: Central Catholic Library Association, 1929).

—. and Desmond Clarke, *Ireland in Fiction: A Guide to Irish Novels, Tales, Romances, and Folklore* (Dublin: Gill & Macmillan, 1985).

Buck, Claire, *Bloomsbury Guide to Women's Literature* (London: Bloomsbury, 1992).

Burke, Sir Bernard, *Burke's Genealogical and Heraldic History of the Landed Gentry of Ireland* (London: Burke's Peerage, 1958).

— *Burke's Irish Family Records*, 5th ed. (London: Burke's Peerage, 1976).

Butler, Patricia, *Irish Botanical Illustrators and Flower Painters* (Suffolk: Antique Collectors Club, 2000).

Byrne, Anne, and Ronit Lentin, *(Re)searching Women: Feminist Research Methodologies in the Social Sciences in Ireland* (Dublin: Institute of Public Administration, 2000).

Caherty, Thérèse, Rita Corley, Patricia Dixon and Catherine MacConville, *More Missing Pieces: Her Story of Irish Women* (Dublin: Attic, 1985).

Carlson, Julia (ed.), *Banned in Ireland: Censorship and the Irish Writer* (London: Routledge, 1990).

Choice, Donald (ed.), *Living Landscape Anthology* (Cork: West Cork Arts Centre, 1990).

Cleeve, Brian, *Dictionary of Irish Writers: Fiction*, vol. 1, 3 vols. (Cork: Mercier, 1967).

—. *Dictionary of Irish Writers: Non-Fiction*. vol. 2, 3 vols. (Cork: Mercier, 1969).

—. and Ann Brady. *Biographical Dictionary of Irish Writers* (Dublin: Lilliput, 1985).

Coleman, J. (ed.), *Windele's Cork: Historical and Descriptive Notices of the City of Cork from its Foundation to the Middle of the Nineteenth Century*, by John Windele (Cork: Guy, 1910).

Collins, Mary, "Bibliography of Munster Writers of the Twentieth Century" Unpublished bibliography. 1969. Cork City Library (Local Studies Section).

Colman, Anne Ulry, *A Dictionary of Nineteenth-Century Irish Women Poets* (Galway: Kenny's Bookshop, 1996).

Connolly, Claire (ed.), *Theorizing Ireland*, Readers in Cultural Criticism series (London: Palgrave, 2002).

Connolly, Linda, *The Irish Women's Movement: From Revolution to Devolution* (London: Palgrave, 2002).

Conrad, Kathryn A., *Locked in the Family Cell: Gener, Sexuality and Political Agency in Irish National Discourse*. (Wisconsin: Wisconsin University Press, 2004).

Coughlan, Patricia, and Alex Davis (eds.), *Modernism and Ireland: The Poetry of the 1930s* (Cork: Cork University Press, 1995).

Cross, Nigel, *The Royal Literary Fund 1790–1918: An Introduction to the Fund's History and Archives, with an Index of Applicants* (London: World Microfilms, 1984).

Cullen, Mary, and Maria Luddy, *Women, Power and Consciousness in Nineteenth-Century Ireland* (Dublin: Attic, 1995).

Delanty, Greg, and Nuala Ní Dhomhnaill (eds.), *Jumping Off Shadows: Selected Contemporary Irish Poets* (Cork: Cork University Press, 1995).

De Salvo, Louise, *et al.* (eds.), *Territories of the Voice: Contemporary Stories by Irish Women Writers* (Boston: Beacon, 1989). [Republished as *A Green and Mortal Sound: Short Fiction by Irish Women Writers* (Boston: Beacon, 1999).]

Donovan, Katie, A. Norman Jeffares and Brendan Kennelly (eds.), *Ireland's Women: Writings Past and Present* (Dublin: Gill & Macmillan, 1994).

Ezell, Margaret J.M., *Writing Women's Literary History* (Baltimore: Johns Hopkins University Press, 1993).

Fenwick, Gillian, *Women and the Dictionary of National Biography: A Bibliography of DNB volumes 1885–1985* (Aldershot: Scholar, 1994).

The Field Day Anthology of Irish Writing, Vols. I–III, ed. Séamus Deane (Derry: Field Day Publications, 1991).

The Field Day Anthology of Irish Writing, Vols IV–V, ed. Angela Bourke, Siobhán Kilfeather, Maria Luddy, Margaret McCurtain, Gerardine Meaney, Máirín Ní Dhonnchadha, Mary O'Dowd and Clair Wills (Cork: Cork University Press, in association with Field Day, 1996).

Fitzpatrick, David, *Oceans of Consolation: Personal Accounts of Irish Migration to Australia* (Cork: Cork University Press, 1994).

Fogarty, Anne, "The Ear of the Other: Dissident Voices in Kate O'Brien's *As Music and Splendour* and Mary Dorcey's *A Noise from the Woodshed*", in Éibhear Walshe (ed.), *Sex, Nation and Dissent in Irish Writing* (Cork: Cork University Press, 1997), 170–201.

— (ed.), *Irish Women Novelists: 1800–1940*, special issue of *Colby Quarterly* 2.36 (2000).

Haberstroh, Patricia Boyle, *Women Creating Women: Contemporary Irish Women Poets* (Dublin: Attic, 1996).

Hayes, Alan, and Diane Urquhart, *The Irish Women's History Reader* (London: Routledge, 2001).

Hogan, Robert (ed.), *Dictionary of Irish Literature* (Dublin: Gill & Macmillan, 1979).

— (ed.), *Dictionary of Irish Literature*, 2 vols., 2nd ed. (London: Aldwych, 1996).

Hoff, Joan, and Moureen Coulter, *Irish Women's Voices Past and Present*, special issue of *Journal of Women's History* 6.4–7.1 (1995).

Hooper, Glenn, and Colin Graham (eds.), *Irish and Postcolonial Writing: History, Theory and Practice* (London: Palgrave, 2002).

Jeffares, A.N., *Anglo-Irish Literature* (London: Macmillan, 1982).

Kelleher, Margaret, *The Feminisation of the Famine: Expression of the Inexpressible?* (Cork: Cork University Press, 1997).

—. and James H. Murphy (eds.), *Gender Perspectives in Nineteenth-Century Ireland: Public and Private Spheres* (Dublin: Irish Academic Press, 1997).

Kelly, A.A., *Pillars of the House: An Anthology of Verse by Irish Women from 1690 to the Present* (Dublin: Wolfhound, 1987, 1997).

—. *Wandering Women: Two Centuries of Travel Outside Ireland* (Dublin, Wolfhound Press, 1995).

Kelly, Cornelius, *The Grand Tour of Cork* (Cork: Cailleach, 2003).

Kirkpatrick, Kathryn, *Border Crossings: Irish Women Writers and National Identities* (Dublin: Wolfhound, 2000).

Leerssen, Joep, *Remembrance and Imagination: Patterns in the Historical and Literary Representations of Ireland in the Nineteenth Century*, Critical Conditions: Field Day Monographs series, ed. Séamus Deane (Cork: Cork University Press, in association with Field Day, 1996).

Leland, Mary, *The Lie of the Land: Journeys Through Literary Cork* (Cork: Cork University Press, 1999).

"List of Cork Authors compiled in connection with An Tostál Exhibition of Books and Pamphlets". 2 vols. Unpublished bibliography. (Boole Library, UCC, 1957).

Loeber, Rolf, and Magda Stouthamer-Loeber, *18th–19th Century Irish Fiction Newsletter* 1 (Jan. 1998): 1.

—. *18th–19th Century Irish Fiction Newsletter* 20 (Aug. 1999): 1–6.

—. "Literary Fiction as a Mirror of the Times: A Guide to Irish Fiction Published in Europe and North America" Unpub. ms. (*forthcoming* Four Courts Press, 2006).

Luddy, Maria, *Women in Ireland 1800–1918: A Documentary History* (Cork: Cork University Press, 1996).

—. and Mary Cullen, *Female Activists: Irish Women and Change, 1900–1960* (Dublin: Woodfield Press, 2001).

—. and Cliona Murphy. *Women Surviving: Studies in Irish Women's History in the 19th and 20th Centuries* (Dublin: Poolbeg, 1990).

Madden Simpson, Janet, *Woman's Part: An Anthology of Short Fiction by and about Irish Women, 1890–1960* (Dublin: Arlen House, 1984).

MacCarthy, B.G., *The Female Pen: Women Writers and Novelists 1621–1818* (Cork: Cork University Press, 1994).

McBreen, Joan, *The White Paper/An Bhileog Bhán: Twentieth-Century Irish Women Poets* (Cliffs of Moher, Co. Clare: Salmon, 1999).

McCoole, Sinéad. *No Ordinary Women: Irish Female Activists in the Revolutionary Years 1900–1923* (Dublin: O'Brien Press, 2003).

McMahon, Seán, and Jo O'Donoghue, *The Mercier Companion to Irish Literature* (Cork: Mercier, 1998).

McRedmond, Louis (ed.), *Modern Irish Lives: Dictionary of Twentieth-Century Biography* (Dublin: Gill & Macmillan, 1998).

Morash, Chris, *The Hungry Voice* (Dublin: Gill & Macmillan, 1989).

Murphy, James H., "'Things Which to You Seem Unfeminine': Gender and Nationalism in the Fiction of Some Upper Middle Class Catholic Women Novelists, 1880–1910", in Kathryn Kirkpatrick (ed.), *Border Crossings: Irish Women Writers and National Identities* (Dublin: Wolfhound, 2000). 58–78.

National Library of Ireland Collection List No. 56. Una Troy Papers. Compiled by Ann M. Butler. July 2000.

Ní Dhuibhne, Eilís (ed.), *Voices on the Wind: Women Poets of the Celtic Twilight* (Dublin: New Island, 1995).

O'Brien, Anthony, Ciarán O'Driscoll, Jo Slade and Mark Whelan (eds.), *On the Counterscarp: Limerick Writings 1961–1991* (Galway: Fourfront Poets / Salmon, 1991).

O'Brien, Joanne, Marie McAdam and Mary Lennon, eds. *Across the Water: Irish Women's Lives in Britain* (London: Virago, 1988).

Ó Céirín, Kit, and Cyril Ó Céirín (eds.), *Women of Ireland: A Biographical Dictionary* (Galway: Tír Eolas, 1996).

Ó Cuilleanáin, Cormac, and Léan Ní Chuilleanáin, "The Eilís Dillon Irish Writing Pages", http://homepage.tinet.ie/~writing.

O'Donoghue, D.J., *Poets of Ireland: A Biographical and Bibliographical Dictionary of Irish Writers of English Verse* (Dublin: Hodges & Figgis, 1912).

Ó Drisceoil, Donal, *Censorship in Ireland 1939–1945* (Cork: Cork University Press, 1993).

Parkinson, Siobhán, *A Part of Ourselves: Laments for Lives That Ended Too Soon* (Dublin: A. & A. Farmer, 1997).

Pettitt, Lance, *Screening Ireland: Film and Television Representation* (Manchester: Manchester University Press, 2000).

Pilkington, Lionel, *Theatre and the State in Twentieth-Century Ireland: Cultivating the People* (London: Routledge, 2001).

Prone, Terry, *A Woman's Christmas* (Dublin: Martello, 1994).

Smyth, Ailbhe (ed.), *Wildish Things: An Anthology of New Irish Women's Writing* (Dublin: Attic, 1989).

Smyth, Gerry, *Decolonisation and Criticism: The Construction of Irish Literature* (London: Pluto, 1998).

Somerville-Arjat, Gilean, and Rebecca E. Wilson, *Sleeping with Monsters: Conversations with Scottish and Irish Women Poets* (Dublin: Wolfhound, 1990).

St Peter, Christine, *Changing Ireland: Strategies in Contemporary Women's Fiction* (London: Macmillan, 2000).

Stars, Shells and Bluebells: Women Scientists and Pioneers (Dublin: WITS, 1994).

Tharu, Susie, and K. Lalita. *Women Writing in India: 600 BC to the Present Day* (London: Pandora, 1991).

Todd, Janet, *The Sign of Angelica: Women, Writing and Fiction, 1660–1800* (London: Virago, 1989).

—. "Introduction", in B.G. MacCarthy, *The Female Pen: Women Writers and Novelists 1621–1818* (Cork: Cork University Press, 1994).

—. *Feminist Literary History* (New York: Routledge, 1998).

—. *Daughters of Ireland: The Rebellious Kingsborough Sisters and the Making of a Modern Nation* (New York: Ballantine Books, 2004).

Tynan, Katherine, *The Cabinet of Irish Literature*, 4 vols. (London: Gresham, 1905).

Urquhart, Diane, and Alan Hayes (eds.), *The Irish Women's History Reader* (London: Routledge, 2000).

Walsh, Joe, "Laura Mary McCraith of Loughloher", in Michael Hallinan (ed.), *Tipperary County: People and Places: An Anthology of the Evolution of County Tipperary, Some Historic Events and the History of the Principal Towns in the County* (Dublin: Kincora Press, 1993), 175–6.

Walshe, Éibhear (ed.), *Ordinary People Dancing: Essays on Kate O'Brien* (Cork: Cork University Press, 1993.)

—. *Sex, Nation and Dissent in Irish Writing* (Cork: Cork University Press, 1997).

Weekes, Ann Owens, *Unveiling Treasures: The Attic Guide to the Published Works of Irish Women Literary Writers* (Dublin: Attic, 1993).

Welch, Robert (ed.), *Oxford Companion to Irish Literature* (Oxford: Clarendon, 1986).

Who's Who / Who Was Who: An Annual Biographical Dictionary (London: Black, 1891 (and subsequent eds.)).

Women's Commemoration and Celebration Committee, *Ten Dublin Women* (Dublin: WCCC, 1991).

Zimmerman, Bonnie, *The Safe Sea of Women: Lesbian Fiction 1969–1989* (Boston: Beacon, 1990).

Bibliography: Irish entries

An Scoláire Scairte, "Scríbhneoirí Móra is Beaga Chorca Dhuibhne", *Agus* XIV.6 (1974): 18–22

Bairéad, Peadar, "Léirmheas ar *Pacáiste Eolais: An Ghaeilge i gCill Chainnigh*", *An tUltach* (1995).

Bourke, Angela, "The Irish Traditional Lament and the Grieving Process", *Women's Studies International Forum* 11.4 (1988): 287–91.

Bourke, Angela. "Performing – Not Writing", *Graph: Irish Literary Review* 11 (1991–2): 28–31.

Bourke, Angela, "'Performing, Not Writing': The Reception of an Irish Woman's Lament", in Yopie Prins agus Maeera Schreiber (eag.), *Dwelling in Possibility: Women Poets and Critics on Poetry* (Ithaca: Cornell University Press, 1997), 132–46.

Boylan, Henry, "Ní Chonaill, Eibhlín Dhubh", *A Dictionary of Irish Biography*, 3rd ed. (Dublin: Gill & Macmillan, 1998).

Breathnach, Diarmuid, agus Máire Ní Mhurchú, *1882–1982 Beathaisnéis a hAon* (Baile Átha Cliath: An Clóchomhar Tta, 1986).

—. *1882–1982 Beathaisnéis a Dó* (Baile Átha Cliath: An Clóchomhar Tta, 1990).

—. *1882–1982 Beathaisnéis a Trí* (Baile Átha Cliath: An Clóchomhar Tta, 1992).

—. *1882–1982 Beathaisnéis a Ceathair* (Baile Átha Cliath: An Clóchomhar Tta, 1994).

—. "Beathaisnéis 1–4 Ceartúcháin agus Eolas Breise", *1882–1982 Beathaisnéis a Cúig* (Baile Átha Cliath: An Clóchomhar Tta, 1997).

—. *1782–1891 Beathaisnéis* (Baile Átha Cliath: An Clóchomhar Tta, 1999).

Breatnach, Pádraig A., "Muircheartach Óg Ó Súilleabháin (+1734): Stair, Traidisiún, agus Marbhnaí", *Téamaí Taighde Nua-Ghaeilge* (Maigh Nuad: An Sagart, 1997). 178–95.

Bromwich, Rachel, "The Keen for Art O'Leary, Its Background and Its Place in the Tradition of Gaelic Keening", *Éigse* V (1948): 236–52.

Cleeve, Brian, *Dictionary of Irish Writers: Writers in the Irish Language*, vol. 3, 3 vols. (Cork: Mercier, 1971).

Coughlan, Patricia, "An Cur Síos ar Shaol na mBan i dTéacsanna Dírbheathaisnéise Pheig Sayers", in Aogán Ó Muircheartaigh (eag.), *Oidhreacht an Bhlascaoid* (Baile Átha Cliath: Coiscéim, 1989).

Cruise O'Brien, Conor, *States of Ireland* (London: Hutchinson, 1972).

Cullen, L.M., "Caoineadh Airt Uí Laoghaire: The Contemporary Political Context", *History Ireland* 1.4 (1993).

—. "The Contemporary and Later Politics of Caoineadh Airt Uí Laoire", *Eighteenth Century Ireland* (1993).

de Hae, Risteárd, agus Brighid Ní Dhonnchadha (eag.), "Clár Litridheacht na Nua-Ghaedhilge 1850–1936" Vol. 1 (Baile Átha Cliath: Oifig Dhíolta Foilseacháin Rialtais, 1938).

De Paor, Pádraig, *Tionscnamh Filíochta Nuala Ní Dhomhnaill*, Leabhair Thaighde 82 (Baile Átha Cliath: An Clóchomhar, 1997).

Donovan, Katie, A.N. Jeffares and Brendan Kennelly (eag.), *Ireland's Women* (Dublin: Gill & Macmillan, 1994).

Éilgeach, Fiachra, "Filí Chorcaighe", *Saothar Suatha: do léigheadh os comhair Dáil na hÉisge, i gCorcaigh, Meadhon Foghmhair, 1907*, vol. 1 (Baile Átha Cliath: Muinntir an Ghoill, Teo., 1908). 26–41.

E.O.N., "Na hAisteoirí", *An Claidheamh Soluis* 8.19 (Aibreán 1913).

Gariníon le Nell Ní Laoghaire, "An Seana-Shaoghal", *An Músgraigheach* 8. Samhradh (1945): 15–22.

Gonzalez, Alexander G., *Contemporary Irish Women Poets: Some Male Perspectives* (Westport / London: Greenwood, 1999).

Gunn, Marion (eag.), *Céad Fáilte go Cléire* (Baile Átha Cliath: An Clóchomhar Tta, 1990).

Haberstroh, Patricia Boyle, *Women Creating Women: Contemporary Irish Women Poets* (Baile Átha Cliath: Attic Press, 1996).

Hardiman, James, *Irish Minstrelsy* (London: Joseph Robins, 1831).

Kelly, A.A. (eag.), *Pillars of the House: An Anthology of Verse by Irish Women from 1690 to the Present* (Dublin: Wolfhound, 1987, 1997).

Kennelly, Brendan, "Poetry and Violence", in Joris Duytschaever agus Geert Lernout (eag.), *History and Violence in Anglo-Irish Literature* (Amsterdam: Rodopi, 1988). 5–27.

Kenny, Edward, *The Splendid Years: Recollections of Máire Nic Shiughlaigh, as told to Edward Kenny* (Dublin: Duffy, 1955).

Lankford, Éamon, *Cape Clear Island: Its People and Landscape* (Cape Clear Museum, Co. Cork, 1999).

Levenson, Leah, and Jerry H. Natterstad, *Hanna Sheehy-Skeffington, Irish Feminist* (Syracuse: Syracuse University Press, 1986).

Mac Conghail, Muiris, *The Blaskets: People and Literature* [*The Blaskets: A Kerry Island*] (Baile Átha Cliath: Country House, 1987, 1994).

Mac Craith, Nioclás, "Peig Turraoin, Bean Uí Réagáin, 1905–1999", Pádraig Ó Macháin agus Aoibheann Nic Dhonnchadha (eag.), *An Linn Bhuí: Iris Ghaeltacht na nDéise*, Vol. 3 (Baile Átha Cliath: Leabhair na Linne, 1999). 135–6.

—. "Polly", in Pádraig Ó Macháin agus Aoibheann Nic Dhonnchadha (eag.), *An Linn Bhuí: Iris Ghaeltacht na nDéise*, vol. 3. (Baile Átha Cliath: Leabhair na Linne, 1999).

Mac Fhearghusa, Pádraig, "Blúiríní", *Feasta* 54.9 (2001): 26.

Mac Mahon, Bryan, "Peig Sayers and the Vernacular of the Story Teller", in Alison Feder agus Bernice Schrank (eag.), *Literature and Folk Culture* (St John's: Memorial University of Newfoundland, 1977). 83–109.

McWilliam Consalvo, Deborah, "Review of 'The Love Riddle'", *Irish Studies Review* (1996): 52–3.

Ní Annracháin, Máire, "Dearbhú Beatha", *Comhar* (1984): 55–8.

Ní Chéilleachair, Máire (eag.), "Peig Sayers Scéalaí 1973–1958", *Ceiliúradh an Bhlascaoid* (Baile Átha Cliath: Coiscéim, 1999). 111.

Ní Chonaill, Eibhlín Dubh, *Caoineadh Airt Uí Laoghaire*. 1961. Eag. Seán Ó Tuama (Baile Átha Cliath: An Clóchomhar Tta, 1963).

Ní Dhomhnaill, Nuala, "Ní Dhomhnaill, Nuala", interviewed by Rebecca E. Wilson, *Sleeping With Monsters: Conversations with Scottish and Irish Women Poets* (Dublin: Wolfhound Press, 1990). 148–57.

Ní Ríordáin, Brenda, "Cérbh í 'Dul Amú'?", *Comhar* (Lúnasa 1993): 40–44.

Ní Shéaghdha, Máire. *Laethanta Geala. Cailín scoile i gCiarraighe [.i. M. Ní Shéaghdha] do scríobh* (Corcaigh: Oifig "An Lóchrainn", g.d.)

Nic Eoin, Máirín, *An Litríocht Réigiúnach*, Leabhair Thaighde 40 (Baile Átha Cliath: An Clóchomhar Tta, 1982).

—. *B'ait leo bean: Gnéithe den Idé-eolaíocht Inscne i dTraidisiún Liteartha na Gaeilge* (Baile Átha Cliath: An Clóchomhar Tta, 1998).

Nic Fhearghusa, Aoife, *Glór Baineann, Glór an Léargais: an tsochaí, an bheith agus dánta Dheirdre Brennan* (Baile Átha Cliath: Coiscéim, 1998).

O'Brien, Frank, "Máire Mhac an tSaoi", *Filíocht Ghaeilge na Linne Seo: Staidéar Criticiúil*, Leabhair Thaighde 17 (Baile Átha Cliath: An Clóchomhar, 1968, 1978). 163–202.

Ó Buachalla, Breandán, *An Caoine agus an Chaointeoireacht* (Baile Átha Cliath: Cois Life, 1998).

—. "Marbhchaoine an Athar Seán Ó Maonaigh", in Pádraigín Riggs, Seán Ó Coileáin agus Breandán Ó Conchúir (eag.), *Saoi na hÉigse: Aistí in Ómós do Sheán Ó Tuama* (Baile Átha Cliath: An Clóchomhar, 2000). 197–208.

Ó Cearnaigh, Seán, *Scríbhneoirí na Gaeilge 1945–1995* (Baile Átha Cliath: Comhar Teoranta, 1995).

Ó Céirín, Kit, agus Cyril, *Women of Ireland* (Gaillimh: Tíreolas, 1996).

Ó Coigligh, Ciarán (eag.), *An Fhilíocht Chomhaimseartha 1975–1985* (Baile Átha Cliath: Coiscéim, 1987).

O'Connor, Mary, "Lashings of Mother Tongue: Nuala Ní Dhomhnaill's Anarchic Laughter", in Theresa O'Connor (eag.), *The Comic Tradition in Irish Women Writers* (Florida: Florida University Press, 1996), 149–70.

Ó Cróinín, Donnchadh, "Filí agus Filíocht Mhúsgraighe", *An Músgraigheach* 1. Meitheamh (1943): 15–20.

Ó Cróinín, Dáibhí (eag.), *The Songs of Elizabeth Cronin, Irish Traditional Singer: The Complete Song Collection* (Baile Átha Cliath: Four Courts Press, 2000).

Ó Crualaoi, Pádraig, *Seanachas Phádraig Í Chrualaoi*, eag. Donncha Ó Cróinín (Baile Átha Cliath: Comhairle Bhéaloideas Éireann, 1982).

Ó Cuív, Brian, *Cnósach focal ó Bhaile Bhúirne* (Baile Átha Cliath, 1947).

Ó Dálaigh, Seosamh, "Cuntas ar ar bhailigh Flower ó Pheig", in Aogán Ó Muircheartaigh (eag.), *Oidhreacht an Bhlascaoid* (Baile Átha Cliath: Coiscéim, 1989).

Ó Donnchú, Donncha, "Lámhscríbhinní an Athar Donncha Ó Donnchú".

Ó Droighneáin, Muiris, *Taighde i gComhair Stair Litridheachta na Nua-Ghaedhilge ó 1882 anuas* (Baile Átha Cliath: Oifig Dhíolta Foilseacháin Rialtais, 1936, 1937).

Ó Dubhda, Seán (eag.), *Duanaire Duibhneach: bailiú d'amhránaibh agus de phíosaibh eile filidheachta a ceapadh le tuairim céad bliain i gCorca Dhuibhne, agus atá fós i gcuimhne agus i mbéaloideas na ndaoine ann* (1933: Baile Átha Cliath: Oifig Dhíolta Foilseacháin Rialtais, 1969).

Ó Duilearga, Séamas, *Leabhar Sheáin Uí Chonaill: Sgéalta agus Seanchas ó Íbh Ráthach* (Baile Átha Cliath: Cumann le Béaloideas Éireann, 1948).

Ó Dúshláine, Tadhg (eag.), "Kruger sa Bhéaloideas", *Is Cuimhin Linn Kruger: Kruger Remembered* (Maigh Nuad: An Sagart, 1994), 56–68.

Ó Fiannachta, Pádraig, "Aiste ar Pheig Sayers", in Aogán Ó Muircheartaigh (eag.), *Oidhreacht an Bhlascaoid* (Baile Átha Cliath: Coiscéim, 1989).

Ó Gadhra, Seán, *Dúchas Pheig Mhóir: tráchtaireacht agus treoir don leabhar "Peig" le Peig Sayers* (Corcaigh: Mercier, 1972).

Ó Gaoithín, Mícheál, *Beatha Pheig Sayers* (Baile Átha Cliath: Foilseacháin Náisiúnta Tta, 1970).

Ó Góilidhe, Caoimhghin (eag.), *Ardteistiméireacht Díolaim Filíochta: Eagrán oifigiúil* (Baile Átha Cliath: Folens, 1974).

— (eag.), *Duanaire na Meánteistiméireachta* (Baile Átha Cliath: Folens, 1975).

Ó hÓgáin, Daithí, *An File: Staidéar ar Osnádúrthacht na Filíochta sa Traidisiún Gaelach* (Baile Átha Cliath: Oifig an tSoláthair, 1982).

Ó hOibicín, Mícheál (eag.), *Réaltra: Filíocht agus Prós don Ardteistiméireacht, Gnáthleibhéal* (Baile Átha Cliath: An Cló Ceilteach).

Ó Loinsigh, Pádraig, *Gobnait Ní Bhruadair: Beathaisnéis* [*The Hon. Albinia Lucy Broderick*], aist. ag Pádraig Mac Fhearghusa (Baile Átha Cliath: Coiscéim, 1997).

Ó Loinsigh, Amhlaoibh, "Diosgán Eile ó Chúil Aodha", *An Músgraigheach* 4 (1944): 19–21.

Ó Luínse, Amhlaoibh, *Seanachas Amhlaoibh Í Luínse*, eag. Donncha Ó Cróinín (Baile Átha Cliath: Comhairle Bhéaloideas Éireann, 1980).

Ó Lúing, Seán, "Cur Síos ar Mharie-Louise", *Journal of the Kerry Archaeological and Historical Society* (1987).

Ó Macháin, Pádraig, agus Aoibheann Nic Dhonnchadha (eag.), "Cáit M. Ní Ghráinne", *An Linn Bhuí: Iris Ghaeltacht na nDéise* (Baile Átha Cliath, 1999). 130.

O'Mahony, John, "Morty Oge O'Sullivan, Captain of the Wild Geese", *Journal of the Cork Historical and Archaeological Society* 1 (1892): 24.

Ó Maoileoin, Pádraig, *Na hAird Ó Thuaidh* (Baile Átha Cliath: Sáirséal agus Dill, 1960).

Ó Milléadha, Pádraig, "Seanchas Sliabh gCua", *Béaloideas* 6 (1936): 192–4.

Ó Muirí, Pól, "Léirmheas ar *Pádraic Ó Conaire: Deoraí*", *Anois* 18–19 (1995).

Ó Muirthile, Diarmaid, *Cois an Ghaorthaidh, filíocht ó Mhúscraí 1700–1840* (Baile Átha Cliath: An Clóchomhar Tta, 1987).

Ó Siadhail, Pádraig, *Stair Dhrámaíocht na Gaeilge 1900–1970* (Indreabhán: Cló Iar-Chonnachta, 1993).

Ó Síocháin, Conchúr (a dheachtaigh), *Seanchas Chléire*, Ciarán Ó Síocháin agus Mícheál Ó Síocháin a chuir i scríbhinn (Baile Átha Cliath: Oifig an tSoláthair, 1940).

Ó Súilleabháin, Seán, *Caitheamh Aimsire ar Thórraimh* (Baile Átha Cliath: An Clóchomhar, 1961).

Ó Súilleabháin, Muiris, *Fiche Blian ag Fás*, eag. Pádraig Ó Fiannachta, 4ú heagrán (Maigh Nuad: An Sagart, 1995).

Ó Tuama, Seán, "Saothar Teann Tíorthúil", *Feasta* (1957).

—. "The Lament for Art O'Leary", *Repossessions: Selected Essays on the Irish Literary Heritage* (Cork: Cork University Press, 1995), 78–100.

—. "The Living and Terrible Mother in the Early Poetry of Nuala Ní Dhomhnaill", *Repossessions: Selected Essays on the Irish Literary Heritage* (Cork: Cork University Press, 1995).

Ó Tuathaigh, Gearóid, "Obituary: An tOllamh Síle Ní Chinnéide, M.A. (1900–1980)", *North Munster Antiquarian Journal* XXII (1980): 79.

Pléimeann, Seán, "Máire Ní Dhonogáin", *The Gaelic Journal* 3 (1889): 105.

—. "Máire Ní Dhonogáin", *The Gaelic Journal* 4 (1890): 29.

Riggs, Pádraigín, *Bua an tSeanchaí: tráchtaireacht agus treoir don leabhar 'Bullaí Mhártain' le Síle agus Donncha Ó Céileachair* (Corcaigh: Cló Mercier, 1974).

—. *Donncha Ó Céileachair: Anailís Stíleach* (Baile Átha Cliath: An Gúm, 1978).

—. "Léirmheas ar *Aoife faoi Ghlas*", *Anois* 26–27 Bealtaine (1990).

Strong, Eithne, "Eithne Strong", interviewed by Rebecca E. Wilson, *Sleeping with Monsters: Conversations with Scottish and Irish Women Poets* (Dublin: Wolfhound Press, 1990), 109–19.

Titley, Alan, *An tÚrscéal Gaeilge*, Leabhair Thaighde 67 (Baile Átha Cliath: An Clóchomhar Tta, 1991).

Tóibín, Nioclás, *Duanaire Déiseach* (Baile Átha Cliath: Sáirséal agus Dill, 1978).

Tyers, Pádraig (eag.), *Leoithne Aniar* (Baile an Fheirtéaraigh: Cló Dhuibhne, 1982).

Ua Cróinín, Seán, "Filí agus Filíocht Mhúsgraighe, 2", *An Músgraigheach* 2. Fóghmhar (1943): 10–13.

—. "Neil Ní Mhurchadha: Ban-Fhile", *An Músgraigheach* 3. Nodlaig (1943): 9–13.

Ua Súilleabháin, Seán (eag.), "Turraoin, Peig", *An Linn Bhuí: Iris Ghaeltacht na nDéise* 4 (2000).

Uí Nia, Gearóidín (eag.), *Eolaire Chló Iar-Chonnachta de Scríbhneoirí Gaeilge* (Indreabhán: Cló Iar-Chonnachta, 1998).

Uí Ógáin, Ríonach, "Máire Ní Dhuibh", *Sinsear* (1981): 101–7.

Wagner, Heinrich, agus Niall Mac Congail (eag.), *Oral Literature from Dunquin, Co. Kerry: Gaelic Texts with Phonetic Transcription, English Summaries and Folkloristic Notes by H. Wagner and N. Mac Congail* (Béal Feirste: IIS, 1983).

Journals and Newspapers

Anois
Comhar
Feasta
Irish Independent
Irish Times

Web pages

University of Liverpool: http://www.liv.ac.uk./irish/staff.htm.
Strokestown Poetry Competition: http://www.strokestownpoetryprize.com/.
www.litríocht.com
www.pgil-eirdata.ie